Reading Eco

Advances in Semiotics

Thomas A. Sebeok, General Editor

Reading Eco

An Anthology

edited by Rocco Capozzi

Indiana University Press
Bloomington and Indianapolis

The paper used in this publication meets the
minimum requirements of American National
Standard for Information Sciences—Permanence
of Paper for Printed Library Materials, ANSI
Z39.48-1984.

Manufactured in the United States of America

Cataloging information for this work is available
from the Library of Congress.

1 2 3 4 5   02 01 00 99 98 97

To Adriana,
        Chiara, Mara, Toni
and Truffle

Contents

Foreword
Thomas A. Sebeok

At the peak of Summer in 1981, I land in Rome from overseas. For the first time, I glimpse *Il nome della rosa,* by my long-time friend and semiotic comrade-in-arms, Umberto Eco, published a few months earlier, displayed wherever books are sold. I buy a copy–"Naturalmente, un manoscritto"– prove the resonance of its Old Testament beginnings, then continue brows-ing at my hotel, wide-eyed from jet lag, late into the night. I finish reading the novel during sleepless times to follow in the course of a dozen train-rides up and down Italy and nights in hotels, until I reach "stat rosa pristine nomine, nomina nude tenemus."

Eventually, I alight in the resort town of Rimini and call up the Ecos from the railway station at their manor nestled inland from the seaside in the region of Alto Montefeltro. Renate answers the phone and tells me to have some refreshments at the station's restaurant while waiting for Um-berto to pick me up. He arrives and drives me to their home. I tell him that I have been nibbling away at his first novel all week long, but he ques-tions whether I can read Italian well enough. As a matter of fact, although out of practice now, I had, as a pre-teen, spent many a holiday in my father's villa in Abbazia (now Opatija) on the Adriatic, and had formally studied Italian for years in the 1930's in an Ujpest gymnasium. In 1936, I was even awarded a medal for my efforts on Benito Mussolini's behalf by Italy's Ambassador to Hungary. Many decades later, while I stopped by to lecture at a North Italian university, my host, whom I recognized as the former Ambassador, now serving as the Professor of Glottology as well as the Rector, needed reminding of our earlier encounter. "Sh," he whispered, "not so loud"!

I ask Umberto to autograph my copy, which he inscribes: "Ad mentem divi Tom, sherlockly. . ." In retrospect, two years afterwards, this last tag becomes emblematic of our book on Dupin, Holmes, and Peirce co-authored, co-edited, and co-published in our respective habitats, Milano and Bloomington, as *Il segno dei tre* (Bompiani) and *The Sign of Three* (Indi-ana University Press).

Surprisingly early next morning after my arrival, the phone rings at the villa. The aged President Alessandro Pertini is on line to congratulate Eco once more for his novel having won the Premio Strega not long before. (The Premio Anghiari, Premio I1 Libro dell'anno, and, eventually, the Premio Viareggio, were all to come later, and the phone hasn't stopped ringing since.) Amidst Presidential felicitations, the line goes dead, but sounds again a few minutes afterwards. I hear Eco shouting (he always roars into the receiver): "You see Mr. President, nothing in Italy works!"

To the public at large, Eco is of course known as the author of three hugely successful novels. Today, his mythical stature as a writer of fiction overshadows his scholarly pre-eminence, but to me, and to most colleagues in our profession, he remains one of the most original and creative contributors to semiotics. Ever constant to our métier, he was quoted in a recent New York Times interview as claiming: "I think semiotics is the only form philosophy can take in the present century." Needless to say, I count myself among those who agree with him, although I tend to regard the last phrase (possibly supplied by a credulous interlocutor) needlessly restrictive.

The omnivorous range of his ceaselessly roving intelligence over far-reaching epochs–especially the twelfth to fourteenth centuries of his Latinate mythopoeic imagination–vast spaces, including a chimerical seventeenth century South Pacific, and an astonishing variety of topics, Ancient and Modern, brings to mind Dr. Johnson's couplet that could serve as Eco's motto: "Let observation with extensive view / Survey mankind, from China to Peru." The essays assembled even in this, Rocco Capozzi's hefty, well-informed book ventilate a mere fraction of his oeuvre to date. And he is, after all, still a productive "medievalist in hibernation" (as he likes to designate himself), with many spring tides in his (to be hoped for) smokeless future.

An admirable, if to some readers minor genre, at which Eco is adept but which is seldom noted in commentaries on the rest of his dazzling work, is exemplified by his many Forewords, Prefaces, Introductions, Commemorations, Palimpsests, and comparably pithy prose pieces, familiar perhaps only to those to whom they matter the most and those who are immersed in the local circumstances. This sort of venture is represented in this volume only by a single item, Eco's perspicacious presentation, in 1990, of three of Yuri Lotman's important articles, including his now classic "The Semiosphere," translated from Russian into English by Ann Shukman. (Key early works by several principal "Soviet" semioticians of the famous Moscow-Tartu School were made accessible to Western readers for probably the first time in a 1969 Italian collection Eco himself had co-edited with R. Faccani.)

The Russian master had been a Vice-President of the International Association for Semiotic Studies (IASS) from its founding in 1969 to his death in the Fall of 1993. And so was Roman Jakobson (d. 1982). What could therefore be more appropriate than for Eco, a co-founder and since 1994 an Honorary President of the same Association, to have constructed another of his invaluable assessments of a senior colleague–one could say, of another elder of the same extended semiotics tribe -titled "The Influence of Roman Jakobson on the Development of Semiotics" (originally published in 1977, then reprinted in a 1987 volume of *Classics in Semiotics*)? It was there that Eco initially proclaimed his thesis that "the entire history of philosophy could be re-read in a semiotic perspective," then going on to demonstrate that, and why, Jakobson was "the major 'catalyst'" in the contemporary semiotics movement. I know that Jakobson grew increasingly fond of Eco after the 1960's, for he spoke of him to me with affection on several occasions and because I happened to be odd man out in a trio of espresso drinkers in a café with Eco and Jakobson when Roman, out of the blue, in an emotionally charged moment, turned to Umberto and said: "Thank you!" Umberto asked: "For what?" "Just for being," Roman replied.

This may be the appropriate spot to allude to the matter of the impact of Charles Peirce on modern sem(e)iotic(s), which came through rather different but converging channels to Jakobson, Eco, and myself. I have related at length elsewhere that I was led to Peirce's thought, successively, by Ogden and Richards (in Cambridge, in the mid-1930s), then via both my teachers, the philosopher Charles Morris and the philologist Roman Jakobson (in the early and late 1940s, respectively). Jakobson told me he himself was first alerted by Morris but then followed up on his own through ready access to the Peirce papers and the Philosophy faculty at Harvard, where he became a Professor in 1949. He first spoke publicly about Peirce, with warm eloquence, at a meeting of anthropologists and linguists in Bloomington in the Summer of 1952, and thereafter cited him regularly (even, some might think, obsessively) to the end of his life.

The advent of Peirce in Italy is, however, a far more complicated story, which was the subject of three lectures at a December 1990 international conference in Naples (attended by both Eco and myself) on the theme *Peirce in Italia*. The reason for this complexity is that Peirce himself had visited that country some half-a-dozen times in the 1870s, and so came to leave his personal imprint on influential segments of Italian scholarship and literature. Mario Quaranta, in one of the Naples talks, traced Peirce's intellectual reception in Italy between 1900 and 1960, as Arturo Martone did in another for the ensuing three decades. I had pointed, in an earlier article, also titled "Peirce in Italia" (in *Alfabeta* No. 35, 1982), to the resulting *confluenza*–or *contaminazione,* a term Martone favors–between Saussurean "semiology" and Peircean "semiotics." This particular trend may, I thought, have been most authoritatively and conspicuously carried forward in Eco's work in the early 1970s—notably in his *Trattato di semiotica generale,* where he already cited the American progenitor about five times more often than the Swiss. This is not to deny the secondary guidance, as it were, of Jakobson. Some years later, in the Fall of 1976, the three of us had a splendid opportunity to exchange views about Peirce among ourselves at a "Peirce Symposium on Semiotics and the Arts," held at The Johns Hopkins University. Eco's formal talk in Baltimore dealt with Peirce's notion of interpretant, wherein he asserted, among many other interesting things: "I want to make explicitly clear that [his] present approach has to be labeled 'Peircist'."

The IASS is of course but one of several of Eco's enduring lettered circles. I do believe it is appropriate for me to note here his involvement with yet another among our mutual friends, the late Giorgio Prodi (1928-1987), Eco's near-contemporary colleague at the University of Bologna, and himself the scion of a very distinguished family of Italian public servants and academics, severally close to Eco. Prodi was a prodigiously busy polymath, in some ways out-Ecoing Eco: "Perché [Giorgio] aveva una giornata di quarantott'ore e noi di sole ventiquattro?," Umberto questioned in mock-peeve. Indeed, Prodi was, on the one hand, one of his country's leading medical biologists in oncology, while he was, on the other, a highly original contributor to semiotics and epistemology, the philosophy of language and formal logic, plus a noteworthy literary figure. An immensely prolific scientist, Prodi was one of a handful of European pioneers in the exploding transdisciplinary field that has come lately to be dubbed biosemiotics. The year before Prodi died, he and Eco together took part in a landmark meeting in Lucca, juxtaposing semiotics and immunology, bringing the two, as it were, under a new interdisciplinary branch of biological sciences, "immunosemiotics," which is now, with a different emphasis, an important branch of biosemiotics. Prodi's earliest contribution to this area, *Le basi materiali della significazione,* was published first in Eco's journal *Vs* (1976), then boldly the following year in one of the well-known Bompiani series also edited by him. Again, his beautiful, characteristically informed and observant *Ricordo* of Prodi's life and accomplishments, "Una sfida al mito delle due culture" (1988), repays close study for what it tells us about Giorgio no less, to be sure, for what it reveals about Umberto.

I cannot pass over mention of a fourth, utterly delightful and amusing piece in this genre by Eco, less well known to his Anglophone readers than it ought to be. This is his amplificatory Foreword to the 1991 Italian edition, by Il Mulino, of Bob Merton's wonderful "humanist and self-winding book," *On the Shoulders of Giants,* which, in the author's own words, "adopts a non-linear, divagating Shandean mode for examining the enduring tension between tradition and originality in the transmission and growth of knowledge along with a variety of related themes." Eco's Foreword, which is remarkable not only for its technical content but, too, for the convergence of its graceful style and wit with Merton's own–as well as, let it be highlighted once again, with those of Borges–has now appeared, in 1993, in a "Post-Italianate" translation by William Weaver, with yet a new Postface by Merton.

In the course of the opening remarks I was asked to improvise al fresco at the 5th Congress of the IASS in Berkeley in the Summer of 1994, I espied Eco standing in the assembly on my immediate right. Recollecting our Association's organizational meeting convened by the French linguist Emile

Benveniste, with Jakobson as the principal *spiritus movers,* at which the IASS was born in Paris on January 21-22, 1969, I pointed out that, of the dozen or so men and one woman (Julia Kristeva, long since immersed in other endeavors) who were present at the founding and still survive, Eco and I alone have tenaciously remained at work in semiotic studies. My off-the-cuff statement was challenged on the spot, but I later checked the record and now confirm it.

Eco has served the affairs of the Association in several important ways: as Secretary General (1972-1979), Vice President (1979-1984), permanent member of the Editorial Committee of, and an early contributor to, *Semiotica* (e.g., in 1972, he wrote a componential analysis of the architectural sign / *Column/); and he is now one of its two Italian Honorary Presidents (Cesare Segre is the other). Eco will always be gratefully remembered by the world-wide semiotics community for having arranged the Association's 1st Congress, held in June 1974 in his home town, Milan. He viewed that Congress as having offered "a semiotic landscape," this phrase reprised in the main title of the bulky *Proceedings* volume (1238 pages) which he co-edited (with Seymour Chatman and Jean-Marie Klinkenberg), and which was published as the 29th volume (1979) in Mouton's Approaches To Semiotics series. Certainly, both the occasion and this resulting publication, displaying the state of the art of the field as of that decade, set a standard for all ensuing quinquennial Congresses to emulate. Incidentally, he attended and made diverse major contributions to each: in Vienna, Palermo, Barcelona/ Perpignan, and most recently Berkeley.

Eco's over-all administrative talents are far from negligible. His (seemingly) effortless organization of the First Congress was foreshadowed by an earlier, seductively lavish multinational and multidisciplinary get-together in October, 1968, which he undertook–pulling the strings unobtrusively from behind the scenes–when he was still a thirty-six year old Professor of Visual Communication in the Faculty of Architecture at the University of Florence. This memorable, high-level symposium, on the theme of language in the broadest sense, comprehending semiotics, designed to "stimulate cognitive contact between the realm of industrial reality and culture," and which is generally referred to among us as the "Olivetti Conference," took place at Milan's Museo Nazionale della Scienze e della Tecnica in October of 1968, in celebration of the centennial of the founder of this most famous of industrial firms of Italy, Camillo Olivetti. Jakobson spoke on "the need for classification of sign systems and corresponding types of messages," I on zoosemiotic structures, and Eco about codes and ideology. But the design and execution of the *Convegno* has Eco's fingerprints all over it, including the excellent volume of proceedings published two years afterwards. Although our unspoken hope that this symbolic homage offered to technolo-

gy and culture would yield immediate tangible rewards failed to material-
ize, the intellectual spinoffs proved, in due course, abundantly fruitful in
several directions, not least for semiotics.

Readers who follow Eco's publishing activities are certainly aware of the
matchless animating role he played as an "editorial adviser" at Bompiani,
somewhat paralleled by my own function at the Indiana University Press.
His "signpost" *Theory of Semiotics* was the inaugural volume in our Advances in Semiotics series, as well as the first of his books to appear in
English. Half a dozen books of his have graced our series since then. However, the American series includes English translations of ten or more works
by Italian colleagues and students of Eco's, who, as I have previously detailed in my Foreword to Segre's book, and would once more observe with
pride, opened up this unique two-way boulevard for bilingual and bicultur-
al semiosis.

Eco's fecund creativity and myriad enterprises, evident as much in his
life as in his writings, are bolstered by charm, wit, and vigor. This book is
offered as an unpretentious iconic index of his persona; the dynamic object
and its multifarious symbols, taken together, certainly spice with exhilarat-
ing brio these propitious times of the sign.

(Bloomington. February 12, 1996)

PREFACE
Rocco Capozzi

As 1993 came to a close, journalists and newscasters began to popularize the expression "information superhighway." Thanks to the increasing prevalence of personal computers, the new catchword refers to our ability to interact more and more, and faster, with the rest of the world, from our homes and from work. "Information superhighway" is in short a metaphor for something which in theory affects all aspects of our life: education, work, entertainment, and, above all, the way we have access to massive amounts of information. We are, after all, becoming the inhabitants of that wonderful postmodern "electronic global village" prophesied by McLuhan. This may be exciting indeed, especially for those who believe that they should be able to get immediate information on everything and everyone.

"Information superhighway" in my course on literary semiotics is an expression also used to define the overwhelming amount of highly diversified information which can be gathered from Umberto Eco's work. In fact, from his first major publication *Open Work* (1962) to *The Limits of Interpretation* (1992), and to *The Island of the Day Before* (1994) Eco has demonstrated that his stimulating essays, lectures and novels are all loaded with witty, informative, fascinating and thought-provoking material on communication, semiotics, theories of interpretation, and, in short, on the most diverse aspects of culture–high and popular.

Speaking of cyberspace and World Wide Web, most recently Eco has edited and prepared *Encyclomedia: Il Seicento* (1995)–a multimedia CD ROM on seventeenth-century culture and aesthetics. This has reinforced even more my theory that Eco's encyclopedic and rhizomatic works (as his mind) can be best illustrated through hyper/cyber-texts, rich with internet features that allow users to move from one topic to another by merely clicking on a word, image, title, or suggested link. Of course this also means having no assurance that in this potentially infinite chain of references and suggestions one will necessarily return "home", to the point of departure, in the same session. This is in essence the problem that one faces when reading Eco's encyclopedic and labyrinthine hypertexts (his novels as his essays) enriched with a myriad of intertextual echoes that stimulate innumerable "inferential walks".

Whenever students ask me to give them an idea of what Umberto Eco is 'really' like, in person, I often follow their inquiry with my own question: what do Augustine, R. Bacon, T. Aquinas, Templars, Baroque, TV serials like "Colombo," movies like "Casablanca" and the trilogy of "Indiana Jones"; thinkers like Peirce, Bakhtin, Derrida, Foucault, Popper, and Wittengstein; writers like Dante, Poe, Joyce, Borges, Barthes, Lotman; as well as, aesthetics, philosophy, structuralism, semiotics, deconstruction, mass media, Superman, Conan Doyle, esoteric texts, kabbalah, irony, humor, intertextuality, reading the classics, philosophy, comic strips, computers, techniques of writing, and interpreting signs/texts, architecture, libraries, labyrinths, palimpsests, the art of writing best-sellers, "global encyclopedia," "inferential walks," "open works," and "model readers," have in common? After a few seconds of silence I end up explaining that this is a partial list of authors, topics, theories, and issues that Eco can examine, discuss and joke about, with various degrees of authority. I add that this is perhaps the best way to begin to describe the unusually voracious mind of a man of many interests—a man whom everyone would certainly like to have on his team if he had to compete in an academic and scholarly trivial pursuit contest in which the future of his tenure was at stake.

To this rather frivolous sketch of Umberto Eco the semiotician, journalist, narrator, editor, mass communication expert, professor, globe-trotting lecturer, and interpreter of modern culture, I add that Eco's great sense of humor plays an important role whenever he writes or lectures in any of the languages that he speaks fluently: Italian, French, German, English, and Spanish. His wit, his intertextual competence and his vivid imagination at times demand that the reader should have a fairly large encyclopedic competence of his own. Humor and erudition are so well fused in Eco's style that they have become the two most familiar trademarks of his enjoyable and insightful work.

In the last three years I have been working on this anthology as a teaching tool for demonstrating how Eco's works—both his theoretical studies and his intertextual novels—provide us with a fascinating interdisciplinary approach to the general study of semiotics. The project originated in a graduate course on "Umberto Eco the semiotician narrator" which I have been offering in the Department of Italian Studies, at the University of Toronto. One of the objectives of my course (and of this collection) is to examine some of Eco's writings together with secondary sources (with his critics) in order to arrive at a more comprehensive critique of his literary theories and of his notions of general semiotics as a cognitive social/cultural practice.

The idea to publish this anthology received its initial support from my colleague Marcel Danesi who encouraged me, assuring me that when he had mentioned my project to his good friend and distinguished semiotician, Thomas A. Sebeok, they had both agreed that this type of collection of readings would be useful for graduate and undergraduate students, and hopefully for Eco scholars as well. Once the selection was finalized, it became a matter of convincing some authors to make revisions to their articles, and of contacting others, like Kevelson, Miranda, and Bondanella, and ask them to submit their essays that would give the anthology greater depth. I have been very fortunate indeed to have found some of the most collaborative authors that one can ask for. I was actually impressed to see how most of them even thank me for having given them an opportunity to rewrite their article.

I must point out immediately that the very fact that my selection focuses mainly on Eco's work from *A Theory of Semiotics* to the present, should indicate that this text does not claim to be an exhaustive study of Eco's theories on semiotics, nor of his *opera omnia*. Sebeok is certainly right when in the "Foreword" he states that with an author like Eco, any text can only "ventilate a mere fraction of his oeuvre." The goal of this anthology is twofold. First, to examine from a variety of perspectives Eco's notions of literary semiotics and interpretation. Second, to bring together some of the best readings on his theories and applications of semiotics –in his essays and in his internationally acclaimed fiction–which could also serve as a pretext to a study of Eco's work and, possibly, to literary semiotics in general.

Part I contains Eco's own writings followed by a selection of critiques of his major works (mainly from the days of *A Theory of Semiotics*, 1976, to the present). Part II is comprised of articles on literary semiotics which focus primarily on Eco, Peirce, Bakhtin, Greimas, Borges, and Derrida. Part III examines several aspects of Eco's fiction. And whereas for his first two novels there was the problem of which articles to choose from the vast selection available, for *The Island of the Day Before* there was very little choice. The English translation had just appeared and Norma Bouchard was the only author who had published a full length article on Eco's third novel. I asked Bouchard for a revised version of her work and then invited Claudia Miranda–one of Eco's research assistants who was studying in Toronto–to submit some of her work on *The Island*. I also decided to include my article on *The Island* (from my work in progress on 'Eco the semiotician narrator') and asked Prof. Zamora to expand her insightful analysis of *Foucault's Pendulum* so that it would include some comments on *The Island* as well.

Here it must be pointed out that several articles in this anthology are revisions of earlier essays that the authors, very graciously, agreed to expand and up-date for *Reading Eco*.

The professional and amicable ties between Eco and Thomas A. Sebeok are well inscribed in the short history of the studies of semiotics in Italy and the USA. I was happy to learn that Sebeok had agreed to write a "Foreword" to this anthology because, even when choosing to give a few anecdotes about Peirce, zoosemiotics, or Eco, he is always a gold mine of information. In this brief tribute to a fellow promoter of the discipline of semiotics, we recognize the mutual love and respect that the two scholars have shared since they first met. My "Introduction to Eco" was added at the last moment when Sebeok suggested that it would be helpful to have a brief bio-monographic picture of Umberto Eco that summarized the most salient features of one of our most exciting observers of contemporary society–in and outside the great walls of academia.

In the selection of Eco's writings on semiotics and interpretation I was faced with the task of trying to avoid material that the author had already published a number of times in different forms (not an easy task when dealing with Eco). I'm most grateful to Eco for having given me "Semiotics and the Philosophy of Language" and "An Author and his Interpreters"– two articles that, as he puts it, so far "have had little exposure." Of course Eco readers may have seen part of these articles elsewhere, for example in *Interpretation and Overinterpretation.* Nonetheless these two lectures serve to open and to close Part One, because they provide us with a clear and succinct picture of his fundamental views on specific elements of semiotics and interpretation. "Semiotics and the Philosophy of Language" also shows how Eco is always revising his notions on grammar, dictionaries, sign, semiotics, and the philosophy of language.

"Innovation and Repetition: between Modern and Post-Modern Aesthetics," is one of Eco's best discussions on seriality, repetition, parody, pastiche, irony, citation, and intertextuality–all familiar elements of our so-called postmodern culture. From the late Seventies to the present this essay has seen a few revisions which in themselves are important for an appreciation of Eco's parodic and ironic presentations of postmodernism. And precisely because I wanted to show how Eco is constantly revising his theoretical works I chose "Two Problems in Textual Interpretation" which also illustrates how he has been elaborating his views on interpretation from the days of *The Open Work* to *The Role of the Reader.* The author's revisions show us how he has gradually intensified his studies on narratology from his earliest examinations, in the Sixties, of Allais, Sue, Fleming, and popular novels in general, to the more theoretical essays in *The Limits of Interpretation* and *Six Walks in the Woods of Fiction.* Here we also find an interesting discussion on Greimas and especially on "topics" vs. "isotopies" (discursive and narrative), and on "dictionary semantics" vs. "encyclopedia semantics."

The introduction to Lotman's *Universe of the Mind* reveals Eco's deep admiration for Lotman's work and, just as pertinent to this anthology, mentions how the author underlines the split between structuralism and semiotics. We remember that from the days of *La struttura assente* and, even more so, after *A Theory of Semiotics,* Eco departs from the dogmatism of "ontological structuralism" because he (like Lotman) could not accept the "rigidity of the structuralist opposition between code and message." Eco praises Lotman's analyses of a variety of social phenomena and his notions of viewing a text (and a culture) as a "set of texts." In this introduction we also find one of Eco's implicit admissions of why he wrote his fiction. As he speaks of David Lodge's novel, *Small World*, Eco states that: "... literary works can often be much more informative about the world and our society than many scientific treatises." From this affirmation it is not hard to assume that here Eco is also alluding to his own novels which are, among many other things, intended as an encyclopedic source of information on a variety of theoretical, literary and semiotic issues.

"An Author and his Interpreters" complements a similar article, "Reading my Readers," that Eco had published in *Modern Language Notes* (1992). While they give us a sample of Eco's reaction to his critics they offer valuable material for a discussion on the whole issue of the interaction between authors, texts and readers. I was personally interested in these two articles because, in the last few years, I have been re-examining Eco's treatment of the role of the "implied author." In "Reading my Readers" the author responds specifically to the writings of de Lauretis, Coletti and Artigiani. Therefore, I have included two of these articles. I should add that the excellent articles of de Lauretis and Coletti may indeed show how critics are often influenced by other critics (e.g., Coletti's reading of de Lauretis), nonetheless here they serve to demonstrate how one of Eco's textual strategies intended to respect historical and cultural factors can (as expected?) arouse the attention of some critics interested in discussing the question of "gender" (in the Middle Ages and in the present). I am speaking of Eco's calculated treatment of the relatively minor role of a peasant woman in *The Name of the Rose* which, beginning mainly with de Lauretis' "Gaudy Rose," acquires a whole new meaning once it is viewed from a feminist perspective. Moreover, Coletti, as she focuses on the "semiotics of female bodies" in *Foucault's Pendulum*, continues her provocative and insightful analysis of "erasure of gender" that she had begun in her brilliant work (Coletti 1988) on *The Rose and the Middle Ages*.

The job of selecting articles for Part II at first appeared to be a never ending (and perhaps unrealistic) undertaking. But, once it was determined that I would focus on writings which discussed material directly related to authors and topics that Eco analyzes in his own works, I continued to give priority to those articles that made specific references to Eco vis-à-vis Morris, Saussure, Hjelmslev, Jakobson, Peirce, Bakhtin, Foucault, Greimas, Rorty, and Derrida. And thus, in selecting articles that dealt with signs, interpretants and interpretation vis-à-vis unlimited semiosis and intertextuality, I favored writings which at the same time discussed Eco's semiotic theories vis-à-vis semiosis, interpretation, narratology, parody, and the cognitive function of postmodern pastiches.

In my search for some of the early criticism published in North America on Eco's theories of semiotics (before he became an international semiotician and a mass media celebrity) I had found of great interest John Deely's review-article on *A Theory of Semiotics*. I asked Deely to revisit his earlier views on Eco with hindsight. A similar request was made to S. Petrilli, L. Doležel and I. Rauch in order to have at least some articles that dealt more specifically with Eco's general theories on language and semiotics. Petrilli, for example, gives an excellent account of Eco's role as Italian semioticians move from Saussurean structuralist semiotics to Peircean philosophical semiotics.

I invited Petrilli and Deely to expand their original articles primarily because to this date the evolution of Eco's theories from *A Theory of Semiotics* to *Semiotics and the Philosophy of Language* has not attracted a great deal of attention. In fact, it is only after scholars began to examine more closely *The Role of the Reader* in relation to *The Name of the Rose* (especially those pages in which critics like Coletti felt that Eco was discussing semiotic practices from the Middle Ages to the present) that Eco's major works on semiotics have become the object of investigation for a diachronical study of the author's overall views on signs, codes, dictionaries, referent, encyclopedias, metaphors, and intertextuality.

Recently extensive material has come out on *The Limits of Interpretation* (1990) and on Eco's reader's reception theories vis-à-vis semiotics, hermeneutics, and deconstructionism (see Buczynska-Garewicz, Petrilli, Doležel, Riffaterre, Rauch, and Tejera). Because in *The Limits of Interpretation* and in *Interpretation and Overinterpretation* Eco seems to argue that his reading of Peirce's "infinite semiosis" is more accurate than that of Derrida, I looked for articles that contained a critique of Derrida's and Eco's reading of Peirce (e.g. Buczynska-Garewicz). In Tejera's article we find some interpretations of interpreter, interpretant, meaning, metaphor, pragmatics, and encyclopedia which actually challenge some of Eco's readings of Peirce's *Collected Papers*. Tejera's criticism can serve as a point of departure for a discussion on how Eco may be "using" or "misinterpreting" Peirce's terms in order to support his own theories on signs and interpretation. Another issue that emerges here is whether or not Peirce's work is really so ambiguous, or, does the problem in reading Peirce's *Collected Papers* derive from the way that the papers have been collected and published?

As he focuses on *The Role of the Reader* and *The Limits of Interpretation* L. Doležel's discusses strategies of "possible worlds" and underlines some of Eco's key points on Model Readers and semiotic theories of literary interpretation. Doležel gives strong support to Eco's criticism against the dangers of "hermetic drift" promoted by J. Derrida, R. Rorty and S. Fish. Extremely interesting are Doležel's observation of Eco's pursuit of a "certain themata" through variation techniques–observations which lead us to the examination of Eco's familiar practice of "repetition and difference."

A. Longoni's article on "paranoid readings" and "hermetic drift," discusses an important introduction of Eco (not very well known by

English-speaking readers) in which the author had first accentuated his views on the dangers of "hermetic semiosis", before writing *Foucault's Pendulum*. Eco's "Introduction" to the seven esoteric readings of Dante, in *L'idea deforme*, are a gold mine of information for anyone who is looking for analogies between *The Limits of Interpretation* and the many intertextual passages on "paranoid readings" in *Foucault's Pendulum* (see Hutcheon, Bondanella, Bouchard and Capozzi).

The brief article by Perron and Debbèche, is an excellent introduction to the relations between Eco and Greimas. And for readers who have not been able to follow Eco's earlier essays (in his eclectic collections like *Diario minimo*, *Sugli specchi* and *Dalla periferia dell'Impero*) "On The Art of lying" provides valuable information on how, since the Sixties, beginning with Eco's contribution to *Communications 8* (1966), the author became deeply interested in narratology, textual strategies and reader reception theories, that is, long before his sensational success with *The Name of the Rose*.

M. Riffaterre's "The Interpretant in Literary Semiotics" is a most perceptive interpretation of Peirce's "interpretant" for literary semiotics. Readers will appreciate the discussion on the relationship between intertextuality, parody and literariness while at the same time will be reminded of how many of Riffaterre's own views on the "self-sufficient text" are very close to Eco's criteria of "intentio operis" and interpretation.

D. Seed examines how "openness" in Eco suggests flexibility, intellectual receptivity and potential. And whereas many critics have discussed the relations between Eco and Borges very few have investigated the equally important presence of James Joyce in Eco's work. Seed's article offers a brief but clear-sighted look at Joyce, entropy, Kitsch and the heuristic nature of Eco's encyclopedic pastiches.

In his criticism of "hermetic semiosis" Eco's speaks of the dangers of extremist positions of deconstructionism. The writings of Rauch and Buczynska-Garewicz contribute to some interesting discussions on what really separates Derrida and Eco in their views on texts, intertexts, endless semiosis, unlimited interpretation, "hermetic drift," and "infinite deferral" of meaning. Rauch's article also deals with "language research" and "semiotic research" within linguistics theories and Eco's *The Search for the Perfect Language*. Furthermore, because Eco has often considered, even if only briefly, the semiotics of cinema and theater in his writings, I asked Roberta Kevelson to submit one of her latest work on "Eco and Drama"– knowing that she had written it during one of her rare pauses during her ongoing studies on Peirce, Law and semiotics. Stimulating indeed are Kevelson's argument that drama is the representation of the semiotic process *par excellence*, and her discussion on "creative abduction *vs.* overcoded abductions."

In Part III, the selection of articles on Eco's novels (especially on *The Name of the Rose*) became even more problematic. The numerous outstanding writings collected in anthologies, such as those edited by M.T. Inge (*Naming the Rose*) and R. Giovannoli (*Saggi sul Nome della rosa*), or journals like *Sub-Stance* and *Modern Language Notes*, are a just a sample of what in essence constitutes the beginning of a long process of interdisciplinary research on some of the most sensational novels of our times.

The moment one thinks of conjectures and abductions in *The Rose* the first text that comes to mind is undoubtedly *The Sign of Three*. Therefore it would have been a crime not to include T. A. Sebeok's brilliant chapter on Eco. And although it has become a canon article, and rather easily available, I could not leave out T. de Lauretis's writing on *The Rose*, which has clearly inspired several critics. From here on, I tried to select essays that had a semiotic component and that provided new insightful critical material on Eco's metatextual and intertextual bestsellers. For example, D. Richter's article goes beyond the familiar remarks on Eco's interplay between historical, philosophical and detective stories, as he reminds the reader of the different echoes of Peirce, Popper, Wittgenstein, Voltaire and Borges. For Richter *The Name of the Rose* is a novel with a specific ideological message while at the same time, through its parody, it is also a "detective-story-to-end-all-detective-stories". Far from being merely a postmodern pastiche *The Rose* is indeed a clever example of the Bakhtinian "carnivalization" of scholarship. In fact, as Richter reminds us, one has to be careful to recognize where and why Eco often plays cat and mouse with his readers with elements of "problematic anachronisms," history, intertextuality and intricate analogies between the Middle Ages and the Modern period.

Foucault's Pendulum confirmed Eco's talent for fusing (blatant) popular postmodern pastiches with erudite literature. But, one has to be careful to examine how Eco may indeed be extremely ironic and parodic in his application of postmodern techniques as he narrates through seemingly endless chains of intertextuality. For a discussion on Eco's ironic representation of "hermetic semiosis," M. Foucault and postmodernism in general, L. Hutcheon's work came immediately to mind. I had read with great interest the first draft of an article that she was submitting to *Diacritics* and I was particularly interested in her deduction that Eco's Casaubon may very well be Eliot's Casaubon from *Middlemarch*. Eco has rejected this association (see "An Author and his Interpreters"), nonetheless Hutcheon's inferences are worth examining in her acute observations on Eco's art of illustrating his various skills as creative writer and critical theorist.

P. Bondanella's article offers a wide view of *Foucault's Pendulum* in light of Eco's criticism of "hermetic drift" and of his discussions on secret sects, alchemy and misinterpretations echoed in the adventures of Casaubon, Belbo and Diotallevi. Bondanella is among the very few readers who have linked the author's theoretical writings on "hermetic semiosis" with a series of Eco's lectures that inspired *L'idea deforme* and the pages of *Foucault's Pendulum*. L. Parkinson Zamora's article on the *Pendulum* reiterates even more Eco's great sense of philosophical and critical coherence in his work, as it also illustrates a definite continuity in topics and narrative strategies from *The Rose* to *The Island*.

For *The Island of the day Before*, as already mentioned, it became a question of having to find some authors who had written, or were working, on Eco's third novel. Fortunately, Norma Bouchard had just published the first North American article on *The Island* in *Italica* (1995). Bouchard makes several valuable observations on the issues of interpretation and hermetic drift initiated in *Foucault's Pendulum* that early reviewers of *The Island* have not taken into consideration at all. Claudia Miranda, one of Eco's research assistants, also came to my rescue. When I asked her if she had anything on Eco's *Island* I was glad to hear that she was just completing an article on the semantic and semiotic mystery of the "Orange Colored Dove" in relation to Eco's theories of interpretation and to his polemics with American deconstructionists (mainly of Derrida and Rorty). Finally, my own writing on intertexuality, metaphors and metafiction in Eco's Neo-Baroque *Bildungsroman* wishes to further demonstrate the author's overwhelming encyclopedic competence–here focusing on the arts, aesthetics, philosophy, language and overall culture of the seventeenth century.

The Integrated Bibliography of References

To avoid duplications and to save space the integrated bibliography has been compiled from the references that appeared in each article. Titles which were mentioned in the notes but were not quoted in the texts may have not been included in the integrated bibliography.

Abbreviations
The following abbreviations appear in parentheses, without a date, in order to eliminate ambiguity whenever the same date pertained to more than one work of Eco:

Island
The Island of the Day Before

Postscript
Postcript to The Name of the Rose

Lector
Lector in fabula

Role
The Role of the Reader

Limits
Limits of Interpretation

Rose
The Name of the Rose

OW
The Open Work

SPL
Semiotics and the Philosophy of Language

Pendulum
Foucault's Pendulum

Travels
Travels in Hyperreality

Acknowledgments

I am most grateful to Umberto Eco and to all the journals, publishers and authors who have granted me permission to include their articles–they are after all the ones who have indeed made possible this anthology. Each author has indicated in an initial endnote if their article is a revision of an original essay and where it was first published.

I would like to thank Thomas A. Sebeok and Marcel Danesi for their encouraging words in support of this project. Whenever projects become "work in progress" for a long time they often risk losing their priority as other plans move to the foreground of one's research. This anthology escaped such a fate thanks to two extremely ambitious and persevering assistants. My special thanks go to Enza Antenos-Conforti and Frances Koltowski for their generous and indispensable help. Their many hours of work in scanning, proof-reading and preparing a camera-ready text enabled me to complete the project in a relatively short period. Last, but certainly not least, I must thank my wife Toni for assisting me with the editing of some of the articles and, most of all, for putting up with me while I was working on this important project.

Part I

Reading Eco

Semiotics and the Philosophy of Language

GRAMMARS AND THE PHILOSOPHY OF LANGUAGE

There are many disciplines–such as linguistics or iconography or musicology–that are concerned with different semiotic systems, of which they represent the rules of functioning. We will call these disciplines *grammars*. In this sense Italian linguistics is a grammar, as is the study of gestural languages, or as it can be the study of different types of road signals. Any theory of signs that assumed to be a general or universal grammar would be a grammar in the above sense in so far as it takes into account only these rules that are allegedly at work in every sign-system, by articulating them into a super-system able to explain how the different sign-systems function as they do.

If the philosophy of language can be thought of as a reflection on language (or, in various ways, on languages, and on the faculty of expression), it could also be said that during this century a "linguistic turn" has taken place, and that philosophy as a whole is now none other than a reflection on language.

But any philosophy of language (be it an analytical or a hermeneutical one) usually takes the grammatical researches for granted. The philosopher is rather interested in the fact that we use grammars in order to speak about the universe (in the widest sense of such term, which includes even these metaphysical assertions that neo-positivists might have excluded from the realm of meaningful propositions). Philosophers of language do not seem directly concerned with the way in which the syntactical or the lexical component of a grammar are organized, but rather with the activity of speaking, that is, with the way in which we use grammars in order to make meaningful statements about actual or possible worlds, with the nature of meaning, or (since even Vico and Condillac were philosophers of language), with the origins of language, with the relationships between language and Being, and so on.

If Heidegger's is a philosopher of language (and there is no doubt that he spent his life speculating on language in general), he represents a good exam-

ple of a philosopher who ignores grammatical questions (and when dealing
with them, at least at the etymological level, is no more rigorous than
Isidore of Seville).

For historical reasons, contemporary semiotics was instead to come into
being as a grammar above all else; be it as universal grammar or as the study
of specific grammars. Undoubtedly this is what did occur with structuralist
semiotics, along that line which runs from Saussure and Hjelmslev and
passes on through to Barthes, continuing from there towards the grammar
of fashion or the grammar of Japanese cooking. Lévi-Strauss's designed a
grammar of parental relations, and it was for this reason that it was to have
so much influence on the development of structural semiotics. Greimas
started out as a lexicographer and then founded an all-too-rigorous
narratological grammar.

But outside of the structuralist current of thought, Peirce, too–although
from the beginning he was to establish his semiotics as a purely philosophical discourse (in which he elaborated a list of new categories, performed a
critique of Cartesianism and sketched out a theory of inference)–contem-
poraneously elaborated a 'grammar' of all the possible types of signs. His
trichotomies belong to his "speculative grammar."

Peirce is, at any rate, an example of how the distinction between philosophical inquiry and grammatical inquiry sometimes blurs. If we reconstruct a history of semiotics as a history of the various doctrines of all the
different types of signs, is it possible to separate a grammatical moment
from a philosophical one in the works of Aristotle or the Stoics? Can one
say that the *Prior Analytics* are a grammar of logic and the *Posterior* ones a
philosophical reflection on our ways of knowing? Should the universal
grammar of Modistae be considered a grammatical analysis of Medieval
Latin or a philosophical reflection on the role and essence of language?
Locke is certainly a philosopher of language, but are the authors of Port
Royal only grammarians? Chomsky is evidently on the side of grammar,
but his Cartesian philosophy of language is the explicit and unignorable
nucleus of his entire project. Where would we place Montague's formal
grammar? Would we take Austin's, Grice's and Searle's pragmatic research
as a philosophical one, or as "grammar" which establishes a set of rules for
using natural languages in different contexts?

GENERAL SEMIOTICS

As repeatedly stated in Eco 1984, I believe that there are *specific semiotics*,
which are *grammars* of a particular sign system, and which Hjelmslev
would have called *semiotics*, in the plural. These grammars would be able to
exist–and sometimes have in fact developed–outside of the general semiotic
picture. But naturally they are more interesting when they take this picture

into account. Now and then the general picture has prevailed over the specificity of the sign system at hand; during the 1970's there were some rather naive attempts to extend the categories of linguistics to every sign system. This occurred because a single specific grammar, that of natural languages, was assigned the task of serving as the parameter for semiotics in general. An example of an even-handed elaboration of the specific grammars of simple systems (road signals, navy flags, bus numbers and so on) is that of Prieto. In *Messages et signaux* (1966), he provisionally adopts the parameters of the linguistic notion of articulation, but precisely in order to demonstrate how the systems he is analyzing do not obey the same rules as natural languages do.

When it is well-constructed, a specific semiotics attains a scientific status, or close to it–to the extent to which this is possible for human sciences. These grammars are descriptive, frequently they also are prescriptive and to some extent they can be predictive, at least in a statistical sense, in so far as they are supposed to successfully predict how a user of a given sign system, under normal circumstances, will generate or interpret messages produced according to that system's rules.

Opposed to these specific semiotics (in the sense that it is superordinate to them) lies a *general semiotics*. Whereas the specific semiotics find their objects as already given (ways of using sounds, gestures, lights and so on), general semiotics *posits* its own theoretical object as a philosophical category. In this sense, the concept of *sign*–or of *semiosis*–which should account for the various kinds of "signs" used by the specific semiotics–is a philosophical concept, a theoretical construct.

The philosophical nature of general semiotics explains the resistance which it encounters from time to time. For the layperson it often seems incongruous that scholars who discuss the syntactical structure of Swahili are grouped under the same aegis as those who analyze the direction of the gaze in a Renaissance painting; not to mention still others who investigate the inferential mechanisms which guide a doctor when diagnosing pneumonia or when investigating the question of whether there is a system of communication among lymphocytes. And not only the layperson but also the scholar sometimes wonders whether semiotics, besides concerning itself with the processes of intentional communication, should really be concerned with those processes in which a natural symptom is treated as if it were intentionally produced for purposes of communication.

We usually feel fairly self-confident about telling the layperson that it is only because of his or her insufficiencies that s/he cannot see the relationship between the word *smoke* and a puff of smoke, between the German language and traffic signals, between the production of a linguistic act and the waving of a flag. Several decades have now passed since the days when we thought that these phenomena should all be investigated using tools provided by linguistics. We no longer think semiotics must concern itself

exclusively with sign systems or signs organized in systems, because we
know it is possible to observe moments in which communication takes
place without, beyond, before and against any system. We know that semiotics can study rules as well as processes–including those processes which
don't follow the rules. Nevertheless, if general semiotics has meaning, it has
it inasmuch as it is able to unify, to subsume under a single set of categories
of all the particular cases in which human beings (and to some extent also
animals, for certain scholars) use phonations, gestures, and natural or artificial objects in order to refer to other phenomena (objects, classes of objects
or states of affairs) that are not perceivable during certain interactions, and
which often do not exist, or exist only in a non-physical form.

Certainly it is easier to recognize the empirical existence of texts written
in Italian (studied by literary history or the history of the Italian language)
or of species of animals, than it is to recognize semiosic processes. It is for
this reason that semiotics works harder to gain recognition than does literary history or zoology; but it took just as much effort to construct a general concept of the atom–and this concept attained the status of a philosophical principle long before any empirical verification was possible.

Therefore, even if a sentence is different from an epic poem, and even if
the way we perceive Morse signals is different from the way we perceive the
form and chromatic shadings of a cloud, we maintain that in all cases,
whether explicitly or implicitly, a common mechanism is at work, no matter how disparate the outcomes may seem on the surface. If it is the same
physiopsychological apparatus that renders us capable of understanding
both the sentence *It will rain tomorrow* and the cloud which announces a
rainshower not yet experienced, then there must be something that allows
us to join these two different processes of perception, elaboration, predic-
tion and dominion over something that semiosis does not place before our
eyes.

In this sense a general semiotics is a branch of philosophy, or better still,
it is the way in which philosophy reflects on the problem of semiosis.

Then one can distinguish a general semiotics from a philosophy of language by stressing two peculiar features of a general semiotics. (1) Semiotics
tends to make its categories so general as to include and define not only
natural or formalized languages, but also every form of expression (even
those which seem alien to any grammatical organization), as well as the
processes for generating grammars that do not yet exist, the operations by
means of which one can break the rules of a given grammar (as it happens in
poetry), and also those phenomena that do not seem to be produced with
the aim of expressing something, but which can be nevertheless seen at the
starting point of an interpretive inference. (2) Semiotics tends to draw its
generalizations from its experience with grammars, to the point that philosophical reflection becomes heavily enmeshed in grammatical description.

In undertaking such an enterprise, semiotics evidently runs certain risks. Under the entry "Semiotics" which appears in the 1970's edition of the Garzanti *Enciclopedia Europea*, Raffaele Simone–after correctly reconstructing the history and problems of the discipline–goes on to cite the enlargement of the semiotic field from Saussure up to the present, extending from literature and logic to animal communication and psychology; an enlargement in which semiotics "goes so far as to aim to be the general science of culture." Simone comments: "In this excessive amplification of its horizon lie the reasons for [semiotics'] diffusion but also the germ of its eventual defeat: if all of culture is a sign, a single science that studies everything with the same concepts and the same methods is perhaps both too little and too much. It would be more useful to look to a variety of independent disciplines, each of which could cover an area of inquiry, even if this area was to be imbued with an awareness of the semiotic nature of the object of study."

There are a number of thinks to think about in this passage. I would eliminate the word "defeat" and replace it with "crisis" (for crises can also be periods of growth). I would like to reflect here on the "germs" of this crisis.

In his delineation of these germs, Simone was a bit optimistic: both in his reduction of the list of fields which semiotics invaded and in his accusation against semiotics–that it aimed to become the general science of culture. In effect–as a look at Simone's bibliography suffices to show–semiotics is actually much worse, going so far as to present itself as the general science of nature. Simone could not have missed the passage (an explicit one in Peirce) from a theory of the sign to a general theory of inference, and from there to the study not only of communication and signification, but also of the perceptive processes. Today semiotics tends to consider perception as a (fundamental) aspect of semiosis. On the other hand, if we take all the studies that have either the word *semiotic* in the title, or which appear in journals with this word in the title, as examples of semiotic research, we find this research extends to the world of nature, from zoosemiotics to the development of a phytosemiotics; to immunologists' interest in cellular semiosis, to the intertwining of brain sciences, artificial intelligence and semiotics. Twenty years ago, in *A Theory of Semiotics*, I placed all of these aspects of semiotics beyond a taboo threshold which I called the "lower threshold of semiotics." But this was above all an act of caution: one can decide, *ex professo*, not to address a series of problems without claiming that these problems do not exist.

Simone suggests that it would be more useful to look for a variety of independent disciplines, even all of them had to be imbued with an awareness of the semiotic nature of their object of study. I have to say that I am fairly inclined to subscribe to this view. I am convinced that semiotics does not exist as a scientific discipline. There are many specific semiotics, and often the same semiosic phenomenon gives rise to a range of theorizations and grammars. To put this in academic terms, "semiotics" should not be the name of a discipline, but rather that of a department or a school–just as there is no single discipline called "medicine" but instead schools entitled "school of medicine." Medicine was a single discipline in the days of Paracelsus and Galen, that is to say when it was in a primitive stage. Today the common object of the medical sciences is the human body, and the methods and approaches, like the specializations, are constantly changing. Under the headings of medicine we have surgery, biochemistry, dietetics, immunology and so on....

If you go to visit one of the best-stock scientific bookstores, the Harvard Bookstore at Harvard University, you will see that in the last ten years the shelves have been reorganized. In many American bookstores books about semiotics are erratically shelved. Occasionally they are under literary criticism; from time to time they are in a section that used to be called structuralism and which now (as Barnes & Noble has done in New York) is called "post-structuralism." At the Harvard Bookstore, however, there is a separate, quite extensive section which includes artificial intelligence, the brain sciences, logic and analytical philosophy, psychology of perception, linguistics and semiotics; and this section is entitled *Cognitive Sciences.*

No one in the United States has ever claimed that the cognitive sciences are a science, or a discipline; and everyone is in agreement about maintaining them as a sort of interdisciplinary aggregate with a common nucleus. And it does not displease me that semiotics has come to be included in this confederation, even if there are those who debate whether semiotics is a cognitive science or the cognitive sciences are a branch of semiotics. Even if we affirm that semiosis has become a central concept for our contemporary scientific paradigm–as the concept of nature or *res extensa–res cogitans* dyads were for other paradigms–then it is certain that many disciplines can derive inspiration from semiotic concepts, without necessarily being *a* semiotics.

But in order to be able to say this, it is necessary that there continue to be this discourse that I call general semiotics; a discourse that addresses the extent to which there is an object of study (or genus generalissimum) common to all these disciplines, and that also outlines the conditions necessary for its theorization. A general semiotics is necessary precisely because semiotics is not a unified science.

THE SITUATION OF THE PHILOSOPHY OF LANGUAGE

Philosophy of language seems to enjoy a more secure status only if one thinks of the classic English or American philosophy department, in which the sole analytical koiné is recognized. But (beyond the fact that even there many scholastic convictions have been challenged by such thinkers as Quine, Putnam, Goodman, and Rorty) a principle of tolerance oblige us to acknowledge, as philosophies of language, various other modes of philosophical reflection on homo loquens.

Many handbooks on philosophy of language are affected by a Fundamentalist Fallacy. The paramount case of Fundamentalist Fallacy is instantiated when one assumes-that his/her own philosophy is the only valid philosophy of language (and demands a universal agreement on such a statement).

We cannot speak of unified disciplinary criteria for the philosophy of language. For instance, on one side, the analytical current primarily deals with statements expressed in a natural language, and either evaluates them in truth functional terms, or tries to describe the linguistic usages and aims at curing the cramps that affect our everyday linguistic interactions; on the other side the hermeneutical oriented philosophies assign a revelatory role to language, analyze not common linguistic usages but poetic texts (where the very presence of semantic or pragmatic "cramps" becomes a condition for a fruitful ambiguity), and recur to a notion of truth that is completely different from the analytical one. To say nothing of deconstructionism, whose nature, as no one would deny, is that of a philosophical reflection on language, which is however born as analytico-repellent and truth-misfunctional.

It is very difficult to escape the Fundamentalist Fallacy. We could say that, when I write a book called, let's say, Talks with God, I have the right to believe that my religious confession is the sole guarantor of truth; whereas if I participate in the Council of Churches I am supposed to be-as the word "council" implies-more conciliatory. Nevertheless, if one decides to participate in the Council of Churches, then even one's personal talks with God should in some way come to be influenced by the tolerance that one has had to demonstrate towards other truths.

An example of the Fundamentalist Fallacy can be found in Greimas' and Courtés' work, Dictionnaire raisonné des sciences du langage (Semiotics and Language: An Analytical Dictionary. (Larry Crist, et al. (Trans). Bloomington, In.: Indiana UP, 1982)-and it is no accident that this is an expression used by the school antonomastically known as the Ecole de Paris). Many terms in use in the field of the sciences of language are redefined here in Greimasian terms; other definitions are omitted, as if extraneous, or else are completely ignored. Take, for example (this will delight the analytical philosophers), the Greimasian definition of "truth":

> Truth designates the complex term which subsumes the terms being and seeming situated on the axis of contraries within the semiotic square of veridictory

modalities. It might be helpful to point out that the "true" is situated within the discourse, for it is the fruit of the veridiction operations: this thus excludes any relation (or any homologation) with an external referent. (p. 353)

I wouldn't say I do not agree with this solution; but I would say it does not seem right to offer this as the only definition in a dictionnaire raisonné, or analytical dictionary, of language. I would raise the same objection to the Enciclopedia Einaudi, in which, under the entry "Semantics," Diego Marconi (after having defined semantics as the study of meaning) assumes that semantics is concerned only with natural languages, then goes on to devote the body of his article to model-theoretic semantics, to possible-worlds semantics and to the dictionary vs. encyclopedia debate. At the beginning of his article Marconi makes a passing mention of the so-called componential semantics, saying that it has enjoyed a certain vogue among linguists, and does not consider any semantics of lexicographic origin–that is to say, that of Trier, Matoré, Pottier, on down through Greimas.

In opting for a single notion of semantics (which leads to an entry that is, however, very satisfactory in terms of the limited sphere it does address) Marconi's article would present us with a manifestation of the Fundamentalist Fallacy, were it not for the fact that (and I know this from direct experience as one of the collaborators on this encyclopedia) it forms part of a work that never tried to be an encyclopedia (except as a commercial fiction) so much as a provocative collection of individual essays organized in alphabetical order. Its collaborators were asked to outline their own theoretical approach, since other authors, in other entries related to the same field (for instance, there is an entry of mine under the title "Meaning") were supposed to express different points of view.

The only way to escape the Fundamentalist Fallacy is Absolute Relativism. I served on the editorial board of another encyclopedia, the Encyclopedic Dictionary of Semiotics (Mouton-De Gruyter). In case of controversial entries the directory board decided to ask more than an author to provide a different approach–as frequently Diderot and D'Alembert did with the Encyclopedie. Thus, for example, the entry on "Semantics" starts with an excellent essay by Bierwisch, which sought to escape the often-fatal embrace between semantics and the study of natural languages. After defining semantics as the study of meaning, Bierwisch proposes a formula of the type "A interprets B as a representation of C," in which B stands for an object or event, not necessarily a phonation or verbal statement. The author lists all the problems and takes into account the various positions, but in the body of the article he provides them with a Bierwischian solution. The editorial board then took up the entry "Seme," by Henry Shogt, in which the positions of the linguists (from Lyons to Lamb and Pottier, from

Aspresjan to Melcuk, from Coseriu to Buyssens, Prieto, Greimas and so on) undergo close scrutiny. A perhaps not-indispensable entry on "Action-Theory Semantics," by Georg Meggle, was also included. I think that this was a pretty satisfactory criterion.

Unfortunately the publisher, for economical reasons, could not accept all the indications of the Board. Consequently some topics have several entries, some have only one whose partiality was left untempered. The total effect instantiated a case of Relative Relativism.

In the dictionary of Greimas we can find interesting cases of Non-Standard, or Limited Fundamentalist Fallacy. For historical reasons attributable to Greimas' background, the section on semantics begins with a review of the various lexicographic theories concerning the conceptual and semantic fields; then componential theories are taken into account. The entry goes on discussing the requirements of a generative semantics (thereby recognizing the work of the post-Chomskian generativists), deals with the necessity of a syntagmatic approach (how to go beyond the limits of a lexical taxonomy in order to outline a possible text-semantics) and ends by advocating a general semantics, which is not limited to the analysis of linguistic meanings but must also study the so-called "semantics of the natural world", insofar as this is manifested through various (and not merely linguistic) semiotic systems.

We cannot ask Greimas to take into account either truth functional semantics (given the position he has taken on the concept of truth) or model-theoretic or possible-worlds semantics (since his notion of modalité can be hardly related to modal logic). The Dictionary unfolds from there with entries devoted to the semantics of discourse, narrative semantics, seme and sememe, all rendered in a strictly Greimasian key. But, with these criticisms made, I believe that even philosophers of language with no interest in grammars would find it fruitful to read this collection of entries in order to know something more about the different senses, according to different schools of thought, of the word "semantics".

I cannot say which of the entries I have cited belong to the philosophy of language and which to semiotics. Marconi's seems to meet the criteria of the analytical koiné; Bierwisch's undoubtedly takes into account a "grammar of Meaning". Interestingly, Greimas's entries–while of course referring to the imposing narrative "grammar" which, for this thinker, presides over every manifestation of meaning–take such a grammar for granted, and seem to be aiming at a more ambitious philosophical project.

I feel that both the philosophers of language and the semioticians would do well to read these three entries, or group of entries, in order to see that the department or school of which the Harvard Bookstore shelves are the concrete allegory undoubtedly includes both these groups of scholars, and that the time has come for exchanges between them to take place above and beyond convenient labels. Besides, when a student asks me what semantics is, I suggest the two volumes of Lyons' *Semantics*, which provide a well-balanced and tolerant approach to the different traditions in this subject area. The fact of being on the one hand a linguist exposed to the Sirens of continental theory and, on the other, an insular Briton, has not been such a bad thing for Lyons.

DIFFERENCE

Structural semiotics has long suffered from two constraints. Of one of these we have already spoken, that is, the strict dependence on one specific grammar, namely that of verbal languages. The second constraint has been the attention to "languages" (verbal or non-verbal) as systems. This constraint can of course also be a point of strength, and is one to which scholars of different provenance should seriously consider.

I believe that when dealing with sentences and with their truth value, and/or their felicity conditions (that is, with linguistic processes), the analytical philosophers risk to forget that these processes are allowed by a linguistic system, or a structured set of semantic rules (even if Davidson would express doubt on this point). One can say that the exasperated attention given to systems has deterred many structuralists from studying process, but this cannot be said–for instance–of Benvéniste's analyses of discoursive processes, and among the Italian structuralists De Mauro was the first to decide that the signifying unit is not the word, but the sentence. Nevertheless, structural semiotics, in general, has preferred to analyze systems of signifying terms, whereas analytical philosophers analyzed series of true or false sentences. On the one hand there is a tradition that wonders if the feature "animal" is part of the meaning of dog, and on the other those for whom the problem is whether or not it is true that dogs are animals. I feel the moment has arrived to overcome this apparent difference of approach.

I am convinced that structuralist semiotics underwent the fascination of pragmatics only because this was introduced via the speech act theory born within the framework of the analytical philosophy of language. Pragmatics, as a term, was invented by Morris, and with Morris we are more on the side of Peirce and of the *Encyclopedia of Unified Science* than on that of Saussure. But I must say that it is the merit of the semioticians to have tackled pragmatics right off the bat, thus showing a great deal of receptivity to problems that at first seemed *extra moenia*.

I no longer know whether the first attention given to case grammars should be attributed to the philosophers of language or to the linguists: in any case the decision to shift from compositionalism to case grammars originated (speaking at least in terms of chronology, if not in terms of direct influence) in Tesnières' linguistics, Kenneth Burke's literary criticism, and in actantial semantics, textual linguistics, and narratology. If one can criticize the semioticians who design abstract systems, thereby ignoring the vicissitudes of our utterances in the concrete flux of daily speech, it is also necessary to reproach the others for continuing to transform everyday utterances into laboratory fictions (an endless series of bachelor-kings of France and bald evening stars...), never trying to approach "real" and complex texts–let's say, the way we are usually telling what happened during our vacations or the whole chapter of a novel.

The semiotic field is full of Formula Adventurers who call "formalization" their habit to use alphabetic symbols instead of words, thus mistaking formal calculus with shorthand. But many philosophers of language, enamored with formalization, remain always outside the actual experience of speaking.

It is a shame that Greimas constructed an entire theory of modalities which takes no account whatsoever of modal logic, but it is equally regrettable that many insular theoreticians of linguistic acts take no account of Bühler or of Jakobson's functions of language.

Much of semiotics, reacting against certain excesses of the truth functional semantics, has expunged the problem of reference from its sphere of study thus encouraging at the final end that semiotic heresy called deconstruction–according to which language is so omnipotent that it can only speak of its own impotence. I think it is fair–even for a formal logician–to succumb once in a while to the anguish of the vanishing of the subject, or to experience doubt about whether any transcendental meaning is possible; provided that the others recognize that life can also hang on the truth value of the statement *there is a storm today*–at least if we are in a plane that is taking off.

I would like to conclude by recalling a book that, ever since it came out, has seemed to me to begin to fill the gap between philosophy of language and semiotics. I am referring to *Languages of Art* by Nelson Goodman. The merit of this book is not only its most evident one of having taken the experience of a philosopher of language (whose job has long been understood as the analysis of verbal utterances) and putting it to work to find ways to legitimatize the existence of visual languages; its real merit is that of being an effort to construct adequate semiotic categories where logical and linguistic categories are unable to determine certain fundamental differences. I am thinking of the sections on "Examples and illustrations", the discussion of autographical and allographical arts, and so forth. There Goodman is starting to outline a *visual semiotics*.

And yet his entire book suffers continual problems when dealing with the representational character of images, because it fails to free itself from the idea of denotation, or to move on to look at the clusters of signification that a visual work can communicate above and beyond the fact that it more or less denotes something.

When Goodman asks if a gray-tone painting representing a landscape, and which certainly denotes a landscape, also denotes the property of grayness or is denoted by the predicate "gray", he tells us nothing about the signification that the color gray in this painting may have for one who views it. He seeks only to make a phenomenon of visual communication graspable in linguistic terms, and he thereby renounces the task of elaborating a semiotics of the visible. When he asks whether a red object *exemplifies* the property of *redness* (and in this case embarrassing questions arise if the object also exemplifies coextensive properties, such as trilaterality or triangularity) or whether it exemplifies the predicate *red* (in which case the problem arises of whether it also exemplifies the predicate *rouge* for a French person), or whether it exemplifies the denotation of this same predicate, Goodman tells us nothing about the signifying function that, for example, a red object has for a viewer of a film who has just watched a bloody scene a few seconds earlier. And to ask what red exemplifies in a priestly garment has nothing to do with the emblematic signification that red assumes (something that is not at all or not always translatable in verbal terms) in the semiotic system of liturgy.

In what is one of book's most interesting chapters, on the denotation of images, Goodman makes subtle distinctions between a "man-picture" and a "picture of a man," and asks multiple questions about the denotative modality of a painting which represents both the Duke and Duchess of Wellington. This painting could be said to denote at one and the same time both the couple and, in part, the Duke; and could thus be seen as a "two-person picture" and also, in part, as a "man-picture," yet would not be a representation of the Duke as two people... and so on. This is an interesting and even amusing set of questions that arise only if the painting is understood as the equivalent of a series of verbal sentences–and therefore, as the visual parasite of a verbal phenomenon. But the viewers of the portrait never worry about these problems (except in the extreme case of when the painting is used for identification purposes, as a photo on a passport is, or for historical-documentary purposes); nevertheless for them the portrait *means* something.

I went looking, somewhat randomly, among the semiotic studies of portraiture, and I found that the categories put into play, above and beyond the question of resemblance (I am citing here from Omar Calabrese's essay "La sintassi della vertigine: Sguardi, specchi e ritratti," VS 29, 1981) are, for example, oppositions concerning the framing of the image, the position of the hands, the relationship between the figure and the background, the direction of the gaze, and consequently the relationship between a portrayed person who looks outside the painting, and seems to know that he/she is being looked at by a viewer, and another one who is looking at something inside the painting but not at the viewer; and so on.

If we wanted to draw an analogy with linguistic questions we could do so by returning to the question of aspectuality. Of course no one would deny that *John is leaving the house, John used to leave the house, John left the house* and *John was leaving the house* all say different things and are not just different sentences expressing the same proposition. In order to find analogous phenomena in a visual work categories specific to this mode of representation would be needed, without short circuiting from the visual image to its clumsy verbal translation. Notice that I am not demarcating a difference between the semantic and the aesthetic functions of the painting; I am saying that either we grasp the semantic modes of the visual statement, or we are forced to deny to the visible the capability of communicating meanings; denying, too, that there are significations not immediately interpretable in linguistic terms.

Goodman's book certainly represents one of the most interesting attempts to build a bridge between theories of reference and theories of visual representation. But it suffers from excessive familiarity with a truth functional approach applied to verbal languages. I am inclined to view with equal severity all semiotic approaches that tend to forget that, if only in sociological terms, a portrait is also painted in order to speak of some aspect of the world.

In my ideal department, or School of the Disciplines of Language, many interconnections are still to be established. If the various currents and schools of thought are able to learn to speak to one another a bit more, it will also become possible to ask what does it mean to speak–whether it be with one's tongue or by some other means.

Umberto Eco

Innovation and Repetition: Between Modern and Post-Modern Aesthetics*

It is not by chance that modern aesthetics and modern theories of art (and I mean by "modern" those born with Mannerism, developed through Romanticism, and provocatively restated by the early-twentieth-century avant-gardes) have frequently identified the artistic message with metaphor. Metaphor (the new and inventive one, not the worn-out catachresis) is a way to designate something by the name of something else, thus presenting that something in an unexpected way. The modern criterion for recognizing the artistic value was *novelty*, high information. The pleasurable repetition of an already known pattern was considered, by modern theories of art, typical of Crafts–not of Art–and of industry.

A good craftsman, as well as an industrial factory, produces many *tokens*, or occurrences, of the same *type* or model. One appreciates the type, and appreciates the way the token meets the requirements of the type: but the modern aesthetics did not recognize such a procedure as an artistic one. That is why the Romantic aesthetics made such a careful distinction between "major" and "minor" arts, between arts and crafts. To make a parallel with sciences: crafts and industry were similar to the correct application of an already-known law to a new case. Art, on the contrary (and by art I mean also literature, poetry, movies, and so on) corresponded rather to a "scientific revolution": every work of modern art figures out a new law, imposes a *new paradigm*, a new way of looking at the world.

Modern aesthetics frequently forgot that the classical theory of art, from ancient Greece to the Middle Ages, was not so eager to stress a distinction between arts and crafts. The same term (*techne, ars*) was used to designate both the performance of a barber or a ship-builder, the work of a painter or a poet. The classical aesthetics was not so anxious for innovation at any cost: on the contrary, it frequently appreciated as "beautiful" the good tokens of an everlasting type. Even in those cases in which modern sensibility enjoys the "revolution" performed by a classical artist, his contemporary enjoyed the opposite aspect of his work, that is, his respect for previous models.[1]

This is the reason why modern aesthetics was so severe apropos the industrial-like products of the mass media. A popular song, a TV commercial, a comic strip, a detective novel, a Western movie were seen as more or less successful tokens of a given model or type. As such they were judged as pleasurable but non-artistic. Furthermore, this excess of pleasurability, repetition, lack of innovation, was felt as a commercial trick (the product had to meet the expectations of its audience), not as the provocative proposal of a new (and difficult to accept) world vision. The products of mass media were equated with the products of industry insofar as they were produced in series, and the "serial" production was considered as alien to the artistic invention.

REDUNDANCE AND REPETITION IN THE MASS MEDIA

According to the modern aesthetics, the principal features of the mass-media products were repetition, iteration, obedience to a pre-established schema, and redundancy (as opposed to information).[2]

The device of *iteration* is typical, for instance, of television commercials: one distractedly watches the playing out of a sketch, then focuses one's attention on the punch line that reappears at the end of the episode. It is precisely on this foreseen and awaited reappearance that our modest but irrefutable pleasure is based.

Likewise, the reading of a traditional detective story presumes the enjoyment of a scheme. The scheme is so important that the most famous authors have founded their fortune on its very immutability.

Furthermore, the writer plays upon a continuous series of connotations (for example, the characteristics of the detective and of his immediate "entourage") to such an extent that their reappearance in each story is an essential condition of its reading pleasure. And so we have the by now historical "tics" of Sherlock Holmes, the punctilious vanity of Hercule Poirot, the pipe and the familiar fixes of Maigret, on up to the famous idiosyncrasies of the most unabashed heroes of the hard-boiled novel. Vices, gestures, habits of the character portrayed permit us to recognize an old friend. These familiar features allow us to "enter into" the event. When our favorite author writes a story in which the usual characters do not appear, we are not even aware that the fundamental scheme of the story is still like the others we read the book with a certain detachment and are immediately prone to judge it a "minor" one.

All this becomes very clear if we take a famous character such as Nero Wolfe, immortalized by Rex Stout. I shall review here the main characteristics of Nero Wolfe and his partners because it is important to ascertain how important they are for the reader of Stout's books. Nero Wolfe, from Montenegro, a naturalized American from time immemorial, is outlandishly fat, so much so that his leather easy chair must be expressly designed for him. He is fearfully lazy. In fact, he never leaves the house and depends for his investigations on the smart and brilliant Archie Goodwin, with whom he indulges in a continuous sharp and tense polemic, tempered somewhat by their mutual sense of humor. Nero Wolfe is an absolute glutton, and his cook, Fritz, is the vestal virgin in the pantry, devoted to the unending care of this highly cultivated palate and equally greedy stomach; but along with the pleasures of the table, Wolfe cultivates an all-absorbing and exclusive passion for orchids; he has a priceless collection in the greenhouse on the top floor of the villa where he lives. Quite possessed by gluttony and flowers, assailed by a series of accessory tics (love of scholarly literature, systematic misogyny, insatiable thirst for money), Nero Wolfe conducts his investigations, masterpieces of psychological penetration, sitting in his office, carefully weighing the information verbally furnished by Archie, studying the protagonists of each event who are obliged to visit him in his office, arguing with Inspector Cramer (attention: he always holds a methodically extinguished cigar in his mouth), quarreling with the odious Sergeant Purley Stebbins, and, finally, in a fixed setting from which he never veers, summoning the protagonists of the case to a meeting in his studio, usually in the evening. There, with skillful dialectical subterfuges, almost always before he himself knows the truth, he drives the guilty one into a public demonstration of hysteria by which he gives himself away.

The gamut is much more ample: Archie's almost canonical arrest under suspicion of reticence and false testimony; the legal diatribes about the conditions on which Wolfe will take on a client; the hiring of part-time agents like Saul Panzer or Orrie Carther; the painting in the studio behind which Wolfe or Archie can watch, through a peephole, the behavior and reactions of a subject put to the test in the office itself; the scenes with Wolfe and an insincere client .... Such is the "eternal" story that the faithful reader enjoys in Stout's novels. To make it palatable, the author must invent every time a "new" crime and "new" secondary characters, but these details only serve to reconfirm the permanence of a fixed repertoire of *topoi*.

Not knowing who the guilty party is becomes an accessory element, almost a pretext. It is not a matter of discovering who committed the crime, but, rather, of following certain "topical" gestures of "topical" characters whose stock behavior we already love. The reader, little interested in the "new" psychological or economic motivations of the "new" crime, in fact enjoys those moments when Wolfe repeats his usual gestures, when he goes up for the nth time to take care of his orchids while the case itself is reaching its dramatic climax, when Inspector Cramer threateningly enters with one foot between the door and the wall, pushing aside Goodwin and warning Wolfe with a shake of his finger that this time things will not go so smoothly. The attraction of the book, the sense of repose, of psychological extension which it is capable of conferring, lies in the fact that, plopped in an easy chair or in the seat of a train compartment, the readers continuously recover, point by point, what they already know, and what they want to know again: that is why they have purchased the book. They derive pleasure from the non-story (if indeed a story is a development of events which should bring us from the point of departure to a point of arrival where we would never have dreamed of arriving); the distraction consists in the refutation of a development of events, in a withdrawal from the tension of past-present-future to the focus on an *instant*, which is loved precisely because it is recurrent.

It seems that mechanisms of this kind proliferate more widely in the popular narrative of today than in the eighteenth-century romantic *feuilleton*, where the event was founded upon a *development* and where the characters were required to march towards their death in the course of unexpected and "incredible" adventures.

If this were true, it would be because the feuilleton, founded on the triumph of information, represented the preferred fare of a society that lived in the midst of messages loaded with redundancy; the sense of tradition, the norms of social life, moral principles, the rules of proper comportment in the framework of a bourgeois society designed a system of foreseeable messages that the social system provided for its members, and which allowed life to flow smoothly without unexpected jolts. In this sphere, the "informative" shock of a short story by Poe or the *coup de théâtre* of Ponson du Terrail provided the enjoyment of the "rupture." In a contemporary industrial society, instead, the social change, the continuous rise of new behavioral standards, the dissolution of tradition, require a narrative based upon redundancy. Redundant narrative structures would appear in this panorama as an indulgent invitation to repose, a chance of relaxing.

In fact, even the nineteenth-century novel was repetitive. Its fundamental patterns were always the same, and it was not so difficult, for a smart reader, to tell before the end of the story if Miss So-and-So was or was not the lost daughter of the duke of X. One can only say that the nineteenth-century feuilleton and contemporary mass media use *different* devices for making the expected appear unexpected. Archie Goodwin is explicitly expecting, with the readers, that Nero Wolfe will act in a certain way, while Eugène Sue pretended not to know in advance what her readers suspected, namely, that Fleur-de-Marie was the daughter of Rodolphe of Gerolstein. The formal principle does not change.

Perhaps one of the first inexhaustible characters during the decline of the feuilleton and bridging the two centuries at the close of *la belle époque* is Fantomas. Each episode of Fantomas closes with a kind of "unsuccessful catharsis"; Juve and Fandor finally come to get their hands on the elusive one when he, with an unforeseeable move, foils the arrest. Another singular fact: Fantomas, responsible for blackmail and sensational kidnappings, at the beginning of each episode finds himself inexplicably poor and in need of money and, therefore, also of new "action." In this way the cycle is kept going.

THE ERA OF REPETITION

I would like to consider now the case of an historical period (our own) for which iteration and repetition seem to dominate the whole world of artistic creativity, and in which it is difficult to distinguish between the repetition of the media and the repetition of the so-called major arts. In this period one is facing the discussion of a new theory of art, one that I would label *post-modern aesthetics*, which is revisiting the very concepts of repetition and iteration under a different profile. Recently in Italy such a debate has flourished under the standard of a "new aesthetics of seriality." I recommend my readers to take "seriality," in this case, as a very wide category or, if one wants, as another term for repetitive art.

Seriality and repetition are largely inflated concepts. The philosophy of the history of art has accustomed us to some technical meanings of these terms that it would be well to eliminate: I shall not speak of repetition in the sense of Kierkegaard, nor of "répétition différente," in the sense of Deleuze. In the history of contemporary music, series and seriality have been understood in a sense more or less opposite what we are discussing here. The dodecaphonic "series" is the opposite of the repetitive seriality typical of all the media, because there a given succession of twelve sounds is used once and only once within a single composition.

If you open a current dictionary, you will find that for "repeat" the meaning is "to say something or do something the second time or again and again; iteration of the same word, act or idea." For "series" the meaning is "a continued succession of similar things." It is a matter of establishing what it means to say "again" or "the same or similar things."

To serialize means, in some way, to *repeat*. Therefore, we shall have to define a first meaning of "to repeat" by which the term means to make a replica of the same abstract type. Two sheets of typewriter paper are both replicas of the same commercial type. In this sense one thing is the same as another when the former exhibits the same properties as the latter, at least under a certain description: two sheets of typing paper are the same from the point of view of our functional needs, even though they are not the same for a physicist interested in the molecular structure of the objects. From the point of view of industrial mass production, two "tokens" can be considered as "replicas" of the same "type" when for a normal person with normal requirements, in the absence of evident imperfection, it is irrelevant whether one chooses one instead of the other. Two copies of a film or of a book are replicas of the same type.

The repetitiveness and the seriality that interests us here look instead at something that at first glance does not appear the same as (equal to) something else.

Let us now see the case in which (1) something is offered as original and different (according to the requirements of modern aesthetics) (2) we are aware that this something is repeating something else that we already know; and (3) notwithstanding this–better, just because of it–we like it (and we buy it).

The Retake

The first type of repetition is the retake. In this case one recycles the characters of a previous successful story in order to exploit them, by telling what happened to them after the end of their first adventure The most famous example of retake is Dumas's Twenty Years Later the most recent ones are the "to be continued" versions of Star Wars or Superman. The retake is dependent on a commercial decision. There is no rule establishing whether the second episode of the story should reproduce, with only slight variations, the first one, or must be a totally different story concerning the same characters. The retake is not strictly condemned to repetition. An illustrious example of retake are the many different stories of the Arthurian cycle, telling again and again the vicissitudes of Lancelot or Perceval.

The Remake

The remake consists in telling again a previous successful story. See the innumerable editions of Dr. Jekyll or of Mutiny on the Bounty. The history of arts and literature is full of pseudo-remakes that were able to tell at every time something different. The whole of Shakespeare is a remake of preceding stories. Therefore "interesting" remakes can escape repetition.

The Series

The series works upon a fixed situation and a restricted number of fixed pivotal characters, around whom the secondary and changing ones turn. The secondary characters must give the impression that the new story is different from the preceding ones, while in fact the narrative scheme does not change. I have said something above on the scheme of the novels by Rex Stout.

To the same type belong the TV serials such as All in the Family, Starsky and Hutch, Columbo, etc. (I put together different TV genres that range from soap opera to situation comedy, and to the detective serial).

With a series one believes one is enjoying the novelty of the story (which is always the same) while in fact one is enjoying it because of the recurrence of a narrative scheme that remains constant. The series in this sense responds to the infantile need of hearing again always the same story, of being consoled by the "return of the Identical," superficially disguised.

The series consoles us (the consumers) because it rewards our ability to foresee: we are happy because we discover our own ability to guess what will happen. We are satisfied because we find again what we had expected, but we do not attribute this happy result to the obviousness of the narrative structure, but to our own presumed capacities to make forecasts. We do not think, "The author has constructed the story in a way that I could guess the end," but rather, "I was so smart to guess the end in spite of the efforts the author made to deceive me."

We find a variation of the series in the structure of the flashback: we see, for example, some comic-strip stories (such as Superman) in which the character is not followed along in a straight line during the course of his life, but is continually rediscovered at different moments of his life, obsessively revisited in order to discover there new opportunities for new narratives. It seems as if these moments of his life have fled from the narrator out of absent-mindedness, but their rediscovery does not change the psychological profile of the character, which is fixed already, once and for all. In topological terms this sub-type of the series may be defined as a loop.

Usually the loop-series comes to be devised for commercial reasons: it is a matter of considering how to keep the series alive, of obviating the natural problem of the aging of the character. Instead of having characters put up with new adventures (that would imply their inexorable march toward death), they are made continually to relive their past. The loop solution produces paradoxes that were already the target of innumerable parodies. Characters have a little future but an enormous past, and in any case, nothing of their past will ever have to change the mythological present in which they have been presented to the reader from the beginning. Ten different lives would not suffice to make Little Orphan Annie undergo what she underwent in the first (and only) ten years of her life.

The spiral is another variation of the series. In the stories of Charlie Brown, apparently nothing happens, and any character is obsessively repeating his/her standard performance. And yet in every strip the character of Charlie Brown or Snoopy is enriched and deepened. This does not happen either with Nero Wolfe, or Starsky or Hutch: we are always interested in their new adventures, but we already know all we need to know about their psychology, their habits, their capacities, their ethical standpoints.

I would add finally that form of seriality that, in cinema and television, is motivated less by the narrative structure than by the nature of the actor himself: the mere presence of John Wayne, or of Jerry Lewis (when they are not directed by a great director, and even In these cases) succeeds in making, always, the same film. The author tries to invent different stories, but the public recognizes (with satisfaction) always and ever the same story, under superficial disguises.

The Saga

The saga differs from the series insofar as it concerns the story of a family and is interested in the "historical" lapse of time It is genealogical. In the saga, the actors do age; the saga is a history of the aging of individuals, families, people, groups.

The saga can have a continuous lineage (the character is followed from birth to death; the same is then done for his son, his grandson and so on, potentially forever), or it can be tree-like (there is a patriarch, then the various narrative branches that concern not only his direct descendants, but also the collateral lines and the kin, each branch branching out infinitely). The most familiar (and recent) instance of saga is certainly Dallas.

The saga is a series in disguise. It differs from the series in that the characters change (they change also because the actors age) But in reality the saga repeats, in spite of its historicized form, celebrating in appearance the passage of time, the same story. As with ancient sagas, the deeds of the gallant ancestors are the same as the deeds of their descendants. In Dallas grandfathers and grandsons undergo more or less the same ordeals: struggle for wealth and for power, life, death, defeat, victory, adultery, love, hate, envy, illusion, and delusion.

Intertextual Dialogue

I mean by intertextual dialogue the phenomenon by which a given text echoes previous texts. Many forms of intertextuality are outside my present concerns. I am not interested, for example, in stylistic quotation, in those cases in which a text quotes, in a more or less explicit way, a stylistic feature, a way of narrating typical of another author either as a form of parody or In order to pay homage to a great and acknowledged master. There are imperceptible quotations, of which not even the author is aware, that are the normal effect of the game of artistic influence. There are also quotations of which the author is aware but that should remain ungraspable by the consumer; in these cases we are usually in the presence of a banal work and plagiarism.

What is more interesting is when the quotation is explicit and recognizable, as happens in literature or post-modern art, which blatantly and ironically play on intertextuality (novel on the techniques of the narrative, poetry on poetry, art on art).

There is a procedure typical of the post-modern narrative that has been much used recently in the field of mass communications: it concerns the ironic quotation of the commonplace (topos). Let us remember the killing of the Arab giant in Raiders of the Lost Ark and the staircase of Odessa in Woody Allen's Bananas. What joins these two quotations? In both cases, the spectator, in order to enjoy the allusion, must know the original topoi. In the case of the giant, it is a situation typical of the genre; in the case of Bananas–on the contrary–the topos appears for the first and only time in a single work, and only after that quotation the topos becomes a shibboleth for movie critics and moviegoers.

In both cases the topoi are recorded by the "encyclopedia" of the spectator; they make up a part of the treasury of the collective imagination and as such they come to be called upon. What differentiates the two quotations is the fact that the topos in *Raiders* is quoted in order to contradict it (what we expect to happen, based on our experience, will not), while in *Bananas* the topos is introduced only because of its incongruity (the staircase has nothing to do with the rest of the story).

The first case recalls the series of cartoons that was published years ago by *Mad* under the heading "a film which we would like to see " For example, the heroine, in the West, tied by bandits to the railroad tracks: the alternating shots show on one side the approaching train and on the other the furious cavalcade of rescuers trying to arrive ahead of the locomotive. In the end, the girl (contrary to all the expectations suggested by the topos evoked) is crushed by the train Here we are faced with a comic ploy which exploits the presupposition (correct) that the public will recognize the original topos, will apply to the quotation the "normal" system of expectations (I mean the expectations that this piece of encyclopedical information is supposed to elicit), and will then enjoy the way in which its expectations are frustrated. At this point the ingenuous spectator, at first frustrated, overcomes his frustration and transforms himself into a critical spectator who appreciates the way in which he was tricked.

In the case of *Bananas* however, we are at a different level the spectator with whom the text establishes an implicit agreement (tongue-in-cheek) is not the ingenuous spectator (who can be struck at most by the apparition of an incongruous event) but the critical spectator who appreciates the ironic ploy of the quotation and enjoys its desired incongruity. However, in both cases we have a critical side-effect aware of the quotation, the spectator is brought to elaborate ironically on the nature of such a device and to acknowledge the fact that he has been invited to play upon his encyclopedic competence.

The game becomes complicated in the "retake" of *Raiders* that is in *Indiana Jones and the Temple of Doom*: here the hero encounters not one but two giant enemies. In the first case, we are expecting that according to the classical schemes of the adventure film, the hero will be disarmed, and we laugh when we discover that instead the hero as a pistol and easily kills his adversary. In the second case, the rector knows that the spectators (having already seen the preceding m), will expect the hero to be armed, and indeed, Indiana Jones quickly looks for his pistol. He does not find it, and the spectators laugh because the expectation created by the first film is this time frustrated.

The cases cited put into play an intertextual encyclopedia. We have texts that are quoted from other texts and the knowledge of the preceding ones–taken for granted–is supposed to be necessary for the enjoyment of the new one.

More interesting for the analysis of the new intertextuality in the media is the example of *E.T.*, in the scene where the creature from outer space (an invention of Spielberg) is led into a city during Halloween and encounters another personage, disguised as the gnome in *The Empire Strikes Back* (an invention of Lucas). E.T. is jolted and seeks to hurl himself upon the gnome in order to embrace him, as if he had met an old friend. Here the spectators must know many things: they must certainly know of the existence of another film (intertextual knowledge), but they must also know that both monsters were created by Rambaldi, that the directors of the two films are linked together for various reasons (not least because they are the two most successful directors of the decade); they must, in short, have not only a knowledge of the texts but also a knowledge of the world, circumstances external to the texts. One notices, naturally, that knowledge of the texts and the world are only two possible chapters of encyclopedic knowledge, and that therefore, in a certain measure, the text always makes reference to the same cultural patrimony.

Such phenomena of "intertextual dialogue" were once typical of experimental art, and presupposed a Model Reader, culturally very sophisticated.[3] The fact that similar devices have now become more common in the media world leads us to see that the media are carrying on–and presupposing–the possession of pieces of information already conveyed by other media.

The text of *E.T.* "knows" that the public has learned, from newspapers or from television, everything about Rambaldi, Lucas, and Spielberg. The media seem, in this play of extratextual quotation, to make reference to the world, but in effect they are referring to the contents of other messages sent by other media. The game is played, so to speak, on a "broadened" intertextuality. Any difference between knowledge of the world (understood naively as a knowledge derived from an extratextual experience) and intertextual knowledge has practically vanished. Our reflections to come, then, must not only question the phenomenon of repetition within a single work or a series of works, but all the phenomena that make various strategies of repetition producible, understandable, and commercially possible. In other words, repetition and seriality in the media pose new problems for the sociology of culture.

Another form of intertextuality is the genre-embedding that today is very common in the mass media. For example, every Broadway musical (in the theater or on film) is, as a rule, nothing other than the story of how a Broadway musical is put on. The Broadway genre seems to require (postulate) a vast intertextual knowledge: in fact, it creates and institutes the required competence and the presuppositions indispensable to its understanding. Every one of these films or plays tells how a Broadway musical is put on, and furnishes us, in effect, with all the information about the genre it belongs to. The spectacle gives the public the sensation of knowing ahead of time that which it does not yet know and will know only at the moment. We stand facing the case of a colossal preterition (or "passing over"). In this sense, the musical is a didactic work that takes account of the (idealized) rules of its own production.

Finally, we have the work that speaks of itself: not the work that speaks of a genre to which it belongs, but a work that speaks of its own structure, and of the way in which it was made. Critics and aestheticians were inclined to think that this device was an exclusive feature of the works of the avant-garde and alien to mass communications. Aesthetics knows this problem and indeed gave it a name long ago: it is the Hegelian problem of the Death of Art. But in these later times there have been cases of productions in the mass media capable of self-irony, and some of the examples mentioned above seem to me of great interest. Even here the line between "high-brow" arts and "low-brow" arts seems to have become very thin.

A Moderated or "Modern" Aesthetic Solution

Let us now try to review the phenomena listed above from the point of view of a "modern" conception of aesthetic value, according to which every work aesthetically "well done" is endowed with two characteristics:

(1) It must achieve a dialectic between order and novelty–in other words, between scheme and innovation;

(2) This dialectic must be perceived by the consumer, who must not only grasp the contents of the message, but also the way in which the message transmits those contents.

This being the case, nothing prevents the types of repetition listed above from achieving the conditions necessary to the realization of aesthetic value, and the history of the arts is ready to furnish us with satisfactory examples for each of the types in our classification.

Retake. Ariosto's *Orlando Furioso* is nothing else but a retake of Boiardo's *Orlando Innamorato* and precisely because of the success of the first, which was in its turn a retake of the themes of the Breton cycle. Boiardo and Ariosto added a goodly amount of irony into material that was very "serious" and "taken seriously" by previous readers. But even the third Superman is ironical in regard to the first (mystical and very, very serious). It appears as the retake of an archetype inspired by the gospel, made by winking at the films of Frank Tashlin.

Remake. I have already suggested that Shakespeare remade a lot of very well-known stories of the previous centuries.

Series. Every text presupposes and constructs always a double Model Reader (let us say, a naive and a "smart" one). The former uses the work as semantic machinery and is the victim of the strategies of the author who will lead him little by little along a series of previsions and expectations; the latter evaluates the work as an aesthetic product and enjoys the strategies implemented in order to produce a model reader of the first level. This second-level reader is the one who enjoys the seriality of the series, not so much for the return of the same thing (that the ingenuous reader believed was different) but for the strategy of the variations; in other words, he enjoys the way in which the same story is worked over to appear to be different.

This enjoyment of variations is obviously encouraged by the more sophisticated series. Indeed, we can classify the products of serial narratives along a continuum that takes into account the different gradations of the reading agreement between the text and the "smart" reader (as opposed to the naive one). It is evident that even the most banal narrative product allows the reader to become, by an autonomous decision, a critical reader, able to recognize the innovative strategies (if any). But there are serial works that establish an explicit agreement with the critical reader and thus, so to speak challenge him to acknowledge the innovative aspects of the text.

Belonging to this category are the television films of Lieutenant Columbo. It is worth noticing that in this series the authors spell out from the beginning who the murderer is. The spectator is not so much invited to play the naive game of guessing (whodunit?) as (1) to enjoy Columbo s detection technique, appreciated as an encore to a well-known piece of bravura (and in this sense the pleasure provided by Columbo is not so different from the one provided by Nero Wolfe) and (2) to discover in what way the author will succeed in winning his bet, which consists in having Columbo do what he always does, but nevertheless in a way that is not banally repetitive. Every story of Nero Wolfe was written by Rex Stout, but every episode of Columbo is directed by a different person. The critical addressee is invited to pronounce a judgment on the best variation.

I use the term "variation" thinking of the classical musical variations. They, too, were "serial products" that aimed very little at the naive addressee and that bet everything on an agreement with the critical one. The composer was fundamentally interested only in the applause of the critical listener, who was supposed to appreciate the fantasy displayed in his innovations on an old theme.

In this sense, seriality and repetition are not opposed to innovation nothing is more "serial" than a tie pattern, and yet nothing can be so personalized as a tie. The example may be elementary, but that does not make it banal. Between the elementary aesthetics of the tie and the recognized "high" artistic value of the Goldberg Variations, there is a gradated continuum of repetitious strategies, aimed at the response of the "smart" addressee.

The problem is that there is not, on the one hand, an aesthetics of high" art (original and not serial), and on the other a pure sociology of the serial. Rather, there is an aesthetics of serial forms that requires an historical and anthropological study of the ways in which, at different times and in different places, the dialectic between repetition and innovation has been instantiated. When we fail to find innovation in the serial, this is perhaps less a result of the structures of the text, than of our "horizon of expectations" and our cultural habits. We know very well that in certain examples of non-Western art where we always see the same thing, the natives recognize infinitesimal variations and feel the shiver of innovation. Where we see innovation, at least in the serial forms of the Western past, the original addressees were not at all interested in that aspect and conversely enjoyed the recurrences of the scheme.

Saga. The entire *Human Comedy* by Balzac presents a very good example of a tree-like saga, as much as *Dallas* does. Balzac is more interesting than *Dallas* because every one of his novels increases our knowledge of the society of his time, while every program of *Dallas* tells us the *same* thing about American society–but both use the same narrative scheme.

Intertextuality. The notion of intertextuality itself has been elaborated within the framework of a reflection on "high" art. Notwithstanding, the examples given above have been taken up provocatively by the world of mass communication in order to show how even these forms of intertextual dialogue have by now been transferred to the field of popular production.

It is typical of what is called post-modern literature and art (but did it not already happen thus with the music of Stravinsky?) to quote by using (sometimes under various stylistic disguises) *quotation marks* so that the reader pays no attention to the content of the citation but instead to the way in which the excerpt from a first text is introduced into the fabric of a second one. Renato Barilli has observed that one of the risks of this procedure is the failure to make the quotation marks evident, so that what is cited is accepted by the naive reader as an original invention rather than as an ironic reference.[4]

We have so far put forward three examples of quotations of a previous topos: *Raiders of the Lost Ark*, *Bananas* and *E.T.* Let us look closer at the third case: the spectator who knows nothing of the production of two films (in which one quotes from the other) cannot succeed in understanding why what happens does happen. By that gag, the movie focuses both upon movies and upon the media universe. The understanding of this device is a condition for its aesthetic enjoyment. Thus, this episode can work only if one realizes that there are quotation marks somewhere. One can say that these marks can be perceived only on the basis of an extratextual knowledge. Nothing *in the film* helps the spectator to understand at what point there ought to be quotation marks. The film presupposes a previous world-knowledge on the part of the spectator. And if the spectator does not know? Too bad. The effect gets lost, but the film knows of other means to gain approval.

These imperceptible quotation marks, more than an aesthetic device, are a social artifice; they select the happy few (and the mass media usually hopes to produce millions of happy few ....). To the naive spectator of the first level, the film has already given almost too much: that secret pleasure is reserved, for that time, for the critical spectator of the second level.

The case of *Raiders* is different. Here, if the critical spectator fails–does not recognize the quotation–there remain plenty of possibilities for the naive spectator, who at least can always enjoy the fact that the hero gets the best of his adversary. We are here confronted by a less subtle strategy than in the preceding example, a mode inclined to satisfy the urgent need of the producer, who in any case must sell his product to whomever he can. While it is difficult to imagine *Raiders* being seen and enjoyed by those spectators who do not grasp the interplay of quotations, it is always possible that this will happen, and the work is clearly open even to this possibility.

I do not feel like saying which, between the two texts cited, pursues the "more aesthetically noble" ends. It is enough for me (and perhaps or the moment I have already given myself much to think about) to point out a (critically relevant) difference in the functioning and use of textual strategy.

We come now to the case of *Bananas*. On that staircase there descend, not only a baby carriage, but also a platoon of rabbis and I do not remember what else. What happens to the spectator who has not caught the quotation from the *Potemkin* mixed up with imprecise ancies about the *Fiddler on the Roof*? I believe that because of the orgiastic energy with which the scene–the staircase with its incongruous population–is presented, even the most naive spectator may grasp the symphonic turbulence of this Brueghel-like kermis. Even the most ingenuous among the spectators "feels" a rhythm, an invent on, and cannot help but fix his attention on the way it is put together.

At the extreme other end of the pole of the aesthetic interests, I would like to mention a work whose equivalent I have not succeeded In finding In the contemporary mass media; it is not only a masterpiece of intertextuality but also a paramount example of narrative metalanguage, which speaks of its own formation and of the rules of the narrative genre: I refer to *Tristram Shandy*.

It is impossible to read and enjoy Sterne's anti-novel novel without realizing that it is treating the novel form ironically. *Tristram Shandy* is so aware of its nature that it is impossible to find there a single ironical statement that does not make evident its own quotation marks. It brings to a high artistic resolution the rhetorical device called *pronuntiatio* (that is, the way of stressing imperceptibly the irony).

I believe that I have singled out a typology of "quotation marking" that must in some way be relevant to the ends of a phenomenology of aesthetic value, and of the pleasure that follows from it. I believe further that the strategies for matching surprise and novelty with repetition, even if they are semiotic devices in themselves aesthetically neutral, can give place to different results on the aesthetic level.

Some conclusions follow:

Each of the types of repetition that we have examined is not limited to the mass media, but belongs by right to the entire history of artistic creativity: plagiarism, quotation, parody, the ironic retake, the intertextual joke, are typical of the entire artistic-literary tradition.

Much art has been and is repetitive. The concept of absolute originality is a contemporary one, born with Romanticism; classical art was in vast measure serial, and the "modern" avant-garde (at the beginning of this century) challenged the Romantic idea of "creation from nothingness," with its techniques of collage, mustachios on the Mona Lisa, art about art, and so on.

The same type of repetitive procedure can produce either excellence or banality; it can put the addressees into conflict with themselves and with the intertextual tradition as a whole; thus it can provide them with easy consolations, projections, identifications: it can establish an agreement exclusively with the naive addressee, or exclusively with the smart one, or with both at different levels and along a continuum of solutions that cannot be reduced to a rudimentary typology.

Nevertheless, a typology of repetition does not furnish the criteria that can establish differences in aesthetic values.

Yet, since the various types of repetition are present in the whole of artistic and literary history, they can be taken into account in order to

establish criteria of artistic value. An aesthetics of repetition requires as a
premise a semiotics of the textual procedures of repetition.

A RADICAL OR "POST-MODERN" AESTHETIC SOLUTION

I realize that all I have said until now still represents an attempt to reconsider the various forms of repetition in the media in terms of the "modern"
dialectic between order and innovation. The fact, however, is that when
one speaks today of the aesthetics of seriality, one alludes to something
more radical, that is, to a notion of aesthetic value that wholly escapes the
"modern" idea of art and literature.[5]

It has been observed that with the phenomenon of television serials we
find a new concept of "the infinity of the text"; the text takes on the
rhythms of that same dailiness in which it is produced, and that it mirrors.
The problem is not one of recognizing that the serial text varies indefinitely
upon a basic scheme (and in this sense it can be judged from the point of
view of the "modern" aesthetics). The real problem is that what is of interest is not so much the single variations as "variability" as a formal principle,
the fact that one can make variations to infinity. Variability to infinity has
all the characteristics of repetition, and very little of innovation. But it is
the "infinity" of the process that gives a new sense to the device of variation. What must be enjoyed–suggests the post-modern aesthetics–is the fact
that a series of possible variations is potentially infinite. What becomes
celebrated here is a sort of victory of life over art, with the paradoxical
result that the era of electronics–instead of emphasizing the phenomena of
shock, interruptions, novelty, and frustration of expectations–would produce a return to the continuum, the Cyclical, the Periodical, the Regular.

Omar Calabrese has thoroughly looked into this:[6] from the point of
view of the "modern" dialectic between repetition and innovation, one can
easily recognize how in the Columbo series, for example, on a basic scheme
some of the best names in American cinema have worked in variations.
Thus it would be difficult to speak, in such a case, of pure repetition: if the
scheme of the detection and the psychology of the protagonist actor remains unchanged, the style of the narrative changes each time. This is no
small thing, especially from the point of view of the "modern" aesthetics.
But it is exactly on a different idea of style that Calabrese's paper is
centered. In these forms of repetition "we are not so much interested in
what is repeated as we are in the way the components of the text come to be
segmented and then how the segments come to be codified in order to establish a system of invariants: any component that does not belong to the
system, can be defined as an *independent variable*. In the most typical and
apparently "degenerated" cases of seriality, the independent variables are

not altogether the more visible, but the more microscopic, as in a homeo-
pathic solution where the potion is all the more potent because by further
"succussions" the original particles of the medicinal product have almost
disappeared. This is what permits Calabrese to speak of the Columbo series
as an "exercice de style" à la Queneau. We are, says Calabrese, facing a
"neobaroque aesthetics" that is instantiated, not only by the "cultivated"
products, but even, and above all, by those that are most degenerated. Apropos of *Dallas*, one can say that "the semantic opposition and the articulation of the elementary narrative structures can migrate in combinations of
the highest improbability around the various characters."

Organized differentiations, polycentrism, regulated irregularity–such
would be the fundamental aspects of this neo-baroque aesthetic, the principal example of which is musical variations à la Bach. Since in the epoch of
mass communications "the condition for listening . . . it is that for which all
has already been said and already been written ... as in the Kabuki theater, it
may then be the most minuscule variant that will produce pleasure in the
text, or that form of explicit repetition which is already known."

What results from these reflections is clear. The focus of the theoretical
inquiry is displaced. Before, mass mediologists tried to save the dignity of
repetition by recognizing in it the possibility of a traditional dialectic between scheme and innovation (but it was still the innovation that ac-
counted for the value, the way of rescuing the product from degradation
and promoting it to a value). Now, the emphasis must be placed on the
inseparable knot of scheme-variation, where the variation is no longer
more appreciable than the scheme. The term neobaroque must not deceive:
we are witnessing the birth of a new aesthetic sensibility much more archaic, and truly post-post-modern.

As Giovanna Grignaffini observes, "the neo-baroque aesthetics has
transformed a commercial constraint into a 'formal principle.' " As a result,
"any idea of unicity becomes destroyed to its very roots."[7] As happened
with Baroque music, and as (according to Walter Benjamin) happens in our
era of "technological reproduction," the messages of mass media can and
must be received and understood in a "state of inattention."

It goes without saying that the authors I have quoted see very clearly
how much commercial and "gastronomical" consolation there is in putting
forward stories that always say the same thing and in a circular way always
close in on themselves. But they do not only apply to such products a
rigidly formalistic criterion, but also suggest that we ought to conceive of a
new audience that feels perfectly comfortable with such a criterion. Only
by presupposing such agreement can one speak of a new aesthetics of the
serial. And only by such an agreement is the serial no longer the poor relative of the arts, but the form of art that can satisfy the new aesthetic sensibility, indeed, the post-post-modern Greek tragedy.

We would not be scandalized if such criteria were to be applied (as they have been applied) to abstract art. And in fact, here we are about to outline a new aesthetics of the "abstract" applied to the products of mass communication.

But this requires that the naive addressee of the first level will disappear, giving place only to the critical reader of the second level. In fact, there is no conceivable naive addressee of an abstract painting or sculpture. If there is one who–in front of them–asks, "But what does it mean?" this is not an addressee of either the first or second level; he is excluded from any artistic experience whatever. Of abstract works there is only a critical "reading": what is formed is of no interest, only the way it is formed is interesting.

Can we expect the same for the serial products of television? What should we think about the birth of a new public that, indifferent to the stones told (which are in any case already known), only relishes the repetition and its own microscopic variations? In spite of the fact that today the spectator still weeps in the face of the Texan families' tribulations, ought we to expect in the near future a true and real genetic mutation?

If it should not happen this way, the radical proposal of the postmodern aesthetics would appear singularly snobby: as in a sort of neo-Orwellian world, the pleasures of the smart reading would be reserved for the members of the Party and the pleasures of the naive reading reserved for the proletarians. The entire industry of the serial would exist, as in the world of Mallarmé (made to end in a Book), with its only aim being to furnish neo-baroque pleasure to the happy few, reserving pity and fear to the unhappy many who remain.

Some Questions in the Guise of Conclusions

According to this hypothesis we should think of a universe of new consumers disinterested in what really happens to J.R., and bent on grasping the neo-baroque pleasure provided by the form of his adventures. However, one could ask if such an outlook (even though warranting a *new* aesthetics) can be agreed to by an *old* semiotics.

Baroque music, as well as abstract art, is "a-semantic." One can discuss, and I am the first to do so, whether it is possible to discriminate so straightforwardly between purely "syntactic" and "semantic" arts. But may we at least recognize that there are figurative arts and abstract arts ? Baroque music and abstract painting are not figurative; television serials are.

Until what point shall we be able to enjoy as merely musical those variations that play upon "likenesses"? Can one escape from the fascination of the possible worlds that these "likenesses" outline?

Perhaps we are obliged to try a different hypothesis.

We can say then that the neo-baroque series brings to its first level of fruition (impossible to eliminate) the pure and simple myth. Myth has nothing to do with art. It is a story, always the same. It may not be the story of Atreus and it may be that of J.R. Why not? Every epoch has its myth-makers, its own sense of the sacred. Let us take for granted such a "figurative" representation and such an "orgiastic" enjoyment of the myth. Let us take for granted the intense emotional participation, the pleasure of the reiteration of a single and constant truth, and the tears, and the laughter–and finally the *catharsis*. Then we can conceive of an audience also able to shift onto an aesthetic level and to judge the art of the variations on a mythical theme–in the same way as one succeeds in appreciating a "beautiful funeral" even when the deceased was a dear person.

Are we sure that the same thing did not happen even with the classical tragedy?

If we re-read Aristotle's *Poetics* we see that it was possible to describe the model of a Greek tragedy as a *serial* one. From the quotations of the Stagirite we realize that the tragedies of which he had knowledge were many more than have come down to us, and they all followed (by varying it) one fixed scheme. We can suppose that those that have been saved were those that corresponded better to the canons of the ancient aesthetic sensibility. But we could also suppose that the decimation came about on the basis of political cultural criteria, and no one can forbid us from imagining that Sophodes may have survived by virtue of a political maneuver, by sacrificing better authors (but "better" according to what criteria?).

If there were many more tragedies than those we know, and if they all followed (with variations) a fixed scheme, what would happen if today we were able to see them and read them all together? Would our evaluations of the originality of Sophocles or Aeschylus be different from what they are currently? Would we find in these authors variations on topical themes where today we see indistinctly a unique (and sublime) way of confronting the problems of the human condition? Perhaps where we see absolute invention, the Greeks would have seen only the "correct" variation on a single scheme, and sublime appeared to them, not the single work, but precisely the scheme. It is not by chance that, when speaking of the art of poetry, Anstotle dealt mainly with schemes before all else, and mentioned single works only for the sake of an example.

Since at this point I am playing what Peirce called "the play of musement" and I am multiplying the hypotheses–in order to find out, maybe later, a single fruitful idea–let us now reverse our experiment and look at a contemporary IV serial from the point of view of a future neoromantic aesthetics which, supposedly, has assumed again that "originality is beautiful." Let us imagine a society in the year 3000 A.D., in which go percent of all our present cultural production had been destroyed and of all our television serials only *one* show of lieutenant Columbo had survived.

How would we "read" this work? Would we be moved by such an origanal picture of a little man in the struggle with the powers of evil, with the forces of capital, with an opulent and racist society dominated by WASPs? Would we appreciate this efficient, concise, and intense representation of the urban landscape of an industrial America?

When–in a single piece of a series–something is simply *presupposed* by the audience, which knows the whole series, would we speak perhaps of an art of synthesis of a sublime capacity of telling through essential allusions?

In other words, how would we read a "piece" of a series, if the whole of the series remained unknown to us?

Such a series of questions could continue indefinitely. I started to put them forth because I think that we still know very little about the role of repetition in the universe of art and in the universe of mass media.

Umberto Eco

Two Problems in Textual Interpretation*

Preface

PREFACE

The two sections below are two further elaborations of the theory of the interpretation of narrative texts presented in *The Role of the Reader* (1979) and then developed further in *Lector in Fabula* (1979).

For the convenience of the reader, I am presenting here the table of levels of textual cooperation (published in *Role* 14). In the box on discursive structures I did not sufficiently develop the voice "chosen of the isotopies," since the concept of isotopy was there understood as used in Greimas' semiotics. As to the deeper intensional levels, in *The Role of the Reader* I have developed only a few aspects of the question since my major interest was in the interpretation of the narrative level (fabula) and in the extensional inferences (=possible worlds). In the two following sections I shall deal explicitly with isotopies and with some problems concerning the intensional interpretation of deep textural structures.

1. ON ISOTOPY

In Eco (*Role*, 0.6.3) I devoted several pages to the notion of topic, defined as a cooperative device activated by the reader (usually in the form of a question) for the purpose of identifying the isotopy for interpreting the text. I wrote: "the topic as question is an abductive schema that helps the reader to decide which semantic properties have to be actualized, whereas isotopies are the actual textual verification of that tentative hypothesis," by which I meant to say that the topic as such is not expressed by the text, while the isotopy is a verifiable semantic property of it. In other words, the topic is a pragmatic device, while the isotopy is a level of possible semantic actualization of the text. Yet in order to analyze that semantic property or indeed that level of meaning that a text manifests, it is necessary to specify more exactly what is meant by isotopy. My hypothesis is that the term, variously defined by Greimas and by his school, is an umbrella term, a rather general notion that can allow for various more specific ones defining different textual phenomena. Only the clarification of these differences will make it possible to throw light on the positive theoretical aspects of the notion.

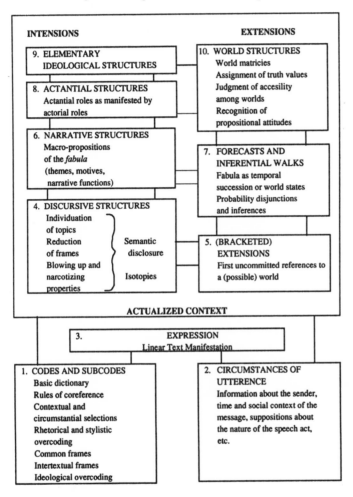

FIGURE 1

Greimas (1970: 188) defines isotopy as "a complex of manifold semantic categories making possible the uniform reading of a story." The category would then have the function of textual or transsentential disambiguation, but on various occasions Greimas furnishes examples dealing with sentences and outright noun phrases. For instance, in order to explain in what sense the amalgam on a single classeme (either semantic category or repeated contextual seme) makes possible a uniform reading, he gives the example of the two expressions *"le chien aboye"* and *"le commissaire aboye."* Given that "bark" has two classemes, human and canine, it is the presence of the dog or the commissioner that reiterates one of the two that decides whether "bark" is taken in a literal or figurative sense. It should be obvious that what are called classemes here are our *contextual* selections (cf. TS, 2.12.2). The human presence of the commissioner introduces a "human" context and makes it possible to make the appropriate selection out of the compositional spectrum of "bark."[1]

But can we say that an isotopy obtains always and only under such conditions? Aside from the fact that if so, it would not differ from normal semantic coherence or from the notion of amalgamation, the lists made of the various meanings of the term either in Greimas or his disciples (cf. Kerbrat-Orecchioni, 1976) do say that at various times there are isotopies that are semantic, phonetic, prosodic, stylistic, enunciative, rhetorical, presuppositional, syntactic or narrative. It is therefore fair to assume that isotopy has become an umbrella term covering diverse semiotic phenomena generically definable as coherence at the various textual levels. But is that coherence obtained at the various textual levels by applying the same rules? That is why it is advisable, if not to work out an isotopic system, to make the term less equivocal and more manageable, at least for the purposes of this present paper, stipulating the minimum conditions for its use. In an initial examination, the meanings shown in Figure 2 seem to emerge. The diagram is not meant to finalize an isotopic system, but to show how the category can assume various forms.

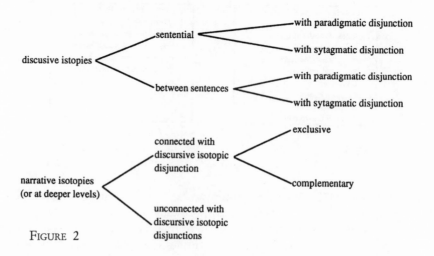

FIGURE 2

Let us now consider a few examples that will support this classification.

1.1. Sentential discursive isotopies with paradigmatic disjunction.[2]

In his essay on crossword writing, Greimas (1970) examines this definition with the correlated denomination

(1)   l'ami des simples = herbalist

in which the clever definition arises from the fact that *simples* has two contextual selections, one common and one specialized, precisely governed by the "vegetable" selection. Only after it is decided (through topicalization) that the term is understood in the second sense is it established that it counts as a substantive and not an adjective, and therefore it is decided to decode *ami* as "lover" or "fan" and not as "friend." The topic has intervened as a reading hypothesis (speaking of plants and not of ethical attitudes), and has pointed toward the appropriate contextual selection, and has imposed a rule of interpretive coherence affecting all the lexemes involved. We can apply the term isotopy to the semantic result of that coherent interpretation, and recognize the actualized isotopy as the "objective" content of the expression (objective in the sense that it is supported by the code. Naturally, in the case of this expression, which is deliberately ambiguous, or, if we like, bi-isotopic, the objective contents are two, both actualizable). It should be noted too that in this case the isotopy does not depend on any redundancy of a semantic type, since *ami* and *simples* do not seem to have semes in common. In truth the final isotopy is realized by the whole syntagm "question + solution": "the herbalist is the friend of simples." That is to say that once the topicalization is made (that the subject is plants) we get the sentence "The herbalist likes herbs" in which "botanist" imposes a vegetal seme which makes it possible to actualize the appropriate contextual selection within the componential spectrum of "simples." Cases of the same kind are demonstrated in those puzzles called mnemonic "cryptographs" studied extensively by Manetti and Violi (1977).

That is the reason these isotopies are defined as sentential although at first glance they seem to apply only to defined descriptions. In each case they are characterized by paradigmatic disjunction: they depend on the fact that the code includes lexical expressions with a multiple meaning. It is evident that the paradigmatic disjunction derives from a cotextual pressure that operates syntagmatically, but that does not eliminate the need to decide what reading passage to assign to one or more componential spectrums.

Moreover, these isotopies are *denotatively exclusive*: the subject is either the evangelical in spirit, or it is herbs. The topic intervenes as a concurrent, cooperative hypothesis to individuate contextual selections.

1.2. Sentential discursive isotopies with syntagmatic disjunction.

Transformational grammar has accustomed us to ambiguous sentences like

(2)   They are flying planes.

which can generate two different deep structures. In disambiguating the
sentence, paradigmatic disjunctions undoubtedly apply (it is necessary, for
instance, to decide whether the verb should be understood as active or passive) but the fundamental decision (always deriving from the prior
topicalization) is whether the subject is humans doing something with the
airplanes, or airplanes doing something. At that point it is necessary to
actuate a coreference and establish to whom or what they refers. We could
say that the coreferential (syntagmatic) decision decides the paradigmatic
choice concerning the meaning of the verb.

   These isotopies too are denotatively exclusive: either the subject is a human action, or it is mechanical objects.

   Here the topic intervenes as a concurrent hypothesis to actualize both
coreferences and contextual selections.

1.3. Discursive isotopies between sentences with paradigmatic disjunction.

Let us examine in this connection the little story of two fellows conversing
during a party, cited by Greimas (1966). The first praises the food, the serv-
ice, the hospitality, the beauty of the women, and finally the excellence of
the "toilettes." The second replies that he has not yet been there. The second speaker, in interpreting the text uttered by the first, blunders because
he superimposes two frames (cf. Role). The frame "party" undoubtedly
includes the hosts' garments, but cannot include the condition of the sani-
tary facilities, or it would have to consider also the electrical system, the
water supply, the solidity of the walls, and the layout of the rooms. These
elements are considered at most as belonging, say, to a frame like "interior
architecture and furnishing." The party refers to a frame that is social in
nature, furnishings to one that is technological. The individuation of the
topic in this case is the individuation of the semantic field, so as to enable
contextual selections to be effected. The French term "toilettes" is undoubtedly polysemic and acquires two meanings according to the disjunction between the selection "fashion" (which in turn belongs to a seme of
"social" nature) and the selection "architecture." In this case we can certainly speak of the presence of a classeme or a dominant semantic category,
since the text of the first speaker in fact abounded in key terms containing
references to the party and to the social nature of the situation. There were
misunderstandings possible, and the story makes us laugh precisely because
it constitutes a case of awkward textual cooperation.

These isotopies have paradigmatic disjunction because, if only on the basis of cotextual (syntagmatic) pressure, they concern contextual selections in lexemes with multiple meaning. These isotopes too are denotatively exclusive: the subject is either clothing or it is bathrooms. The topic intervenes as a concurrent cooperative hypothesis, to individuate contextual selections that hypothesize frames.

1.4. Discursive isotopies between sentences with syntagmatic disjunction.

This is the case of the ambiguous sentence

(3)   Charles makes love with his wife twice a week.
      So does John.

The point is whether this short text should be read as the story of two couples, or the story of a triangle. In this case too we have discursive isotopies with alternative denotations. In extensional terms, it is a matter of deciding whether there are three people involved or four. In order to do so, it is necessary to decide how "so" should be interpreted, but then it is a matter of establishing a coreference. The choice concerns the syntactic structure of the sentence, and only through a syntactic decision is the one or the other semantic result obtained. As already seen, it is through the topicalization operation that the decision is made as to whether the subject is two couples or a triangle: in the first case the logical structure of the text would be A:B = C:D while in the second it would be A:B = B:C. It is a problem of interpretive coherence; if four individuals are concerned and A and B are compared in the first sentence, "so" means that in the second sentence C and D should be compared; if, on the other hand, three people are involved and A and B are compared in the first sentence, "so" means that in the second B and C should be compared. But it is not obvious how the two interpretive decisions derive from the redundance of semantic categories. Here the connection is between the topic and coreferential decisions, without the mediation of contextual selections. At the most, as already seen, presuppositions of frames are involved.

The two isotopies are characterized by syntagmatic disjunction. They are mutually exclusive (the subject is either the Kinsey report, or it is the story of adultery) but they are by no means denotatively alternative: some of the individuals remain the same in each case, only they are ascribed different actions and intentions.

The topic intervenes as a cooperative concurrent hypothesis to establish the coreferences, thus orienting the structurization of different narrative worlds.

1.5. Narrative isotopes connected with isotope discursive disjunctions generating mutually exclusive stories.

The following text is the French translation of an extract from Macchiavelli and it is irrelevant whether the original Italian text shows the same ambiguity as the French;3 the French text will be examined as if it were an anonymous original:

> (4) Domitian surveillait: l'âge des senateurs, et tous ceux qu'il voyait en position favorable pour lui succéder il les abattait. Il voulut ainsi abattre Nerva qui devait lui succéder. Il se trouva qu'un calculateur de ses amis l'en dissuada, va que lui même (my italics) était arrivé à un âge trop avancé pour que sa mort ne fût toute proche; et c'estainse que Nerva put lui succéder.

It is immediately evident that here we have first of all a choice between two transsentential discursive isotopies with syntagmatic disjunction: lui-même can refer to either Domitian or Nerva. If it refers to Domitian, the death referred to later (sa mort) is the imminent death of Domitian; otherwise it is Nerva's death. It is therefore necessary to decide on the coreference on the basis of topicalization: is the subject Domitian's age or Nerva's? Once the coreference is decided, there is a denotatively alternative discursive sequence in respect to the other. In effect in one case the advisor tells Domitian not to kill Nerva because he–Domitian–will soon die and it is therefore useless to eliminate his possible successors–in the other, the advisor tells Domitian that Nerva will probably die soon and therefore does not present a danger for Domitian.

But it is clear that two different stories can be derived on the basis of the two discursive isotopies. The two discursive isotopies generate two possible narrative recapitulations. In one case it is the story of a friend of Domitian's giving him an argument about Power. "In dying you risk losing Power, but by sparing Nerva and implicitly designating him your successor, though dying you retain control of the Power, you generate the new Power." In the other case it is the story of a friend of Nerva's making Domitian the victim of a courtier's wiles: "O Domitian why do you want to kill Nerva? He's so old that he'll soon die by himself!"–and thus the courtier puts Nerva on the throne.

Thus, two mutually exclusive stories emerge, whose individuation depends on the discursive actualization. Not only that, but at a deeper level (cf. Figure 1) there emerge different actantial structures and different ideological structures. According to Greimas' categories, the advisor can be seen as the Opponent of Domitian and Helper of Nerva, or as the Helper of Power and the Opponent of Domitian as a mortal, or a Helper of

Domitian and neutral in regard to Nerva. And it can be decided that what is defined here is an ideological opposition of Power versus Death (in which Power overcomes even Death) or Power versus Shrewdness, where the courtier's wiles overcome the brutality of Power. It can also legitimately be asked whether it is the choice of coreferences that generates the different deep structures, or a preliminary hypothesis regarding the deep structures that in suggesting a specific topic controls the actualization of the coreferences at the discursive level. The interpretive cooperation is made of leaps and short-circuits at the different textual levels where it is impossible to establish logically ordered sequences.

In each case we have seen that here the narrative isotopies are connected to these discourses (or vice versa).

The two narrative isotopies are mutually exclusive but they are not at all denotatively alternative: in both cases the narration is about Nerva and Domitian, except that different actions and intentions are attributed to them. The individuals remain extensionally the same, but change some of their intensional features. Different possible worlds are developed.

The topic intervenes to orient the structurization of these narrative worlds.

1.6. Narrative isotopies connected with isotopic discursive disjunctions that generate complementary stories.

That is the case of the medieval theory of the four senses of the scriptural verses, also cited by Dante. Given the text

(5)   In exitu Israel de Aegypto–domus Jacob de papolo barbaro–facta est Judea santificatio ejus–Israel potestas ejus.

We know that "if we look only at the letter it means the exodus of the children of Israel from Egypt in Moses' time; if we look at the allegory it means our redemption through Christ; if we look at the moral sense it means the conversion of the soul from the struggle and misery of sin to the state of grace; and if we look at the mystical sense it means the departure of the holy spirit from the servitude of this corruption to the freedom of eternal glory." Let us consider, in order to simplify matters, just the literal and moral senses. Once again everything depends on the topic hypothesis: Is the statement about Israel or about the human soul? The decision on this affects the discursive actualization: in the first case Israel will be understood as a proper name of a people, and Egypt as a proper name of an African country; in the second case Israel will be the human spirit, but then by interpretive coherence, Egypt will have to be sin (the reading levels cannot be mixed).

Here, however, alternative senses of a componential spectrum will not be chosen, because we must foresee that in as rich an encyclopedia as the medieval one Israel denoted the chosen people and connoted the soul. Thus it is not like the case of "toilette" that has the sense of either x or y; here the expression connotes the sense y precisely because it denotes x. The relationship and implication is not one of disjunction. Consequently isotopic disjunction exists, but it is not based on disjunction but rather on semantic implication.

Once the preferred reading at the discursive level is decided, various stories can be inferred from the actualized discursive structures, the the moral story will derive from the moral discursive actualization just as the literal one will from the literal discursive actualization. But the two stories (and we know in reality there are four) are not mutually exclusive; they are rather complementary, in the sense that the text can be read simultaneously in two or more ways, and one way reinforces the other rather than eliminates it.

Thus narrative isotopies are connected with discursive isotopies, but are not mutually exclusive. On the contrary, they are denotatively alternative; the subject is either the chosen people, or it is the soul (and in fact the option is between various denotations and connotations). By virtue of this choice various possible worlds developed.

The topic (both the discursive and the narrative) intervenes to choose between denotative and connotative semes, and orientate the structure of the narrative worlds.

1.7. Narrative isotopies not connected with discursive isotopic disjunctions that generate complementary stories in each case.

Greimas (1970) in his analysis of the Bororo myth of the *aras* [a Brazilian name of a bird] speaks of another type of narrative isotopy.

The myth in effect contains two stories, one about the search for water, and the other about the problem of diet. So it is the "natural" isotopy versus the "alimentary." But in both cases we perceive that whatever the story (or the *fabula*) that we actualize, *there is no change on the discursive level.* The stories always tell of certain people and certain events. At the most, according to the narrative isotopy, we select certain actions as more pertinent than others, but the actions and people doing them remain the same, even if there is a change in the value we attribute to them in the narrative arrangement. It is a matter of elaborating a hypothesis with a narrative theme and relying on key terms or sentences without, however, paradigmatic disjunctions as to the sense of the lexemes, or syntagmatic disjunctions as to the sense of the coreferences.

The persistence of a single discursive coherence results in this case in the two narrative isotopies not annulling each other, *the relation between them not being exclusive or alternative, but complementary.* Although Greimas chooses the alimentary isotopy as best, this does not mean that the story cannot be read through the natural isotopy as well. In fact the two isotopies reinforce each other.

The toilet story is characterized by two opposing readings, of which one is clearly inferior, and if the first speaker had really wanted to speak of bathrooms, his utterance would have been conversationally inept because it violated the rule of relevance. That cannot be said about the myth of the *aras.* Thus we have here narrative isotopies unconnected with discursive disjunctions.

The two or more narrative isotopies are not mutually exclusive. They are not even denotatively alternative; at most, different necessary features are attributed to different individuals (cf. *Role,* 8.7). Therefore, different possible narrative worlds are proffered.

The topic intervenes only to orient the evaluation of the narratively pertinent features, and thus the structurization of those worlds.

1.8. Provisional Conclusions

According to what has been said, it is permissible to assert that isotopy is an umbrella term covering various phenomena. Like all umbrella terms (such as iconism, presupposition, code) this one shows that the diversity conceals some unity. Indeed, isotopy refers almost always to constancy in going in a direction that a text exhibits when submitted to rules of interpretive coherence, even if the rules of coherence change according to whether what is wanted is to individuate discursive or narrative isotopies, to disambiguate definite descriptions or sentences and produce coreferences, to decide what things certain individuals do, or to establish how many different stories the same deed by the same individuals can generate.

What should be clear in any case is that the identification of the topic is a cooperative (pragmatic) movement guiding the reader to individuate the isotopies as semantic features of a text.

2. Use and Interpretation

An isotopy is a semantic feature of a text even when the text is open to several possible interpretations. We have seen that a given interpretations can choose one of two or more alternative isotopies or allow complementary isotopies to live together. It appears difficult to assert, on the other hand, that isotopies which a text *does not allow* can be attributed to it. This obviously negates Valery's statement that "il n'y a pas de vrai sens d'un texte." But that does not mean to say that there is just *one* and *only one* interpretation of a text. Between the theory that the interpretation is wholly determined by the author's intention and the theory that it is wholly determined by the will of the interpreter there is undoubtedly a third way. Interpretive cooperation is an act in the course of which the reader of a text, through successive abductive inferences, proposes topics, ways of reading, and hypotheses of coherence, on the basis of suitable encyclopedic competence; but this interpretive initiative of his is, in a way, determined by the nature of the text. By the "nature" of the text I mean what an interpreter can actualize on the basis of a given Linear Manifestation, having recourse to the encyclopedic competence toward which the text itself orients its Model Reader (cf. *Role*).

However, we must distinguish between the free *use* of a text taken as imaginative stimulus and the *interpretation* of an "open" text. It is on that dividing line that the possibility of what Barthes calls a text of "jouissance" is grounded, without theoretical ambiguity: the decision must be taken as to whether the text is *used* as a text of "jouissance" or whether a certain text considers the stimulation of the freest possible use a constituent of its own strategy (and thus of its *interpretation*). But we believe that some restrictions obtain, and that the notion of interpretation always involves a dialectic between the strategy of the author and the response of the Model Reader.

Naturally, aside from procedure, it is also possible to provide an esthetic of the free, deviant, desirous and malicious use of texts. Borges suggested reading the *Odyssey* as if it came after the *Aeneid*, or the *Imitation of Christ* as if it were written by Céline. These are splendid, exciting and realizable proposals, very creative indeed, because in effect a new text is produced (thus Pierre Menard's *Quijote* is quite different from Cervantes' which it accidentally corresponds to word for word). And then in the writing of that other text, it happens that the original is criticized, or hidden possibilities and values discovered in it. (Nothing is more revealing than a caricature because it resembles, but is not, the caricatured object, and on the other hand certain retold romances become more beautiful because they become "other" romances.)

From the point of view of a general semiotics and in the light of the complexity of the pragmatic processes and contradictory nature of the Global Semantic Field, all these operations are theoretically explainable. But if the range of interpretations can be infinite, as Peirce has shown, the universe of discourse itself operates to limit the size of the encyclopedia. And an "other" text is nothing more than the strategy constituting the universe of these among its interpretations which, if not legitimate, are legitimizable. Any other decision on using a text freely amounts to a decision to expand the universe of discourse. The dynamics of unlimited semiosis (cf. TS) does not prevent it, but rather encourages it. But it is necessary to know whether what is wanted is to have the semiosis function, or to interpret a text.

Proust could read a railroad timetable and find in the names of the Valois region sweet, labyrinthian echoes of the Nervalian voyage in search of Sylvie. But it was not a matter of the *interpretation* of the timetable but rather of an almost psychedelic use of it. As a matter of fact, a railway timetable postulates only a specific type of Model Reader, able to deal with Cartesian orthogonal axes (vertical and horizontal) and with a vigilant sense of the irreversibility of temporal sequences.

It seems, nevertheless, in the light of the table reproduced at the beginning of this article, that there are levels of actualization in which the reader seems more bound, with respect to a certain encyclopedic competence than in others. The reader who actualizes discursive structures is undoubtedly restricted by the nature of the lexicon (if the text says "a dog appeared" it cannot be made to say "a cat appeared"); similarly, it seems that on the level of narrative structures he has to recognize the worlds of the fabula as the text organizes them (if "there was once a woods with a little house where a little girl lived," it cannot be read "there was once a mountain with a castle where a king lived"). But what happens when, after the discursive and narrative structures are actualized, the readers advance hypotheses on deeper structures (actantial structures, ideological values)?

Once the narrative structures are actualized, while the reader makes forecasts about the states of the fabula (delineating possible worlds), he can (before, after, or at the same time) formulate a series of macropropositions even more abstract than the narrative ones. That is, he can individuate the actorial roles (Greimas) or narrative sequences. He can deprive the actorial roles of their residual individuality and reduce them to actantial oppositions (subject/object; helper/opponent; sender/addressee) deciding that in some cases a single actantial role is covered by more actors.

What makes it difficult to define the theoretical placement of this cooperative mode is that, on the one hand, the reader has already to have precalculated hypotheses regarding the actants in order to be able to define certain narrative structures, and on the other hand, already to have delineated possible worlds with their individuals, in order to be able to determine the actors in the game. Take, for instance, a text like Gérard de Nerval's *Sylvie*. Each of the three women in it–Sylvie, Aurelia and Adrienne–enters into a game of ever-changing opposition with one of the others, donning various actantial roles, with one or the other becoming the real presence, as opposed to memory, according to the state of the fabula and the time section (present, immediate past, remote past) of which the narrator is speaking. Thus, on the one hand, the reader should already have proffered a hypothesis on the role of the character in that part of the fabula so as to formulate narrative macropropositions. On the other hand he should have recognized the states of the fabula in their logical sequence so as to determine whether a given discursive passage represents a fact that is happening, that happened, that is remembered, that in the past was believed and then was contradicted by subsequent reality, and thus lives. Obviously, possible worlds cannot be identified without the discursive structures having been actualized; but at the level of these latter, to disambiguate certain complexities of verb tenses, it would be necessary to have already formulated hypotheses not only about the worlds,but also about the actantial frame and the roles played by the characters.

When we read Hugo's *Quatre-vingt-treize* at what point do we decide, on the explicit and repeated declarations of the author, that it is the story of a grandiose subject, Revolution, as the voice of the people and of God, that is projected against its exact opposite, Reaction? When is it fully understood than Lantenac or Cimourdain, Gauvain or the Convention, Robespierre or the Vandée aresuperficial manifestations of a deeper conflict about which and of which theauthor is chiefly speaking? And when does it happen that when this is understood, the reader foregoes individuating the characters, some "historical" and some fictitious, that populate the novel beyond the limits of the memorizable? It is clear that in an operation of that sort, the actantial hypothesis emerges not inresolution of a series of successive abstractions, from discursive structures to thefabula and from it to ideological structures, but rather establishes itself very quickly in the course of the reading, and guides the choices and forecasts, and determines macropropositional filterings.

An action or an event can be left to fall, while the author's long philosophical perorations come to be part of what really pertains to the fabula, because across a multitude of aspects, gestures, and events we need to retain only what tells uswhat the revolution is doing to pursue its design, and how it works on the individuals and directs their actions.

The same can be said for what we have called ideological structures, to which so much space is devoted in the textual research of the past decade. While an actantial framework preexists as an encyclopedic apparatus (even before it is realized in the text) like a system of oppositions, that is as an S-code (cf. TS), an ideological structure (whether at the level of encyclopedic competence or in its textual actualization) presents itself as a code in the true sense and that is as asystem or correlations. We could thus say that an ideological structure manifests itself when axiological connotations are associated with actantial roles inscribed in the text. And it is when an actantial framework is provided with value judgements and the roles convey axiological oppositions like Good versus Evil, True versus False (or even Life versus Death or Nature versus Culture) that the text exhibits its ideology as if by a watermark.

At that point the Model Reader's ideological competence comes in to direct the choice of the actantial framework and of the great ideological oppositions. For example, a reader whose ideological competence consists of a coarse but effectiveopposition between Spiritual Values (with the connotation of "good") and Material Values (with the connotation of "evil") might be tempted in a tale like *Death in Venice* to actualize two large oppositions on the actantial level; Aschenbach's esthetic vocation against his carnal desire (and thus Spirit versus Matter), assigning on the level of ideological structures a mark of "positive" to the first and "negative" to the second. Rather poor and hardly problematic reading, but an example was sought of how ideological competence determinesthe actualization of the deep textual structures. Naturally, a text can anticipate such competence in the true Model Reader and work–at all the appropriate lower levels–to bring it to a head and induce the reader to individuate morecomplex ideological and actantial structures.

Then there are the cases of deviant (more or less happy) decoding: a typical one is that of the *Mystères de Paris* in which the ideological propensity of the proletarian readers functioned like a code shifter and induced them to actualize in revolutionary key a discourse made in a socio-democratic one. Ideological competence does not necessarily act as a restraint on the interpretation but may function as a stimulus as well. And, as such, it is conducive to finding in the text whatthe author was unaware of but which the text in some way conveyed.[4]

But what happens when the reader, while identifying the deep structures, brings to light something that the author could not have wanted to say but that the text nevertheless seems to show with absolute clarity? Obviously, here we are touching on the subtlest limit separating interpretive and hermeneutic cooperation. Furthermore, is it not proper to assume that it is the hermeneutic thatdiscovers in the text the truth that it offers, discloses, allows to appear?

Obviously there are hermeneutics and hermeneutics. The etymologies of Isidor of Seville–and many of Heidegger's–make words say what they cannot say if the encyclopedia has its own objective social existence; and the medieval readings of Virgil treated as a prophetic text did violence to the Virgilian discourse. These are the cases in which a text is not interpreted but rather used in absolute freedom, as if it were a pack of Tarots. But the case is different when a person peruses a text to draw conclusions from it on the deep impulses of the author or to find traces in it of his unavowed ideology. Sue wanted to be a revolutionary and wrote a book that was blandly reformist. But his working-class readers found calls to revolution in it. Who was right? Poe wished to tell the story of an extremely lucid mind, Dupin, and in theDupin trilogy many have found the setting of a theatre of the unconscious. Is it right to disregard the author's numerous explicit assertions of Dupin's lucid and controlled rationality?

Let us suppose there is a narrative text produced in recent years in which there are manifested obsessively–not only on the level of individuals, properties and relations but also on the level of the syntactic structures

themselves–actantial impressions, anaphoric substitutions, abrupt switches
from first to third person, in a word, difficulties in recognizing and making
recognizable the subjects put into play by the *énoncé*, and the same subject-
author understood as enunciative strategy. It is not hard to apply this description to a long series of experimental or avant-garde texts. In such cases
it may confidently be assumed that the author had in mind all those aspects
of the current encyclopedia by which such expressive phenomena are related to dissociative elements and identity crises. The text is invested with
and expresses as its proper content a schizomorphic vision–not described
but *manifested* as style, as the organizational modality of the discourse. The
author as empirical subject of the *énoncé* may be more or less conscious of
what he was doing, but textually he did do it, in the same way in which I
may not know that a particular word has a particular meaning, but if I
pronounce it, I've said what I've said. Just as on the psychological level one
would speak of a "slip," it could be said that I spoke in a state of mental
cloudiness, that I am stupid, that I made a mistake.

At this point we come, however, to a different situation. Let us illustrate
it with another text, from an epoch in which so many psychiatric and psychoanalytical discoveries were not yet in the public domain (or by a contemporary author but with a very limited encyclopedia). The text tells an
ostensibly irrelevant story, but gives the clear impression that through the
use of obsessive metaphors or the particular syntactic arrangements, the
picture of a schizoid attitude or Oedipus complex is being constructed as if
in a watermark. Could we say that this structure is part of the contents of
the text that the Model Reader is called upon to actualize?

By interpretation is meant the semantic actualization of what the text as
strategy wants to say with the cooperation of its own Model Reader–in the
ways and on the levels outlined above. It could then be maintained that a
text that through its own structures manifests the schizoid personality of
the author, or the fact that he suffers from an Oedipus complex, is not a
text that requires the cooperation of an ideal reader to make its unconscious
tendencies evident. The revelation of those tendencies has nothing to do
with the process of textual cooperation. It has to do rather with a subsequent phase of approaching the text in which, after semantic actualization,
it is evaluated and *criticized*. The criticism can evaluate its "esthetic" success
(whatever definition is given of that effect) and the relations between the
ideology and stylistic solutions of the author and economic situation, and
can search for the unconscious structures manifested through the actantial
structures (without their having been the content understood by the author). However, such psychological, psychiatric or psychoanalytic inquiry,
though important and fruitful, would belong with the *use of the text* for
documentary purposes, and is located in a phase subsequent to semantic
actualization (even if the two processes can in turn affect each other). It is as

if in the expression "I confess everything" there were a matter of textual cooperation to actualize all its semantic implications, to define its topic, and to single out its remote presuppositions. On the other hand there is also a matter of documentary utilization to use this expression as the judicial evidence that the speaker was guilty. But that would mean that in the expression "Come here, please" it is not a matter of textual cooperation to infer that the speaker is motivated by the evident desire to have me go to him. On the contrary, it appears that this type of inference is an essential part of the actualization of the message. We posit that there does exist a text in which the author could clearly not have been aware of encyclopedic data through which a whole series of actions or relations express given psychic contents, and yet it appears quite evident that the entire textual strategy leads inexorably to invest it with contents of that nature. A typical case could be Sophocles' *Oedipus Rex*, at least the way Freud read it. It is clear that we today can read the tragedy as related to an encyclopedia containing, across its own sub-codes, the results of the Freudian overcoding, but it must be said that neither Sophocles as subject of the utterance nor Sophocles as textual strategy could relate to that encyclopedia. Nevertheless, the very blind obstinacy of Oedipus in dismissing the truth that is offered to him at various times in such an incontrovertible manner, seems the primary content of the Sophoclean text. Let us say that in this case the author was instituting new encyclopedic data. The text as an act of invention (see the definition of that category in TS, 3.6.7.ff) institutes a new code, and for the first time establishes a relationship between the expressive elements and the content data that the semantic system up to that point had not yet defined and organized. In that case, the Freudian reading constitutes a legitimate operation of textual cooperation, which actualizes what there is in the text and what the author as expressive strategy puts there. For after the empirical Sophocles as subject of the utterance was more or less aware of what he was doing textually, it is a matter of use, of symptomatological reading, and extraneous to the activity defined by a theory of textual cooperation; it applies, if we like, to Freud as Sophocles' personal physician and not to Freud as Model Reader of *Oedipus Rex*. And that leads us to say (or reiterate) that the Model Reader of *Oedipus Rex* was not the one Sophocles was thinking of, but the one Sophocles' text postulates.

It is likewise clear that the Sophoclean text, in postulating the appropriate Model Reader as cooperative strategy, constructs a reader capable of bringing out those content data which up to then remained concealed (if one admits that Sophocles was the first to take note of the manifestations that are called the Oedipus complex, and the encyclopedia of Greek culture of the period did not yet have competences organized for the purpose, say intertextual traditions). In other words, the Model Reader of *Oedipus Rex* is required to carry out cooperatively the same operations of recognitions of relations that Oedipus as a character is asked to carry out–and that he does somewhat late. In that sense certain narrative texts in telling the story of a character meantime provide pragmatic semantic instructions to their Model Reader, whose own story they tell. It is reasonable to suppose that to a certain extent this happens in any narrative text, and perhaps in many others that are not narrative. *De te fabula narratur.*

To illustrate better the difference we are trying to isolate, let us take an example from the interpretation Maria Bonaparte (1949) gives to Edgar Allan Poe's work. She demonstrates that Poe (already defined by Lauvrière as an extreme degenerate and by Probst as an epileptic) was totally impotent. He was dominated by the impression he felt as a child when he saw his mother, dead of consumption, on the catafalque. Thus, in adult life he always felt morbidly attracted, in fiction as well as fact, to women with the unhealthy and funereal features of his mother. From this memory came his necrophilia, his love for diseased child-women, and his stories populated by living corpses.

Naturally, the data is taken indiscriminately from the poet's life and from his texts, a procedure that is not incorrect for a psychological study of a person called Edgar Allan Poe, but is to be rejected for a study on the Model Author that the reader of those texts imagines and needs to imagine even if he has no biographical data on Edgar Allan Poe. In that case we can safely say that Maria Bonaparte is *using* Poe's texts as documents, symptoms, and psychiatric reports. It is a pity she could not do so with Poe alive, and thus help to cure him of his obsessions. Be that as it may, the fault is not hers, and as Poe is dead, we retain the very human and also scientifically productive satisfaction of reflecting on the exemplary case of one of the greats, and on the mysterious connections between disease and creativity.

All that has nothing to do with a semiotics of the text or an analysis of what the reader can find in Poe. But Maria Bonaparte also knows how to do a textual semiotics, and splendidly. In the same essay, she analyzes the poem "Ulalume": the poet wishes to reach the planet of Venus-Astarte; earth-bound Psyche holds him back. He follows his path nonetheless, but at the end of the journey finds the tomb of his loved one. Maria Bonaparte observes that the poet's symbolism is very transparent, and makes a sort of actantial analysis *ante litteram*: a dead actor prevents Poe from approaching love that is psychically and physically normal, symbolized by Venus. Transform the actors into plain actantial polarities and we have a subject observing an object, a helper and an opponent.

When Maria Bonaparte examines the tales "Morella," "Ligeia" and "Eleonora" she finds that all three have the same fabula (following in this respect some intuitions of Baudelaire). Aside from a few differences, we always have a husband in love with an exceptional woman. She dies of consumption, the husband swears eternal grief, does not keep his promise, and becomes attached to another person; but the dead one reappears and wraps the new woman in the mantle of her funereal power. From that fabula (a true intertextual "script") it is easy to pass to actantial structures, and Maria Bonaparte does so instinctively when she considers the second woman of the third tale dead as well: though she does not die, in some manner she plays the role of love object who escapes from the lover, and thus identifies herself with the first woman. Maria Bonaparte perceives in the three tales the structure of an obsession, and perceives it first of all as a textual obsession.

But this beautiful analysis is continuously interwoven with biographical remarks that connect the textual evidences with the various aspects of Poe's private life. So Maria Bonaparte takes a ethodological detour that diverts her attention from the interpretation of the texts to their *use* on a clinical plane. The image of the mother, which does not appear *in the texts,* is introduced within their framework from extratextual sources.

Let us now see reading of an opposite type more akin to our conception. It is the one done by Jacques Derrida on "The Purloined Letter" in *Le facteur de la vérité* (1975), dealing with both the reading of Bonaparte's and the celebrated one by Lacan (which on the other hand he criticizes). Starting with an appropriate ideological competence that leads him to favor the discourse of the unconscious in the text, he identifies in it more general subjects of the actors that represent them. He does not count so much the nature of the letter as the fact that it gets back to the woman from whom it was taken, or that it was found hanging from a nail under the center of the fireplace ("on the immense body of the lady, between the posts, between the legs of the fireplace"); and he does not count so much the actor Dupin as the fact that he displays a *deceitful* character by which "he identifies successively with all the characters." It is not a matter here of deciding whether Derrida's interpretation satisfies the plurality of possible contents exhibited by Poe's text. What is interesting here is that Derrida wishes to uncover, as he says (and in opposition to the position he imputes to Lacan) the "textual structures"; he does want to "question Poe's unconscious" but "not the author's intentions," and in order to do so he seeks to identify it from time to time "with this or that position of its characters."

In doing so Derrida proceeds from the fabula (chosen according to his own ideological leanings, which guide him in individuating what for him is the topic of the whole event, a story of castration) to the actantial structures, showing how they are manifested at the deep levels of the text. Good or bad, the process is *legitimate.*

It remains to be said whether this method of proceeding should not be viewed more as critical interpretation than interpretive cooperation. But the borderlines between these two activities are very narrow and are set in terms of cooperative intensity and of clarity and lucidity in expounding the results of an actuated cooperation. The critic in this case is a cooperating reader who, after actualizing the text, relates the appropriate cooperative steps and renders evident the way in which the author, through the proper textual strategy, led him to cooperate in that way. Or else, he evaluates in terms of esthetic success (however theoretically, he defines it) the modality of the textual strategy.

The methods of criticism are varied, we know: there is philological criticism, esthetic criticism, sociological criticism and psychoanalytical criticism; criticism that expresses value judgements and criticism that throws light on the direction of a piece of writing. And others besides. The difference that is of interest here is not that between textual cooperation and criticism, but between criticism that relates and yields the modalities of textual cooperation, and criticism that uses the text, as we have seen, for other purposes.

Umberto Eco

Universe Of The Mind.
A Semiotic Theory Of Culture*

In the course of his intellectual career, Yuri M. Lotman has applied his mind to a wide range of disciplines: aesthetics, poetics, semiotic theory, the history of culture, mythology, and cinema, in addition to the principle themes of the history of Russian literature of which he is Professor at the University of Tartu in Estonia. His works range from the analysis of cultural phenomena such as blue jeans, and observations on demonology, through readings of poetic texts and consideration of the problems of interpretation, to references to mathematics and biology. However, even readers unfamiliar with the entire range of Lotman's work will be able to identify in this book the broader theoretical approach on which Lotman's work is built. It may be useful, however, to outline here certain aspects of Lotman's work which contribute to a fuller understanding of the themes and methods at work in this book.

During the Sixties, two disturbing words erupted into the calm waters of the European academic world: semiotics (or semiology) and structuralism. The centre of this research paradigm was Paris, although the phenomenon spread steadily throughout Europe and to many North and Latin American universities. The devastating effect created in Britain by these new approaches to language (and, as a result, to the study of the languages of art) is recorded by David Lodge's novel *Small World*, (clear proof that literary works can often be much more informative about the world and our society than many scientific treatises).

Small World was published in 1984, at a time when the series of English translations of Russian and Soviet semiotic texts produced by L.M. O'Toole and Ann Shukman, *Russian Poetics in Translation*, had already been in progress for several years. However, during the Sixties and Seventies, Lotman's works were more widely known on the Continent than in Britain. Interest in structural studies of language had led (particularly through the influence of Roman Jakobson) to an interest in the works of the Prague School, and at the same time to the rediscovery of the Russian Formalists of the Twenties. Up until this time, the Formalists had been known only at second hand through the seminal text *Russian Formalism* by

Victor Erlich.[1] In 1965, Tzvetan Todorov translated many of the Russian Formalist texts into French,[2] and little by little, in steady progression, the most important works of Shklovsky, Tomashevsky and Tynyanov were translated into the European languages (especially into Italian).

Alongside this growth of interest in Russian Formalism, during the early Sixties scholars in Italy and France were beginning to discover the semioticians at work during this period in Russia–principally in Moscow and Tártu. These were such figures as Ivanov, Revzin, Uspensky, Zolkovsky, Sceglov, Segal, Toporov and Egorov, as well as two names from the earlier generation, the linguist Saumijan and the mathematician Kolmogorov. However, at the centre of this new field of research, as both link and fulcrum (through the series *Trudy po znakovym sistemam [Works on Sign Systems]*, produced in Tartu) stood the figure of Yuri Lotman .

According to the teachings of the Formalists, a work of art was a semiotic *device* which could be analyzed as a set of rules and inventions, of pre-fixed effects and conscious modifications of socialized codes. The new Russian and Estonian semioticians took up the notion of 'device' and 'de-familiarization' and took one step further the techniques involved in the creation of a work of art as an individual re-construction of the store of procedures which go to make up the social fabric in which communication works.

Unfortunately, in their attempts to explain the artistic 'mystery' in terms of an analyzable device, the Formalists had become entangled in a series of contradictions. They had been unable, for example, to free themselves completely from the aesthetics of the image as an ineffable event. In addition, as may be seen in the work of Lévi-Strauss and Propp in particular,[3] they were not able to achieve the passage from formal analysis to full structural awareness. They had not fully understood that the putting into form of a work of art has also to involve the organization of content; they had therefore been working on signifying systems without taking into consideration those semantic systems which the new Russian semioticians were able to re-discover at the level of religious systems and world views. A final difficulty may be evidenced by Tomashevsky's or Shlovsky's theories on the structure of the novel. Here it becomes clear that the Formalists had at most brought to light individual devices or systems of rules which were valid only within the confines of one specific genre.

In this sense, then, the neo-semioticians went a step further. The advent of Information Theory, of Game Theory and of structural analysis in Linguistics and Cultural Anthropology allowed them to distinguish and postulate a universal field of communication phenomena. It is not possible to distinguish the rule system appropriate to a given communicative phenomenon without at the same time postulating a structural homology with the rule systems which apply to all other communicative phenomena. The new Russian semioticians developed a universal semiotic theory (and method) whereby the rules governing each communicative sector were to be seen as variations of more general codes.

In order to understand the interest aroused by these critics, who had been up until now unknown in the West except to a few Soviet Studies experts, it must be remembered that semiotics and structuralism form a highly complex pair of terms. Semiotics aims to study the entire range of sign systems (of which verbal language is the most important) and the various processes of communication to which these systems give rise. Such a study also involves the demonstration of the existence of sign systems even where least immediately apparent or expected. Structuralism is a method which has been shown to be extremely useful in the explanation of linguistic systems, in the work of Saussure and, later, of Hjelmslev and Jakobson. In the Sixties, especially in France, this method was also used to explain other systems, one of which was (and the work of Lévi-Strauss is pre-eminent here) the system of cultural phenomena. However, not all semioticians used the structuralist method. Charles Sanders Peirce and Charles Morris, for example, propounded a semiotic theory which was by no means structuralist. This is a point which bears emphasis, for Lotman, in my view, is a critic who started from a structuralist approach to the phenomena of signification and communication, and indeed retains much of this method, but who does not remain bound by it. This may be seen clearly in this book. For example, the first theoretical problem which the structuralists of the Sixties found most difficult to deal with was the fact that certain systems, through communication processes (which are historical processes, that is processes which take place in time) changed. The second problem was that given that a semiotic system was seen as a code, or rather as a system of rules, how could there be communication processes in which it was difficult to identify codes or where there seemed to be a conflict between different codes? It is these problems which hold the key to an understanding of the evolution of Lotman's thought.

In the Sixties, Lotman stressed the usefulness of the structural approach and the application of exact methods to the study of literature. That is, he remained faithful to Saussure's opposition of *langue* and *parole*, and to that proposed by Jakobson and Information Theory of code and message. In 1967, Lotman wrote an article on 'Exact Methods in Russian Literary Science' for the Italian journal *Strumenti critici*. This article repeated the positions already taken in his other writings and expounded some of the main principles of his research methods. These are outlined briefly below:

1. The opposition of exact sciences and humanistic sciences must be eliminated.
2. The study of literature, if carried out in a purely historical way, blends into the history of social thought.
3. The Russian Formalists of the Twenties had initiated the study of the 'techniques' of literary phenomena but it was now time to introduce into the

study of literary texts the methods of linguistic structuralism, semiotics (and he was thinking here of Peirce too), of Information Theory, cybernetics and mathematical-statistical analysis.

4. Semiotic systems are *models* which explain the world in which we live (obviously, in explaining the world, they also construct it, and in this sense, even at this early stage, Lotman saw semiotics as a cognitive science). Among all these systems, language is the *primary modelling system* and we apprehend the world by means of the model which language offers. Myth, cultural rules, religion, the language of art and of science are *secondary modelling systems*. We must therefore also study these semiotic systems which, since they lead us to understand the world in a certain way, allow us to speak about it.

5. If texts represent models of the world, the set of texts which is the culture of a period is a secondary modelling system. It is thus necessary to attempt to define a *typology of cultures*, in order both to discover universal aspects common to all cultures and to identify the specific systems which represent the 'language' of Medieval culture or the 'language' of Renaissance culture.

6. When a culture is analyzed as a code or system (as also happens with natural languages), the processes of use are richer and less predictable than the semiotic model which explains them. Reconstructing the code of a culture does not mean explaining all the phenomena of that culture, but rather allows us to explain why that culture has produced those phenomena.

Lotman realized, however, that seeing a text as a message elaborated on the basis of a linguistic code is by no means the same as seeing a text (or a culture as a set of texts) as a code. For Lotman was and is aware of the fact that no historical period has a sole cultural code (even if the construction of a model-code can be a useful abstraction) and that in any culture there exist simultaneously various codes. It seems to me that in attempting to deal with this problem, Lotman is moving beyond structuralist dogmatism and offering a more complex and articulated approach. Faced with the rigidity of the structuralist opposition between code and message, Lotman introduces, even within the same culture, a difference between grammatical learning and textual learning.

Cultures can be governed by a *system* of rules or by a *repertoire* of texts imposing models of behaviour. In the former category, texts are generated by combinations of discrete units and are judged correct or incorrect according to their conformity to the combinational rules. In the latter category, society directly generates texts, which constitute macrounits from which rules can eventually be inferred, but which initially and most importantly propose models to be followed and imitated.

A grammar-oriented culture depends on 'Handbooks', while a text-oriented culture depends on 'The Book'. A handbook is a code which permits further messages and texts, whereas a book is a text, generated by an as-yet-unknown rule which, once analyzed and reduced to a handbook-like form, can suggest new ways of producing further texts.

Lotman recalls the customary twofold experience of language learning. Adult learners are usually introduced to an unknown language by means of rules. The receive a set of units along with their combinational laws and they learn how to combine these units in order to speak. On the other hand, a child, when first learning to speak, is trained through exposure to a continuous textual performance of pre-fixed strings of language and s/he is expected to absorb competence even though not completely conscious of the underlying rules.

The difference between grammatical learning and textual learning had led Lotman to look at the various texts which are current in a culture in order to see that culture as a set of texts and a *non-hereditary collective memory*. 4

On this basis, Lotman has effected subtle analyses of cultures, some interesting examples of which are included in this book. A particularly rich example of this kind of analysis is offered by 'The Notion of Boundary'. In this way, Lotman has managed to fuse the structural method (which takes a synchronic approach, that is, the description of a culture system at a given moment in time) with his vocation as historian, a historian interested in explaining how a culture is formed and how different culture systems, distant from one another in time, can be compared.

Even when different cultures seem to be using the same terms, they fit into a different system. Lotman gives us a brilliant example of typology of cultures with his comparison between the cultural language of the Middle Ages and that of the Enlightenment. On the one hand, we have a culture in which everything (not merely words but also things) signifies a higher reality and where objects themselves are important not for their physical nature or their function, but rather in so much as they signify something else. On the other, we have a cultural system where the world of objects is real, while words and signs in general are conventional constructions and vehicles of falsehood, and where only the 'noble savage', who is not aware of the constructions of culture, can understand reality.5 Another example is given in the analysis of the concepts of 'honour' and 'glory' in medieval Russia. Whereas we may think that the terms are more or less synonymous, in medieval Russian culture 'honour' represents a recognition and a favour granted to an inferior by a superior and 'glory' pertains rather to those at the highest levels of the social order.6

In these studies of the typology of cultures, the analytical method is structural in the sense that honour and glory are opposed in just the same way that two phonemes are opposed and are reciprocally given their appropriate value within a phonological system. However, in the course of his research Lotman realized that a code identified in a culture is much more complex than that which can be identified in a language and his analyses became increasingly subtle and took on a rich, complex historical awareness.

Even in the Sixties, Lotman understood clearly that the multiplicity of codes in a given culture gives rise to contrasts and hybrids, or 'creolizations'. In his later works, and particularly in what he has written during the last decade, he has worked out the concept of the semiosphere, in analogy with the concept of the biosphere.

The present work sets out clearly what Lotman intends by the semiosphere, and here I would like to draw attention to a crucial definition:

> . . . imagine a museum hall where exhibits from different periods are on dis-
> play, along with inscriptions in known and unknown languages, and instruc-
> tions for decoding them; there are also the explanations composed by the mu-
> seum staff, plans for tours and rules for the behaviour of the visitors. Imagine
> also in this hall tour-leaders and visitors and imagine all this as a single mecha-
> nism (which in a certain sense it is). This is an image of the semiosphere. Then
> we have to remember that all elements of the semiosphere are in dynamic, not
> static, correlations whose terms are constantly changing. We notice this spe-
> cially at traditional moments which have come down to us from the past.

Thirty years ago, Lotman was already considering the concept of the text as a unity. This concept forms the basis of his Lessons on Poetic Structure of 1964 which was then re-issued as The Structure of the Poetic Text in 1970. However, in more recent work, this interest has been extended to cover the entire semiosphere. In his 'O semiosfere' (Trudy, 17:1984), Lotman states that the whole semiosphere (culture as semiosphere) must be considered as a single mechanism and it is only in this way that we will be able to understand its various aspects. He concludes by saying that 'if we put together lots of veal cutlets, we do not obtain a calf. But if we cut up a calf, we obtain lots of veal cutlets.'

In case this metaphor disturbs the squeamish reader unwilling to consider art and culture in terms of calves and raw meat, I can attempt to, translate it with a more 'noble' equivalent (though by doing so, the basic concept which Lotman has so forcefully expressed remains the same). If we put together many branches and great quantity of leaves, we still cannot understand the forest. But if we know how to walk through the forest of culture with our eyes open, confidently following the numerous paths which criss-cross it, not only shall we be able to understand better the vastness and complexity of the forest, but we shall also be able to discover the nature of the leaves and branches of every single tree.

This book gives an indication of both the vastness and the allure of the forest and helps us to understand the form and the colour of the leaves and branches through which the forest lives.

Umberto Eco

An Author and his Interpreters

I have repeatedly tried, in the course of the last 15 years, not to speak about my novels. First of all I decided not to answer silly questions and once I made a list of 12 stupid questions for which I have already provided 12 stupid answers. I remember that the first question was "Why did you choose this title?" and the answer was "Because *Pinocchio* and *Snow White* were already copyrighted".

Then I think that a narrator, as well as a poet, should never provide interpretations of his own work. A text is a machine conceived for eliciting interpretations. When one has a text to question, it is irrelevant to ask the author.

In 1962 I wrote my *Opera aperta* (now *The Open Work*, 1989). In that book I was advocating the active role of the interpreter in the reading of texts endowed with aesthetic value. When those pages were written, my readers mainly focused the 'open' side of the whole business, underestimating the fact that the open-ended reading I was supporting was an activity elicited by (and aiming at interpreting) a work. In other words, I was studying the dialectics between the rights of texts and the rights of their interpreters. I have the impression that, in the course of the last decades, the rights of the interpreters have been overstressed.

In various of my writings I elaborated upon the Peircean idea of unlimited semiosis. But the notion of unlimited semiosis does not lead to the conclusion that interpretation has no criteria. First of all, unlimited interpretation concerns systems not processes. A linguistic system is a device from which, and by using which, infinite linguistic strings can be produced. If we look in a dictionary for the meaning of a term we find definitions and synonyms, that is, other words, and we can go to see what these words mean, so that from their definition we can switch to other words–and so on potentially ad infinitum. A dictionary is, as Joyce said of *Finnegans Wake*, a book written for an ideal reader affected by an ideal insomnia.

But a text, in so far as it is the result of the manipulation of the possibilities of a system, it is not open in the same way. In the process of producing a text one reduces the range of possible linguistic items. If one writes "John is eating a...." there are strong possibilities that the following word will be a noun, and that this noun cannot be *staircase* (even though, in certain contexts, it could be *sword*). By reducing the possibility of producing infinite strings, a text also reduces the possibility of trying certain interpretations.

To say that the interpretations of a text are potentially unlimited does not mean that interpretation has no object. To say that a text has potentially no end, does not mean that every act of interpretation can have a happy end. I have proposed a sort of Popper-like criterion of falsification by which, if it is difficult to decide if a given interpretation is a good one, and which one is better between two different interpretations of the same text, it is always possible to recognize when a given interpretation is blatantly wrong, crazy, farfetched.

Some contemporary theories of criticism assert that the only reliable reading of a text is a misreading, that the only existence of a text is given by the chains of the responses it elicits and that a text is only a picnic where the authors brings the words and the readers the sense. Even if that was true, the words brought by the author are a rather embarrassing bunch of material evidences that the reader cannot pass over in silence, or in noise.

In my book *The Limits of Interpretation* I distinguish between the intention of the author, the intention of the reader and the intention of the text.

A text is a device conceived in order to produce its Model Reader. This Reader is not the one who makes the 'only/ right' conjecture. A text can foresee a Model Reader entitled to try infinite conjectures.

How to prove a conjecture about the intention of a text? The only way is to check it upon the text as a coherent whole. This idea, too, is an old one and comes from Augustine (*De doctrina christiana*): any interpretation given of a certain portion of a text can be accepted if it is confirmed and must be rejected if it is challenged by another portion of the same text. In this sense the internal textual coherence controls the otherwise uncontrollable drives of the reader.

When a text is put in the bottle–and this happens not only with poetry or narrative but also with the *Critique of the Pure Reason*–that is, when a text is produced not for a single addressee but for a community of readers, the author knows that he/she will be interpreted not according to his/her intentions but according to a complex strategy of interactions which also involves the readers, along with their competence of language as a social treasury. I mean by social treasury not only a given language as a set of grammatical rules, but also the whole encyclopedia that the performances of that language have implemented, namely, the cultural conventions that that language has produced and the very history of the previous interpretations of many texts, comprehending the text that the reader is in the course of reading.

Thus every act of reading is a difficult transaction between the competence of the reader (the reader's world knowledge) and the kind of competence that a given text postulates in order to be read in an economic way.

The Model Reader of a story is not the Empirical Reader. The empirical reader is you, me, anyone, when we read a text. Empirical readers can read in many ways, and there is no law which tells them how to read, because they often use the text as a container for their own passions, which may come from outside the text, or which the text may arouse by chance.

Let me quote some funny situations in which one of my readers has acted as an empirical and not as a Model reader. An old childhood friend of mine, whom I hadn't seen for years, wrote to me after the publication of my second novel, *Foucault's Pendulum*: "Dear Umberto, I do not recall having told you the pathetic story of my uncle and aunt, but I think you were very indiscreet to use it for your novel". Well, in my book I recount a few episodes concerning a certain uncle Charles and an aunt Catherine, who in the story are the uncle and aunt of the protagonist, Jacopo Belbo, and it is true that these characters really did exist: though with a few alterations, I told a story from my childhood concerning an uncle and aunt, who had, however, different names. I wrote back to that friend of mine saying that Uncle Charles and Aunt Catherine were my relations, not his own (therefore I had the copyright), and that I was not even aware that he had had any uncle or aunt. My friend apologized: He had been so absorbed by the story that he thought he could recognize some incidents that had happened to his uncle and aunt, which is not impossible because in wartime (as was the period to which my memories went back) similar things happen to different uncles and aunts.

What had happened to my friend? He had sought in my story something that was instead in his private memory. He was not interpreting my text, but rather *using* it. It is not forbidden at all to use a text for day-dreaming and we do it frequently, but this is not a public affair; this means to move within a text as if it were our own private journal.

There are certain rules of the game, and the Model Reader is someone eager to play such a game. My friend forgot the rule of the game and superimposed his own expectations as empirical reader on the expectations that the author wanted from a model reader.

In Chapter 115 of my *Foucault's Pendulum* the character called Casaubon, on the night of the 23rd to the 24th of June 1984, having been at a occultist ceremony in the Conservatoire des Arts et Metiers in Paris, walks, as if possessed, along the entire length of rue Saint-Martin, crosses rue aux Ours, arrives at Centre Beaubourg and then at Saint-Merry Church. Afterwards he carries on along various streets, all of them named in my book, until he gets to Place des Vosges. I have to tell you that in order to write this chapter I had followed the same route for several nights, carrying a tape recorder, taking notes on what I could see and the impressions I had.

Indeed, since I have a computer program which can show me what the sky looks like at any time in any year, at whatever longitude or latitude, I had even gone so far as to find out if there had been a moon that night, and in what position it could have been seen at various times. I hadn't done this because I wanted to emulate Emile Zola's realism, but I like to have the scene I'm writing about in front of me while I narrate: it makes me more familiar with what's happening and helps me to get inside the characters.

After publishing the novel I received a letter from a man who had evidently gone to the National Library to read all the newspapers of June 24, 1984. And he had discovered that on the corner of rue Réaumur, that I hadn't actually named but which does cross rue Saint-Martin at a certain point, after midnight, more or less at the time when Casaubon passed by there, there had been a fire, and a big fire at that, if the papers had talked about it. The reader asked me how Casaubon had managed not to see it.

I answered that Casaubon had probably seen the fire, but he hadn't mentioned it for some mysterious reason, unknown to me, pretty likely in a story so thick with mysteries both true and false. I think that my reader is still trying to find out why Casaubon kept quiet about the fire, probably suspecting of another conspiracy by the Knights Templars.

Now let me tell you another story concerning the same night. Two students from the Parisian Ecole des Beaux Arts once came to show me a photograph album in which they had reconstructed the entire route taken by my character, having gone and photographed the places I had mentioned, one by one, at the same time of night. Given that at the end of the chapter Casaubon comes up out of the city drains and enters through the cellar an oriental bar full of sweating customers, beer-jugs and greasy spits, they succeeded in finding that bar and took a photo of it. It goes without saying that that bar was an invention of mine, even though I have designed it thinking of the many bars of that kind in the area, but those two boys had undoubtedly discovered the bar described in my book. It's not that those students had superimposed on their duty as model readers the concerns of the empirical reader who wants to check if my novel describes the real Paris. On the contrary, they wanted to transform the "real" Paris into a place in my book, and in fact, of all that they could have found in Paris, they chose only those aspects that corresponded to my descriptions — or, better, to the descriptions provided by my text.

In these dialectics between the intention of the reader and the intention of the text, the intention of the empirical author becomes rather irrelevant. We have to respect the text, not the author as a person so and so. Frequently authors say something of which they were not aware and discover to have said that only after the reactions of their readers.

There is however a case in which it can be interesting to resort to the intention of the empirical author. There are cases in which the author is still living, the critics have given their interpretations of his text, and it can be nice to ask the author how much and to what an extent he, as an empirical person, was aware of the manifold interpretations his text supported. At this point the response of the author must not be used in order to validate the interpretations of his text, but to show the discrepancies between the author's intention and the intention of the text. The aim of the experiment is not a critical one, but rather a theoretical one.

There can be, finally, a case in which the author is also a text theorist. In this case it would be possible to get two different sorts of reaction from him. In certain cases he can say "No, I did not mean this, but I must agree that the text says it, and I thank the reader who made me aware of it." Or: "Independently of the fact that I did not mean this, I think that a reasonable reader should not accept such an interpretation, because it sounds uneconomical".

A typical case where the author must surrender in face of the reader is the one I told about in my *Reflections on the Name of the Rose*. As I read the reviews of the novel, I felt a thrill of satisfaction when I found a critic who quoted a remark of William's made at the end of the trial: (page 385 in the English-language edition). "What terrifies you most in purity?" Adso asks. And William answers: "Haste." I loved, and still love, these two lines very much. But then one of my readers pointed out to me that on the same page, Bernard Gui, threatening the cellarer with torture, says: "Justice is not inspired by haste, as the Pseudo Apostles believe, and the justice of God has centuries at its disposal." And the reader rightly asked me what connection I had meant to establish between the haste feared by William and the absence of haste extolled by Bernard. I was unable to answer. As a matter of fact the exchange between Adso and William does not exist in the manuscript, I added this brief dialogue in the galleys, for reasons of concinnity: I needed to insert another scansion before giving Bernard the floor again. And I completely forgot that, a little later, Bernard speaks of haste. Bernard's speech uses a stereotyped expression, the sort of thing we would expect from a judge, a commonplace on the order of "All are equal before the law." Alas, when juxtaposed with the haste mentioned by William, the haste mentioned by Bernard literally creates an effect of sense; and the reader is justified in wondering if the two men are saying the same thing, or if the loathing of haste expressed by William is not imperceptibly different from the loathing of haste expressed by Bernard. The text is there, and produces its own effects. Whether I wanted it this way or not, we are now faced with a question, an ambiguous provocation; and I myself feel embarrassment in interpreting this conflict, though I realize a meaning lurks there (perhaps many meanings do).

Now, let me tell of an opposite case.

Helena Costiucovich before translating into Russian (masterfully) *The Name of the Rose*, wrote a long essay on it.[1] At a given point she remarks that there exists a book by Emile Henriot (*La rose de Bratislava*, 1946) where it can be found the hunting of a mysterious manuscript and a final fire of a library. The story takes place in Prague, and at the beginning of my novel I mention Prague. Moreover one of my librarians is named Berengar and one of the librarians of Henriot was named Berngard Marre.

It is perfectly useless to say that, as an empirical author, I had never read Henriot's novel and that I ignored that it existed. I have read interpretations in which my critics found out sources of which I was fully aware, and I was very happy that they so cunningly discovered what I so cunningly concealed in order to lead them to find it (for instance the model of the couple Serenus Zeitblom-Adrian in Mann's *Doktor Faustus* for the narrative relationship Adso-William). I have read of sources totally unknown to me, and I was delighted that somebody believed that I was eruditely quoting them (recently a young medievalist told me that a blind librarian was mentioned by Cassiodorus). I have read critical analyses in which the interpreter discovered influences of which I was unaware when writing but I certainly had read those books in my youth and I understood that I was unconsciously influenced by them (my friend Giorgio Celli said that among my remote readings there should have been the novels of Dmitri Mereskovskij, and I recognized that he was correct).

As an uncommitted reader of *The Name of the Rose* I think that the argument of Helena Costiucovich is not proving anything interesting. The research of a mysterious manuscript and the fire of a library are very common literary *topoi* and I could quote many other books which use them. Prague was mentioned at the beginning of the story, but if instead of Prague I mentioned Budapest it would have been the same. Prague does not play a crucial role in my story.

Finally, Berengar and Berngard can be a coincidence. In any case the Model Reader can agree that four coincidences (manuscript, fire, Prague and Berengar) are interesting and as an empirical author I have no right to react. O.K.: to put a good face upon this accident, I formally acknowledge that my text had the intention to pay homage to Emile Henriot.

However, Helena Costiucovich wrote something more to prove the analogy between me and Henriot. She said that that in Henriot's novel the coveted manuscript was the original copy of the *Memorie* of Casanova. It happens that in my novel there is a minor character called Hugh of Newcastle (and in the Italian version, Ugo di Novocastro). The conclusion of Costiucovich is that "only by passing from a name to another it is possible to conceive of the name of the rose".

As an empirical author I could say that Hugh of Newcastle is not an invention of mine but a historical figure, mentioned in the medieval

sources I used; the episode of the meeting between the Franciscan delega-
tion and the Papal representatives literally quotes a medieval chronicle of
the XIV century. But the reader is not obliged to know that, and my reaction cannot be taken into account. However I think to have the right to
state my opinion as an uncommitted reader. First of all Newcastle is not a
translation of Casanova, which should be translated as New House, and a
castle is not a house (besides, in Italian, or in Latin, Novocastro means New
City or New Encampment). Thus Newcastle suggests Casanova in the
same way it could suggest Newton. But there are other elements that can
textually prove that the hypothesis of Costiucovich is uneconomical. First
of all, Hugh of Newcastle shows up in the novel, playing a very marginal
role, and has nothing to do with the library. If the text wanted to suggest a
pertinent relationship between Hugh and the library (as well as between
him and the manuscript) it should have said something more. But the text
does not say a word about that. Secondly, Casanova was–at least in the light
of a commonly shared encyclopedic knowledge–a professional lover and a
rake, and there is nothing in the novel which casts in doubt the virtue of
Hugh. Third, there is no evident connection between a manuscript of Casanova and a manuscript of Aristotle and there is nothing in the novel which
alludes to sexual incontinence as a value to be pursued. To look for the
Casanova connection does not lead anywhere.

Obviously, I am ready to change my mind if some other interpreter
demonstrates that the Casanova connection can lead to some interesting
interpretive path, but for the moment being–as a Model Reader of my own
novel–I feel entitled to say that such a hypotheses is scarcely rewarding.

Once during a debate a reader asked me what I meant by the sentence
"the supreme happiness lies in having what you have". I felt disconcerted
and I swore that I had never written that sentence. I was sure of it, and for
many reasons: first, I do not think that happiness lies in having what one
has, and not even Snoopy would subscribe such a triviality. Secondly it is
improbable that a medieval character would suppose that happiness lies in
having what he actually had, since happiness for the medieval mind was a
future state to be reached through present suffering. Thus I repeated that I
had never written that line, and my interlocutor looked upon me as an
author unable to recognize what he had written.

Later I came across that quotation. It appears during the description of
the erotic ecstasy of Adso in the kitchen. This episode, as the dullest of my
readers can easily guess, is entirely made up with quotations from the Song
of Songs and from medieval mystics. In any case, even though the reader
does not find out the sources, he/she can guess that these pages depict the
feelings of a young man after his first (and probably last) sexual experience.
If one goes to re-read the line in its context (I mean the context of my text,
not necessarily the context of its medieval sources), one finds that the line
reads: "O lord, when the soul is transported, the only virtue lies in having

what you see, the supreme happiness is having what you have." Thus happiness lies in having what you have, but not in general and not in every
moment of your life, but only in the moment of the ecstatic vision. This is
the case in which it is unnecessary to know the intention of the empirical
author: the intention of the text is blatant and, if English words have a
conventional meaning, the text does not say what that reader–obeying
some idiosyncratic drives–believed to have read. Between the unattainable
intention of the author and the arguable intention of the reader there is the
transparent intention of the text which disproves an untenable interpretation.

An author who has entitled his book *The Name of the Rose* must be ready
to face manifold interpretations of his title. As an empirical author (Reflections 3) I wrote that I chose that title just in order to set the reader free:
"the rose is a figure so rich in meanings that by now it has no meaning left:
Dante's mystic rose, and go lovely rose, the Wars of the Roses, rose thou
art sick, too many rings around Rosie, a rose by any other name, a rose is a
rose is a rose is a rose, the Rosicrucians..." Moreover someone has discovered that some early manuscripts of De Contemptu Mundi of Bernard de
Morlay, from which I borrowed the exameter "stat rosa pristina nomine,
nomina nuda tenemus", read "stat Roma pristina nomine"–which would
look more coherent with the rest of the poem, which speaks of the lost
Babylon (event though, since the o of rosa is short and the o of Roma is
long, only the first term can meet the quantitative requirements of the
exameter). Had I come across another version of Morlay's poem, the title
of my novel, could have been The Name of Rome (thus acquiring fascist
overtones).

But the text reads The Name of the Rose and I understand now how
difficult it was to stop the infinite series of connotations that word elicits.
Probably I wanted to open the possible readings so much as to make each
of them irrelevant, and as a result I have produced an inexorable series of
interpretations. But the text is there, and the empirical author has to remain silent.

There are however (once again) cases in which the empirical author has
the right to react as a Model Reader.

I have enjoyed the beautiful book by Robert F. Fleissner, A Rose by any
other name–A survey of literary flora from Shakespeare to Eco (1989) and
I hope that Shakespeare would have been proud to find his name associated
with mine. Among the various connections that Fleissner finds between
my rose and all the other roses of world literature there is an interesting
passage: Fleissner wants to show "how Eco's rose derived from Doyle's
Adventures of the Naval Treaty, which, in turn, owed much to Cuff's admiration of this flower in The Moonstone" (p.139).

I am positively a Wilkie Collins' addict but I do not remember (and certainly I did not when writing my novel) mention of Cuff's floral passion. I believed to have read the opera omnia of Doyle but I must confess that I do not remember to have read The adventure of the Naval Treaty. It does not matter: in my novel there are so many explicit references to Holmes that my text can support also this connection. But in spite of my open-mindedness, I find an instance of overinterpretation when Fleissner, trying to demonstrate how much my William 'echoes' Holmes' admiration for roses, quotes this passage from my book:

"Frangula," William said suddenly, bending over to observe a plant that, on that winter day, he recognized from the bare bush. "A good infusion is made from the bark..."

It is curious that Fleissner stops his quotation exactly after bark. My text continues, and after a comma reads: "for hemorrhoids." Honestly, I think that the Model Reader is not invited to take frangula as an allusion to the rose–otherwise every plant could stand for a rose.

Let me come now to Foucault's Pendulum. I named one of the main characters of my Foucault's Pendulum, Casaubon, and I was thinking of Isaac Casaubon, who demonstrated that the Corpus Hermeticum was a forgery. If one reads Foucault's Pendulum one can find some analogy between what the great philologist understood and what my character finally understands. I was aware that few readers would have been able to catch the allusion but I was equally aware that, in term of textual strategy, this was not indispensable (I mean that one can read my novel and understand my Causaubon even though disregarding the historical Casaubon — many authors like to put in their texts certain shibboleths for a few precocious readers). Before finishing my novel I discovered by chance that Casaubon was also a character of Middlemarch, a book that I had read decades ago and that in Italy is not as frequently quoted or studied in schools as in anglo-saxon countries. Thus I had obviously forgotten the names of the characters. That was a case in which, as a Model Author, I made an effort in order to eliminate a possible reference to George Eliot. On p.63 of the English translation can be read the following exchange between Belbo and Casaubon:

"By the way, what's your name?"
"Casaubon."
"Casaubon. Wasn't he a character in Middlemarch?"
"I don't know. There was also a Renaissance philologist by that name, but we are not related."

I did my best to avoid what I thought to be a useless reference to Mary Ann Evans. But then came a smart reader, David Robey, who remarked that, evidently not by chance, Eliot's Casaubon was writing a Key to all mythologies. As a Model Reader I feel obliged to accept that innuendo. Text plus encyclopedic knowledge entitle any cultivated reader to find that connection. It makes sense. Too bad for the empirical author who was not as smart as his readers.

In the same vein my second novel is entitled Foucault's Pendulum because the pendulum I am speaking of was invented by Léon Foucault. If it were invented by Franklin the title would have been Franklin's Pendulum. This time I was aware from the very beginning that somebody could have smelled an allusion to Michel Foucault: my characters are obsessed by analogies and Foucault wrote on the paradigm of similarity. As an empirical author I was not so happy with such a possible connection. It sounds like a joke and not a very clever one, indeed. But the pendulum invented by Léon was the hero of my story and could not change the title: thus I hoped that my Model Reader would not have tried a superficial connection with Michel. I was wrong, many sharp readers did it. The text is there, maybe they are right, maybe I am responsible for a superficial joke, maybe the joke is not that superficial. I do not know. The whole affair is by now out of my control.

Giosue Musca[2] wrote a critical analysis of my second novel that I consider among the best I have read. From the beginning he confesses however to have been corrupted by the way of thinking of my characters and goes fishing for analogies. He masterfully isolates many ultraviolet quotations and stylistic analogies I wanted to be discovered, he finds other connections I did not think of but that look very persuasive, and he plays the role of a paranoiac reader by finding out connections that amaze me but that I am unable to disprove--even though I know that they can mislead the reader. For instance it seems that the name of the computer, Abulafia, plus the name of the three main characters, Belbo, Casaubon and Diotallevi, produces the series ABCD. Useless to protest that until the end of my work I gave the computer a different name: my readers can object that I unconsciously changed it just in order to obtain an alphabetic series. It seems that Jacopo Belbo is fond of whisky and his initials make JB. Useless to confess that when my work was in progress his first name a different one and that I changed it into Jacopo at the last moment.

The only objection I can make as a Model Reader of my book is that (i) the alphabetical series ABCD is textually irrelevant if the names of the other characters do not bring it until X,Y and Z, that (ii) Belbo also drinks Martini and furthermore his mild alcoholic addiction is not the most relevant of his features. On the contrary I cannot disprove my reader when he also remarks that Pavese was born in a village called Santo Stefano Belbo and that my Belbo, a melancholic piedmontese, can recall Pavese. It is true Recife who intermarried with Indians and Sudanese blacks--with her Jamaican face and Parisian culture–had wound up with a Spanish name." This means that I took the name Amparo as if it came from outside my novel.

Months after the publication of the novel a friend asked me: "Why Amparo? Is it not the name of a mountain, or of a girl who looks at a mountain?" And then he explained: "There is that song, *Guajira Guantanamera*, which mentions something like Amparo."

Oh my God. I knew very well that song, even though I did not remember a single word of it. It was sung, in the mid fifties, by a Latin American girl with whom I was in love at that time. She was not Brazilian, not Marxist, not black, not hysterical as Amparo is, but it is clear that, when inventing a Latin American charming girl, I unconsciously thought of that other image of my youth, when I was the same age as Casaubon. I thought of that song, and in some way the name Amparo (that I had completely forgot) transmigrated from my unconscious to the page.

This story is fully irrelevant for the interpretation of my text. As far as the text is concerned Amparo is Amparo is Amparo is Amparo.

Second story. Those who have read my *Name of the Rose* know that there is a mysterious manuscript, that contains the lost second book of Aristotle *Poetics*, that its pages are ointed with poison and that (at p.570 of the paperback edition) it is described like this:

> He read the first page aloud, then stopped, as if he were not interested in knowing more, and rapidly leafed through the following pages. But after a few pages he encountered resistance, because near the upper corner of the side edge, and along the top, some pages had stuck together, as happens when the damp and deteriorating papery substance forms a kind of sticky paste...

I wrote these lines at the end of 1979. In the following years, perhaps also because after the *Name of the Rose* I started to be more frequently in touch with librarians, I became a regular rare books collector. It had happened before, in the course of my life, that I bought some old book, but by chance, and only when they were very cheap. Only in the last decade I have become a serious collector, and 'serious' means that one has to consult specialized catalogues and must write, for every book, a technical file, with the collation, historical information on the previous or following editions, and a precise description of the physical state of the copy. This last job requires a technical jargon, in order to precisely name foxed, browned, waterstained, soiled, washed or crisp leaves, cropped margins, erasures, rebaked bindings, rubbed joints and so on.

One day, rummaging through the upper shelves of my home library I discovered an edition of the *Poetics* of Aristotle, commented by Antonio Riccoboni, Padova 1587. I had forgotten that I had it; I found on the endpaper a *1000* written in pencil, and this means that I bought it somewhere for

1000 liras, less than a dollar, probably twenty or more years before. My catalogues said that it was the second edition, not exceedingly rare, but I was happy to have it because the commentary of Riccoboni is less known and less quoted than those, let say, of Robortello or Castelvetro.

Then I started writing my description. I copied the title page and I discovered that the edition had an Appendix "Ejusdem Ars Comica ex Aristotele". This means that Riccoboni had tried to re-construct the lost second book of the *Poetics*. It was not however an unusual endeavor, and I went on to set up the physical description of the copy. Then it happened to me what had happened to a person described by Lurja, who, having lost part of his brain during the war, and who with part of the brain the whole of his memory and of his speaking ability, was nevertheless still able to write: thus automatically his hand wrote down all the information he was unable to think of, and step by step he reconstructed his own identity by reading what he was writing.

Likewise, I was looking coldly and technically at the book, writing my description, and suddenly I realized that I was re-writing the *Name of the Rose*. The only difference was that from page 120, when the Ars Comica begins, the lower and not the upper margins were severely damaged; but all the rest was the same, the pages progressively browned and dampstained at the end stuck together, and looked as if they were ointed with a disgusting fat substance. I had in my hands, in printed form, the manuscript I described in my novel. I had had it for years and years at my reach, at home.

At a first moment I thought of an extraordinary coincidence; then I was tempted to believe in a miracle; at the end I decided that *who Es war, soll Ich werden*. I bought that book in my youth, I skimmed through it, I realized that it was exaggeratedly soiled, I put it somewhere and I forgot it. But by a sort of internal camera I photographed those pages, and for decades the image of those poisonous leaves lay in the most remote part of my soul, as in a grave, until the moment it emerged again (I do not know for what reason) and I believed to have invented it.

This story too has nothing to do with a possible interpretation of my book. If it has a moral it is that the private life of the empirical author is in a certain respect more unfathomable than their texts. Between the mysterious history of a textual production and the uncontrollable drift of its future readings, the text *qua text* still represents a comfortable presence, the point to which we can stick.

Umberto Eco

Part II

Readings on Eco. A Pretext to Literary
Semiotics and Interpretation

The *Open Work* in Theory and Practice

Reviewing the early works of George Eliot in 1866 Henry James reflected on the possibility of foreshadowing later events in narratives without every describing them. This possibility leads James to make the following statement about the composition of novels: "In every novel the work is divided between the writer and the reader; but the writer makes the reader very much as he makes his characters. When he makes him ill, that is, makes him different, he does no work; the writer does all. When he makes him well, that is, makes him interested, then the reader does quite half the labour."[1] With astonishing prescience James here anticipates reader response theory in generalizing the novelist's responsibility to situate the reader in the text at points where s/he can respond to the text's inferential cues.

The germ thrown out briefly by Henry James comes to its logical fruition in Umberto Eco's seminal 1959 essay "The Poetics of the Open Work" which sets the keynote for two collections: *The Role of the Reader* and more recently *The Open Work*. Taking his starting point from the musical compositions of Stockhausen, Henri Pousseur and others, Eco identifies a new art-form characteristic of the modern age where a work is entirely explicit about it own lack of completion. Instead of requiring assent to a structural sequence with a firm conclusion such works construct a "field of possibilities," to borrow a phrase from Pousseur, within which the performer can make a choice. Where most works of art limit their potential area of response, this new kind of art deliberately refuses to make prescriptive limitations on its own consumption and Eco stresses the importance of the Symbolists here because they developed a program of exploiting verbal suggestion at the expense of direct statement. Eco approaches the position of Wolfgang Iser and the other reception theorists in making the reader the co-producer of a work: "every reception of a work of art is both an *interpretation* and *performance* of it, because in every reception the work takes on a fresh perspective for itself"[2] (Eco's emphasis). Here at least three distinct but related processes are run together. There is firstly the realization of a musical score through performance, secondly the process of interpretation which as it were actualizes a text for the reader, and more implicitly a suggestion that in interpreting the reader is resolving what Iser designates the "indeterminacies" of a work. Eco at this point anticipates Roland Barthes who has argued that the text "asks the reader for an active collaboration."[3] Both critics have as a common purpose the desire to re-energize the act of reading to remove it as far as possible from the passivity of conventional consumption and Eco puts such a high premium on a work's inexhaustibility that elsewhere he goes as far as identifying the "poetic effect" of literature with a works' limitless suggestiveness, "The capacity that a text displays for continuing to generate different readings, without ever being completely consumed."[4] It is not entirely clear here whether this is a general property of all texts or a qualitative judgment on their relative richness.

In foregrounding the importance of performance, Eco takes his initial examples from music but his commentary helpfully opens up an avenue for approaching the postmodern fiction of such novelists as Raymond Federman and Ronald Sukenick who explicitly write the processes of composition into their novels. Where Eco draws particular attention to mobiles Federman and Sukenick construct texts in motion, exploiting different forms of type and unusual page arrangements to jolt the reader out of conventional grooves of response. For this reason Federman has declared that the "elements of the new fictitious discourse . . . must become digressive from one another, in the sense of using discontinuity to disrupt the flow of reading."[5] If every element is digressive no single one can maintain hegemony over the flow of discourse and the reader is forced willy-nilly to scrutinize the relations between the different elements. This kind of fiction responds well to performatory analysis and, as we shall see, contains the kinds of discontinuity Eco values in Joyce.[6]

In order to explore the quality of openness Eco makes what he calls a lengthy 'detour' into information theory partly because it sheds light on our reactions to indeterminacy and partly to ask whether the methods of that discipline could be transposed on to aesthetics. Taking as a premise that works of art are messages, 'organized systems governed by fixed laws of probability' (p. 50), Eco summarizes attempts at quantifying information and then cautiously introduces into his discussion the notion of entropy. In his 1950 study *The Human Use of Human Beings* Norbert Wiener sets up what Eco finds to be too stark a contrast between information's dependence on order and the relation of entropy to disorder. Eco, however, posits a distinction between meaning and information whereby the former emerges from simple denotative statements and the latter from unpredictability and suggestion. A clear message is efficient in conveying meaning but low in information, whereas if we take poetical examples by Petrarch and Ungaretti we find that their informational value increases as new readings of these poems multiply. For Eco poetical value emerges from unorthodox or unpredictable literary messages and so we return to the aesthetics of openness which demonstrates a "tendency toward *controlled* disorder" (p. 65; Eco's emphasis). Meaning correspondingly becomes a measure of order and predictability whereas information, because it is less predictable, becomes a measure of freedom of choice in interpretation.

It is no longer as unusual as Eco suggests to relate entropy to literature. Given his interest in systems (he defines style as a "system of probability"), it is surprising that Eco has not paid more attention to the fiction of Thomas Pynchon which abounds in humorous views of the structures we erect to make sense of the world. Pynchon's early story "Entropy" (1960) distances itself from the apocalyptic implications the term carried for Henry Adams by constructing a layered presentation of its different meanings without committing itself to any. Rudolf Arnheim's *Entropy and Art* (1974) attempts to clear up the confusions surrounding the term. He notices first of all a shift in its application from explaining the "degradation of culture": "it now provides a positive rationale for "minimal" art and the pleasures of chaos."[7] Like Eco Arnheim homes in on the question of unpredictability and disqualifies the application of entropy to aesthetics on the practical grounds that it would necessitate impossibly laborious calculations. He then refuses the application on the second grounds that entropy does not explain sequence but rather distribution within given systems. The same highly randomized sequence could be described by an entropy theorist as highly probable and by an information theorist as highly *im*probable. Arnheim implies that this discrepancy could only disappear if a work of art were hypostatized into a static system whereas Eco's concern is to show the dynamics of how these systems come into being.

Eco draws on information theory to argue that poetical expression by its very nature risks disorder in diverging from grammatical and syntactic rules. Extreme examples of this process could be found in nonsense poetry but Eco is careful to stress that they are only particular cases of a general principle of unorthodoxy that governs literary expression. The aesthetic value of a work is therefore related to its divergence from a pattern and some of Eco's wittiest and most perceptive essays have been those where he identifies the patterns underlying popular culture. In his analysis of Bond narratives, Eco points out how characters are placed in opposition to each other (most notably Bond vs. Villain), thereby reflecting a Manichean ideology.[8] When discussing the film *Casablanca*, Eco realized that the action had so efficiently drawn on previous cinematic techniques that the film became a compendium of clichés. *Casablanca* thus "cites countless other films" and becomes in effect "an anthology."[9] The popularity of this work involves the recognition of familiar devices which in the postmodern cinema would be used more self-consciously, as sit were within quotation marks.

Eco identifies the art which exploits its own familiarity as Kitsch, a category which would involve the Bond narratives. In his essay in *The Open Work* "The Structure of Bad Taste" Eco attempts to investigate the general features of Kitsch, taking issue with those critics who superciliously dismiss it as a deplorable side to mass culture. More neutrally Eco argues that Kitsch engages in a constant dialectic with the avant-garde, adopting methods which have already become familiar and diverting them towards immediate and effortless comprehension. It makes more sense to speak of *re*consumption here since artistic techniques are essentially being recycled. Whereas a poetic message requires the decipherment of a new code Kitsch relies upon codes which are already known. But there is a further characteristic. Kitsch borrows from other works in such a way that the borrowing does not blend into a new homogeneous whole.

It should be clear by now that Eco gradually maximizes the connotations of the term 'open' as suggesting flexibility, intellectual receptivity, and potential. Each succeeding essay in *The Open Work* examines the central idea in relation to particular contexts—serial music, television drama and so on. Eco gradually extends its applicability so that it comes to suggest a paradigm of the mind's activity. Here, for instance, is how Eco, with some help from Dewey and Piaget, explains the working of the intelligence: "The subject, guided by experience, proceeds by hypotheses and trial-and-error to find. . .reversible, mutable structures that allow him, after he has linked two elements in a relationship, to pull them apart again and go back to where he started" (p. 73). This gives us a reasonable account of how Eco's own essays work. He delights in speculating about links between diverse phenomena (typically skipping from Stockhausen to Merleau-Ponty and Brecht within the same page). Analogies are of paramount importance to Eco's syncretism because he is constantly probing after a master-code, a unified way of explaining signification. It is predictable for him to turn to structuralism for help in this search since he defines a work of art as a "system of relationships." And it was only a matter of time before he drew on semiotics for more sophisticated help in explaining the generation and interrelation of all signs. Eco proceeds dialogically in his discussions, quoting writers and then taking issue with them, or hypothesizing objections which might arise to his own assertions. One particularly clear instance of the latter tactic occurs in his essay on Luigi Pareyson who was Eco's adviser when he was writing his thesis on Aquinas at the University of Turin. Pareyson played an important role in Eco's intellectual development by helping him to move away from Croce's idealism but Eco's tribute to a former mentor asserts awkward identifications (the creator *is* the content of a work of art), by questions of intention, and blurs together a work's potential and completed structure. Worst of all, Pareyson's influence can be seen in Eco's references in these essays to organic form whose connotations of closure sit very oddly with Eco's main emphases on the openness of the work art, its status as an intertext, and its dependence on the reader as co-creator.

The trial-and-error sequence helps to explain why Eco should be drawn so repeatedly to narratives of detection, although his attitude to the genre seems sometimes rather ambivalent. At one point he takes the detective story as the "most extreme example" of traditional narrative structure because here he finds his paradigm of the reading process so clearly confirmed: the reader "eliminates all the false clues, whose main function is that of keeping the reader in a state of suspense, and, by and by, he discovers the real causes of the crime. . ." (p. 147). Eco expresses an ironic weariness over the ways in which the stereotyped detective narrative confirms social order and therefore, by implication, the reader's comfortable assumption of order - civic and literary. But elsewhere in *The Open Work* Eco also admits the unusual semiotic importance of this genre. A poetic message, he declares, is a "constant invitation to cryptanalysis" (p. 198), a proposition which would have been absolutely congenial to one of the founders of the genre–Edgar Allan Poe. Several of Poe's narratives like "The Gold-Bug," for example, read like semiotic exercises *avant la letter*, and Poe constantly weaves an awareness of different systems of signifying into his tales of detection. Indeed it could be argued that the detective genre uniquely foregrounds the arbitrary nature of signs sometimes to such an extreme degree that a character can non longer use any means to prove her own existence, as happens in *The Woman in White*. The very name of Eco's protagonist in *The Name of the Rose*, William of Baskerville, pays tribute to the Sherlock Holmes stories and forewarns the reader that the narrative is going to revolve round investigation. When William discovers a document containing fragments of Greek script with yet more signs which become visible only after heat is applied, the document stands as a synecdoche for the whole novel. William functions like a surrogate for Eco himself, trying to extrapolate a "general law" from disconnected data, and he demonstrates the same semiotic awareness which Eco expresses theoretically in *The Open Work* when he asserts that a "book is made up of signs that speak of other signs" (*The Rose*: 396). Eco himself locates the nature of poetic language as the "multiform" and "plurivocal" interdependence signs which therefore need to be read differently. Eco designates some modern works of art "epistemological metaphors" in so far as their structure suggests ways of knowing, and the library in the novel has a similar function to perform. It is structured as an octagonal labyrinth whose secrets of access are handed down from one librarian to the next. Eco has explained in *Reflections on 'The Name of the Rose'* that the 'crime novel represents a kind of conjecture' and that the labyrinth represents "an abstract model of conjecturality."[10] The labyrinthine library thus depicts in concrete (and Borgesian) form the site for such a play of mind.

This library, however, is caught up within a second play of meaning to understand which it is helpful to take brief bearings from the writings of Mikhail Bakhtin. When formulating his theory of "heteroglossia" where different kinds of discourse traverse the texts of novels Bakhtin argues that authoritarian regimes tend to centralize discourse in a single official mode whereas cultures always possess counter-discourses from different minorities which tug anarchically against this tendency.[11] Eco similarly proposes an opposition between open and closed literary works which carries comparable political undertones. For him the very antithesis of the open work is the fourfold stratification of meaning in allegory which Dante puts forward in his famous thirteenth letter. As if summarizing Bakhtin, Eco comments: "it is obvious at this point that all available possibilities of interpretation have been exhausted. The reader can concentrate his attention in one sense rather than on another. . . but he must always follow rules that entail a rigid univocality." The restricted possibilities of interpretation thereby reflect state control of texts and society alike: "The order of a work of art in this period is a mirror of imperial and theocratic society" (p. 6). It is no accident therefore that the action of *The Name of The Rose* should take place in a period of transition when that central ecclesiastical authority was weakening. The struggle between William of Baskerville and the aged librarian takes on a clear historical symbolism as a conflict between a conservative and reactionary authority which confirms its own prejudice that knowledge is dangerous by making a manuscript literally poisonous, and a new open-minded secularism represented by William. The term "open" is never used neutrally by Eco. It always carries connotations of heuristic freshness, freedom from prescription, and so on. Indeed he speculates that, if modern art takes the consumer through repeated ruptures of patterns, the result might have consequences reaching far beyond art alone. This process "would come to represent modern man's path to salvation, toward the reconquest of his lost autonomy at the level of both perception and intelligence" (p. 83).

In pursuit of this openness Eco diverts from his stance as a neutral 'cultural historian' in a number of ways. Although he is skeptical about direct literary activism this does not mean that literature has no social role. A wry retrospective essay looks back at the "Gruppo 63" which was set up to attack the complacency of the then Italian avant-garde. This purpose burgeoned into the more grandiose aim of making a critique of Italian culture as a whole until the student upheavals of 1968 reduced the group to silence. Eco has a well-developed sense of media pressure gained partly from first-hand experience since after completing his book on Aquinas, he secured a job as television writer for RAI (the Italian equivalent of the BBC). His essays refer repeatedly to media projection, to the processes by which a culture imposes images on its members and thereby anaesthetizes them. At times Eco insists that openness can lead to cultural pluralism and dialogue. Contemporary art, he continues, violates the conventional patterns of a culture and by so doing demystifies those patterns, allowing the consumer to question or avoid them. Postmodern art is given a crucial moral role in that it could "come to represent modern man's path to salvation, toward the reconquest of his lost autonomy at the level of both perception and intelligence." Eco constantly stresses that works of art are embedded in their cultural contexts, reacting against already existing patterns of discourse. Alienation is described as a narcosis brought on by a conventionalized cultural system, a state which can only be countered by deliberate acts of nonconformity.

The writers which Eco highlights as pursuing multiple and indeterminate meaning are characteristically those whose works resist closure or who pursue diverse systems of signification like Kafka and Mallarmé (discussed in *The Open Work*) or Poe and Borges (alluded to in *The Name of the Rose*); but standing out above all these writers is the figure of James Joyce. Joyce occupies pride of place in Eco's discussion of the open work and *The Middle Ages of James Joyce* (1982) can be read as a brief companion to *The Open Work*.

Running through Joyce's fiction like a connecting thread Eco locates a dialectic between a "classical conception of form and the need for a more pliable and 'open' structure of the work and of the world."[12] Eco follows in a long line of critics when he argues that Joyce lost his faith in Catholicism but retained a nostalgia for the massive intellectual order of Catholic thought. Accordingly there results a tension in Joyce between the medieval and the modern, between a poetics culled from Aquinas and a rival attitude to art deriving from the Symbolists. Eco shows that in his theorizing Stephen Dedalus uses Aquinas to smuggle heresy into his theories which the clerics fight shy of contradicting because this would involve them in refuting the authority of Aquinas himself. These "medieval garments" cloak Stephen's growing aestheticism. Secondly Eco compares Stephen's use of Aquinas with the latter's theories as a whole, contrasting the notion of catharsis as purgation (which Joyce wittily used in "The Holy Office") and catharsis as an arrest of feeling, which would shed light on Stephen's puritanical streak. Eco concludes that Stephen (and Joyce?) had no direct knowledge of Aquinas and finds strong and unacknowledged echoes of Mallarmé in Stephen's discussion. The other main topic which Eco discusses in early Joyce is the epiphany which involves an arbitrary decision to

surcharge an event or image with gratuitous significance. The notion carries its own circular justification: the fact "appears worthy of being
epiphanized because, in fact, it has been epiphanized."[13] By lifting such
moments out of context Joyce denies them the pivotal significance of
Wordsworth's spots of time, instead using them to reflect implicitly on the
sensibility of the registering consciousness.

When Eco moves on to *Ulysses* his primary concern is to show how it
reflects Joyce's medievalism by constructing a "work-as-cosmos." The
novel, he argues, assembles a massively complex system of symbolic relationships which lacks the accessibility that would be furnished by a homogeneous culture: "the organizing key to this circuit does not rely upon an
objective code lying outside of the work but upon an internal set of relationships which are embedded in its structure."[14] Eco quickly disposes of
the reader's forlorn hope that there may be a single figure in this carpet,
suggesting rather that Joyce has superimposed a series of quasi-medieval
orders on his material. Because no single system is privileged over another
(not even the much-discussed Homeric parallels) the reader is confronted
with a hermeneutic field around which s/he can move at will. Each signifier
is thus charged with a multiple reference that startles the reader by incomplete gestures towards meaning.

Eco reads *Ulysses* as a *summa*, an encyclopedic work whose elaborate
arrangement of data implies a desire for intellectual and social integration
which can never be fulfilled. In the preface which he wrote for a reissue of
The Aesthetics of Thomas Aquinas (1954) Eco singles out Joyce for special
mention as the "main example of an avant-garde writer whose aesthetics, in
his youth, was based upon Scolasticism."[15] For Joyce and for the moderns
in general, however, God is unavailable as a fixed point of origin and the
Bible as an ultimate textual authority. Even beauty in Aquinas' world became a transcendental entity carrying an "unchanging objectivity," which
contrasts starkly with its appearance in *Portrait* as the central issue of
heated debate. For Eco *Ulysses* expresses a yearning for a lost totality
whereas Edward Mendelson has hypothesized a special encyclopedic genre
stretching from Dante's *Divine Comedy* through Rabelais and *Moby-Dick* to
Ulysses and *Gravity's Rainbow*.[16] These works, he suggests, appear at moments of heightened national self-consciousness and attempt to incorporate
the data and forms of knowledge used by their societies. Mendelson's argument suggests a more political reading of *Ulysses* by means of highlighting
just those aspects of its organization which Eco too had stressed. Taking the
"Proteus" episode as a synecdoche, Eco finds a poetics of "expressive form"
in *Ulysses* whereby the form itself articulates the work's meaning. He arrives at this McLuhanesque position by positing a radical shift of emphasis
from content to expression and in the process supplies a distorted and over-
stated account of the novelty of *Ulysses*. In his eagerness to establish its

historical importance Eco resorts to a crude contrast between form and content, implying that modernism exploits the one and traditional realism the other; but no-one would dream of reading realistic works only with reference to their contents. Eco suggests rightly that *Ulysses* is criss-crossed by a series of correspondences and suggests that the reader generates meaning by maneuvering among these systems. Similarly he could have argued that the reader's transitions from one genre to another, from one discourse to another, within the same work account for its originality rather than a simple shift from content to form.

Finnegans Wake for Eco culminates Joyce's career and gives us the paradigmatic open work of the modern sensibility where 'the author intends his book to imply the totality of space and time' (p. 10). Now the basic unit is the pun embedding different lexemes within each other, every single one of which can generate a series of associations. With due acknowledgment to Joseph Frank, Eco spatializes both *Ulysses* and *Finnegans Wake*, demonstrating that the latter juxtaposes different semantic fields.[17] *Finnegans Wake* shows an isotropic universe which can be entered at virtually any point because no individual perspective is privileged. By this account each single word sets up a different perspective on the book: "in each thing is realized everything and everything is in each thing. Each thing finally appears as a perspective on the universe and a microscopic model of it."[18] The only way to account for this kind of work, it seems, is by such circular statements. So *Finnegans Wake* becomes the "poetics of itself" and now we can see why another title for Eco's book on Joyce is *The Aesthetics of Chaosmos*. This title strikes just the right note of tension between order and disorder which is implicit in Eco's notion of the open work.

David Seed

Looking back on *A Theory of Semiotics:*
One Small Step for Philosophy,
One Giant Leap for the Doctrine of Signs

In 1976, Umberto Eco's *Trattato di semiotica generale*, published by
Bompiani the year before, appeared in the English translation of David
Osmond-Smith[1] under the title *A Theory of Semiotics*. This volume was the
first in the Advances in Semiotics series begun with the Indiana University
Press under the editorship of Thomas A. Sebeok. The series now exceeds
forty-six volumes, and the *Theory of Semiotics* has appeared in perhaps as
many languages as the series has volumes. A general study heretofore pursued mostly by writers of solitary genius (such as John Poinsot in the seventeenth century and Charles Peirce in the nineteenth) suddenly found in
Eco's work a voice which would ring throughout the intellectual world of
the late twentieth century, in practically every culture and every language.
It was a giant leap for the doctrine of signs.

It was my privilege to review the book that year for *Semiotica*, the official journal of the International Association for Semiotic Studies. Professor
Capozzi has invited me to revisit the work in the light of intervening developments in semiotics, and to emphasize the points of contact between
Eco's book and my own writings. Accordingly, I will re-examine Eco's
Theory of Semiotics here in three dimensions: as a work of transition in the
emergence of semiotics as a contemporary intellectual movement, as a piece
in the historical puzzle of how the way to contemporary semiotic consciousness was prepared, and as a theoretical proposal that needs to be met
on its own terms as well.

I. A WORK OF TRANSITION

If we juxtapose the title of Eco's 1975 book with the subtitle of his 1968
book, *Introduzione alla ricerca semiologica*, the contrast in the choice of
terms is of the greatest interest to the sophisticated reader. For history accu-
mulates in language, and the historical cargo of these two terms,
"semiology" and "semiotics", is profoundly different (Sebeok 1971; Deely
1995). Eco has become a giant of pop culture as well as of semiotics. After

The Name of the Rose made him a best-selling novelist over and beyond his
academic work, it is not surprising that the editors[2] and reviewers[3] of Eco's
work persist in perpetuating the popular confusion that surrounds the derivation and destiny of these two profoundly different terms. As we shall see,
not without some reason do Eco devotees, in particular, cling to this confusion. Yet is it well to note from the start that "the intellectual ambience
evoked by each [of these two terms] is so different that Hill's dictum about
synonymy"–that perfect synonyms do not exist (Hill 1958:412)–"is recon-
firmed once again."[4]

At the time of writing my review in 1976, I considered the most noteworthy feature of this book to be the immensity of Professor Eco's achievement in covering the range of the contemporary literature on signs, and in
showing the semiotic import of a good deal more of the then-current writings in language, scientific linguistics, anthropology, aesthetics, ethology,
and other 'traditional' specialized disciplines that had so far developed outside the orbit of an explicitly semiotic understanding. The degree of sophistication and comprehensiveness of the book put it in a class by itself. That
favorable impression and judgment stays with me, twenty years later. This
is a book for every semioticians' bookshelf. Although more limited than its
author imagined, *A Theory of Semiotics* is not only a classic of the period but
makes as well vital and permanent contributions, especially with its notion
of "code".

From a philosophical point of view, what we have learned about the
nature and historical development of semiotics as an intellectual enterprise,
both possible and more and more actual, enables us to see this landmark
book of Eco's in quite a new light, no less favorable, but one that brings out
now its colors as a work of transition, a work that reaches the boundary
between late modernity and postmodernity without completely crossing
the line. While Eco's choice of title, in retrospect, signaled the end of the
dominance of the Saussurean paradigm in the studies of sign, the work itself, in its text, notwithstanding its authors intentions to the contrary, remains within the orbit of an idealist understanding of sign as exclusively the
work of thought and culture, as examination of the details of Eco's theoretical proposals will shortly reveal.

Some rectification of terms is in order before proceeding further.[5]

By idealism I mean the distinctive epistemological position proper to
modern philosophy as it developed from Descartes to Kant in revealing, by
a series of logical consequences, that the common assumption of the early
moderns (that ideas of the understanding are the direct objects of experience) leads inevitably to the conclusion that whatever the mind knows the
mind itself makes.

By postmodernism, or postmodernity, I do not mean that collection of
quintessentially idealist writings which revel in deconstruction and Her-

metic drift. [6] I mean quite simply the development of the consequences for human thought of the demonstration that ideas as signs do not and cannot consist in being the direct objects of experience and apprehension, as the moderns assumed. Ideas serve merely to found relations to objects signified which, as such, are indifferent to physical existence without precluding such existence on any general or a-priori grounds (Santaella-Braga 1994). This demonstration preceded modernity, but the founders of modernity had no cognizance of it. Since ideas are the principal form of sign, in the sense that all other signs depend, in differing ways, on the signs that are ideas, the realization the "all thought is in signs", as Peirce put it (1868:5.253; cf. Poinsot 1632:271/28-35), may be regarded as the beginning of semiotic consciousness. This consciousness, vis-à-vis modernity, returns to the fork in the road where the moderns began their trek down the way of ideas, and follows rather the way previously less taken, the way of signs. [7]

By taking up where Latin thought left off on this point, semiotic consciousness constitutes a definitive break with modernity and, at the same time, manifests a continuity with the early modern milieu out of which modernity first took rise. The doctrine of signs restores continuity to philosophical tradition and history, something that had been lost for three-hundred years in the wake of Descartes. Postmodernity, in its positive content, consists first of all in that recovery, or rather, in the step outside the epistemological limits of modernity presupposed for fully entering upon the way of signs.

In taking this step semiotics definitively transcends modern idealism, something that Eco's *Theory of Semiotics* tried but, for reasons we shall here examine, did not quite manage to do. No more realist than idealist, and no less idealist than realist, to the extent that it achieves fully the perspective proper to itself and relies on no previous philosophical paradigm in establishing its own paradigm rooted directly in the action and understanding of sign, semiotics begins from a standpoint superior to this classical and quintessentially late modern opposition. The *Theory of Semiotics* does not quite achieve this standpoint, at least, so to speak, not "with both feet". Instead, from within the realist-idealist opposition, Eco's book develops, with consummate clarity[8] and rigor, the nature and role in human experience of that type of sign which the Latins called ad placitum, but fails to visualize the place and role of that other type of sign the Latins (with less clarity than one could wish) called, all too simply,[9] naturale.

So much for preliminary clarification of terms. We need now only to frame our discussion of the theoretical details of Eco's landmark book by a brief outline of what we have learned about the history of semiotics, almost entirely since 1976, an unfolding in which the continuing research of Eco and his students has been a decisive influence.

II. The History of Semiotics as it Appears Today

Semiotics is nothing more or other than the knowledge we develop by studying the action of signs, and it receives its various divisions from the various ways and regions in which that action is verified.[10] This study presupposes nothing more than a notion of sign as one thing standing for another in a relation of renvoi (Jakobson 1974; Deely 1994a:201-244), that is to say, an irreducibly triadic relation, actual or virtual, but in the case of cognitive life, it seems, always actual. Such a general notion of sign is verified, at the extremes, in phenomena we call "natural" and in phenomena we call "cultural", as well as in the intermediary phenomena of social interaction (for example, such as sociology studies it). But—and this is one of the more surprising upshots of contemporary semiotic research—the actual proposal of such a general notion of sign appears to be no older than Augustine, and a creation of the specifically Latin Age of philosophical history.[11]

Proposed in the fourth century, the semiotic point of view did not receive a warrant until the early seventeenth century (Herculano de Carvalho 1969, 1970, 1973), when it was for the first time demonstrated how the early Latin proposal for a general notion of sign, applicable in a single sense to the extremes of nature and culture, could be vindicated through the fact that relation according to the way it has being is indifferent to whether its subjective foundation or ground be taken from both the being of physical interaction and from cognitive activity, or from either alone. This establishment of a unified object or subject matter for semiotic investigation was in principle revolutionary for our understanding of human experience and the knowledge which derives therefrom. For it unified in a single instrument or medium the otherwise diverse products of speculative knowledge about the natures of things, on the one hand, and, on the other hand, practical knowledge about human affairs and the application thereto of speculative knowledge. [12]

The privilege of naming the idea of the doctrine of signs as a new and distinct philosophical discipline was John Locke (Sebeok 1971; Romeo 1977; Deely 1994a:109ff.). But the first author who succeeded in giving voice to the underlying unity of the being in relation upon which all action of signs as such depends was John Poinsot (1589–1644), an Iberian philosopher of mixed Burgundian and Portuguese descent. In the text of his Tractatus de Signis, published in 1632 (reviewed by Sebeok 1986a; Fisch 1986; FitzGerald 1986, 1986a; Bird 1987, Deely 1988, Santaella-Braga 1991, inter alia), the new beginning implicit in the adoption of the semiotic point of view was in two ways indirectly symbolized. First, the text expressly noted that the sign requires a standpoint superior to the division of being into what is and what is not independent of cognition, which translates, in modern parlance, into a standpoint superior to the confrontation of realism with idealism. Second, the compass of the Tractatus de Signis text united what were, in the then-traditional liberal arts curriculum of the European universities, the opening discussions of logic with the concluding discussions of the theory of knowledge.[13]

This new beginning, the way of signs, was not, however, the new beginning that the authors of what was to become the classical modern mainstream of philosophy actually undertook. Instead, they chose to follow what Leibniz (1704:62) summarily and accurately characterized as the way of ideas. This historical path was predicated on the assumption that the very ideas formed by the human mind are as such the immediate and direct objects of experience at every level of cognitive activity—that is to say, in sensation no less than in intellection as the activity proper to human understanding. This assumption, the heart of the modern epistemological paradigm, is impossible in semiotic terms, because it depends upon a reduction of signification to representation. Such a reduction had already been shown to be a confusion by a whole series of late Latin authors, principally Hispanic, who had undertaken in the sixteenth century the initial exploration and development of the requirements of semiotic consciousness. But their work in this regard was ignored by, perhaps unknown to, the founders of philosophical modernity. In the glare of attention focused on the way of ideas, the way of signs, which had been barely adumbrated by authors of a waning Latinity, soon became lost in the shadows of modernity. The way of signs remained forgotten until a confluence of scholarly coincidences, themselves mostly occasioned by the contemporary interest in semiotic studies, brought them to light. [14]

In the ancient world dominated by Greek philosophy, the notion we translate as sign, μ ("semeion"), should actually be translated rather as "natural sign", for this term in antiquity referred only to natural phenomena such as meteorological occurrences and symptoms of disease. When attention was finally turned to the phenomena of signification in late modern times–in the very twilight of modernity in which mainstream philosophy of the twentieth century persists in dwelling–there was hardly any place left for a viable notion of natural phenomenon. It was therefore no accident that the original popular success of contemporary attempts to develop a theory of sign was not under the designation of semiotics, a name redolent of the natural origins of signification in physical processes anterior to human cognition. The attempts which caught the public eye went rather under the designation of semiology, a name taken from linguistic studies and intended to signify that the paradigm for any theory of signs should be not the early Latin general notion but a specifically modern notion of sign as determinately arbitrary and linguistic, that is, cultural, in derivation.

Only slowly and against the greatest resistance on all sides did semiotic research, indebted especially to the powerful impulse given it by the philosophical investigations in this area by Charles Sanders Peirce, compel the gradual recognition that any notion of sign as inherently arbitrary, however valid and necessary in specific areas, was incapable of providing an adequate foundation for the possible field of investigations opened up by the action of signs.[15] The progress of this grudging recognition was signaled in the literature on signs, iconically, as it were, by the shift in terminology from "semiology" to "semiotics" as the proper designation for the point of view under development.[16]

Thus, by the most unexpected of turns in philosophical history, semiotics as the way of signs puts us back at a point where modern philosophy began, and compels us to look anew at those late Latin-early modern texts, ignored by modernity, wherein was achieved the first establishment of the foundations for what we today call semiotics. From this curious standpoint, at once antiquarian and postmodern, as I have elsewhere explained (Deely 1994a), Eco's book appears today as a definitive step in the muddled transition from semiology (as a final stage of the idealism of modernity) to semiotics proper and postmodern times.

III. THEORETICAL HEART OF ECO'S BOOK

It remained for our own times effectively to recognize, in Saussure's words (i.1906–11), the "right to existence" and "place staked out in advance" for a unified approach to the phenomena of signification with their characteristic effect—communication, in whatever mode or on whatever levels it occurs. But we can no longer say with Saussure that "since it does not yet exist, one cannot say what form will take". It will take the form of a definitely postmodern development, because it calls for an epistemological paradigm incompatible with that which defines modernity, and begins, as we saw, at a point beyond the quintessentially modern controversies between realism and idealism.

The characteristically contemporary attempt to realize such a perspective has emerged from nowhere, as it were, since the first World War, originally under the charismatic influence of the Swiss linguist Saussure, but more properly and later under the aegis of the American philosopher Charles Peirce, and along a truly supra-national front (see the surveys of Sebeok 1974, 1975a, 1976). In a field burgeoning with such a bewildering array of pursuits as seemed to all but belie its claim to the possibility of an over-arching, systematic perspective or doctrine, the publication of Professor Eco's book provided a clarifying landmark .

For the purpose of discussing here the theoretical details of Eco's book, I will make use of Eco's own system of internal division and punctuation.

Thus, all references to the work will be in terms of the chapters and numbered divisions within each chapter, usually followed by page numbers, or, occasionally, in terms of page numbers alone. "0", in Eco's numeration, is for "Introduction", followed by four chapters numbered 1 through 4, giving a total in effect of five major divisions or sections for the book. For reasons of space, I will here consider among these details only those which bear directly on my main concern, which is also the main concern of the book. Eco proposes that signum as the defining notion of semiotics can be adequately replaced by (or translated into) his notion of sign function. For my consideration of other technical details (notably the ratio facilis and ratio difficilis) I refer readers to the original review (Deely 1976).

1. Field or Discipline?

What Professor Eco undertook in this work was not "to explore the theoretical possibility . . . of a unified approach to every phenomenon of signification and/or communication" in an abstract and definitive way, such as Poinsot envisaged, but rather to make only "a *preliminary exploration* of such a theoretical possibility" in terms of "*the present state of the art*" (0.1.1, 3; italics added).

I have emphasized this qualifying phrase in order to give it the sense and importance I think is due it in connection with the question Eco raises quite early, and in which any reader is certain to have an especial interest:"'Semiotics': field or discipline?" (0.2, 7–8).

Eco himself, in 1976, did not attempt fully to settle this question—a prudent enough stance before the complexity and remaining obscurity shrouding the history of semiotics at that time. Even Sebeok, of whom Steiner (1975:vii) remarked that his "knowledge of the whole range of current language studies may well be unrivalled", assumed at that period that Peirce "was heir to the entire tradition of philosophical analysis of signs" (Sebeok 1974:220; also Sebeok 1975). What Eco did make clear was that his work had been conceived in view of semiotics more as a field than as a discipline. But this point was not as clear as might at first seem, since Eco's manner of making it gives the appearance of assuming, in line with the then-prevailing fashions in the analytic philosophy of science, that a discipline as such requires a deductive model at its center.

Yet even at the time such an assumption should not have passed unchallenged in a major work. [17] In subsequent years, within American semiotics at least, discussion shifted more from the "field-discipline" polarity, with its implied scientific model, to a discussion of the expression "doctrine" in the classical formula *doctrina signorum*.[18] This formula, "doctrine of signs", was used in common by Poinsot, Locke, and Peirce. It proved to have far more clarifying power with regard to the philosophical status of semiotics, in no small part because it avoided the trap into which Eco's discussion had fallen of buying into the regnant assumptions of an already stagnant, but institutionally dominant, school of late modern philosophy, as Sebeok expressly noted in a work coeval with the book of Eco under discussion (Sebeok 1976:ix):

> The expression *doctrine of signs*, for the title of this collection, was selected with deliberation to emblematically align the arguments embodied in these eleven essays with the semiotic tradition of Locke and Peirce rather more closely than with others that prefer to dignify the field—often with premature strategic intent—as a 'theory' or even a 'science'.

Yet the "field-discipline" polarity, like the medieval distinction between "material and formal logic" adopted from the Arabs, provoked much useful discussion without ever receiving a clear and agreed upon sense, and still warrants further discussion today, since it both was one of the seminal points in Eco's book and directly contributes to a better situating and fuller understanding of that work. Let me try once again at giving this distinction its best sense.

In my own review of 1976, I proposed to use as semantic markers for the parts of this distinction the two terms "semiotic" and "semiotics", the former to name the foundational and philosophical disciplinary aspect, the latter to name the interdisciplinary field of studies to which the fundamental notion of sign as the medium of all thought (and therefore in whatever discipline) naturally gives rise. Like Russell's earlier attempt (1905, 1910, 1919) to tie his theory of descriptions to the historical accident of the linguistic difference between "the" and "a" as definite and indefinite articles of contemporary English (although I hope with better theoretical grounds), this attempt on my part soon enough proved to be too provincial from a linguistic point of view. Even though it worked quite well in English, it proved unworkable within the international context of the contemporary semiotic development.[19]

But the sense of the distinction as thus unsuccessfully marked still seems to me valid today, so I will try to represent it here under the auspices of some new semantic markers. Let us today speak rather of a difference between semiotics *theoretical* and *applied*,[20] where the qualifying terms have the Aristotelian sense of the difference between what cannot be and what can be brought under human control.[21] "Theoretical semiotics" refers to the doctrine of signs in its foundational sense. In this sense it authorizes, legitimizes, and gives rise to a whole field of investigations which follow the action of signs in carrying understanding across disciplinary lines as well as in establishing disciplines in the first place. But it also, and more importantly, establishes the structures of experience out of which the possibility of disciplines arises in the first place and against which disciplinary structures, like the structures of understanding in general, have constantly to recur for inductive verifications. "Applied semiotics", then, takes the results of such researches and tries to make use of them in various specific contexts of human thought and action, especially in those areas over which the human understanding has the relative maximum of voluntary control, which is to say in the areas of society and culture and the "arts" generally— whence "visual semiotics", "semiotics of film", "semiotics of gesture", "facial semiotics", "semiotics of culture", and so forth. Success in the former investigations would constitute semiotics as a discipline in the philosophical sense, while the play of the latter investigations would constitute the interdisciplinary and transdisciplinary field of semiotic inquiries, many of them "scientific" in the manner of the social and humanistic sciences.

Semiotics *as a discipline*, therefore, refers primarily to the development of what Peirce and Locke called the "doctrine" or theory of what a sign is, and the conditions for anything to be a sign. [22] As *a field*, on the other hand, semiotics consists in the development of attempts to isolate and pursue the implications of specifically signifying aspects and elements of phenomena that are studied in their own right by the range of traditional specialized pursuits (music, architecture, ethology, etc.), or that are involved in the specific production of signifying phenomena in the various areas. [23]

Thus the 'field' conception of semiotics brings into focus the inherently interdisciplinary ramifications of the possibility of success in developing a unified theory of signs. Since all thought is in signs, and, moreover, all the objects of our experience both presuppose and are themselves comprised of signs, the range of implications and applications of a theoretical semiotics successfully grounded are practically unlimited. Prior to semiotics, "interdisciplinary programs", so essential to compensating for the myopic tendencies of specializations in modern academe, have always required deliberate contrivance to develop, and, as a consequence, have had a rather tenuous (often "personality dependent") status vis-à-vis the specialties. Within the perspective of semiotics, this situation changes radically and for the better. For the first time an interdisciplinary outlook ceases to be something contrived or tenuous. Such an outlook appears now rather as something built into semiotics, simply by virtue of the universal role of signs as the vehicle of communication, within and between specialties, as everywhere else.

Clearly, theoretical and applied semiotics so understood are distinct but only imperfectly separable pursuits. Foundations call for superstructures as much as superstructures (if they are to endure) require foundations. But there is more than this. Unlike material constructions, which require that foundations be completely laid before superstructures are raised, the constructions of understanding are such that superstructures derive from foundational intuitions not only in advance of the perfect clarification (or "completed laying") of these foundations, but also in such a way that the foundational clarification itself proceeds (if at all) only by a backward glance (*Blickwendung*) from such superstructures as it enables. This is a Heideggerian point much more germane to the success of Eco's project than any disciplinary models to be found in the literature of analytic philosophy.

In this way, it becomes clear how and why the laying of foundations (in our case, theoretical semiotics, the establishment of what it is for anything to be a sign) and the study of a field (in our case, applied semiotics, the study of the production and functioning of particular signs and classes of signs) are only *relatively* independent. What also becomes clear is how and why this *relative* independence is such that the understanding of foundations must be achieved through a *preliminary* investigation of what those foundations have already made possible, namely, the interdisciplinary (or transdisciplinary[24]) field. Thus the prior, though independent of the posterior, is nonetheless *known* by its adumbration therein, and must be so approached, even though this epistemological dependence obtains only in a preliminary way, and by no means ties the foundational inquiry to the full grasp of the development of the field in all its possible ramifications. Were that the case foundational inquiry would be rendered impossible, since the grasp and development in question—being positive science—are an asymptotic affair in time. Heidegger's description of the process is still the best (1927:10):

> Basic concepts determine the way in which we get an understanding beforehand of the area of subject-matter underlying all the objects a science takes as its theme, and all positive investigation is guided by this understanding. Only after the area itself has been explored beforehand in a corresponding manner do these concepts become genuinely demonstrated and 'grounded'. But since every such area is itself obtained from the domain of entities themselves, this preliminary research, from which the basic concepts are drawn . . . must run ahead of the positive sciences, and it *can*. . . .. Laying the foundations for the sciences in this way is different in principle from the kind of 'logic' that limps along after, investigating the status of some science as it chances to find it, in order to discover its 'method'. Laying the foundations, as we have described it, is rather a productive logic—in the sense that it leaps ahead, as it were, into some area of Being, discloses it in its constitution of Being, and, after thus arriving at the structures within it, makes these available to the positive sciences as transparent assignments for their inquiry.

Study of the field in its own right and, as it were, for its own sake (the case of semiotics as Eco principally envisages it for the present work), is thus tied to the state and diversity of the positive sciences (what Eco calls "the present state of the art"), whose state and diversity are themselves functions of a *use of signs* (Locke 1690:460-463). Study of the discipline proper, on the other hand (also the case of semiotics, but envisaged now directly in terms of the action of signs as rooted in and stemming from the being proper to any sign), is *necessarily* first adumbrated in viewing the field in some overall sense, but is not itself tied through this adumbration to any permanent or thoroughgoing dependence upon the vagaries of scientific research. Semiotics adumbrates what it in turn springs from: the *Sein* proper to signs.

The distinction I have just outlined is not stated thus within Professor Eco's book. Yet it nonetheless applies thereto and is finally implied thereby. Understanding Eco's work in the light of the distinction between field and discipline taken in the manner just outlined demonstrates the appropriateness of his chosen title, while internal analysis of the book's structure leads toward a critical justification of the proposed distinction so grounded. Thus, as befits a new theory, Eco envisions no more than a *preliminary* exploration of the possibility of a unified approach to signification. He envisions not an exploration leading to *the proper foundation* of the very possibility of the field of semiotics, but a preliminary exploration rather of (or 'belonging to') *the field as such*–and as yet finally presupposing such a foundation as this book does not pretend to give.

By the de facto angling of his work in this way, Professor Eco is able to satisfy a need in some respects even more pressing at the time he wrote than the need for a purely philosophical establishment of the foundations of a doctrine of signs. What was at the time most sorely needed, and what this book magnificently supplied, was the need of a demonstration of the *common relevance* of the staggering array of writings that had proliferated in recent years under the banner of semiotics and its congeners (as including "semiology"). In achieving this much, Eco gave effective answer to those mistaken, but forgivably bemused, critics who so far had seen in semiotics only a nominal unity concealing a hopeless nest of jargon and equivocation, anything but the nascent form of a perspective and discipline of philosophy powerful and encompassing enough to achieve a major revolution in our understanding of the intellectual life and its diverse roles in nature and culture.

2. *Sign or Sign-Function?*

The theoretical difficulties which constitute the book's challenge are precisely what continues to be most interesting about the book. Of these various difficulties, one in particular is keyed to the book's overall structure. It crops up in the opening paragraphs of the very first chapter, as Professor

Eco explains how he proposes to realize the aim of exploring in preliminary fashion "the theoretical possibility and the social function of a unified approach to every phenomenon of signification and/or communication" (0.1.1, 3). "One must first take into account", Eco writes, "the all-purpose notion of 'sign'", not just to distinguish signs from objects signified, say, but, more importantly, "to translate the notion of 'sign' into the more flexible one of *sign-function* (which can be explained within the framework of a theory of codes)" (0.1.1, 34). As we shall see over the course of this discussion, this amounts to proposing the elimination of semiotics in the name of semiotics, or, what amounts to the same thing, the restriction of semiotics to the horizon of semiology.

Sebeok had already commented, approaching what proved to be the apogee of the transition from "semiology" to "semiotics", that "semiotics must surely be one of the rare provinces of knowledge the very practitioners of which have failed to reach a consensus even about what to call their discipline" (1975a:156). He might have noted, more substantively and with even greater justice, that semiotics must surely be one of the rare provinces of knowledge the practitioners of which begin by denying the very existence of their proper subject matter. In July of that very year, at the First North American Semiotics Colloquium held at Tampa, Florida, on the campus of the University of South Florida (see Sebeok Ed. 1976), I had listened to Professor Henry Hiz deliver the first Presidential Address of what was to become, in the following year at the Atlanta, Georgia, meeting, the Semiotic Society of America. In that memorable address, Professor Hiz, who, so far as I know, has not been heard from again on the American scene, solemnly proposed that the first *desideratum* for the nascent new society should be to do away with the notion of "sign". Here, then, in Eco's work, for the second time in a short interval, I found myself in the presence of an authority pronouncing, in the very name of semiotics (the *doctrina signorum*), elimination of *signum* as the basic theoretical and analytic category.

That such a translation as Eco proposed should truly be necessary is puzzling at first glance. Yet so radical a proposal from an author so prominent in the very field for which the proposal is made can be dismissed, if at all, only after examination in detail. This demand for examination in detail in the present case was all the more pressing as it became apparent that, though introduced with minimal preliminaries, the proposed "translation" doing away with *signum* as a theoretical notion is the key conceptual move for the book as a whole. The sequence of chapters in the book, as well as the boundary-definitions of Eco's research, are directly related to and largely consequent upon the substitution of sign-function for sign as the basic semiotic category.

2.a. Eco's notion of sign-function

What, then, is a *sign-function*? Eco defines this term at a number of points. "A sign-function arises when an expression is correlated to a content" (2.1, 48); "the sign-function is nothing more than the correspondence between a signifier and a signified" (2.2, 52-54). But perhaps his fullest and most formal statement occurs on p. 191:"a sign-function is the correlation between an expression and a content based on a conventionally established code (a system of correlational rules)". Thus the effort to understand signification, for Eco, "entails a theory of codes" (0.1.1, 4), because "codes provide the rules that generate sign-functions" (3.5.1, 191). And since communication "presupposes a signification system as its necessary condition" (0.3, 9), it is clear both why the "discriminating categories" of semiotics are *signification* and *communication*, and why the theory of codes must precede the theory of sign (function) production as the instrument of communication's actual occurrence (0.1.1, 4):

> . . . there is a signification system (and therefore a code) when there is the socially conventionalized possibility of generating sign-functions. . .. There is on the contrary a communication process when the possibilities provided by a signification system are exploited in order to physically produce expressions for many practical purposes.

Hence the structure of Eco's book, as follows. After an introductory chapter stating the aim and bounds of the research (0.), there comes a first chapter (1.) on signification and communication, wherein an elementary communication model is proposed that serves mainly to clarify what is *properly* called a code (namely, a rule coupling a set of signals with a set either of notions or of behavioral responses [1.2, 36-37]) as against what is–by homonymy–*commonly* called a code (namely, the notion of purely combinational systems, whether of signals, notions, behaviors, or whatever). This common notion of code, since it is *improperly* so called, Eco proposes to rename as an *s-code*. He proposes by this terminological clarification "to avoid the considerable theoretical damage" that can be produced by such homonymous equivocation (1.2, 37) as obtains when both code properly so called (coupling rules, which are purely relational) and code improperly so called (an *s-code*, combinational systems of whatever elements founding relations, what the Latins called "transcendental relatives") are simply referred to by the same character-string "code" (1.2, 37-38):

> I shall therefore call a system of elements such as the syntactic, semantic and behavioral ones . . . an s-code (or code as system); whereas a rule coupling the items of one s-code with the items of another or several other s-codes . . . will simply be called a code.

This clarification is followed by a second and much longer–103 as opposed to 16 page–chapter (2.) on the theory of codes proper as the key to and basis for sign-functions, which leads to another lengthy 163 page chapter (3.) on the actual production of sign-functions in communicating. After this there is, in conclusion, only a very short–5 page–chapter (4.) on the subject of semiotics. But "subject" here does not mean the subject-matter, but rather the "empirical subjects which display labor in order to physically produce expressions" (4.0, 317), i.e., you and me. This chapter seeks to make the purely methodological point that if "semiotics recognizes as the only testable subject matter of its discourse the social existence of the universe of signification" (4.0, 317),[25] then it "is entitled to recognize these subjects"–you and me–"only insofar as they manifest themselves through sign-functions" (4.0, 317). Whether, "by accepting this limit, semiotics fully avoids any risk of idealism", as Eco posits (4.0, 317), is a point to which we shall have to return.

For the present, it is clear from the above that by far the bulk of Eco's work–266 out of 318 pages, or, if we count the preliminary clarification of code as correlating rule in Chapter 1, 282 out of 318 pages–is occupied with the discussion of topics whose importance is directly tied to the "translation" of the notion of *signum* into that of *sign-function*. Hence, equally for understanding and for criticizing Eco's transitional work, we must carefully look above all into this move.

In Eco's own framework, the importance of the move from sign to sign-function cannot be over stressed. "The notion of 'sign' is a fiction of everyday language", Eco asserts–just the sort of assertion that philosophers have gotten used to after Wittgenstein. This particular "linguistic fiction" is one "whose place should be taken by that of sign-function" (3.1.3, 158). Or again, using Eco's own italics: "*it is the very notion of sign which is untenable*" (3.5.10, 216).

2.b. The classical notion of sign

Claims such as these, however familiar in the context of analytic and "ordinary language" philosophy, are not obviously true, and should be argued for directly rather than simply posited as point of departure. Although short of a direct argument on this point, a remark Eco makes in passing about the supposed 'ordinary language' and 'classical' notion of sign provides important insight into his decision to replace *signum* with his conception of sign-function. The ordinary notion, he asserts, is "naive and non-relational" (0.1.1, 4), whereas a sign-function is relational, "realized when two *functives* (expression and content) enter into a mutual correlation; the same functive can also enter into another correlation, thus becoming a different functive and therefore giving rise to a new sign-function" (2.1, 49;

Eco's italics). Thus "if the theory of codes and the theory of sign production succeed" (p. 4) with the translation of sign into sign-function, "the classical notion of 'sign' *dissolves* itself into a highly complex network of changing relationships" (2.1, 49; Eco's italics).

That is all well and good, and certainly a complex network of changing relationships fits our experience of signifying incomparably better than any non-relational item or category possibly could. So true is this that, were it necessary to go from signs to sign-functions in order to achieve at the level of theory the identification of signification with some form of thoroughly relative being, Eco's translation would be *ipso facto* justified.

Such, however, is not the case. Let us suppose that there is, as Eco alleges, some "ordinary language" notion of sign that is "naive and non-relational". Even if that be true, such a notion can hardly be equated with anything that can credibly be called the "classical" notion of sign. Historical research has shown, on the contrary, that "a sign is something relative" is a proposition that has always been a point of common agreement wherever the notion has been thematized, certainly among the Latin discussants of signifying from Augustine (5th century) and Boethius (6th century) to Poinsot (17th century)–the full extent of the Latin Age in philosophy (Deely 1994a:39-52; Williams 1985). So it is hard in the first place to know on what grounds Eco can speak of a "classical" notion of sign that is *non*-relational. [26]

In the sixteenth and seventeenth century scholastic discussions of *signum*, for example, which were commonplace in the Iberian world especially, [27] there was never any question as to *whether* signs were relative "because nothing signifies itself, although something may represent itself", as Poinsot put it. [28] *That* signs are *aliquid relativum* was the starting point of discussion and controversy. So central was this realization in the Latin consciousness that Poinsot made it the point of departure for his epochal *Tractatus de Signis* (see Book I, Question 1, esp. 117/18-118/18), which was the first successful attempt historically, as we mentioned above, to establish a unified subject matter for semiotic inquiry. The question has always been *how* signs are relative, what sort of relative being, precisely, belongs to signs as such. That signs are relative there was never any doubt.

Therefore I think that Eco is definitively moving in the right direction when he proposes that signs are neither physical nor fixed entities (2.1, 49 top; cf. Deely 1994:32[29]), but wrong as a matter of historical fact in thinking that the classical notion of *signum* was not already pointed in this same direction. Moreover, any non-relational notion of sign, being a self-contradictory pseudo-notion, would prove no more suitable for colloquial than for technical semiotic discussions (except where irresolvable paradox were the subject being discussed). It would appear that, by opting for sign-functions to replace signs on this ground, Eco has either been frightened by or opted for the convenience of a straw man.

2.c. Overlaps and differences in the two notions

An *indirect* argument in support of Eco's rejection of the notion of sign in favor of that of sign-function as the basic semiotic category can be construed from Eco's "Critique of iconism" (3.5, 191-217). Yet, even considered as an indirect argument for the untenability of the very notion of sign, this critique of iconism (essential details of which we shall have occasion shortly to discuss) is so embedded in the code/sign-function theoretical context as to remain doubtful to one not already persuaded of the need for the suggested "translation".

The absence of detached argumentation for such an early and key conceptual move must be adjudged a serious flaw in the theoretical execution of this book. The flaw is underscored by Eco's own admission–tacitly in conflict with his insupportable claim that the "classical" notion of sign was non-relational–that "this notion [of] sign appears to be so suitable in ordinary language and in colloquial semiotic discussions that it should not be completely abandoned" (0.1.1, 4-5). Accordingly, Eco writes, "I shall continue to use the word /sign/ every time the correlational nature of the sign-function may be presupposed" (0.1.1, 5), even though "properly speaking there are not signs, but only sign-functions" (1.1, 49). Thus, except where context clearly stipulates otherwise, as in the passages from pp. 158 and 216 quoted above, the word "sign" occurs in Eco's framework as a short-hand synonym for the expression "sign-function". For example: ". . . everything can be understood as a sign *if and only if* there exists a *convention* which allows it to stand for something else" (0.7.1, 19; italics added). Or again:"I propose to define as a sign *everything* that, on the grounds of a previously established social convention, can be taken as *something standing for* something else" (0.5.2, 16; Eco's italics).

This centrality of *convention* as part and parcel of the notion of sign-function ("*every* pattern of signification is a cultural convention" 1.1, 32)–indeed, as its *essential ground* (*iff:*"if and only if")–by itself suffices to challenge not only the necessity of translating the notion of sign into that of sign-function, but even more the *adequacy* of such a translation. I shall explore this matter shortly. But first I want to conclude the discussion of a point made earlier.

3. Political or Natural Boundaries?

I have said that not only are the order and content of the main divisions or chapters of Eco's book basically consequent upon the adoption of sign-function in place of sign as the fundamental category of semiotics, but also that his conception of the *boundaries* of semiotics is in important ways tied to this same decision. We have already set out warrant for the first part of this claim. I would now like to extend that warrant to cover the rest of the assertion.

Eco distinguishes between *political* and *natural* boundaries for semiotics. Political boundaries are more immediately important even if ultimately less interesting inasmuch as they are provisional and subject to change. They are chiefly the result, as Eco's discussion makes quite clear (pp. 5-7, 9-14), on the one hand, of the comparative infancy of the semiotic movement, and, on the other hand, of the fact that the great panoply of academic specialties—formal logic, analytic philosophy, linguistics, information theory, rhetoric, aesthetics, behavioral psychology, etc.—de facto arose and have come to relative maturity in a pre-semiotic environment of understanding. Thus "the semiotician may express the wish that one of these days there will be a general semiotic discipline of which all these researches and sciences can be recognized as particular branches" (0.1.2, 5-6); but a more realistic interim approach would be the proposal of "a unified set of categories in order to make . . . collaboration more and more fruitful" (p. 6), keeping in view also the "whole group of phenomena which unquestionably have a semiotic relevance even though the various semiotic approaches have not yet completely succeeded in giving them a satisfactory definition" (p. 6).

3.a. Information Theory vs. Semiotics

In particular, information theory is one of the more immediate objects of Eco's concern to distinguish "politically" from semiotics, and for this his distinction between "codes" and "s-codes" serves nicely. At the "lower threshold" of semiotics, Eco points to the sort of "communicative process" improperly so called that involves merely the transmission or exchange of physical signals, in order to distinguish it from the sort of communication properly so-called that involves signification whereby one item not merely triggers but *stands for* another (1.3, 40, and 1.4.1, 41, respectively):

> . . . the elements of an informational 'grammar' explain the functioning not only of a syntactic system, but of every kind of structured system, such as for example a semantic or a behavioral one. What information theory does not explain is the functioning of a code as a correlating rule. In this sense information theory is neither a theory of signification nor a theory of communication but only a theory of the abstract combinational possibilities of an s-code.

> . . . a theory of codes . . . will use categories such as 'meaning' or 'content'. These have nothing to do with the category of 'information', since informa-

tion theory is not concerned with the contents that the units it deals with can convey but, at best, with the internal combinational properties of the system of conveyed units, insofar as this too is an s-code.

In general, "the phenomena on the lower threshold" indicate "the point where semiotic phenomena rise from something non-semiotic" (0.7.2, 21). Thus, in Eco's view, "neurophysiological and genetic phenomena", for example, "are not a matter for semioticians, but . . . neurophysiological and genetic informational theories are so" (0.7.3, 21; also 47 n. 5).[30]

3.b. Eco vs. Peirce

The *natural* boundaries of semiotics, more interesting for the long run, on the other hand, "those beyond which a semiotic approach cannot go" (0.1.2, 6), precisely because of their definitive character, must be prescissed very carefully. In approaching this matter, Eco proceeds by way of a limited comparison of the basic thrust in the semiotic conceptions provided respectively by de Saussure and Peirce (0.5, 14-16). He concludes by preferring the conception of Peirce as far as it has been presented, because "it does not demand, as part of a sign's definition, the qualities of being intentionally emitted and artificially produced" (0.5.2, 15). Yet he does not hesitate to part company with Peirce's conception in another respect: "It is incorrect to say that every act of inference is a 'semiosic' act—even though Peirce did so. . . . straightforward identification of inference and signification . . . needs to be corrected by adding the expression 'when this association is culturally recognized and systematically coded" (0.6.1, 17).

What is the reason this qualification "needs" to be added? Why must the identification of inference and signification be "corrected" in this way? It turns out that no reason is apparent *other than Eco's thesis* that a sign-function, the correlation between all expression and a content, must be based on a convention, i.e., a cultural link (3.5.1, 191). The thesis requires it; therefore it must be—classic *petitio principii*.

4. Iconism or Indexicality?

Eco is not unaware of the difficulty at the heart of his proposed translation, or substitution, of sign-function for sign. In his "critique of iconism", 3.5.1, 191, he attempts to meet the difficulty head-on:

If there exist signs that are to some degree motivated by, similar to, analogous to, naturally linked with their object, then the definition given in 2.1 [48; Eco's italics: "a sign is always an element of an *expression plane* conventionally correlated to one (or several) elements of a *content plane*"; "every time there is a correlation of this kind, recognized by human society, there is a sign."] should no longer be tenable.

The only way to maintain it is to demonstrate that even in these types of signs a correlational convention is in operation. The core of the problem is obviously the notion of convention, which is not co-extensive with that of arbitrary link, but which is co-extensive with that of *cultural* link.[31] If one examines the mode of production of signs one must not only analyze the mode of production of the signal in itself but also its mode of correlation to its content, the correlating operation being part of the production.

Careful choice of examples at this point is crucial, and the simpler the appropriate illustration the better, for the less chance there is of losing our way in the analysis of irrelevant variables.

Let us begin by noting that "motivated by, similar to, analogous to, naturally linked with", may be roughly equivalent expressions in the case of icons, but in themselves "similar to" and "analogous to" form one set of related terms, "motivated by" and "naturally linked with" quite another, such that it is possible to sharply detach the two sets. Images that function as representational signs are sometimes said to be "naturally linked with" the object signified by virtue of their similarity or analogicity (=correspondence) to that object. But this constitutes a case radically distinct from effects such as smoke or causes such as clouds that are also classically said to be "naturally linked with" an object signified, fire in the former instance, rain in the latter, despite their complete lack of similarity or analogicity to the signified objects in question, as appears in the following table:

"naturally linked"

Set A		Set B
similar to (icon)	analogous with (symbol)	motivated (index)

Eco clarifies his notion of "motivates" (p. 221) by indicating it has the basic sense of "determines": "For example the size of the imprinter determines (or motivates) the size of the imprint . . ." (see also the usage context provided on pp. 188-189). But this is the notion of a natural linkage which is primarily indexical, not of one that is primarily iconic or symbolic. In deciding therefore that the sign-function definition of 2.1 is tenable after effectively considering the role of culture only in the Set A sort of "natural linkage", or, perhaps better to say, after confounding and assimilating to the linkage of Set A the irreducibly different linkage proper to Set B, it can be said that Professor Eco is guilty of what he subsequently defines as a piece of "ideological discourse" (3.8.1, 278):

> I mean by ideological discourse a mode of argument that, while using probable premises and considering only a partial section of a given semantic field, pretends to develop a 'true' argument, thus covering up the contradictory nature of the Global Semantic System and presenting its own point of view as the only possible conclusion (whether this attitude is deliberately and cynically adopted by a sender in order to deceive a naive addressee, or whether the sender is simply the victim of his own one-sidedness).

I suspect that the last is the case. But, in any event, with the above distinction of cases in mind, it is clear that the "critique of iconism" is a matter of special pleading so far as concerns the tenability of the definition from 2.1.

Before proceeding further, it is crucial to note the feature of signs that underlies the possibility of such an assimilation and confusion as Eco seems here to have made, namely, the fact that "signs" are classified only indirectly, through their sign-vehicles, so that "it is not signs that are actually being classified", as Sebeok put it (1985:120), "but, more precisely, aspects of signs" (1985:121):

> Aspects of a sign necessarily co-occur in an environment-sensitive hierarchy. Since all signs, of course, enter into complex syntagmatic as well as paradigmatic contrasts and oppositions, it is their place both in the web of a concrete text and the network of an abstract system that is decisive as to which aspect will predominate in a given context at a particular moment, a fact which leads directly to the problem of levels, so familiar to linguistics–being an absolute prerequisite for any typology–but as yet far from developed in the other branches of semiotics. This important issue . . . cannot be dealt with here, beyond underlining it, and making an ancillary terminological assertion: that a sign is legitimately, if loosely, labeled after the aspect that ranks predominant.

Hence, in speaking of an "icon", an "index", or a "symbol", for example, along with the dominant aspect according to which the identification has been made, there are normally also subordinate aspects exhibiting differences in gradation which could also be emphasized to justify alternative cross-classifications legitimate from other points of view in conflict with the original one. There is probably no icon which is not *also* an index and *also* a symbol: yet it remains that, in cultural phenomena as such, a symbolic dimension preponderates; in physical occurrences, an indexical one; while icons more straddle both; etc.

Bearing in mind, then, that a hierarchic principle is inherent in the architectonic of any species of sign, let us proceed to consider the neglected sort of case of "natural linkage", namely, where that proper to Set B pre-ponderates, in order to assess for ourselves the tenability of the definition in question and, more generally, of the proposed translation-without-loss of "sign" into "sign-function". I recognize some clouds as "signs" of rain: there is no doubt that certain clouds are *naturally linked with* rain. When I become aware of and *recognize* that link, I no doubt do so on the basis of experiences. In this sense, as Eco argues, the sign is something that always must be produced and, in the human case, is therefore always formed in terms that can be expressed also on the basis of a 'conventional code'.[32] But *what* I am recognizing, *what it is* that I become aware of in such a case, is *not fully* based on the code. To the contrary, *what* I am recognizing, *the linkage that constitutes what is properly described as natural about the signification*, is precisely antecedent to and independent of the "recognition codes" whereby I am here and now aware of it. Moreover, it seems false to say in such a case, as Eco contends in the passage cited from p.191, that "the corre-lating operation is a part of the production of the signal in itself". For the correlating operation resulting in signification which takes place is indeed wholly dependent upon my experience, but the production of the signal in itself takes place principally independently of my experience. What is needed is precisely an account of the manner in which what depends upon my experience incorporates into my experience some things which as such do not depend upon my experience, and this Eco's theory does not provide for.[33]

The notion of sign-function as Eco employs it, therefore, fails to take account of a fundamental distinction among signs. All signs have the rela-tion to what they signify here and now through experience. But some of these signs turn out, upon sufficiently controlled observation, to be con-nected with what they signify wholly due to the social action whereby they became signs (became assimilated as significantly relative within cognition) in the first place. Yet others, such as symptoms, clues, and imprints, in addition to being conjoined to something signified through experience (and therefore partly in terms of codes), also turn out to be conjoined–and knowable as so conjoined–independently of our experience of (and codes concerning) their conjunction. Recognition of the connection in every case depends upon our experience. But *the connection recognized* sometimes transcends that dependence and *is recognized so* to transcend. Part of what is recognized is the transcendence, the irreducibility to our experience.

Moreover, if culture functioned in the recognition of all natural struc-tures and significations in the way that Eco's definition of the sign-function requires it to do, then clouds could be signs of rain and smoke a sign of fire *only for humans*, whereas we have every reason to believe that they function as natural signs for many species of animals besides our own. It is not enough to show that culture *is at work* in the recognition of such signs as such, as Professor Eco does rightly and with little trouble (3.6.2. Recognition. esp. 222-224). It would be necessary to show further that it is at work *in the way required by the definition of the sign-function*, that is, as the sole essential ground of the correlation itself under every consideration, and not merely as the essential ground of the recognition of the correlation. Such a demonstration, to the extent that it might be possible, would be yet counterfactual.

5. Conclusions and Basic Problems

I conclude that the notion of sign-function is not an adequate—let alone necessary—substitute for the classical notion of *signum*, precisely inasmuch as the classical notion was proposed as a genus to which significant natural and cultural phenomena *alike* are species.

5.a. Mind-Dependent vs. Mind-Independent Relations

The basic problem in Eco's analysis of recognition and natural signs would seem to devolve upon the irrelevance in his theory of mind-independent or physical occurrences of relations and the role such relations play in signifying. Eco nowhere discusses the subject of relation for its own sake. It is not that he denies the existence of physical relations. Yet the irrelevance of such relations to semiosis as he theorizes it is implicit in his definition of sign-function as dependent on a "previously established social convention". The irrelevance of physical relativity to semiosis is something required by his theory but gratuitous in terms of our experience of the action of signs overall.

5.b. Sensation vs. Perception

The tacit failure to recognize the role of physical relations in semiosis is further borne out by his reference (3.3.4, 165; Eco's italics) to "the vast problem of *perception as interpretation of sensory disconnected data* . . . organized . . . by a cognitive hypothesis based on previous experiences". This way of couching the problem profoundly confuses the phenomenologically interdependent but logically distinguishable (through prescission) and ontologically distinct levels of sensation and perception, what the Latins called *sentire* as distinct from (although presupposed to) *phantasiari* (see Deely 1994:41–43, 45, 120, 296, 298, 300; 1994a:73–88; 1996).

Eco states: "I connect together some stimuli coming from an as yet unstructured field and I produce a *perceptum* based on a previously acquired experience" (3.5.2, 193). In so stating, he seems to take for granted the hoary empiricist and rationalist conception of sense data as discrete and atomic in character (the "myth of the given"), achieving any least measure of correlation and synthesis only and wholly in the comparatively unreal constructions of perception and understanding, what the Latins called "negationes et non entia" (Deely 1996).

Yet a more careful analysis of what actually transpires in experience suggests that sensory data are never given in a simply disconnected way. For example, "a sense impression representing a colored thing also represents the profile and movement and other common sensibles there contained and adjoined, yet does not on this account pass beyond simple cognition, even though the thing cognized is not simple, but plural: otherwise, we would not be able to see a plurality of objects by a simple vision. But if we are able to see many objects in a single vision, why not also an ordered plurality and one thing through another, and, consequently, a significate through a sign and as contained in the sign?"[34] Sensation, analytically considered, differs from perception precisely in that it makes the organism aware only of the immediate physical surroundings insofar as they are proportioned to the biological cognitive powers or organs of the organism by a series of physical relationships introduced through the physical interaction of organism and environment. Perception will further structure this "data" according to the desires and needs specific to the organism, which may have no counterpart as such on the side of the environment. But to miss the fact that the data of sensation are already naturally structured through the determinate character of the stimulus acting on the determinate character of the cognitive dispositions of the organism is to miss a great deal that is important for understanding the dependency of anthroposemiosis on zoösemiosis and physiosemiosis generally.

We do not get sensory stimuli "from an as yet unstructured field" of simply "disconnected sensory data" subsequently organized *only* "on the basis of previous experience." *Already* in the sensory manifold as *here and now* stimulating, there is a *naturally determined* structure of objectivity–however minimal and underdetermined respecting perception and understanding as gestalt wholes–which is 'then' *further* but *not wholly* structured by the intervention of constructive activities and previous experiences. And this naturally determined macrostructure, common across a broad range of biological species (e.g., the anthropoids), is precisely a system of relations physically relative to the constructive networks of perception and understanding based upon them and interwoven with them.

The "first interpretants" of phenomena thus are not ideas (percepts and concepts), but naturally determined patterns labile and in motion at the base and core (the "first immediate denotation," roughly, in Eco's terms) of the constructs that ideas elaborate in order further to interpret and give a "logical" sense to the larger phenomenal fields of unanalyzed experience. Whence the process of cultural semiosis is not an unlimited one in all directions (cf. Ch. 2.7, 68-72). It is susceptible of a "reality-check" through critical control exercised over variables in the direct experience and progressive objectifying of the environment, [35] including those various bubbles within the environment that semiotics has come to recognize as *Umwelten*, species-specific objective worlds distinct from the physical environs as common to all the life forms.

5.c. Invention vs. Invented

My analysis of the inadequacy of Eco's notion of sign-function as a full (let alone necessary) substitute for the classical notion of *signum* is borne out by Eco's own analysis of *invention* as a mode of sign production. "How is it possible", he asks (3.6.7, 249-250), "to represent a man standing and a lady sitting under a tree, a calm landscape with clouds and a corn field behind them, a given light and a given mood—as happens in Gainsborough's *Mr. and Mrs. Andrews?*". I add some italics to Eco's own (p. 250):

> Nevertheless, *if such a phenomenon seems to escape the correlational definition of sign-function: it certainly does not escape the basic definition of a sign as something which stands for something else:*for Gainsborough's painting is exactly this, something physically *present* which conveys something *absent* and, in certain cases, could be used in order to mention a state of the world.

If something can escape the correlational definition of sign-function without escaping the basic definition of *signum*, however, what other conclusion is possible than the conclusion that sign is a more fundamental category for semiotic analysis than that of sign-function? Far from translating the notion of sign, the notion of sign-function is subordinate (inferior in the logical sense) to the notion of sign. "Sign-function" is but a partial transcription of *signum*, co-ordinate with but irreducibly distinct from the natural phenomena of signification which are also products of semiosis, but a semiosis more fundamental than the semiosis (and semiotics) of culture.

5.d. Modes of Sign-Production vs. Typologies of Sign

Here I should mention that, coupled with the attempted substitution of sign-function for sign, Eco proposed to substitute the identification of modes of sign production for the more traditional typologies of signs. Of course, in his text, this was a necessary move, inasmuch as everything began with the assumption that "there are not signs". But even in the absence of this assumption, counterfactual as it seems for the reasons stated, a study of the modes of sign-production is an essential development of semiotics. The initiation of such an inquiry is much to Eco's credit. For it is not enough simply to note, as we have seen among the Latins, [36] that in no case does a sign as such consist in the physical relation of cause to effect or effect to cause. It is further necessary to explain how such relations are incorporated through experience into the semiotic web of perception and understanding, and this is one of the most important tasks for the theory of sign production. For such a task, an account such as Eco's, *exclusively* in terms of socio-cultural convention, can hardly suffice.

We note, therefore, two things in Eco's undertaking to formulate an account of sign production: first, that the explicitation and thematization of this topic is an essential advance in the development of the doctrine of signs; second, that more is necessary than an account adequate exclusively to the *signum ad placitum* or sign as sign-function, for the sign in general extends to *signa naturalia* as well. To have taken the first step, nonetheless, is already an advance in the doctrine of signs, one of the several important advances signalized in Eco's pathmarking book.

Yet, granted the theoretical importance of this move toward a recognition of the necessity of developing a study of the modes of sign production, it is at the same time necessary to realize that this move is additional to, not, as Eco proposes, substitutive for, more traditional typologies of sign. The move is similar to that of Peirce in shifting the focus from the being of signs to their action (see Deely 1990:Ch.3, 22ff.). For just as action follows from being, so a typology of signs is essential to the study of sign-production, in order that we might know what it is the production of that we seek to discover. To study a mode of production with no idea of what it is that the mode of production will produce would be a blind process indeed, incapable of being initiated for want of a clue in which direction to proceed.

Neglect of this basic point, at least as old as the *naturalia* of Aristotle (Deely 1965–6:notes), leads Eco to commit a kind of howler, or what Ryle might have termed a category mistake, in the context of his Gainsborough analysis. "If 'invention' were a category within a typology of signs . . .", Eco writes (3.6.8, 256). But what would be a category within a typology of signs would be *invented signs*, not *invention*—i.e., the product not the process. And *invented signs* belong to the subspecies *signum ad placitum* of the genus *signum*, co-ordinate with such other subspecies as the *signum ex consuetudine*, verified in zoösemiosis and anthroposemiosis alike, and *signa naturalia*, whose action is displayed further in phytosemiosis and physiosemiosis.

There are plenty of problems with traditional typologies (cf. Sebeok 1974:26–45, 1975b), but these are problems of the sort that semiotics cannot avoid. Improvement of the typologies and investigation of the modes of sign-production are lines of research that cannot proceed but in tandem. It is not fully clear then, how Eco can think that, in this part of his work, "the idealistic fallacy is avoided" [256], especially as that fallacy is proper to modern philosophy, by the flight from typology to modes of production.

"Idealism" in modern philosophy, as stated above, is the thesis that everything the mind knows, in precisely what the minds knows of it, owes its basic constitution to the mind. Professor Eco goes out of his way, more than once, in an effort to avoid any risk of idealism (pp. 22, 256, 317). Yet into idealism is precisely where his theory takes him with its claim that there are not signs but only sign-functions, inasmuch as these are grounded entirely in cultural linkages. A giant step for the doctrine of signs in the terminological move from semiology to semiotics and on many particular points, Eco's theory as a whole is yet one small step within philosophy itself, because it does not succeed in leaping the chasm which separates the basic standpoint of semiotics from the pre-semiotic epistemological paradigms tied to the modern standpoint of idealism. It is not a question of any realism *versus* idealism. It is a question of a doctrine of signs which, when fully aware of its origins and proper standpoint, is able to begin at a point beyond the modern controversies. And this standpoint is the cognizance of the being in relation proper to signs as such, the *renvoi* by which every sign, natural, social, or cultural, is constituted.

6. The Theory of Codes and Anthroposemiosis

The theory of codes at the heart of Eco's analysis of *signum* in its *ad placitum* guise, what he calls the "sign function", seen in its proper dimension, is an analytical tool of permanent importance for analyzing the more typically cultural elements at work in human experience, and especially the predominantly linguistic aspects of those elements. Parmentier's twin insistence–doubly correct–on the absence of a notion of code in Peirce and on the importance of the concept for anthropology doubly justifies the approach of Eco's tract. But his tract does not go far enough, for "cultural semiotics needs both Peirce's notion of indexicality and Saussure's notion of code" (Parmentier 1994:xiii). Eco's notion of code, unparalleled in sophistication, to be sure, is not simply that of Saussure. Still less is his notion of indexicality that of Peirce. But by drawing the Peircean notion of interpretant into the theory of codes, Eco accomplishes, especially by judicious illustrative passages, some interesting clarifications of what we might call the *experimental ground* of this difficult notion (e.g., see the discussion of theological notions over pp. 61-68) so central to the doctrine of signs.

The notion of the interpretant, at the time Eco wrote (also Eco 1972), was not a notion well understood in the secondary Peirce literature, thanks to the "many scholars who proceeded to exorcise it by misunderstanding it (interpretant = interpreter or receiver of the message)" (pp. 69–70). [37] In Eco's own understanding, "the idea of the interpretant makes a theory of signification a rigorous science of cultural phenomena, while detaching it from the metaphysics of the referent" (p. 70) such as that appears in the philosophers and linguists inspired by Frege (1892) and Ogden and Richards (1923) (see Eco, 2.5.1 and 2.5.2, 58-61). But of course, these are very late authors in their own right, and very extraneous in their mode of conceptualizing to the Latin origins of semiotic consciousness in the sixteenth century Hispanic authors traced by Beuchot (1996). Nor did Peirce see his notion of interpretant as restricted by any means to cultural phenomena (Deely 1994a:Chs. 7 and 8).

In particular, the "metaphysics of the referent" about which Eco speaks amounts to little more than the modern blunder of confusing physical things and events with objects, whereas in fact the two concepts are as distinct in principle as is the Peircean category of brute force and secondness from the realm of thirdness constituted through signs. This is a terminological point of the greatest importance for semiotics, but I can do no more here than refer the reader to my own book-length discussions of the problem.[38]

The basic insight of Eco's book on this point, probably even the motivating one for the theory of codes, is the fundamental contrast between *units of nature*, on the one hand ("things"), and *units of experience and of culture*, on the other (2.5.3, 61-6):

> . . . codes, insofar as they are accepted by a society, set up a 'cultural' world which is neither actual nor possible in the ontological sense; its existence is linked to a cultural order, which is the way in which a society thinks, speaks and, while speaking, explains the 'purport' of its thought through other thoughts. Since it is through thinking and speaking that a society develops, expands or collapses, even when dealing with 'impossible' worlds (i.e., aesthetic texts, ideological statements), a theory of codes is very much concerned with the format of such 'cultural' worlds, and faces the basic problem of how *to touch* contents.

This insight belongs to the bedrock of Eco's book; and, if the earlier testimony of Poinsot on the point is accurate, it is an insight which belongs to the bedrock of semiotics itself.[39] "Units of nature" and "units of experience", what Poinsot would call "physical unities" and "objective unities", are by no means the same; and though they may occasionally coincide, and constantly intertwine in experience, the fact remains that, as Eco puts it (p. 66), "social life did not develop on the basis of things, but on the basis of cultural units", that is to say, objective as opposed to physical divisions. Thus, even at those points where the universe of objects and the universe of things intertwine, the significations in different phases or moments of anthroposemiosis—either within one culture or between different cultures—need be by no means the same. "The multiplicity of codes, contexts, and circumstances shows us that the same message can be decoded from different points of view and by reference to diverse systems of conventions" (2.15, 139).

Of course, the simple notation of this *fact* is hardly new. To cite but a single classic example among many which could be given, any reader of Gibbon (i.1776-1788) will find in the notes dozens of concrete and colorful illustrations of the fact made in terms of the competing Lebenswelts of antiquity. But awareness of the fact is one thing; the attempt to assign express *reasons for* the fact quite another. This latter Eco achieves as yet another groundbreaking advance in the formulation of a doctrine of signs (see the example of the case of whales in 2.11.3, and Table 19, 113).[40] I think there can be no doubt of the need to work the notion of code into the fabric of the Peircean notion of semeiosy and of the Latin notion of *signum* on which semiotics relies, to achieve a viable notion of textuality coextensive with the possibilities of objectification seen in the full scope of its dependence on the action of signs (Eco 1972; Baer 1992; Deely 1994:Part II).

Cultural units are, precisely, "the meaning to which the code makes the system of sign-vehicles correspond" (2.6, 67), even though these themselves first appear in the garb later known to be proper only to *res transcendentales*, environmental phenomena in their physical dimension. This is why language—the universe of discourse—is able to display a relative autonomy vis-à-vis so-called "facts"—the universe of being (2.5.2, 60-61). Eco's statement "that an expression does not, in principle, designate any object", where 'object' is taken to mean some actual existent or event, however, needs to be immediately qualified, for here our author has fallen into the trap of accepting the established usage of the term "object" to designate in principle a physical referent of some kind. This notion is inviable in semiotics, as I mentioned shortly above.[41] The expression "*does not*" should read "*need not*" to achieve an exactness which is not misleading. "The fact that *semiosis lives as a fact in a world of facts* limits the absolute purity of the universe of codes" (p. 158; Eco's italics), indeed, but Eco seems not to notice that it limits as well the proposition that "*Semiosis explains itself by itself*" (p. 71; Eco's italics).[42]

It remains that the relative independence of discourse from being stands as the first and most basic characteristic of signs to be reckoned with, and not only as including the sign-systems of species-specifically human language (I have argued this point in a variety of contexts since 1975, having first learned it from a *Tractatus de Signis* antedating that of Eco by three hundred-and-forty-five years). This point, so central for semiotics, Eco trenchantly underscores by remarking: "The possibility of lying is the *proprium* of semiosis" (p. 59; cf. 7, 64, 116). This is well put, if one sided, since the possibility of expressing any truth is equally the *proprium* of semiosis. Since the sign is that which every object presupposes, and since semiotics studies the action of signs, perhaps the best definition of semiotics would be: the study of the possibility of being mistaken.

IV. Concluding Remarks

Enough has been said to persuade readers of these remarks in retrospect that Eco's book set a standard of comprehensiveness fairly early in the game for further work in the field. I have concentrated in my remarks on this classic work on the critique of the alleged adequacy of the sign-function as a translation of the notion of *signum*, because, as a matter of fact, the notion of *signum* is broader and more fundamental than Eco's notion of sign-function, and nothing is more important in the long run than a proper clarification and laying of the foundations for the enterprises of semiotics.

Without such a clarification, the array of semiotics' pursuits would eventually become in fact just what it has always appeared to be in the eyes of obtuse critics: a disarray. Semiotics would risk dispersion and eventual assimilation of its pursuits back into the already established specialties for want of the critical awareness and development of its own foundation. The whole range of attempts to isolate and analyze the specifically *signifying* aspects and elements of disciplines as diverse as architecture, music, theater, ethology, etc.–the *field of semiotics*–must therefore never fail to reflect upon and succeed in grasping ever more surely the insight that underlies and gives justice to (*founds*) the entire panoply of semiotics' concerns. This is the realization that the sign is the universal instrument of communication, within oneself or with others equally.

Principally in this direction has Eco's work been "gone beyond", but without being "left behind", for the many reasons I have indicated. With such a focus, the inherently interdisciplinary character of semiotics is bound to reveal itself with increasing vitality and persuasive power. Professor Eco's fine study was one of the most important recent steps along the way. Albeit that it was one small step for philosophy, as appears from what we have since learned of the history of semiotics. Even so, as an intellectual movement of contemporary culture, *A Theory of Semiotics* was one giant leap for the doctrine of signs.

———————————

John Deely

The Themata of Eco's Semiotics of Literature

In a key passage of *The Book of Laughter and Forgetting* Milan Kundera poses the question why the mature Beethoven "committed his most beautiful meditations" to the form of variations. At first glance, variations might appear to be "the most superficial of forms, . . . a work suited for a lacemaker rather than a Beethoven". But when the son-writer deciphers the unfinished gesture of his dying father-musicologist, he comes to understand that the form of variations is a voyage "into the infinite internal variety which is hidden in every thing". The variation technique, a tenacious pursuit of certain themata with a view to a distant resolution, is characteristic of the master semiotician Umberto Eco. And let us emphasize that the themata he has pursued are at the core of the concerns and controversies of our epoch. Eco has his own image for this method–spiral repetition: every new exploration elevates the solutions to a higher level by expanding the thema's cognitive context. This is Eco's way of responding to the incessant theoretical challenges posed by contemporary philosophy, science and scholarship.

The basic ideas of Eco's semiotics have been formulated in *A Theory of Semiotics* (1976). He re-assessed and refined them in several books which form the corpus of his literary semiotics. Only a study the size of a dissertation (or two) could do justice to this impressive and still growing output. I can give no more than a summary of the themata of Eco's literary semiotics.[1]

1. THE OPPOSITION CLOSED/OPEN WORK IS ECO'S EARLIEST CONCERN.

The variations of the thema express his agonizing over the fundamental problem of literature–the contrast between innovation and stereotype, originality and repetitiveness. Eco's conception of the closed work is stimulated by the "narrative grammar" of the closed "fabula", initiated by Vladimir Propp's "morphology" and other theorists of stereotyped narrative genres (Beadier, Jolles). In the main, his contribution is situated in the framework of French structuralist narratology (which was in part inspired by Propp). His representative study of the closed text, "Narrative Structures in Fleming," first appeared (in an incomplete version) in the programmatic volume of French structuralism, *Communications 8* (1966). Eco is within this epistemological paradigm in the selection of his material–works of popular, mass literature, in his analytic strategy–search for narrative "deep" structures, and in his bringing forth the ideological manipulation of the reader subtly effected by trivial literature. The critique of the modern "mythologies" is most penetrating in "The Myth of Superman" (*Role* 107-24), where the force of Eco's debunking is comparable only to the great demascating exercises of Roland Barthes. Eco reveals the absurdity of the myth by pointing out the inexplicable discrepancy between the hero's virtual omnipotency and the small-scale field of his operations. If we consider the gigantic, historical deeds that Superman could accomplish, his activities are "a paradoxical waste of means." But this paradox is inevitable, if the myth is to carry its basic ideological message: "Superman must make virtue consist of many little activities on a small scale," because he is "a perfect example of civic consciousness, completely split from political consciousness" (*Role* 123). Eco thus reveals that narrative submitted to ideology is stereotyped by necessity: ideology creates a well-serving narrative structure and this structure is perpetuated *ad infinitum* by the never-ending demand for ideological reinforcement.

But when Eco proceeds to investigate narrative time in the iterative structure of the "serial", a new perspective on the closed work opens up. The standard concept of time as a unidirectional vector "breaks down": the serial's time is "an ever-continuing present". With acute insight, Eco perceives an analogous "disintegration of temporality" in many "sophisticated" works of modern literature and art (Joyce, Robbe-Grillet, the film "Last Year in Marienbad"). This analogy would seem to put into question the validity of the opposition closed/open work. But it need not be abandoned, it just has to be reinterpreted: even a closed narrative structure offers "infinite variations of the theme". In the detective novel, for example, "each crime has new psychological and economic motivations, each time the author devises what appears as a new situation" (*Role* 119). The poetics of the closed work is deceptively simple, but in fact the work satisfies not only the "hunger for redundancy," but also the need for change. It might be that the balance between familiarity and novelty is the very source of the mass appeal of closed works.

Eco's further contributions to the poetics of the closed text take account of this precarious dialectic. In "Rhetoric and Ideology in Sue's *Les Mystères de Paris*" (*Role* 125-43) the dialectic is posed as a contrast between the invariant "sinusoidal structure" of the serial novel and Sue's stylistic innovation, his inventing "a Kitsch for the poor" (*Role* 135). Interestingly, a much more recent writer, Fleming, whose Bond cycle is the subject of the study mentioned above (*Role* 144-172), relies on a very similar strategy. While the narrative structure of the cycle is perfectly iterative, Fleming's "mastery" is in his ability to foist "a clever montage of *déjà vu*" as "a stylistic invention". Reinventing Kitsch for the modern reader, Fleming, who repeats the same story again and again, can also be numbered "among the cleverest exploiters of an *experimental technique*" (*Role* 163, 168; emphasis-L.D.). Fleming's descriptive digressions, his intense attention to detail and verbal embellishment, elevate the Bond novels to the status of Literature (the capital letter is Eco's).

These and similar observations re-affirm the feature of closed narrative texts uncovered already by Propp: while in their fabula they implement a stereotype, in their other dimensions, especially in their descriptive passages, they offer a "field of freedom" where the story-teller displays his imagination, his art of improvisation, his stylistic mastery. These variable elements, such as the "attributes" of the characters, "provide the folk tale with its brilliance, charm, and beauty" (Propp 1928:79). We have some excuse for reading Sue, Fleming, Ruth Rendell and others of that ilk, at least as bedtime reading. But Eco leads us further. In *The Limits of Interpretation* he finds a role for trivial literature as the intertext of "high" literature. Borges's and Casares's appropriations and transformations of the detective story (Ch. 10) testify to the de-automatization of the stereotype in experimental (avant-garde) literature. This intertextuality shows once again that literary history is not a history of two isolated parallels. The closed works of popular literature and the open works of "high" literature have engaged in centuries-old exchange.

The "opening" of the closed work does not, however, invalidate the notion of the open work. Just as the closed fabula served Eco well as a starting point for understanding the features of the closed work, so the aesthetics of the open work is stimulated by experimental pieces of contemporary music. Using an analogy–though emphasizing also the difference–between the "performer" of music and the "interpreter" (reader) of literature Eco draws from this special case a general definition of open works: they "reject the definitive, concluded message and multiply the formal possibilities of the distribution of their elements. They appeal to the initiative of the individual performer, and hence they offer themselves not as finite works which prescribe specific repetition along given structural coordinates, but as 'open' works, which are brought to their conclusion by the performer at the same time as he experiences them on an aesthetic plane" (*OW* 3). In modern literature, the open work triumphs in the *oeuvre* of Franz Kafka, James Joyce and in the utopian project of Mallarmea's *Livre*. The open work of literature is "a communicative strategy" which already at the moment of its generation envisages, presupposes, a role for the reader. While the reader of the closed work is passive, lulled and ideologically manipulated, the reader of the open work is an active coproducer of the literary meaning and structure. "An open text is a paramount instance of a syntactic-semantico-pragmatic device whose foreseen interpretation is a part of its generative process" (*Role* 3). Reaching the concept of active reader, Eco is able to finish the circle from the closed to the open work and back: "Every work of art, even though it is produced by following an explicit or implicit poetics of necessity, is effectively open to a virtually unlimited range of possible readings, each of which causes the work to acquire new vitality in terms of one particular taste, or perspective, or personal performance" (OW 21). Or, as he puts it in a different variant: "So-called open texts are only the extreme and most provocative exploitation–for poetic purposes–of a principle which rules both the generation and the interpretation of texts in general" (Role 4-5).

With his concept of open work (the Italian original dates to 1962, the French translation to 1966), Eco, the fellow-traveler of French structuralism, became also a dissident, at least within a structuralism that saw the poetic work as "an object which, once created, had the stiffness–so to speak–of a crystal" (Lévi-Strauss, qtd. from *Role* 4). It is highly significant for the history of poststructuralism, that Eco does not see the introduction of a pragmatic concept, the reader, as contradictory to structural analysis: "To postulate the cooperation of the reader does not mean to pollute the structural analysis with extratextual elements. The reader as an active principal of interpretation is a part of the picture of the generative process of the text" (*Role* 4). After all, did not Morris's classical model of semiotics provide a place for pragmatics? Communication in general and literary communication in particular requires a receiver as much as it requires a sender.

2. MEANING AND INTERPRETATION.

This thema of Eco's literary semiotics is closely related to the open/closed work thematic. One of the potential dangers that the introduction of the reader (and any other pragmatic concept) into literary theory brings, is a radical relativization of the literary work's meaning and of the procedures of interpretation. Indeed, if the reader coproducts the literary work's meaning, then there is no limit to the coproductions. Every reader makes his/her own Kafka, Joyce, Hesse and so on. No criteria of interpretation, no distinction between interpretation and misinterpretation can be postulated.

Eco's assessment of this possible interpretation of interpretation is negative. Having perceived that "in the course of the last decades, the rights of the interpreters have been overstressed", he re-evaluates his *Opera aperta*: "I was studying the dialectics between the rights of the texts and the rights of their interpreters" (*IO* 23). Now he postulates, along the intentio auctoris and the intentio lectoris, the intentio operis. If a semantic intention is inscribed in the text, then there is such a thing as "bad" interpretation; even if only one case of it could be found, it "is enough to disprove the hypothesis that interpretation has no public criteria" (*IO* 25).

In fact, the "criteria for limiting interpretation" are assumed in the very foundations of Eco's semiotics (as, indeed, they are assumed in semiotics simpliciter). *A Theory of Semiotics* provides a background for a theory of interpretation by making a distinction between signification and communication and establishing a clear hierarchy between them: "A signification system is an autonomous semiotic construct that has an abstract mode of existence independent of any possible communicative act it makes possible. On the contrary (except for stimulation processes) every act of communication to or between human beings–or any other intelligent biological or mechanical apparatus–presupposes a signification system as its necessary condition" (*TS* 9). Transferred to text interpretation, the hierarchy asserts the "rights" of the text vis-à-vis the interpreter. Eco's semiotics views interpretation as an interplay between the addressee and the work as an objective fact. As a signification system, the text restricts the range of its possible interpretations: "Before a text is produced, every kind of text could be invented. After a text has been produced, it is possible to make that text say many things–in certain cases a potentially infinite number of things–but it is impossible–or at least critically illegitimate–to make it say what it does not say".2 For this reason, it is legitimate to adjudicate different interpretations in a way that reminds us of Popper's evaluating of scientific hypotheses: "It is impossible to say what is the best interpretation of a text, but it is possible to say which ones are wrong" (*Limits* 148).3

Eco's semiotic conception of literary text interpretation is strengthened by two contrasts. The first opposes interpretation and use. Of course, readers or nonreaders can use literary texts for many different purposes, some of them quite usual–as historical documents, psychiatric reports, ideological manifestoes etc. (1980:153-61), others more bizarre (as, say, plagiarized love letters). But Eco insists, and rightly so, that use is not interpretation, that it appropriates the literary text for purposes it was not designed to serve.

The second opposition is within the concept of interpretation itself. Ever since A Theory of Semiotics Eco has been staking out a reasoned position between the postulate of a single interpretation and unlimited semiotic drift: "On one side, it is assumed that to interpret a text means to find out . . . its objective nature of essence, an essence which, as such, is independent of interpretation. On the other side it is assumed that texts can be interpreted in infinite ways" (*Limits* 24). Calling both of these positions "epistemological fanaticism", he spends no time on refuting the first one. The reason may be that in recent decades the view has been given such a pounding that it survives only in a few underground shelters. In contrast, the second view is something of an "official" position today. Therefore, Eco faces it squarely and his criticism is informed by a far-seeing historical per-spective. Semiotic drift is situated within the Hermetic tradition (its history is sketched in *Limits*, Ch. 1 and *IO*, Ch. 1), whose interpretative praxis is based on the principle of "universal analogy and sympathy": the elements of the "sublunar world" are matched with the elements of the "superior world". Such matching requires "a very flexible notion of resemblance" which causes Hermetic drift, "the uncontrolled ability to shift from mean-ing to meaning", to connect everything with everything else "by a labyrin-thine web of mutual referrals" (*Limits* 24-27).

But are not structuralism and semiotics, with their postulates that "tout se tient" and that the meaning of a sign is just another sign, children of the Hermetic tradition? Eco is aware of the connections, but is trying to disso-ciate semiotics or, at least, Peirce's unlimited semiosis from the Hermetic drift. He claims that by Peirce's method "the sign is more and more deter-mined both in its breadth and in its depth. In the course of unlimited semiosis the interpretation approximates (even though asymptotically) the final logical interpretant" (*Limits* 24-28), a communal depository (Habit, convention) of meaning. But a possible take-over of semiotics cannot be so easily prevented. As long as semiotics locates the generation of meaning in the sign-sign axis only, as long as it rejects the notion of reference, that is the sign-world axis, it can and will produce again and again its own Hermetism.

Without doubt, Eco's theory of interpretation is the best that the semi-otic tradition can offer with respect to this topic. But can it convince or, at least, influence a Richard Rorty or a Stanley Fish? I think not. Because for these people interpretation is an intuitive byproduct of reading, it is read-ing expressed in a written, spoken or thought paraphrase. No theory is necessary for this enterprise to proceed. Interpretation is practical activity, just as reading is. Here is what Rorty has to say about reading: "Reading texts is a matter of reading them in the light of other texts, people, obses-sions, bits of information, or what have you, and then seeing what hap-pens" (*IO* 105). But if reading is guided by factors enumerated by Rorty, then the multiplicity of interpretations is necessarily given in the activity itself. Interpreting is the production of a potentially infinite number of incompatible and incommensurate interpretations. No "objective" crite-rion belongs into this game. Since interpretation is a byproduct of reading, then Rorty's "reading" of Foucaults' Pendulum (*IO* 89-93) has no more, no less legitimacy than that of a housewife from Peoria.

Interpretation resulting from the praxis of reading is a hit-or-miss game. It can lead to something "weird and idiosyncratic", just as it can yield inter-pretations "so exciting and convincing that one has the illusion that one now sees what a certain text is really about". But it is not any criterion of interpreting that determines how convincing an interpretation is, it is "the needs and purposes of those who are being excited and convinced" (IO 105) In other words, you find convincing an interpretation which confirms your doxa. Evaluation of interpretation is self-confirmation of a closed mind.

But who is really playing this game of interpretation? Who decided that it is the central concern of the discipline of literature? Is it the core of literary semiotics, or was it imposed on it?. At the end of Eco's "Reply" (IO 139-51), in connection with his seminar on Nerval's "Sylvie", the concept of analysis makes its appearance: "We hope to have explained–after a quasi-anatomical analysis of every line of that text, scoring the verbal tenses, the different role played by the pronoun je as referred to different temporal situations, and so on and so forth–by which semiotic means that texts creates its multiple and mutually contradictory effects . . . Due to the fallibilism of knowledge I assume that some further descriptions will discover further semiotic strategies that we have underestimated, just as they may be able to criticize any of our descriptions as effected by an excessive propensity toward hermeneutic suspicion. In any case I presume to have understood better how Sylvie works" (IO 147-48) "How Sylvie works" sounds remarkably like "how Don Quijote is made" (Swklovskij) or "how Gogol's 'The Overcoat' is made" (Ejchenbaum), and that is a completely different project in a completely different tradition than to ask what does Sylvie, Don Quijote or "The Overcoat" mean. Fueramus Pergama quondam. But not all is lost if today's literary semiotician remembers, at least at the end of his reflection on meaning in literature, that in our academic youth Jakobson, Ejchenbaum, Mukarwovskya, Barthes and others did not teach us to assign this or that meaning to a literary text, but to analyze the text in order to discover its overt and covert strategies of meaning-production.

3. POSSIBLE WORLDS

The thema of possible worlds entered Eco's semiotics in *The Role of the Reader*. There is no better proof of Eco's sensitivity to theoretical innovation than his efforts to appropriate possible-worlds semantics, originating in logic and analytic philosophy, for the needs of literary semiotics. Eco has immediately perceived its potential but also recognized the basic problem connected with the introduction of formal concepts into empirical disciplines: easily handled in logical or mathematical formalisms, they become remote (some would say, empty) symbolic representations of empirical phenomena. Indeed, very often mathematical and logical models have been applied in linguistics, text theory, poetics and semiotics as pure formalisms, without any regard for the heuristic needs of empirical study. Some theorists tried to impress us with complex formal models (often just copied from textbooks of logic or mathematics) whose concepts, however, were impotent to solve empirical problems or describe empirical data. Formal theory has become a cumbersome giant whose cognitive power is minuscule.

Eco's adaptation of formal (logical) possible-worlds semantics to the needs of literary semiotics is an example to follow. He starts with the suggestion, expressed in one of his apposite metaphors, that the possible worlds of text theory and literary semantics cannot be "bare", but must be "furnished". "We shall speak not of abstract types of possible worlds that do not contain a list of individuals . . ., but, on the contrary, of 'pregnant' worlds of which one must know all the acting individuals and their properties" (*Role* 218). Later on, in Ch. 4 of *The Limits of Interpretation* (which is a revised version of Eco's contribution to Nobel symposium 65, see Allén 1989), he finds useful Jaakko Hintikka's concept of "small world"–"a relatively short course of local events" (Hintikka 1989:55). If fictional worlds of literature are thought of as small furnished possible worlds, then the formal concept becomes a theoretical concept of literary semantics, without losing all the stimulating features which have come with it. Literary semantics now has at its disposal such notions as extension and intention, modalities, accessibility, transworld identity and so on. And, last but not least, Eco's own powerful concept of "cultural encyclopedia", the shared communal or cultural knowledge about the world, the cognitive background of world-construction and world-reconstruction.[4] Already in Eco's study of a very puzzling text, Alphonse Allais's "Un Drame bien parisien", some of these conceptual tools were successfully tested (*Role* 200-60).

Eco's original formulation of the possible-worlds semantics of literary fiction is not without problems. He interprets all possible worlds as "cultural constructs" and that necessarily leads him to conclude: "Even a so-called 'actual' or 'real' world of reference must be taken as a possible world, that is, as a cultural construct" (*Role* 222). Eco thus aligned himself with an ontology which he felt to be very close to philosophical idealism. Yet the idea of possible worlds does not commit us to ontological idealism. Already in Saul Kripke's original formalism, one of the worlds (G) was privileged by being called "actual". Robert Adams (1974) recognized that possible-worlds semantics can operate in two different ontologies. One ontology, called "actualism" by Adams, deems the actual world to be ontologically special–the realm of actualized possibles; the second ontology, "possibilism", treats all possible worlds as ontologically uniform, as mental constructs, for example. Actualism is defended by Alvin Plantinga (1974:45-51; 1979:257-72), Nicholas Rescher (1975:90-92), Robert Stalnaker (1984), and even David Lewis's "indexical" theory of possible worlds is inscribed within his realist (materialist) ontology (1983;1986).[5] I have serious doubts that possibilist ontology can sustain the distinction between fictional and factual texts, a distinction which, I believe, Eco does not want to give.

The dynamism of the thema of possible worlds in Eco's literary semiotics is best attested by his changing attitude to the concept of "impossible worlds". At the beginning, Eco was hesitant to give "full status" to worlds which violate two-value logic: "They undermine the world of our encyclopedia rather than build up another self-sustaining world" (*Role* 234). But later he accepted impossible worlds into literary semantics and contributed to their theoretical understanding. He adopts the view that they cannot achieve the status of authentic worlds (Doležel 1989), but they can be "mentioned", i.e. can be suggested by fictional texts: "We cannot conceive of worlds furnished with square circles that can be bought for an amount of dollars corresponding to the highest even number. However, . . . such a world can be mentioned" because "language can name nonexistent and inconceivable entities" (*Limits* 76; see also *Walks* 81-83). Eco thus lends theoretical support to the modernist and postmodernist fiction makers who have been stubbornly challenging the two-value logic and expanding the domain of sense beyond the limits of the logically possible (see Doležel forthcoming)

CONCLUSION

I have already mentioned that the themata of Eco's literary semiotics are substantive contributions to contemporary intellectual debates. This engagement is most clearly revealed in Eco's preoccupation with contemporary pragmatics and with deconstruction.

Contemporary pragmatics is a rapidly developing field of semiotics in general and of literary semiotics in particular. In the form of radical pragmatism it not only encroaches on the domain of semantics, but absorbs it. Eco, wary of any dogmatism, warns against this extreme position. He notices that Charles Morris's useful division of semiotics into syntactics, semantics and pragmatics might lead to a rigid division of labor and, ultimately, to a sterile "splendid isolation" of the three branches. So he refuses to assign the study of signification exclusively to semantics and that of communication exclusively to pragmatics. There is a pragmatics of signification, which will "represent in a semantic system pragmatic phenomena", just as there is a pragmatics of communication which will "analyze pragmatic phenomena that take place in the course of a communicative process". Similarly, Eco's preferred semantic theory—the encyclopedia model—introduces into the domain of semantics "a great deal of idealized pragmatic phenomena". In such a way, pragmatics and semantics, instead of striving to swallow each other, supplement each other in "a new, unified semiotic approach" (*Limits* 212, 219).

A similar aversion to dogmatism characterizes Eco's engagement with deconstruction. Every critic is, of course, aware that deconstruction by its very nature is impervious to any theoretical challenge or philosophical analysis. Deconstruction thus can be criticized only indirectly, by being placed in a certain interpretive tradition and by observing the past practices and consequences of that tradition. Eco places deconstruction in the Hermetic tradition. Having distinguished Hermetic drift from Peircean unlimited semiosis (see sec. 2), he finds Derrida's (and Rorty's) appropriation of Peirce unjustified. Deconstruction is not a form of Peircean semiosis: "Deconstructive drift and unlimited semiosis cannot be equivalent concepts" (*Limits* 36). What, ultimately, differentiates Peirce from Derrida is Peirce's recognition of a communal base of meaning, expressed in the "final logical interpretant" (see sec. 2). "From the moment in which the community is pulled to agree with a given interpretation, there is, if not an objective, at least an intersubjective meaning which acquires a privilege over any other possible interpretation spelled out without the agreement of the community" (*Limits* 40).

Eco's attitude to deconstruction might seem rather critical, but, in fact, he gives it much credit when he summarizes its contribution to contemporary semiotics: "Derrida has a fascinating penchant for saying things that are nonobviously true, or true in a nonobvious way. When he says that the concept of communication cannot be reduced to the idea of transport of a unified meaning, that the notion of literal meaning is problematic, that the current concept of context risks being inadequated (sic!); when he stresses, in a text, the absence of the sender, of the addressee, and of the referent and explores all the possibilities of a nonunivocal interpretability of it; when he reminds us that every sign can be cited and in so doing can break with every given context, engendering an infinity of new contexts in a manner which is absolutely illimitable–in these and in many other cases he says things that no semiotician can disregard" (*Limits* 36). Yet does this enumeration–-expressed as it is in "logocentric" language and "traditional" conceptualization–capture the subversive theory and practice of deconstruction? I suggest that it is rather a summary of postulates and assumptions which have been reached in contemporary semiotics irrespective of, and outside of, deconstruction.

Lubomir Doležel

Toward Interpretation Semiotics

1. Eco's contribution to the transition from decodification semiotics to interpreation semiotics in Italy.

The mid 1970s onward have been decisive years in Italian semiotics considering both the development in general sign theory as well as the flourishing of the various specific semiotics. In fact, these years mark a transition from decodification semiotics, which was influenced either directly or indirectly by Saussurean linguistics, to interpretation semiotics, largely a derivation of the Peircean-Morrisian tradition. Two books by Umberto Eco–A *Theory of Semiotics* of 1975 and *Semiotics and the Philosophy of Language* of 1984–may be viewed as expressions of this transition. Indeed, Eco's *A Theory of Semiotics* may be taken as the point of arrival of the initial phase in Italian semiotics and the point of departure of current orientations, which are strongly

Peircean as compared with the previous phase (It is no coincidence that the second edition of Ferruccio Rossi-Landi's 1953 monograph on Charles Morris also appeared in 1975). However, Italian semiotics is rich with many other problems and perspectives beyond the Saussurean influence or even the Peircean, which renders the semiotic scene during the years mentioned rather complex and varied. We are alluding to such factors as the work of M. Bakhtin, the rediscovery of Victoria Lady Welby, and the pioneering work inaugurated in the early 1950s by Feruccio Rossi-Landi.

The recent ferment in critical thought and theory in Italy should be seen in the context of intellectual developments at the European and world levels, and in relation to serious fields. Such interconnections led to the flourishing of such a great multiplicity of semiotic methodologies, theories, and practices that to speak of the 'adventures' of the sign as does the Italian philosopher of language and semiotician Augusto Ponzio (cfr. Ponzio 1990; part 1) is no doubt appropriate. Furthermore, semiotic studies have developed interdependently on the vertical axis of historiographical reconstruction, with numerous contributions tracing the life of signs through ancient and medieval thought (see for example Corvino et al. 1983; SPL;

Manetti 1987; Peter of Spain 1986 (1230?); Ponzio 1985a; *Versus* 50/51, 1988), and on the horizontal axis populated by the dissemination of the various specific semiotics.

An important issue taken into consideration by Eco in *Semiotics and the Philosophy of Language* is the relation between the specific semiotics, general semiotics, and philosophy of language. As already indicated in the title of this book of 1984, Eco significantly associates in his introduction:

> I believe that semiotics is philosophical in nature given that it does not study a particular system but proposes general categories in the light of which different systems may be compared. And for general semiotics philosophical discourse is neither advisable nor urgent: it is simply constitutive. (*SPL*:xii).

Besides signaling a connection between general semiotics and philosophy, the title of Eco's book also underlines the fact that semiotics and philosophy of language, a field not easily distinguished from general semiotics, do not coincide. For a fuller understanding of the specificity of semiotic discourse, it is important to look at semiotics through the eyes of philosophy, and particularly the philosophy of language (which is not only verbal language). This concept is further clarified by Ponzio:

> Philosophy of language may be described as exploring the external margins, protrusions and excesses with respect to the 'semiotic field', or science–or 'theory' (Morris) or 'doctrine' (Sebeok)–of signs. Recalling the expression 'metalinguistic' as used by Bakhtin to characterize his own reflection on language insofar as he transcends the limits of linguistics, we could characterize the philosophy of language as 'metasemiotics' (Ponzio 1988b:228).

On the other hand, in Eco's opinion, the specific semiotics, as grammars of particular sign systems, need not concern themselves with philosophical reflection on the categories in which they are grounded, which does not mean denying their philosophical foundations. This statement is also made as a reply to Emilio Garroni (cf. Garroni 1977, and his polemic response to Eco in Mincu 1982), who takes the opposite stand. Garroni maintains that even though the specific semiotics may privilege empirical research, they must be fully conscious of the categories through which they operate. Cesare Segre (in Marrone 1986: 153-163) also believes that so-called 'specific semiotics' must deal directly with problems of philosophical order, for they work within a specific theoretical framework and therefore at some stage must inevitably deal with the general problems of semiosis as well.

The practitioners of semiotics in Italy work in a great variety of different fields including aesthetics, psychology, information theory, literary theory, literary criticism, philology, mathematics, biology, etc., in addition to philosophy and linguistics. Semiotic theory has benefited from the contribution of theories and methods imported from different territories, which in turn have been enriched through their use of semiotic instruments. In response to the request that he identify the major Italian representatives of semiotics and underline their originality with respect to other European schools, Eco (in Mincu 1982: 68) mentions the field of architecture, reflection on iconic signs and on literature, the importance of philosophical speculation ("it was precisely in Italy that the transition was achieved from a structuralist semiotics of Sassurean derivation to a philosophical semiotics of Peircean derivation.), and the stronger characterization of Italian semiotics as social semiotics (with interesting graftings from Marxism) as compared for instance with French semiotics, which is decidedly oriented toward studies in psychology, with graftings from psychoanalysis.

Semiotics today may be described as transcending the phase designated as decodification (or, if we prefer, code, or equal exchange) semiotics (cf. Banfantini 1984:28ff), with its subdivision into communication semiotics (Saussure, Buyssens, Prieto) and signification semiotics (Barthes), and as working in the direction of so-called interpretation semiotics (Peirce, Bakhtin, Barthes, etc.). Code semiotics in Italy had already been seriously called into question in such books as Rossi-Landi's *Semiotica e idelogia* (1972–though his critique dates back as far as 1961 with *Significato, comunicazione e parlare comune*), Eco's *A Theory of Semiotics* (1975), Ponzio's La *semiotica in Italia* (1976), and Garroni's *Ricognizione della semiotica* (1977). These writings, and others still, including articles and monographic issues of journals, anticipate subsequent publications all of which were to work in the direction of interpretation semiotics. These include Eco (1984, 1990), and Bonfantini (1984, 1987), Rossi-Landi (1988), Ponzio (1985b, 1990a), and Bonfantini et al. (1985), and two Peircean anthologies (edited by Bonfantini) in Italian translation: *Semiotica* (1980), and *Le leggi dell'ipotesi* (1984).

2. On Signs Models Between Semiotics and Philosophy of Language

In *Semiotics and the Philosophy of Language* Eco reviews and reconstructs semiotic thought with a focus on problems of a theoretical order. To this end he examines five fundamental concepts in semiotics and philosophy of language: sign, meaning, metaphor, symbol, and code. The project of describing the development of twentieth-century semiotics with reference to the various phases in the development of sign model is announced in the introduction, in which Eco makes the following statement:

> First of all, it must be observed that contemporary semiotics would seem to be troubled by the anguish of an alternative. Is its founding concept the sign of semiosis? (. . .) On reading the history of the birth of semiotic thought in this

century, let's say from Genevan structuralism to the sixties, it would seem that semiotics initially emerged as reflection on the sign; but subsequently this concept gradually put in crisis and dissolved, and interest shifted to the engendering of texts, their interpretation, the drift of interpretations, productive pulsions, to the pleasure itself of semiosis. (*SPL*: xiv-xv).

Moreover, in Eco's view there is a need to push beyond the alternative between sign and semiosis, a need for "rediscovering that the original notion of sign was not founded on equality, on fixed correlations established by a code, on equivalence between expression and content, rather on inference, interpretation, the dynamics of semiosis" (*SPL*:xv).

The semiotics of Charles S. Peirce covers many aspects that direct a dialogic sense on the one hand, and contribute toward a more profound understanding of dialogic structures and practices on the other. His very thought-sign theory may be read as evidencing the dialogic structure of the self, which we might imagine as developing in terms of dialogue between a thought acting as a sign and another sign acting as interpretant. The Peircean sign model is today gaining wide consensus in both semiotics and the philosophy of language. This particular sign model is now gradually supplanting the Saussurean model, which thanks to the diffusion of structuralism has spread from linguistics (and semiology) to influence other human sciences as well.

We know that the Saussurean sign model is rooted in a series of dichotomic pairs comprising the notions of *langue* and *parole*, *signifiant* and signifié, diachrony and synchrony, and the syntagmatic and paradigmatic axes of language (Saussure 1916), which has favored its connection with the mathematical theory of communication [cf. Shannon and Weaver 1949) and its reformulation, therefore, in such terms as code and message, transmitter and receiver which explains why the semiotics of Saussurean derivation has been described as 'decodification semiotics' (Rossi-Landi 1968), code and message semiotics (cf. Bonfantini 1981), or 'equal exchange' semiotics (Ponzio 1973, 1977b). Despite their reductive character with respect to signifying and interpreting processes, for quite some time it was thought that such concepts as those just mentioned could adequately describe all kinds of sign processes–not only the simple sign processes of the signal type relative to information transmission, but also the complex type, the sign in the strict sense relative to human communication in its globality and in its different aspects (for the distinction between sign and signal, cf. Bakhtin-Volosinov 1929; Ponzio 1985b).

In the framework of 'decodification semiotics' the sign is divided into two parts: the signifier and the signified (respectively, the sign vehicle and its content). These are related on the basis of the principle of equal exchange and of equivalence–that is of perfect correspondence between communicative intention, on the one hand (which leads to codification), and interpretation (intended as mere decodification), on the other. In Italy, this sign model has already been criticized by Rossi-Landi (1961), who described it ironically in terms of this 'postal package theory'. As Rossi-Landi points out, decodification semiotics proposes an oversimplified analysis of communication in terms of messages (the postal package) complete in themselves, which pass from a sender to a receiver (from one post office to another) ready for registration: all the receiver need to is decipher the content, decode the message. Furthermore, as amply demonstrated by Rossi-Landi and subsequently by his collaborator, Ponzio, the Saussurean sign model which is the main reference point of decodification semiotics) is heavily influenced by the marginalistic theory of economic value as developed the School of Lausanne (Walras and Pareto), and is largely the result of applying the point de vue statique of pure economics to the study of language. Assimilation of the study of language to the study of the marketplace in an ideal state of equilibrium gives rise to a static conception of the sign. In fact, the latter is viewed in a synchronic framework and is described as being dominated by the paradigms of the logic of perfect correspondence between what is given and what is received–that is, by the logic of equal exchange currently regulating all social relations in today's dominant economic system (cf. Rossi-Landi 1968, 1975; Ponzio 1991).

Interpretation semiotics today puts into evidence the inadequacy of the sign model subtending decodification semiotics. Our 'rediscovery' of interpretation semiotics has no doubt been favored by new orientations of a socio-cultural order arising from signifying practices which are intolerant of the polarization between code and message, langue and parole, language system and individual speech. The flourishing of such signifying practices is concomitant with the weakening of the centripetal forces in linguistic life and socio-cultural life generally, which privilege the unitary system of the code over the effective polylogism, plurilingualism, multiaccentuativity and pluriavailability of signs. Moreover, by comparison with the claim to totalization implied by the dichotomies characterizing decodification semiotics, the categories of interpretation semiotics also account for the 'irreducibly other' as theorized by Bakhtin as well as by such philosophers as Emmanuel Lévinas (cf. Ponzio 1989).

As Bakhtin-Voloshinov had already demonstrated in Marxism and the Philosophy of Language (1929; Engl. trans. 1973), the instruments provided by decodification semiotics are inadequate for a convincing analysis of the distinguishing features of human communication such as plurilingualism (especially that internal to a single so-called 'national language'), plurivocality, ambiguity, polysemy, dialogism, otherness: as such verbal communication cannot be contained within the two poles of langue and parole, as had been theorized by Saussure. Far from being reduced to the status of mere signality, what characterizes the sign in general in a strong sense with respect to pure and simple signals is the fact that its interpretive potential is not exhausted in a single meaning. In other words, the signifier and the signified do not relate to each other on a one-to-one basis. As mentioned above, meaning is not simply a message that has been expressed intentionally by the sender according to a precise communicative will, and consequently the work of the interpretant sign is not limited to the very basic operations of identification, mechanical substitution, or mere recognition of the interpreted sign. By contrast with signals, signs at high levels of signness, of semioticity, cannot be interpreted by simply referring to a fixed and pre-established code, through mere decoding processes.

Sign models are also intimately related to our conceptions of the subject: in the perspective of the semiotics of decodification or of equal exchange, the subject is rooted in the concept of identity with a very low margin of otherness or dialogism. According to this approach, the subject coincides perfectly with its own consciousness in that it fully manages its own sign processes, subjecting what it communicates to its own will as a sender and coder.

On the contrary, in those trends in semiotics which refer to the Peircean model of sign and which generally come together in what has been called the 'semiotics of interpretation' (as distinct from the 'semiotics of decodification'), the production of sense and meaning is described in terms of an ongoing, open effort without the guarantees offered by appeal to a code with the function of regulating exchange relations between signifiers and signifieds (cf. *SPL*, Limits; Peirce, CP 5.284; Ponzio 1988, 1989, 1990). In a paper of 1984 (now in Ponzio 1990) entitled 'Semiotics between Peirce and Bakhtin'. Ponzio makes use of categories developed by these two thinkers to demonstrate how the sign model proposed by decodification semiotics, by the semiotics of equal exchange, is oversimplified and naive, maintaining as it does that

> the sign: (1) is at the service of a meaning pre-established outside the communication and interpretation process, (2) is a flexible and passive instrument in the hands of a subject who is also given, pre-established, and capable of controlling and dominating the sign, and furthermore, (3) is decodifiable on the basis of a pre-existent code common to both partners in the communicative process (Ponzio 1990 [1984]: 252)

The sign model proposed by interpretation semiotics is constructed on the basis of such categories as Peirce's tripartite division of interpretants into 'immediate interpretant', 'dynamic interpretant', and 'final interpretant', his subdivision of the object into 'immediate object' and 'dynamic object', and his main triadic division of signs into 'symbol', 'index', and 'icon', etc. Peirce places the sign in the dynamic context of semiosis, developing the concept of 'unlimited semiosis', and of its relationship with the interpretant, which emerges as a dialectic and dialogic relationship (cf. Peirce's Collected Papers, vol. 2). Considering such aspects then, Ponzio's association of Peirce and Bakhtin appears highly relevant, for Bakhtin too places the sign in the context of dialogism in which alone it may flourish as such, using in his study of signs such categories as 'text', 'otherness', 'responsive understanding', and 'intertextuality' (cf. Bakhtin 1970-71; Barthes 1981; Todorov 1981). Though working independently and in different directions (Peirce being primarily concerned with questions of a cognitive order, Bakhtin with literary language), both scholars recognize the fundamental importance of dialogism.

3. DIALOGISM AND INTERPRETATION IN THE STUDY OF SIGNS

What ensues is a sign model that is dialectic or 'dia-logic' (intended as dialectic founded on dialogue) according to which the sign and semiosis coincide. Considered dialectically, the sign no longer appears as an autonomous unit endowed with a well-defined meaning, with a value of its own as determined in the relationship of mechanical opposition with the other units forming the sign system:

> Once signs are no longer reduced to a single element, or broken down into their component parts, it is difficult to say where they begin and where they end. Signs are not things, but processes, the interlacing of relations which are social relations. . . .. (Ponzio 1990 [1984]: 260)

Bakhtin's notion of the text is no doubt broader than his notion of the sign taken as an isolated unit; nonetheless, like the sign, the text can only flourish and be understood in the light of a still broader context: the intertextual context of dialectic/dialogic relationships between texts. The sense of a text develops through its interaction with other texts along the boundaries of another text. As Bakhtin says: 'The dialogic relationships among texts and within the text. The special (not linguistic) nature. Dialogue and dialectics' (Bakhtin 1959-61 in 1986:105).

This approach gives full play to the centrifugal forces of linguistic-cultural life, theorizing otherness, polysemy, and dialogism as constitutive factors of the sign's very identity. The categories developed by decodification semiotics have often proven to be oversimplifying, especially in their application to discourse analysis, writing, and ideology. On the other hand, interpretation semiotics, with its theories of sense, significance, and interpretability ('interpretanza', as Eco says–cf. 1984:43), with its broad, flexible and critical conception of the sign, is able to account for signification as much as for communication, thus furnishing us with a far more exhaustive description of human communicative interaction. The sign model developed by interpretation semiotics is a dynamic model no longer founded on the notion of equivalence between one sign and another, between the signifiant and the signifié, on the logic of equal exchange and of equivalence between the language system on one side and the utterance on the other (langue/parole). It is based, instead, on the idea of deferral forming the open chain of signs, on the idea of renvoi from the interpreted sign to the interpretant sign. These two factors of semiosis (the interpreted sign and the interpretant sign), which can only effectively emerge in semiosic processes, are theorized as being connected by a relation of non-correspondence determined by the logic of excess, of otherness. According to this logic the interpretant sign never corresponds exactly to the previous sign, the interpreted sign, but says something more (cf. SPL 1984; Peirce, CP 2.228), developing and enriching it with new meanings. The interpreter/interpretant responds to something, and in so doing becomes a sign which in turn gives rise to another interpretive response, etc. In such a perspective, the function of the interpretant sign is not limited to the mere identification of the previous sign, but rather is taken to various levels of 'responsive understanding' (cf. for example Bakhtin 1959-61), which implies the existence of a concrete dialogic relationship among signs regulated by the principle of reciprocal otherness. As Bakhtin says (1986:127): 'Being heard as such is already a dialogic relation. The word wants to be heard, understood, responded to, and again to respond to the response, and so forth ad infinitum'. Semiosis ensues from this live relation and certainly not from any abstract relationships among the signs forming a sign system. Bakhtin's concept of 'responsive understanding' is analogous to Peirce's 'dynamic interpretant'. And like Peirce, Bakhtin believes that the human being is a sign (cf. also Sebeok 1986) in the sense that, as explicitly emerges in Bakhtin-Voloshinov (1927; Engl. trans. 1976), both the conscious and the unconscious are made of sign material–that is, of dialogically structured verbal material.

In the situation of impasse characterizing decodification semiotics, Peirce's approach represents a means of escape. His *Collected Papers*, which include studies on signs going back to the second half of the nineteenth century, only began appearing in 1931 and have the merit, among other things, of recovering the forgotten connection with the detailed sign studies of the Middle Ages (in the *Collected Papers*, for example, Peirce makes frequent reference to Peter of Spain's *Tractatus*). In his famous paper of 1867, 'On a new list of categories', Peirce describes the concepts he believed most suitable for a satisfactory analysis of the polyhedric nature of sign life. However, an even more articulate version of this description is generally considered to be his letter of October 12th, 1904 to his correspondent Victoria Lady Welby, in which, with reference to the relationship between signs and knowledge, he expresses himself as follows:

> a sign is something by knowing which we know something more. With the exception of knowledge, in the present instant, of the contents of consciousness in that instant (the existence of which knowledge is open to doubt) all our thought & knowledge is by signs. A sign therefore is an object which is in relation to its object on the one hand and to an interpretant on the other in such a way as to bring the interpretant into a relation to the object corresponding to its own relation to the object. I might say 'similar to its own' for a correspondence consists in a similarity; but perhaps correspondence is narrower. (Peirce, in Hardwick 1977:31-32)

According to Peirce, a *sign* stands to someone for something in some respect or capacity. The sign stands to someone in the sense that it creates 'an equivalent sign, or perhaps a more developed sign', in the *interpreter*; that is, it creates an *interpretant* sign (CP 2.228). Moreover, the sign stands for something in some respect or capacity in the sense that it does not refer to the *object* in its entirety (*dynamic object*), but only to some part of it (*immediate object*). A sign, therefore, subsists for Peirce according to the category of *Thirdness*; it presupposes a triadic relation between itself, its object, and the interpretant thought, itself a sign. A sign always plays the role of *third party* precisely because it mediates between the interpretant sign and its object.

Peirce's semiotics focuses on the concept of interpretation, identifying meaning (which Saussurean semiology leaves unexplained) in the interpretant–that is to say, in another sign which takes the place of the preceding sign. Insofar as it is a sign, the interpretant only subsists by virtue of another interpretant in an open-ended chain of *renvoi* rooted in the potential creativity of interpretive processes. According to this perspective, semiosis is not guaranteed *a priori* thanks to the possibility of appealing to a code that is fixed previously with respect to semiosis, for the code itself does not subsist outside interpretive processes which indeed establish it and maintain it in force. 'Mediation', which is closely interrelated with interpretation and unlimited semiosis, is another fundamental concept in Peirce. The sign is in fact mediated by the interpretant, without which it cannot express its meaning, and in turn mediates the relationship with the object in any interpretive act whatsoever, from the simplest levels of perception to the most complex levels of knowledge. Meaning resides not in the sign, but in the relationship among signs. Peirce's semiotics is primarily a cognitive semiotics in which logic and semiotics are related on the basis of the assumption that knowledge is mediated by signs, indeed is impossible without them. Interpretation semiotics substitutes the dichotomy between the signifier and the signified for the triadic relationship between the object, the sign, and the interpretant and the type of sign produced (whether symbol, index, or icon) is determined by which of the relationships regulating the connection between the sign, object, and interpretant is dominant; but whichever prevails the role of the interpretant remains fundamental. Meanings evolve dynamically in open interpretive processes: the greater the degree of otherness in the relationship between the interpretant sign and the interpreted sign, and therefore of dialogism, the more interpretation takes place as active dialogic response, creative reformulation, inventiveness, rather than as mere repetition, literal translation, synonymic substitution, identification.

The description of signifying processes in terms of unending semiosis, of interpretive processes characterized by dialogic responsiveness, in terms of deferral or *renvoi* from an interpreted sign to an interpretant sign, has consequences for the theory of identity and of the subject. In fact, contrary to their description in the perspective of decodification semiotics, in interpretation semiotics the concepts of identity and the subject no longer emerge as coherent and unitary entities. In this perspective otherness is placed at the very heart of identity, is constitutive of identity as the latter develops in the dialectic and dialogic dynamic between the sign and its interpretant in the thought processes forming a single consciousness and in the relationship among different consciousnesses. Identity, the subject, consciousness develop in open semiosic processes, evolving through the dynamic of responsive understanding, dialogism, and otherness in the interchange between the thought-sign and the interpretant. For both Peirce and Bakhtin, then, the self is constructed dialogically in the translative/interpretive processes connecting thought-signs with interpretants in an open-ended chain of deferrals: in such a framework the self is always other, is never definitively present to itself, and in this context alone can effectively subsist as self. Therefore, the self-other relationship subsists not only in the more obvious case of the relationship between different consciousnesses, but also between the multiple 'selves' forming a single, 'individual' consciousness:

> The subject does not contain interpretative processes, he is not pre-existent to them nor does he control them from the outside: he is the chain of sign-interpretant relations in which he recognizes himself, to the point that experience of the self of another person is not a more complicated problem than that relative to the recognition of certain sign-interpretant relations as 'mine', those through which 'I' become aware of myself. Consequently, says Peirce, just as we say that a body is in movement and not that the movement is in a body, we should say that we are in thought and not that thoughts are inside us. (Ponzio 1990 [1984]:268)

A sign subsists and develops in the dialectic among *symbolicity*, *indexicality*, and *iconicity*, which accounts for the different degrees of dialogism in the relationship between signs and interpretants, and between the premises and the conclusion of an argument. A sign is never a pure symbol, but also contains traces of indexicality and iconicity; in the same way, as much as a sign is prevalently indexical or iconic, it will always maintain a certain margin of symbolicity. In other words, as with symbols in the case of indices and icons as well mediation by an interpretant and recourse to a convention are necessary. It follows that all signs simultaneously share in the character of symbolicity, indexicality, and iconicity in varying degrees: for example, verbal signs, though fundamentally conventional, also contain a certain degree of iconicity.

Symbolicity is an expression of the conventional character of the sign—that is, of the relation of *constriction by convention* between a sign and its object as established on the basis of a code, of a law. The symbol is not related to its object if not through the interpretant, without which it could not subsist as a symbol. However, even if the symbol is founded on a code, a convention, a law, the latter in turn is also founded on an open process of unending deferral and *renvoi* from one sign to the next: consequently, even in the case of symbols, the sign's relationship with the object is never completely univocal. Symbolicity is present in all signs in varying degrees, and not just in the symbol (which of course it characterizes). In the above-mentioned letter to Welby, Peirce gives the following definition:

> I define a Symbol as a sign which is determined by its dynamic object only in the sense that it will be so interpreted. It thus depends either upon a convention a habit, or a natural disposition of its interpretant, or of the field of its interpretant (that of which the interpretant is a determination). (Letter from Peirce to Welby of October 12, 1904; in Hardwick 1977: 33)

Furthermore, according to Peirce, in signs of the conventional type where the relationship with the object is established by an external law and necessarily depends on the interpretant, the category of Thirdness dominates. Thirdness is ultimately concerned with the sign in its relation to the interpretant.

Indexicality refers to the compulsory nature of signs, to the relationship of cause and effect, of *necessary contiguity*, of spatio-temporal contiguity between a sign and its object. As Peirce puts it: 'I define an Index as a sign determined by its dynamic object by virtue of being in a real relation to it' (in Hardwick 1977: 33). In the case of indices, unlike symbols, it is not the interpretant that decides the object. Rather, the relationship between the sign and the object preexists with respect to interpretation as an objective relationship, and in fact conditions interpretation. The sign and what it is a sign of are given together, independent of the interpretant. This does not exclude the inevitability of resorting to a convention, however, for the relationship between a sign and its object to become a sign relationship. The indexical character of signs prevails, for example, in traces, symptoms, and clues, in the relationship between fire and smoke, between the spots on the skin and a liver disease, between a knock at the door and the fact that someone is behind the door and wants to enter. Given that the relationship between the sign and the object is here of cause and effect, of necessary contiguity (natural contiguity, inferential contiguity, etc.), and as such subsists independently of the interpretant, indexical signs are characterized by the category of Secondness.

The icon is characterized by a relation of *similarity* between the sign and its object which takes on different forms as in the case of images, metaphors, and graphs: "I define an Icon," says Peirce, "as a sign which is determined by its dynamic object by virtue of its own internal nature" (in Hardwick 1977: 33). The dominating factor in iconic signs is no longer a system of conventions, natural causality, or any other form of contiguity, but rather individual intentionality. The iconic sign signifies without depending on a code, a convention, on conferral of sense by an interpretant. The iconic sign is self-signifying, has meaning in itself, imposes itself on its own account: its virtue of signifying is simply due to its quality. Here the sign achieves a maximum degree of independence with respect to its object, while the interpretant may occur in a distant system, and in extreme cases even be invented *ex novo*–neither through a relation of necessary contiguity (index), nor of conventionality (symbol), but of hypothetical similarity. Though containing traces of symbolicity and indexicality, the iconic relation is distinguished by the character of affinity, attraction, innovation, creativity, dialogism, and otherness. Given its relative signifying independence with respect to the object and the interpretant, the icon expresses the reality of Firstness.

Iconicity and dialogism are intimately connected (Bonfantini and Ponzio 1986; Ponzio 1993); indeed, the highest degrees of dialogism are reached in iconic signs. Not being the expression of a convention, the mechanical effect of a cause, etc., iconicity is connected with the concepts of responsive understanding, active participation, dialogic evaluation, point of view, semiotic materiality, resistance on the level of signification, irreducibility to a situation of identity, and otherness (cf. Petrilli 1990c). Indeed, on considering icons and dialogism together, a useful expedient is to imagine them as rejoinders in a dialogue–that is, in terms of a creative response to the verbal or nonverbal standpoint of another interlocutor, whether a provocation, prayer, threat, question, etc.

Necessity characterizes signs of both conventional and indexical types, with the difference that in the first case the relation of necessity ensues from accepting a convention, while in the second it is passively endured as the result of an external effect. Consequently, in both symbols and indices dialogism is relatively reduced. However, we also know that signs generally depend on their relationship with interpretants, but while such dependency is a determining factor in symbols owing to the dominance of conventionality, it carries less weight in indices and icons, which, among other things, Peirce classifies as *degenerate* signs (a term taken from the language of mathematics) in contrast to symbols–that is, to relatively *genuine* signs.

A fundamental characteristic of interpretation semiotics in contrast to decodification semiotics is the light it sheds upon inferential processes. Inferences are developed in the passage from a sign to its interpretant, which, as mentioned above, are related *dialogically*. Inferences (or as Peirce also calls them, arguments) may be divided into three types: deduction, induction, and abduction–each being characterized by the predominance of either indexicality, symbolicity, or iconicity. In deduction the relationship between the sign and the interpretant is dominated by indexicality, in induction by symbolicity, in abduction by iconicity.

Considering sign processes as open chains formed by the unending deferral of interpretants leads, sooner or later, to a need to consider the terms and sense of this opening; or, as Eco says in the title of one of his most recent books (1990), it leads to a need to examine the question of "the limits of interpretation." In his book, Eco singles out two conceptions of interpretation: on the one hand, to interpret means to highlight the objective nature of a text, its essence independent of interpretation, on the other, the text is described as being subject to infinite interpretation. Eco criticizes the latter, which he classifies as 'hermetic semiosis', maintaining that (contrary to appearances and to the opinion of certain scholars) the Peircean theory of unlimited semiosis is something altogether different, the main object of his criticism being Jacques Derrida's notion of 'infinite deferral' as taken up by 'deconstructionism'. Eco argues that Derrida's and, above all, the deconstructionists' idea of 'infinite drift' differs from Peirce's own concept of infinite semiosis, and does so on the basis of Peirce's notion of *habit*. The latter is connected to the intersubjective character of interpretation, for it is always fixed by community convention:

> from the moment in which the community is pulled to agree with a given interpretation, there is, if not an objective, at least an *intersubjective* meaning which acquires a privilege over any other possible interpretation spelled out without the agreement of the community. (*Limits*: 40)

Eco's specifications concerning the Peircean notion of 'unlimited semiosis' would seem to point to the dialogic character of interpretation. The relationship between interpretants is dialogic (in other words, the logic of interpretants is a dia-logic–cf. Bonfantini and Ponzio 1986) in the sense that an interpretant sign cannot impose itself arbitrarily, authoritatively, or unconditionally upon the interpreted sign: understood in terms of a dialogic chain, the Peircean chain of interpretants escapes the risk of being considered as the equivalent to a free reading in which the will of the interpretants (and with them of the interpreters) beats the interpreteds 'into a shape which will serve their own purposes' (cf. *Limits*: 42).

This makes the connection established by Ponzio between Peirce and Bakhtin even more interesting, for indeed the latter also places particular emphasis on the dialogic aspect of signs. Ponzio demonstrates how the three different types of argumentation (induction, deduction, and abduction), considered by Peirce in terms of the relationship among interpretants, are obtained thanks to a differentiation in the degree of dialogism between the premises and conclusion, or between the interpreted sign and the interpretant sign. From this point of view, on proceeding from the highest to the lowest degree of dialogism and otherness, abduction classifies first, followed in order by induction and deduction (see also Ponzio 1993).

In deduction, as in indexical signs, the relationship between the premises and the conclusion is regulated by necessity, more precisely by *necessary contiguity*: the facts asserted in the premises oblige us to accept the interpretant-conclusion. Such a relation of constriction is necessarily characterized by an extremely low level of dialogism and otherness. In induction the conclusion is not imposed unconditionally by the premises: on the contrary, what we have is an *inclination* to accept the conclusion once the premises have been accepted, the conclusion neither depending on nor deriving directly from the premises. The relationship between the premises and the conclusion is of a symbolic order, so that inference is largely determined by interpretation and by convention. In other words, given the margin of *free consensus*, the relationship between the premises and the conclusion is conventional and corresponds to symbolicity. Induction allows for a quantitative increase in cognition. Ponzio (1990 [1984]: 267) comments as follows:

> In this case, we do not have the predetermination of a given dialogic part in an argument in virtue of another part as occurs in deduction, here there is a certain relation of autonomy between the parts in question: however the distancing between the premises and the conclusion is only of a quantitative type: similarly to deduction, the inductive process is unilinear, it develops according to a precise order of succession extending from the point of departure to the point of arrival without discontinuities or retroaction.

By contrast, in abduction or retroduction, as Peirce also calls it, inference proceeds backwards from the consequent to the precedent. The law in abduction is searched for *a posteriori* with respect to observation and interpretation, on which it depends. Such dependence renders the law confutable and implies that, given a certain context, one law may be referred to instead of another. In some cases the law is founded on the existing cognitive encyclopedia; in others it must be completely invented. This implies the possibility of passing from the highest levels of novelty and abductive creation to the lowest. In abduction the relationship between the premises and the conclusion is determined neither by the obligation of contiguity nor by the arbitrariness of conventionality. The premises *suggest* the conclusion, and simply through a relation of *relative similarity*: we start from a result which evokes a given law on the basis of which it is possible to explain the case in question. In this kind of inference the relationship between the premises and the conclusion is only probable: it is dominated by conjecture, by the inclination to guessing, and is variously risky. The interpretant-conclusion is relatively autonomous with regard to the premises: the higher the level of creative abductivity, the higher the degree of dialogism and otherness, and whatever the degree of innovation, novelty, and creativity, the terms of the argument in abduction are always connected dialogically and are characterized by high levels of otherness. Furthermore, given the role played by similarity, abduction is predominantly associated with iconicity. By contrast with trends in communication analysis, where the task of the linguistic worker is viewed simplistically as consisting in the effort of decodification and recognition, where signs are largely reduced to the status of signals, in the perspective of interpretation semiotics theorization about the interconnection between semiotics and logic is inevitable.

Peirce's two main typologies–his typology of signs, with its main division into symbols, indices, and icons; and his typology of the forms of inference, with its division into deduction, induction, and abduction–are not simply lists or classifications whose contents are reciprocally separate from and indifferent to each other. On the contrary, the different types of signs and inferences or arguments are in fact interconnected in varying degrees relative to their dialogic import; and we have seen that such dialogic consistency concerns the relationship between the sign and its interpretant. As pointed out by Ponzio, Peirce theorizes a relationship between these two terms similar to that between the rejoinders in a dialogue. The connection between Peirce's semiotics and his logic (that is, between his typology of signs and his typology of inferences or arguments) is also, therefore, the connection between semiotics and dia-logic.

Considering together Peirce's semiotics and Bakhtin's philosophy of language not only enables us to place the sign in the dynamic context of inference, interpretation, and the dialogic processes of semiosis, but also helps to evidence still other aspects of the relationship between signs in different signifying practices. For example, in an essay entitled 'Signs to talk about signs' (1985b). Ponzio himself, through reference to these two authors, considers the problem of meaning in both verbal and nonverbal signs in terms of an *interpretive route*. Motivated by the ambitious aim of setting up verbal instruments useful for talking about signs, with this essay Ponzio recalls Morris's own project as proposed in *Foundations of the Theory of Signs* (1938). In his effort at theoretical and terminological systematization, Ponzio's description of both verbal and nonverbal meaning in terms of an 'interpretive route' is noteworthy: to understand meaning as an 'interpretive route' means to place it in the context of dialogic relationships which, while responding to both the Peircean and Bakhtinian conceptions of the sign, represents an original aspect of his research. Meaning is described as a possible interpretive route in a dense sign network, a route interweaving with other routes, with other meanings branching out from the same sign. On taking off from the sign intersection, one may choose and shift among a multiplicity of alternative itineraries. Meaning emerges as a signifying itinerary in a sign network, as an interpretive route simultaneously well defined and yet subject to continual amplification and variation by virtue of continual dialogic contacts with alternate interpretive routes. This explains the indeterminacy, openness, and semantic availability of the sign, which thereby finds its place in the context of dialogic relationships. These emerge: (1) in the relationship between the sign and its interpretant, which in argumentation is (2) the relationship between the premises and the conclusion, characterized by a minor or major degree of dialogism in deduction, induction, and abduction (Peirce); (3) in the relationship among the multiple interpretants, verbal and nonverbal, forming the open trajectory of the interpretive route; and (4) in the relationship among the interpretants of different interpretive routes (cf. Ponzio 1985b, 1990). Such a description makes a valid contribution to the understanding of the distinguishing features of human communication (see also Petrilli 1990a, 1990e), which include, as mentioned at the beginning of this paper, such aspects as ambiguity, polysemy, plurivocality, heteroglossia, dialogism, and the 'semiotic materiality' of signs–that is, the otherness, resistance, and semiotic autonomy of signs and their meanings with respect to other signs as well as to the subject who produces, uses, and interprets them.

Susan Petrilli

Openness, Eco, and the End
of Another Millennium

ANALOGY: ANOMALY

The origin and nature of language as an object of human curiosity is entering its third millenium of study in the Western world. Discussion of this premier semiotic system, language, has ever been suspended in a tension between historiographically so-called Analogists and Anomalists (cf. Colson 1919), be they from among, e.g., the Greek Ancients or from among, e.g., the contemporary Cognitivists. Whether to understand the nature of language as natural or conventional, rule driven or usage bound, regular or irregular and the myriad proximate and distal implications deriving from these Western metaphysical bifurcations remains thus an unabated subliminal, if not overt obsession of language research, and *ceteris paribus,* semiotic research. Indeed, the perennial identity question of semiotics arises deep within the analogist way of thinking, which, e.g., Eco (1978) addresses in the title question "Semiotics: A Discipline or an Interdisciplinary Method?" On the side of Analogy, so to speak, Eco proposes five criteria for legitimizing semiotics as a science/discipline (p. 76): ". . . a precise subject. . ., a set of unified methodological tools. . ., the capability of producing hypotheses. . ., the possibility of making predictions. . ., the possibility of modifying the actual state of the objective world." On the side of Anomaly, Eco renders judgments concerning these five requirements of a science/discipline, such as (pp. 81-82):

> Every discipline at a certain stage of its metatheoretical development should be concerned with semiotic phenomena, and if one does not want to consider semiotics as a discipline *per se,* one should at least consider it as a methodological approach serving many disciplines. . ..I can see your disappointment and frustration: lured by the promise of the revelation whether semiotics is indeed a science or an interdisciplinary method, we find that it is in fact *three* sciences. . ..i.e., the ones propagated by Peirce, Morris, and Hjelmslev. . ..At present there are many semiotic methods, each of which is focussing on the same object and yet is organizing the same set of categories differently.

However, the ultimate Anomalist view as to the nature of semiotics is likely verbalized by Eco even more strikingly when he writes (1975:17): ". . . we may say that there does not yet exist a single unified semiotic theory, and that we hope there never will. . .." to be sure, this expressed hope is doubly spectacular by its faint echoing of one of semiotics' most illustrious historical Anomalists, viz. Locke, who (Rand 1927:156) wrote "Natural philosophy, as a speculative science, I think we have none, and perhaps I may think I have a reason to say we never shall. . .." Needless to say, the drive toward legitimization of a field of study as a science was especially vigorous in our immediately preceding nineteenth century, in which the natural sciences did indeed evince a previously unparalleled rigor that penetrated a great many fields directly and indirectly.Thus, e.g., Saussurean *langue,* which encapsulates scientifically focused structuralism (cf. Rauch 1984) imbued linguistics with its paradigm, but also semiotics, as well as seemingly antistructuralist paradigms such as deconstruction, germane to recent literary approaches, and prototype theory, cultivated in latter-day linguistic method. However, remember that the notion *parole* was never far behind.

A short hundred years later, as the twentieth century wanes, a somewhat counter-development has emerged which is a trend toward a willingness to openness, to also look at other approaches. Broadly speaking we may say it bespeaks Anomalists. Richard Tarnas (1990) judges the pulse of the times well by his query: "And why is there evident now such a widespread collective impetus in the Western mind to articulate a holistic and participatory world view, visible in virtually every field?" That the nature of scientific inquiry as such has changed and is changing is voiced also by F. E. Yates, who chooses semiotics, that apparently all-encompassing, loosely fitting paradigm, as central to both natural and humane sciences. He writes (1986:359):

> Science has been softened up by deep problems raised concerning quantum reality . . . and seems to be open to new discussions of the nature of inquiry, models, theories, intentionality, explanation and meaning. Those hoary issues that in the past had to be set aside to clear the way for scientific advance, now come back to haunt us once again. They are not technical issues susceptible of durable resolution in the same sense that quantum mechanics itself has been to any other idea ever conceived by man. But as we build information processing machines that rival or surpass many of our own cognitive faculties, the persistent tension between linguistic [information] and dynamic views of complex systems . . . generates extraordinary opportunity for semiotics to meld the sciences.

That semiotics has a natural bent toward openness, tolerance, affability is hardly disputable (cf. further Rauch 1991, 1996). In the following we observe trends that might be construed as characterizing openness in literary deconstruction and in linguistic prototype theories; we demonstrate their interdigitation and their compatibility with the semiotic paradigm via a fresh set of empirical linguistic data. Finally we observe what can be considered Eco's subversion of the Anaolgy: Anomaly controversy.

OPENNESS: LITERATURE

Jacques Derrida, indisputably a premier theorist of deconstruction, builds his paradigm on the deconstruction of Saussure himself by uncovering the flaw in Saussure's paradigm, i.e., that feature which subverts Saussurean thought, namely, the fact that Saussure does not develop his concept of difference far enough. Thus, for Saussure the linguistic sign derives its existence and accordingly its meaning from differences, i.e., relationships within a system, and Saussure holds that the meaning or signified is as inalienably united with the form of the signifier in the sign as are, to use Saussure's well-known metaphor, two sides of a piece of paper. This view leads to the linguistic principle of biuniqueness or isomorphism, whereby a linguistic entity may be unequivocally disambiguated and identified. Derrida challenges the possibility of an absolute, univocal meaning, as well as the distinction between signifier and signified, which reflects the traditional metaphysical division between matter and spirit or thought. He states:

> ... it was necessary to begin thinking that there was no center, that the center could not be thought in the form of a present being, that it was not a fixed locus but a function, a sort of non-locus in which an infinite number of sign substitutions come into play. This was the moment when language invaded the universal problematic, the moment when, in the absence of a center or origin, everything became discourse ... that is to say, a system in which the central signified, the original or transcendental signified, is never absolutely present outside a system of differences. The absence of the transcendental signified extends the domain and play of signification infinitely (1978:280).

There is no absolute meaning, no center, since in order for one to exist, either the signifier or the signified must be final (Derrida says "transcendental"), i.e., incapable of referring to or differing from another signifier or signified. Each signified becomes in turn a signifier, thus muting the distinction between the two entities and extending a signification into the infinite. The maintaining of an absolute signified is called by Derrida the "metaphysics of presence", whereas infinite signification is a metaphysics of past and future as well. Presence is merely absence of what it is not, i.e., difference. Thus, meaning is continually deferred, extending as he says, "the play of signification infinitely". This process frees the reader, Derrida maintains, from nostalgia for origin and a center and offers instead the joyful Nietzschean affirmation of free play and the innocence of becoming (Derrida 1978:278-93).

In the interrelatedness or system of differences, the signs, whether viewed as signifiers or signifieds, carry "traces" of one another. Derrida states:

> There has never been anything but writing, there have never been anything but supplements, substitutive significations which could only come forth in a chain of differential references, the "real" supervening, and being added only while taking on meaning from a trace and from an invocation of the supplement, etc. And thus to infinity, for we have read, *in the text,* that the absolute present, nature, that which words like "real mother" name, have always already escaped, have never existed; that what opens meaning and language is writing as the disappearance of natural presence (1976:159).

Beyond speaking to trace and supplement (proliferation of signifiers from an ever-deferred signified), this passage once again encapsulates fundamental concepts of Derrida and it brings to the fore his quasi- dissolution of Saussure's distinction between speech and writing, which, as with form and meaning, is derived from Western metaphysics. Plato assigned priority to speech; Derrida, however, holds this priority to be bonded with the metaphysics of presence. For him, writing exemplifies well the concept of deferral or endless commutation, the displacement of one signifier by another in an endless chain. Beyond this, writing is not fleeting; speech is fleeting and thereby tends to suppress, by its being present, the play of endless differences. Similarly, Roland Barthes speaks to the endless commutation of meaning in any text observing (1977:146) that "the text is not a line of words releasing a single 'theological' meaning (the message of an Author-God) but a multi-dimensional space in which a variety of writings, none of them original, blend and clash. The text is a tissue of quotations drawn from innumerable centers of culture." So too, Michel Foucault explains the intertextuality, i.e., the endless "differentially interrelated fabric" (Merrell 1984:126) in which the text moves, as follows:

The frontiers of a book are never clear-cut; beyond the title, the first lines, and the last full stops, beyond its internal configuration and its autonomous form, it is caught up in a system of references to other books, other texts, other sentences; it is a node within a network. . ... The book is not simply the object that one holds in one's hands; and it cannot remain within the little parallelepiped that contains it: its unity is variable and relative. As soon as one questions that unity, it loses its self-evidence; it indicates itself, constructs itself, only on the basis of a complex field of discourse (1972:23).

OPENNESS: LINGUISTICS

Prototype theory, presently widely applied in cognitive studies of various disciplines, owes part of its recent refinements to current linguistic methods of categorization which deal a severe blow in particular to classical distinctive feature theory. In the tradition of Western metaphysics, an entity is characterized according to Aristotelian necessary and sufficient features which are binary in nature, i.e., either absent or present, and which allow absolute and clear-cut disambiguation from another entity. In the strongly language user-oriented paradigm which prototype theory reflects, atomistic objective, and often, abstract features are taken as unrealistic perceptions attributed to the putative user. The flesh and blood language user and not the language theorist assigns an entity to a category. The entity may not at all be perceived by the user as a distinct item; it may be categorized subjectively, i.e., relative to the user's experience, and it might be quite concretely, i.e., physically experienced. To quote Ronald Langacker:

> Experimental work in cognitive psychology. . .has demonstrated that categories are often organized around prototypical instances. These are the instances which people accept as common, run-of-the-mill, garden-variety members of the category. They generally occur the most frequently in our experience, tend to be learned the earliest, and can be identified experimentally in a variety of ways. . ..Nonprototypical instances are assimilated to a class or category to the extent that they can be construed as matching or approximating the prototype. Membership is therefore a matter of degree: prototypical instances are full, central members of the category, whereas other instances form a gradation from central to peripheral depending on how far and in what ways they deviate from the prototype. Moreover the members are not necessarily a uniquely defined set, since there is no specific degree of departure from the prototype beyond which a person is absolutely incapable of perceiving a similarity (1987:16-17).

Prototype may be perceived as an entity, i.e., a particularly good example of a category, or as an abstract schema or network which represents shared features of entities or members of the category. Goodness is determined empirically by the perceiver who infers entities as gestalts and judges some entities as more representative of a category than others. The inferences of the perceiver derive from quasi-encyclopedic, i.e., all his/her experiential knowledge within his/her culture rather than from isolated abstractions, so that entities are categorized by Wittgensteinian "family resemblance", described by Eleanor Rosch and Carolyn Mervis (1975:575) as a "relationship [which] consists of a set of items of the form A B, B C, C D, D E. That is, each item has at least one, and probably several, elements in common with one or more other items, but no, or few elements are common to all items." On the one hand, family resemblance could suggest infinite relationship; on the other hand, infinite resemblance is curtailed by the necessary distinctions between category membership status and degree of representativeness within a category. To be sure, John Taylor writes (1989:50): "Categorization makes it possible for an organism to reduce limitless variation in the world to manageable proportions."

The fact that language users speak with considerable frequency in figurative rather than in literal terms leads to category extension particularly through metaphor and metonymy. More basically, and as input to both metaphor and metonymy, however, the language user conceptualizes his/her experience through image schemes, George Lakoff's (*Woman, Fire and Dangerous Things* 1987:283) "Spatialization of Form Hypothesis . . . [which itself] requires a metaphorical mapping from physical space into a 'conceptual space'". Lakoff explains:

> Recall for a moment some of the kinds of image-schemes. . .: schemes for CONTAINER, SOURCE-PATH-GOAL, LINK, PART-WHOLE, CENTER-PERIPHERY, UP-DOWN, FRONT-BACK. These schemes structure our experience in space. What I will be claiming is that the same schemes structure concepts themselves. In fact, I maintain that image schemes define most of what we commonly term "structure" when we talk about abstract domains. When we understand something as having an abstract structure, we understand that structure in terms of image schemes (pp. 282-83).

MUTUAL OPENNESS

Let us extract, by recalling particularly salient insights from the citations given above, some surprisingly clear analogies, indeed similarities, to which deconstruction, prototype theory and semiotics are mutually open. The destruction of a monolithic signification which permeates the given citations is voiced e.g., in Derrida's "extends the domain and play of signification infinitely" (sect. 2 above) beside e.g., Langacker's "there is no specific degree from the prototype beyond which a person is absolutely incapable of perceiving a similarity" (sect. 3 above) beside Peirce's (1932:§302) simple aphoristic encapsulation "symbols grow". That signification is grounded in experience is reflected e.g., in Derrida's "not a fixed locus but a function. . . the absence of a transcendental signified" (sect. 2 above), beside Langacker's "prototypical instances . . . occur the most frequently in our experience" (sect. 3 above) and Lakoff's (1987:154) negative reply to the question "Are concepts and reason 'transcendental', that is, independent of the nature and bodies of the reasoning beings?" beside Uexkull's autoambience theory which holds that (Uexkull 1940:61, translation mine): "The body likened to a house is, on the one hand, the creator of meaningful signs, which inhabit its garden, and, on the other hand, it is the creation of these signs, which intervene as motifs in the construction of the house." Notice the interplay with prototype theory, which also espouses various kinds of both biological and linguistic relativity (cf. now Lakoff 1987:335 "I am convinced by Whorf's arguments that the way we use concepts affects the way we understand experience"). The concretization of features within endless signification is a common motif, thus e.g., Barthes' "the text is not a line of words releasing a single 'theological' meaning (the message of an Author-God) but a multi-dimensional space" and Foucault's "it is a mode within a network" (cf. sect. 2 above), beside Lakoff's "image-schemes" (cf. sect. 3 above) and Langacker's (1987) "trajector/landmark" schema, beside René Thom's (1975) "archetypal morphologies" or "elementary catastrophes".

Needless to say, these few commonalities alone whet the appetite. In closing, let us briefly test the mutual interaction of the three paradigms on a fresh, albeit small, sample set of linguistic data taken from the very physical linguistic component, phonology. The evidence is part of Phase Four of the San Francisco Bay Area German Linguistic Fieldwork Project (Rauch et al. Forthcoming). In eliciting the pronunciation of the German word *leid* "painful" from five children of German descent living in the San Francisco Bay area, each fieldworker transcribed phonetically the word as s(he) heard it on the tape of the recorded informant. The informant spoke each word twice by reading it from a card; accordingly, the phonetic transcription should yield two entities, each of word length. However, the fieldworkers, averaging seven to eight per transcription session, did not perceive the taped evidence uniformly. All perceptions recorded by two or more fieldworkers were considered viable. Two different methods led to the extraction of the phonetic bits. Method A yielded five phonetic transcriptions for the five informants by opting for the simple majority perception of the fieldworkers, thus: [la'd , l > a'd, li t, lisymbol 43 \f "WP Phonetic" \s 10 t, li symbol 44 \f "WP Phonetic" \s 10?] in the case of the informants' first reading. Method B applied to the recorded data yielded six transcriptions perceived by at least two or more fieldworkers: [la'dsymbol 47 \f "WP Phonetic" \s 10 (14%), la't (6%), li symbol 44 \f "WP Phonetic" \s 10?(22%), lisymbol 43 \f "WP Phonetic" \s 10 t (14%), li t (25%), l > a'd(14%)]. Six instead of five transcriptions for five informants demonstrates beautifully how perception may influence reality. The prototype schema on the data differ accordingly, although both may well differ from a possible third set, if the taped data were subjected to sound spectrography. The question is, what are the phonetic realia? Might an informant have in fact actually pronounced [la't] or still other phonetic configurations? We are inclined to rely on machines rather than on the human ear, yet the newer wave, as argued above, also recognizes human perception as a factor in science. Compare Kelly and Local (1989:8) who "do" phonology by ear: "Instrumental findings, though crucial to our understanding, in quantitive terms, of phonetic exponency, do not in themselves contribute to the elaboration of phonological entities."

The deconstructionist enterprise not only comes to the fore in the variable interpretation of the leid data by the fieldworkers, but also by three speakers' displacement of a hypothesized prototypical pronunciation of the vocalic nucleus of the word. The two [i symbol 44 \f "WP Phonetic" \s 10] and one [i symbol 43 \f "WP Phonetic" \s 10] pronunciations are certainly not central to the prescribed standard [a'] actually spoken by at least one of the first generation speakers in the word leid. The deconstruction takes place by the graphic confusion of <ei> with <ie> (possibly through interference from English) as found in the German word Lied 'song'. Needless to say, the Peircean categories underlie all of the above observations; thus, e.g., while a prototype as an instantiation of goodness fit is Secondness, the <ei> <de> analogy is by way of abduction, Firstness, and the majority perception of the fieldworkers results in Thirdness or convention.

ECO'S SUBVERSION

Questions of openness have long informed Eco's writings. Literary scholars in particular will be familiar with Eco's insights into the nature of his so-designated "open" and Uclosed" texts relative to the "Role of the Reader," in which he concedes (Role 40) that: Everything can become open as well as closed in the universe of unlimited semiosis." The fine-tuning, clarification, of Eco's views on the openness of a text, the "Limits of Interpretation," is encapsulated in a statement (somewhat reminiscent of ordered chance theories in the natural sciences):

> A text is a place where the irreducible polysemy of symbols is in fact reduced because in a text symbols are anchored to their context. The medieval interpreters were right: one should look for the rules which allow a con textual disambiguation of the exaggerated fecundity of symbols. Modern sensitivity deals on the contrary with myths as if they were macro symbols and–while acknowledging the infinite polysemy of symbols–no longer recognizes the discipline that myths impose on symbols they involve. Thus many modern theories are unable to recognize that symbols are paradigmatically open to infinite meanings but syntagmatically, that is, textually, open only to the indefinite, but by no means infinite, interpretations allowed by context (Limits 21).

It is, accordingly, not totally surprising that in the area of linguistic studies and openness Eco confronts the challenge of one of linguistic historiography's most notorious Analogist controversies, viz., the "Search for the Perfect Language." One immediately associates perfection with uniqueness and exclusivity, in short, with a type of closedness which comes perhaps only with death in the experiential world. So basic is language to human needs that the striving for a perfect language is as natural as the desire to be "queen/king of the hill," so to speak. The search for the perfect language arises out of the human condition, since language is associated as a quasi-psychosomatic feature of the body, similar to essential food, water, and air.

Eco brings the perfect language discussion, strongly cultivated in the JewishChristian tradition, into prominence at the end of yet another millennium to pursue this very search. Two and one-half millennia ago the Greeks were convinced that their language represented the truth, and thus the perfect language, and that all other languages were quasi-Greek or Greek in nature. Adamic language dominated discussion, in particular of language origin; it was the perfect creation in the Garden of Eden and only subsequently became obscure, muddled,* as witnessed in the confusion of tongues at the Tower of Babel.

To be sure, one of the more interesting questions in this two and one-half century quest is what constitutes "perfection" and does "perfection" require exclusivity. Exclusivity simply does not bespeak the human condition. So it is that Eco considers the genetic/immunological code as some sort of "language which could be defined as the primitive one par excellence . . .[and] would nest in the roots of evolution. . .before the dawn of humanity (Search 116). And so it is that the dominant leitmotiv of Eco in presenting what he terms "the story of a dream" (p. 5), "of a myth and of a wish" (p. 352) is exactly that. Eco is clearly sympathetic to the Renaissance mindset that would, so to speak, represent Babel at least as a felix culpa and at best as a felicitous occurrence, a celebration. Language is never singular; it is always plural. (In fact, Troubetzkoy had the insight to view the nature of Proto-lndoEuropean, to be sure the handiwork of many an Analogist Neogrammarian, as an adjective rather than a noun, writing (1939:81): ". . . die Vermutung einer indogermanischen Ursprache. . .ist aber auch gar nicht notwendig. . .") At the same time, Eco is, e.g., sympathetic to linguistic relativity as well, which rejects isomorphism or biuniqueness between and among languages, and, accordingly, speaks to the integrity of each language. We thus observe singularity in plurality, whereby Eco subverts the millennia-old Analogy: Anomaly controversy. Notice, this subversion is inherent in reading Eco, whether on linguistics or on literature. Consider finally Eco:

> Medieval interpreters were wrong in taking the world as a univocal text; modern interpreters are wrong in taking every text as an unshaped world. Texts are the human way to reduce the world to a manageable format, open to an

intersubjective interpretive discourse. Which means that, when symbols are inserted into a text, there is, perhaps, no way to decide which interpretation is the "good" one, but it is still possible to decide, on the basis of the context, which one is due, not to an effort of understanding "that" text, but rather to a hallucinatory response on the part of the addressee (*Limits* 2).

Irmengard Rauch

Eco, Peirce, and the Necessity of Interpretation

1. Semeiotics, Literary Theory, and *The Limits of Interpretation*.

At a time when the lines between literary theory, literary criticism, and literature have been deliberately blurred by so many critics and theorists–it is good to have a book on the problems of contemporary text theory from the learned littérateur and semeiotician Umberto Eco[1]. The essays that make up his book, he tells us, "study. . .the dialectics between the rights of texts and the rights of their interpreters;" they also seek to "stress the limits of the act of interpretation." He finds that, having "advocated an active role of the interpreter in the reading of texts. . .with aesthetic value, in *Opera Aperta*" (1962; *The Open Work* 1989), his readers "underestimat[ed] the fact that the open-ended reading [he] supported was an activity elicited by (and aimed at interpreting) *a work*." So he now also wants "reader-oriented theory" to realize that readers cannot escape submitting to *some* constraints: in general, to those that arise from or "coincide with the rights of the text" (*Limits* 6f.). So Eco labors to show that

> An open text is always a text, and a text can elicit infinite readings without allowing any possible reading. It is impossible to say what is the best interpretation of a text, but it is possible to say which ones are wrong. . ..Texts frequently say more than their authors intended to say, but less than what many incontinent [i.e. hermeticist or deconstructionist] readers would like them to say (*Limits* 148).

Eco rightly wants (as does this reviewer) more respect for "the text as a system ruled by an internal coherence" (*Limits* 151).[2]

This, it must be agreed is a worthy project, and one that Eco is certainly most competent to undertake. However, the very first example of such constraints that he gives (on the previous page) is a puzzle and a bit foreboding: this is the constraint on a reader of a tendency *to begin* by granting the "literal meanings" they appear to have to "sentences" and "lexical items." The literal meaning, Eco says here, "is the one listed first by dictionaries as well as the one that Everyman would first define when requested to say what a given word means" (*Limits* 5). But given that works so often call for non-literalist responses, and that such a tendency, as something cultural or psychological, is more a matter of the reader's personal make-up than of the work and, as such, something that should be under the control of the reader's *literary competence*, isn't Eco putting the cart before the horse here--especially since he distinguishes later on between the "naïve reader" and the "appreciative reader" who, together, make up his Model Reader?

To anticipate: in this book we can take Eco's model reader to be someone who proceeds as if "any act of interpretation is a dialectic between openness and form, initiative on the part of the interpreter and contextual pressure." On one hand the model reader does not "support the 'repressive' idea that a text has a unique meaning guaranteed by some interpretive authority" (*Limits* 21), nor does s/he, on the other, support the regressive idea that a text has infinite interpretations. Most interesting to critics and theorists should be Eco's showing that the postmodernist line of support for the latter "epistemological pole" or extreme dovetails with the Hermetic tradition of the allusive inexhaustibility of symbols.

Readers of Eco's creative output will be aware that, like his subject-matter, his theories and viewpoints are ever in a state of flux and development. But Eco's research is always focused; the characteristic which attaches his readership to him is its ability both to entertain and teach while remaining exploratory and interrogative. The one disadvantage of Eco's approach is its compulsive need to concede too much to aspects of the-state-of-the-question--and the vocabularies of their exploiters--which on his own principles are marginal or regressive. In a commercialized and careerist-ridden intellectual environment, the impulse to explore and the need to dialogue do not require giving equal time to *all* directions, regardless of whether they are dead-ends, or to *all* fashions that are bureaucratically entrenched. This is not to say that Eco's outreach in so many directions is not deserving: it is, and that it does not serve its readership: it does, and does so most stimulatingly--whether what we highlight is one of his aesthetic insights or an occasional semeiotic lapse. By lapses I specifically mean *only*, lapses from the semeiotic of the acknowledged founder C.S.Peirce. In any case, Eco's book must be seen against the background of postmodern text theory, and in relation to current work in the semeiotics of literature. This review will examine Eco's book from the point of view of Peirce's theory of signs and the largely unexploited possibilities of its application to the literary arts and the problem of metaphor.

We can say at once that Eco's *excursi* in the field, long or short, are all enlightening, but that the semeiotics and distinction-making which accompany his otherwise apt incursions into literature are often, from Peirce's point of view, assumptively or *categorially* loose. The counter-semeiotic or categorial difficulties, nonetheless, can be separated from the spirit and drift of Eco's advances with a minimum of damage to what is positive in them. The difficulties must be attended to for the sake of good theory in semeiotics.

A serious cause of distortions in Eco's theorizing is his repeated appeal to the notion of "semantics." The term is not found anywhere in Peirce; for pragmaticism the field 'semantics' is supposed to demarcate, simply *does not* and *cannot* exist. Eco's own critique of Charles Morris, who first brought the notion into semeiotics via his misunderstanding of Peirce, calls it "dangerous" and part of a misdefinition–or pseudoscientific definition–of the domain of semeiotics (p. 204f.)[3] Morris's definition of the field is tripartite, into "pragmatics," and "syntactics," as well as "semantics."[4] So Eco rightly points out that this turns semeiotics into a high-level or generic label for "a mere confederation of three independent sciences, each of them dealing with three independent objects." Since "pragmatics," for Morris is "the science of the relations of signs to their interpreters" (1938:5), Eco also sees that Morris has now got a self-contradictorily defined science on his hands; for, this has the consequence of making the definitions of the objects related (i.e. signs and interpreters) independent of each other, at the same time that Morris has said that "something is a sign only because it is interpreted as a sign of something by some interpreter." He has also agreed to the truism that "semiotics is concerned with. . .objects insofar (and only insofar) as they participate in semiosis." Morris's "only," here, brings out his assumption that there can be extra-semeiotic objects; Morris believes that there are objects that are not part of a semeiosis.

Now though Eco knows, unlike some neopositive linguists, that there can be extra-linguistic objects he does not balk–as he should–at Morris's iterated "insofar's." For, in Peirce's semeiotic, to be an object at all is to be a semeiotic object, namely, a significate object. Morris has no grounds for his qualifier other than the correspondence-theorist's belief that there are things out there, which are recognizable as what they are, independently of our idea of them. This allows him to privilege what he calls "ordinary objects" or any "particular kind of object" as external to semeiosis, and as if our access to them was different from the kind of access we have to objects that come under semeiotic scrutiny. But critical as Eco is of Morris's work, he unfortunately shares Morris's assumption that language and art can have extra-semeiotic "referents," as he calls them.[5]

While Eco sees that "pragmatics cannot be a discipline with [a] proper object as distinguished from th[at] of semantics and syntactics," he does not–as a Peircean should–question the notion itself of "pragmatics" as the study of the relations of signs to their interpreters. In Peirce it is the focus on the relation between signs and their interpretants that can be called pragmatic: "pragmatics" is not a term or notion of Peirce's any more than "semantics" is. Eco doesn't seem to see that what he and Morris call pragmatics is really sociology: part of a study of the use made by the interpreters (human agents) of the interpretant (the conceptional pivot relating the sign to the object in the triadic process of signification). An interpreter is not an interpretant. Even though Eco quotes Peirce's insistence at 5.488, that semeiosis "involves a cooperation of three subjects. . .a sign, its object and its interpretant, this tri-relative influence not being in any way resolvable into action between pairs," he persistently (though not always) talks in terms of interpreters rather than interpretants. We have to ask, how operative are these vestiges of Cartesian dualism and positivistic correspondence theories of truth in Eco's semeiotics; are they central and generative, or only called out by a climate of opinion in which both common-sense and the two orthodoxies of Analysis and phenomenology still talk about language and knowledge in the dualistic terms we have inherited from Descartes.

The answer is, briefly, that while many of his essays or sketches and both his big novels remain true to the creative spirit of expressive art, in Eco's formal theoretical work the tension persists according to which he wants to make Peirce's semeiotic intelligible in Cartesian or "analytic" terms when, in fact, it is the terms of Peirce's pragmaticism and semeiotics that can dissolve the misformulations shackling Cartesian or neopositivist approaches and solve the problems of meaning and representation that they address. In regard, for example, to his cherished project of clarifying the limits of interpretation we see already that by speaking of constraints but not of interpretants Eco deprives himself of a most important systematic limiting principle (constraint) of interpretation, namely, the constraints of the interpretants that mediate the effective object of the literary sign and the constructed work of art which is that sign.

Interpreters are free to do or say whatever they like; but if they are to speak to the work and the experience it informs, rather than about other things, and if they are to verbalize that informed experience, they must speak out of, or according to, the interpretants determined by the work-as-the-literary-sign that it is. These interpretants arise in the interaction or transaction between the reader's literary competence and the (complex) design of the (composed) work. When readers assent to a proposed interpretation it is because they share interpretants with its propounder: their responses, including their aesthetic responses, will be differential and not quite verbalized in the same way.

In connection with the problems of the identity of the literary work, Eco also needs a better definition or conceptualization of "identity" than the unarticulated one to be found in his book. Because he decides to treat identity as a primitive term (*Limits* 176), and believes (i) that when it does get defined in relation to "such concepts as Truth and Falsity, Authentic and Fake, Identity and Difference," the definition is circular, and (ii) that our general criteria for identity are very "hazardous" (Limits 201), his entertaining chapter on "Fakes and Forgeries" is less interesting intellectually than it could have been. It does have an interesting subsection (4.3. "Forgery Ex-Nihilo") on works composed "in the manner of," on apocrypha, pseudoepigrapha and creative forgeries. When a claimant falsely attributes a work Oj to a given author, one must know, Eco says, of a set a of different objects (Oa1, Oa2, Oa3. . .) all produced by the author A who is well-known. From the set a can be derived an abstract type, which can't take account of all the features of the individual members of a but displays "a sort of generative rule assumed to be the description of the way in which A produced every member of a . . .. Since Oj looks as if. . . produced according to this type, it is then claimed that Oj is a previously unknown product of A."

Briefly and in very broad outline this gives us the form according to which a claim to authenticity is couched. From it we can derive the outline of the form which demonstrations of *inauthenticity* will follow. Namely, the claimant's challenger will have to show that the literary design and textural attributes of work Oan do not coincide with those of a in general or of Oa1, Oa2,. . .Oa4. . . in particular, i.e. that properties of Oj are incompatible with Oa. Difficulties will certainly arise in connection with the choice of traits that are literarily, historically, and materially relevant to defining the generalized type Oa of a work by A. Thinking of Plato's dialogical works, for example, if the word-play, the humor, the wit, the irony, and the subtle characterizations found in the undoubted dialogues are not included as attributes, then any number of works lacking these traits–as long as they are dialogues in language that can pass for fourth century Greek–can be claimed to be Plato's.[6]

Any thing or process, any literary work, discriminandum or complex can be found or placed in many contexts. So we distinguish, with Justus Buchler, between the *integrity* and the *identity* of a complex; and this for two reasons. It is the integrities of a complex that are plurally located; and, accurately viewed, identity is a relation or set of relations.[7]

> A complex has an *integrity* for each of its ordinal locations. The continuity and totality of its locations, the interrelation of its integrities is the *contour* of the complex. The contour is itself an integrity, the gross integrity of that which is plurally located, whether successively or simultaneously. A contour is the integrity of a complex not in so far as the complex transcends all orders but in so far as it belongs to many orders (1966:22).

Since the integrities of a complex are a function of their ordinal location or context, the totality and continuity of a complex's locations is the *gross integrity* or contour of the complex.[8] This leads to the definition we need: "*the continuous relation that obtains between the contour of a complex and any of its integrities*" is "*the identity of a complex*" (1966:22).

For example, in the context of cultural or historical sociology, a work can be said or appear to have the integrity of a symptom, in general history, that of a document or archaeological artifact; while, as part of the material or intellectual history of publishing, it will evince the traits belonging to an integrity in the order of publishing and marketing. But in the order of literary art, or the aesthetic order, it will have the integrity and design, the unity of a work-of-art. It is just because the work's *literary* integrity is distinct from its aspects as a symptom, document, or marketable product that we are at advantage in distinguishing between the integrities of a work and its identity as a literary composition or complex utterance. This means that successive or different interpretations are integrities that qualify or redefine the identity of the work-of-art. If they are literary integrities they augment or spoliate the literary integrity of the work. Economistic, sociohistorical or psychoanalytic characterizations, as contributing to the scope of the work, are also constitutive of its gross integrity; but they do not strongly affect its literary integrity. Interpretations, as interpretations, are educed by further *collateral information* and renewed or else distinct contextualizations. Granting a gross integrity or contour to works also grants them the continuity and relatedness among their integrities which they need to have in order to be understood in their histories and appreciated in their present fullness or ramifications.

We also see that economistic or psychoanalytic critiques of a literary work are reductive and miss its aesthetic integrity. So, too, do logicalist analyses of verbal works-of-art (like Plato's dialogues or Thucydides' history) *constructed* to be *exhibitive* judgments *of* their subject-matter not assertive claims *about it*-bypass and miss the integrity, the experience and point of such works. As dramatizations or narratizations of their subjects they give determinacy to them by putting them on exhibit in the same transformation that the verbal *work* of art (the informative *skill* of the artist) turns language into an expressive medium. And the assertions that may be found in a drama, a dialogue, or a dramatized narrative history are held in the suspension of that medium and the allusional universe of the work: they may not be treated as categorical truth-claims without violating the literary integrity of the work. We may not attribute to Eco as his own, for instance, the claims made by the hermeticists in *Foucault's Pendulum*, nor may we take Adso's stated beliefs in *The Name of the Rose* to be necessarily the author's.[9]

2. DUALISTIC "SEMANTICS" VERSUS THE MODEL READER

We must face one more difficulty in Eco's conceptualization and terminology. He calls *semantic* interpretation "the result of the process by which an addressee, facing a . . .Text. . . fills it up with a given meaning." He adds, "Every response-oriented approach deals first of all with this type of interpretation, which is a natural semiosic phenomenon" (*Limits* 54). But *critical* interpretation, Eco says,

> is, on the contrary, a metalinguistic activity–a semiotic approach–which aims at describing and explaining for which formal reasons a. . .text produces a given response (and in this sense it can also assume the form of an aesthetic analysis).

The next paragraph shows that Eco intends a contrast between "ordinary sentences" and "aesthetic texts" or texts under formal linguistic scrutiny: the latter "foresee a critical interpreter," the former "only expect a semantic response." In other words Eco is distinguishing between merely practical or merely *semiosic* (i.e., meaning-grasping) responses and aesthetic, rationalizing responses:

> many texts aim at producing two Model Readers, a first level, or a naive one, supposed to understand semantically [i.e. semiosically]what the text says, and a second level, or critical one, supposed to appreciate the way in which the text says so. . ..[For example] a mystery tale displays an astute narrative strategy in order to produce a naive Model Reader eager to fall into the traps of the narrator. . . but usually wants to produce also a critical Model Reader able to enjoy, at a second reading, the brilliant narrative strategy by which the first-level, naive reader was designed.

We need to ask, here, is Eco keeping track of his terminology? On Eco's dualistic understanding of "semantic," the term represents the interest in the extra-semeiotic "referents" of words. But if "semiosic" means simply assimilating or manipulating the everyday or dictionary meanings of syntagms, then "semiosis" doesn't have to be extrasemeiotic in the neopositivist sense of referring to external "referents," even if these meanings are also called "literal." That Eco equates *semiosic* with *semantic* implies that he continues to think–in spite of his extensive knowledge of Peirce–of meaning-processes as involving reference to objects external to the semeiosis, and therefore pre-given or immediately recognizable in themselves –At the same time, moreover, that he seems able to forget that in Peirce's pragmaticism the world itself and every object discriminated in it is a *significate object*, Eco has also forgotten that there is no response that does not have an aesthetic component. No respondent can be alive and not feeling; that respondents in our culture don't correlate their feelings with–or raise them to consciousness as generated by–the semeiotic object, simply means that they've suppressed them. But that doesn't give the semeiotician the right to also suppress the aesthetic dimension of any experience, no matter how practical it may be thought to be.

While Eco's own practice of interpretation addresses particular works in a stimulating and substantive way, the belief that "critical interpretation" must be "a meta-linguistic activity" is, as theory, surely a trap. For, strictly, metalinguistic discourse is about the concepts or exploratory notions in terms of which we appreciate and reflect upon literary works; it is talk about our verbal response, not the verbal response itself. The latter is our critical interpretation. Since, however, Eco's practice proceeds as if verbalizing the response itself is somehow metalinguistic,[10] then it must be either because he is thinking of *the interpretants* as already linguistic or that thinking about or with the interpretants is already self-reflective. So, though his habit of focusing on the interpreters or readers of works allows him to elide mention–at the level of methodology and self-reflection–of the interpretants which the complex literary sign is determining, he has nonetheless operationally proceeded as if there was *no way* of detouring *past* the *interpretant*. He has only unstatedly both over-intellectualized it, and conflated it à la Saussure with the "union of" the aesthetic *object* of the literary sign and the complex *sign* itself. For, what *different* readers who are said to share the *same* "interpretive response" in fact share is the same *interpretants*; and they will articulate these in terms that suit themselves, that reflect different personalities, varying literary competence, and noncongruent amounts of collateral information.

"Semiosic competence," Eco says, is the ability "to interpret verbal and visual signs, and [sic] to draw inferences from them, by merging the information they give with background knowledge" (*Limits* 204). Does Eco's *and*, here, mean that he is missing Peirce's point that just as all inference is interpretive, so all interpretation is inferential? This is a point that ought to be as dear to hermeneuticists and phenomenologists as it is to pragmaticists. In any case–for reasons already rehearsed–what Eco calls *semiosic* he also calls *semantic*. This hampers Eco's critique of the anti-contextualism of analytic "truth-conditional semantics."[11] But it does not lessen his agreement with Quine that

> 'analytical' truths as well as synthetic ones, depend on a system of cultural assumptions, that is, they represent the more resistant – but by no means eternal– core of a system of social expectations."

But since his view of semantics entails a dualistic non-Peircean need for pragmatics, Eco is led, in his effort to foster the importance of context, into a (supererogatory) distinction between "signification" and "communication." We need, he says, what he calls "a pragmatics of signification (how to represent in a semantic system pragmatic phenomena)," as well as "a pragmatics of communication (how to analyze pragmatic phenomena. . .in the. . .communicative process" (*Limits* 212). And this has to do, in Eco's overall purview, with his idea of the function of a "Dictionary" and "Encyclopedia" in semeiotics. The latter idea, in turn, is a consequence of Eco's habit of thinking of signification in terms of coding and decoding.

This signification/communication distinction goes back to Eco's *A Theory of Semiotics* (1976); it would seem that he hasn't seen past it because he still thinks of "significations" as "sign-functions established by a code" (*TS* 16). Eco believes that a theory of signification entails a theory of codes because it is codes which assure that a given sign (sign-function) is correlated to or with its "connotation" or "content" (*TS* 86), and that "the very complexity and unpredictability of sign production springs from the [topological, rhizomic] format of the semantic [!] universe as it must be outlined by a theory of codes" (TS 142). The theory of codes will generate properly open, networking dictionaries and encyclopedias which systematically apportion "sign-vehicles" or *"expressions"* to "contents" (the "elements conveyed").[12]

But, given his encyclopedias, why does Eco still need a "pragmatics" to grasp "significations" or meaning-processes fully? Because, having *semanticized* semeiotics and *atomized* meaning-processes, "communication" for him is about interpreters and what they do: so that significations (which Eco thinks should be storable) do not encompass all aspects of *the ways and context in which* they are "communicated." The net effect of all this, the Peircean reader can already see, is first of all to reify significations and make signs seem like "entities" (things which Eco has said he doesn't want to do), and detaches the sign or representamen from its *ground*. Next, it not only bypasses the interpretants of the sign but also reassigns *constituents of both the sign and the interpretant*–such as tone of voice, accompanying gestures, interactional effects upon characters and their situation, silently implied irony or inferable by-play–*to the interpreter or the collateral context.*

That this bit of theoretical slippage can be serious is quickly perceived in connection with the reading of works from oral-aural cultures in which the speaking voice is always pivotal, or works in which voice is in some way constitutive of the meanings in and of the text. Such, for instance, is the case with Plato's dialogues. This is a pity, given that Eco is well aware that many works provide internal clues, "self-focusing appeals" to the ideal reader, that elude naïve or first readings (*Limits* 52; and *Role*, Ch. 8). It is a weakness also because the context of the transmission of given works can be so tightly guarded that a tradition of sustained *misinformation* about the works can be passed off *as* relevant *collateral* information. And experienced readers know that one of the biggest causes of misreading is collateral misinformation about the work, just because (as with Plato's dialogues), the misinformation distracts from or overrides the internal clues.

So, however much they might help Artificial Intelligence work, we should not expect that either tables for encoding and decoding texts or Eco's encyclopedias of atomized (non-denumerable but non-processual) entries will help the actual practice of the art of good reading, because the skill required to handle them–assuming they could be created–is not itself a storable item, and because however they are handled lexical markings of texts wouldn't by themselves assure a proportionate or aesthetic response to the work-as-a-whole. What encyclopedias and dictionaries supply is, in Peircean terms, collateral information; they help the reader's response only as they are applied in clarifying *the interpretant*. The "code" or system of "signification" does *not by itself* perform the "communication." Nor does Eco deny that encyclopedias are, after all, practical devices, fallible, labyrin-thine, and hypothetical, neither unitary nor all-inclusive, and "rhizomic."[13] Bakhtin's reminders are apposite, here, that "a word may never be precisely defined, exhausted and, finally, stored;" and that

> one and the same word will belong simultaneously to two languages, two belief systems that intersect in a hybrid construction–and, consequently, the word has two contradictory meanings, two accents. . ..hybrid constructions are of enormous significance in novel style (1981: 305).

Encyclopedias will reflect some model of what Eco calls "an organized semantic universe" (*Limits* 147); and this model may be incompatible with the semeiotic or allusive universe presupposed or implied by the work in hand, as for example, the Ptolemaic or Newtonian universes are with the ecosystems implicit in the literature and fragments of Archaic Greek litera-ture, the paintings of Van Gogh, or transcribed Native American myths.[14] Fruitful in some respects as Eco's suggestion might be that we try applying Emanuele Tesauro's *Il cannocchiale aristotelico* to the reading of *Finnegan's Wake*, we should do it with the reservations suitable to intercultural studies and with a care to avoiding mechanistic violations of the aesthetic life or integrity of the work.

Because of his continued *literalist* application to theory of the *metaphor* of language as a code, readers may look for light on the subject of metaphor itself in *The Limits of Interpretation*. They will find none, although since Eco came to the conclusion in more recent work that (*SPL* 127),

> No algorithm exists for the metaphor, nor can a metaphor be produced by means of a computer's precise instructions, no matter what the volume of or-ganized information to be fed in,

some readers had hoped there would be an advance, in the new work, into the aesthetics of metaphor. In *The Role of the Reader* Eco had already acknowledged that "the semantic aspect does not explain how metaphor can also have an aesthetic function" (*Role* 69), thus granting that mechani-cally correlated lexical operations are aesthetically blind. It follows that the "semantic" understanding of prose is *reductive*. Since Eco nowhere explicitly denies the Deweyan point that nothing discriminated is without an aesthetic dimension, his analyses of literature will continue to be at risk from the two defects in his theorizing about meaning that are anti-aesthetic and anti-Peircean, namely, his literalism and his semanticism, so to call them.

3. The Model Reader, and the Problem of Metaphor

Eco the literary critic is certainly a Model Reader but, well-read as he is in classic American pragmaticism, the semeiotic theorizing in *Limits of Interpretation* continues to suffer from the gap between theory and practice that is an operative residue of the rationalist-empiricist heritage from which the assumption comes that a syntagm's first or basic meaning is its so-called literal meaning.[15] In *Semiotics and the Philosophy of Language* (p. 88) Eco had put it this way: every discussion of metaphor faces an initial choice,

> either (a) language is by nature or originally metaphorical, and the mechanism [sic] of metaphor establishes linguistic activity. . ..or (b) language (and every other semiotic system) is a rule-governed mechanism [yes], a predictive machine that says which phrases can be generated and which not, and which from those able to be generated are 'good' or 'correct,' or endowed with sense;. . ."

And this does not seem an over-stated dilemma. He continues with an apposition,

> a machine with regard to which the metaphor constitutes a breakdown, a malfunction, an unaccountable outcome, but at the same time the drive toward linguistic renewal."

The difficulty here is that, though Eco knows that metaphor "is in fact a semiotic phenomenon permitted by almost [?] all semiotic systems," namely, that metaphor negates the linguist's mechanistic alternative he opts for the literalist horn of the molecular premise. He does this with the weaseling "almost," which makes the syllogistic alternative non-deductive, and also because he sees (with unnecessary panic) that

> "If it is metaphor that founds language, it is impossible to speak of metaphor unless metaphorically."

But Eco himself speaks metaphorically about theory and semeiotic phenomena so often that he cannot say he has dealt with his subject-matter with uniform literality, even on his own understanding of the literality of the pronouncements among which his metaphors are embedded. And if there are degrees of literality in the running prose, then non-literality is a *regular* not a "deviant" feature of language– so pervasive, in fact, that literalists don't notice it in their own prose. Just look back above at my most proximate four or five citations from Eco: "founds," "machine," "breakdown," "mechanism," "drive," "says," "instructions," "fed," "hybrid," "accent," "intersect," "construction," are all used metaphorically. I would therefore take Eco's attitude to particular theories of interpretation to be more authentically expressed by what he does with them exhibitively in his two big novels, than by the way he asserts and qualifies them, over-uses or drops them, in the investigative essays in which he thinks he is being categorically assertive.[16] Also, finally, if metaphor is the method by which language "renews" itself, as Eco admits, doesn't that create a presumption for the inquirer that it might also be the principle by which language is ever *newing* itself ?.[17]

In any case the way in which Eco frames the question that will guide his investigation, simply begs the question itself: "The question we want to discuss here is. . .on what encyclopedic rules must the solution of the metaphorical implicature base itself" (*SPL* 89)? The interrogative does not generate a research program that is basic *enough*. A previous question obtrudes itself, namely, in what ways is speech or language operating when meanings arise in it? In this investigation the distinction between metaphoric and literal speech is left till later. Here the interrogation does not begin by granting that there can be a conveyance of meaning–sign activity–without a *transference* of some kind, as if *to convey* meant something other than to transport, transfer or, in Greek, *metavore n*. And if meaning is a kind of transference, then literal meaning, to be meaning at all, must be a species of transference.

Now the species of transference which we call metaphor demands *functional* treatment just because it is felt, or defined, to be something of a semeiotic *event*, a happening. That metaphors stand out as "unusual," however, does not entail that they have to be understood in terms of what is not metaphor, any more than the compellingness of art calls for art to be explained in terms of what is not art. And just as art is not understood if it is not also seen to be the germ and productive principle of the culture that produces art, so metaphor cannot be explained if it is not seen to be also the principle which produces meaning. Bad art is not non-art, and passable art that has faded into near invisibility, like the uglinesses to which city-dwellers are inured, is also not non-art but dead art. As a species of transfer with the power to compel, metaphors are also a species of art; they are *expressive*. And this in two senses; first in the sense that speaking or writing at all are skills or arts and, secondly, in the sense that they are what Dewey calls "expressions" in distinction from "statements" (1934, Ch. 5). Expression is a completive or "consummatory" activity; it contrasts with statement which is directive or assertive as in the experimental and deductive sciences. Expressions do not make categorical truth-claims, statements do.

When language is a means of expression it, of course, becomes a *medium*, a medium to be shaped and configured in accordance with the meanings and effects which the maker or sender hopes to convey. Poems and paintings do not function like scientific statements that guide experiments or deductions; they operate in a different mode altogether. Poetry deals as directly as possible with the *qualities* of situations, in such a way as to create an unhindered response informed by just these meanings or qualities. And this is what metaphor does too. So metaphor, like art and poetry, operates in what has to be called the *exhibitive* mode of judgment. *Assertive* judgments create new determinacies by claiming to be true or false. But a construction or contrivance is an *exhibitive* judgment; it creates new determinacies through its shaped meaningfulness. It does not claim to be true or false, but rather to be effective, good or fitting. Similarly, with *active* judgments; they implement new determinacies in the environment by the doing of something, through action seeking presumably to be appropriate, successful or adequate. Scientific symbols in the assertive mode are not iconic, they are dicent thirds; when they are hypoiconic, it is in a sublated way. Scientific statements are properly subject to logical analysis because their terms are, by stipulation, univocal. But artistic symbols and metaphors, which operate in the exhibitive mode, are fully hypoiconic and polysemic, pregnant with allusiveness and therefore not legitimately subject to logical analysis. They require, not logical but aesthetic or poetic analysis.

In semeiosis, it is the mediating and unifying function and power of the interpretant which produces the metaphor and its aesthetic or semeiotic effectiveness. The thirdness of the interpretant guarantees the consonance and unity of the transference and representing processes or "referring." The locus of metaphor is the signitive nexus–the *rheme*–which mediates the terms, creating the unity between them. Peirce explains metaphor in terms of parallels which don't intersect but come either already fused (prebridged), turn on each other as a unity, or else *fuse* into a unity. Peirce calls metaphor hypoiconic ("sub-iconic") because the similarity need only be minimal or abstractible in any way as a matter of parallelism. This is to say, a metaphor is a new sign made up of a parallelism "contain[ing] signs whose meaning is only explicable by icons" (2.278). Speaking generally Peirce says, in this and the next paragraph, that

the only way of directly communicating an idea is by means of an icon; and every indirect method of communicating an idea must depend for its establishment upon the use of an icon. Hence every assertion must contain an icon or set of icons. . . .[even] an algebraic formula is an icon (2.279).

Peirce divides hypoicons into *images, diagrams,* and *metaphors.* So, though metaphors are iconic in the minimal sense explained, icons are not necessarily metaphors. Iconic signs resemble their object in some respect; whereas parallels don't necessarily involve what is usually called a resemblance. In Peirce's terms metaphors are, technically, *rhematic interpretants*. Thus, to invoke resemblance or substitution based on resemblance is trite; it doesn't explain the element of surprise or novelty in metaphor any more than transference alone can explain the difference between dead metaphor and metaphor.

Metaphors, for Peirce, are a species of hypoicon which functions to feature or represent, by means of a parallelism with something else, the representative nature of the representamen (2.277). What a metaphor *brings into exhibition* is a fusion of the unstated traits of one term of the metaphor with the unstated traits of the other term. And the terms of the metaphor are *fusible*, not necessarily because they resemble each other in some easy sense, but because they are abstractively parallel. Moreover, the sign-complex, the metaphor produced by the fusion can also stand for the (anthropomorphized) relation between the terms of the metaphor. A metaphor features or exploits the representative potentialities of its terms, each becoming a representamen of the other, in such a way that the interpretant constitutes an exhibitively suggestive (expressive) whole. And it can do this because successful metaphors, like art, are self-validating. It is the parallels extractable from the end-terms that are the *ground*, in the new metaphorical *object*, of the ingenious *sign* which has created for the *interpretant* the evocativeness of the sign.

The connotations of a metaphorical sign are rather more open-ended than not; their suggestiveness is a function of this open-endedness. Notice the difference with Homeric similes which, in elaborating a comparison get quite specific: thus keeping the two terms from fusing because the comparison is limited to *specified* traits. In paragraph 7.590 Peirce states that metaphors are apt because they are the opposite of specific. Properly understood, he says, metaphor ought to mean "broad comparison on the ground of characters of a highly abstract kind," such as practiced by Cuvier's categorizations in zoology. He adds that the common idea of metaphor as the assertion of a similarity as if it were an identity is "literal" and imprecise. As we are seeing, it is just because metaphors are taken to be assertive, instead of exhibitive, judgments that past theories have been inadequate to the subject.

As unexpected units grounded in abstractible, expressive parallels metaphors are rightly taken to be pivotally *rhematic* interpretants in semeiosis. A Peircean proof that a perfect metaphor is a good fusion is that, though metaphor involves at least two terms, it is never taken as a *dicent* by the reader or auditor, not even when the metaphor is an oxymoron.[18] Putting it in a negative way, we could say that the more a purported metaphor is received as dyadic or as an assertion, the less of a poetic success is it going to be. A Buchlerian way of phrasing this would be to say that, in a good metaphor, neither of the fused elements is *alescent*: the interfused terms only *augment* each other. For example, in Pascal's metaphor of man as a "thinking reed," the second term is somewhat *spoliative* of the first; and, to that extent the second term ("reed") does not fully fuse with the first ("thinker" or "man"). Contrariwise, Shakespeare's "Shall I compare thee to a summer's day" is a full equation, with no residue between the two terms which augment and resonate with each other.

In verbal metaphors the words are legisigns, they mean what they mean by convention. But at the sign-pivot of semeiosis they are *arguments*, in Peirce's technical sense of the *tenth* class of signs, based on some poetic or invented convention that is not educible till after the fact of the metaphor's creation. At 8.337 Peirce says,

> Holding. . .that a Dicent does not assert, I naturally hold that an Argument need not actually be submitted or urged. I therefore define an argument as a sign which is represented in its signified interpretant not as a Sign of that interpretant. . .but as if it were a Sign of the Interpretant or perhaps as if it were a Sign of the state of the universe to which it refers, in which the premises are taken for granted.

This entails that metaphors are not asserted as existential identities or oppositions, but are the semeiosic exploitation of the representative potentialities–the pregnancy–of the poetic materials. The metaphor is the exhibitive judgment which calls out these potentialities. It feels like a breakthrough both because it seems to deny the principle of contradiction,[19] and because it (magically) harmonizes the tensions which the poem is informing, by assuming for the nonce an alternate universe in which they become a natural compatibility. Moreover, even if there is inference or some poetic counterpart of inference in metaphor, no conclusions are asserted. But in the new context they are convincingly exhibited as real possibilities in the implied alternative universe. And, since metaphors are no more iconic than any other kind of sign–because they are only so insofar as they are a species of hypoicon, then standing criticisms of iconism become irrelevant to the Peircean understanding of metaphor.

It is not a stumbling block to our theory that so many metaphors are *unstable* in their cultural context–in contrast to the store of successful metaphors whose freshness survives in the works which they helped to create. For now we are speaking of metaphorical usage that become "lexicalized" by passing into everyday use, thus becoming *sleeping* metaphors or standard terms. The life-cycle in which such metaphors are banalized can be and has been circumstantially traced by more than one grammarian. Michael

Shapiro's Peircean *The Sense of Grammar* traces in this way the life of a syntagm, "back door manouver" (1983:193f.), borrowed from basketball. This kind of metaphor clarifies poetic or successful metaphor by contrast: in the latter the dynamic quality of metaphor translates into durable liveliness, instead of into the eventual dormancy of dead metaphor.

Victorino Tejera

Semiotics and Deconstruction*

Semiotics and deconstruction deal with the question of text, its meaning and interpretation. They both are significant and influential contemporary theories of meaning. However, the sense of meaning and interpretation provided by them is very different. They are contradictory rather then complementary theories. Semiotics is general theory of signs which intends to clarify signs and to "make our ideas clear", while deconstruction stresses the notion of "indecidability" of meaning and intends to refutation of logocentrism. If the rational analysis is still the main method of semiotics, certainly deconstruction focuses on the limits of reason and opens a venue for irrationalism. The purpose of this article is to demonstrate some radical oppositions between semiotics and deconstruction.

The following analysis has been provoked by Derrida's manner of speaking about Peirce and his semiotics. This manner seems to suggest that Peirce's semiotics helped to pave the road to the deconstruction or even was already the first step to deconstruct sign. Derrida's writing about Peirce makes an illusion of affinity between deconstruction and semiotics what, according to the present author, can be only a misinterpretation of Peirce. Certainly, the thesis that there is a misinterpretation of Peirce in Derrida comes already from without the deconstruction. Who speaks about misinterpretation he must presume a possibility of interpretation, as well as, the fact that reading is different from writing, i.e., that finding a meaning in existing text is different from creating a new text with its new meaning, even if reading is an interpretation rather than simple repetition. Interpretation certainly provides a new elucidation of the text but whatever new is brought into it by an interpretative act it must be grounded on an already formerly existing meaning.

Derrida in his criticism of Husserl's philosophy of meaning juxtaposes Husserl and Peirce. In a conclusion of his analysis, he claims Peirce's superiority over Husserl. Peirce, according to him, made a significant contribution to overcoming logocentrism. The main moments of Peircean semiotics underlined by Derrida in this context are:symbols are growing out of symbols; identification of logic and semiotics; the notion of pure grammar;

the infinitude of sign universe. Moreover, Derrida claims that Peirce has deconstructed the sign and that he has undermined the significance of logic through liberating semiotics from logic.

Some of the main points of Derrida's interpretation of Peircean semiotics can be clearly seen in the two following fragments from Derrida's *De la grammatologie*. The first fragment speaks about the sign and representation:

> Peirce va très loin dans la direction de ce que nous avons appelé plus haut la déconstruction du signifié transcendental, lequel, à un moment ou à un autre, mettrait un terme rassurant au renvoi de signe à signe. Nous avons identifié le logocentrisme et la métaphysique de la présence comme le désir exigeant, puissant, systématique et irrépressible, d'un tel signifié. Or Peirce considère l'indéfinité du renvoi comme le critère permettant de reconnaître qu'on à bien afaire à un système de signes. Ce qui entame le mouvement de la signification, c'est ce qui en rend l'interprétation impossible. La chose même est un signe. (1967:71-72)

And in the second fragment Derrida suggests that Peirce has overcome logic:

> La sémiotique ne dépend plus d'une logique. La logique, selon Peirce, n'est qu'une sémiotique./. . ./ Et la logique au sens classique, la logique 'proprement dite', la logique non-formelle commandée par la valeur de vérité, n'occupe dans cette sémiotique qu'un niveau déterminé et non fondamental. (1967:70-71)

The last quotation stays simply in a disagreement with Peirce's concept of semiotics in its relation to logic. However, the purpose of this article is not just to criticize Derrida's misinterpretation of Peirce. Rather, I would prefer to focus on some principal oppositions between semiotics and deconstruction. The crucial fact is that semiotics wants to find the logic of signs, while deconstruction rejects such logic at all. From a clear concept of what semiotics is, Derrida's misinterpretation of Peirce will become evident as well.

The distance dividing semiotics from deconstruction is marked by such Peirce's terms and concepts as:sign-representamen, object of representation, immediate interpretant, final interpretant, speculative grammar, destiny, truth, as well as Derrida's terms and concepts:deconstruction of sign, écriture, signifiant du signifiant, indecidability, intertextuality, trace, dissemination.

I want to analyze some of the problems implied by these terms.

First, in semiotics, historically (Peirce) as well as presently (Max Bense, Umberto Eco), the concept of sign constitutes the main category. The sign is a specific entity which semiotics tries to define. Semiotics does not deal with only accidental features of sign, or with a selected group of signs, but it is a theory of sign as such, i.e., it clarifies what essentially belongs to sign. As Eco writes:semiotics as a general theory is "able to explain every case of sign-function in terms of underlying systems of elements mutually corre-lated by one or more codes" (*TS* 1976:3). Semiotics is a theory of categorical 'something':the sign. Semiotics defines sign as a triadic relation between sign itself (a vehicle of meaning), its object as it is represented by sign and its meaning grasped by another sign. This type of triadic relation is a phenom-enon of representation and it is essential for sign to be such. When there is no representation there is no sign at all. This categorical sense of sign, with-out which semiotics is not possible as such, is radically rejected by deconstruction. Derrida's main point is to de-construct the concept of sign, that is, to discover its hidden meaning, to find some unspoken presump-tions which are grounding the concept, etc., in other words, to find in sign something else than its essential being. Deconstruction of the sign simply means that "sign" is no longer a category. Deconstruction implies a decategorization of the sign. Deconstruction rejects all essential questions as wrongly asked ones. (It is a refutation of phenomenology as well.) So, in the case of sign it suspends the essential problem:what sign is? and replaces it by searching for what sign is not. Such a decategorization of sign cer-tainly implies that a theory of sign becomes impossible.

Through deconstructing the sign Derrida negates the notion of represen-tation. The concept of representation is, according to him, only a disguised metaphysics of presence. Representation is only a metaphysical construct. After a criticism of de Saussure and Husserl, after a refutation of the con-cepts of sign and meaning, Derrida replaces them by a new term "gramme" and grammatology. Grammatology stays in an opposition to semiotics. Since semiotics is a theory of signs, grammatology is a non-theory of non-signs. Gramme is not a sign, it is not a categorical something and since it is not a category a theory of it is not possible. Grammatology wants to escape all characteristics of a science exploring the essentially of some objects. At this point Derrida applies to the realm of signs Heideggerian criticism of traditional metaphysics, which reduces Being to something. However, the notion of Being is quite different from the concept of sign (representation) and what can be an inspiring criticism in metaphysics, not necessarily has a reasonable application to the question of representation. Certainly, Being is not something; the notion of Being comes from ontological differentiation between the things which are (all entities) and the common to them "to be". Being, to be, cannot be grasped either by description or by name with-out a distortion, i.e., without turning it to an entity, to something which is. And then, when named, it is no longer the Being but only its particular case:an entity, a something. However, the sign or representation does not have the general dimension of 'to be'. The sign IS 'something'. The repre-sentation is the triadic relation; so, it always has a dimension of an entity (a being) and never of Being, which cannot be named without a distortion. Briefly, Derrida's attempt to apply Heideggerian "destruction" of history of metaphysics to theory of signs is grounded on a wrong presumption that sign is like Being. However, grammatology, which has ambitions to be a kind of negative theology of meaning, may be only a poor replacement for semiotics. It has a vague and arbitrary presumption that sign "is not a something". Semiotics, on the contrary, presumes that sign is a categorical something. It would be hard to find an argument against this presumption. This something which is explored by semiotics Eco defines as human activity of interpreting signs. "A general semiotics studies the whole of the human signifying activity" (*TS* 12).

Secondly, semiotics and deconstruction differs radically in their relation to the signans/signatum problem. Neither Peirce, nor the contemporary semiotics abolish the distinction between the sign and the signified. Derrida, however, makes the refutation of this distinction a one of the main points of his deconstruction.

Peirce's numerous definitions of sign as a triad always mention the object of sign. No triadic relation is possible without an object. Sign necessarily stands for "something else". The fact that Peirce correctly refuses the naive realistic understanding of object in no way implies a possibility of a sign which would not be a REPRESENTAMEN, that is, which would not stand for something else. Semiosis is not an objectless process. For a sign it is essential that it "stands for something else." Peirce demonstrates the referential character of sign and semiosis when he identifies the object with a cause of sign. He speaks about the signans/signatum relation in a deterministic language. The object has "its mode of being as an independent agent determining the sign."[1] The ontological status of an object is another question and Peirce agrees that there are many different types of objects. But clearly, there are some objects through which the bridges between the realm of signs and the realm of actual facts are built. Peirce claims not only that semiosis has necessarily a referential character but also that signs stay in a relation to the real empirical realm. This, as Eco reminds us, is clearly stated by the pragmatic maxim which points out to a final interpretant of a sign as a habit of action and finally the action itself. "The action is the place in which the **haecceitas** ends the game of semiosis" (*Role* 195).

Peirce's classification of signs into icons, indices and symbols is grounded on the three different types of referring to an object. Sign is related to its object either by similarity, or by real interaction, or by symbolic, abstract denotation. This classification emphasizes the referantial nature of sign as well.

Thus, Peirce has the same logocentric concept of a sign as one can find in Husserl's analysis of meaningful expression. Meaningful sign is not possible as objectless. Representation is a triadic relation from which the independent object cannot be eliminated without annihilation of the whole relation,

what would cause the destruction of meaning itself, as well. Peirce undoubtedly belongs to logocentrism. Derrida, however, wants to have signification without signatum. He introduces non-referential "gramme".
Deconstruction of sign, which rejects its referential character, implies a
notion of "signifiant du signifiant." Sign replaces only another sign and it
has no relation to anything else than sign.

"Écriture" is Derrida's term for this non-referential process, which is so
totally different from semiosis. "Signifiant du signifiant" expresses
Derrida's refutation of de Saussure's distinction of *signans* and *signatum*.

Thirdly, equally radical opposition between semiotics and deconstruction may be found in the question of meaning. For Peirce, meaning is
within the sign, not beyond sign. It belongs to the sign rather than to be
only in-between signs. This intrinsic meaning of the sign Peirce names its
"immediate interpretant". This is "the interpretant as it is revealed in the
right understanding of the sign itself , and is ordinarily called the meaning
of the sign." (CP 4.536). And also:interpretant is ". . .all that is explicit in
the sign itself apart from its context and circumstances of utterance." (CP
5.474).

The interpretant, or meaning of the sign is the third relate of the triadic
relation of representation. It is not external to the sign but is an intrinsic
component of the sign itself. Each sign has its interpretability preceding the
real interpretation. This real interpretation, which can be accomplished
only by another sign, Peirce calls the "final interpretant". Between the immediate interpretant and the final one there is only a difference of mode of
being:the first is pure possibility while the second is necessity. Peirce speaks
in this sense also about different "grades of interpretants". The final
interpretant is the interpretation, to which every interpreter "is destined to
come," when the sign is sufficiently considered. The meaning of sign manifests itself through another sign:the final interpretant unveils the meaning
of sign but does not constitute it. Deconstruction, however, negates any
intrinsic meaning of the text and locates meaning only outside it, only in-
between. Meaning, for Derrida, is that which is not present in the text. It
must be remade in the infinite process of differing/deferring. This is the
process of écriture. And the concept of écriture replaces those of text or
sign. Text means nothing at all, it has no decidable meaning. Only a parodying play with meaning exists. Reading is only writing a new text, it is
making the meaning which disappears in the same moment when it is
made. The text is an enigma which cannot be deciphered, it brings nothing
except open possibilities of differentiation. There are only traces, never
meanings. To deconstruct is to go beyond the meaning, beyond the sign,
beyond the text. Deconstruction means to take that which was supposed to
be a meaning as a vague trace only and to abandon any attempt to understand it. Derrida negates any identity of meaning, he makes meaning abso-

lutely ambiguous and claims its "indecidability". Semiotics, on the contrary, is a theory of meaning and interpretation, as well as, a methodology of deciphering meaningful signs. There is a radical opposition between semiotics and deconstruction in the question of meaning. It can be characterized as the distinction between 'within' and 'without'. Semiotics as a theory of signs develops a method of clarifying meanings, while grammatology of écriture offers a "chute dans l'extériorité du sens" (1967:24).

Fourthly, Derrida, after liberating sign from its object and its meaning, deconstructs all logical syntax. Subsequently, he gives a different sense to the whole semiotic realm and the process of interpretation. When the meaning is only an enigma, only a vague trace, it cannot stay in a clear relation to another meaning-enigma. In-between two enigmas may be only another enigma. The in-between is only an accidental, indetermined happening. That is how deconstruction replaces interpretation by intertextuality, regularity by spontaneity. Interpretation is not possible between non-existing meanings. Intertextuality is a play of the traces, and as such is a mystery. It is a senseless and endless process of differentiations, which is not bound either by determination or by a goal. Every text emerges as intertext and this accidental play of traces is called "dissemination". Intertextuality and dissemination mean a full spontaneity:the former text in no way is bounding the emerging new one; the new one has no relation whatsoever to the former one. Dissemination proclaims the perfect chaos.

The idea of dissemination stays in a radical opposition to the sense of semiosis. Peircean semiotics is a theory of sign production, which means searching for and defining principles ruling over the generation of signs.

Semiosis is a process of a continuous self-reproduction of signs. Sign as a triadic relation necessarily implies other signs. "The whole purpose of sign is that it shall be interpreted in another sign" (CP 8.191). "Thought must address itself to some other thought" (CP 7.356). This self-generating nature of sign is a core point of Peircean semiotics. However, this generation of signs is totally different from Derridaen dissemination. An interpretant of sign is a kind of logical conclusion. Every sign generated by former signs is determined by them, as well as, it determines further signs. Semiosis is a process of continuity of meanings. Each sign finds its foundation in another sign of which it is an interpretant and, consequently, it creates by itself the basis for a subsequent sign, i.e., its interpretant. Semiotical generation is a rational process in which every step, on the one hand, is bound by its past and, on the other hand, is defining the future meanings.

So, the idea of self-reproduction of signs has in semiotics a radically different sense than that of dissemination. Derrida's presentation of the game of differing/deferring shows its arbitrary character:

Le jeu joue toujours la différence sans référence, ou plutôt sans referent, sans extériorité absolue, c'est-a-dire aussi bien sans dedans./. . ./ Dans cette allusion perpétuelle au fond de l'entre qui n'a pas de fond, on ne sait jamais à quoi l'allusion fait allusion, sinon à elle-même en train de faire allusion, tissant son hymen et fabriquant son texte. (1972:248)

To this only accidental, irrational movement of unfolding differences semiotics opposes the implication of signs by signs, i.e., the rational process of thinking.

The distinction between semiosis and dissemination becomes even more clear from the point of view of the relation between semiotics and logic. Peircean tradition emphasizes the identity or at least close affinity between semiotics and logic. Such an approach is presently strong in the logical semiotics and in the Stuttgart School.

Peirce writes:"Logic in its general sense is /. . ./ only another name for semiotic, the quasi-necessary or formal, doctrine of signs" (CP 2.227). And: "Logic is the science of general necessary laws of Signs and especially of Symbols" (CP 2.93). He divides it into three branches:critical logic, which is a theory dealing with the general conditions of the reference of signs to objects, speculative grammar, the doctrine of general conditions of signification, and speculative rhetoric, a theory of interpretants. That what was appealing to Peirce in logic was the fact of its "exactness". It is an exact science. And his identification of semiotics with logic is stressing this exact character of semiotics as science of signs. So, when Derrida says that for Peirce semiotics no longer depends on logic, he just reverses Peirce's point. The fact is, that Peirce not only does not liberate semiotics from logic, but, on the contrary, he wants to create semiotics which is as exact as logic itself. One could say that he wants to have semiotics "ordine logico demonstrata." Semiotics is a broader logic. Peirce says:"I extend logic to embrace all the necessary principles of semeiotic, and I recognize a logic of icons, and a logic of indices, as well as a logic of symbols" (CP 4.9).

This point of logic and semiotics is important not only because it shows Derrida's misinterpretation but even more because it makes apparent the deep chasm between semiotics and deconstruction. Semiosis is a process of logical implications, while dissemination is an accidental play of traces and differentiations. Eco speaks about semiotics as a "logic of culture."[2]

Fifthly, semiotics understands semiosis as the process of growing knowledge. More developed signs bring better cognition. "A sign is something by knowing which we know something more."[3] And ". . .every reasoning connects something that has just been learned with knowledge already acquired, so that we thereby learn what has been unknown" (CP 7.536). At this point Peirce clearly continues the tradition of stoic semiotics, which says that a sign provides a new knowledge. Derrida's écriture, however, is not a cognitive process at all. And no growth in any sense can be accomplished by it. The later écriture is in no way better than the former one, there is no growth, no declining either, because essentially no comparison and no evaluation can be made. What does matter in dissemination is only the present immediacy without any relation to the past or the future. Ecriture is showing only the present:"l'écran réfléchissant ne capte jamais que l'écriture, sans arrêt, indéfiniment, et le renvoi nous confine dans l'élément du renvoi" (1972:229). Deconstruction claims that all writing is simultaneously erasing:the old text is substituted by the other. Subsequently, there is no continuity of interpretation, only punctuality of nows. Historicity of interpretation (a hermeneutical point) is negated by deconstruction as well, because the lack of continuity deprives every now of its historical content (inherited from the past) and turns it into an empty spatio/temporal point of the present. When Peirce emphasizes the growing nature of semiosis he does not mean only the accumulation of knowledge but also an intrinsic continuity of interpretation. Interpretation is a continuous development where the former element implies the present and the present makes a ground for the next step. Derrida is right when he says that Peirce well understands the flowing nature of sign realm, however, Derrida misinterprets the nature of this flowing due to his concepts of erasing and immediacy. That which really, at this point, differentiates semiotics from deconstruction is the opposition between accumulating and erasing. According to Peirce, the past is "our sole store-house of premises,"[4] and all our present and future signs are grounded on it. While for deconstruction, the past is simply erased by a new écriture and never present in it.

Subsequently, what is our sixth point, we find two different understandings of temporality of sign/text in Peirce and Derrida. According to Peirce, temporal duration is intrinsic to sign and it differs it from simple intuition. A sign, in order to be a sign, requires an interpretant and that makes of semiosis a temporal process. Semiosis is necessarily developing in time. It can not be instantaneous. There is an essential openness of the sign to the future:meaning is disclosed by the future interpretation of the sign. An interpretant is a future sign. Subsequently, something is a sign only from the perspective of the future. The question of the future is crucial in semiotics. The concept of sign presumes the time flowing. Peirce says:"The rational meaning of every proposition lies in the future" and pragmatism "locates the meaning in future time."(CP 5.427). The pragmatic maxim speaks about the future habit of action as a criterion of meaningfulness. This future habit is defined by the present sign in the same way as a result is determined by its cause. However, écriture emphasizes only the present. From the point of view of deconstruction the past is erased and the future "undecided" and hidden beyond endless possibilities. There is only the immediacy of the present and the moving, which is nothing else than leaping, from one to another present, through the play of contingent allusions.

Derrida's concept of time, implied by the sense of intertextuality and écriture, is close to what Bergson calls the scientific distortion of time. This scientific concept of time is a linear sequence of spatio/temporal points of "now", which has no real continuity. To such a sense of time Bergson opposes the notion of duration which captures the moment of flowing as crucial in time. Flowing, experienced in memory, means existence of essential interconnections between three phases of temporality. However, deconstruction negates memory and affirms forgetting. Écriture, intertextuality, dissemination, all these concepts are grounded on the fact of forgetting. Memory is not a faculty of mind used in deconstructing:erasing, disseminating. Intertextuality is a sheer present moment, free of any relations to an old (past) text, as well as, to a new one (future). If earlier in this article the anti-logical aspect of dissemination was stressed:that there are no rules for intertextuality but it is only a spontaneous accidental play, here, the anti-temporal, anti-historical aspect of dissemination is revealed. Écriture is not a historical process, it is rather a constantly repeated act of an independent making of the presence. Deconstruction is dominated by the present immediacy and the other times:past and future, are beyond it. So, the flowing of time in the sense of duration is missed in Derrida. Écriture is possible only as a leap from one present immediacy to another present immediacy. Such an imprisonment of thought in the presence must imply a refutation of history, what really is the case in deconstruction.

If the question of the present text in its relation to the past one is differently solved in semiotics and deconstruction, the difference between them becomes perhaps even more radical when we ask about its relation to the future texts. Semiotics affirms that the only purpose of a sign is to be interpreted by another sign. The immediate presence of the sign is for the sake of the interpretant, i.e., the future. Semiosis is a teleological process:every sign has its goal in another sign but also a process of interpretation as such intends towards the growth of cognition. Derrida negates the both moments: defining the future interpretation, as well as, existence of any goal of écriture. Nothing is stronger stressed by him than the lack of any telos in écriture. And there is an aspect of "dissemination" which means a negation of telos as well. So, if semiosis is intrinsically teleological, deconstruction proclaims a radical refutation of any telos. This question of telos brings us to the last, but not least, opposition between semiotics and deconstruction, which we find in the problem of truth.

So, seventhly, semiotics is a truth-directed process, its growth approximates truth and truth is its ultimate telos. As Peirce writes:". . . the interpretant is nothing but another representation to which torch of truth is handed along" (CP 1.339). Truth is the goal as well as the destiny of interpretation. Peirce's final interpretant ". . .is that which would finally be decided to be true interpretation if consideration of the matter were carried so far that an ultimate opinion were reached" (CP 8.184). While truth is the main concern in Peircean semiotics, Derrida's main intention is to make intertextual process independent of telos and truth. The écriture has no goal at all and does not aim at truthfulness. Truth is the concept which belongs to the condemned logocentrism and must be overcome. Ecriture is a play, which means not only suspension of any rules, but also suspension of any goal. It is a sheer purposeless immediacy, a Nietzschen innocence of becoming. So, in this way, the thinking becomes liberated from the tyranny of logos and telos. The only question remains:is it still a thinking? It seems clear, that deconstruction offers a game which goes beyond rationality.

So, there is a radical theoretical and methodological difference between semiotics and deconstruction. The shortest way to characterize it is to say that this is the chasm between rationalism and irrationalism. Deconstruction, which defines écriture as a play, is itself only a play. While semiotics, what recently was so strongly demonstrated by Max Bense,[5] aspires to be "als strenge Wissenschaft".

Hanna Buczynska-Garewicz

The Interpretant in Literary Semiotics

This essay is an attempt at adapting Peirce's semiotic model to the analysis of literary texts. It could not have been written without Umberto Eco's seminal contributions to semiotics and to the theory of interpretation.

Semantic and formal constant features of literature can be identified that may help define a literary kind of sign. Intertextuality[1] offers an effective model for the understanding of the relationships between these features. No definition of a specialized literary sign can have any validity, however, unless it can be integrated in a general theory of signs. I propose therefore to test poetics against semiotics by fitting intertextuality into the triadic model that C.S. Peirce proposed for semiosis, and to show in particular a parallelism between his interpretant and the type of intertext that generates the literariness of a text.

Intertextuality is the reader's perception that a literary text's significance is a function of a complementary or contradictory homolog, the intertext. The intertext may be another literary work or a text-like segment of the sociolect (a fragment of descriptive system [Riffaterre 1978: 39-40, 1983a: 39-41, 49-56, 200-1], for instance) that shares not only a lexicon, but also a structure with the text.

Significance is understood as the interpretation the literary text forces upon the reader. It combines two factors, a semiotic transformation and the inference the reader draws from it. The transformation affects simultaneously a sequence of discrete meanings identified through a first heuristic reading. A second reflexive, comparative, retroactive reading makes the reader discover that the sequence must be seen rather as a network or system which converts its components into variants of a single representation. The inference is that this overall shift is verbal art. We sense that the text is an artifact because it displaces natural or habitual semantic relationships with an ad-hoc system that deprives words of their presumed referentiality, making them signify together, as a whole, something other than what they would mean sequentially. The artifact presupposes in turn the presence of an author, and we unavoidably assume that its dependence on the writer's real or imagined intention modifies and supersedes its dependence on linguistic usage and on the users' consensus about reality.

The reader has to read twice and look for semiotic relationships other than the rules of the sociolect's grammar because he encounters phrasings that appear unacceptable or unexpected in the light of his linguistic competence. These "ungrammaticalities" prompt him to look for a solution elsewhere, that is, in the intertext. For these do not result from untraceable random verbal collocations. Quite to the contrary, such ungrammaticalities depend on perverse references to usage, verisimilitude, and plain logic, for they always are the reverse side of a web of established sign-systems, the other face of a coin whose obverse is the sociolect's grammar, lexicon, and corpus of commonplaces. Everything that is ungrammatical in a literary text, any constituent of its idiolect that seems a departure from usage has a reassuringly familiar sociolectic correspondent.

The link which leads a reader back to that correspondent is not vulnerable to his absentmindedness or ideological blind spots, for the very logic of language controls his response. First, the text's anomaly is such that no coherent interpretation can be arrived at without solving the problem it poses. Second, the solution cannot be a lucky, random discovery, nor can it be the privilege of those sharing in the culture of an elite, for the reader is directed to it by the fail-safe mechanism of presupposition. Thus, intertextuality generates literariness either in absentia or in actuality, since it either indicates that a significance is yet to be found, or it guarantees that the significance ultimately uncovered does fulfill the premises of presupposition.

The presupposed constituents of the intertext are awaiting discovery either in the sociolect's sign systems, as I suggested above, or in other literary works. In the latter, the intertext is already the product of a first departure from the sociolect. Presupposition still works, although it does so at a remove. But the ungrammaticalities in the text we are reading have a greater impact, for the literary intertext interposed between the sociolect and our text adds to the latter's further or secondary ungrammaticality the authority of a primary one, the authority of the already said, of a tradition, of a canonic rather than isolated artifice.

As significance results from a coupling of components of the text with their intertext(s), a unit of significance cannot be the same as a unit of meaning. What delimits a unit of meaning (the lexematic or syntagmatic actualization of a sememe) is its coupling with a referent. Consequently, the second or retroactive, interpretive reading is done through a new segmentation of the text. The new segments' boundaries encompass several words or sentences, and may ultimately extend to the whole length of a text, a situation mostly encountered in poems. In longer texts, significance units will be "subtexts," i.e., segments that are not coterminal with lexemes and syntagms, but function like these, as embeddings in the overall verbal sequence (tropes may be such subtexts).

The advantage of this model is that it accounts at once for two basic features of literariness that we perceive empirically: catachresis and monumentality. By *catachresis* (the basic figure of inappropriateness in ancient rhetoric), I designate any indirection of meaning, any displacement or deviation from the sociolect, in short the whole system of ungrammaticalities described above, including traditional categories like tropes and figures but by no means limited to them. Whereas catachresis is a fact of the text, its perception as *artifice* is the reader-response counterpart of that fact (especially the reader's rationalizations about the writer's intentions, evaluations such as "originality," etc.). As for *monumentality*, it compensates for catachresis by linking the verbal scandal of the text to its precedents or to the rule it violates. In other words, monumentality is that constant authority or guarantee that the intertext offers for the text. Intertextuality bespeaks the indissoluble union of scandal and conformity, rule and rulebreaking, norm and anomaly. Because there cannot be an aberrant text without its corresponding ad-hoc intertextual norm, the peculiarities of literary discourse, however extreme they may be, do not appear gratuitous. This single fact goes a long way towards explaining why a literary idiolect exerts the same imperative sway over its reader as the sociolect or literary precedents it challenges. The text cannot cancel or upset the intertext without compelling the reader to refer back to that intertext's authority and to acknowledge its pertinence.

Furthermore, this same authority makes itself felt in yet another way, more germane still to an understanding of the irreducible uniqueness and difference of the literary text. Not only does intertextuality make up for the waywardness of catachresis, it also regulates and legitimizes the very mode and manner in which catachresis itself operates, the selection of the devices it utilizes to challenge the intertext. For these devices owe their authority to a second intertext that interferes with the first, a second intertext just as solidly backed up by the sociolect or by other literary works as the first intertext against which it is targeted.

The model I have just described posits a three-way relationship between the text (or subtext), its intertext, and the second intertext that the text brings to bear on its relationship with the first. Since the text cannot exist as a system of signs without differentiating itself from the sign system it reflects (otherwise there would be no way of distinguishing between the textual sign system and its object, the intertextual sign system), the text necessarily dictates to its reader an interpretation for which a new sign system is employed. This new system, the second intertext, actualizes in verbal form, for all readers to decipher, the ad-hoc grammatical rule whereby the first intertext determines the production of the text. The second intertext, by producing a sign system equivalent to the first but couched in a different code, provides the reader with the means properly to decipher what significance results from or must be attached to the text's departure from the first intertext.

Let us compare this interaction of text and intertexts with one of C.S. Peirce's more developed definitions of the sign:

> A sign, or representamen, is something which stands to somebody for something in some respect or capacity. It addresses somebody, that is, creates in the mind of that person an equivalent sign, or perhaps a more developed sign. That sign which it creates I call the interpretant of the first sign. The sign stands for something, its object. It stands for that object, not in all respects, but in reference to a sort of idea, which I have sometimes called the ground of the representation (Peirce CP 2.228).[2]

In the light of Peirce's categories, the intertextual model may be tentatively reformulated thus: the literary sign or representamen is that subtext (or segment of the text) that is perceived as the homolog of an intertext. It stands to the reader for the intertext in this respect that the meaning it conveys depends on the text's mode of actualization of the intertext (completing, negating, reversing, etc. the representations composing the intertext). The object of the literary sign is that first intertext. The literary interpretant is a second intertext, equivalent to, or more developed than, the text. It therefore also stands for the object, but from another perspective indicated by, and derived from, a feature of the literary sign i.e., a lexical or syntagmatic component of the text (Riffaterre 1979: 133-135). This derivation is encoded in the text, enabling the reader permanently to retrieve the interpretation that generated it.

I shall now test the applicability of the above model to literature[3] by analyzing a fictional subtext, a fragment of narrative that tells its story, a very minor incident, in plain English. So plain, in fact, and about so little, that the literariness in the telling of it cannot possibly depend on pre-established or pre-textual esthetic values, nor could it be said that the literariness results from an intrinsic importance of the object. The only way that such factual insignificance, and verbal neutrality in representing it, can attain significance in the literary sense is by mobilizing a powerful intertext.

The subtext, from Kurt Vonnegut Jr.'s 1968 novel, *Slaughterhouse Five*, tells the aftermath of a daughter's wedding. Now that the celebration is over and the guests and newlyweds are gone, the depressed father wanders about in the empty house until he chances upon a bottle of champagne left over:

> Drink me, it seems to say.
> So Billy uncorked it with his thumbs. It didn't make a pop. The champagne was dead. So it goes.

It is possible, of course, to find the incident symbolic because of a "natural" (non-verbal) parallelism between the bottle left over and Dad left behind, or because the flat wine is a last straw. That makes for pathos, not for literariness, and the reader is free to be amused and to sympathize, to be amused without sympathizing, or to remain indifferent. The reader, on the contrary, is hooked, and his interpretation strictly controlled, as soon as he perceives the incident as a parody, and the form in which it is recounted as the agent of meaning. Indeed, the form permits us to equate this subtext and others that precede it, setting up the conditions of a retroactive reading which will make this subtext a negative conversion of the others. Its significance (the parody) results from the fact that the previous, comparable subtexts now function as its intertext.

Early in the novel, the reader is obliged to notice that the phrase *so it goes*, popping up frequently, regularly comments on a death. This colloquial equivalent of *the way of all flesh* expresses at first fatalistic resignation, starting with page two where a Dresden cabbie seems to say that life in Communist East Germany is not so bad ("He had a pleasant little apartment, and his daughter was getting an excellent education. His mother was incinerated in the Dresden fire-storm. So it goes"). Then, nineteen times in the seventy pages preceding our subtext, *so it goes* concludes with a shrug, as it were, stories in which death struck down someone who should not have died because he was lovable (a father, the Lamb of Scripture, a dog), or had done no wrong (a prisoner of war, Private Slovik). Better still, *so it goes* comes to draw the lesson of deaths symbolizing the irony of fate (a bridegroom killed because his ring gets caught in machinery, a military chaplain chosen to go when we would have expected the Lord of Hosts to protect his own), or poetic justice (soldiers in ambush are themselves ambushed).

Repetition clearly makes each recurrence the equivalent of the others, and it goes on to the end of the novel where *so it goes* glosses the pointless bombing of Dresden. Each recurrence therefore is a variant on a serious use of irony - the message, of course, being the futility of heroics, of war, of life. But our subtext cancels out this seriousness, now indicting even the moral attitude and mocking the commonplace wisdom that so far had been a guarantee of simple truth. The moral lesson is just as futile as everything else.

This canceling out is achieved by the simple trick of appending *so it goes* to a metaphorical death (*dead* as flat), no longer a tragic one. This is the more parody because *dead* here is a dead metaphor, totally devoid of sad connotations. Such irreverence is bolstered by another series (the recurrence of a desultory *and so on* throughout the book), and by the mocking song of birds amidst ruins of war at the end. Significance rests on Intertextuality. If this dead champagne did not negate a whole intertext of dead bodies, so it goes would only express the trivial disappointment of someone's thirst - this was not his day.

Now our subtext does indeed constitute one single sign not a sequence of signs, since every variant of the series is opposable to the others as a whole comprising three inseparable components (an innocent actor or act, death, morality), and since their order of succession itself is significant. Such is the pertinent segmentation.

It would not do to analyze the components as separate signs. If we did, and took the predicate in the champagne was dead to be a separate sign, its object would be "no bubbles" and its interpretant flat. Again, taken separately, so it goes would have a shrug or a deprecating smile for its object, and some sign for "cynicism" or "defeated acceptance" as its interpretant. The two signs following each other sequentially would reduce interpretation to the trivial reading I have just alluded to.

But since the sign is the subtext - the whole story, a full-fledged narrative unit - its object is not a bubbly wine that is spent, its object is not a thing, nor even a representation of a thing. Its object is the intertext composed of recurrent variants of a narrative invariant in which innocence in action or desire earns death as its retribution, and in which a metalinguistic comment underscores the habitual, and therefore meaningful, nature of this recurrence.[4]

As for the interpretant, the idea the text-sign gives rise to is that of parody, a verbal irony at the expense of the irony of Fate. An interpretant, however, is a sign, and parody is actually encoded in the text so as to insure that the proper interpretation will be repeated from one reading to the next. This encoding is done through the second intertextuality (as opposed to the first which determines the object).[5] The interpretant intertextuality here affects two intertexts, one for each of the successive events that betray the hand of destiny. The first parodies the representation of death, and the other parodies the representation of the initial guileless step that unleashes a nemesis. Here the innocent act or desire that unaccountably triggers retribution is replaced with an intertext from Alice in Wonderland[6] –a playful version of innocence yielding to harmless seduction, not without consequences: the mock animation of the bottle, its enticing voice ("Drink me," it seems to say). This is obviously outside the pedestrian universe of the character. The realism of the sketch (Billy, the cork. the thumbs) underscores by its contrast with the intellectual allusion to Lewis Carroll's magic bottle that this touch of whimsy shows the hand of the author. Intertextuality therefore not only generates the parody by poking fun at the primary intertext, but clearly focuses on the art of the work of art, rather than just on its ethical content.

The other parodic factor (the mock version of death) is encoded in the deceptive synonymy that can fool no one, in the metaphorization (the adjective dead in "sparkling[sic] wine" context) that annuls at one blow the literal mimesis of actual deaths in the primary intertext. The interpretant states that the whole subtext is a play on words, that the futility of the text compounds the futility of life which it claims to represent–the ground[7] for this sign could be "Vanity of vanities, saith the Preacher."

The preceding discussion suggests that the concept of intertextual interpretant can account for literariness in texts that hardly depart from non-literary discourse. Such texts are so devoid of rhetorical features that they would fall through the net of conventional poetics. I will now turn to the more extreme instances of the artifice as reader-response to the catachretic interpretant. Such instances are commonly dismissed as failures or as excesses of ephemeral esthetic fashions, if the texts in which we observe them belong to periods so remote that we have lost touch with their sociolect. Such has been the fate of a celebrated line from a sonnet of the Italian Baroque poet, Achillini:

Sudate, o focchi, a preparar metalli.
[Sweat, ye fire, in preparing metals.]

Ever since seventeenth-century Marinism has fallen out of fashion, an image that switches the sweat from the blacksmith's brow to the fire of his smithy has been censured as egregiously pointless. Umberto Eco picks on it as a metaphor that must disappoint because its form is feebly motivated and teaches us nothing new despite the gap between tenor and vehicle at the level of content. Eco finds the metonymic sequence fire-heat-sweat a wearisome tautology: the fire receives as its own seme the effect it has on whoever is subjected to its action (. . .) No expressive necessity (. . .) justifies the use of the verb sudare. One might very well have said, without detracting from the rhyme or the meter bruciate, o focchi (burn oh fires) . . . (the reader refuses) so much exertion in order to learn what was already known - that fire causes sweat" (*Role* 83-84). Achillini's laborious metaphor, however, no longer appears an idle exercise when it occurs to us to read it literally. For if we do, sweating is not a metonym for hard work but a plain factual statement about metal working. For sweat here only appears to mean body perspiration. In a metallurgical context, it refers to an age-old welding process used before modern soldering came in, as does German Schweitzing or French chaude suante, Italian sudare, like French chauffer à chaude or just suer as a transitive verb, and like English sweat used with apredicate, is the precise technical word for heating a metal just enough to liquefy its surface, making it sudat, so that it can be stuck — glued as it were — to another metallic surface.

The apparent metaphor thus results from the reader's misreading of a literal statement. But, of course, privileging the literal interpretation would also result from a misreading, for the sentence is so constructed as to make *sudare* a syllepsis. Grammar alone would prevent us from choosing between two mutually incompatible meanings. However, the rules of the literary genre the poem belongs to tip the scales in favor of a figurative interpretation. The literal meaning, therefore, occurs to the reader (at least to the reader still familiar with a dying sociolect) only as an afterthought. The conventions of lyric poetry (and even more so those of didactic poetry) demand that the inanimate be animated, and the animate arranged into a tableau of mythological or allegorical personae. The imperative mode of *sudate o focchi* results from a transformation similar to that which derives Tennyson's "Break, break, break/ At the foot of thy crags, O Sea!" from an implicit or potential, prosaic or objective, description like "I hear the sea endlessly breaking at the foot of the cliff." The imperative then generates a ghost personification of the fires as blacksmiths, or, to keep up with convention, of the fires as Cyclopes glistening with sweat and hammering in Vulcan's forge. I specify "ghost personification" because it never comes into its visual own. It is merely a linguistic presupposition of the verb in its normal or obvious sense of human perspiration. The mythological intertext is, if not actualized in the text, at least activated by a combination of human implication of the verb in the sociolect and superhuman implication in the genre-induced idiolect. Whereupon the literal meaning is rediscovered because the conventional figurative meaning appears to tax credibility; it is blocked by the basic sememic polarity that makes fire and water exemplary opposites. This rediscovery–retrieving the other face of the syllepsis–makes the technical acceptation into an intertext. It is now to this intertext that the ludicrous image owes compelling truth.

Clearly, this is a happy discovery. The metaphor is mimetically true instead of being conventionally true. It is mimetically true since *sweat* imputed to perspiration only disguises technical accuracy, hiding the no-nonsense discourse of applied sciences behind allegorical discourse. Contrariwise *sweat* at as perspiration is only conventionally true, true only within the logic of grammatical coherence. Its grammar enacts the rules of a game, the overtly lucid convention whereby fires are to play blacksmiths. Far from being unilluminating at the cognitive level, the metaphor is but a step (however fancifully sidestepping. however catachretic it may be) towards truth, or rather towards an image of truth. It meets therefore Aristotle's criterion for a good metaphor (SPL 101-2). Furthermore, this cognitive content is enhanced by its concealment: as a riddle, metaphor hides its teaching.

But it must be equally clear that the discovery would be an unhappy one if reading ended with it. For our find would be reductive in that we could then forget about the catachresis, drop it the way we shrug off a lie after it has been exposed. A pity, since getting there was all the fun.

Fortunately, the fact that the sign which triggers this semiosis is a *(sub)textual sign* rather than a lexical one (and that an intertext-object rather than a thing-object determines it) prevents the reading process from ending with the discovery. For the sign is generated by a syllepsis, that is, by two meanings whose competition or conflict constitutes the significance, not the triumph of one over the other (an alternation typical of intertextuality: each meaning takes turns playing intertext to the other). The sign delimits a verbal space wide enough to distribute clues to both meanings, and structured enough to permit the interpreter to oscillate to and fro between the two, without ever finding a reason to stop. Oscillation must continue because undecidable reading leads to rereading. To and fro here swings from the transitive to the intransitive construction of the verb (from the fires/Cyclopes sweating metals to fires/Cyclopes sweating, period) and back. To and fro swings the verb between being alternately the tenor and the vehicle of the metaphor.

The intertextual model suffices to show that such is indeed the reading strategy imposed upon any user of the text, and that it is endlessly circular. But in order to demonstrate that this circularity is also the test of truth that restitutes to the texts catachresis the grammaticality of its intertext, we must again try a semiotic rewrite.

As a sign, the *sudate* metaphor (or apparent metaphor, or better, the figurative-literal ecliptical trope that Achillini's conceit parades as a bona fide metaphor) is determined by one single object–the metallurgical intertext (i.e., the words designating metal working practices, each of which is the nucleus of a descriptive system).

Sudate gives rise to three interpretants: one generated by its grammatical function; the second by the homonymy of its transitive and intransitive modes of existence as a lexeme, which homonymy begets a syllepsis; and the third by the actualization of the syllepsis that divides the homonymous form into two (transforming the latter into two variants, lexical and syntagmatic, or the verb itself and the clause issuing from it).

The *first interpretant* stems from the verbal ending (*-ate* as opposed to infinitive *-are*), an index of the imperative mode. Since the verb expresses a command, it entails diegetically the characters that ought to obey it. Within the rules of the literary genre, these characters will be the mythical smiths. The first interpretant therefore implies a *Cyclops* intertext. This intertext is now the authority for Achillini's line to function as a frame, within which a conventional transcoding is permissible–the implicit translation of metalworking into mythological discourse. It is thus that the conceit is now possible, that the text is given license not to get straight to the point, to obfuscate through catachresis, to transform communication into an exercise in riddles.

The catachresis itself is produced by the second interpretant, the one arising from the homonymy of the transitive and intransitive forms of *sudare*. This undecidability is now actualized as syllepsis, that is, as two readings privileging alternately the two competing sememes hidden in one lexeme. The first sememe to be actualized is entrusted, so to speak, to the verb proper, as it begins the line, and the other sememe, being displaced outside of the verb, finds its opportunity for actualization in the sentence derived from it.

The first sememe, our *second interpretant*, imputes human sweat to the fires and these are personified as a result. The second sememe, the one that is displaced into the syntagm (a syntagm therefore equivalent to the verb, but picking up only its alternate content), generates a narrative of the consequences of the action (*a preparar metalli*). Thus bringing to the fore diegetically the idea of welding, it must be considered as the *third interpretant*.

As the third interpretant, the second sememe represents the technical sweating, that is, a synecdoche of metal working, a component of the descriptive system constituting the *object* that had determined the textual sign in the first place. In effect, the third interpretant ultimately functions as a sign referring back to that object. The circle is now closed on a return to the point of departure. Catachresis's real function is to make an obnoxious image into a circuitous route from interpretant to interpretant, towards the vindication of that image. Since the continuity of the semiosis is experienced in the circularity made possible by feedback from the interpretant to the text-sign, it takes only rereading to set the whole wheel of significance in motion.

In conclusion, I should like to make three points that have to do with the way a literary text is generated both as a continuous reference to the intertext and as a series of departures from it. As I have suggested, the gap between the two, the conflict between the text's idiolect and the grammar of the sociolect, is signaled by the imprint left on the verbal sequence by interpretants. This imprint insures the durability of their impact and their continuous perception by any reader (monumentality).

I have explained this impact by incompatibilities between the intertext-interpretant and the intertext-object. This, my first point, may seem at variance with Peirce's incontrovertible assertion that "a Representamen mediated between its Interpretant and its Object, and that which cannot be the Object of the Representamen cannot be the Object of the Interpretant" (CP 2.311). There is, however, no contradiction. Indeed, while it is true that the interpretant generates verbal sequences that interfere with those born of the intertext-object, this derivation nonetheless issues from the word that is first to encode the interpretant in the text. This lexical generator therefore does refer to the object of the representamen (i.e., to the intertext-object), but in so doing it selects and isolates a quality of that object and represents it by another sign. Thus, this interpretation makes use of a code other than that of the intertext-object. Consequently, the

interpretant generates a derivation that conflicts with that intertext, or selects a set of ungrammaticalities by the mere fact that the derivative words
belong to that other code. But despite its difference, the code does not cease
to be an amplification (in the rhetorical sense) or textual transformation of
an equivalent of the object. The resulting idiolectic peculiarities are
ungrammatical only in the sense that they are not regulated by the mimesis
of the object, but owe allegiance only to the word from which they are
derived. Ungrammaticalities are especially striking when the only connection of that word with the object is a homonymy, while its derivatives issue
from its semic content. The connection, however, whatever it may be, is
what counts and it remains intact.

   The lexical traces left by the interpretant in the text and the derivations
from these constitute a recording, a written representation of the interpretant, which may seem at odds with Peirce's insistence on the mental
nature of the interpretant (an idea, a reaction excited by the object upon the
brain. etc.: e.g. Peirce CP 2.274, 2.276). But, and this is my second point no
text literary or not can be produced without the signs registering an interpretation as well as a representation of their objects. This follows necessarily from the fact that a text is generated from a matrix by developing words
into sentences, sentences into texts, smaller units of meaning into larger
units. This is the consequence of the ad-hoc segmentation I described at the
beginning, of the creation of (sub)textual units of significance. Whether the
mode of generation is descriptive or narrative, the diegetic translation of a
sememe into a text produces isotopies and paradigms of synonyms or anto-
nyms, whose successive components run the gamut of the characteristic
features of the matrix sign (like a dictionary definition, and a dictionary
definition is an interpretant), of its presuppositions and of its entailments
(*Role* 175, 184-6; Riffaterre 1978:13, 19-21,47-80). Each actual selection and,
even more so, each gap or omission represents an interpretant (Riffaterre
1983b). To decipher these is to retrace the interpretation that gave rise to
the signs, the writer's specific view of objects that are common knowledge,
or his determination, or creation. of imaginary objects starting from signs
(Peirce CP 2.261; *Role* 181). Needless to say, the departures that separate
the text's idiolect from the sociolectic intertext or from a canonical literary
intertext insure that little will be missed of the ideas about the object that
the signs elicited and that the interpretants recorded. The only difference
between the mental interpretant, as we experience it in producing our own
messages, and the recorded interpretant of the literary text is that, in reading such a text, we reverse the sequence of mental events that resulted in its
being written. As the derivation from the intertext-interpretant opens
enough textual space to allow lexical feedback from the interpretant to
modify the direct derivation from the sign, the interpretant itself is par-
tially inscribed in the verbal sequence–a monument to the semiosis that

took place in the author's mind. A monument, but also a set of constraints on the reader's freedom, a model for *his* interpretation, that programs him to retrieve the original semiosis by decoding upstream from the genesis sequence. As a consequence of this reversal, the recorded interpretant becomes in its turn a sign of which the initial (written) sign is now the interpretant in the reader's mind.[8] Thus, text production (that is, the reader's decoding of the text) reverses the order followed in the creative process, during the genesis of the work of art.

Finally, the circularity created by feedback from the interpretant to the text suggests a compatibility between two concepts that appear at first to be mutually exclusive: that of unlimited semiosis,[9] and the definition of text as a set of constraints imposing uniform reader responses and consistent interpretation that endure despite changes in esthetic or ideological fashions. Syllepsis is by no means the only mechanism that dictates a circular reading. Much more general in its application, the concept of a new segmentation producing units of significance obeys the same law: whenever the reader is compelled by intertextuality to relate together signs that their ordinary meanings kept separate, the awareness of a semiotic transformation peculiar to the text causes him to re-read, to double-check. Each re-reading forces him to go through the hurdles of a new unacceptable decoding at meaning level. Each re-reading forces him to work at retrieving the elusive significance. This alternation is therefore a form of unlimited semiosis, but one taking place within the text's closure. Paradoxically, this instability of the decoding, this repeated inability to stop and be content with a reductive reading does not threaten the text's monumentality. In fact, the best evidence we have for this universal is that it manifests itself in the endless instability of reading, but one that, remaining circular, cannot escape the orbit of the text.

Michael Riffaterre

On Truth and Lying: Umberto Eco and Algirdas Julien Greimas

"Before that, Paul of Rimini was abbot, a curious man about whom they tell strange stories. . ... he had a strange infirmity: he was unable to write. They called him Abbas agraphicus. . . He became abbot when very young; it was said he had the support of Algirdas of Cluny" (*Rose* 421-22).

Fellow travelers and long term acquaintances, Umberto Eco and Algirdas Julien Greimas' friendship and collaboration date from the beginning of the 1960s. Indeed, they both published a chapter in the seminal volume, *Communications 8, L'analyse structurale du récit*, edited by Roland Barthes, along with Claude Bremond, Christian Metz, Tzvetan Todorov and Gérard Genette, to name but the most prominent of the contributors who were to have a major impact on the shaping of theory and methodology in the social sciences and the humanities. Greimas' contribution, "Eléments pour une théorie de l'interprétation mythique," consisted in working out the descriptive procedures for the interpretation of the narrative of myth. Within a structuralist stratificational framework, contrary to Barthes and Bremond who evacuated temporality for a logic of actions, he attempted to account for both the temporal dimension of narrative and the articulation of the form of its content. Hence, he concentrated on the problem of segmenting the text into content sequences, based on formal criteria determined at the level of expression; he defined the narrative units, paradigmatic and syntagmatic, borrowing from Claude Lévi-Strauss for the former and Vladimir Propp for the latter, and introduced the concept of isotopy, a reiterated set of semantic categories that made it possible to give a specific reading of a text; he also identified the general theoretical problem of the existence of two distinctive modes, the *deceptive mode* and the *veridictory mode*, and finally sketched out an intermediate narrative grammar, interactional in nature, between subjects, objects of value, and anti-subjects, based on the concept of the polemic and/or contractual. In short, Greimas put into place a number of elements that would lay the foundations for his semiotics of action, cognition and, ultimately, passions.

Whereas Greimas' contribution provided a micro-analytic approach to a specific myth, in his study, "James Bond: une combinatoire narrative," Umberto Eco adopted a more macro-analytic perspective, when he examined 11 novels of Ian Fleming's major oeuvre, the James Bond series. He began by situating the author's work within the tradition of the detective action novel, notably Mickey Spillane, and showed how, by abandoning psychology as the mainspring of his narrative and transposing characters and situations to the level of objective and conventional strategies, much like what occurred in many disciplines in the early sixties, Fleming unwittingly passed from the psychological method to the formal one. His next move was to focus on the first novel, *Casino Royal*, and construct a model made up of a small number of rather elementary units organized by rigorous combinatory rules. This narrative apparatus was then examined in detail, in order to determine the reasons for Fleming's widespread international success. Contrary to Greimas, who bracketed off the problematics of the receiver when describing the narrative structures of the works, Eco deliberately evaluated their probable effect on a hypothetical reader's sensitivity. He determined a combinatory of fourteen series of oppositions that allowed for a limited number of changes and interactions. These semantically invested pairs were defined as invariables around which minor pairs (variables), that were modified from novel to novel, gravitated. His penultimate move was to view the series of opposing pairs as the elements of an *ars combinatoria* governed by elementary rules, which enabled him to interpret the plot line in terms of game theory. He then linked narrative structures to ideological positions that result not as much from the structured content but from the way content is structured in the narration, ending up with considerations on the role of the reader.

From this time on, Greimas and Eco's paths continued to converge and diverge on the way to semiotics, each discussing and taking into account the other's projects as they considerably modified their initial theoretical and methodological positions. Moreover, Eco played a role in the publication of *On Meaning* (1987) by the University of Minnesota Press when, with Fredric Jameson, he encouraged one of the co-authors of this chapter to undertake the translation of a selection of some of Greimas' more important essays, in order to present the English reader with an overview of this theory and methodology. Two further volumes, *The Social Sciences: A Semiotic View* (1990), and *The Semiotic of Passions* (1993), subsequently appeared in the same series.

One of the last published homages to Eco by Greimas was his preface to "Notes sur la sémiotique de la réception" (1987), which opened with the declaration that "Umberto Eco is not an author for whom one writes a preface. He is present, he speaks. All the more so when dealing with Eco the semiotician and, as is the case here, with the interpreter of interpreters of interpretants: what shadow of meta-power could authorize this."

Greimas then stated that he reread Eco's text three times, two seriously and the third with pleasure. His first reading was "literal", and he noted how closely they coincided on essential things: "...the text exists, it is supported by its internal coherence, the purpose of its reading is both the 'identification of the author's strategic matrix' and the construction of object, text." His second reading, this time "critical", to better understand Umberto Eco's "strategic matrix": "A serious academic style, carrying along twenty or so university thinkers, shored up with references and quotes, first; the summoning up of other authorities, ranging from Saint Augustine to Ronald Regan, but along the way inviting James Joyce, Agatha Christie and Louis Borgès; an intended jumble of overlapping, complementary, contradictory opinions. A matrix of the best Baroque, in short, made up of amplifications, enumerations, of mixed styles." In his third reading, for pleasure this time, but also a profound one, Greimas stressed "The paradox of deconstruction: How a 'pretext-reading', a 'philosophical practice', that is 'magical and evocative' happens to transform itself into a 'method of textual explication'. In other words, how starting from the innocent pleasure of saying that sometimes drives the philosopher, he succeeds in establishing the status of a serious scholar while maintaining an 'everything goes'." A further pleasure was identified, this time aesthetic, that arises from the "derisory questioning that underscores Eco's text: What makes all of us run–besides the legitimate concern for our careers and vainglory–to squabble on the edge of the abyss of 'the irreducible ambiguity of the text', and of the world?" When one is aware of Greimas' deep and long lasting friendship with another Italian writer of genius[1], an essay of whose he also published and prefaced in this very same series, then one can gauge the import and the intensity of his closing comments: "This is where I join Umberto Eco, my brother in Italo Calvino. This is why I love his gesticulation and his truth" (pp. 4-5).

Although we wish to remain true to Greimas and Eco's semiotic projects, in this brief study it is impossible to cover all the points of convergence or divergence of their respective undertakings, or to dwell on the more technical aspects of the former's thought, that Fredric Jameson, in his brilliant, ludic gambit, or opening sentence of his "Foreword" to *On Meaning* (1987), describes as "..the last of the great thinkers and theoreticians of French structuralism and poststructuralism to be translated into English and presented to the American public, and perhaps in many ways the most difficult and forbidding–bristling with scientificity, as these texts are, and breaking out at all points into the graphics of formalization (equations, schemata, nonverbal symbols of variables and invariables) that always seem to the 'humanist' to draw a boundary across which one looks with frustration at the forbidden promised land of mathematics or symbolic logic, or of musical theory." (p. vi). Rather, we have chosen to examine an essay by Eco, "Strategies of Lying" (1985), in which Richard

Nixon's famous televised speech of 30 April 1973 is analyzed, and over-write it from a Greimassian perspective, thereby raising issues that are at the very heart of both their semiotics. We shall also not take into account all of Greimas's multiple readings of "Notes sur la sémiotique de la réception" but, instead, focus more on the "strategic matrix" and the "pleasure" of reading Eco.

The proper name, Umberto Eco, prefacing this essay is not an empty or innocent signifier and, without reducing it to the referent, or extralinguistic world, we would like to suggest that such a name, or signature, instead, should be considered from the point of view of referentialisation, or the procedures through which the referential illusion–what Barthes describes as the meaning effect "reality" or "truth", is constituted. At this level of analysis the signature has both an anaphoric and a cataphoric function, that is to say, on the one hand, it refers back to a series of discourses on and by Eco that attest to the competence and the performance of the subject who has written widely read, highly acclaimed fiction and theoretical work and, on the other, to the event that is about to take place, the essay announced by the title. Obviously, anyone who comes across "Strategies of Lying" for the first time will bring her/his own prior experience of reading generally, and of Eco, in particular, to bear on this specific text. In other words, to summarize Paul Ricoeur (1984-88), for whom time becomes human time only when it is articulated through narrative; and, as a corollary, narrative is meaningful insofar as it configures temporal experience through personae who act, think and feel, the reader, who narrativizes the experiential and has a pre-comprehension of the temporalized actional of daily life, *Mimesis I*, will take Eco's configuration of the mimesis of action, *Mimesis II* and, through the act of reading, will reconfigure this narrative by means of her/his pre-comprehension of the actional, *Mimesis III*. However, in reading Eco, there is no pre-comprehension, or first order rationality, without a second order rationality, that consists in schematizing the synthetic operation, in understanding the procedures that integrate multiple and dispersed actions and events in his narrative, and unify the circumstances and means, the initiatives, the interactions and the events and all the non-willed consequences that are projected in his text. In short, the signature both witnesses prior highly successful texts already appraised, and an-nounces a discursive performance to come that will be sanctioned by the reader.

Yet, how will Eco, the author, construct the "strategic matrix" that informs this particular piece? He begins with brio by elaborating two narratives. The first, entitled *Cardinal Mazarin Tells How to Simulate a Self*, deals with a seventeenth century politician of Italian origin who ruled France under the Regency of Anne of Austria in the 1640s and remained absolute master of the country until his death in 1661; the second, *The Leader of the Free World Tried, But. . .*, with Richard Nixon's aforementioned televised speech. The first is a sort of "mise en abyme", or micro-narrative that, in Gérard Genette's (1972) terms, has a proleptic function, insofar as it plays, replays, prepares and programs, at another level and another time, the manipulative strategy set in place in the second one dealing with President Nixon. In itself, this is not an uncommon literary or narrative tactic, but what sets this text apart is the way in which the enunciator constructs his very own specific meaning effect, or "truth", that will make him eminently believable as a credible witness and analyst of historical events, past and present.

First of all, one notes that the enunciator, "I", syncretises the roles of the originator of the discourse as well as that of an observer who actively evaluates and sanctions the narrative on Mazarin. Hence, the numerous deictics of person that position both the enunciator and the enunciatee with respect to the topic under discussion. However, these deictics are not simply positions, but invested, personalized, cognitivized and pathemized positions. The very first sentence, "Let's face it.", to paraphrase Émile Benveniste (1966), simulates the appropriation of all the resources of language by which the subject defines itself in an intersubjective relation. And here the relation is one of inclusion and connivance. This is immediately reiterated in the following sentence with, "What we know...", "we learned". The very same pattern of deictization occurs in the last few lines of the first paragraph, "we knew that Dumas...just imagine him...And so we trusted him." Other narrative and rhetorical devises are at play in this introductory section: recourse to the doxa, "whose name popular tradition has spelled with a single 'z'"; indirect discourse; brief non localized discourse, "whom Beaufort caricatures in charcoal and calls the 'illustrissimo facchino Mazarini'"; immediately followed by the enun-ciator's translation, "the illustrious scoundrel"; interrogations and evalu-ations that could be attributed to Alexandre Dumas himself. Furthermore, as soon as a coherent account of Mazarin is given it is immediately deconstructed, putting into doubt the relation between social reality and its repre-sentation. The enunciator's judgmental, "But can Mazarin have been such a bastard?", is at once followed by a discussion of Dumas' art of the novel, who, when speaking "of historical figures did not invent, he embellished and dramatized, yes, but he paid attention to sources, chroniclers, and memorialists, even when dealing with fictional characters" (p. 3). After this initial simulation of a real dialogical situation, in which enunciator and enunciatee are assimilated in the form of an "us" and a "we", the enun-ciating subject can assume its identity as independent ego, "I do not know whether Dumas knew. . ." Henceforth, at the level of enunciation, this first narrative on Mazarin will continue to position at a vertiginous rate enun-ciator and enunciatee, creating a level of complicity and trust. However, numerous other procedures contribute to the meaning effect, "reality", and especially, "truth". For example, the reference in the subtitle to Cardinal

Mazarin is promptly followed in the first paragraph by his Italian paronym "Cardinal Mazzarino", alluding to his country of origin. Historical and literary figures, university thinkers, politicians, philosophers, from very different times and places, are summoned up as needed in the demonstration: Mazarin, Dumas, Richelieu, the Duc de Beaufort, Anne of Austria, Buckingham,, Machiavelli, Ugo Foscolo, Croce, Baltazar Gracian, Torquato Accento, The Jesuits, Erving Goffman, and Giulio Andreotti are all mentioned in the first four pages of the tale. In addition, events such as the Thirty Years War, the Reformation, the Counter Reformation, along with titles and the dates of published works: *Vingt ans après*; the *Politician's Breviary*, 1684; *The Prince*; *The Manual Oracle or Art of Prudence*, 1647; *On Honest Dissimulation*, 1641; other toponyms, chrononyms are cited in no particular chronological order.

Yet, this strategic matrix serves two specific purposes, both of the order of cognitive manipulation. The first is, that after having positioned, re-positioned, de-positioned, manipulated and invested the enunciatee, the enunciator has progressively assimilated, the past and the present, Mazarin and the current political and socio-historical situation. This kaleidoscopic deictic machine also displaces events and personae, so that the discourse on Mazarin is projected into the now of the act of reading, into the historicity of the act of writing. And so, for example, we find Mazarin, labeled as a XVIIth century semiotician linked to a XXth century social scientist specializing in human interaction: "Mazarin is what he succeeds in appearing to be to others: he has a clear notion of the subject as a semiotic product. Erving Goffman ought to have read this book. . ." (p. 4); Mazarin the manipulator linked to actual situations in the modern world, but on closer study of the phraseology, in actual fact, the American work place: "Mazarin gives us a splendid image of how to obtain power through the sheer manipulation of consensus. How to please your own boss (a fundamental precept) and not only your friends, but also your enemies. . ."; the Manipulator folded into America's everyday life: "In this sense it is not only a portrait of Mazarin; you can use it as a catalogue of mug shots in your daily life. In it you will find people you know, whether seen on TV or met at the office. At each page, you can say, 'But I know this man!'" (pp. 4-5). The second purpose is to present the reader with a whirligig of information, a dazzling control and display of facts, figures, dates, events that, on the one hand, confirm the enunciator in his role of faultless erudition, which is indeed the case and, on the other, authentifies and sanctions the meaning effect "truth", so that what Eco writes of Dumas holds both for him and the implied reader: "And so we trusted him" (p. 3).

For us, this "piece of High Baroque theatre" of enunciatory bravado, stages complex narrative programs of "lofty theoretical rigour" (p. 4) of deceit and of simulation. In short, the text sets in play and theoretizes a semiotics of manipulation, by enacting a series of dramatizations in the mode of micro-sequences reiterating more or less the same scene. A number of dislocated sequences, at least chronologically, narrativize a succession of actions undertaken by an agent, S(1), figurativized as Mazarin, who systematically tests, and then dominates other agents, (S2). However, the success of these tests rests on implied contractual relations of a fiduciary nature, respected by the agents (S2), who are made to believe by (S1) that he too honours the trust which founds intersubjective exchange. All of (S1)'s acts are deemed morally and socially reprehensible: "Mazarin lies, breaks his promise, is late in paying debts, poisons the Duc de Beaufort's dog. . .He is cowardly base, a perjurer. . ." (p. 3), yet they always have a positive outcome. But how does he do this? What is the secret of his success? Contrary to other theoreticians of manipulation who set in place a semiotics of deception and dissimulation based on "what is does not appear", or the secret[2] as a strategy of survival–both Gracian and Accetto, two other XVIIth century political theoreticians who wrote on the topic of manipulation,[3] we are told, fall into this category–(S1) practices a semiotics of simulation, whereby "what does not appear is not", or falsehood. As a corollary though, in order for (S1) to be successful, (S2) must be persuaded that "what does not appear is not", in effect, "is what appears", or truth.

Eco opens his text with a series of micro-narratives, or performances, attesting to Mazarin's competence, before comparing him to others who wrote on the same topic. He then goes on to examine somewhat in detail the work attributed to Mazarin, made up of a string of maxims that are so many precepts on how to construct one's external image and manipulate consensus in order to obtain power. At first glance, this might amount to a semiotics of cognitive manipulation, whereby (S1) manipulates his image in order to make the other, (S2), believe that "is what appears". And obviously, this presupposes a series of modalities that inform (S1)'s performance, i.e. a certain kind of knowing-how-to, of wanting-to, of having-to and of being-able-to. Here again, (S1) has succeeded admirably, as his power and hold over the other, (S2), though often challenged, is never relinquished, until his actual death. On further examination, however, this semiotics of manipulation is, in fact, a semiotics of perception: "There is not, in this first fundamental chapter, a single maxim that does not contain a verb having to do with appearance: to show signs, to give the impression, to reveal, to look, to pass for. . . or towards symptoms or revealing signs. . ." (p. 5). In this "manual for the theatricalization of the 'self'" (p. 4), (S1), for whom seeing is, indeed, the differential trait of knowing, has become the master of signs for he knows not only how to produce them for (S2) but also how to read those generated by (S2). But again, what types of signs are these and how do they circulate? What we are dealing with here is not the unincorporated Saussurian sign made up of a simple signified and signifier, but a sign made flesh, a sign mediated by the body, the body of the self and the other. Hence the numerous references to corporality: "Don't stare at others, don't twitch your nose or wrinkle it. . .Let your gestures be few, your head straight, offer few words, allow no spectators at your table" (p.5). All signs in this universe are by definition socialized, since they are incorporated in a body politic that sets into motion regulatory mechanisms of self and other. Here, to master the sign is not only to control the body, but to stage the self by neutralizing, desensitizing, depathemizing and even attempting to disincorporate the socialized embodied sign, in order to produce the self as an external image, readable only as pure exteriority. The originality of this strategy of simulation in this world, where "is not what does not appear", is that one can attain, exercise and maintain social control only through the manipulation of the disembodied sign.

The second part of this diptych regarding Nixon's speech, as has been suggested, builds on and plays out both the enunciative strategies of the Mazarin section, and the narrative programs of manipulation. As such, it echoes and reiterates the same problematic, but with the difference that Nixon's, (S1), narrative programs do not lead to a consolidation of the Subject's situation but, on the contrary, to its dissolution. It should also be noted that the enunciative strategies of the first section, position and condition the enunciatee in such a way that Eco's analysis of Nixon's speech will be favourably received. Although Mazarin's situation and strategies of simulation have been progressively and imperceptibly assimilated and conflated into that of the American Way of Life in the first part of this analysis, it is legitimate to ask how Eco convincingly passes from an Absolute Monarchy to a Democracy in the final one?

In effect, at the very beginning of the second section, after having immediately established the homology: Dumas is to Mazarin what the mass media are to Nixon; the transition from the XVIIth to XXth century is ensured by the evocation of myth. It should be noted, though, that the homology is in itself problematic insofar as Dumas, an exemplary writer of fiction who, "when he spoke of historical figures, did not invent: he embellished and dramatized" (p. 4), is equated with the mass media, who when it speaks of historical figures. . . Yet, the homologation is not without foundation, since Alexandre Dumas (Sender, Se), the most successful and popular serial writer of the Romantic period who signed over three hundred works many of which were historical, greatly contributed to the formation of public opinion (Receiver, Re), about past European historical figures. However, contrary to Dumas who could only enter into a mono-logical relation with the historical figures in question and, hence simply act as an interpreter for posterity, the mass media, on the contrary, plays the dual role of interpretant of the interpreter (Sanction, Sa) with respect to public opinion[4] which, in a democratic system, is both Sender (Se) and Receiver (Re), as well as antisubject (S2) that enters into a dialogical relation with the actual subject (S1): ". . .faced with pressure from the media, which as yet had no specific proof, the President of the United States, unable to resist the rising tide of mere suspicion, should have to justify himself before 200 million citizens, by baring his own weaknesses and (a highly dramatic characteristic of televised speeches) his own fears and anguish." (p. 6)

The semiotic status of the President (S1) is presupposed, since he is elected by the people (Se) and must account to the people (Re). The hero, (S1), who is granted a mission of governance and is positively valorized, must exercise his authority within a sphere of actions having cognitive and pragmatic dimensions. What is also presupposed is that there exists an a priori cognitive sanction of the American people, or a recognition of the type (S1) has, or has not, up till now successfully carried out his mission. Moreover, the hero is accredited with the modal values of competence: knowing-how, being-able, wanting-to and having-to carry out his mission for the good of the people and is moralized, which as Greimas and Courtés (1982) remark "has the effect of homologizing the term euphoria with the subject with the subject and the term dysphoria with the anti-subject (hero/villain)." (p. 197).[5]

Whereas in the Mazarin section Eco dazzles the reader with his erudition and enunciative virtuosity, and brilliantly demonstrates his competence as master of narrative and expert, reliable witness, in the second episode he conjures up only a single authority, Hitchcock and three types of exemplary stories: "Little Red Riding Hood, Pearl Harbour, and The Press's 'Western'", before focusing on Nixon's speech. The enunciator's presence fades into the background, with a minimal number of inter-ventions or intrusions of any sort. Deixization is limited so much so that the enunciatee is invited to occupy a quasi static position and observe the drama as it relentlessly and inexorably unravels. In brief, we pass from the deictic extravaganza of telling to the sobriety of showing and, here, Eco's "strategic matrix" shifts from what we called "High Baroque Theatre" to sober, simplified "Classical Drama".

Furthermore, Eco analyzes the relation between Nixon and the press as a struggle between narratives with the American people, the implied sender, syncretizing the role of receiver. To counter the narrative (N1) con-structed "with the skill of Hitchcock by the press (Sa + S2), Nixon (S1) tried to regain public trust (Re) by staging a counter-story" (p. 6) (N2), that follows the traditional patterns of the mass media. The press, its narrative staged as a Western, as well as the President's tale, constructed from stories emanating from "the narrative unconscious" (p. 6) of the American public, are examined within the context of a simple Proppian perspective. From our semiotic point of view, the President's narrative program is to convince or "make-believe" his electorate that the errors attributed to him should be ascribed to careless collaborators, since he was preoccupied by negotiations with China and Vietnam and, therefore, he could not closely supervise what was happening during the election campaign. His task is to convince public opinion that he was not the "villain" but the "hero", albeit an imprudent hero, who was defending the American way of life. Nixon, to whom can be attributed Mazarin's "how to please not only your friends but also your enemies" (p. 5) certainly attempts and succeeds in pleasing his enemies, the press, with the "substitution of chess pieces. . .He did not dare to cast the reporters as 'villains'; rather, he reserved them a place among the rescuer's helpers. . ."(p. 8), thus setting in place a semiotics of cognitive manipulation, deception, where "what appears is not", or lie. This discursive machine of manipulation, characterized by Eco as "a masterpiece of rhetorical manipulation" (p. 11), on the one hand, displaces the President from the role of villain to that of hero, but on the other, though it remoralizes him by shifting the dysphoria linked with the villain to that of euphoria equated with the hero, it nevertheless has a disastrous effect.

Before the speech, public opinion in the main trusted Nixon, after the speech, in which before a "public accustomed to the narratives of the mass media. . .[he] replaced one story with another, equally spellbinding one" (p. 11), contrary to all expectations, the majority distrusted him. Examining the persuasive mechanism set in place by the President's narrative to manipulate public opinion, nothing could lead one to believe it would fail. What happened?

Eco reminds us that "the narrative construction would have been perfect had the discourse been a written text. But it was 'spoken'" (p. 11), the word was made flesh, and the passage from the medium of writing to that of multi-media institutes a different, more complex sign system. All the parameters of intersubjective enunciation come into play, including the most important one, the body, which results in a number of consequences. If, on the one hand, moralization shifts from the domain of the text to the enunciatee (Re), bringing about the possibility of dysphoric identification with the visually observed subject, on the other, the embodied sign becomes the locus, not of the coagulation of meaning, but of its seepage. In short, the character Nixon would have been completely inscribed in the narrative if, and only if, he had corresponded absolutely with the personage he was attempting to portray. What the public observes is an actor who, though he knows and speaks his lines, misses his cues and cannot control his projected image, thereby enabling the body–in the interstices of the riddled spoken text–to insert and assert itself in collusion with, and in reaction to, the unraveling narrative. As the subject's (S1) competence is grounded in the written form of another era he does not succeed in mastering the polysign system of the age of multi-media. Playing his role in front of the public (Re), the perceiving and sanctioning receiver; (S1) is unable to act out the part cast for him. Contrary to Mazarin, who exercised a body politic of control, "is not what does not appear", falsehood, here the activity of the body is not, as desired, in contradiction with the affective state of the subject. Paradoxically, we could say that the body is in perfect symbiotic relation with the instance of enunciation, "Is what appears,"[6] truth. For (S1) to convince or cognitively manipulate (Re) it would be necessary to carry out an enunciative disengagement making it possible to inscribe a body in the discourse distinct and distant from (S1)'s state of mind, or affect, "is not what appears", lie. However, the enunciator's body identifies with his state of mind, a process that imposes itself independently of all desires.

Although "The press won the first round" (p. 11), the President is not yet done. So successful is Eco's own "masterpiece of rhetorical" construction that the editor of the volume, Marshall Blonsky, is won over, convinced and, in turn, sanctions the master narrative. Not only does he project Eco's analysis into the future with his footnotes, euphorically moralizing the enunciator, but he also adds a pictorial dimension to the scriptural by inserting two complementary series of photographs that could not both have appeared in the original: the first dealing with Nixon's 30 April 1973 speech and, the second with the one of 8 August 1974.[7]

What could, at first glance, be considered a simple commentary or a palimpsetic overwriting, actually complexifies the text by introducing a new semi-symbolic sign system within a symbolic one. The editor, the subject of an effective cognitive manipulation, assumes and plays out the role of the implied reader, "And so we trusted him", by reiterating, continuing and even duplicating Eco's own analysis of the incorporated sign. He therefore serves as interpreter of the interpreter of interpretants: "The second round is almost over now. Nixon is projecting himself as the elder statesman: sagging face (the fright lines gone), pondered or ponderous declarations and the visits to China to remind his audience of the main success of his administration. The media is going along, on another American myth: 'Don't step on the fallen', or 'Give the man a break'" (p. 11). Nixon the statesman, Nixon the public figure learned through his experience with the media and staged a new strategy of cognitive and pathemic manipulation, a body politic which, according to the editor, succeeds in convincing the public and the media that "is what appears". However, the editor underscores that this is simply a role "Nixon is projecting himself as..." and that the President remains, in effect, a persona of duplicity, more at home behind the scenes of power with its secrets, falsehoods and lies than up front on the stage of truth.

Paul Perron and Patrick Debbèche

Eco and Dramatology

1. Introduction: Of Agon, a Trace

That Eco makes frequent recourse to narrative fiction is not surprising since the semiotician and the author of fictive narrative are two of the most public faces he presents to us who adore and admire him from whatever portion of himself he gives freely and with great gusto. But what is a surprising fact, to use Peirce's notable term for that which comes to us from experience and shakes us out of old habit into new play, is Eco's occasional mention of the dramatic text as representing through the work of some twentieth-century playwrights a prototype of the indeterminacy, non-finiteness, overcoding, continuous transformation, and, indeed, those marked characteristics which describe, especially, the Peircean theory of sign-process. This dynamical process is what happens to an idea or complex sign-system when the pragmatic method is used to perform its operations upon selected, featured thought-signs, so that the thought or representation of an object-thought moves, grows, becomes new meaning in the world of human values.

The reference to dramatic text which occurs now and again, in passing, in the rich corpus of Eco's work, is most often to Brecht: –his theories on drama, and especially on the *Galileo*. I have read the playscript often and have had the good fortune to see it performed several times, each with markedly different interpretations in staging, on props, and on all aspects of those personnae which, in their entirety, constitute the players of this (and every) stage-play. Whether we want to call the Brechtian voice authorial or something else in the nature of a continuum, is not my concern in this paper. Rather, I want to suggest here that Eco's inclusions of the drama in his work are not sufficiently frequent to permit one to quite imagine the drama as a configuration in his own work, however elliptical. But perhaps it is more likely that each of his mentions and uses of the drama–Brechtian or other–appears at intervals, or interludes, and then submerges in the Eco-ic mind, leaving fresh evidence of its existence and effect, or pragmatic consequences, *as a trace*.

To my knowledge Eco does not discuss the notion of trace, not as it occurs in linguistics nor in the discourse of the biological sciences: in the former, trace is that which is no longer evident in that sample of natural language under examination; and in the latter the concept of trace refers to some bit of living matter which came into existence, effected the cell which was its context and exerted such influence upon its context that a cell division occurs: it does its job and disappears, leaving only a 'trace' as consequence (Hamburgh 1971).

Eco veers close to affirming the characteristic structure of all semiotic processes as dramatistic. But to actually do so would require that he abandon his edenic — adamic — implied or tacit wish to hold onto a belief in the predictability of the world. Moreover, at the crux of this near affirmation is Eco's wanting to hold onto a kind of perfectibility, or aesthetic closure, of any complex idea regarded as a universe of thought. I am not sure, but I think Eco has ambivalent feelings on this matter: the wish for perfectibility and closure is never far from his observations of the semiotic process as nonfinite and without fixed limit.

It is my point, however, that the narrative model of discourse which Eco chooses over the dramatistic model is, at bottom, a sustained preference on his part of the *hypertactic* structure of the novel, however complex and sustaining it is of many voices. By contrast, the drama–dramatic play–is dialogic, interactive, and *paratactic* in its structure (Kevelson 1987). The hypertactic model is in western cultures identified with determinable events, whereas the paratactic model has been relegated to mere or trivialized recreation, an idea which has become attenuated to the notion of nonsignificant 'past-time.'

For Eco to shift from one model to another would require that he undertake, as his leading principle, a *paradigmatic shift*. This would be nothing short of an ideological revolution, since the structures and the values each symbolizes are antagonistic if not mutually exclusive discourse types. This is not to say that segments of dialogue are absent from predominantly hypertactic texts, or conversely, that monologue is not be found in dramatic play. But the style or type of each of these discourses are not compatible, and to espouse one, in effect, is to subordinate the other. Except, and this exception is in point, *the Peircean project, or 'quest of quests' aims to bring into new, more comprehensive relationship discrete universes of discourses and thus to create a new synthetic world of meaning.* This point would expect Eco to qualify his analysis of the use of hypothesis in discovery/detecting and to especially focus on its role in a logic of paradox. Eco does not go quite this far.

Eco does not quite affirm a genuine revolution in human values, nor does he give up the 'quest' for certainty. To do so would be to take risk as a serious matter, and to accept the irreversibility of the significant world.

Not even in his 'playing' of Sherlock Holmes and Charles Peirce against one another, with respect to the type of deduction each characteristically represents, does Eco *endorse* that which is the most 'revolutionary' or creative of the abductive possibilities he so brilliantly describes (*"Horns"* 207).

It might be noted that the risk-taking which characterizes dramatic play, especially the play of anarchic comedy, is not hypothetical, or 'overcoded abduction,' in Eco's terms; nor is it 'undercoded abduction' which Eco sees as the selection of one option from among others, all of which are 'known' and hence available for re-cognition and re-discovery but not as a sign of a genuine Becoming out of Nothing. But Peirce *does* distinguish between two kinds of nothings, or Zero Signs: the first is a result of the process of sub-traction, in which nothing signifies 'other'; whereas the second Nothing is that potentiality and possibility from which the Firstness of all quality–all perceivable general ideas–emerges. This last Nothing is boundless, free, risky, undetermined. This is not the nothing which features in Eco's analy-sis of hypothesis, but it is the bottom line–an oxymoron, I concede–a Nothing which may become Some Things and thereby turn traditional logic on its head as in a logical wonderland: a paradox revisited, a Primal Play (Kevelson 1989, 1996).

Yet Eco does again come very close to this position when he discusses the last and most important (in terms of evolving meaning out of the proc-ess of making meaning more meaningful) of his kinds of abduction. This he calls 'creative abduction.' Eco emphasizes the paradoxical nature of this kind of adducing process. He argues that it is in defiance of all traditional logic, since it brings, or invents, *'ex novo'* (*"Horns"* 207).

This genuinely creative abduction leads to and requires that the players/actors propose (or 'pose' in a quasi-positivist sense) that which may be as-sumed to support the creative Becoming. In this manner the process of accepting the element of genuine novelty — of risk and chance happening — leads to a reinforcement of an emergent future, by using the past or precedent as an invented instrument. The past is invented in order to act as a post-present and thus as a platform for a possible future. This is not a revision of the past, of history, but is an abducted historical frame of refer-ence upon which to set a *possible* future as it emerges from a *postfuture present*. The present is then set in place, is staged, subsequent to the making of future and past, in that respective order. *The present is the last piece to be set in place.*

Contradictory to traditional wisdom, the past is not a prologue, but rather, it is the future which is invented as prological. The drama is be-tween two worlds: the future and the past. The will to the future is protago-nist, and the will of the past is antagonist in this abductive drama, a drama as aboriginal as the *hieros gamos* in the primal encounter of earth and hu-man culture.

According to Eco, creative abduction differs from 'overcoded abduc-tion' precisely on the dramatic character of the former. Or so I extrapolate. The overcoded mode of abduction proceeds by connecting 'imprints' or found marks with possible causal forces which are 'known,' i.e., defined and named. Such marks are significant in a synechdocical manner (*"Horns"*

210-11). But by contrast, the creative process of abduction *makes* the very marks it uses in order to carry forward the abductive process itself.

But even this inventive creative abduction is not yet the method of a dramatistic semiotics, Eco points out. The dramatic mode is, he suggests, a meta-abduction. It is this meta-abduction which, he notes, is that which Peirce himself understands as 'an accord between mind and course of events . . . more evolutionistic than rationalist' (*"Horns"* 218).

Whereas Sherlock Holmes is always eventually 'correct,' Peirce is ever fallibilistic and 'iffy.' I am not suggesting that the Peircean abduction is a 'kabuki' play, turning in all directions, endlessly, as permitted/determined by its referent conventions. Rather it is open-ended, as kabuki is: the structure is neither ziggurat nor labyrinth, but closer to the mid-twentieth century notion of a dramatic 'happening.' Surely there is little or no resemblance between this drama-type and the so-called 'well-made play' with *its* Aristotelian beginning, middle and end: a finite curve with appropriate closure. Yet it is the older form which is the background and which serves, symbolically, as an obsolescent judgment in the wake of a Peircean 'surprising fact,' an event which calls the whole of what has been assumed to be known into question, into new perspective. In some respects, as Eco suggests, the process of meta-abduction is representative of, or a *verisimilitude* of, a Brechtian 'epical' piece of theater. The Peircean meta-abduction, as the Brechtian drama, begins by focusing on a significant issue or problem, the concern of which draws the play's personnae into unprecedented relationships. The problem catalyzes the performance. What is at stake, as becomes clear, is not the resolution of the problem, but rather the nature of the relationships brought into play. By contrast, in the well-made play it is the problem brought to light which needs to be resolved and/or redefined.

Indeed, Eco's last word on the Conan Doyle/Charles Peirce contest is that they are not telling the same kind of story after all, but they are playing different roles, representing different types of discourse, different kinds of hypotheses and possibilities. A semiotic approach, which Eco takes, reveals that at bottom there are two incomparable scripts. He then goes on to suggest that a better fit is between Galileo and Peirce rather than Sherlock Holmes/Doyle and Peirce. It is the Brechtian Galileo to which Eco explicitly refers. Thus Peirce and Galileo play out their respective misadventures, with the proverbial 'nerve for failure,' and even perhaps the will, if not to lose, yet to keep the game going.

Eco says that the main difference between Aristotelian monologic deductive argument and the Peircean dialogic abductive argument is that the former attempts to understand 'surprising facts' by working out 'a hierarchy of causal links,' whereas Peirce lifts out the middle term of the Aristotelian syllogism and recasts it as a new, noncausal function, as a hypothetical force or 'triggering device of the whole process.' According to Aristotle, the purpose of invention was to establish a 'good middle term,' while by contrast Peirce selects an arbitrary middle term as a relational nexus, a dramatic occasion, I might add, *between terms*. The Peircean hypothesis is mediator or semiotic fulcrum.

This creative abduction is a kind of protagonist, in dialogic and dramatistic defiance of traditional logical hypothesis, since it invents/creates out of nothing (*"Horns"* 207).

Such oppositional relationship is the very nature of drama, the meaning of which is the existential, experiential 'struggle' which Peirce assigns, as semiotic function, to Indexicality and Secondness. The drama is quintessentially a battle of wills, of worlds. The outcome is never given, but comes out of the interaction. The drama, as significant conflict, creates a yet-to-be encoded phenomenon. As such it is at play until classified and evolved from factive representation into symbolic representation or tool, i.e., from Index to predominantly Symbolic sign. The dramatic event is, therefore, radically distinct from both 'overcoded' and 'undercoded' abductive processes, as Eco shows us.

For my purposes here it is enough to recognize this pattern of emergence of the topic of drama in Eco's writings without at the same time feeling obliged to investigate, at this time, why it is as it is and not otherwise.

My interests in theater and the dramatic text go deep, and my experiments with writing dramatic script precede and underscore the points of view I bring to semiotics, to Peirce's pragmatic method in particular, and to Eco's important concepts of openness and overcoding in aesthetic texts, in point in this paper.

Given my orientation and well-known Peircean agenda I wish to turn the spyglass around, as it were, and look through the other end. I attempt to gain insight into some significant platforms of concurrence between Eco and Peirce with respect to the dynamical indeterminacy and openness of semiosis by using the drama as a many-faceted lens: an instrument for observing how signs grow, rather than for using selected principles of semiotic theory to explicate dramatic texts.

In brief, I want to note that in my early studies of drama, from the perspective of semiotics, I classified the system of dramatic dialogue as one paradigm among others within an over-arching concept of aesthetic paradigms (Kevelson 1975). At that time I was focusing on the special influence of the Prague Linguistic School and cross-referentiality, on distinctions between closed and open texts. I made good use of Veltrusky's and Karcievski's notable studies on theater and the significant interaction of all players. All actors including props, audience and the several styles of stage link or mediate audience with actors (Veltrusky, in Garvin 1964).

Without digressing too far here, I want to say at the outset that I still hold the view that drama, in its dominant feature, is characterized by interactions and patterns of plots or transformations and mutations (*muthos*, Ridgeway 1904/ 1915:406). I go further and suggest that the drama is the representation of the semiotic process, par excellence, with respect to the special relations which connect artworks with events and institutions of actual human affairs. On the level of human affairs and social life I see The Law as linked with drama, as related with drama via the medium of human disputes and antagonisms (Kevelson, 1991, 1993, 1994). Indeed, The Law as idea and in its practice represents the idea of theater, especially of the Indexical sign-function manifest in dialogue, i.e., in adversarial and inquisitorial interactions. Brecht's Galileo, as many of his plays, is foregrounded against the context of conflict of law, of ideological oppositions between instantiated law and other legitimations. Eco's references to Brecht constitute a pattern of his thought, I suggest, so broad that the design is visible only in part, that is, to one who presumes to take Eco at mere face-value, as an iconicity.

Just as some undercurrent of Eco's continuing concern with the function of the drama in semiotics percolates as an irrepressible insight, if I may so fancy, my own experience in scripting and exploring the many masks of drama also surfaces through this paper as a recollection, a recognition, a trace. Again, the Peircean emphasis on the dialogic, interactional nature of all semiosis is clearly dramatistic, but mostly by implication.

2. TENSION AND SIGN-PRODUCTION

When Eco speaks of sign-production we may, with minimal modification, substitute the Peircian term, pragmatic method. Eco says, "We may define as invention a mode of production whereby the producer of the sign-function chooses a new material continuum not yet segmented for that purpose and proposes a new way of organizing (of giving form to) it in order to map within it the formal pertinent element of a content type . . . a semiotic mode of production (is defined as that action) . . . in which something is mapped from something else which was not defined and analyzed before the act of mapping took place. We are witnessing," he goes on to say, "a case in which a significant convention is posited at the very moment in which both the functives of the correlation are invented" (*TS* 345, 350).

The "we" refers, presumably, to the inquirers–us–who perform the role of addressee or audience in relation to that which is before our eyes, which is appearing or 'featured' as players. The idea which we are attending is phenomenal, imagistically and iconically present–re-presented or made present–as Peirce uses the term 'dialogism' in the sense that Vico did, to refer to an evidentiary complex piece of significance that is brought into the judgment theater (court of law, specifically) to transform the virtual icon into a virtual fact or index (Kevelson 1987). The notion of 'mapping' in Peirce is, as it is used here by Eco, only in some respects (Kevelson 1993).

Mapping and staging are related. The former refers to a choice of iconic representations which do not replicate the object but which model it in ways that point up selected purposes for seeing it and for establishing a frame for a point of view. The latter marks the ground or locus–the space as a bounded context or frame–upon which an action is to be performed. Both map and stage, or ground, permit configurations since they are topical:–definable topics (as in both the Topics of traditional rhetoric and in the surfaces of geometry). Plots, then, are patterns upon a ground, or transfigurations: shifts and rises and turns on a terrain.

The order of a play–its associating or paradigmatic arrangement–is a communicative sign to its audience at a level different from the way signs communicate information between the participants on stage. Within the play, the dramatic relations are equivalent to a semiotics of syntax; at a higher level, dialogue semantically reinforces its syntactic structure; at the level where the play influences the judgment of the audience, that is, conditions its habitual mode of perception (in Peirce's sense of 'judgment') its semiotic function is pragmatic.

In effect, the structure is not be viewed as a State, but as a process of Becoming; this implies a continual shift in perspective from functions which appear as interactions, extending in space, as alternately stabilizations and deformations, relative to their before and after positions, syntagmatically. The purpose in constructing 'models' of language is to be able to use them as ciphers–as Signs–which relate to the real world. The meaning of 'use' here corresponds to the meaning of 'function' in Prague School theory and method. Because the word function is homonymous with the term for 'correspondence between two mathematical variables,' its intended meaning of 'task' and 'role' becomes obscured.

Cartography and mapping play an explicitly important role in Peirce's semiotics (see mss 1349-1355, and, in passing, throughout his other writings). But staging is not explicitly used by him. I take liberty in suggesting we may presume that in Peirce's thought a stage refers to any space — graphed, bounded, defined–upon which ideas are shown to interact, as he himself shows with respect to his Existential Graphs (see Kevelson 1987).

The concept of a stage, or place of performance, implies a distinction between that which is staged and that which is unstaged, i.e., between the marked actors and the audience, between the framed inner and the outer. In the experimental drama of the 20th century this 'line' between players and viewers is blurred, and becomes almost immaterial when we move from absurd theater, to 'happening,' to the cyberstage.

This precarious balance or semiotic tension is presupposed, however imperceptible it may be. Eco says, in point, that this tension is an aspect of

aesthetic openness, and thus is integrally involved in the process of significance evolving, changing, growing. This tension is always an interactional
process. This process is that same dynamical method of process of Peircean
semiotics. The display of this tension is described by Eco as an infinite
complex of significance that grows n-dimensionally, and is not at all confined to the elemental, to the emotional. Rather, as he refers to Brecht's
theoretical writings, Eco indicates that 'dramatic action is conceived as the
problematic exposition of specific points of tension' (Role 55).

In Brecht's plays it is not the play which solves the posited problem, i.e.,
'devises solutions,' but it is the audience which 'draws its own conclusions'
from what it has observed, from how it has interpreted the map or has
estimated the amount of meaning so staged (see Role, above, at p. 55). But
the problem, laid out upon a noneuclidean topography, is not a fixed and
unchanging problem; it shifts and moves, and is, therefore, not ever wholly
solvable, says Eco. The problem is indeterminate and 'open.' Its encoded
paradigms are, therefore, open as well. They are infinitely interpretable,
like a Peircean idea which grows endlessly, as long as inquiry continues.

Eco goes on to say that drama such as Brecht's is an example of an intentional ambiguity, or so I extrapolate. It does not lead to a certain goal or
conclusion, but to a provisional and ad hoc judgment only. This provisional solution may be reopened at any time, each time the play is performed. So the process of inquiry is continuously activated and reactivated.
"In every century," says Eco, "the way that artistic forms are structured
reflects the way in which science or contemporary culture views reality"
(Role 57).

The systems of 'play space,' 'logical space,' and living space (in daily,
ordinary life) are assumed to co-relate in any historically-framed total social
system; the relationship between systems is considered to be hierarchically
ordered, but ordered differently at different times. Each type of space-
frame, for example, functions as a sign but the predominant sign feature of
each specific space-frame is sometimes iconic, sometimes indexical, and
sometimes symbolic in relation to the overall social system. Analogous
with the function of the aesthetic text as a marked sign in a 'defined' social
system, each system competes for dominance, or foregrounding, against
the background of the entire social network (Kevelson 1977).

Further, I observe that systems of Law and Order conceal their play
origins by translating the terms of 'play space' to the discourse of 'logical
space.' The element of play is apparent when we note how juridical systems
contain, as integral with their total structures, the means of healing their
own ruptures, and of acting in self-restorative and self-generative ways.
Conflict and opposition are implicit in any code of law; periodic reconciliation of the legal contest is implicit also. Ultimately, all functioning, operative bodies of Law rest upon public consensus and the people's acceptance

of rule-governed, rule-generating social behavior. Language, law, and social organization were the bones, brains, and blood of medieval society. The nerves, as the centers of sense, are signified by play activity (Kevelson 1977).

The dramatic play, as Appearance, is simultaneously illusion and disclosure, I suggest. The play as Sign frames the structure of the action on the dramatic stage–frames its plots–so that it achieves its intention, its deliberately ambiguous intention, by disrupting a conventionalized or symbolic appearance of order, of an ordered habit of expectation. It accomplishes a 'dissociation of sensibilities' which brings about recognition of an emergent new order, new meaning or value.

The appearance of a new order appears strange and unfamiliar. Since it is seen as grotesque it elicits for the viewer a protective pleasure. That which seems incongruous, foolish, absurd, belongs to the realm of the Comic. Comedy both affirms and undermines the State. In the indeterminate drama of this century the mode of the Comic is anarchic comedy: it is the voice of the rebellious puppet, in Durrenmatt's sense, who cuts free from the puppetmaster and says, 'nobody plays us' (Kevelson 1965).

In Peircean terms, the action on the stage is analogous with a sign or representamen in relation to its referent ground. The personnae play against a ground. This ground is the Immediate Interpretant to which the interacting protagonist and antagonist refer. The viewer, or addressee, connects with the play. In the mind of the viewer is created a new idea. The action between players and audience is predominantly Indexical, just as the performance is predominantly Appearance or Iconic. The relation between problem and solution is provisionally final, as an emergent Symbolic value representing consensual compact between observer and observed.

The Peircean interpretant–Immediate, Dynamic, or Final–in any and all stages of its process never represents its object completely, but always leaves open a question, a possibility, a surplus meaning. In Peirce's words, the interpretant illuminates an idea of the object as seen against an idea or 'ground of the representamen.'

The Peircean pragmatic method, which is the way ideas evolve, as relations seen against a ground and transmitted to another who recreates and reinterprets, i.e., re-presents the idea against its ground, proceeds by certain movements. These stagings are rhetorical strategies or tactics–ploys of the pragmatic method–which Peirce identifies with what he called Speculative Rhetoric, or the theory of that Methodology which constitutes the Praxis of the Theory of Signs: Semiotics (see Kevelson 1995).

This Speculative Rhetoric or Methodology, is the *doer* of certain acts: 'Its tasks is to ascertain the laws by which in every scientific intelligence one sign gives birth to another, and especially one thought brings forth another' (see Peirce, mss 318; and Kevelson 1987, 1990).

Referring to the role of dilemmatic constructs in evolving new ideas, Eco recalls that it is the principle of nonresolved disfunction which permits open inquiry to continue. He says disjunction permits open inquiry to continue. . ... He further says that the term, 'perceptive ambiguities' is used to indicate "the availability of new cognitive positions which fall short of conventional epistemological stances and which allow the observer to conceive the world in a fresh dynamics of potentiality before the fixative process of habit and familiarity comes into play" (*Role* 59).

In similar fashion Peirce also discusses how new ideas force their way through interstices, mere possibilities or cracks in the edges of existing, settled habits of thought understood as defined universes of discourse. The emergence of new ideas is always a struggle or an Agon. It is predominantly indexical, representing experience. Such struggle between habitualized states and revolutionary possibles is dramatic. New experience forces itself upon us, superimposing the novel on the known, creating a climate or ground of ambiguity. Surprise destabilizes, unsettles. Our whole system responds in effort, as a bracing, a tension, a mobilizing of all our existential forces, such that the physical feeds into the nonphysical, and visceral response is translated into an image, an appearance, a something inwardly pictured. The new appears as spatial, as is the ground spatial. But this space is also non-linear upon which the *quality* of the surprising thing occurs.

Although pragmatists are divided in their approach to many ideas, they are unified in the notion that the physical and the mental are but two kinds of *organizations* of the significant. But at the conceptual level of organization significant meaning becomes accessible to the operations of pragmatic/rhetoric tactics and transformations. The physical response to the unexpected represents a receptivity, an openness. The conceptual openness equivalent is inquiry: a waking to the idea of the possible (CP 5.478-79). Inquiry takes the form, first of all, of a conjecture, a free and unbound guess. Every new idea begins as a conjecture. "Every conjecture is equivalent to and is expressive of such a habit, that having a certain desire one might accomplish it if he could perform a certain act" (CP 5.480).

Although Eco is not speaking of the drama in particular, but of the aesthetic work in general, his thought is especially pertinent to dramatic performance: "The moment that the game of intertwined interpretations gets under way, the text compels one to consider the usual codes and their possibilities . . . the aesthetic text becomes a multiple source of unpredictable "speech acts" whose real author remains undetermined, sometimes being the sender of the message, at others the addressee who collaborates in its development" (TS 272-76).

Throughout this entire section on sign production Eco and Peirce, to whom he refers, seem to be engaged themselves in a kind of interchange, where the differences between them are subtle but important. I don't think that at this point in his exposition of Peirce that the full impact of Peirce's dynamic pragmatism is accepted by Eco. Thus, the drama as vehicle and as representation of the drama as sustainable, indeterminate tension, is not confronted by Eco, head-on. But it surfaces, now and again.

In some respects, it seems to me that Eco is reluctant to give up the hold on stative grasps of semiotic 'moments' or events. For example, where he closely, with acute sensitivity, examines the Peircean concept of openness, he observes that the 'depth' of a term–a universe of discourse represented by a complex sign in other words, "refers to its intension, or the sum *total* of its intensionality," which is the sum total of its semantic content. And he continues, by noting that each term or system of marks or features increases as our knowledge of the idea grows. The rheme of each term is like a lodestone, Eco says, which draws into it "all the new marks that the process of knowledge attributes to it" (*Role* 186). What he misses, in my view, is the dramatic process as such, since it is the action which, as *interaction*, carries the meaning of its motion–*e-motion, com-motion, motivation* etc.–in an ever-evolving, opening, spiraling configuration, in contemporary but not in classic drama or even in the so-called well-made play. It is only when we come to the mid-twentieth century that the Peircean notions, together with the significance of a quantum science with no fixed referent, can be touched as it passes, but not grasped, not quite. . .. In my opinion it is Peirce's logic of relatives which is the appropriate logic of dramatic art in general, and it is his logic of paradox which is the structure of the drama of our own times.

Eco's chapter on "Peirce and the Semiotic Foundations of Openness" (*Role* 199) is itself quintessentially a dramatic exchange between two powerful players. It is a dialogue of which we hear but one voice. Eco's. I hear, in the background, an unexpressed but clear allusion (or so I create in my mind) to Strindberg's unforgettable one-acter: *The Stronger*.

3. INNER AND OUTER

Peirce begins his serious work with early testimony to the protosemiotic thought of the poet Schiller whose essays on aesthetic play came to constitute for Peirce the basis of his life's work (Kevelson 1987, 1993). The idea of play — of what he later called 'pure Musement' — came to represent the connective force between so-called states of ideas, states of symbolized concepts, as *interludes*. The rational sequence of numbers represented in Peirce's schema fixed and statal ideas defined for the *time being*, while the 'subterranean' or subsurface level represented a-lineal continua. The sequence of enumerated states on the surface were 'rational,' according to Peirce. The cohesive force was irrational, not confinable to bounded states. This dialogue between rational and fluid playtime occupied Peirce and constituted a theme that ran through his work, even through his last writings.

As late as 1906, in the last decade of his life, Peirce observed that "Every sane person lives in a double world, the outer and the inner worlds, of percepts and the world of fancies. . . ." (cited by Buchler at page 283, and printed also in *Collected Papers*, 5.11-2; 464-8, 470-96).

This observation occurs in the context of yet one more attempt for Peirce to explain what he means by the pragmatic method, and how this method of pragmatism is dramatistic, agonistic, engaging inner and outer in the problem of transforming/renewing/creating habits of truths, i.e., habits of value and meaning.

Indeed, Eco takes up this conflict of inner and outer in his own memorable discussion of the 'subject of Semiotics.' Here he asks what the role of the 'acting subject' is, since it is this 'acting subject' which has a kind of 'ghostly presence' throughout his *Theory of Semiotics*, he says, and must finally *Appear* (TS 314).

Let us be clear about what is meant by the term 'subject' as Eco uses it here: It is not a person. It is not a grammatical function. It is not an egoistic self-reference. It is not a static concept. It *is*, says Eco, a position in relation to something. He says that "This subject is a way of looking at the world and can only be known as a way of segmenting the universe and of coupling semantic units with expression-units: by this labor it becomes entitled to continuously destroy and re-structure its social and historical systematic concretions" (TS 315).

It is the empirical, externally observable, perceivable 'subject' which is the maker of such processes that permit communicative and other signifying process to happen, Eco says. To say that the empirical subject is not dual, but is doubled, is his way of emphasizing the basic relational reality of all semiosis. He stresses that this doubleness is not a metaphysical 'given' but is a 'methodological one' (TS 316). The external, or the manifestation of the 'subject,' is relational with, and not merely the obverse of, the whole interactional process which constitutes the process of all semiosis.

At this important point he affirms, and is affirmed by, Peirce, who remarks that it is the external symbols of language which provide the materiality of thought. But this material could not exist if it were not for their having been invented and produced by the semiotic persons who first imagine them, out of conjecture, out of response to the world.

We begin with some aspect of the Hieros Gamos, Peirce suggests: a rupturing of the bonded surface of the earth, and a celebration of that rupture which is both reparation, mourning, and something else: a surplus that comes out of the cultivation of this breach, this Game or Agon. We begin with the fiction of the Person and the fiction of the World, and with our dramatization of the juncture of these fictive personnae. People and their words reciprocally interact to teach one another, Peirce said. And "the word or sign which man uses IS the man itself. For, as the fact that every thought is a sign, taken in conjunction that life is a train of thought, proves that man is a sign; so that every thought is an *external* sign, proves that man is an external sign . . . the man and the external signs are identical . . . the man is the thought" (CP 5.313-314).

But in the sense that each semiotician gets outside himself/herself, it is especially the dramatic production which shows us how it is to violate the ancient laws of thought, the old static laws of identity, *such that one may be and not be*, such that it is possible to both be the 'Subject' and to be 'outside the Subject,' in Levinas' notion (see Levinas 1987/1993:151-158).

It is the agon which re-presents relations of perception to fantasy in its primitive forms: We relive the moment of significance emerging, of Firstness in Relation, Value experienced as the overflow of Freedom (see Levinas, above, at 155).

Peirce transforms the 'I-It' relation to an 'I-Thou' relation: — a subject/ object relation to a subject-subject relation — early in his long career (see Kevelson 1987, 1993). This semiotic shift of viewpoint (in Jakobson, Veltrusky and others, in 1967, 1964 respectively) transforms stage props into 'subjects' for the actors, and converts actors into referent or focal subjects or 'properties' of situations and events: ". . . a given object in one situation is part of the set or costume and in the next becomes a prop. . .. In reality, however, its function is determined by the antinomy of two opposing forces contained within it: the dynamic forces of action and the static forces of characterization. Their relationship is not stable; in certain situations one predominates, in others the other. Sometimes they are in balance" (Veltrusky, at 83-91). In tension we know a precarious dramatistic balance. When Eco speaks of the double aspect of codes (*TS* 299, n. 3) he emphasizes that iconic codes in particular are complex and 'double' (*TS* 302, n. 18).

The motion of inner and outer occurs also in relation to the performance as such, as medium between player and audience. Every performance is a kind of rehearsal: a reliving of a death or a solution that never comes to be, I suggest. Bloch, for example, refers to the concept of rehearsal, in the Brechtian sense, in which the role of the play-maker is to create the drama as a pragmatic instrumental crafter of paradigms, i.e., of value-systems (see Bloch on Brecht, 1988:225-26).

This inner-outer relationship, especially in the Brechtian play, is explicated in a splendid paper by Tom Beebee, in which he discusses how the play moves from its outer frame to its internal plays, where each sub-play is a plot, continuously transforming, changing. Beebee describes also the 'doubling process' in Brecht, in particular in the *Good Woman of Sezuan* (Beebee 1992:47).

Beebee explores the Brechtian corpus to show the plays within the play. The several outers and inners of the subject, Play, is a way of infusing the 'Theaters' of Law with a dramatic "crises in legimation" that the playwright sets in motion. Beebee makes his case that it is the 'judicial wrangle' which provides the possibility to "create a picture of reality" (Beebee, above, 48). Thus the fantastic court, representing the actual law courts or judgments of the people, brings a perceptual sharpness into a juncture with apparent fictionalized inner trial of *Azdak the Judge/Actor*.

In point here Eco, referring to Lotman's theory of codes, describes Lotman's notion of code as a manual or how-to handbook with rules for generating meanings in endless, nonfinite productions. This results in overcoding or extracoding which enables participants in the sign-making performance to select from among a variety of possibles a *selected set of possibles*. Extracoding results in such freedom of choice: "the multiplicity of codes, contexts and circumstances shows us that the same message can be decoded from different points of view and by reference to diverse systems of inventions" (*TS* 139).

I want to conclude here with a question raised by Eco, which is as unsoluble as the questions raised by any indeterminate play: He asks, "Is it possible to use the concept of possible worlds in the analysis of the pragmatic process of actualization of narrative structures without assuming it in a merely metaphorical way?" (*TS* 218).

My response, as I suggested earlier, is that narrative depends upon the metaphoric connection to join possible worlds, whereas drama itself *becomes* a relation of possible worlds by means of its cross-reflexivization moving *between* the inner and outer, in the manner of a moebius strip, with no clear demarcation of either as outer or inner.

In brief, the connection between Eco and drama must be seen as one of implication, of ellipses and even of the 'occult.' Yet in what he chooses to connect with Peirce it is clear that the dialogic, interactional mode or style of semiosis is one he fully engages with.

Eco says of Peirce: "The system of system of codes, which could look like an irrealistic and idealistic cultural world separate from the concrete events, leads men to act upon the world; and this action continuously converts itself into new signs giving rise to new semiotic system" (*Role* 195).

We know today that there is no turning back, that time is not reversible, that we are not medieval characters, but are actors with many masks. And we know that parallel lines *do* meet, that space *does* bend, that we may come face to face with ourselves in a time-space Euclid never dreamt of. Thus we are, indeed, dramatistic. Our semiosis represents such conflictual, indeterminate, massive-productions of meaning, and always a firstness and a Freedom and a plot.

Eco wisely reminds us to look at Peirce as "not only a contradictory thinker," but, he says "he is a dialectical one, and more so than he is usually believed to be" (*Role* 195).

Roberta Kevelson

Esoteric Conspiracies and the Interpretative Strategy*

The present critical debate focuses on the role of the interpreter who can be seen shifting between two extremes, dangerously near the edge of the deconstructionist whirl or firmly anchored to the objectivity of the text.

In this debate the literary theories interlace with the philosophical ones, and criticism is in danger of getting lost in the labyrinth of its numerous and divergent tracks, which can lead to the unique and absolute textual truth or, in the opposite direction, to the never-ending replacement of meanings.

The predominant question is: does there exist a legitimate interpretation and therefore a watershed which would distinguish a true and verifiable reading from the metastatic explosion of an analysis which spreads *ad libitum*?

Eco, looking for an answer, has chosen to work experimentally with a group of scholars on a number of texts which turned out to be most useful in verifying the theory: the esoteric interpretations of the *Divina Commedia*, a chapter of Dante criticism which is peculiar although not negligible, never legitimated and always left aside by the official critics. The esoterics give in fact an unmistakable evidence of a kind of analysis to be regarded as illegitimate: a misreading which induces in readers (of esoteric writings and of Dante) an instinctive distrust. Their excess makes it easy to identify the mechanism underlying the analysis, the macroscopic distortions which arouse suspicion in those who are not esoterics, the waste of energy of a reader who doesn't respect, in the interpretative strategy, the *intentio operis*.

Eco's research about '*semiosi ermetica*' begun in the academic year 1986-1987, during a course held at the University of Bologna. The first results of this study appear in the introduction to the book under review (edited by Maria Pia Pozzato) which brings together the essays of seven authoresses (Cinzia Bianchi, Sandra Cavicchioli, Maria Lacalle, Helena Lozano, Claudia Miranda, Maria Pia Pozzato, Regina Psaky); the complete research is discussed in *I limiti dell'interpretazione*, published by Eco in 1990.

However, Eco's studies about *'criteria to legitimate an interpretation'*[1] date back to 1962, when his book *Opera aperta* is issued in Italy. During this long period, the three roles proposed by the theory of communication–the author, the text and the reader–have been considered by Eco in different ways. In *Opera aperta*, opposing the contemporary critics who believed in the absolute supremacy of the text, he shows that it is necessary to emphasize the interpretative function of the reader who has to collaborate with the text. Eco confirms this in *Lector in fabula* (1979), while today, facing the performance of deconstructionism, he makes it a point to balance the interaction between *intentio auctoris*, *intentio operis* and *intentio lectoris*.

In *I limiti dell'interpretazione* the scholar declares this strange situation: in 1962 he was accused of allowing too much freedom to the reader, now of emphasizing the textual objectivity.

Actually, in Eco's opinion criticism has to reach a balance in order to avoid being caught either in the web of fundamentalism, which searches for the ultimate meaning, or in the web of skepticism, which only finds uncertain signals, doubts that have to be explained with other doubts.

Therefore, Eco says that Valery's verse 'il n'ya pas de vrai sens d'un texte' doesn't mean that one can 'use' a text as he wants. It's possible, and perhaps amusing, to read *De imitatione Christi* supposing it is by Céline (following Borges's invitation), but it is useless: this kind of reading in fact is completely arbitrary, because it isn't supported by *intentio operis*. Valéry's verse suggests on the contrary that it is possible to interpret a text in a plurality of ways (sometimes also contrasting), searching for the plurality of meanings that the author has instilled (*Limits* 23).

So, once again the matter hinges upon the relationship between the reader and the text: how far can the interpretation of the reader, who interacts with the text, legitimately go? What is legitimacy of interpretation?

Reading the interpretations of the *Commedia* offered by the esoterics, the non-adept becomes convinced that if 'it is impossible to say which one is the best interpretation of a text', it is nevertheless 'possible to say which ones are wrong' (*Limits* 107).

Proceeding in line with the indications given by this sort of negative theology, the seven co-authoresses of *L'idea deforme* seek to find proof of excess in the interpretative drift. The fact that the answers given by the seven scholars are not always univocal, and that sometimes they are clearly contrasting, confirms the complexity of the semiotic problem analyzed.

Let us consider first of all one of the reasons Eco chooses the field of what he calls *'semiosi ermetica'* as the model of unlimited interpretation (*unlimited* not according to the idea of Pierce, but as theorized by the deconstructionist school, with its various positions).[2]

Hermetic thought is based on an analogic vision that connects the micro- and the macrocosmos; the chain of associations that can be created (between natural world–sublunar world–spiritual world) becomes a never-ending process which leads one to read behind each aspect of reality (to whatever sphere it may belong) a further meaning which in turn recalls something else, in an unlimited process.

The text of the world–and the world of the text–thus becomes the object of an endless reading and interpretation, in the effort to search for the secret there implied: the words conceal hidden meanings, which are associated with prima signa in an endless process; anything can refer to anything.

The hermetic critic, often in bad faith, is adept at discovering unexpected associations, playing with the text, deliberately concealing what does not appear to be functional, underlining, even distorting, what serves his ends.

The process is one which Eco, with an evocative image, defines as a 'theatre of mirrors': to the eyes of an esoteric the universe appears to be a continuous mirroring of everything in everything; it is underneath this interplay that the Secret is hidden.

Only the adept can approach the secret, but at the same time (and here the paradox of hermetic positions becomes plain) the secret must continuously elude understanding; comprehension would automatically reveal the error. In fact, the secret must never cease to be such, otherwise the whole construction would collapse. The interpreter has become the reader of that which is not interpretable because it is a secret, and not because the truth doesn't exist, as in the opinion of deconstructionists.

His enthusiasm leads the esoteric critic to lay his cards on the table so that it becomes possible to single out quite easily the false steps which were necessary for him to arrive at so misleading an interpretation.

The esoteric has a specific method when he chooses examples or quotations: he may opt to quote continuously in order to overwhelm the reader; or to rewrite the text studied using an oriented paraphrase; or to remove a quotation to a different context so that it loses its original meaning. Furthermore, a corollary of statements, which demonstrates that it is the texts speaking for themselves and not the interpreter that is reading subjectively, confirms that the interpretation is obvious. Another device of the hermetic is to start his research by proposing to the reader a number of suppositions which are then gradually made to seem certitudes, although no demonstration is provided; or he may use what is called 'anaforizzazione discorsiva', whereby he continues to repeat or anticipate his argument, convincing the reader, through redundance, that his assertions are legitimate simply because they have been put forward from the outset.

So, in line with such strategy, the trick is to present as true that which is not–i.e., by including in the final reconstruction of the interpretative journey elements which the reader in fact never encountered during that journey.

The interpretation therefore inevitably tends to an aim which is unrelated to the work studied, which means that the lector projects his intentio–with strong ideological motivation–on that of the opera and of the auctor (and Dante becomes a mason or an initiate of the most diverse and peculiar secret sects).

As underlined by Eco, it is obvious that not only in hermetic criticism, but in any interpretative process the reader must start from a hypothesis which inevitably engenders a system within which some elements of the text–otherwise inexplicable–make sense. Let us, like our seven authoresses, give an example from the reading of Dante.

When a critic like Maria Corti (1989), analyzing Canto XXVI of the Inferno (the Ulysses canto), shows the link that connects three metaphors found in these verses–sailing, flight, fire -, she starts from an interpretative hypothesis which leads her to look for the influence of a particular philosophical current (that of Averroism) in Dante's poem.

Having found in many passages evidence that Dante had read the philosophers concerned, she goes on to compare their texts with the episode of the 'folle volo' of Ulysses. Enlightened by those new sources, the three elements–sailing, flight, fire (which were at first sight unrelated)–can be related to each other, since all three elements are used to represent intellectual transgression.

The legitimacy of interpretations is effected by the textual verification that shows unambiguously that Dante had indeed read the texts in question.

In conclusion, a hypothesis, in order to become a legitimate interpretation, must be built upon clear proofs given to the reader.

This particular canto of the Inferno has been interpreted by the official critics in a variety of ways–sometimes contrasting, all more or less legitimate3.

But what is it that gives them the mark of legitimacy? The fact that they are always within what Eco calls 'l'isotopia semantica pertinente': the context must give the reader a guideline that will set the boundaries within which to move in the oscillation of interpretation (which becomes wider the more complex the interpreted text is).

To return to our example from Corti, the isotopia upon which the analysis is based is pertinent, as sailing, flight, and fire are a metaphorizing of the same metaphorized: the speculative transgression of those who go beyond orthodoxy. On the contrary, the isotopia of an esoteric like Guénon is not pertinent: he makes so bold as to explain the symbolism of the Graal in terms of an unrestrained eteropica enunciation, saying that it is 'the heart of Christ; a vase; the cup containing the blood of Christ; the third eye of Shiva; the center of the world; the garden of Eden; a book; a triangle with the point facing down; a heart in a triangle; a rose; a crescent'.

214 ESOTERIC CONSPIRACIES AND THE INTERPRETATIVE STRATEGY

Earlier we spoke of the complexity of the semiotic problem discussed in Pozzato's volume. Considerations on the relationship between reader and text convince Eco that it is necessary to deny an excessive interpretative freedom, as the text itself sets some limits (Eco adds that even the wildest deconstructionist must admit that some interpretations are unacceptable); however, we find in *L'idea deforme* that this exhortation to balance and caution is not followed all the time.

Thus, Sandra Cavicchioli, who studies Pascoli's work on Dante, appears to be more susceptible to relativity of interpretation: she denies that there exist objective constraints on the interpretation of a text, and is convinced that the readings depend on 'a look, on the questions put, on the observation angle' and thus on the intentio of the reader: she concludes that 'our knowledge can be only hypothetical'.

The statement of Regina Psaki is stronger: in the last essay she studies the relationship between official and esoteric critics of Dante's work; she compares *good* and *bad* interpretations, coming to the conclusion that 'the validity of a method and of the result is contractual and agreed, rather than inherent and ontological' (recalling the Kuhnian notion that a community that shares similar interpretative strategies shares the same way of reading). This is a relativist position from which we can infer that any interpretation is legitimate, as long as it is supported by an agreement.

This way the focus is moved to the reader, simplifying (we think excessively) interplay between the *intentiones* of author/readers/cultural context. The consequence of placing legitimacy within the consensus of the readers is a weakening of the bond represented by the literal meaning, by the coherence of the text, and by the will of the author.

There is in this book a convincing conclusive chapter to the volume by Alberto Asor Rosa, who, from a different point of view and according to principles different from those assumed by semiotic research, brings the argument back to the wise caution of Eco.

Asor Rosa does not accept the interpretation which underlines many of the seven essays, according to which the neglect suffered by esoteric criticism is caused by its excess. He attributes such neglect to the *arbitrio* that comes into play every time an interpretative strategy does not achieve documented verification, recovering the necessary link between author, reader and text.

Although it is true that interpretation of a text is a continuous approaching and approximation to its meaning, according to Asor Rosa it is nevertheless possible each time to search for the truth of the text: 'the hermeneutic can not leave out of consideration an ontology of poetic creation: if it does, it is a reading of nothing'. Eco asks himself why Guénon and company don't have as much credit as other scholars who studied allegorism in the *Commedia*, as Gilson or Pound. According to Asor Rosa, it is because Dante's reader meets a mystery (the mystery of 'the sign which has enclosed the world into a whole of *plurisense* images') which is 'incomparable with the worthless mystery with which Aroux and Guénon competed'.

To confirm the thesis of Asor Rosa that it is more appropriate to speak of *arbitrio* than to speak of excess, a further consideration may be useful. The unsatisfactory nature of the esoteric criticism of the *Commedia* arises from an initial infringement, or betrayal: Dante conceives the literary text and the text of the world as a plurality of meanings enclosed within a knowledge which is limited; he belongs in every way to medieval culture, which considers knowledge to be a *Summa*–encyclopedic, but not boundless.

This is why the hermetic interpretative model that uses a boundless associative chain will not work if used to read a text like Dante's: it cannot be applied to a text of this kind, which must be placed by the reader in its historical-cultural context, without which any interpretation becomes delirium.

Let us now leave Dante and take as the object of interpretation contemporary works such as those of Joyce or Kafka: they *impose* on the reader a plurality of interpretations, because for them there no longer exists a *unique* interpretation of the world. Reality itself is fragmented, and it is represented in the literary text by fragments that can be endlessly reassembled.

It is in cases like these that the interpreter must make a reconstruction that will always recall something else, in a kaleidoscope of constantly changing images.

Consequently those arguments that are 'beside the point' when used in the esoteric criticism of Dante become appropriate when applied to Kafka or Joyce by an official interpreter.

According to Stefano Agosti, i.e., the work of Joyce is a striving toward freedom from the schemes of traditional narrative because, having lost its origin, meaning 'can be continuously thrown back from far away places (the word can be split indefinitely)'. With regard to Kafka, the critic states that the indecipherability of his representations does not arise from the fact that they are 'hanging above a vacuum of meaning', but rather from the fact that 'the meaning is not given, it is indecipherable'.

Why does a statement very similar to this one become illegitimate when it is the esoteric critic who continuously splits the word, and when the word split, which is considered indecipherable, is that of Dante?

It is not only because that kind of interpretation is sometimes wrong in itself, but because it is arbitrary when applied to the text read: the *intentio* of the *Commedia* is not that of a never-ending reading, while this is (but always within certain limits) the *intentio* of *Finnegans Wake*. In fact Joyce imagines a reader who is able to arrange units of sense, to discover endless potential messages by interpreting the ambiguity of the meaning; he doesn't propose 'a text which determines its own reading' but 'a text which demands an activity of reading' (MacCabe 1978: 28).

Literary works send us some signals, and even starting from the most incongruous clues it is possible to reconstruct the course of events. Chesterton's priest-detective Father Brown can explain in many ways the tobacco, the diamonds, the candles, and the metal device found in a castle. The owner could have an interest in the *ancien régime* and in the Bourbons; or criminal activity may be involved; or perhaps a search for diamonds: 'Ten false philosophies will fit the universe; ten false theories will fit Glengyle Castle. But we want the real explanation of the castle and the universe'.

While it is difficult to define what a legitimate interpretation is, it is easier to say what a misreading is; therefore, although in decoding the literary text it is not possible to find the true interpretation, it is the duty of the interpreter to look for a pertinent one: his aim is to grasp a fragment of truth.

Research will not then be an illusive combinatorial game, but the positive answer to the challenge the author and the text issue to us to discover in the narrative universe the cipher-key of Existence.

Therefore, rather than to the din of hermetic 'disco-music' preference should be given to the 'Adagio' of a research which, without eluding the plurality of meanings, is able to be always–according to the advice of Gianfranco Contini–'Auditor of itself'.

Anna Longoni

Interpretation and Overinterpretation:
The Rights of Texts, Readers and Implied Authors*

The sensational "success story"[1] of Umberto Eco's first internationally acclaimed best-seller novel *The Name of the Rose* (1980), followed by *Foucault's Pendulum* (1988) and *The Island of the Day Before* (1995), has been accompanied by an increasing amount of attention given to the author's writings on interpretation vis-à-vis his views on semiotics, textual analysis, narratology, postmodernism, and reader response theories. In North America, Eco's role among contemporary theorists of literary criticism became noticeable after the publication of *A Theory of Semiotics* (1975; 1976) and *The Role of the Reader* (1979). Today, after the appearance of *Semiotics and the Philosophy of Language* (1984), *The Open Work* (1989), *The Limits of Interpretation* (1990) and *Interpretation and Overinterpretation* (1992), and *Six Walks in the Fictional Woods* (1994), critics have started to (re)examine the author's theories on "open works," interpretation, and "unlimited semiosis" in relation to his earlier observations on the "rights" of texts and readers.

The Limits of Interpretation and *Interpretation and Overinterpretation* (the publication of Eco's "Cambridge Tanner Lectures"[2]), reopen some debates on the so-called "rights" "intentions" and "freedom" of texts and readers. These essays also encourage us to review some of his previous works, like *The Role of the Reader,* where the author talked extensively on *intentio auctoris, intentio operis* and *intentio lectoris* and on the difference between "using" and "interpreting" a text. In short, his two recent works on interpretation entice us to re-examine many questions about a reader's (unlimited) "rights" in interpreting a text, and to discuss whether or not the whole issue of interpretation can be limited to an analysis of the interaction between texts and readers that excludes, completely, the role/presence of the "model author." In the opening remarks of the "Tanner Lectures" Eco asserts:

> In some of my recent writings I have suggested that between the intention of the author (very difficult to find out and frequently irrelevant for the interpretation of a text) and the intention of the interpreter who (to quote Richard Rorty) simply "beats the text into a shape which will serve his purpose," there is a third possibility. There is *an intention of the text* (*IO* 25).

Throughout the lectures, as he addresses those rights of the text that must be respected by the reader, we find several remarks on the role of the author. This is not surprising, it is in fact another confirmation that Eco has never disregarded the importance of the role of the author (implied or model) in a text.

In the opening pages of *Semiotics and the Philosophy of Language*, the author maintains that there are two extreme positions in contemporary theories of interpretation: a) those who "assume that every text. . . can be interpreted in one, and only one, way, according to the intention of its author." b) those who "assume that a text supports every interpretation–albeit I suppose that nobody would literally endorse such a claim, except perhaps a visionary devotee of the Kabalistic temura" (*SPL* 3). Moreover, echoing the "Peircean notion of semiosis," he adds that a more logical solution can be found in "a continuum of intermediate positions" (p. 3). In essence, a position that Eco has held on interpretation from the days of *The Open Work*.

I should clarify immediately that throughout this paper I am speaking about the presence of a model or implied author and not about the empirical author that naturally a reader may never meet in or outside the text. Moreover, this is not meant to be an analysis of different critical views on the role of the implied author–from the days of Wayne Booth's application of the term, in *The Rhetoric of Fiction* (1961) to the present. Critics like Seymor Chatman can provide us with some excellent criticism on this topic (see Chatman 1978 and 1990). For a chronological account of Eco's theories on interpretation one could resort to a comparative analysis of his notions of authorial intentions vis-à-vis Husserl, Iser or other theoreticians of reader response criticism that the author mentions in his first Norton Lecture. This, I would add, is something that critics have yet to pursue fully.

Here, as I focus on a few statements from *Interpretation and Overinterpretation*, *The Limits of Interpretation* and *Six Walks in the Woods of Fiction*, I will deal primarily with what Eco calls "circumstances of utterance" (information about the sender, time and social content of the message, suppositions about the nature of the speech act, etc.).[3] In the process I shall discuss the implied presence of the author in a text, and why he is a part of the "intentions/constraints" of the text. Intentions and constraints that, as Eco has frequently suggested, should be taken under consideration whenever a reader's interpretation risks becoming "overinterpretation" as a result of a free-wheeling application of associations, similarities, sympathy, connotations, infinite chains of signifiers, and uncontrolled unlimited semiosis. The same dangers of "hermetic semiosis" that we find discussed in his "Introduction" to *L'idea deforme* (1989), and cleverly narrated throughout *Foucault's Pendulum*.

It must be stated that in *The Limits of Interpretation* Eco never speaks of, nor does he allude to, the existence of an authorial intention which should be reconstructed in the reading/interpreting of a text. And he certainly does not suggest that texts contain some quintessential "truths" that every interpretation must try to disclose. Instead, Eco has always maintained that: "no text can be interpreted according to the utopia of a definite, original and final authorized meaning" (*Limits* 2). Moreover, we know that he has never supported the primacy of the author over that of the text, or of the reader. And yet, as we review Eco's theories on the rights of the text we see that from the days of *Opera aperta* (written between 1957 and 1962– just before he became interested in semiotics) and of *La definizione dell'arte* (written between 1955 and 1958), to those of The Role of the Reader and of *The Limits of Interpretation* (and naturally to those of his brilliant intertextual novels), he has not forgotten the teachings of Pareyson, nor has he ever abandoned his original views that during the creative process the "model author" implants the "limits of interpretation" of his text. This is clearly underlined in the introduction to *The Role of the Reader*:

> An author can foresee an 'ideal reader affected by an ideal insomnia' (as happens with *Finnegans Wake*), able to master different codes and eager to deal with the text as with a maze of many issues. But in the last analysis what matters is not the various issues in themselves but the maze-like structure of the text. You cannot use the text as you want, but only as the text wants you to use it. An open text, however 'open' it be, cannot afford whatever interpretation.
>
> An open text outlines a 'closed' project of its Model Reader as a component of its structural strategy (p. 9).

Also, let's examine from *Six Walks in the Fictional Woods* two statements on the importance of the model author:

> The model author, on the other hand, is a voice that speaks to us affectionately (or imperiously, or slyly), that wants us beside it. This voice is manifested as a narrative strategy, as a set of instructions which is given to us step by step and which we have to follow when we decide to act as the model reader (p. 15).

> Only when empirical readers have discovered the model author, and have understood (or merely begun to understand) what it wanted from them, will they become full-fledged model readers (p. 27).

My contention is that Eco has never embraced the Barthesian notions of "the death of the author" or of the modern author that has become a mere *scriptor* (Barthes 1986:52). Before moving on to demonstrate how for Eco the implied presence of an author is taken for granted, it is worth pointing out that throughout the first two Norton Lectures, after having emphatically stated that he is not interested in the role of the empirical author, as he speaks repeatedly about the textual strategies of model authors, we notice that he cannot resist (avoid?) making references to empirical authors (such as Poe and Nerval). And, from the third lecture on, we see how often Eco returns to one of his favorite topic from *The Role of the Reader*: the "inferential walks" (p. 50) planned by a model author.

A BRIEF SUMMARY

Throughout the last three decades, beginning with *Opera aperta* Eco has often argued that the encyclopedic competence of a text opens up the text to different interpretations and that at the same time it supplies the criteria for limiting the interpretations of the text. In *Lector in fabula* we are reminded that the chain of interpretations is not infinite because the universe of discourse intervenes and limits the format of the encyclopedia (*Lector* 59-60). More recently, in *The Limits of Interpretation*, Eco asserts that even though the deliberate ambiguity of a text allows for different interpretations–making it difficult to say which one is the privileged one–it is possible to decide which one is not acceptable because it cannot be legitimated "contextually."

Eco's first comments on "open texts" and on the reader's cooperation in giving voice to the implied intentions that an author plans in a text, go back to the days when he was studying "aesthetics" and philosophy at the University of Turin, under the guidance of Luigi Pareyson. In fact, studies of Eco's evolution of his theories on aesthetics, open texts and interpretation, should take into consideration the author's early essays which appeared in *La definizione dell'arte*.[4] One needs only to read the opening essay of this collection, "L'estetica della formatività e il concetto di interpretazione," written between 1955-58, to see how Eco has remained a strong supporter of Pareyson's theories of interpretation. By the same token, one should also examine the essays of *Apocalittici e integrati*[5] (a fundamental work at the foundation of many of Eco's postmodern writings) which illustrate how the author has viewed erudite and popular culture as complementary elements within the universal encyclopedia of culture.

After the appearance of *A Theory of Semiotics* and *The Role of the Reader*, English-speaking critics have begun to quote Eco (at times *vis-à-vis* R. Barthes) on the role of the reader as a "collaborator" who helps a text to disclose its meanings.[6] We should note that most of the writings in *The Role of the Reader* (and *Lector in fabula*) were written in light of the increasing popularity of reader reception theories connected with critics such as Iser and Ingarden, and in response to the hermeneutic writings of Hirsh, Gadamer and Ricoeur. Soon after, as critics began to discuss (and, in some cases, to be divided by) the theories of interpretation associated with Derrida (1976) and Yale deconstructionists (H. Bloom, P. de Man, G. Hartman, and J.H. Miller)[7] we see Eco focusing on "hermetic semiosis" and "hermetic drift" as he discusses the dangers of radical deconstructionist readings which–at the expense of the rights of the text–give unlimited freedom to the interpreter.

In *Interpretation and Overinterpretation* we find some interesting reactions of Richard Rorty ("The Pragmatist's Progress"), Jonathan Culler ("In Defense of Overinterpretation") and Christine Brooke-Rose ("Palimpsest History"), to Eco's suggestions of having to put some "limits" on the theoretically infinite semiosis that "radical" deconstructionist readings seem to encourage. The challenging responses of these critics (some see Eco betraying his original spirit of "openness" presented in *The Open Work*) would certainly merit a separate lengthy discussion.[8]

The Tanner Lectures and *The Limits of Interpretation* are the result of Eco's many years of studies on the process of generating and interpreting signs and texts. Here Eco appears to advocate the "rights" of the text over those of the reader, nonetheless, even when he calls the intentions of the empirical author "irrelevant" he continues to refer to the question of whether or not the presence (and, to a lesser extent, the intentions) of the author should not also be taken into consideration, if one wishes to arrive at a more comprehensive interpretation of a literary text.

As I briefly review some of Eco's statements on the "freedom and determinacy" of the text I intend to show how nearly thirty years after having pronounced his controversial views on the interaction between "open texts" and readers (see the opening chapter of *The Open Work*), Eco determines that he must clarify his position, not on the autonomy–on the "self-sufficiency" (Riffaterre 1973)–of the text, but on the unrestricted freedom of the reader in interpreting a text. In so doing, he also confirms that the author's intentions are inherent in the linguistic and textual strategies that a reader must keep in mind when interpreting a text. Furthermore, we have to wonder if Eco does not feel partly responsible, because of his poetics of the *Open Work*, perhaps not so much for Barthes' notion of the "death of the author," as for the unlimited freedom given to readers in interpreting a text by Derrida and by deconstructionists in general. And thus, we can only ask: could this be what he is trying to rectify with *Interpretation and Overinterpretation*?

Towards the end of his second Tanner lecture, "Overinterpreting texts," as he continues his discussion on the relations between the *intentio operis* and the *intentio lectoris*, Eco reiterates:

A text is a device conceived in order to produce its model reader. . . A text can foresee a model reader entitled to try infinite conjectures (p. 64)

To recognize the *intentio operis* is to recognize a semiotic strategy. Sometimes the semiotic strategy is detectable on the grounds of established stylistic conventions (pp. 64-65).

Clearly recalling *The Role of the Reader* Eco reminds us of his fundamental belief (inherited from Pareyson's *Estetica*) that in every work there is an author who "conceives" a text and establishes its "stylistic conventions" and its "semiotic strategies"–that is, an author who plants all the textual strategies. In the concluding statements of the second lecture he even mentions the intentions of the author (empirical and model):

> I realize that, in the dialectics between the intention of the reader and the intention of the text, the intention of the empirical author has been totally disregarded [. . .] My idea of textual interpretation as the discovery of a strategy intended to produce a model reader, conceived as the ideal counterpart of a model author (which appears only as a textual strategy), makes the notion of an empirical author's intention radically useless. We have to respect the text, not the author as person so-and-so. Nevertheless, it can look rather crude to eliminate the poor author as something irrelevant for the story on an interpretation (pp. 65-66).

And, in the second part of the third lecture he adds:

> I hope my listeners will agree that I have introduced the empirical author in this game only in order to stress his irrelevance and to reassert the rights of the text.
> As I draw to the end of my lectures, however, I have the sense that I have scarcely been generous to the empirical author. Still, there is at least one case in which the witness of the empirical author acquires an important function. Not so much in order to understand his texts better, but certainly in order to understand the creative process (pp. 84-85).

It is questionable that with the above statement Eco is trying to please everybody, or that he regrets not having been "too generous" towards the "empirical author," because, after all, he himself is an author well known for his talent and cleverness in "devising" textual strategies. His reluctance to overlook, completely, the role of the author may in fact be a way of not having to refute his (and Pareyson's) basic views on "form" and "style."[9] But it is also a way of reinstating his earlier assertions in *Lector in fabula* and *The Role of the Reader,* where he underlines that an author foresees his model reader and the "infinite conjectures" which can be made about his text:

> The author has thus to foresee a model of the possible reader (hereafter Model Reader) supposedly able to deal interpretatively with the expressions in the same way as the author deals generatively with them (*Role* 7).

Speaking of *The Role of the Reader,* I find it most interesting that whereas in the English text, section 0.2.4, "Author and reader as textual strategies," is two pages long, in the Italian text, *Lector in fabula,* the corresponding section 3.5, "Autore e lettore come strategie testuali," continues in section 3.6, "L'autore come ipotesi interpretativa," where the creative process and the role of the Model Author are elucidated much better (see *Lector* 62-66).

Throughout the *Role of the Reader* Eco speaks specifically about the intentions of the author. For example, referring to Allais' strategies in "planning" and "provoking" the reader's inferences, Eco affirms: "Allais is telling us that not only *Drame* but every text is made of two components: the information provided by the author and that added by the Model Reader" (p. 206). For our discussion it is important to see how in 1979, as he (re)proposes his "Poetics of the open work" to English-speaking readers, Eco points out that the author endows the text with specific "rights" and "intentions":

> . . .*the work in movement* is the possibility of numerous different personal interventions, but it is not an amorphous invitation to indiscriminate participation. The invitation offers the performer the chance of an oriented insertion into something which always remains the world intended by the author [. . .] The author is the one who proposed a number of possibilities which had already been rationally organized, oriented, and endowed with specifications for proper development (p. 62).

In *A Theory of Semiotics* (see section 3.7.8, "Aesthetic text as a communication act") Eco is even more specific in suggesting a reader's responsible collaboration with the author, warning that the reader must never completely betray the author's intentions. So that in the interpretive reading a dialectic between *fidelity* and inventive *freedom* is established. On the one hand the addressee seeks to draw excitement from the ambiguity of the message and to fill out an ambiguous text with suitable codes; on the other, he is induced by contextual relationships to see the message exactly as it was intended, in an act of fidelity to the author and to the historical environment in which the message was emitted (. . .). A responsible collaboration is demanded of the addressee. He must intervene to fill up semantic gaps, to reduce or further complicate the multiple readings proposed, to choose his own preferred paths of interpretation, to consider several of them at once (even if they are mutually incompatible), to re-read the text many times, each time testing out different and contradictory presuppositions. Thus the aesthetic text becomes a multiple source of unpredictable 'speech acts' whose real author remains undetermined, sometimes being the sender of the message, at others the addressee who collaborates in its development (p. 276).

In "Two Problems in Textual Interpretation" (1980), as Eco revises some of his earlier notions on "discoursive" and narrative isotopies which had appeared in *The Role of the Reader*, he carefully underlines that "the notion of interpretation involves a dialectic between the strategy of the author and the response of the Model Reader."[10]

These statements dealing with the role of the "author" suggest that while in *Interpretation and Overinterpretations* Eco seems to have shifted his focus onto the intentions and rights of the text, in reality he is fully aware that the internal coherence of a text is constructed with the different strategies (semantic, stylistic, psychological, semiotic, structural, etc.) that an author plans, very carefully, for his readers. In fact, a careful reading of Eco's work shows that in discussing general issues of linguistics and semiotics (with references to Jakobson, Peirce, Lotman, or Derrida) he views the production of meaning and interpretation within the parameters of an interaction between author, text and reader.

Anyone who has worked on Eco has quickly learned that it is almost impossible to discuss his writings without also mentioning how the author has already commented on the same issues. This is because Eco has an uncontrollable temptation in wanting to expound (with plenty of footnotes and bibliographies) on everything that he writes. Consequently he often reveals some of the intertextual references in his writings and at times even responds to a few controversial reactions coming from his critics. Also, because he likes to work with his publishers and translators, he usually makes sure that the translations, or revised editions, include his own prefaces in which he can explain[11] how and why the English and Italian texts do not contain identical material. For example, in the introduction to *The Limits of Interpretation* the author explains how he published this text shortly after the appearance of the English edition of *The Open Work*:

> In that book I advocated the active role of the interpreter in the reading of texts endowed with aesthetic value. When those pages were written, my readers focused mainly on the "open" side of the whole business, underestimating the fact that the open-ended reading I supported was an activity elicited by (an aiming at interpreting) a *work*. In other words, I was studying the dialectics between the rights of texts and the rights of their interpreters. I have the impression that, in the course of the last few decades, the rights of the interpreters have been overstressed. In the present essays I stress the limits of the act of interpretation.
> It is neither accidental nor irrelevant that these essays follow my previous writings (*A Theory of Semiotics, The Role of the Reader, Semiotics and the Philosophy of Language* . . .) in which I elaborated upon the Peircean idea of *Unlimited semiosis* (p. 6).

And in the closing lines of this introduction, speaking of the textual "constraints" which (should) prevent readers from arriving at some "blatantly unacceptable" interpretations, he reiterates:

. . . the interpreted text imposes some constraints upon its interpreters. The limits of interpretation coincide with the rights of the text (which does not mean with the rights of its author) (pp. 6-7).

It is true that readers do not need to know the author's intentions in writing a text. Nonetheless, some questions remain: if we accept that most of the constraints which are not of a linguistic nature (e.g.: ideological, cultural and historical ones) are important elements of the author's textual strategies, then, should we not try to identify these constraints? After all, they are an integral part of the text's internal coherence that should be respected (along with all the other text's rights) during the process of interpretation. Of course, once the author publishes his text he ceases to have a direct hold on how his work should/will be read and interpreted. But, does this mean that he disappear completely after the act of writing is finished? This may not be the place to debate how the author's subjective and historical consciousness are integral elements of the overall consciousness of the text, nonetheless we must ask if the author's "encyclopedic competence"–underlined so frequently by Eco–can be ignored entirely? Because Eco has spoken so frequently about authorial strategies his work forces us to ask these and other questions about the role of the author in general.

"Contextualization" (Thibault 1991) is a familiar basic principle in Eco's work because (like Lotman 1990) he considers it an essential element of semiosis. When speaking of the dialectics of "fidelity" and "inventive freedom" during interpretations, he reinforces his views that in an interpretive act, the reader must follow the internal coherence (semantic, structural, cultural, etc.) of the text. A coherence which is intentionally planted by an author who foresees everything, including the possible misinterpretations of his text.[12]

The full extent of Pareyson's influence[13] on Eco's philosophical, aesthetic and literary theories has yet to be investigated. However, beginning with the essays in *La definizione dell'arte* we can see that Pareyson's *Estetica. Teoria della formatività* has played a major role in the formulation of Eco's theories on interpretation. A close investigation of Eco's formative years would certainly be helpful for a richer understanding of his writings in which he has objected to Crocean aesthetics and to any form of "grasshopper criticism" and farfetched interpretations that he later associates with "hermetic drift." In these formative years we would also have to take into consideration the strong influence of Peirce's *Collected Papers* (and to some degree C. Morris's writings) and see how they relate to Eco's notions of the pragmatics of semiosis. Pragmatics, I may add, which would exclude Derrida's views on unlimited semiosis (whereby one is caught in an endless chain of signifiers).[14]

The Name of the Rose firmly confirmed how well Eco combines in a most clever fashion his theoretical and creative writings. Most of his theories of interpretation underlined in *The Limits of Interpretation* have in fact been illustrated in his narratives through a gamut of colorful and witty characters, stimulating images, highly imaginative situations, and innumerable intertextual echoes. One of the outstanding features in his novels is undoubtedly the attention given to the narrative strategies of a "model author" who narrates semiotic and literary theories on generating and interpreting texts. The same strategies that we find discussed at great length in essays like *The Role of the Reader* and *Six Walks in the Fictional Woods*.

Eco's novels are, as they should be, autonomous and "self-sufficient" (Riffaterre) "possible worlds." However, the nature of his fiction is such that readers will certainly appreciate the novels much better if they make some conjectures about the intentions of the empirical author Umberto Eco–or of his *persona* which is often easily recognizable in his novels. As we know, his ironic and parodic postmodern metafictions make extensive and explicit use of intertextual references not only to numerous authors, but also, through intratextual and self-referential allusions, to most of his own theoretical studies. Of course, this type of argument leads to a vicious circle of author explaining text explaining author etc. etc.. Nonetheless, because in Eco's novels we are dealing primarily with "books made of" and that "speak of" other books, it helps to read his fiction while also trying to determine the intentions of the author's strategies in using unlimited intertextuality. In the process we may ask: is his intertextuality a form of pure *divertissement*–a Barthesian *jouissance* of *writerly* texts? Are we confronted by a parodic and ironic exploitation of intertextuality which verges on "hermetic drift"? Furthermore, how do we cope with the ironic and parodic voices in Eco's novels? Does the reader dialogue only with the voices of the written text, or does he also automatically converse with the ironic voice(s) of the implied narrator/author? In fact, in *The Rose*, as in *Foucault's Pendulum* and in *The Island*, the (model?) reader soon discovers that he must dialogue with all of these voices if he wishes to grasp more than one level of meaning in these intricate and rhizomatic intertextual pastiches.

In the process of interpretation, we all agree, it should never be a question of having to get the author's approval, but this does not imply that we should not be concerned with the author's encyclopedic competence, his historical consciousness, his coherence, and his possible intentions in using specific textual strategies. The reader's interaction with the *intentio auctoris* not only may help him to arrive at a more comprehensive interpretation of the different meanings planted in the text, but it should also prevent him at the same time from making the text say something that the author could have not possibly have known and/or meant.

In *The Limits of Interpretation*, Eco contends Derrida's (mis)inter-
pretation of Peirce's unlimited semiosis without stressing sufficiently how
a complete disregard of the interaction between *intentio operis* and *intentio
auctoris* can encourage an endless chain of "slippage of meaning" and a "language caught in a play of multiple signifying games" (*Limits* 33).[15] In his
novels, on the other hand, Eco puts into practice his own interpretation of
unlimited semiosis and infinite intertextuality and illustrates very well his
belief that "a text is a device conceived in order to produce its model
reader." A concept, we should add, quite different from Derrida's view that
"a written text is a machine that produces an indefinite deferral" of meaning
(1990:32). Therefore, it is rather surprising that a critic like Norman N.
Holland, in his excellent work *The Critical I*, does not see a difference between Eco and Derrida on the interpretation of unlimited semiosis.[16]

It should be noted that Eco's criticism is not directed against Derrida's
or deconstructionism in general.[17] Perhaps, as suggested by Robert Scholes
(1992), Eco should have targeted more specifically the writings of Stanley
Fish and Richard Rorty. Nonetheless, in *The Limits of Interpretation* Eco
chooses to focus on the "hermetic semiosis" and "hermetic drift" that he
finds extolled in *Dissemination* and *Of Grammatology*[18] maintaining that
"infinite semiosis" (as brilliantly demonstrated throughout *Foucault's Pendulum*) does not give a reader the license to practice unlimited interpretation through an endless series of connotations that words and names elicit.
This is because Eco has always been against a type of criticism whereby *tout
se tient*–that is, whereby "everything bears relationships of analogy, contiguity and similarity to everything else."[19]

ECO'S "POSSIBLE WORLDS". THEORIES AND PRACTICE OF UNLIMITED SEMIOSIS AND INTERTEXTUALITY.

In *The Role of the Reader* Eco speaks of texts in which the reader is expected
to take as many "inferential walks"[20] as possible–walks suggested by paradigmatic associations and intertextual references which lead to the
reading(s) of many other texts which in turn add to our understanding of
the different meanings which have been planted in the text. Eco's novels
invite (I would even say, require) this type of "inferential walks," precisely
because his fiction is an excellent example of how "books speak of" and "are
made of other books."

On the inside cover of *Il nome della rosa* we find the witty pun: "di ciò di
cui non si può teorizzare, si deve narrare" (literally: "what cannot be theorized must be narrated"). This is just one of the author's several ironic statements which steer us into a rhizomatic intertextuality from which––
depending on our encyclopedic, literary and overall cultural, competence–

may be difficult to exit. In short, the more the reader is intertextually competent, the deeper he will get into the labyrinth/library at the center of Eco's fiction.

A brief "inferential walk" in our encyclopedic competence of literature shows that Eco's above witty assertion on the back-cover of *The Rose* is an echo of Wittgenstein's closing statement from his *Tractatus logico-philosophicus*: "What we cannot speak about we must consign to silence" (Wittgenstein 1971:151). Naturally, Wittgenstein's words, like those of numerous other thinkers, writers and poets present in Eco's novel, must be carefully examined within the sharp parodic tone of the implied narrator, or better yet, within the ironic vision of the "empirical/model author" of *The Rose*. As we discover in the novel, through the intertextual echo of Wittgenstein our author is really saying: that which I have already theorized now I must narrate. This is precisely what Eco says in *The Role of the Reader* when, speaking of his closing chapter on *Un drame bien parisien*, he states:

> To conclude a book of textual explorations with a metanarrative text that speaks ambiguously and with tongue-in-cheek of its own ambiguity and of its own derisory nature seems to me an honest decision. After having let semiotics speak abundantly about texts, it is correct to let a text speak by itself about its semiotic strategy (p. 40).

The Name of the Rose, Foucault's Pendulum and *The Island of the Day Before*, in addition to being three of the most fascinating popular intertextual metanarratives to come out of Italy, are also stimulating and captivating essay-novels in which Eco discusses, in narrative form, some of the most polemicized theories of interpretation of the last three decades: semiotics, structuralism, deconstruction, hermeneutics, hermetic semiosis, and postmodernism.[21] Here I do not discuss Eco's pragmatic views on postmodernism but I should mention that in his novels while one can examine how Eco associates certain practices of postmodernism with those of hermetic drift, unlimited semiosis and intertextuality, he should also notice that the author does not rejecting the various practices of postmodernism.

In articles and interviews Eco has acknowledged that in *The Rose* he wanted to pay some of his debts to Borges.[22] This is evident from the central role of the parodic character Jorge da Burgos who dominates the labyrinthine library (of *Babylon*?) in the abbey. Eco has never mentioned that he may have arrived at a deeper appreciation of Borges' work with the help of Calvino's fictions. Notwithstanding, there are good reasons to believe that in Calvino's brilliant possible worlds–from the days of *Cosmicomics* (1965) to those of *If On a Winter Night a Traveler* (1979)[23]– Eco finds some excellent examples of highly imaginative narrations on the same themes and topics which he will in turn fabulate. By the same token Eco's *Lector in fabula* is also appreciated by Calvino who from the sixties on, as he practices his own style of *docere et delectare*, narrates literary theories (semiotics, structuralism, narratology) in the middle of his inventive and entertaining short stories. In the opening pages of *Six Walks in the Fictional Woods* we find Eco speaking precisely about this.

Eco in Fabula

When I first began to work on *The Name of the Rose*[24] I was immediately fascinated with Eco's talent in illustrating the intricate process of unlimited semiosis and intertextuality. Being familiar with Eco's love for humor and wit, and with his belief (like Calvino's) that the art of literary *divertissement* is a serious business,[25] I was also interested in examining the possibility that in addition to providing different degrees of linguistic and literary *pleasure* to different types of readers, Eco's novel was also presenting a clever answer to those critics who were skeptical about the applications of literary semiotics. And thus, the more I became concerned with Eco's superb play with intertextuality, the more I found myself re-reading his earlier theoretical works on semiotics, literary texts and mass culture.

Like many other readers, I followed Eco's suggestion that one level of reading entailed the challenge of taking as many "inferential walks" as possible. This also led me to ask a number of questions about *The Rose*. For example: were these "walks" mainly a question of trying to identify how many quotations came from Eco's own works and how many from those of other authors? Were (model) readers being asked to become detectives on a mission to find, identify and footnote all the intertextual references hidden by the model author? Was the pleasure of reading *The Rose* limited to the author's cunning verbal skills and to his ability to write one of the most polyphonic (Bakhtinian) dialogical narrative discourse? Moreover, was Eco illustrating his own practice of Barthes' notion of "jouissance" – that indescribable "bliss" which can be derived from an endless chain of orgasms experienced in "writerly texts"?

Considering that *The Name of the Rose* is not really what Barthes would define as a "writerly text"–in fact, *The Rose* resembles more a "well made" "readerly" novel than a writerly open text–then, what is Eco's novel about? As I discussed in my first article on *The Rose*, if we focus excessively on the play of (unlimited) intertextuality we end up examining Eco's "anxiety of influence," which in my estimation is not one of the (intended) central points of the novel.[26]

With *Foucault's Pendulum* I tried to follow a path of reading which would not stir me too deeply into the labyrinth of esoteric texts mentioned in the novel. Instead, I looked for a link between the obvious and abundant variety of intertextual references and Diotallevi's and Casaubon's final realization that one does not escape, unharmed, from the webs of extreme, paranoid and obsessive interpretation. This is the lesson that they learn from their mistakes. The main characters get entangled in a web of unusual and farfetched connections between Jesus Christ, the Templars, the Holy Grail, Dante, Hitler, IBM, the Eiffel tower, "Les protocoles des Sages de Sion," Kabbalah, Masons, various esoteric groups, astrology, alchemy, *ars combinatoria*, terrorists, and the "pendulum" of Foucault (just to mention a few). Belbo, Casaubon and Diotallevi, with their *tout se tient* attitude, had concluded that everyone and everything, in one way or another, can be linked to the "secret plan."

Eco's essays on "hermetic semiosis," and on "paranoid readings" ("la critica sospettosa")–published shortly before his second novel–convinced me to reread both novels in an attempt to see if *Pendulum* was a logical sequence to *The Rose* (without necessarily having to be its sequel). Convinced that the two novels showed a progression which followed Eco's evolution of theories on semiotics and interpretation, I looked for specific connections between *The Name of the Rose* (being mainly about abductions, interpreting signs, structures, intertextuality, and manneristic labyrinths) and *Foucault's Pendulum* (dealing primarily with reading/interpreting texts, unlimited semiosis/intertextuality, the infinite relations of rhizomes, and hermetic drift). Among Eco's ingenious narrative strategies I noticed that in addition to offering another (narcissistic but stimulating) example of his vast encyclopedic competence, his second novel was saturated with intertextual references which elicited "inferential walks" among texts which dealt specifically with general issues of interpretation. Thus, I began to re-examine some of the mistakes admitted by William and Adso in *The Rose*–mistakes which dealt with abductions and with interpretation in general–keeping in mind similar mistakes made by Casaubon, Belbo and Diotallevi in *Pendulum*.

In short, I was also looking for some obvious clues that in his second novel Eco was in fact expanding his fabulation of semiotic and structuralist strategies to include observations on practices of hermetic semiosis and deconstructionism.

Throughout *Foucault's Pendulum* appear specific references to Hermes, *The Corpus Hermeticum*, scriptural hermeneutics, the studies on Kabbalah by Moishe Idel and Harold Bloom,[27] and Bloom's notion that there are no interpretations, but only "misinterpretations." Moreover, the fact that the references to kabbalah, Torah and Holy Scriptures (see especially Belbo's files in his computer "Abulafia") are linked with the various themes of authority, secrets, veiled messages, alchemy, claims to knowing the truth, the quest for the Holy Grail, vanity presses, popular films like *Casablanca* and *Indiana Jones*, and above all with the dangers of misinterpreting texts, persuaded me to look into Eco's earlier writings for related clues. The pages on "dictionary *vs.* encyclopedia" (see *Semiotics and the Philosophy of Language*) and the articles on "hermetic semiosis" (now in *The Limits of Interpretation*) proved to be excellent guides. However, what gave me new insight was Eco's preface to the esoteric readings of Dante, in *L'idea deforme* (1989). Today, the publication of *Semiotica: Storia, teoria, interpretazione* (1992) makes it much easier to search among Eco's lectures and writings for specific issues linked to topics of intertextuality, interpretation and "hermetic drift" narrated in *Pendulum*. And I would add that the recent publication of *La ricerca della lingua perfetta* (1993; *The Search for the Perfect Language*)[28] clarifies even more the presence of Abulafia, Casaubon, Kabbalah, Torah, and *ars combinatoria* in the novel.

The different methods and abuses of interpretation narrated in *The Rose* and *Pendulum* deal with semiotic strategies and with the notions of "signs as texts," "texts as signs," "the world as a text," "text as a [possible] world," and naturally with the idea that: "To interpret means to react to the text of the world or to the world of a text by producing other texts" (*IO* 23) This explains why in *The Rose* a good part of the dialogues between William and Adso deal with William's intention to educate Adso in the art of reading and interpreting signs. In one of these "lessons" (see the end of "Day Five") Adso learns a most important point about books: "The good of a book lies in its being read. A book is made up of signs that speak of other signs, which in their turn speak of things. Without an eye to read them, a book contains signs that produce no concepts, therefore it is dumb" (*Rose* 393). And thus, together with Adso, readers of *The Rose* learn mostly about the Middle Ages, nominalism vs. realism, signs, symbols, libraries, labyrinths, Peirce's art of making abductions, and most importantly that a text invites (and needs) dialogical relationships with a reader. But as we read William and Adso's conversations aren't we also reading and interpreting Eco's own reading/interpretation of the Middle Ages, Augustine, Bacon, Ockam, Peirce, Wittgenstein, etc.?. In other words, depending mainly on our "inferential walks," our dialogical relationship extends beyond the text in order to include a dialogue with Eco and with the many authors (and in turn with their world and/or encyclopedia) recalled through the intertextual references.

A written text is a form of dialogical discourse (Peirce, Bakhtin, Barthes, Eco, etc.) But, how does a reader approach this dialogue? How does a reader's encyclopedic competence condition the dialogue? And with whom does the reader ultimately dialogue?[29] Simply with written words (with chains of signs and signifiers)? Furthermore, if signs, as Peirce tells us, are signs which stand for other signs which in turn stand for something in some capacity for someone, doesn't the something go beyond the endless chain of unlimited semiosis? This is where Eco and Derrida disagree in their reading of Peirce. Eco believes that at one point–in the chain of the possibly, infinite semiosis–the realist and pragmatist Peirce had in mind a "final logical interpretant," and thus some kind of a referent related to the "immediate object" and the "dynamical object"? (see Johansen 1993).

In re-reading *The Rose*, side by side with *Foucault's Pendulum*, I kept in mind how William's final admission that there was no "apocalyptic plan" in the abbey, was quite similar to Casaubon's final acknowledgment that there was no "secret cosmic plot" dating back to the Templars and Rosicrucians. And in *The Island* we see that a "punto fijo" (a fixed point) is all relative. We recall that at the end of *The Rose*, realizing that he had made a mistake in applying the structure of an apocalyptic plan in his attempt to solve the mystery of the murders, William confesses: "there was no plot. . . And I discovered it by mistake" (p. 487). William admits that it was a mistake to abandon the science of signs and the art of making abductions in order to pursue, instead, an ontological structuralist approach whereby a fixed and conditioning structure (namely the apocalyptic plan of an antichrist) could explain the sequence of murders in the abbey. William concludes "I behaved stubbornly, pursuing a semblance of order, when I should have known well that there is no order in the universe" (p. 488). And, recalling Wittgenstein's famous ladder, he adds: "The order that our mind imagines is like a net, or like a ladder, built to attain something. But afterwards you must throw the ladder away, because you discover that, even if it was useful, it was meaningless" (p. 488). In paraphrasing Wittgenstein's maxim that the "ladder" after being used must be thrown away, because it is merely an instrument, we see that William is convinced that specific 'structures' may be useful in trying to arrive at a particular meaning but they are not necessarily useful when trying to arrive at other meanings in different situations, and even better, in other texts and in other contexts.

The themes of order, relations, coincidences, plans, secrets, labyrinths, authority, fear, suspicion, and control for power return in *Pendulum*. And as far as labyrinths are concerned, whereas in *The Rose* Eco uses the traditional form of a labyrinth which has only one or two paths to get in and out, in *Pendulum* he presents us with the structure of a rhizome, with its innumerable possible paths that (can) connect any point with any other one.

In *Foucault's Pendulum* Eco advocates a return to common sense as a way to avoid the many dangers associated with "paranoid interpretation" (*dietrologia*) and with the freewheeling associations of unlimited interpretation whereby *tout se tient*. As we recall, it is Lia who explains to Casaubon, Belbo and Diotallevi how in their eagerness to reconstruct an allegedly old and powerful secret plan, they ended up interpreting a "laundry list" as a coded message of a secret group who wanted to control everything and everyone with a "cosmic" plan. The three protagonists did not consider the dangers in playing too long and too seriously with the idea/game that it is easy to find a "connection" or association between anything and anyone. Consequently, their initial curiosity and subsequent love for "Hermetic semiosis" (their fascination with the "alchemy" of unlimited semiosis and intertextuality?) proves to be a dangerous game which leads them to their deaths.

The fact that in both novels Eco fabulates about the mistakes of characters who impose a fixed plan, plot or order, where there isn't one, could suggest that the author is also revisiting his views expressed in *La struttura assente*-a text in which he had tackled some of the issues of ontological structuralism. William's and Casaubon's final statements seem to suggest this. But my overall contention remains that Eco's two fictions are essentially a way of narrating how and why his reading of Peirce's "unlimited semiosis" (*The Rose*) is different from Derrida's interpretation of the same notion (*Pendulum*). Furthermore I feel that Eco's basic belief in some degree of extratextual referentiality of signs helps him in his playful exploitation of unlimited semiosis (and of Bakhtin's intertextuality) in such a way that while he uses it for constructing his fantastic possible worlds and for entertaining his readers with the encyclopedia of texts and culture, he also uses it very cunningly to make allusions to our modern society (terrorism, power struggles, literary criticism, postmodernism, growing interest in esoteric sects, apocalyptic paranoia, Popper, Derrida, deconstructionism, etc.).

One of the suggestions in *Foucault's Pendulum* is that the dangers of the "syndrome of suspicion" exist in society as they exist in literary criticism, and that people who are thirsty for power and authority can be found in socio-political institutions just as in the world of academia. Indeed it would not be an exaggeration to affirm that among the different connotations of the so called "plan" in *Pendulum* we should consider Eco's intentions of talking about the struggles for power and control in the fortresses and ivory towers of academia (in this case, among professors of theories of literary criticism). The whole question of secrets, ambiguity of meaning, closed circles, intellectual arrogance, suspicion, and of power and control in the hands of a chosen few (the initiated and privileged ones) who feel that they have the answer (their own?) to coded messages can certainly be applied to the academic world (in itself a self-sufficient possible world?).

In *The Name of the Rose* William of Baskerville is portrayed in such a way that while he can easily recall Conan Doyle's famous detective, Sherlock Holmes, he can also reflect Eco's own detective semiotician persona (throughout the novel we find plenty of self-referential allusions which can substantiate this conjecture). A main character who is a detective semiotician returns in *Foucault's Pendulum*. We recall that Casaubon opens his own detective agency "of cultural information" (see section 34). In Casaubon we can also see Eco's intentions of wanting to link his fictitious persona with that of the real author Isaac Casaubon who historically demonstrated how the *Corpus Hermeticum* was a forgery. Diotallevi also summarizes many of these issues linked to the abuses of interpretation (see especially Ch. 110). Realizing why he is dying, Diotallevi regrets having tempered with Torah, with history, with words, and with texts, stating:

> There must be a right meaning and a wrong meaning: otherwise you die (p. 566).
>
> I'm dying because I convinced myself that there was no order, that you could do whatever you liked with any text. . . I'm dying because we were imaginative beyond bounds (p. 567).

In *The Limits of Interpretation* we have a perfect example of how the same written text can elicit different interpretations. Eco tries to convince us that Derrida is the one who misreads/ misinterprets Peirce's text. But how does Eco go about arguing his point? First, he draws our attention to Peirce's scientific discourse (a call for logic?), then he speaks about Peirce's overall intentionalities in speaking about signs and unlimited semiosis (insisting on context; on the internal coherence of Peirce's work), and finally (as we can see much better in his third Tanner Lecture) he brings into the discussion some comments on some misreadings of *Foucault's Pendulum,* and in particular about Casaubon and the *Corpus Hermeticum* (and thus resorting to his own ingenious fiction to discuss the intentions of the author vis-à-vis the (mis)interpretations of some readers).[30]

Is this just another example of Eco's clever strategies? Or is it an attempt, by an author, to implicitly show that sometimes the "rights of the text" must be reinforced by the intentions of its model/empirical author? My conclusion is that Eco the semiotician and Eco the narrator show characteristics of the same author who, from *Opera aperta,* continues to make his presence felt (through his encyclopedic competence–his intelligence–and his humor) as a model author, in all of his texts. A presence that readers do not mind having to cope with, once they begin to interact with the author's witty practices of always entertaining his readers while at the same time informing and teaching, regardless of the subject matter under scrutiny. A presence, I must conclude, that Eco himself will not easily part with, because it has become an authorizing trademark of his encyclopedic "model author" for his international "model readers."

Rocco Capozzi

Part III

Reading Eco's Possible Worlds

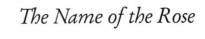

The Name of the Rose

Gaudy Rose: Eco and Narcissism

SCENE I. THE BALCONY

What's in a name? asks Juliet, who is a woman and knows the tide, the ebb and flow, the pull of the real. Eco answers her question simply, yet implicating the whole of philosophy and the vicissitudes of Western epistemology: everything and nothing. *Stat rosa pristina nomine. Nomina nuda tenemus* (*Rose* 503). But Juliet's, of course, was a rhetorical question, and Eco's answer is not what she wants. We leave Juliet at the balcony unfulfilled, as she must be, and go on to scene two.

SCENE II: THE GARDEN

Imagine now Adam and Eve in the garden of Eden, naked, without guilt and (naturally, you might think) without language. But no, these Adam and Eve do have a kind of language, a rudimentary code made up of two sounds which combine to form a restricted set of signifiers and their corresponding semantic units or signifieds. The sounds are A and B, and with them Adam and Eve express their appreciation of the lush nature that surrounds them. Theirs is a happy life, unmarred by conflict or uncertainty, a world of simple, lasting values. Things are either edible or inedible, good or bad, beautiful or ugly, red or blue. But one day God speaks and he says:

BAAAB.BAB–BAAAB.BAAB
(apple inedible, apple bad)

That is, he proclaims that the apple, which they considered beautiful, edible, and good (because red), and therefore a yes, is actually a no, in fact a no-no (in the Edenic language, evil–the serpent–is BB). God thus introduces a contradiction in their semantic universe, one which will cause a major crisis in the Garden. For at that very moment Adam and Eve, who cannot doubt the truth of God's assertion since he is AA *par excellence* ("I am that I am," or you might say the transcendental signified), realize that denotation may be in contrast with connotation and, what is even more astonishing to them, that contradiction or ambiguity on the semantic level brings about the possibility of making new expressive forms, new signifiers; for example, of saying and writing "bluered" (BAAAAABABBBBBA). They are literally fascinated by the unusual sound of the new sequence. They repeat it over and over, not even looking at the apple: for the very first time, they are looking at words instead of things.

And so it happens that Adam and Eve come to taste the pleasure of the text, to know desire in language. And they begin to invent new word forms: they write "red" with blueberry juice, line up words in columns or with graphic emphasis, discover rhyme, rhythm, anaphora, *recitar cantando, parole in libertà*, and concrete poetry. In short, together with the arbitrariness of the sign, they have found out the structure of the code and so can instantaneously retrace the history of poetics. Adam rediscovers, after Jakobson, the poetic function of language and experiences Derrida's Heideggerian penchant for false etymologies. The thought crosses his mind that *nomina sunt numina*, the gods speak through language, and language is therefore part of nature, not of the super-structure; and he feels closer to God and his eternal laws. Closer to God than Eve, in fact, and that, he believes, must be the difference. On her part, Eve has other reasons to pursue linguistics and poetics: the meeting with the serpent has intimated the existence of prelinguistic factors in the semiotic domain, and she is now deeply engaged in *sémanalyse*.

To make a long story short, whether or not Adam will eat the apple offered or not by Eve is finally irrelevant. They have left the Garden since the moment they began to play with language and discovered that the univocal correspondence between signifiers and signifieds presumed by the Edenic code did not exist. At that moment, too, history began. For in His wish to test His creatures by instituting a prohibition, and by affirming His own Authority and the positivity of His Enunciation, God introduced a contradiction in the natural order of things, and that contradiction produced a condition of perpetual scrambling in the semiotic order. One moral of the story might be, God made a mistake. But there are at least two other equally possible hypotheses: 1) that God did not make a mistake, but rather, having read Lévi-Strauss, purposely instituted the universal taboo in order to create culture; or 2) that God did not exist, and the myth of the interdiction was arrived at later as a rationalization or *a posteriori* explanation of the event.

This is roughly the sense of an essay which Eco published in 1971 with the title "Generazione di messaggi estetici in una lingua edenica."[1] It was included in *Le forme del contenuto* (1971), a book that marks the transition from the aesthetic and broadly philosophical concerns of *Opera aperta* (1962) and *La struttura assente* (1968) to the more formally defined inquiry of *A Theory of Semiotics* (1976). The essay itself, however, is representative of a third type of discourse, with which only the Italian readers of Eco are familiar, that of his journalistic writings–political commentary, essays in popular culture, reviews, interviews, and interventions in nearly all aspects of Italian life and mores. It is also exemplary of a particular form of the semiotic imagination which shapes all of Eco's writing, from the most abstract and theoretical to the most occasional and fictional.

This Genesis *sub specie semiotica* belongs neither to the former nor to the latter genre, but is constructed, according to the author, as a laboratory model, a practical demonstration of the work of semiosis, of the mechanics of the open work, of the aesthetic use of codes, and especially of invention as a mode of sign production. At the same time it is also a demonstration of the work of semiotics–as Eco sees it–as a potentially demystifying practice of signs, a sort of permanent critique of ideologies. But even more, the essay demonstrates the pleasure of both semiosis and semiotics: the first as pure play, *jouissance*, sense of wonder, Marino's *meraviglia*; the second as self-vindication or affirmation of the human(istic) subject who, by the semiotic activity, enters into a play-off with God, so to speak, and rather than cursing or repressing him, can scale him down to human size and transcode his mighty thunder into bleat or babble (BAAAB.BAB).

Not inconsistently, then, will Eco maintain in later works that semiotics is "a theory of the lie" and man the only animal capable of both lying and laughing (*TS* 6). A text is thus always a lie, often premeditated, and its greatest force is laughter. Long before writing the novel which turns on the quest for the mysterious Ur-text on comedy, the text of the truth of laughter, Eco had written of De Amicis's popular feuilleton Cuore: "Either one laughs at [the bourgeois] Order from within, or one must curse it from without; either one feigns to accept it so as to be able to expose it, or one feigns to reject it only to bring it about again in other forms; either one is Rabelais or one is Descartes."[2] In *The Name of the Rose*, I will suggest, Eco would want to be both.

If there is one text to which the designation of writing as a premeditated lie applies, that must be *The Name of the Rose*, a novel built in the vast laboratory of his critical studies and politico-cultural activities of over two decades and properly a "summation" of the particular vision of history and culture, cognition and creativity, the world and the text, that emerges with consistency from his entire work. For this novel by (let us not forget) the disciple and admirer of Aquinas is also intended to be a narrative summa–the novel most novelistic, the mystery most insoluble, the Bildungsroman most picaresque, the text most intertextual, the manuscript found, not just in a bottle but in a Chinese box. At the same time, this is also the most "personal" of Eco's works, in the sense in which only narrative fiction, or narrativity in fiction, can be. For, however well contained by an elaborate scaffolding of narrative and metanarrative codes the writer's affective investment comes through the fiction as sure as daylight, and in the historical scenario, barely dissimulated by the scholar's astute manipulation of the rules of the genre, one can distinctly glimpse the trappings of another scene.

History and story, the public record of interpreted events and their traces in a subject's personal history, do not always fit so smoothly together. For some, indeed, they clash–Elsa Morante, for one, as *La storia* painfully testifies–producing ruptures and tears in the fabric of both life and text.[3] But here, in this "tale of books" (*Rose* 5), personal and critical history merge in the literary topoi of the journey, the sentimental education, the descent into Hades, the remembrance of things past, the wake of reason; here the political inquest and the mythical quest are twined securely with the Socratic dialogue, the conte à Voltaire, the Conan Doyle mystery story. Our scene iii, then, is the library, as the novel opens with "naturally, a manuscript."

SCENE III. THE LIBRARY

In what appears to be the realm of historical fact, someone (presumably Eco) is handed a book by someone else (unspecified) on "August 16, 1968." The book purports to be the 1842 French translation of a seventeenth-century Latin edition of a manuscript written in Latin by a German monk toward the end of the fourteenth century. The first someone, having left Prague when "six days later Soviet troops invaded that unhappy city" (*Rose* 1), meets up with his "beloved" in Vienna, and together they travel up the Danube to the monastery of Melk, where the presumed author of the manuscript had lived. There, not only is the original manuscript not to be found, but the French book also disappears "one tragic night," abducted by the "beloved," neither one ever to be seen again. By January 1980, the first someone has decided to publish his own manuscript, a modern Italian translation of the memoirs of Adso of Melk. Why? "Let us say it is an act of love. Or, if you like, a way of ridding myself of numerous, persistent obsessions" (*Rose* 5).

Adso's memoirs, written by the Benedictine monk toward the end of his life, at the close of the century, relate events that happened in his youth, in the A.D. 1327. His manuscript begins with a Prologue, and the Prologue begins with the words of John, "In principio erat Verbum," in the beginning was the Word and the Word was with God, and the Word was God." Then the narration of the events, divided in seven days (chapters) and told by Adso in the first person, begins with what may well appear to us as a quotation from Peanuts, the beginning of Snoopy's novel-in-progress: "It was a beautiful morning at the end of November" (*Rose* 21). The three embedded beginnings contain and imbricate three references, three registers of discourse–the literary-historical, the theologico-philosophical, and the popular-cultural–which are not only the major areas of Eco's critical work, but also the field of his writing practice. This is, in short, his semiotic and poetic manifesto. This text, we are to understand, demonstrates how Pierre Menard, in Borges's story, wrote his Don Quixote.[4] It is a novel made up almost entirely of other texts, of tales already told, of names either well known or sounding as if they should be known to us from literary and cultural history; a medley of famous passages and obscure quotations, specialized lexicons and subcodes (narrative, iconographic, literary, architectural, bibliographical, pharmaceutical, et cetera), and characters cut out in strips from a generic World Encyclopedia.

Here are some. An abbot by the name of Abo; a fiftyish Franciscan monk and former inquisitor, Brother William of Baskerville, given to chewing grass in moments of nervous tension; and a young novice, his disciple and scribe named Adso who is often addressed by his better as "my dear Adso." Thus forewarned, the reader who will go and reread *The Hound of the Baskervilles* will find there not only the same investigative and inferential structure governing *The Name of the Rose*, not only the dry humor and the ambiguous relationship that binds Sherlock and Watson, like William and Adso, in an affectionate, homoerotic, master-slave dialectic; but even the exact physical description of characters (e.g., Dr. Mortimer) and locations (the castle, Baskerville Hall) which Eco lifts from Conan Doyle and inserts into his text unchanged. In the English novel, the ancient curse haunting the present owners of the castle is inscribed in an eighteenth-century manuscript; in Eco's, a manuscript more ancient and more elusive is responsible for the murders most foul evenly distributed one in each day or unit of narration. And just as Watson begins his story describing Sherlock Holmes and Dr. Mortimer, so does Adso describe his beloved master in almost the same words and certainly with the same loving attention to his body, his hands, his look.

Further, both novels open with a feat of deductive brilliance: the large quantity of information Sherlock is able to infer from Dr. Mortimer's walking stick is more than matched by the detailed description of the abbot's horse, which William can produce from the bare evidence of a few marks left by its passage on the ground and adjacent shrubs. Here Eco appropriates almost verbatim an episode from Voltaire's *Zadig*–about the queen's dog and the king's horse–which is often cited as an example of semiotic inference, but he coyly goes one step beyond the great Encyclopedist by making his hero deduce the very name of the horse:

"All right," I said, "but why Brunellus?"

"May the Holy Ghost sharpen your mind, son!" my master exclaimed. "What other name could he possibly have? Why, even the great Buridan, who is about to become rector in Paris, when he wants to use a horse in one of his logical examples, always calls it Brunellus."

This was my master's way. He not only knew how to read the great book of nature [as Voltaire's hero did], but also knew the way monks read the books of Scripture, and how they thought through them. (*Rose* 24-25)

Moreover, as Doyle ends his novel with a "retrospection" chapter in which on a cold and foggy night at the end of November, two weeks after the events narrated, Watson and Holmes draw out their final implications, the "Last Page" of Adso's memoirs shows him, "years later," as he returns on the scene of the story. Both texts end in the present tense, the time of writing.

What of the hellish hound, Victorian projection of human lust and excess? Eco wouldn't miss him for the world. He is, of course, the Antichrist, the "foul beast" whose imminent arrival is incessantly announced by the blind seer Jorge of Burgos (!) with words of fire and brimstone. But it is the latter, representative of the dark age's darkest dogmatism and religious zeal, who will cause the apocalyptic fire that destroys the library and who will devour (literally) the much-coveted manuscript–that second volume of Aristotle's *Poetics* which the tradition alleged to be a treatise on the comic.

Fear prophets, Adso [warns Brother William], and those prepared to die for the truth, for as a rule they make many others die with them, often before them, at times instead of them. . ... Jorge feared the second book of Aristotle because it perhaps really did teach how to distort the face of every truth, so that we would not become slaves of our ghosts. Perhaps the mission of those who love mankind is to make people laugh at the truth, *to make truth laugh*, because the only truth lies in learning to free ourselves from insane passion for the truth. (*Rose* 491)

As his first name characteristically suggests, our hero is also modeled on the historical figure of William of Occam, the empiricist philosopher and Franciscan politician who taught at Oxford and who, having been called to Avignon by John XXII on charges of heresy, sought shelter at the court of Louis the Bavarian and became his supporter. Similarly, the learned *disputationes* on the poverty of Christ, on the allegorical meaning of semi-precious stones on the properties of herbs, or the political debates among the factions of papal and imperial supporters are all painstakingly derived from actual medieval texts, the transcripts of heretics' trials, and so on.

Eco's particular mix of history and story, of semiotics and fiction, is summarized in the words of Sherlock Holmes: "It is the scientific use of the imagination, but we have always some material basis on which to start our speculations."[5] This is what leads our hero to a perfectly rational explanation of the mystery of the library, and thus to be on the exact spot where the yarn finally unravels. Once there, however, Eco leaves Conan Doyle and steps into the postmodern condition. The crimes, William finds out, were not determined by an individual's scheme or by a single plot–Jorge's, for instance, which William (and the reader, with some degree of smug self-satisfaction) had believed patterned on the text of the Apocalypse: seven murders, occurring in seven days, and predictable by the guideline of the revelations of the seven seals. That was not the key to the chain of murders. In fact, there was no key: every crime had a different author or perhaps no author at all; there was no single plan, but rather a multiplicity of causes whose relations depended less on the design of an author than on the project of a reader–in this case, William.

> "There was no plot," William said, "and I discovered it by mistake." . . . "Where is all my wisdom, then? I behaved stubbornly, pursuing a semblance of order, when I should have known well that there is no order in the universe."
> "But in imagining an erroneous order you still found something. . .."
> "What you say is very fine, Adso, and I thank you. The order that our mind imagines is like a net, or like a ladder, built to attain something. But afterward you must throw the ladder away, because you discover that, even if it was useful, it was meaningless. Er muoz gelichesame die leiter abewerfen, sô er an ir ufgestigen. . . . Is that how you say it?"
> "That is how it is said in my language. Who told you that?"
> "A mystic from your land. He wrote it somewhere, I forget where. .. ." (*Rose* 492)

The quote, which Eco retranslates into medieval German, is from Wittgenstein.

SCENE IV. THE TEXT

A taste for the apocryphal, the fake, the anachronistic, the pseudo-allegorical, the unwonted analogy, as well as the parodic employ of hyperbole and baroque imagery as distancing devices, are a stylistic constant in Eco's occasional writings since the very popular and funny short pieces of his *Diario minimo*. Sustained through five hundred and some pages, their effect is something of a literary equivalent of pop art, a pop novel. *The Name of the Rose* has no authorial voice, and hence no authority of its own, for every scrap of discourse–every description, incident, or character, every turn of phrase, narrative style, metaphor, or metonymy–is an *objet trouvé*, whether it has been found in mass culture or high art, in an obscure patristic work or a contemporary text of French theory. One more example will suffice: the description of Adso's dream, which, according to Eco, is practically his translation of the medieval *Coena Cipriani* (and I must take his word for this, since I have never read or seen or heard of it before), but which I read as an imposing pastiche of Voltaire, Brueghel, Buñuel, Lyotard, and who knows who else, seasoned with comic book iconography and the liturgical cadence of litanies. At the end of the ten-page account of the dream or vision he had while the choir chanted the "Dies Irae," Adso says: "My vision, rapid like all visions, if it had not lasted the space of an 'amen,' *as the saying goes*, had lasted almost the length of a 'Dies irae'" (*Rose* 435, my emphasis).

I am reminded of Eco's own response to the film *Casablanca*, which he points out as a modern example of the sublime:

> When all the archetypes erupt indecently and unrestrained, Homeric depths are reached. Two clichés will make us laugh, but one hundred will move us. For one senses somehow that the clichés are speaking among themselves and celebrating their reunion. Just as the acutest pain trespasses into pleasure and perversion can touch the threshold of mystical energy, the utmost banality discloses the possibility of the sublime. Something has spoken [in the film] in the place of the director. This occurrence deserves. if nothing else. our veneration.[6]

In *The Name of the Rose*, too, something speaks in the name of the author. But what? The very term "rose," as Eco obviously chose it, is so dense with literary allusions, references, and connotations that it no longer has any, and thus appears to refer to what Baudrillard has called the implosion of meaning: a rose is a rose is a rose is a black hole, as it were. The writing itself, in the "Last Page," seems rather to stop than to end.

> It is cold in the scriptorium, my thumb aches. I leave this manuscript, I do not know for whom; I no longer know what it is about: stat rosa pristina nomine, nomina nuda tenemus.

However, does the book not aim to be like *Casablanca*, a thrust toward the modern, or perhaps the postmodern, sublime? Despite this ending–as low-key, self-denying, and non-authorial as the Prologue was lofty and resounding with the joint authorities of God and History–narrativity and laughter have been deployed in full force, the pleasure of the text and the "pure love of writing" have been consummated, and there is even some room left for writing a sequel. And is it not true, as Maria Corti observed, that this novel by the major theorist of the open work "is so lucidly constructed and so 'closed' as to respect the Aristotelian unities of time, place, and action in a manner that is nowadays all but exceptional"?[7]

Eco's formulation of the "open work," dating back to the period of his direct involvement with the Italian *neoavangardia* movement in the years 1958-63, was prompted by the necessity to find a critical language and new aesthetic categories that would account for certain contemporary artistic works produced by the second avant-garde, as it was called–the music of Berio, Boulez, Pousseur, Stockhausen, Calder's mobiles, as well as their precursors, notably Mallarmé, Joyce, and Brecht. He defined these "works in movement," argued that they should be seen as "epistemological metaphors," and related them to Einsteinian physics and the theoretical constructs of Husserl and Merleau-Ponty (See *Role* 47-66). The emphasis on indeterminacy, which at the time appeared to be the quintessence of "openness" and the *conditio sino qua non* of a radical avant-garde art, was historically motivated by the specific texts considered and the general intellectual climate. But the concern with form, if not yet structure, was equally strong in Eco, as the subtitle of *Opera aperta: forma e indeterminazione nelle poetiche contemporanee* more than suggests.

The notion of "open work," then, was one that applied equally to *The Divine Comedy* and to *Finnegans Wake*, though yielding different interpretive results, and though only the latter was a "work in movement." When Eco returns to it in *The Role of the Reader* (1979), reformulating it in terms of a pragmatics, rather than an aesthetics, of reception, he also renames it "open text."

> An author can foresee an "ideal reader affected by an ideal insomnia" (as happens with *Finnegans Wake*), able to master different codes and eager to deal with the text as with a maze of many issues. But in the last analysis what matters is not the various issues in themselves but the maze-like structure of the text. You cannot use the text as you want, but only as the text wants you to use it. An open text, however "open" it be, cannot afford whatever interpretation.
>
> An open text outlines a "closed" project of its Model Reader as a component of its structural strategy. (*Role* 9)

In other words, the Reader's role in interpreting the text is a "collaboration" demanded by the text's "generative structure," for the Reader is already contemplated by the text, and is in fact an element of its interpretation, a set of particular competencies and conditions which must be met if the text is to be "fully actualized" in its potential content. Much like Althusser's account of the subject's relation to ideology, Eco's recent theory of textuality at once invokes a reader who is already "competent," a (reading) subjectfully constituted prior to the text and to reading, *and* poses the reader as a term of the text's production of certain meanings, as an effect of its structure.[8] Writer and reader do have interpretive "freedom" (the term is Eco's), but that freedom is conditional and overdetermined: for the writer, by the (historically specified) universe of discourses available, which Eco calls at different times "the world of the encyclopedia" and "the format of the semantic space"; for the reader, it is overdetermined as much by the reader's knowledge of codes and frames as by the text's own project. But, if both reader and author are "textual strategies," pre(in)scribed or "foreseen" in the "maze-like structure of the text," then the question, What speaks in the name of the rose?, may indeed have already been answered by Eco against himself.

SCENE V. THE NAME

As Dorothy Sayers could have said, in *The Name of the Rose* Eco wants to "have his carcase"–he wants a mystery both with and without solution, a text both open and closed, an epistemology with and without truth. He wants, that is, to be an author-function (the term is Foucault's), but also and concurrently Rabelais and Descartes. He hints at the implosion of meaning and openly thematizes the abyss, classificatory difference, the "arche-writing" and the originary "violence of the letter"; yet does he not finally side with Lévi-Strauss against Derrida, as William educates Adso in their progress through the babelic labyrinth of the abbey, and as the text takes the reader through the maze of its "writing lesson"?[9]

The labyrinth, like the text, is an abstract model of inference or conjecture. In an essay written after the publication of the novel and in response to its initial reception, Eco states his conviction that the appeal of the detective story lies neither in the representation of murder and guilt, nor in the final triumph of justice and order, but in its being an instance of pure conjecture, on a par with "medical detection, scientific research, even metaphysical inquiry."[10] He then describes three types of labyrinth. In the Greek labyrinth "no one could get lost: you enter, reach the center, and from the center the exit. That's why at the center there is the Minotaur; otherwise the story would make no sense, it would be just a stroll." In the mannerist labyrinth there are a lot of dead ends and only one exit; however, "you can miss it. You need Ariadne's thread in order not to get lost. This is a model of the trial-and-error process." The third type of labyrinth is "the network, or what Deleuze and Guattari call rhizome, "built in such a way that every road connects with every other. It has no center, no periphery, and no exit, and is virtually infinite.

> The space of conjecture is a rhizomatous space. The labyrinth of my library ill still a mannerist labyrinth, but the world in which William lives, as he realizes, is already structured like a rhizome: that is to say, it is susceptible to being structured but never definitively. (*Postcript* 21)

The detective novel, Eco continues, poses and seeks to answer the "basic question of philosophy (as well as of psychoanalysis): whose fault is it?" In order to find out, "one must hypothesize that everything happens according to a logic, a logic imposed by the murderer. . . .. Thus my basic story (who is the murderer?) sends out as off shoots many other stories, all of them stories of conjectures and all having to do with the structure of conjecture as such." Now, if Eco is asking the question of philosophy, and if the result of his "inferential walk" through the rhizomatous space of the novel is the discovery of the "truth of nontruth," as Derrida claims for Nietzsche's styles in *Spurs*, are we to understand that writing in the name of the rose is but another form of "the becoming -female" of the idea?[11] In short, is Eco deconstructing here?

In her reading of *Spurs*, Derrida's reading of Nietzsche, Gayatri Spivak suggests that such feminization of philosophy–philosophy as a practice of writing, or "philosophizing"–as serves the male deconstructor "might find its most adequate legend in male homosexuality defined as criminality."[12] In *The Name of the Rose*, a story of books and monks, fathers and sons, the search for the name of the murderer could hardly lead to anything else. The brothers murder one another to secure the father's text, which is at last ingested, incorporated by the oldest of the horde, Jorge of Burgos, he who aspires, but alas all too literally, to be the body of the Word, to be what Derrida might call "the vocative absolute," or Eco the definitive edition of the world encyclopedia. But he will burn, and not in a bush, for his presumption to incarnate the Law, truth, and the phallus; for that would reduce difference and unlimited semiosis to (as one brother would say) a pound of flesh. The blind seer should have known–he, of all people–that the symbolic murder of the father finally cannot be achieved. What can be achieved instead, and with less effort, is the real murder of the mother.

Eco's lie may be premeditated and built in a modern, critical-scientific laboratory that has little to share with Mary Shelley's "workshop of filthy creation." Yet the novel does not escape the supreme law of modern fiction, the ultimate pop scenario in which the work, once created, turns against its creator and runs away with him. Like Pirandello's six characters or Frankenstein's monster, Eco/Adso's manuscript looses itself from its metanarrative moorings, exceeds the triply-embedded constraints of its "generative structure," breaks out of the author's elaborate *mise-en-scène*, and stages its own performance of desire.

It is in the name of the Father that Adso writes his memoirs (entitling us to read it as amanuensis), and Eco rewrites it as "an act of love," actually a falling in love ("un gesto di innamoramento"), a transference ("per liberarmi da numerose e antiche ossessioni"). He rewrites it after having lost it on the same "tragic night" in which he also lost his "beloved" and ended up with "a great emptiness in my heart." More accurately, he rewrites it having lost it to that person whose name and, more significantly, whose gender, remain unstated.[13] Of that person, however, we will encounter the displaced image (*en âbime*, to be sure) in Adso's manuscript: on another "tragic" and gaudy night, in a nameless young woman in whose body Adso experiences the "igneous ardor" and "splendid clarity" of the "vital spurt." Gaudeamus, igitur! Predictably enough this will be followed, for Adso, by the loss of "all memory in bliss" and the dispersal of identity in the abyss of *jouissance*, as well as *post coitum* depression, giving Eco the opportunity to replay various common places of religious mystical, and metaphysical erotica from The Song of Solomon to Bataille–and making one yearn for the *concinnitas* of a Jerry Lee Lewis. As for the woman the single female character in this story of monks and men, Adso's "igneus ardoi" and "vital spurt" will be followed, just as predictably, by her being burned at the stake.

SCENE VI. THE STAKE

Nameless and speechless body, she (it) stands for *natura naturans*, the presymbolic or presemiotic realm of, as Kristeva would call it, the maternal *chora*. Not coincidentally, upon waking, Adso will find her absent and in her place "dead but still throbbing with the gelatinous life of dead viscera, lined by livid nerves: a heart, of great size" (*Rose* 250). So the woman too, like Jorge and like the faithless and corrupt Mother Church embodied in the Abbey, will burn for all eternity. Less obviously, however, she is also the figure of the abyss. As Adso laments the fate of his only earthly love, and the prohibition that bars him from calling out the beloved's name, he discovers, Eco tells us with another wink toward Derrida, "the power of proper names" (*Rose* 397). Once more, at the end of his years and of his writing, will Adso fantasize her, this time as the mystic body of death: "I shall sink into the divine shadow, in a dumb silence and an ineffable union . . . and all differences will be forgotten. . . .. I shall fall into the silent and uninhabited divinity where there is no work and no image" (*Rose* 501). This is the abyss at the end of meaning's infinite regression, the empty (w)hole around which whirl the signifiers, the utterly unsignifiable double of a lost transcendental signified.

The associative chain woman-mother-church-truth-death could not be etched more sharply. But this dead, inert maternal body is not our story's obscure object of desire. Eco is not Poe. Just as with Poe's purloined letter, however, the object of desire is right on the surface of *The Name of the Rose*. It is the text itself, metonymically mirrored in the legendary text of the father of philosophy, all the more desired the more it is unattainable, and in the other texts it *generates*: Adso's manuscript and its various "translations," interpretants which together constitute the palimpsest of the symbolic body of the father, the inscription of the father's code and of the name of the father across the cultural history of Western Europe. For indeed, what sustains the master-disciple dialectic of William and Adso is the latter's desire for the father's knowledge, vision, and power: his learning–so often exhibited; his glasses–the better to decipher signs; his hands–delicate yet powerful to build wondrous machines; in short, his possession of the code, the magical instrument that transforms things into signs, nature into books (*natura naturata*), and books into history–actions, practices, events of the world.

As for William, then, what he desires is Adso's desire, the writing which inscribes it and the manuscript which signifies that desire and produces it as meaning. William, as we know, is an ex-inquisitor, a politically powerful man who has sought to give up his power and to devote himself instead to the pleasure of the text, the pleasure of constructing his semiotic machines. Yet, in spite of himself, power and knowledge stick to him and confer upon him a social role, a responsibility which he cannot refuse, being the democratic and progressive man that he is. Thus, in the difficult political conjuncture, he takes on the function of mediator between the various agencies of the left and the reactionary establishment. But his political mission fails, the pope and the emperor are going to end up in a stalemate, and the inquisition will continue to squelch dissention. And his work as cultural mediator would seem perfectly useless, were it not for Adso to whom he can bequeath his knowledge, his "writing lesson." For each of them, the possibility of existing in history is founded on the other's desire and recognition.

In this sense, finally, the name of the rose is the name of the father, and Eco's *homo semeioticus* may find his most adequate legend in homosexuality defined as pedagogy. In this sense, too, one might append to his work the words that Barbara Kruger collages over a blown-up detail of the creation scene from the Sistine Chapel: "You invest in the divinity of the masterpiece."[14] If Adam, semiotic subject of the Edenic language, had succeeded in turning myth into history by showing God out of the Garden door, his writing counterpart Adso effectively lets him back in through the open (window of the) text, by turning history into fiction. For the book written in the name of the father is always a testament, whether old or new. It is a book without author, but drenched in an authority that comes no less from the ambiguity of the gospels than from the certainty of the tables of the law, an authority bearing the weight of the obsessions of a great, millenary, and moribund patriarchal tradition.

If writing is an act of love, it is because it works to disavow that death and to allay its threat in the imaginary narrative of male self-creation. The stake of writing, then, is the endless reconstruction of the fetish, and the novel an ancient labor of love: the reconstruction of something lost (stolen) in a primal night, on another scene, and forever pursued across countries, years, and books–and the agony and the ecstasy of that pursuit.

SCENE VII. THE QUESTION

A propos of contemporary art, Craig Owens writes that the "official" production (by men) seems "engaged in a collective act of disavowal," whether it stimulates mastery or it contemplates and advertises the artist's loss of it. This he attributes to the emergent voices of the conquered "Third-World nations, the 'revolt of nature' and the women's movement."

> Symptoms of our recent loss of mastery are everywhere apparent in cultural activity today–nowhere more so than in the visual arts. The modernist project of joining forces with science and technology for the transformation of the environment after rational principles of function and utility (Productivism, the Bauhaus) has long since been abandoned; what we witness in its place is a desperate, often hysterical attempt to recover some sense of mastery via the resurrection of heroic large-scale easel painting and monumental cast-bronze sculpture–mediums themselves identified with the cultural hegemony of Western Europe. Yet contemporary artists are able at best to *simulate* mastery, to manipulate its signs; since un the modern period mastery was invariably associated with human labor, aesthetic production has degenerated today into a massive deployment of the signs of artistic labor–violent, "impassioned" brushwork, for example. [15]

A massive deployment of the signs of writing is certainly an apt description of *The Name of the Rose*, a work which may well be the updated version of the "master narrative," the patriarchal *grand récit* of all times (look at the sales on the international market, including the sale of the screenplay rights); yet it is are make clever enough to admit that the récit has lost credibility, a masterwork invested in divinity, but clever enough to disguise itself as a Text.

If this is true of Eco's writing, however, is it less true of those other writers to whom he constantly alludes, his contemporary intertextual referees, his brothers of the discursive fellowship? Is the postmodern condition not reconstructing its own fetishistic economy in *La Condition postmoderne*?[16] Isn't a metaphysical drive engaged in the critique of metaphysics? Isn't the discourse of power rhetorically reversible in the power of discourse? Ironically, these questions were once asked by Eco himself in his critique of structuralism–of Lévi-Strauss's "ontological structuralism" as well as its opponents and/or epigones, Lacan, Foucault, and Derrida, in *La struttura assente*. For in denying any origin, presence, or ontological foundation to the structure(s) of signification, the latter would also constrain the question of meaning production, and hence the social practices of signs, within a purely discursive dimension. They would cast the semiotic inquiry in the terms of a metaphysics of absence.

Their question, Eco charged, is Who speaks?–the question of philosophy, which has been asked for several thousand years and can be said to constitute thought itself. However, who has been asking that question? "A category of men who could afford the contemplation of Being because of the slave labor of others, and who thus held this question as the most urgent of all."

> Let us suppose there is another question, an even more constitutive one, that is asked not by the free man who can afford "contemplation," but by the slave who cannot; for the slave the question "who dies?" is amore urgent question than "who speaks?" . . .
>
> For the slave the *proximity of being* is not the most radical kinship: that *proximity of his own body and the bodies of others* come first. And in perceiving this other kinship, the slave does not leave the domain of ontology to regress (or to remain without consciousness) in the realm of matter: rather, he accedes to thought from another, equally worthy, pre-categorical situation.
>
> By asking "who dies?" we have not entered an empirical dimension in which all philosophies are worthless, but rather we have set out from another pre-philosophical presupposition in order to found another philosophy.[17]

Eco's proposal thus to reground philosophy was made in 1968. Read in the present context, it may seem either facile or, with regard to his most recent work, to have come to nought. But the sense of his gesture, a rhetorical cutting of the Gordian knot, still retains its polemical charge of negativity and critical productivity. In his own work, these should be looked for rather in the theoretically crucial, but regrettably unrecognized, achievement of *A Theory of Semiotics*, where indeed the question of meaning production is posed not from within the philosophical brotherhood or in the name of the father, but from the field of social practices in their materiality and historicity.

As for the slave's and other bodies burnt at the stake, they do not ask who's dying–that, they know. What they are asking, instead, is Juliet's question, What's in a name? And Eco's answer in *The Name of the Rose*, nothing and everything, is not what they want, is not enough.

EPILOGUE

Just a few weeks after I completed this paper, the *Boston Globe* reported on Eco's recent visit to Cambridge. "On the first of two lectures Monday and Tuesday, he told 500 people wedged into a Harvard lecture hall that he sees a 'new medieval wave' in America and Europe," wrote Richard Higgins, quoting Eco.

> In the Middle Ages, he said, lie the roots "of all our contemporary 'hot' problems." Both our "so-called post-modern era" and the Middle Ages are periods of political, cultural and technological transformation in which "the whole deck of historical cards is shuffled. All the problems of the Western world come out [then]: modern languages, merchant cities, banks, the prime rate, the rising of modern armies, the national state, as well as the idea of a supranational federation . . . the struggle between the poor and the rich, the concept of ideological deviation . . . the clash between state and church, worker unions, the technological transformation of labor [through such as windmills, horseshoes, oxen collars, more advanced rudders, compasses and stirrups] . . . the rise of modern ways of computing with the acceptance of Arab mathematics . . . even our contemporary notion of love as a devastating unhappy happiness."[18]

Need I point out the one "problem" that is not mentioned? Indeed, the one issue of political, cultural, and technological transformation that did not rise in the Middle Ages–or, if it did, was handled most effectively by burning its proponents at the stake (as shown in *The Name of the Rose*)? The problem, in short, of gender: the issue of a difference that divides the social subjects and imposes the question of the relation of subjectivity and experience to meaning, social formations, and power; a question only implied in Juliet's, but critically and politically articulated by feminism. And hence the "problem" of women, a contradiction in the semiotic universe which metaphysics and poetics can no longer hide, or patriarchal fictions reconcile.

The awareness of that contradiction as well as the improbability of reconciliation are not new to literature or even to the fictional genre chosen by Eco. Although not acknowledged contextually as Conan Doyle is, Dorothy Sayers's classic, *Gaudy Night*, comes immediately to mind.[19] What is remarkable there is not just the similarity in setting; the extensive, integral use of literary reference; the topos of the investigator being called into a closed, monastic, single-gendered community and finding there her or his own imaginary, and her or his real complicity in its crimes (Oedipus, once again?); or the double point of view and dialogic manner in which conjecture is worked out and the evidence sifted by the couple Harriet Vane and Peter Wimsey, heterosexual version of Adso and William. What is more remarkable in Sayers's novel is that the relationship between Harriet and Peter, explored within the frame of the narrative, is itself explicitly inscribed in the theme of the mystery and thus intrinsically compromised, despite the happy ending, by the plot's resolution. For the threat posed by the unknown offender to the college female community is revealed to be exactly reversible in the threat that a community of women scholars poses to the institution of heterosexuality. Conversely, as Eco demonstrates, semiotics poses no threat to the Word.

While Eco's gaudy *Rose* pretends to have no master plot and alleges to be a story of books, a game of conjecture in which the referent, historical reality, is always already infinitely mediated, and truth ultimately beside the point, what the book finally affirms is the truth of discourse, the *Name* of the rose, and thus the continuity of the very institution it seems to challenge: the Name of the Father. Sayers's *Gaudy Night*, on its part, admits to a double plot (with fewer murders) whose narrative resolution exposes the very contradiction constitutive of women as subjects in a social reality instituted in the name of the father and, beyond that, points to the contradiction of plot itself, the compromise of narrative discourse as it exists historically in that reality.

The point of this brief reference to *Gaudy Night* is not the futile one of giving Sayers's novel one label and Eco's another, but modestly to propose that some things have happened in America and Europe, as well as in literature and criticism, since the Middle Ages, and one of them is that one now knows that the "logic" of the murderer or of the writing is not the same when the gender is different. In both novels, the motives of the murderers are the same: a conservative, misconceived, even pathetic, last-ditch attempt to salvage the status quo. Yet the logic is not. For, as I read them, the romance of William and Adso emerges unscathed, comforting and everlasting from their journey through history and murder, whereas the romance of Harriet and Peter ends up on the shore of that contradiction which, the novel has shown, brings a woman to murder. Thus, if the mystery story's true achievement is its successful demonstration that the murderer is the reader, as Eco suggests, that "we are the guilty ones,"(*Postcript* 22) then from at least some readers he should expect the question:

Who's we, white man?–a question not unbecoming *The Name of the Rose*, after all.

Teresa de Lauretis

The Mirrored World: Form and Ideology
in Umberto Eco's *The Name of the Rose*

Devoted scanners of the *New York Times* lists of best-selling books were probably mystified in the summer of 1983 by the apparition at the top of the fiction charts of *The Name of the Rose*, a first novel by Umberto Eco. Eco might have been a household word to semioticians and structuralist critics of narrative, but his name meant nothing to the general public. The popularity of his novel must have had a great deal to do with its being a mystery novel; neither of Eco's later novels has done as well. But despite its superficial genre, *The Name of the Rose*, set in the year 1327, was an intricate postmodern metafiction, contained snatches of prose and poetry in Latin, Greek and Middle High German that readers had to translate for themselves or do without, and insisted that they learn more about imperial-papal politics, medieval herbal lore, and religious iconography than most general readers wanted to know. A colleague of mine called it "the book most likely to be left in the Hamptons"–to be purchased, in other words, out of ill-conceived enthusiasm, and then to perish of damp, ignominiously unread, at one's summer beach house.

He was wrong: *The Name of the Rose* lingered on the best-seller list through the spring of 1984, sold millions of paperbacks and inspired a popular (and relatively faithful) Hollywood movie. On the other side of the cultural divide, *The Name of the Rose* became a textual icon, subjected to scrutiny at literary conferences and in special issues of critical journals. In the dozen years since its publication, the academic community produced nearly two hundred books and articles on *The Name of the Rose* exploring "Eco's eclectic debts. . . to William of Occam, Roger Bacon, Alessandro Manzoni, Jorge Luis Borges, Conan Doyle, Mikhail Bakhtin, Charles S. Peirce, Yuri Lotman, Roland Barthes" and so on.[1] In his famous *Encounter* essay, Eco had called his novel "a machine for generating interpretations," and he seems to have hit the nail on the head.[2]

Such attention greets few detective stories. Most exemplars of that genre, subordinating character and motivation to that moment of apocalypsis, depend so much on the astonishment they hope to provoke when the solution to the mystery is revealed that there is little left to enjoy on a second reading unless the consumer can develop a convenient case of amnesia. In his *New Yorker* review of *The Name of the Rose*, John Updike noted an "empty feeling" within him as he finished the novel. Fans of detective fiction know the sensation well–of an enjoyment that can never be recaptured.

So in a way the most signal triumph of Eco's *The Name of the Rose* is way it bears rereading. Indeed, like other novels with surprises in them from *Emma* to *The Brothers Karamazov* to *Lolita*, *The Name of the Rose* is not precisely the same book the second time through. As with any detective story, there is no urgency any more about locating the villain, or in matching wits with the author. And this may in places create a few longueurs, largely because the solution to the novel's most superficial problem–who done it?–sticks so prominently in the mind. There is no chance of forgetting Eco's villain. But other aspects of the novel, through which one may have rushed hurriedly the first time through, impatient to reach the solution, take on new life on a second reading. The following essay concerns some of the issues that become important on a second reading of *The Name of the Rose*, issues of causal connection and narrative form that have occupied the author as a semiotician and as a literary theorist and issues of social and political ideology that have concerned him as a private citizen.

STRUCTURE I. ECO AND THE SEMIOTICS OF DETECTION

omnis mundi creatura
quasi liber et pictura
nobis est in speculum
Alain de Lille (1130-1202): "Anticlaudianus"[3]

The Name of the Rose traces the stages in the long line between Alain de Lille, the twelfth-century antischolastic, and modern structuralists like Umberto Eco himself. Separated by eight centuries, Alain and Eco would agree that the world is like a vast text, "quasi liber et pictura," and that our task on earth is learning the rules for reading it.

The Name of the Rose has been treated as an unusually clever pastiche of the Sherlock Holmes novels. This is a misreading, but one that Eco has courted. He has, after all, named his protagonist William of Baskerville, made him a native of Ireland (like Doyle's ancestors), given him the height, the sharpness of eye and beakiness of nose associated with the sleuth of Baker Street.[4] The narrator's name, Adso, is the middle four phonemes of "Watson" (as close as one could come in a Latinized name), and though a cloistered monk, Adso shares Watson's unascetic gusto for the pleasures of the table and his predilection for romance, along with a talent for muddling up the clues.

The structure of Eco's novel, however, owes very little to Doyle, whose longer detective fictions usually tended to split into two novelettes: one a tale of crime and detection, the other a sensational melodrama about Mormons or East Indian convicts or labor racketeers in industrial Pennsylvania. (Only *The Hound of the Baskervilles*, to which William's name obviously alludes, has the unity of plot and tone Eco has achieved here). In its plotting *The Name of the Rose* seems to owe less to Doyle than to Dorothy Sayers, John Dickson Carr and Ellery Queen. Despite the medieval setting Eco has collected the complete paraphernalia of a classic mystery of the 1930s: maps, cryptograms, unbreakable alibis, a locked room, a labyrinthine library, clues in a variety of foreign languages, all surrounding a series of grisly murders, carefully spaced one per day with an elaborate textual patterning to them. It was apparently Eco's intention to write the mystery to end all mysteries.

But there is another sense in which *The Name of the Rose* is a mystery to end all mysteries: it is also a critique and a parody of the form. This is true in obvious ways–merely setting a murder mystery in the late middle ages suggests either more or less than entirely serious intentions. Part of the book's pleasure comes from watching the conventions of the form crop up, regular as fate, in the most unexpected settings. As a result, the reader seems to be reading two novels at once: a classic detective story, and a detective story in quotation marks–the latter a post-modern fiction which calls attention to its very fictionality.

Perhaps Eco is merely spoofing the mystery form. But the parody has its serious side where it connects with Eco's professional interest in detection as a semiotic activity. It is only in a superficial sense that *The Name of the Rose* presents a Holmes-figure in characteristic action: for William of Baskerville is far more self-conscious and self-critical than Doyle's self-aggrandizing detective who, in A Study in Scarlet (his debut novel), writes a magazine article boasting of his infallibility.[5] As a philosopher, Eco is more aware than Doyle was of the logical status of detective ingenuity.

Throughout the Holmes stories, the detective's abilities are explained as "the science of deduction." One locus classicus explaining the Holmesian method occurs in *The Sign of Four*:

> "But you spoke just now of observation and deduction. Surely the one to some extent implies the other."
> "Why, hardly," [Holmes] answered. . ... "For example, observation shows me that you have been to the Wigmore Street Post-Office this morning, but deduction lets me know that when there you dispatched a telegram."
> "Right!" said I. "Right on both points! But I confess that I don't see how you arrived at it . . ."
> "It is simplicity itself," he remarked, chuckling at my surprise–"so absurdly simple that an explanation is superfluous; and yet it may serve to define the

limits of observation and of deduction. Observation tells me that you have a little reddish mould adhering to your instep. Just opposite the Wigmore Street Office they have taken up the pavement and thrown up some earth, which lies in such a way that it is difficult to avoid treading in it in entering. The earth is of this peculiar reddish tint which is found, as far as I know, nowhere else in the neighbourhood. So much is observation. The rest is deduction."

"How, then, did you deduce the telegram?"

"Why, of course I knew that you had not written a letter, since I sat opposite to you all morning. I see also in your open desk there that you have a sheet of stamps and a thick bundle of postcards. What could you go into the post-office for, then, but to send a wire? Eliminate all other factors, and the one which remains must be the truth" (pp. 138-39).

Holmes–and Doyle–probably thought that this was a perfect demonstration of deductive logic, but when one examines it a bit, it is rather less than impeccable. The syllogism upon which Holmes's inference relies would run, according to his explanation, as follows:

> Men who enter the Post Office will invariably get red mould on their boots.
> Watson has red mould on his boots.
> Therefore Watson has entered the Post Office.

But this syllogism is invalid: the middle term is undistributed. A syllogism in barbara could be constructed if the major term were given as "All those and only those who enter the post office have red mould on their boots." But this is not what Holmes actually asserts, and detectives in general do not make their assertions in such a form. One might step in red earth walking past the post-office; one might step into it and clean one's boots afterwards. Similarly with Holmes's "deduction" of the telegram: if there were three and only three reasons for entering a post office (sending a letter, buying postage, dispatching a telegram), then eliminating the first two possibilities would demonstrate the third. But is it possible to catalog and eliminate all the possible reasons for entering a post office?

The point is not that Holmes is a charlatan, or that Doyle was, but that logical deduction of the sort whose regulations are presented in Aristotle's *Posterior Analytics*, has very little to do with what Holmes is doing. It is noteworthy that the philosopher who best described the art Holmes practiced–the art upon which scientists, doctors, and real detectives all depend–was a contemporary of Doyle's, the American Charles Sanders Peirce.[6] To the previously established logical methods of deduction and induction, Peirce added a third, which he gave the perhaps unfortunate name of "abduction." Whereas deduction proceeds from a general rule (or a definition) to a particular case, and whereas induction proceeds from a series of facts to a general rule, abduction' is "the provisional entertainment of an explanatory inference, for the sake of further testing." ("Horns" 206) In abduction–a mode of reasoning we all probably use far more often than strict syllogistic deduction–both the general rule and the particular conclusion are held only tentatively; they are conjectures to be confirmed or refuted rather than certain truths.

One does not need to read Eco's philosophical essay on abduction to understand its relevance to detective fiction. Much of it is explicitly presented in *The Name of the Rose*:

> "Adso," William said, "solving a mystery is not the same as deducing from first principles. Nor does it amount simply to collecting a number of particular data from which to infer a general law. It means, rather, facing one or two or three particular data apparently with nothing in common, and trying to imagine whether they could represent so many instances of a general law you don't yet know, and which perhaps has never been pronounced. . . .. Take the case of animals with horns. Why do they have horns? Suddenly you realize that all animals with horns are without [incisors] in the upper jaw. This would be a fine discovery, if you did not also realize that, alas, there are animals without [incisors] in the upper jaw who, however, do not have horns: the camel, to name one. And finally you realize that all animals without [incisors] in the upper jaw have four stomachs. Well, then, you can suppose that one who cannot chew well must need four stomachs to digest food better. But what about the horns? You then try to imagine a material cause for horns–say, the lack of teeth provides the animal with an excess of osseous matter that must emerge somewhere else. But is that sufficient explanation? No, because the camel has no upper teeth . . . but does not have horns. And you must also imagine a final cause. The osseous matter emerges in horns only in animals without other means of defense. But the camel has a very tough hide and doesn't need horns. . .. The search for explicative laws in natural facts proceeds in a tortuous fashion. In the face of some inexplicable facts you must try to imagine many general laws, whose connection with the facts escapes you. Then suddenly, in the unexpected connection of a result, a specific situation, and one of those laws, you perceive a line of reasoning that seems more convincing than the others. You try applying it . . . to use it for making predictions, and you discover that your intuition was right. But until you reach the end you will never know which predicates to introduce into your reasoning and which to omit. . .."(pp. 304-305)[7]

William's theory here is one of the major "problematic anachronisms" that I shall discuss in the next section of this essay. As a theory, it owes a great deal to Peirce, and nearly as much to Sir Karl Popper's explanation of the scientific method as a series of conjectures and refutations in *The Logic of Scientific Discovery* (1952). But the example William gives is straight out of Aristotle's *On the Parts of Animals*, a text Eco also analyzes at length in "Horns, Hooves, Insteps," showing that 2300 years ago Aristotle, "the master of those that know," intuitively understood the essential tool of scientific method which Eco calls "creative abduction" (*"Horns"* 215).

In *The Sign of Four* Holmes is permitted suavely to assure Watson, "I never guess. It is a shocking habit–destructive to the logical faculty" (p. 138). But in *The Name of the Rose* Eco's detective, the superficially Holmesian William of Baskerville, is well aware that in the exercise of his logical faculty he needs to guess constantly, and that the world–made up as it is of " everything that is the case"–will confirm or deny his hypotheses, make him seem a genius or a fool.

It is significant that the opening demonstration of William's detective abilities–his description and location of the abbot's horse Brunellus (pp. 23-25)–though a convention of the detective novel since Doyle, does not directly allude to the Sherlock Holmes canon. Instead of using a displaced version of one of Holmes's feats, Eco began *The Name of the Rose* with a revision of part of chapter 3 of *Zadig*. There the Chaldean hero of Voltaire's *conte philosophique* dazzles the servants of the King of Babylon by telling them that the horse they are looking for, which Zadig himself has never laid eyes on, "is the fleetest horse in the King's stable. . . . He is five feet high, with very small hoofs, and a tall three and a half feet in length, the studs on his bit are gold of twenty-three carats, and his shoes are silver of eleven pennyweights."[8]

My first notion was that, in this detective-story-to-end-all-detective-stories, Eco thought it clever to begin with a proto-detective fiction written a century before Poe's pioneering tales. But after looking at "Horns, Hooves, Insteps," it becomes clear that Eco had something else in mind as well–what he calls "meta-abduction," the problem of testing for correspondence the world of one's mental constructs against the world outside one's head. The reason *Zadig* is only one of the forerunners of the detective story and not its first exemplar is that Zadig himself refuses to take that final step. When the huntsmen ask where the horse is, Zadig refuses to guess as Holmes would do, but instead replies " I have not seen him . . . and never heard talk of him before" (p. 11). And, Zadig is first condemned for stealing the horse and then, when the horse is found, for lying to the huntsmen about not having seen the beast whose characteristics he had actually abduced. Eco's meditation on *Zadig* is that, while the philosopher is willing to speak about his abductions as mental constructs of his own, he resists being trapped into asserting an identity between the possible horse of his inferences and the actual horse the huntsmen are seeking: "Unable to accept his fate as a Sherlock Holmes, Zadig was frightened by meta-abduction" (*"Horns"* 215).

Holmes, of course, is never frightened. Though as Eco points out, he often guesses with far less reason for certainty than Zadig had, he never guesses wrong. This is because "he has the privilege of living in a world built by Conan Doyle to fit his egocentric need, so he does not lack imme-

diate proofs of his perspicacity" ("*Horns*" 218). There is always faithful
Watson, ever ready to admit to having acted or thought as Holmes guesses;
nor is the outside world of crime ever so unkind as to falsify Holmes's
abductions. Eco goes on to suggest that, "Whereas in criminal stories an
omnipotent God verifies the hypotheses forever, in 'real' scientific inquiries (as well as in real criminal, medical, or philological deduction) meta-
abductions are a frightening matter. *Zadig* is not a detection story but a
philosophical tale because its deep subject is exactly the vertigo of meta-
abduction" ("*Horns*" 219).

As we shall see more clearly in the last section of this essay, *The Name of
the Rose* stands midway between the detective story and the philosophic
tale. More like a Sherlock Holmes than a Zadig, William of Baskerville
defies the "vertigo" and volunteers his guess about what Brunellus looks
like and where he has gone. And as though he were in a literary world
protected by Doyle, the guess is right on target. But unlike the detectives
who attribute their infallibility to logic rather than authorial kindness,
William knows that his was merely a lucky guess:

> In the case of the horse Brunellus, when I saw the clues I guessed many comple-
> mentary and contradictory hypotheses. . . . I didn't know which hypothesis
> was right until I saw the cellarer and the servants anxiously searching. Then I
> understood that the Brunellus hypothesis was the only right one, and I tried to
> prove it true, addressing the monks as I did. I won, but I might also have lost.
> The others believed me wise because I won, but they didn't know the many
> instances in which I have been foolish because I lost, and they didn't know that
> a few seconds before winning I wasn't sure I wouldn't lose. (*Rose* 305)

While the Holmesian whodunit proceeds on the Cartesian assumption
that there is an order to the universe that can be mirrored in the constructs
of an orderly mind, Eco's mystery takes a more modern, post-Kantian tack.
William never doubts that mental constructs may possess clarity and order:
but there is always a leap of faith to the decision that the outside world
does. And Eco, as we shall see, is less kind to William than Doyle is to
Sherlock Holmes. In this sense *The Name of the Rose* is based upon a
postmodern semiotic theory that is essentially subversive of the mystery as
a genre. In setting such a semiotic quest within the middle ages, Eco's novel
is structurally underpinned by a global anachronism, within which local
instances of intellectual time-warp are set as textural motifs.

TEXTURE I. PROBLEMATIC ANACHRONISMS

In *The Name of the Rose* we are never allowed to lose ourselves in a historical
novel. We are again and again made self-consciously aware, through the

work's inherent contradictions–or apparent anachronisms–that we are reading a construction of history. In a sense, there was no way Eco could have preserved "suspension of disbelief." The reader is bound to be brought up short from time to time by the inescapable anachronism of a whodunit set in the middle ages. The strategy taken up by many contemporary historical novelists (e.g., Mary Renault or Robert Graves), of attempting as far as possible to convey the life of the narrative past in language and narrative technique roughly appropriate to that period, is foreclosed for Eco. To be a detective at all, his protagonist, William of Baskerville, must be essentially a modern man, but he must also be placed within a medieval setting that is as authentic as possible. There is an inherent self-contradiction in this, but instead of trying to deceive the reader about this, Eco chose a playful way of writing historical fiction that would keep the reader off balance; it would fall somewhere between pastiche and serious narrative.

One way of playing with the reader is the phony anachronism. The game to which Eco invites us involves matching wits with the author, and so is structurally similar to the author-vs.-reader game in the standard detective story except that it can be played over and over again. The pattern runs in this way: the author allows the "thoroughly modern" William of Baskerville to use a phrase that recalls a quotation from a later date, or to mention some fact or some process we associate with a more modern period. Then the reader recalls–or looks up–the historical facts, and the apparent anachronism is eliminated.

Take, for example, William's statement: "We are dwarfs . . . but dwarfs who stand on the shoulder of those giants, and small though we are, we sometimes manage to see farther on the horizon than they" (p. 86). This is an all-too-familiar quotation. The classic formulation is: "dwarves that stand on the shoulders of giants can see farther than the giants themselves," and it is usually ascribed to Isaac Newton in the late seventeenth century. As a medievalist, Eco is probably familiar with these earlier sources. But even a nonmedievalist like me might be familiar with an entertaining book by the sociologist of knowledge Robert K. Merton, *On the Shoulders of Giants*. Merton's book traces the quotation back considerably *before* 1327–to the twelfth-century philosopher Bernard of Chartres–and Eco even includes the detail that his William of Baskerville had studied at Chartres.

A more convoluted instance involves Adso's heartfelt remark on Jacques of Cahors, later Pope John XXII: "and heaven grant that no pontiff take again a name so distasteful to the righteous" (p. 12). The first level of the joke is fairly obvious: it was well known that Angelo Giuseppe Roncalli, on ascending the throne of St. Peter, took the title of John XXIII as a way of disinfecting a papal name that had remained unused since the middle ages. The second level of the joke is rather more obscure: the bad smell in the name of John had been left at least as much by a previous John XXIII (Baldassare Cossa, 1410-15) as by the John XXII who appears in *The Name of the Rose*. The fifteenth-century pope (he was one of two anti-popes–the other was Benedict XIII–who had been elected by a faction during the official Pontificate of Gregory XII) was accused of so many crimes, including heresy, simony, piracy, sodomy, rape, incest and the assassination of his predecessor, that he was deposed by the Council of Constance as *scandalizor ecclesiae*.

Not all the anachronisms turn into jokes on the half-learned reader. Some of them remain anachronisms. Most of these are intertextual jokes, like the hints (p. 16) that William gets high chewing the leaves of some mysterious forest herbs (whose effects–lethargy and visions–sound suspiciously like those of cannabis). Here, of course, the point is an allusion to Sherlock Holmes's dalliance, at times of intellectual vacuity, with the cocaine-bottle. Substituting cannabis for coca is at least mildly anachronistic, since around 1327 Indian Hemp was used as a drug only in the Orient and was apparently unknown in the West till the 1580s. We could make the favorable assumption that William is familiar with Eastern sources now forgotten, but cocaine itself would have been utterly impossible as the coca plant is native to the Americas and would be unavailable in Europe for nearly two hundred years.

Some of the anachronistic jokes, though, are not intertextual in any very specific sense: they pertain rather to the general tradition of learned wit to which this novel belongs. At one point William recites a few gnomic lines from a text called *Hisperica . . . famina*, apparently a medieval poem about the Irish Potato Famine of the 1840s (p. 311). At still another point William makes what we cannot fail to interpret as a mocking allusion to Freud ("We have so many truths in our possession that if the day came when someone insisted on deriving a truth even from our dreams, then the day of the Antichrist would truly be at hand" [p. 438]). And on what is nearly the novel's last page (p. 492), William quotes for Adso "a mystic from your land" [Germany], who wrote "somewhere, I forget where" about philosophical constructs: "'*Er muoz gelichsame die leiter abwerfen, sô er an ir ufgestigen*'" (p. 438). It means "One must throw down the ladder as soon as he has climbed up it," and it was written–though not in Middle High German, of course–by Ludwig Wittgenstein in the *Tractatus Logico-Philosophicus* (1921).[9]

The novel is filled with this sort of amusement–a sort of Ph.D.-level Trivial Pursuit. Out of hundreds possible let me give one last example, which is not a joke but rather an homage to the greatest master of the learned wit tradition, François Rabelais. The "maguffin" of *The Name of the Rose*, the manuscript containing Aristotle's lost treatise on comedy, is bound together with several other manuscripts in various languages; one of these is "Expositio Magistri Alcofribae de coena beati Cypriani Cartaginensis Episcopi" (p. 439)–a commentary on the porno-satiric *Coena Cypriani* by one "Master Alcofribas." "Alcofribas Nasier," of course, was the anagrammatical pseudonym under which Rabelais began in 1532 to publish his porno-satirical histories of Gargantua and Pantagruel. There are a number of connections here: like William of Baskerville, Rabelais was a Franciscan friar who transferred for political reasons to the Benedictines. Adso and William's pleasure in lists–lists that go on long after you expected them to be exhausted–comes directly from Rabelais. But the central issue, I suspect, is the "carnivalization" (as Mikhail Bakhtin puts it) of history and scholarship Rabelais brings to fiction. This carnivalization is precisely what Eco is attempting in *The Name of the Rose*: not a parody of the detective story, precisely, nor a pastiche, but a witty and learned game which not only solicits but demands the participation of the reader, and deals out rewards in proportion to his own learning and wit.

TEXTURE II. TIME IN *THE NAME OF THE ROSE*: THE BLACK DEATH

In *The Role of the Reader*, Eco has analyzed the way Time is structured in series detective stories, like those involving Sherlock Holmes or Nero Wolfe: he calls this "the iterative scheme"(*Role* 117-120). In each novel or story, the "event takes up again from a sort of virtual beginning, ignoring where the preceding event left off" (*Role* 119). A popular detective series, like the Nero Wolfe stories of Rex Stout, contains a vast number of *topoi*, which can be repeated again and again. On the one hand there are "infinite variations of the theme" in that each new crime "has new psychological and economic motivations" (*Role* 119); on the other hand, the memorable moments are the ones that recur from book to book (e.g., Wolfe getting up to tend his orchids when the case is at an obvious crisis point). Eco's main point is given the "virtual beginning," the series is free to ignore the way time is consumed by the events of each separate story. Stout's novels were written over a period of more than forty years–from the early 1930s when the series began to the late 1970s when it ended– but Wolfe always seems to be a man in his forties, Archie Goodwin in his late twenties. Rare cases may fall into an ordered series, and occasionally a novel will refer to one of its predecessors or to a topical event, but generally each novel constitutes a new beginning that is connected only vaguely to historical time or to the continuous pasts of the series characters.

Historical detective stories like *The Name of the Rose* must be set at some definite time (i.e., they cannot be set in a vague narrative present like the Nero Wolfe series), but there is no reason that Eco's "iterative scheme" may not apply to them. Indeed, the "Sergeant Cribb" series of Peter

Lovesey is a sequence of Victorian *romans policiers* with eminently predictable *topoi*. Most historical whodunits, even when they happen to be single-
tons (like John Dickson Carr's *The Demoniacs*), fail to consume the lives of
the narrator and/or the detective; unlike most novels, they might be continued indefinitely, in that nothing unalterable occurs to characters other
than the disposable victims and villains.

In *The Name of the Rose*, however, Eco reverses this narrative convention
of the detective story. Though the story takes up only a week or so in the
lives of William and Adso, the novel is set within a restrictive time-frame
that "consumes" the characters and prevents any sense of possible continu-
ation. Most important for this aspect of the story is the framed beginning
and ending of the story, in which Adso the narrator, old and perhaps dying
toward the end of the fourteenth century, places in context the events of
the novel, which are set within his youth in the year 1327. The effect is not
solely a matter of age and youth: between Adso the writer and Adso the
character there looms the great event of the fourteenth century, the Black
Death of 1348-50. Before the Black Death were the high middle ages, the
renaissance of learning of the twelfth and thirteenth centuries; after it came
a century of chaos as Europe recovered from the death of over one third of
its population. Like his namesake, William of Ockham, William of
Baskerville perished during the plague–perhaps a less than tragically prema-
ture end for a man who is well into his fifties in 1327. The point, though, is
that Adso, who survived, tells us of a society that largely did not: he tells us
of "the disaster of an aging world" (p. 15).

In terms of the "distant mirror" aspect of *The Name of the Rose*, the
intertextual play between the fourteenth and twentieth centuries, the Black
Death equated to the potential atomic holocaust that was somewhere in the
back of everyone's mind throughout the Cold War. It was not a bad metaphor, except that the atomic holocaust would not leave monkish survivors
to record it. What is probably most important about it, for Eco's purposes,
is that in Adso's retrospective narrative (and the reader's historical perspective) the echo of the Black Death invests the action with the sense of im-
pending chaos, of an apparently ordered and balanced intellectual and social system whose doom is already pronounced.

TEXTURE III. THE "DISTANT MIRROR" THEME

Barbara Tuchman's popular history of the fourteenth century was entitled
A Distant Mirror and she was by no means the first historian to see "phenomenal parallels" between that age and our own. When this century was
only two decades old, James Westfall Thompson was ready to compare the
aftermath of World War I with that of the Black Death. Thompson saw
both the fourteenth and the twentieth centuries as exceptionally disor-

dered: in both he found running rampant "economic chaos, social unrest, high prices, profiteering, depraved morals, lack of production, industrial indolence, frenetic gaiety, wild expenditure, luxury, debauchery, social and religious hysteria, greed, avarice, maladministration, decay of manners."[10] The advent over the past forty years of weaponry capable of depopulating the world faster and more dependably than the bubonic plague has only deepened the sense that we have something to learn from that unhappy period.

Just as the tone of *The Name of the Rose* owes a good deal to the overhanging shadow of the Black Death, Eco's secondary purpose in setting his detective entertainment in the early fourteenth century may have had more to do with the pestilential politics of Emperor and Pope than with the apocalypse of rats and lice that came later. The suggestive analogy, I think, for a liberal European socialist like Eco, is the cold war between Louis the Bavarian and John XXII on the one hand, and the one that ran from 1949 to 1989 on the other between capitalism and communism, America and the Soviet Union, NATO and the Warsaw Pact. Eco was no neutral. He deplored the insistent division of the political and moral powers of the known world, a division that implicitly brooks neither independence nor neutrality, which claimed that all who are not for me are against me. I would argue that Eco has drawn such an analogy, and has developed it at a length that–detracting formally from *The Name of the Rose* as it does–indicates the strength of his personal commitment to it.[11]

The general structure of the political allegory, which is not explored with absolute consistency, would equate the party of Holy Roman Emperor Louis of Bavaria with the massive might of the old USSR, with the ideology of socialism, perhaps with the alliance of Warsaw Pact and socialist movements in Europe and the Third World; conversely, the party of Pope John XXII might be identified with the USA, with the ideology of capitalism, with the NATO alliance. This alignment would put the Franciscans–who were in doctrinal opposition to the Pope, though ostensibly his own order–in the approximate position of the European socialist movements. Or the analogy might work another way. Since the Emperor had the habit of using, then abandoning his allies and since the Pope was the more obviously ruthless of the two men, it may be that we are to link Louis with the Western and John with the Eastern bloc. In fact the orientation of the allegory makes very little difference. What is important for Eco is the absolute and totalized nature of the confrontation, the way the political battle raged over Europe for decades with final victory ever elusive, and the fact that the outcome of the battle, for both sides, was the destruction of the authority of the institutions they represented.

For an Italian socialist like Eco, in fact, the central problems of the international scene had to do less with the USA and the USSR. with their half billion inhabitants, than with the impact of their struggle on the three billion people elsewhere in nations that might have preferred to remain unaligned but who were inexorably forced to take sides, if only to give them standing to help mediate the conflict. While there are no certain limits to the application of Eco's political allegory in *The Name of the Rose*, I think there are at least three major issues that haunted him: (1) the nominally "socialist" revolutionary movements in the Third World, (2) the attraction of intellectuals to terrorism,' and (3) the international penetration of other nations by clandestine political organizations like CIA and KGB. Let me briefly indicate the connections between Eco's fiction and these three problems.

1. The fourteenth century was a fertile period for heresies of various sorts: Fraticelli, Catharists, Waldensians, Arnoldists, Patarines, and countless other groups sprang up and were ruthlessly extirpated by the Papacy. Around pp. 196-207, William holds a platonic dialogue with Adso on what he calls "the great river of heresy." William rejects the idea that most heretics are convinced adherents of particular mistaken doctrines. In fact, he points out, most heretics are simple folk who might join the Catharists in one village and the Waldensians in another–though the two heresies are doctrinally quite distinct. In the Church's view a heretical doctrine is first proclaimed by a renegade cleric and then taken up by the simple. In William's view it is the condition of being "simple" rather than the doctrine that causes heresy, for the simple–those landless peasants without a stake in the State, who were equally excluded from the intellectual and social protection of the Church–join heretical movements not because they believe but because the movements give them hope: the hope at least of violently overthrowing the order that excludes them.

The parallel is obvious between William's "simple" heretics and the peasants who willingly joined to fight and die for socialist or communist movements in the Third World. Their doctrinal commitment to Marxism may have been scant. They believed in whatever opposed the native or colonial powers, in whatever gave them hope to overturn the order that kept them hungry. Eco seems to suggest that the West, and the USA in particular, were paranoid about such "communist" movements, that it misunderstood them as an overt threat to join the Soviet enemy, when the real issue was the hunger of the people–not merely a hunger for bread but a hunger inclusion within the international polity.

2. One rather memorable character Eco took from the pages of history and transferred to *The Name of the Rose* is Fra Ubertino of Casale, author of the *Arbor Vitae Crucifixae*. Ubertino was one of the Spirituales,

a rather mystical religious movement deriving from the prophecies of the twelfth-century apocalyptic thinker Joachim of Floris. Ubertino's personal history and that of his movement appear in *The Name of the Rose* at pp. 41-64; for most of the rest of the novel, Ubertino is relatively undeveloped as a character, neither a suspect nor a victim. He can be fully understood only after the passages on heresy, for Ubertino is an intellectual whose preaching led the "simple" to join heretical movements (like the Dolcinians and the Fraticelli), movements that the Papacy crushed with fire and the sword. Nevertheless Ubertino somehow managed to keep himself clear of the taint of heresy, speaks with horror of the Fraticelli, and evidently believes that there is some quintessential difference (a difference not obvious to this reader) between the beliefs of Fra Dolcino, who suffered at the stake. and his own.

I can make sense of this episode only as displaced commentary on a group of European leftists who glorified revolution but who had little stomach for the violence of the terrorists that would have been willing to put their programs into practice. These "limousine liberals," like Ubertino, had no intention of losing their privileged academic places in the societies they attacked, much less of suffering for their beliefs. Eco may have had in mind the crowds that idolized Herbert Marcuse or Frantz Fanon in the sixties; perhaps Ubertino is a satire on the greatest of them all: Michel Foucault. In any case, Eco quietly exposes their hypocritical habit of theoretically advocating anarchic violence while remaining noncommittal about terrorism of the Black September type.

3. Finally there is another character out of history: the Papal Inquisitor Bernard Gui (1261-1331), author of the *Practica Inquisitionis*. In a sense, Bernard assumes a place within *The Name of the Rose* that the traditional structure of the detective story assigns to the dumb cop, the unimaginative official policeman who flails about helplessly, baffled by his inability to solve the crime. But Bernard is more than a structural locus and a foil for William. While the aimless brutality of the cops in whodunits is usually limited to bad language and the occasional swat with a rubber hose, Gui has three people put to death in a memorably horrifying manner for crimes they have not committed. One point Eco makes about Bernard's methods is that, seeking out heresy, he invariably finds it, as the accused's words and deeds will ineluctably be twisted against him. The other point is that the Inquisition, in trying to extirpate heresy by the most arbitrary and limitless methods, ends by causing more heresy than it destroys. Eco's analogue could be simply to the twentieth-century version of the Inquisition, the secret po-

lice, which, under various names in both Eastern and Western bloc nations (FBI, KGB, Securitate...) provoked the opposition it aimed to still. But given the international slant to Eco's analogues, Gui and the Inquisition may also stand for the international organizations (like the CIA and MI5) specializing in covert activities whose effect was equally perverse. As with Bernard, failure (as in Cuba and Nicaragua) bred contempt, while success (as in Chile) turns potential friends into renegades. Meanwhile the institution was an international embarrassment to the nation that wielded it.

There are surely many more topical parallels between the events and institutions in *The Name of the Rose* and those in the world within which Eco was writing. But Eco has created neither a mere history lesson nor a sermon on contemporary international politics, but a system of mirrors by which the present and the past are allowed to reflect, distort and parody each other.

STRUCTURE II. THE DENOUEMENT OF THE NAME OF THE ROSE:
BETWEEN THE MODERN AND THE POST-MODERN DETECTIVE STORY

There is a peculiar tension all through *The Name of the Rose* between creation and parody, between the apparently sincere imitation of the *topoi* of the classic mystery novel and the carnivalization of its forms. This tension explodes in the denouement. It requires a backward glance, though, at the standard ending of the detective story and the way its postmodern revisionists have turned it inside out.

In its standard manifestations the form of the detective story is almost entirely ritualized: a murder is committed, the detective is called in to investigate, clues are followed up, stories checked, hypotheses presented and discarded; finally the villain is unmasked and the crime explained to the subsidiary characters–and to the reader. Or as Dennis Porter has put it: "In the process of telling one tale, a classic detective story uncovers another. It purports to narrate the course of an investigation, but the 'open' story of the investigation gradually unravels the 'hidden' story of the crime."[12]

The ultimate *desideratum* of the final explanation–the obligatory section of the novel that turns the fragmented clues of the original crime into the material of narrative–is that it be both astonishing and predictable at once. In the "golden age" of the detective story between the wars, when its writers belonged to guilds and wrote up sets of rules governing the form,[13] the chief point of the regulations was fairness–allowing the reader to match wits with the author on terms that both parties could understand. In more modern terms, Roger Caillois tells us that the author of the whodunit "triumphs by *explaining the impossible*. He first presents an event as inadmissible, and then accounts for it easily, elegantly, without forcing anything or using elaborate contrivances. . ... At bottom the unmasking of a criminal is less important than the reduction of the impossible to the possible, the inexplicable to the explained, the supernatural to the natural."[14] When the explanation is over, the detective hands the criminal over to justice or, not infrequently, allows the criminal to take his own life.

This pattern is so strongly marked that it was parodied almost as soon as it was established. Even before the so-called "golden age" between the wars, E. C. Bentley's *Trent's Last Case* (1913) had exhibited a false-bottom ending, in which the detective's explanation of the death of Sigsbee Manderson turns out to require several major revisions. In the conventional first ending Trent reveals that what at first had appeared to be a political gang murder was actually a sordid domestic crime. But then the tables are turned: after confronting the young man he had accused, Trent admits error and instead comes to the conclusion that the death was a suicide, till in the final chapter it is revealed to have been the result of an accident.

All this, however, makes less difference than it might seem, for while *Trent's Last Case* was fatal to the convention (derived from Poe and Doyle) of the superman-detective, Bentley had not really rejected the conventional ending; he had triplicated it. For each new ending confirms the essential process of detective hermeneutics, merely adding a few extra clues that had been previously produced within the purview of both detective and reader, clues which Trent had not taken into account.

Throughout the golden age and after, practitioners of the whodunit worked out variation upon variation on the static topos of the deductive denouement. Where the case is genuinely altered is in the postmodern versions of the detective story–what I have called the antimystery. In the major avatars of this subgenre–including works like Alain Robbe-Grillet's *The Erasers*, Friedrich Dürrenmatt's *The Pledge* and Jorge Luis Borges's "Death and the Compass"–the expected conclusion is wrenched around, not merely to a surprising twist, but to a deconstruction of the form.

Borges and Robbe-Grillet use opposing gambits. In "Death and the Compass," the detective carries out the deductions in the purest Holmesian fashion and predicts a fourth murder to complete a complex geographical. mystical and numerological scheme: what he does not foresee, fatally, is that the murder will be his own.[15] The Robbe-Grillet *nouveau roman* is longer and less lucid, involving the play of surfaces and distortions of time and space. But within that surrealistic texture the plot, reminiscent of the *Oedipus*, concerns a detective who is sent to investigate a shooting. He is misinformed that the assassin's target is dead: twenty-four hours later the victim is indeed shot dead, but it is the detective who has become his accidental assassin.

Dürrenmatt's version is less slick and more pathetic. In *The Pledge* the super-detective, Inspector Matthaï, despite being already packed to leave Switzerland on an overseas assignment that was to have been the climax of his career, begins investigating a set of gruesome sex murders of children. In a moment of genuine passion, he swears to the mother of the latest victim that he will not rest until he has brought the monster to justice. Obsessed with his pledge, Matthaï sacrifices fame and success to stay on the case: he sets a trap for the killer using another little girl as the bait. But Matthaï waits and waits and the killer does not appear. Years pass, and Matthaï himself goes to seed, while the little girl grows into a warped and unhappy adolescent. The ending bespeaks hideous waste of life and energy. But what has gone wrong? Were Matthaï's deductions mistaken? Not till long after both detective and girl have in effect been destroyed by Matthaï's zeal is the truth revealed: that Matthaï had been a perfect detective, had been correct in every detail, but that the killer's rendezvous with justice was prevented by that most banal of chance events, a fatal auto accident.

In Robbe-Grillet, the detective's semiotic investigations lead him to an inadvertent murder; in Borges, to a triumph that is his own destruction; in Dürrenmatt, to a dead end. The denouement of *The Name of the Rose* partakes of all three topoi of the antimystery.

First of all, William and Adso had been called in to investigate a case of sudden death at the nameless abbey where the story is set for what might be called political reasons. The Benedictine order is hoping to stay neutral and more or less independent of the struggles between Pope and Emperor, Ghibelline and Guelf, and the abbot fears that the disorder of an unexplained homicide will put the abbey into the power of the Pope's inquisition. But the effect of the investigation is to stir up suspicions that lead to further homicides, and to the false and irrelevant but politically damaging arrest of two monks for heresy and witchcraft by the papal inquisitor.

This is only a foreshadowing of the eventual solution of the crimes, which leads to the destruction of the entire abbey. This ending, as dramatically gripping as it is philosophically fascinating, involves the final confrontation of William, the apostle of positivism and enlightened rationality, with the blind sage Jorge of Burgos, who like Dostoevsky's Grand Inquisitor seeks to enslave his fellow-creatures' minds in order to rescue them from too much knowledge and freedom. While the Abbot himself suffocates in a coffin-like passage below them, the confrontation takes place in the *finis Africae*, the secret room in the monastic library where Jorge has hidden the Aristotelian treatise on comedy, emblem of his fear of laughter and truth. There Jorge proudly admits that he poisoned the book's pages to keep its contents forever from spreading, thereby entailing the deaths of two monks who insisted upon reading it. But to the book-loving reader, the horror of this confession pales before what follows. In the course of the struggle and the darkling pursuit through the midnight library, Adso's oil lamp is dashed from his hands, lands on a dry pile of parchment, and "as if for centuries those ancient pages had been yearning for arson and were rejoicing in the sudden satisfaction of an immemorial thirst for ecpyrosis," the Aristotle manuscript and with it the entire library–the wonder of Europe–burns to the ground. Jorge is dead, and in a technical sense justice has been done, but William's is a pyrrhic victory in which no one could take any satisfaction.

But the principal victim of the denouement is neither the Abbot nor the library itself, but the hermeneutic process of detection that underlies the novel and its entire genre. As William himself is honest enough to admit to Adso, amid the burning carnage of the library, he discovered Jorge's guilt via a train of reasoning that was in fact completely mistaken. While there were many clues that William read rightly, the trail that led him most directly to Jorge was an intertextual pattern–the connection that seems to be woven between the successive deaths in the abbey and the prophecy of the seven angels with the seven trumpets in the book of Revelation (8:6 to 10:10).

The first death, that of Adelmo the illustrator, who is found fallen from a high window into a bloody patch of snow, resembles the first angel whose trumpet brings "hail and fire mingled with blood" (p. 159). The next day Venantius is found drowned in a tub of blood, recalling the prophecy of the second angel, at the sound of whose trumpet "the third part of the sea became blood." And similarly through the three mysterious deaths that follow: the third angel poisons "a third of the rivers" and Berengar is found poisoned in the balneary; with the fourth trumpet "a third of the sun was struck and a third of the moon, and a third of the stars" and Severinus is found with his head bashed in by an armillary sphere portraying the sun, moon and stars; the fifth trumpet brings locusts with "power like the power of scorpions of the earth," and on the fifth day Malachi falls dying of poison, with the mysterious last words " he told me . . .truly . . . it had the power of a thousand scorpions. . . .."

Eco's use of the seven angels of the apocalypse is itself intertextual. This literary pattern recalls many classic detective stories: including S. S. Van Dine's *The Benson Murder Case*, where a series of murders is based on nursery rhymes; Agatha Christie's *The ABC Murders*, with an alphabetical pattern; Ellery Queen's *Ten Days Wonder*, where the crimes follow the Ten Commandments. In classic mysteries, the pattern is a red herring: it is a way of concealing another, more significant pattern. This is what Borges parodies in "Death and the Compass," where Lönnrot the detective sees through a specious numerological pattern of threes to a genuine pattern of fours–and so keeps the appointment in Samarrah with his own murderer.

In *The Name of the Rose*, it is the connection of the deaths with the book of Apocalypse and with Jorge's violently apocalyptic sermon that leads William to link the Spanish monk and the murders. To a reader familiar with the topoi of detection, it seems quite reasonable: Jorge is, as a blind man, the "least likely person" to have committed the crimes, and therefore, by the conventions of mystery an excellent candidate. Furthermore, Jorge is one of very few monks with the temperament to have committed a ruthless series of crimes and the only one made on sufficiently grand an intellectual scale to be a worthy foe to William: no one else could have played Moriarty to his Holmes.

The penultimate revelation, of course, is that William's reasoning is based on paralogism. If the murders are a connected and concerted plot, then Jorge must be behind it. But as William admits to an astonished Adso, "There was no plot . . . and I discovered it by mistake" (p. 491). Jorge poisoned the *Poetics of Comedy*, right enough, but the apparent connections among the deaths–and of the deaths to the prophecy–were meaningless coincidences:

> I arrived at Jorge through an apocalyptic pattern that seemed to underlie all the crimes, and yet it was accidental. I arrived at Jorge seeking one criminal for all the crimes and we discovered that each crime was committed by a different person, or by no one. I arrived at Jorge pursuing the plan of a perverse and rational mind, and there was no plan, or rather Jorge himself was overcome by his own initial design and there began a sequence of causes, and concauses, and of causes contradicting one another which proceeded on their own, creating relations that did not stem from any plan. Where is all my wisdom, then? I behaved stubbornly, pursuing a semblance of order, when I should have known well that there is no order in the universe. (p. 492)

Like Matthaï in *The Pledge*, William has been cheated by chance, and though evil is not finally triumphant, the semiotic rationale of literary detection is decisively defeated.

What I hesitatingly would call the ultimate revelation is something that occurred to me after I had completed the novel–and while one perhaps might grasp it as it happens, it is not marked out for the reader in the text. I am referring to the fact that the phony apocalyptic pattern William follows on the trail of Jorge continues unbroken right to the end. The sixth victim, the abbot, suffocates, as we said, in a sealed passageway–recalling the prophecy of the sixth angel and death by suffocation, the monstrous horsemen who kill by "smoke and sulphur" which "issue from their mouths." And the last death is appropriately that of Jorge himself, who succeeds in killing himself and foiling William's desire to read the lost manuscript by cramming the poisoned pages down his own throat. This recalls the last angel of Revelation, who gives John a scroll and tells him "Take it and eat. . . . And I . . . ate it; it was sweet as honey in my mouth, but when I had eaten it my stomach was made bitter."

In a playful way, then, Eco rejects the semiotic faith that one may accurately read the world through patterns, but continues nevertheless to impose upon the story the patterns we are warned against trusting. Has Eco rejected the play of signs or affirmed it? Is this an anti-mystery–or an anti-anti-mystery? If I am correct, in the ending of this astonishing novel the careful reader is set uneasily adrift between the radical rationalism of the detective story and the radical deconstruction of that rationalism. And the purpose of the reverberation between these ways of reading might be to make us conscious of the special kind of text this is and the way we must decode it.

Here as elsewhere in *The Name of the Rose* one may detect an enactment of Eco's earlier criticism, in this case the 1975-77 essay "Lector in Fabula," first printed in *The Role of the Reader*. After an analysis of the contradictory demands made on the reader's inferential capacity made by the sign-structures within "Drame" (a short metafiction by Alphonse Allais), Eco concluded that

> There are different types of fictional texts. Some ask for a maximum of intrusion. . . and are called "open" works. Some others are mealy-mouthed and, while pretending to elicit our cooperation, in fact want us to think their way and are very "closed" and repressive. "Drame" seems to stay half-way: it lures the Model Reader into an excess of cooperation and then punishes him for having overdone it. (*Role* 256)

Now what I have here called mystery and anti-mystery are, in effect, what Eco has called "closed" and "open" texts. *The Name of the Rose* is neither; like "Drame," it "is neither open nor closed: it belongs to a third category of works, to an exclusive club whose chairman is probably *Tristram Shandy*. These works tell stories about the way stories are built up . . ." (p. 256). Like "Drame," *The Name of the Rose* "asks us . . . to extrapolate from it the rules of the textual discipline it suggests" (p. 256). Learning these rules has always been what Eco's work has been about.

David H. Richter

Give Me Another Horse*

The form of the horse's hoof is just as much an image of the steppe it
treads as the impression it leaves is an image of the hoof.
(Lorenz 1973:xi)

There hangs in London's National Portrait Gallery a 1926 cartoon by
Bernard Partridge, depicting Sir Arthur Conan Doyle as "the slave of his
creation, Sherlock Holmes.

Because "The Adventure of the Lion's Mane" (Doyle 1967:776-89), first
published in the same year, 1926, represents a singularly radical stylistic
experiment on the part of its author, then age 67, this, of all his mysteries,
surely became one the most intriguing in the entire Sherlock Holmes corpus of 56 short stories: for Holmes, then living in retirement in his Sussex
home, necessarily conducts his investigation there in the absence of
Watson. As the great detective notes at the outset of this account, he must
therefore serve as his "own chronicler".

What is lacking here is the venerable cliché of the naive, unreliable narrator, a hoary literary device that Doyle reanimates throughout the rest of his
oeuvre with consummate finesse. He uses it, among other goals, to cover
up some of the more improbable aspects of his stories.

Apropos of the "Lion's Mane", its creator was quoted remarking that,
among all his tales, he himself "should put" this very one, about a death-
dealing marine coelenterate, "in the front row"- although, he qualified,
"that is for the public to judge". "The Lion's Mane", in Doyle's own self-
assessment, was admittedly "hampered by being told by Holmes himself, a
method which . . . certainly cramps the narrative. on the other hand", he
deemed "the actual plot . . . among the very best of the whole series"
(1967:789).

This text alone, then, sets limits to the generalization that all the
Sherlock Holmes stories are variants of "one story" (cf. Zholkovsky
1984:76). Viktor Shklovsky so claimed (1925) in the sense in which all Russian fairy tales, for example, were said to be uniform in their structure
(Propp 1928); or as, for another, a myth can be defined "as consisting of all

its versions" (Lévi-Strauss 1958:92). While the plot of "The Lion's Mane" is indeed as ingenious as it is entertaining, this story's thematic development (cf. O'Toole 1975:148) continues to disconcert in that it largely fails to conform to its readers' presuppositions and expectations. What is the essence of the missing ingredient that troubles the readership of this far from favorite tale?

Absent here is Doyle's otherwise inviolate structural principle of *nesting*, omnipresent throughout his other short stories, and accentuated even in such novellas as "The Hound of the Baskervilles". By "nesting" I refer to the organization whereby an ever-variable inner story stands apart from the invariant basic story in which the former lies embedded. "The basic story is what we call that part of the story where Holmes and Watson", the stable pair of foreground characters, "are in action or at least present. The inner story is the client's narrative, i.e., the gradually unfolded train of events which has brought him [or, as in "The Speckled Band", her, one may add] to turn to Holmes for help" (Scheglov and Zholkovsky 1975:56).

The basic story frames the inner story. Within this elegant but standard touchstone chassis, Doyle was able to put forward and encompass, by way of a "description of the repertoire of images, objects, characters, properties, setting, etc." (Scheglov and Zholkovsky 1975:59), a great many atmospheric and other effects realized in the ensuing linear action, constituting his variegated detective plots as such. Many of these semiosic devices are listed by Scheglov and Zholkovsky (1975:60-65), notably including Holmes's celebrated histrionic demonstrations of abduction from apparently trifling clues (Sebeok and Umiker-Sebeok 1980, Eco and Sebeok 1983) - in short, the method that Holmes himself dubbed "The Science of Deduction" (e.g., Doyle 1967:152-64). What characterizes all mystery stories, a genre to which detective stories belong a fortiori (although the reverse is by no means the case), is that the action progresses with an investigation from indexical signs (Sebeok 1991b) by means of abduction to an analysis and solution of the problem in question.

A particularly pertinent instance of this (in "A Study in Scarlet") is Holmes's observation of two ruts in the dry ground from which he proposes a startling abduction, eventually confirmed ("There is no room for a mistake"), that the murder victim Enoch J. Drebber had arrived at the site of the investigation "in a four-wheeled cab, which was drawn by a horse with three old shoes and one new one on his off foreleg". Afterwards, Holmes explains to the incredulous Watson: "There were the marks of the horse's hoofs . . . the outline of one of which was far more clearly cut than that of the other three, showing that that was a new shoe" (Doyle 1967:172-73).

In his novel *Il nome della rosa* (1980/1983), Eco displaces the Baker Street master and his ingenuous friend and aide, Watson, in time and place from

Victorian London to an Italian 14th-century monastic setting, in the guises
of William of Baskerville and Adso. Eco's initial frame opens with what can
concisely be designated, after the name of the abbot's favorite horse, as "the
Brunellus episode" (1980: 30-33; 1983: 22-25; see also the commentary in
Cohen 1988: 66-67 and Daddesio 1990). In this cameo prologue, Eco is able
to rapidly but effectively sketch, for his narrator's (Adso's) as well as his
readers' benefit, his protagonist's personality and habits of abductive thinking. The cellarer asks William:

"When did you see Brunellus?"...
"We haven't seen him at all, have we, Adso?" William said, turning toward me
with an amused look. " But . . . it is obvious you are hunting for Brunellus . . .
fifteen hands, the fastest in your stables, with a dark coat, a full tail, small
round hoofs, but a very steady gait; small head, sharp ears, big eyes. He went to
the right . . .". (*Rose* 3; 1983:23)

It is interesting that Adso's master, William, elucidating his abductions,
immediately goes on to instruct his young pupil: "My good Adso . . . during our whole journey I have been teaching you to recognize the evidence
through which the world speaks to us like a great book. Alanus de Insulis
said that

omnis mundi creatura
quasi liber et pictura
nobis est in speculum

and he was thinking of the endless array of symbols with which God,
through his creatures, speaks to us of eternal life " (*Rose* 31; 1983:23-24) .
Eco's allusion here to the pervasive Western metaphor of the Book of
Nature (Blumenberg 1986) - Carlyle (1987:194f.) referred to it both as "the
complete Statute-Book of Nature" and the "Volume of Nature . . . whose
Author and Writer is God"- was in fact deployed in a magazine article,
titled "The Book of Life", written by none other than Sherlock Holmes
himself: "From a drop of water . . . a logician could infer the possibility of
an Atlantic or a Niagara without having seen or heard of one or the other.
So all life is a great chain, the nature of which is known whenever we are
shown a single link of it" (Doyle 1967: 59) .
William's display of "habits of observation and inference which
[Holmes] had already formed into a system" (Doyle 1967:109) mimics the
structure and spirit, if not the substantive content, of similar passages
throughout the Holmes canon. Thus, for example, at the beginning of
"The Red-Headed League" (1967:418-38),

Sherlock Holmes' quick eye took in Watson's preoccupation, and he shook his
head with a smile as he noticed my questioning glances [at Mr. Jabez Wilson].

"Beyond the obvious facts that that he has at some time done manual labour, that he takes snuff, that he is a Freemason that he has been in China, and that he has done a considerable amount of writing lately, I can deduce nothing else". (1967:419)

As for the content of the Brunellus episode, Eco found his immediate inspiration for this incident of the abbot's horse in Voltaire's *Zadig* (1926:9; discussed at length in Eco and Sebeok 1983:207-15), where the Master of the King's Hounds asks Zadig "if he had not seen the king's horse pass by":

The horse you are looking for is the best galloper in the stable.... It is fifteen hands high, and has a very small hoof. It tail is three and a half feet long. The studs on its bit are of twenty-three carat gold, and its shoes of eleven scruple silver." "Which road did it take? . . . Where is it?" . . . "I have not seen the horse," answered Zadig, "and I never heard speak of it."

The retroduction practiced here was unequivocally designated in an 1880 lecture delivered by Thomas Huxley (1881) at the Working Men's College as "Zadig's method". But long before Voltaire, there were Arabic, medieval, and other variants of Zadig's abductive exploits, where the authors' rei signum of choice (Quintilian 8,6,22) involved one horse or another. Among recent post-Voltaire but pre-Eco illustrations of this equine intertextuality, my last parodic pick fastens upon Dorothy L. Sayers's book, *Have His Carcase* (1932:209-10). In Chapter XVI of this novel, Harriet Vane hands over to Lord Peter Wimsey a horseshoe she has just found on the beach. He then proceeds to reconstruct yet another horse - *ex alio aliud etiam intellegitur* (Quintilian 8,6,22) - in this sparkling cascade of synecdoches:

He ran his fingers gently round the hoop of metal, clearing the sand away.

"It's a new shoe - and it hasn't been here very long. Perhaps a week, perhaps a little more. Belongs to a nice little cob, about fourteen hands. Pretty little animal, fairly well-bred, rather given to kicking her shoes off, pecks a little with the off-fore."

"Holmes, this is wonderful! How do you do it?"

"Perfectly simple, my dear Watson. The shoe hasn't been worn thin by the 'ammer, 'ammer, 'ammer on the 'ard 'igh road, therefore it's reasonably new. It's a little rusty from lying in the water, but hardly at all rubbed by sand and stones, and not at all corroded, which suggests that it hasn't been here long. The size of the shoe gives the size of the nag, and the shape suggests a nice little round, well-bred hoof. Though newish, the shoe isn't fire-new, and it is worn down a little on the inner front edge, which shows that the wearer was disposed to peck a little; while the way the nails are placed and clinched indicates that the smith wanted to make the shoe extra secure which is why I said that a lost shoe was a fairly common accident with this particular gee. Still, we needn't blame him or her too much. With all these stones about, a slight trip or knock might easily wrench a shoe away."

"Him or her. Can't you go on and tell the sex and colour while you're about it?"

"I am afraid even I have my limitations, my dear Watson.". . .

"Well, that's quite a pretty piece of deduction...."

Animals of the most various ilk - since Poe's errant orangutan (1841) of the Rue Morgue, identified by abduction (then called "ratiocination") - abound in detective fiction, notably Doyle's, as well as in Eco's novel. A privately printed paper by Ewing and Patrick (1965) attempted to list every speechless creature, of which there are many, actually appearing in the Sherlockian zoo, under headings such as "Stables", "Kennels", "Cattery", "Aviary", "Menagerie", "Reptile House", "Aquarium", "Insect Cases", "Farmyard", and even heraldic and tavern-inn beasts, as well as a "worm unknown to science" and the unfathomable "giant rat of Sumatra", along-side the Sussex vampire.

"Give me another horse . . . ! Great reason why", cried out Richard III. Horses are especially common in the Holmes saga. They have also been featured in literally scores of modern detective novels, since Doyle's Shoscombe Prince, and notably his chronicle of Silver Blaze, John Straker's race-horse "from the Isonomy stock" (a real horse, by the way), pictured by Sidney Paget in the December I 892 issue of *Strand Magazine*.

To cite just a few by others, these include Creasey's *Death of a Racehorse* (1959), Giles's *Death at the Furlong Post* (1967), Gruber's *The Gift Horse* (1942), Palmer's *The Puzzle of the Red Stallion* (1937) and *The Puzzle of the Happy Hooligan* (1941) Philips's *Murder Clear, Track Fast* (1961), Platt's *The Princess Stakes Murder* (1973), Van Dine's *The Garden Murder Case* (1935), Wallace's *The Flying Fifty-Five* (1922) and *The Green Ribbon* (1929), and, of course, some three dozen racing books, through his current *Longshot* (1990), by Dick Francis.

Indeed, horses - about fifty in all, in rich synonymic assortment - "bay", "cab-horse", "chestnut", "cob", "gray", "mare", "mule" "mustang", "pack-horse", "pony", "trotter" - turn up in so many roles in the Sherlock Holmes cycle that they have engendered quite a respectably secondary literature, including a 31-page illustrated Danish monograph (Lauritzen 1959) . They have also inspired all kinds of speculative meditations about Holmes's private life - "that his young days were spent among circles which were interested in the turf" and that, like Watson, Holmes perhaps patronized book-makers (Bridgeman 1969:59-60); or at least that the stories provide ample

indication of Holmes's "full knowledge of and interest in the equine branch
of the animal kingdom" (Holstein 1970:112).

Why are horses, which were, during the late Neolithic era, the last
among the five most common livestock animals to be domesticated, yet
which remain the least affected by human manipulation and artificial selection, featured with such predilection and detective fiction? "The horse
evolved as a fast-moving ungulate capable of migrating over great distances"
(Clutton-Brock 1981:80). The earliest accounts of riding and the manage-
ment of horses date from the Iron Age; especially noteworthy are the essays
on hunting and horsemanship from the 4th century BC, by Xenophon, an
adviser of Philip of Macedon, the father of Alexander the Great, who, together with his war horse Bucephalus, conquered the world.

In his remarkably rewarding study titled "Clues: Morelli, Freud, and
Sherlock Holmes", Carlo Ginzburg (in Eco and Sebeok 1983: 95-136) has
sown that the "conjectural or semiotic paradigm" - embracing divination
through tracks and eventually the scientific analysis of footprints,
gnawings, hairs, scat, and comparable pointers (body parts, separable or
not)–is connected with Mesopotamian divination and ancient hunting techniques:

> For thousands of years mankind lived by hunting. In the course of endless
> pursuits, hunters learned to reconstruct the appearance and movements of an
> unseen quarry through its tracks - prints in soft ground, snapped twigs, drop-
> pings, snagged hairs or feathers, smells, puddles, threads of saliva...successive
> generations of hunters enriched and passed on this inheritance of knowledge.
> (Eco and Sebeok 1983: 88)

In the mythic landscape of the Indian world of the American wilderness,
the Prairie (Lawrence 1985: 57-77), as depicted by, for one, James Fenimore
Cooper, the last of the Mohicans, Uncas, and his friend Leatherstocking
practiced the art of pathfinding (discussed in Sebeok 1991a) as the real-life
Indians used to track in the Old World of their forefathers. And Peirce's
most striking instance of an indexical symbol was, as well, of this kind:

> The. . .Perceptible may. . .function doubly as a Sign. That footprint that
> Robinson Crusoe found in the sand. . .was an Index to him that some creature
> was on his island, and at the same time as a Symbol, called up the idea of a man
> (1935-1966:4 .531)

Thomas writes: "Tracking is an ancient science. It was probably
practiced to a far greater extent by prehistoric man than it is today simply
because it was a skill necessary for survival.... Tracking or learning to read
signs is no easy task" (1985:129, 131). The distinguished field-naturalist
Niko Tinbergen, ever mindful of the powerful Book of Nature metaphor,

called tracking "countryside detection", based on "a vast map of such records, printed overnight . . . tracks and traces of immense variety, often of wonderful clarity . . . written in footprint code . . ." (Ennion and Tinbergen 1967:1). The track of a horse - an animal with non-cloven hoofs - is well recognizable, either shod or not, as pictured in Bang and Dahlstrom's abundantly illustrated, useful guide: when shod, "one sees only the impression of the shoe and identification is easy" (1972:64, 74). Without shoes, a horse leaves large, almost circular tracks, each more or less deeply indented at the back; but the size varies considerably, depending on the race, which takes an expert to tag.

The survival of all species, and of each individual member of every species, depends on the correct decipherment of indexical signs ceaselessly barraging their Umwelt. The tracker of horses or of other animals, the augur and diviner, the detective, the art historian, the physician and psychoanalyst, and the modern scientist are, each in his own way, avid readers and interpreters of natural metonyms in the Book of Nature - just as the rest of us experience signs throughout our daily lives, only in a perhaps less concentrated, less specialized way. As the Italian physicist Giorgio Carreri wrote (1984:156),

> Our senses pick up . . . events that cannot be arranged within . . simple measurable framework, thanks merely to the yardstick and the clock. For these events, the signs are the most appropriate expressions, and so the correlation among these signs can be perceived as a sense of immeasurable order, for example, in the unity of a work of art.

Thomas A. Sebeok

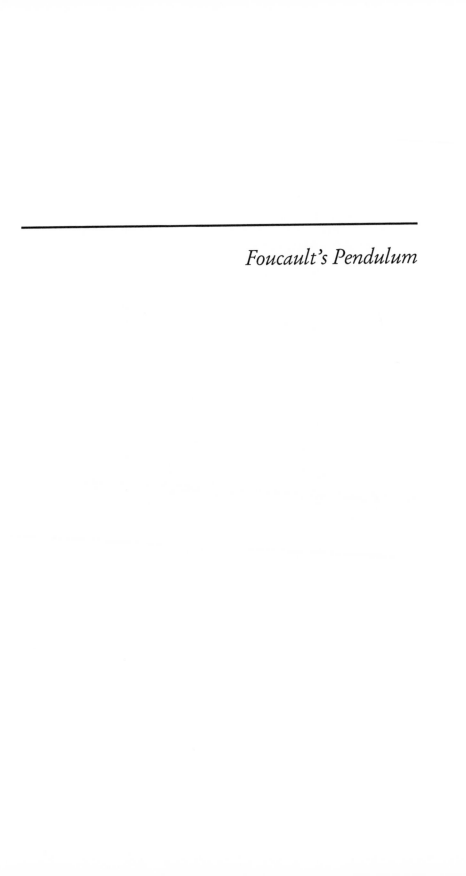

Foucault's Pendulum

Interpretation, Overinterpretation, Paranoid Interpretation and *Foucault's Pendulum**

Only a very naive reader of *Il pendolo di Foucault* (1988, *Foucault's Pendulum*) would not presume that Umberto Eco's second novel can be enriched by reference to Eco's theoretical works on narrative theory, semiotics, and popular culture. But the most important clue to Eco's thinking while he composed this difficult work is infrequently cited by his critics. It is a theoretical introduction to a collection of Italian essays on esoteric interpretations of Dante from the nineteenth century–*L'idea deforme: interpretazioni esoteriche di Dante* (1989, *The Distorted Idea: Esoteric Interpretations of Dante*)–research carried out by Eco's students in a seminar at the University of Bologna on "hermetic semiosis" that took place in 1986.[1] This anthology actually contains a relatively complete and well developed outline of Eco's historical contextualization of contemporary theories on interpretation and overinterpretation, views that constitute the core of two books widely distributed both in Italian and in English –*I limiti dell'interprtazione* (1989, *The Limits of Interpretation*)[2] and the collection of Tanner Lectures Eco presented at Cambridge University in 1990, published as *Interpretation and Overinterpretation* and subsequently translated into Italian in 1995.[3]

Because of the close interconnection between these three separate theoretical or critical books that serve as an intellectual background to Eco's second novel, I believe it is justified to discuss them *en masse* for the purposes of simplicity and economy. We shall subsequently discuss how they enlighten our understanding of *Foucault's Pendulum*.

After spending much of his intellectual life arguing for the "open" work and textual interpretation in which the reader's response plays an active, even a dominant role, Eco now claims that "in the course of the last decades, the rights of the interpreters have been overstressed" and rejects an idea humorously suggested by Tzvetan Todorov that "a text is only a picnic where the author brings the words and the readers bring the sense"(*IO* 23, 24). His argument involves three different concepts: the intention of the author (*intentio auctoris*); the intention of the reader (*intentio lectoris*); and what he calls the intention of the text (*intentio operis*). In common-sense terms almost entirely free of the kind of scholarly jargon typical of some of his earlier theoretical works, Eco argues that while the intention of the work cannot be reduced to a pre-textual intention of the Empirical Author (thereby agreeing with both New Critics and Deconstructionists), an understanding of this Empirical Author's intention nevertheless may serve to assist the Model Reader (that reader posited by the intention of the text, the *intentio operis*) in excluding or discarding certain unlikely, improbable, or even impossible interpretations of a text. The Empirical Author is never, in Eco's view, a privileged interpreter of his or her text but becomes a potential Model Reader offering possible explanations for his or her creation. Unlikely, improbable, or impossible readings constitute overinterpretation and in certain extreme instances–best reflected by the crack-pot theories held by many of the "diabolicals" in *Foucault's Pendulum*–such readings may become paranoid overinterpretations.

The readings of Dante by the "Followers of the Veil" (the "Adepti del Velame"), as Eco calls these critics, were by no means insane and many spent their lives in dedicated scholarship, writing numerous learned tomes to prove their theories. Beginning with Dante's own statements that his poetry contained a non-literal sense under the "veil" of difficult verse, interpreters such as Gabriele Rossetti (1783-1854), Eugène Aroux (1773-1859), and Luigi Valli (1878-1931), read Dante's admittedly complex poetic work for hints of secret messages, secret societies, and elaborate conspiracies. Rossetti and Aroux, in particular, find in Dante a host of symbols and images that, according to them, reflect Masonic and Rosicrucian traditions and even evidence of Dante's link to the Knights Templars (all of which groups play a prominent role in Eco's second novel). The problem with such an interpretation, of course, is that it runs directly counter to a host of historical evidence which argues that Rosicrucian philosophy originated at the beginning of the seventeenth century and that Freemasonry derives from the first part of the eighteenth century. From a historical perspective, Dante could not have known anything about either group, but conversely either group could have seen in Dante a precursor and actually have incorporated elements of Dantesque imagery into their rituals .[4]

Eco believes that many aspects of contemporary literary theory–in particular Deconstructionist theory identified with Jacques Derrida and practiced by numerous American literary theorists–have licensed arbitrary interpretations of literary texts in their desire to establish the fact that an author's intentions have no privileged position. Eco's position is relatively simple and is neatly summarized in his rebuttal to objections raised by his Tanner Lectures: "I accept the statement that a text can have many senses. I refuse the statement that a text can have every sense"(*IO* 141) His critique of postmodern theories of interpretation actually pays little attention to specific works (although Derrida or Foucault are obviously in his mind and are noted briefly). Instead, Eco's primary objective is to demonstrate that "most so-called 'post-modern' thought will look very pre-antique"(*IO* 25).

Eco then proceeds to provide a historical context for understanding the attitudes present in some contemporary thinking about textual interpretation, going back in time to the ancient world and to Renaissance humanism. He offers a magisterial tour of the classical contribution to Western thought, underlining how the two rules inherited from ancient Greece and Rome still shape intelligent reading and should serve as criteria to separate rational ideas from irrational ones. From Greece, we derive our methods of understanding causes, which presuppose several logical rules: the principle of identity (A = A), the principle of non-contradiction (it is impossible for something to be both A and not A at the same time); and the principle of the excluded middle (either A is true or A is false and *tertium non datur*). These logical principles from Greek philosophy produce the "typical pattern of thinking of Western rationalism, the *modus ponens*: 'if p, then q; but p: therefore q'"(*IO* 26-27).[5] The Romans transformed Greek philosophical rationalism into an ethical and legal rationalism with more obvious social dimensions, in particular identifying irrationality with lack of moderation, while rationality was identified as standing within the modus, within limits or within measure. This notion became an ethical principle best expressed by Horace in his Satires (I. 1. 106-7): "There is a mean in things, fixed limits on either side of which right living cannot get a foothold."[6] The Greek world produced other less rationalistic philosophical traditions, particularly in the first several centuries of the Christian era, where Eco sees the triumph of Hermetic philosophy. Hermetic ideas constitute a complex set of syncretic ideas symbolized by the myth of Hermes, a myth that basically denies all the logical principles discussed earlier (identity, non-contradiction, the excluded middle), as well as the causal chains such logical principles imply. Needless to say, such a syncretic philosophy also violates the Latin notion of moderation, of a mean, and stresses the most immoderate kinds of philosophical positions.

Second-century Hermeticism, in particular, rejects the law of the excluded middle and asserts that many things may be true at the same time even if they stand in contradiction to one another. To hold this position, books must be transformed into complex allegories–they say one thing but mean something quite different, often something secret and "hermetically" sealed from the non-initiated. Thus truth becomes identified with what is implied (but not explicitly stated) or what is concealed under the surface, much as the esoteric readings of Dante ignored the obvious literal meaning of Dante's poem and looked, instead, for a reading more conducive to their conspiracy theories. But as Eco asserts:

where the coincidence of opposites triumphs, the principle of identity collapses. Tout se tient. As a consequence, interpretation is indefinite. . . . Hermetic thought transforms the whole world theatre into a linguistic phenomenon and at the same time denies language any power of communication (*IO* 32)

Tout se tient–everything is connected: this French phrase becomes the key to the plot of Foucault's Pendulum (pp. 152, 252, 512) and represents for Eco a view of reality that he fundamentally rejects. In The Limits of Interpretation, Eco provides an excellent, if playful, example of this kind of thinking by analogy, what he calls "hermetic drift" or the uncontrolled ability to shift from meaning to meaning, from similarity to similarity, from a connection to another" (*Limits* 26-27). It is a word game where one moves in six steps from one term (his example is peg) to another (Eco selects Plato as his target). Any connection will do–metaphorical, metonymical, phonetic. Thus we connect peg to pig by sound; pig to bristle (because pigs have bristles); bristle to brush (because Italian masters used pig bristles to make paint brushes); bristle to Mannerism (because bristles used for paint brushes suggest an artistic movement made famous by great Italian painters); Mannerism to Idea (because Mannerism employed a notion of concetti or abstract concepts or ideas in its artistic theory); and finally Mannerism to Plato (since Plato is a philosopher concerned with ideas). As Eco says, with this kind of reasoning, "one can always win."

It is thus perfectly consistent with Eco's theoretical thinking that the main character in his novel is named Casaubon, since Isaac Casaubon (1559-1614) was a Swiss philologist at the beginning of the seventeenth century who established that the Corpus Hermeticum celebrated by Renaissance humanists as a mystical text composed by Hermes Trismegistus living in Egypt before the time of Moses had to be composed after the Christian era and therefore had absolutely nothing to do with ancient Egypt. The kind of ahistorical thinking that would identify a text written after the Christian era with ancient Egypt is exactly the kind of textual interpretation Eco would call, at the very least, overinterpretation, and would more likely term paranoid interpretation. In discussing the origin of the name (Casaubon) for the narrator of his second novel, in the Tanner Lectures Eco specifically underscores the fact that as an empirical author, he was in fact less clever than one of his readers (David Robey) who, in a review of the novel, suggested another explanation for Casaubon–a reference to a character in George Eliot's Middlemarch who is (very appropriately) composing a book entitled A Key to All Mythologies. Robey's suggestion would seem to be as heuristic as Eco's explanation, but Eco contends not only that he did not intend a reference to George Elliot but that he specifically rejected it in the novel itself to make sure the link to Isaac Casaubon was that perceived by the careful reader. In spite of the fact that Eco himself discusses Michel Foucault's ideas about the paradigm of similarity as parallel to the conspiracy theories of his novel's characters, Eco also specifically rejects any intentional reference to Michel Foucault, insisting that Léon Foucault (1819-68), the inventor of the famous pendulum proving experimentally the rotation of the earth, is the only Foucault he meant to signify (*IO* 81-83).[7]

Eco does not reject a clever reader's right to see an allusion in a text the empirical author did not intend. He merely believes that some sort of reality check needs to be imposed upon textual interpretations, and he suggests the "consensus of the community" as a possible answer (IO 144). In effect, Eco argues that an interpretative community (a group of Italianists reading Eco, for example) functions as a check upon outlandish or paranoid interpretations. Suggestive interpretations will engender other equally heuristic readings of a text, while overinterpretations or paranoid interpretations will eventually be refused by the community. Comparing non-useful interpretations to the sterility of a mule, Eco suggests that such non-heuristic textual interpretations will be

> unable to produce new interpretations or cannot be confronted with the traditions of the previous interpretations. The force of the Copernican revolution is not only due to the fact that it explains some astronomical phenomena better than the Ptolemaic tradition, but also to the fact that it–instead of representing Ptolemy as a crazy liar–explains why and on which grounds he was justified in outlining his own interpretation (*IO* 150-151).

In his discussion of the esoteric Dante scholars who read the epic poem as a compendium of secret knowledge, Eco closes his remarks with an interesting discussion of the relative merits of these scholars providing paranoid interpretations, on the one hand, and those more traditional scholars (Gilson, Eliot, Pound, the New Critics, Dante scholars who read Dante's text through the prisms of the *Patrologia Latina* or Medieval poetics). Why, Eco asks rhetorically, were these "Followers of the Veil" abandoned to the dustheap of academic footnotes? Perhaps, Eco suggests, because the latter group of textual readers, forming a community of consensus and employing what he calls the "healthy sense of [textual] economy, went to seek out the secret of Dante where it had lain clearly in view for some time, like the purloined letter"(Pozzato 1992:37).[8] Textual interpretation and learning in general have some characteristics in common with the detective novel, the *whodunit* invented by Edgar Allen Poe (whose tale, "The Purloined Letter," is Eco's obvious point of reference). The common-sense point Eco makes in all of his discussions of overinterpretation is that in many instances, the most sensible interpretation of a text, like the purloined letter, may be found directly under our noses.

Foucault's Pendulum requires more of its reader than did *The Name of the Rose*, in part because Eco's encyclopedic knowledge in the first novel was more sharply focused upon a single historical period (the Middle Ages). In addition, the various theoretical problems that shaped the narrative, most already outlined in Eco's other theoretical works, had already paved the way for a positive reception of the novel among the intelligentsia. For the general reader, the fact that such a complex work of literature could be packaged within the popular genre of the detective story, the *whodunit*, ensured a large audience for the work by appealing to several kinds of Model Readers–both high brow and low brow. With *Foucault's Pendulum*, Eco adopts a far more complex narrative strategy, employing a narrator (Casaubon) and other central characters (Diotallevi, Belbo) that have important autobiographical links to the author's experience as a young man during the war and as an associate of major publishing firms in Turin and Milan in the early years of Eco's career.[9] Moreover, the narrative grants an important role to a computer named Abulafia (or Abu for short). Belbo's computer is named after Samuel ben Samuel Abraham Abulafia (1240-circa 1292), a thirteenth-century Jewish mystic who studied the infinite combinations of the Torah and developed a system of number and letter symbolism that was influential in the development of Kabbalistic thinking. We have previously discussed Eco's interest in his theoretical essays on narrative in writing as a combinative process, a thesis associated with the Paris Oulipo group which included such major writers as Italo Calvino, Georges Perec, and Raymond Queneau (whose important work, *Exercises de style* [1947, *Exercises in Style*] Eco himself translated into Italian).[10]

Now, Eco incorporates the essentially "postmodernist thematics of mechanical reproduction," as one recent critic has called it (McHale 1992:182),[11] directly into the novel by using large narrative blocks (twelve in all)[12] written by Casaubon's friend Belbo and hidden within the locked computer files of Abulafia.

Belbo's computer files allow Eco to provide points of view that may be compared or contrasted to the first-person narrative of Casaubon, and it also allows him to change the time sequences of the story with relative ease. In fact, Eco's novel opens on the night of 23–24 June 1984 with Casaubon hiding inside the Conservatoire des Arts et Métiers in Paris, waiting for the denouement of events that have begun some 14 years earlier. Employing a technique not unlike that in film flashbacks, the story shifts abruptly to two days before when Casaubon broke the code lock to Belbo's computer and discovered his files. Casaubon's life during the last fourteen years thus intertwines with the various computer files left behind by a Belbo who will eventually be killed on the night of 23–24 June 1984 (the night opening the narrative). The conclusion of the novel takes place shortly after Belbo's death as Casaubon goes to Belbo's native village in Piedmont, attempts to understand not only Belbo's past during the Resistance but also his death, and awaits the arrival of the Diabolicals who have caused Belbo's death and who will surely bring about his own demise.

The dangerous situation that results first in Belbo's death and in Casaubon's imminent death derives from a long, interconnected chain of overinterpretations that transcends the category of creative overinterpretation (the kind of creative misreading that critics such as Harold Bloom or others have recommended) and lands squarely inside the boundaries of paranoid interpretations. At Pilade's Bar, a local watering hole that Casaubon compares to Rick's American Café from the film *Casablanca*, Casaubon, writing his university thesis on the history of the Knights Templars, meets Belbo, who is employed at the nearby Garamond Press. Belbo is obsessed with his computer Abulafia, and the two men become friends, with Belbo introducing Casaubon to his colleague at the press, Diotallevi, an albino who aspires to be Jewish (even though his name is a traditional one given to orphans in the Middle Ages and afterwards (Bloom 1975a:27)), and who is himself obsessed with the combinative potential of the Kabbalah, the mass of esoteric and mystical writings that the Jewish religion has produced through the centuries.

Originating as far back as the third century of the Christian era, Kabbalah became an important intellectual phenomenon in medieval France and spread into Spain and Italy. Within the literature of this movement, the Sefirot or the ten complex images of God become crucial. These ten concepts are also employed by Eco as ten major divisions in his novel: Keter ("the supreme crown"); Hokhmah ("wisdom"); Binah ("intelligence"); Hesed ("love"); Gevurah ("power"); Tiferet ("beauty"); Nezah (""victory" or "lasting endurance"); Hod ("majesty"); Yesod ("foundation"); and Malkhut ("kingdom"). I cite Harold Bloom's translations of these terms from his work of critical theory, *Kabbalah and Criticism*, because it is quite likely that Eco himself was influenced by this book and by Bloom's lectures at the University of Bologna which took place before the composition of *Foucault's Pendulum*. Bloom himself discusses textual interpretation in this work in the light of Peirce's semiotic theory (something that would have attracted Eco to the book in the first place), and his theory of strong readings of literary works that of necessity constitute "misreadings" must certainly have occurred to Eco when he began to fashion the overtly paranoid textual interpretations that fill the pages of his second novel.[13]

Eco's use of the ten parts of the Kabbalistic Sefirot to structure his novel continues a practice begun with *The Name of the Rose*–the citation of passages in a variety of languages (including ancient Hebrew) that are practically incomprehensible to any but the most erudite of readers. It is possible to construct some general meaning to the ten-part structure of the Sefirot,

292 INTERPRETATION, OVERINTERPRETATION, PARANOID INTERPRETATION

and Eco plays with his reader, tantalizing him or her into attempting such a textual interpretation. Some critics, but not many, have even attempted to see some order in the selection of these ten concepts.[14] The temptation is enormous to begin to fashion an overarching interpretation of the entire novel based upon these ten Kabbalistic concepts.

However, I believe Eco employs them to draw the reader into his cleverly woven web that will inevitably tempt the reader to overinterpret these Kabbalistic notions. We may remember that the moment of truth for William of Baskerfield came when the monk-detective understood that the secret entrance to the labyrinth was found in the *suppositio materialis*, one of the theories of William of Occam: William had construed the phrase *tertius equi* to refer to a real horse in the real world when, in fact, the phrase merely referred to the third letter of the word for horse, not to a real horse. The Sefirot functions in much the same fashion in his second novel. While attacking paranoid interpretations, Eco wants his reader to experience how easily they may be created, and there is no better or simpler method of doing this than to use these concepts to divide his book, just as the canonical hours (certainly a logical thing to find in a medieval monastery) divided the chapter headings of the first novel without necessarily offering something crucial to the book's meaning. My suspicion that Eco is putting his reader on, in the vernacular sense, finds some textual backing in the preface that Eco ironically places at the beginning of the novel:

> Only for you, children of doctrine and learning, have we written this work. Examine this book, ponder the meaning we have dispersed in various places and gathered again; what we have concealed in one place we have disclosed in another, that it may be understood by your wisdom (*Pendulum* xvii).

The quotation is taken from the *De occulta philosophia* of Heinrich Cornelius Agrippa von Nettesheim (1486-1535), a Renaissance philosopher of the occult whose book dealt with magic, numerology, and the power of sacred names. In my view, Eco's citation of this passage is a completely ironic invitation to his Model Reader to become bogged down in the very kinds of paranoid interpretations Eco's book attacks. As Bloom suggests, "the *Sefirot* fascinate because they suggest an immutable knowledge of a final reality that stands behind our world of appearances" (Bloom 1975a:28).[15] It is precisely this fatal fascination for an immutable, final reality that Eco attacked in *The Name of the Rose* and which he continues to reject in *Foucault's Pendulum*.

The references to such critics as Bloom, Derrida, or Foucault, a recent and most persuasive critical reading of the novel reminds us, point to the fact that Eco's second novel "participates in the genre of academic novels practiced during the late 1970s and throughout the 1980s by British authors

David Lodge and Malcolm Bradbury . . . labeled *critifictional*," novels which provide both fictional accounts of academic life and polemics directed against various schools of literary theory, especially Deconstructionists (Bouchard 1995:50). In *Foucault's Pendulum*, this relatively contemporary genre popular among academic readers merges with the detective novel genre so appealing to the general public, since the entire narrative of Eco's second novel suggests that there is an enormous cosmic plot organized by some very sinister groups of individuals that has existed for some centuries–a kind of cosmic *whodunit*. By joining two normally separate narrative genres, Eco once again hopes to bridge the gap between two very different kinds of audiences and, as with the Model Reader he envisioned for *The Name of the Rose*, Eco has envisioned a Model Reader for his second novel that is equally at ease among diabolical conspirators, literary theorists, and occult philosophers as with detectives.

One of the aspects of *Foucault's Pendulum* that the novel shares with many of the *critifictional* novels of recent publication (particularly those by David Lodge) and which was less apparent in *The Name of the Rose* is Eco's humorous portrait of publishing houses, universities, and academics in general. The three main characters in the novel–Casaubon, Belbo, and Diotallevi–all work for the Garamond Press, supposedly a serious publishing house which houses another less serious and far more lucrative publishing operation, the Manutius Press, which is a vanity press for Self Financing Authors (SFAs). The cynical manner in which the three men and their publisher Garamond, manipulate the hapless SFAs in order to squeeze money out of them for their useless and usually unreadable manuscripts speaks volumes about a certain atmosphere within the publishing industry that Eco knows very well from first-hand experience. The humor is bittersweet when one realizes that Claude Garamond (1499-1562) and Aldo Manuzio or Manutius (1450-1515) are among the heroic early pioneers of European printing: Garamond invented the elegant type still employed today by the world's best publishers; Manutius established the famous Venetian printing press identified by the colophon of anchor and dolphin still used today by Doubleday Books, a pioneer printing firm in creating editions of the classics in small, affordable formats. The owner of the Garamond Press, named after a Mr. Garamond, is an unsavory figure who eventually is revealed to be one of the diabolicals responsible for the death of Belbo and the pursuit of Casaubon.

Eco's portrait of work inside the Garamond publishing firm, his discussion of Casaubon's research, and his description of Belbo's computer also provide him with occasions for wry wit. For example, there are the witty discussions within the Garamond firm among the three protagonists of the novel about an educational reform involving a School of Comparative Irrelevance, where useless or ridiculous courses are given. This school would consist of a number of departments. The Department of Tetrapyloctomy (the art of splitting a hair four ways) would serve an introductory function to inculcate a sense of irrelevance in the students. Possible courses here would include Potio-section (the art of slicing soup); Pylocatabasis (the art of being saved by a hair); or Mechanical Avunculogratulation (how to build machines for greeting uncles). Then there is the Department of Adynata or Impossibilia, where students will be taught to understand the reasons for a thing's absurdity by studying empirical impossibilities. Here, the student might follow seminars on Urban Planning for Gypsies, Morse Syntax, the History of Eastern Island Painting, the Phonetics of the Silent Film, or Crowd Psychology in the Sahara. Another important academic unit would be the Department of Oxymoronics, or self-contradictions. Here, typical courses would include Nomadic Urban Planning for Gypsies, Tradition in Revolution, and Democratic Oligarchy (*Pendulum* 64-65).

Belbo's theory of the four kinds of people in the world is a wonderful example of the sense of humor Eco usually reserved for his occasional essays and which have since been collected and translated as *Diario minimo (Misreadings)* or the *Secondo diario minimo (How to Travel with a Salmon & Other Essays)*. According to Belbo, the world may be divided into four groups: cretins; fools, morons, and lunatics. Cretins are not worthy of discussion (examples are people who hit themselves in the face with ice cream cones or enter a revolving door the wrong way). Fools are more interesting, for they put their foot in their mouth (they ask how one's wife is just after she has left her husband). Belbo's hilarious example of a fool is Joachim Murat reviewing troops returning from Martinique: Murat asks an obviously black soldier "Are you a negro?" and when the man replies in the affirmative, Murat responds: "Good, good, carry on!"(*Pendulum* 55-58).[16] Morons, on the other hand, never make a mistake but mix up their reasoning. Their thought runs in the following pattern: all dogs are pets; all dogs bark; cats are pets; therefore cats bark. Morons are tricky and may even win Nobel prizes, and as Belbo says, the entire history of logic represents an attempt to define an acceptable idea of moronism. Lunatics are morons without a logic behind their thinking, even the kind of false syllogism that concludes cats bark. Lunatics believe everything proves everything else, everything is connected. Lunatics, in other words, believe that *tout se tient*, and according to Belbo, they always bring up the subject of the Knights Templars.

Lunatics are thus at the focal point of *Foucault's Pendulum*, and Eco considers any textual interpretation based upon the concept of universal connectedness as bordering on the insane or the paranoid. As Casaubon, Diotallevi, and Belbo discuss the strange theories of those who are obsessed with the Knights Templars (Causabon's thesis topic), they devise an elaborate parody of the interpretative paranoia of the various diabolicals, what they call "The Plan." This Plan is born after a meeting with a Colonel

Ardenti, an old Fascist officer who believes that the Templars had a plot to conquer the world: after their order was destroyed by the King of France in 1307, Ardenti believes the Templars went underground, and his attention is focused upon the city of Provins (a site with a maze of underground caves, perfect–according to Ardenti–for a group plotting to take over the world). Visiting Provins, Ardenti meets the daughter of a man named Ingolf (another believer in the Templars as conspirators), and in Ingolf's library, Ardenti discovered several interesting documents, including one written in old French but missing some crucial letters (see *Pendulum* 114-115).

Beginning with this intriguing document, the three friends at Garamond begin an elaborate parody of the various conspiracy theories that are held by the numerous crack-pot authors they encounter among the Self Financing Authors who frequent the Manutius Press. These Diabolicals, as they are called, have various ideas concerning not only the Templars but also Freemasons, Rosicrucians, the Jesuits, the Jews, the Nazis, the search for the Grail, the existence of telluric currents that can control the world, and so forth–all of which reflect the paranoid brand of textual interpretation Eco discusses in his theoretical works. The mega-conspiracy they construct with the assistance of Abulafia constitutes an amalgamation of all possible conspiracies, and "The Plan" concentrates upon making "sense" out of Ingolf's document by spinning out every conceivable connection between one conspiracy theory and another. Thus, Ingolf's document can be read to mean that the Templars had planned to meet every 120 years in six different locations, and when these meetings were missed due to various simple events (such as the reform of the calendar), various groups of conspirators spend the next several centuries attempting to contact each other to return to the original planned meetings.

Needless to say, Casaubon, Belbo, and Diotallevi are extremely amused with the cleverness of their imaginary construction, since it is arranged in such a way that the interconnectedness of their material explains everything from the Crusades to the Holocaust. As Diotallevi, puts it: "Not bad, not bad at all . . . To arrive at the truth through the painstaking reconstruction of a false text" (*Pendulum* 381) The governing principle of their creation rests upon a point of view best expressed by Belbo:

> Any fact becomes important when it's connected to another. The connection changes the perspective; it leads you to think that every detail of the world, every voice, every word written or spoken has more than its literal meaning, that it tells us of a Secret. The rule is simple: Suspect, only suspect. You can read subtexts even in a traffic sign that says 'No littering' (*Pendulum* 314).

To prove his point, Belbo then proceeds to demonstrate how a driver's manual can be interpreted to represent the Tree of the Sefirot (ten parts of the engine equal the ten Sefirot)!

In constructing "The Plan," the three intellectuals have forgotten a basic axiom of social behavior: things perceived as real (such as their elaborate meta-conspiracy) are real in their consequences. The Diabolicals of every description, upon hearing of this plan, naturally assume that there is a "Truth" behind it that only the three men possess: Diotallevi dies of cancer and is therefore beyond their reach, but Belbo meets his death literally on Foucault's pendulum in Paris, refusing to reveal the "secret" of the plan to the frenzied Diabolicals, and as the novel concludes, Casaubon awaits their arrival to interrogate him as well in Belbo's home in Piedmont. As he waits, he summarizes the "rules" of their Plan:

> Rule One: Concepts are connected by analogy. . . . Rule Two says that if tout se tient in the end, the connecting works. . . . Rule Three: The connections must not be original. They must have been made before, and the more often the better, by others. Only then do the crossing seem true, because they are obvious. . . . But if you invent a plan and others carry it out, it's as if the Plan exists. At that point it does exist (*Pendulum* 314).

Eco's novel presents an intriguing overview of the mishaps that can oc-cur when paranoid reading takes control of interpretation. Yet, as Eco is surely aware (and as Brian McHale has rightly pointed out), this kind of textual interpretation is practiced not just by the lunatic fringe but by "other, thoroughly 'respectable' and mainstream interpretative communi-ties as well" (*Pendulum* 512-513). Policemen and intelligence organizations collect information in a paranoid manner, amassing it without necessarily knowing a priori that connections exist between their data. Often, the most absurd bits of information in espionage, counter-espionage, or simple detective work prove invaluable to the solution of a problem. In like man-ner, professional readers, McHale reminds us–including students, profes-sors, reviewers, and Eco himself–have acquired "paranoid reading skills in response to the challenge of modernist verbal art, through the process of learning how to read modernist texts properly and, by extension, how to read pre-modernist text modernistically"(McHale 1992:169).

Casaubon, Diotallevi, and Belbo first treat Ingolf's cryptic text with de-rision, but as they develop their Plan, their parodic intentions begin to be transformed into belief, as they, too, like the Diabolicals, are mesmerized by the interconnectedness they can posit between any bit of information, following the principle *tout se tient*. Casaubon's girlfriend Lia (the Italian for Leah) provides what Eco as narrator clearly regards as a non-paranoid, common sense interpretation of the document. We are first introduced to Lia in chapter 35 of the novel, the opening of which is a citation from Dante's *Purgatorio* XXVII (100-102), the key to Lia's function in the novel but a key which requires a knowledge of the next two tercets in Dante's poem.[17]

As Eco knows, the biblical story of Leah and Rachel (Genesis 29:10-31) was interpreted in Dante's day as underlining two different ways of living as a Christian: leading an active life (Leah's gathering of flowers), on the one hand; or following the contemplative life (Rachel's contemplation of herself in the mirror), on the other. In Eco's novel, Lia/Leah not only produces a child (the ultimate reality in the entire novel is represented by this birth, producing "The Thing" which is a fact juxtaposed to "The Plan" that is merely a figment of a paranoid fantasy). She also offers the most sensible explanation of Ingolf's document in chapter 106 of the novel. Using both common sense (contacting the tourist agency of Provins), traditional philology (she construes the repetitious word *item* as the standard manner in which medieval merchants made a list), and just common sense (Provins turns out to have been a major center for the trade of cloth and roses), Lia comes to the extremely reasonable conclusion that Ingolf's mysterious document is, in reality, a kind of laundry list drawn up by a merchant of the period: he is paid in 36 coins for some hay; he delivers some fabric to a street that still exists in the town; he delivers six bunches of roses to six different locations, each costing 20 "deniers" for a total of 120; and the six different locations are still on the town map (see *Pendulum* 440).

It would be difficult, indeed almost impossible, for a professionally trained reader not to jump to the kinds of conclusions Casaubon and his friends first imagined. Like the biblical character Rachel, they believe in contemplation, in textual readings that are metatextual readings and which reflect upon themselves rather than derive confirmation from inferential walks outside their imagination. Lia/Leah, on the other hand, anchored in the corporeal reality of giving birth, keeps her interpretative feet based solidly upon common sense and believes (like Eco) that the simplest and most economical explanation generally constitutes the best one.[18]

Unfortunately, neither Belbo nor Casaubon can tell the frenzied Diabolicals that there is no Plan. Their paranoid perspective assumes the existence of a secret: to tell them that the secret consists in knowing that there is no secret (a version of the Socratic wisdom that the wise man is he who realizes he is not wise) would destroy the foundation upon which their hermetic semiosis is based. If the Diabolicals had been asked (as Casaubon was when he tried to break into Belbo's Abulafia), "Do you have the password?", they would have been incapable of providing the proper response: "NO" (*Pendulum* 37).

The various hair-brained views that constitute the Diabolicals' distorted perspectives have naturally attracted the lion's share of commentary on *Foucault's Pendulum*, especially since Eco's unflattering portrait of overinterpretation or paranoid interpretation in his second novel also involves a devastating value judgment (even if one that is based upon relatively little specific argumentation or extensive documentation) upon certain contem-

porary trends in literary theory associated with Jacques Derrida, Deconstructionism, and Michel Foucault, to name only the most obvious names.
Little interest has been paid to what Eco undoubtedly intended to be one of
the high points of his novel, the death of Belbo upon the pendulum in Paris
and Causabon's subsequent discovery of what Eco calls the "Key Text," a
manuscript that Casaubon examines while he is waiting for the Diabolicals
to come for him in the study of Belbo's Uncle Carlo. This manuscript,
abandoned or hidden long after Belbo came to the depressing realization
that he did not have the talent to be a serious writer (perhaps the ultimate
reason Belbo enjoyed the experiments with mechanical writing and
Abulafia), provides some explanation of why Belbo stood firm and died
rather than reveal the truth that there was no Plan to the Diabolicals.
Belbo's manuscript describes events which took place at the end of April
1945, the end of the war and the partisan experience–the defining moment
in Italian history that gave birth to postwar neorealist culture.

As a young boy, Belbo had always wanted to play the trumpet, and
when the partisans decided upon a grandiose funeral for some of their fallen
comrades, Belbo seemed to have found his chance. At the appointed moment, Belbo had played a single, solitary note on the trumpet, holding it
for what seemed like eternity. In that moment, fixed forever in the "Key
Text" that Belbo abandoned, along with his vocation as a writer, Belbo had
come as close as he ever would to a revelation of truth. As Casaubon puts it:

> You spend a life seeking the Opportunity, without realizing that the decisive
> moment, the moment that justifies birth and death, has already passed. It will
> not return, but it was–full, dazzling, generous as every revelation. That day,
> Jacopo Belbo stared into the eyes of Truth. The only truth that was to be
> granted him. Because–he would learn–truth is brief (afterward it is all commen-
> tary). So he tried to arrest the rush of time. He didn't understand. Not as a
> child. Not as an adolescent when he was writing about it. Not as a man who
> decided to give up writing about it. I understood it this evening: the author has
> to die in order for the reader to become aware of his truth (*Pendulum* 525).

Casaubon describes this magic moment in Belbo's narrative in mystical
terms–as the conclusion of the Great Work discussed by the mystics, as the
essence of Malkhut or revelation. Eco's remark that the author must die
before his work can have meaning agrees with a famous remark that Pier
Paolo Pasolini made on numerous occasions. The passage cited above also
represents Eco's homage to the influence of James Joyce, since Belbo's
"Key Text" describes an epiphany, a concept that Joyce made famous in A
Portrait of the Artist as a Young Man and which Eco himself analyzes in an
important section of The *Aesthetics of Chaosmos: The Middle Ages of James
Joyce*.[19] Readers of *Foucault's Pendulum* have no doubt ignored commentary
on the novel's conclusion because, at first glance, it seems curiously out of

place in a book that has concerned itself almost entirely with various types of crackpot or paranoid interpretations not only of texts but of the world in general. But Belbo's "Key Text" also becomes Casaubon's key text as well (and, I believe, that of the Model Author constructed by this novel, if not the empirical author himself): "But that moment, in which he froze space and time, shooting his Zeno's arrow, had been no symbol, no sign, symptom, allusion, metaphor, or enigma: it was what it was. It did not stand for anything else" (*Pendulum* 525). Casaubon, too, experiences a similar epiphany during the final two sentences of the novel: "So I might as well stay here, wait, and look at the hill. It's so beautiful" (*Pendulum* 533).

Eco's conclusion is an extraordinary ending for a novel written by one of the world's authorities on semiotics. It paradoxically praises a moment in which things represent, signify, symbolize, stand for, or allude to nothing but themselves–in short, a state of grace in which there is absolutely no need for semiotics! It would be an edenic moment in which comprehension and apprehension would coincide completely and ideally. Such a conclusion seems perfectly consistent with the lessons both Belbo and Casaubon learn from their disastrous tinkering with paranoid overinterpretation and the various conspiracy theories held by the different Diabolicals. Of course, the Model Author remains aware that Casaubon's conclusion, so seemingly at odds with the general theory of semiotics (not to mention the entire career of the empirical author, the man Umberto Eco) itself represents the Model Author's interpretation of Casaubon's interpretation. As such, it constitutes yet another step in the process of unlimited semiosis. Earlier in his academic career, Umberto Eco fervently pursued the discipline of semiotics as a means of ferreting out not one Truth but many different truths coexisting in our sublunary condition. The discipline of semiotics had been presented as an appropriate philosophical response to mankind's perennial epistemological questions. In The *Name of the Rose*, however, Eco followed Wittgenstein's dictum, turning to fictional narration presumably when the important truths he wished to discuss could not be adequately treated by philosophical means. At the conclusion of *Foucault's Pendulum*, Eco continues what is in actuality an exaltation of the philosophical potential of fiction. Now, however, the fact that the human condition cannot avoid interpretation and the search for meaning within a jungle of confusing and often contradictory signs represents a fundamentally tragic state to which we, like the author, are eternally condemned.

Peter Bondanella

Bellydancing: Gender, Silence, and the Women of *Foucault's Pendulum*

Shortly after the European publication of Umberto Eco's second novel, the noted historian Jacques Le Goff wrote an essay in which he argued that *Foucault's Pendulum*, despite the modernity of its historical setting, was as profoundly anchored in the Middle Ages as its predecessor, *The Name of the Rose*.[1] Detailing the many ways that Eco's novels represent their complicated debts to medieval discourses, ideas, and social practices, Le Goff observed a decisively medieval quality in their respective figurations of gender: "The Middle Ages was an epoch of men . . . the novels of Umberto Eco are men's novels. This is clear in *The Name of the Rose*. But it is also the case, it seems to me, in *Foucault's Pendulum*, despite the presence of several female characters with strong personalities who often represent the power of reason contrasted to the weakness of the male characters. However, it is the latter who are the heroes, even though they are generally carried away by the flow of history. The women . . ., as in the Middle Ages, are the ones who, for better or worse, bring disorder into this masculine world."[2] While Le Goff's characterization of the gender politics of *Foucault's Pendulum* is accurate to a point, his provocatively succinct invocation of the category women as the troubling other of masculinist culture begs to be interrogated. In what sense are the women of *Foucault's Pendulum* sources of disorder? What is at stake–for narrative and politics–in this gendering of disorder? What does it mean to say that such disorder is "for better or worse"? Better or worse for whom?

If I make Le Goff into something of a straw man with this opening, it is for the purpose of emphasizing how important the unspoken terms of his formulation are to the representations of gender in *Foucault's Pendulum*. Despite the enormous amount of commentary that Eco's novels have inspired, relatively little has focused on questions of gender, even though constructions of masculinity and femininity are central to the fictional worlds and events that these works depict.[3] This essay speaks to that gap by addressing the questions implied by Le Goff's characterization of gender in *Foucault's Pendulum*.[4]

Although *Foucault's Pendulum* warns of the unfortunate fate that befalls those who are tempted to find resemblances where a healthy sense of difference should more properly prevail, I want to pursue for a moment the ways in which Eco's second novel revisits the figurations of gender he pursues in *The Name of the Rose*. The single female character in that novel makes but a few brief appearances in a narrative that she nevertheless oddly inhabits by virtue of Adso's hermeneutic preoccupation with her. The poor peasant girl of the novel becomes for Adso a figure for the signifying processes of language itself, offering him the experience of difference, desire, and the play of meaning that enables his multiple inscriptions of her. She is the beloved of his allegorized eros, the heretic constructed by exclusionary politic discourse, and the symbolic repository of transgressive meanings associated with constructions of the feminine which have predominated in Western culture. A figure of the forever unattainable transcendent signified, she is also preeminently a body, simultaneously an absence and a material presence whose erasure is imaged in her multiple disappearances. She flees from the site of kitchen lovemaking (Adso awakens from his "igneous ardor" to find the girl gone and the discarded heart of an animal in her place). She is removed from the course of historical events by an inquisitorial condemnation ending in certain death. She is glorified yet dismembered, "shattered into plural and separate accidental forms," by monastic theology's parodic dream of reversal and corporeal excess (*Rose* 432-33).[5]

According to Teresa de Lauretis, these figurative and literal disappearances of the girl from the narrative in which she paradoxically plays such an important role coincide with the erasure of gender from the novel as a whole. In *The Name of the Rose*, she argues, the "obscure object of desire" is not the "dead, inert maternal body" of Adso's beloved. Rather, it is "the text itself, metonymically mirrored in the legendary text of the father of philosophy, all the more desired the more it is unattainable, and in the other texts it *generates*: Adso's manuscript and its various 'translations,' interpretants which together constitute the palimpsest of the symbolic body of the father, the inscription of the father's code and of the name of the father across the cultural history of Western Europe." Adso desires William's "knowledge, vision, and power," his "possession of the code," and William desires his disciple's desire, "the writing which inscribes it and the manuscript which . . . produces it as meaning."[6]

If the semiotic universe of *The Name of the Rose* occludes gender as a problem, that is, as "a difference that divides . . . social subjects and imposes the question of the relation of subjectivity and experience to meaning, social formations, and power," what is the fate of this problem in *Foucault's Pendulum*?[7] *Foucault's Pendulum* is more densely populated with women characters whose differences are recognized as a principal aspect of their shared fictional destiny–which is, Le Goff observes, to be at the side of men.[8] To the extent that they are given names–Amparo, Lia, Lorenza Pelligrini–and have quite a lot to say, the women characters of Foucault's Pendulum would appear to fare better than the nameless and silent girl of the Rose. But these differences are ones of scale more than of kind, and like the ostensible differences between the medieval and modern worlds of the two novels, they mask more fundamental similarities of signification.[9] Despite the presence of the computer Abulafia, the dusty offices of Garamond are not unlike the scriptorium and library of the Rose's Benedictine monastery. In both communities men produce books and ponder the meaning of words and things. Foucault invokes the architectural design of the Rose's medieval library with the chapter epigraph from Artephius stating that hermetic philosophy is like a labyrinth. The fate of gender in *Foucault's Pendulum* is proleptically imaged in Gudrun, the misfit mainstay of the Garamond Press, whom Belbo introduces to Casaubon in this way: "Her name isn't really Gudrun. We call her that because of her Nibelung look and because her speech is vaguely Teutonic" (*Pendulum* 72). In *Foucault's Pendulum* gender as a problem is occluded once more, as its women are marginalized by the male-authored Plan, and, like Gudrun's true name, ultimately erased.[10]

This essay focuses on the three women who figure prominently in the novel: Belbo's elusive lover, Lorenza Pelligrini; the hybrid Brazilian Marxist feminist Amparo, whom Casaubon follows to her homeland; and Lia, the practically-oriented interpreter of Casaubon's intellectual obsessions and bearer of his child. Each women is figured principally as a body whose material form is associated with a particular corporeal practice. Lorenza's muscular playing of pinball causes Belbo to fall in love with her (pp. 222-23); Amparo is decisively overcome by indigenous Afro-Brazilian spirits that enter her body at the umbanda rite (pp. 214-45); Lia furnishes the alchemical vessel of gestation in which Casaubon's "good primal matter" steeps (p. 437). The locus of corporeal significance for all three may be further particularized: while each woman is identified as a body, she is more specifically a groin, or a womb, or a belly. According to Belbo, Lorenza owes her success at pinball to the artful movements of her groin (p. 222), while Amparo claims a special knowledge of her country through her womb, not her mind (p. 177). Lia is a veritable expert on the belly, interpreting and epitomizing its significance in the order of things (pp. 361-65; p. 438). But, like the nameless girl in the Rose, these highly individuated corporeal female presences all disappear from the world of the novel.

It could be argued–I shall return to this point at the end of this essay–– that *Foucault's Pendulum* shows an interest in the fundamental materiality of the body which is not limited to the gendered meanings which I single out here. The novel's various bodies are inscribed by a range of discourses. Still, even though the body itself is not essentialized in *Foucault*, the novel's women are essentialized as bodies.[11] The remainder of this essay reflects on the female bodies in novel, the discourses that construct them, and the spaces they occupy in the hermeneutic and hermetic worlds the narrative sets forth.

But first–most people foolish enough to offer interpretations of Eco's fiction feel compelled to preface their readings with a disclaimer. I say "foolish" for the obvious reason that the novels themselves are so utterly self-conscious about the multiplicity and irreducibility of meaning and the impossibility of authorizing it. Structurally and semiotically, *The Name of the Rose* and *Foucault's Pendulum* are ever undoing themselves. Though Casaubon observes at the end of *Foucault* that "the author has to die in order for the reader to become aware of his truth" (p. 633), Eco's novels suggest something quite different: that it is readers and interpreters, not authors, who die in the pursuit of what they think is true.

To advance a reading of *Foucault's Pendulum* addressing the problem of gender, then, poses the additional difficulty of setting priorities of signifi-cance for a work that advises wariness about all such gestures. To whom or what should we (can we?) attribute the "meanings" I am about to describe: the author, the narrator(s), the discourses that create them and the dis-courses they invoke, the text itself, the reader?[12] Rather than endorse a single theory of interpretation by privileging any one of these, I prefer to think that the interpretive effort undertaken here operates as "a dialectic between openness and form, initiative on the part of the interpreter and contextual pressure." My initiative is to explore the possibilities for a read-ing of gender in *Foucault's Pendulum* that is responsive and responsible to the "contextual pressures" of that work. Eco has said that texts "are the human way to reduce the world to a manageable format, open to an intersubjective interpretive discourse"(*Limits* 21). On the problem of gen-der, the contextual pressures of *Foucault's Pendulum* invite such a dialogue.

LORENZA

Of all the women in *Foucault's Pendulum*, Lorenza Pelligrini fulfills the role most like that of the nameless peasant girl of Adso's interpretive reveries, for she is most thoroughly laden with multiple and contradictory significations, most completed mediated by male desire. Elusive and inscru-table, Lorenza is mirrored in the locked computer files accessible only to one who possesses the password (pp. 41-2). She is for Belbo the last in a series of what his computer file calls a "A bevy of fair women," whose number includes the Virgin Mary, one "Marilena (Marylena? Mary

Lena?)," and Cecelia, and whose primary significance for Belbo is their unavailability.

Lorenza's unavailability is incarnated in the way she plays pinball, me-
morialized by Belbo in a computer file of the same name:

> You don't play pinball with just your hands, you play it with the groin too.
> The pinball problem is not to stop the ball before it's swallowed by the mouth
> at the bottom, or to kick it back to midfield like a halfback. The problem is to
> make it stay up where the lighted targets are more numerous and have it
> bounce from one to another, wandering, confused, delirious, but still a free
> agent. And you achieve this not by jolting the ball but by transmitting vibra-
> tions to the case, the frame. . ... You can only do it with the groin, or with a play
> of the hips that makes the groin not so much bump, as slither. . ... The ball is
> intoxicated with vis movendi, remaining in play for memorable and immemo-
> rial lengths of time. But a female groin is required, one that interposes no
> spongy body between the ileum and the machine, and there must be no erectile
> matter in between, only skin, nerves, padded bone sheathed in a pair of jeans,
> and a sublimated erotic fury, a sly frigidity, a disinterested adaptability to the
> partner's response . . . the Amazon must drive the pinball crazy and savor the
> thought that she will then abandon it. (p. 222)

In Belbo's account of effective pinball technique, success at the
game–imaged in the production of sustained but unfulfilled desire–depends
upon sexual difference. Belbo's fixation with Lorenza's pinball playing repeats a childhood scene, when he learns from his mother "that little girls
don't grow wee-wees" and suddenly realizes that Mary Lena "is blond and
haughty and inaccessible because she is different. No possible relationship;
she belongs to another race," he writes in "A bevy of fair women" (p. 57).

The discontinuous story of Belbo's computer files and childhood recollections records the eroticized idealization of otherness and failed attempts
at transcendence that Lorenza's pinball playing represents for him. By
Casaubon's account, that is why Belbo falls in love with her: because "she
could promise him an unattainable happiness," a promise which is also "the
promise of the Pendulum" (p. 223). Standing in for all the lost objects of
desire, Lorenza bears the burden of Belbo's metaphysical quest.

It is especially ironic that Lorenza and her pinball playing should be
identified with the pendulum's promise of transcendent fixity, since pinball
in its own right utterly contradicts such a signification. Rather, as Belbo's
account of the game makes clear, pinball epitomizes change, chaos, and
uncertainty, all of which more properly apply to the character of Lorenza
as depicted in Belbo's computer files and Casaubon's narrative.[13] In this
respect, Belbo's difficulty with Lorenza is the result of the contradictory
meanings he ascribes to her; his emotional pain is a function of his mixed
metaphors.

Belbo does not exhaust Lorenza's potentiality as a contradictory signifier. She is also subject to inscription by her several other suitors, notably Aglie and Riccardo, and she inhabits Casaubon's own narrative as an absence and a censored image (pp. 343-48; p. 41). Whereas Riccardo pursues her purely as a sex object, Aglie assigns Lorenza multiple yet predictable identities, rooted in the binarism through which Western patriarchy has constructed the female.

Aglie lures Lorenza's attention with the promise of an "intellectual partnership" in which she assumes the role of the Gnostic Sophia in conflict with her male counterpart over the creation of the world. As the latter, she replays the mythic identification of woman with matter, the primordial stuff in which "Sophia was caught. . . .. Prisoner of the world," as she tells Belbo (p. 300). Lorenza's drunken account of herself as the avatar of Sophia proves that a little bit of Gnosticism is a dangerous thing. In her amusing version of her travels through history in that form, Lorenza appears unaware of the disturbing identities that have been assigned to her, even though her own misunderstanding provides momentary resistance to the very discourses that would mythically contain her. Relating to Casaubon how Aglie found her when she was a prostitute in a brothel in Tyre, she defends herself: "in those days when they said prostitute, they meant a woman who was free, without ties, an intellectual who didn't want to be a housewife. She might hold a salon. Today she'd be in public relations" (p. 301). But Lorenza more readily embraces, or at least parrots, the mythic identities Aglie gives her. "'I am the saint and the prostitute,'" she cries out as Belbo tries to take control of her one evening (p. 303), proclaiming the angelic and demonic roles in which she also haunts his fiction.

Were she not so naively courageous at the bizarre sacrificial circus at the end of the novel, when she steps forward to stand by her man and utters with stark lucidity, "'Are you all crazy?'" (p. 595), Lorenza would almost seem a parody of the dualistic construction of a mythic femininity, a Venus in blue jeans. Yet, though she is always on the move, in and out of Pilade's, on a train to somewhere, there is nothing elusive about her death. At Belbo's ultimate heroic moment, Lorenza makes her unfortunate final appearance, dazed and diaphanous, fulfilling the role that the hermetic brotherhood has defined for her (p. 586). Though Lorenza and Belbo are both prisoners, Belbo at least has the dubious privilege of having authored his own end, even to the point of anticipating how the pendulum will swing with a human weight attached to it. Lorenza is accorded no such privilege; coerced and, until the penultimate moment, in a trance, she experiences instead a very generic death as the "sacrifice humain" (p. 595). Nor is her death accorded any other meaning beyond itself, while Belbo's horrific if ingenious demise is dignified by Casaubon's philosophical ruminations.

Belbo leaves behind a living record–his computer files, his juvenilia, his childhood memories of a time rich with meaning. But Lorenza is simply gone, as Casaubon states, "as if she had never existed. . . .. In that world of the dead, she was the most dead" (p. 601).

AMPARO

Amparo's disappearance from the novel is less dramatic, certainly less brutal. She simply wanders off from Casaubon with "a volume of political economy under her arm" (p. 216), embarrassed and disgusted for having allowed herself to be incarnated by the indigenous spirit that possesses her at the umbanda rite. "Called by deep voices," as Casaubon reports it, "she had stripped herself of all defenses, of all will" (p. 213). Amparo's loss of control signals her inability to reconcile her leftist politics and her feminism with the bodily imperatives of her native culture, a world she clings to, Casaubon states, "with the muscles of her belly, her heart, her head, her nostrils" (pp. 162-63).

Although Amparo's belly bears a different semiotic burden from Lorenza's pinball-playing groin, her bodily experience, like that of Lorenza, also becomes a trope for her otherness. On the evening of her possession by Pomba Gira, Casaubon registers this difference: "It was as if there were an unknown being next to me" (p. 216). It is a difference founded in a dualistic view of mind and body and replicated in the male/ female binary. For Casaubon, despite his own powerful attraction to the smells and the drums of the umbanda, runs no risk of being overcome. He plays the agogo offered to him, and by "becoming part" of the event, controls it: "I found relief by moving my legs and feet, I freed myself from what surrounded me, I challenged it, I embraced it," he states (p. 213). Amparo, not similarly fortified, may have been "guarding her mind tenaciously," as Aglie explains to him, "but she was not on guard against her body" (p. 215).

Amparo shares her experience of bodily possession with her native sisters. Though she mocks with "sarcastic asides . . . the sensitivity of her sex" as the women begin to fall under the spell of the umbanda rite (p. 211), later she apologizes for them all as she struggles to understand what has happened to her: "I really must have eaten something I shouldn't have. All those women tonight must have. I hate my country" (p. 214). Even the failure to be overcome by spirits is presented as unique to female bodily experience. Amparo's self-disgust is ironically mirrored in the disappointment of the blonde German psychologist, "who had been participating in the rites for years . . . but . . . the trance never came. . . .. The German woman's eyes were wide, and every movement of her hysterical limbs begged for oblivion. . ... However much she tried to lose control, she constantly regained it." "Poor Teuton," Casaubon remarks, "sick from too many well-tempered clavicords" (pp. 211-12).[14]

The ecstatic abandon of distinctively female flesh encodes a fate that is not Amparo's alone. For hers is the political story, disguised as romance. As Casaubon puts it: "Loving Amparo was like being in love with the Third World. Amparo was beautiful, Marxist, Brazilian, enthusiastic, disenchanted. She had a fellowship and splendidly mixed blood" (p. 158).[15] A "descendant of Dutch settlers . . . who intermarried with Indians and Sudanese blacks," Amparo, with her Jamaican face, Parisian culture, and Spanish name (p. 161), offers a paradigm of the syncretism that is so central to Casaubon's experience of Brazilian culture. To him Amparo is as perplexing in her "splendid contradictions" as the "unbridled hybridizations" of Brazil and its people, which after a time make him feel "like a walking blender mixing strange concoctions" (p. 171).[16]

Amparo thinks like a Marxist but feels things inspired by her native culture that she doesn't even understand. This is not an unusual combination among her comrades, who meet in houses adorned with portraits of Lenin and Amerindian fetishes and who punctuate conversations on the class struggle with references to Brazilian cannibalism and African deities (p. 162). But Amparo is unable to negotiate these differences. While she at one point laments having forgotten the stories of her grandmother for "a bit of Europe and a bit of historical materialism," (p. 182) when the import of those stories overcomes her at the umbanda, she is full of self-condemnation: "'I'm still a slave. . . .. I'm a poor dirty black girl. Give me a master; I deserve it!'" (p. 214).

Amparo's inability to sustain her leftist politics in the face of her native religious impulses signifies not merely a personal failure but also the lamentable prospects for Third World reform. It also portends the collapse of revolutionary politics and the ascendancy of the unconscious which Casaubon discovers upon returning to Italy from Brazil. Signor Garamond puts the matter succinctly as he offers his justification for establishing a new series of occult texts, Project Hermes: "Brazil is right here" (p. 261). Casaubon resists this transformation in historical and political consciousness, just as he recoils from Amparo's possession. But like his companion editors Belbo and Diotallevi, he eventually finds that he too is vulnerable to the temptations of a syncretic fantasy that he will not be able to control by striking the agogo.

In an interview given at the time of the publication of *Il Pendolo di Foucault*, Eco commented on the importance of the Brazilian episode in his novel in terms similar to the analysis offered here.[17] In fact, the entire episode appears to draw heavily upon an account of Brazilian Candomble and umbanda rites which Eco first published in 1979.[18] Eco's description and

history of the Afro-Brazilian rites return in the novel–coincidentally, both
Casaubon and his creator are sons of Oxala (p. 188)–and *Foucault* credits
Amparo with a cultural critique of the practice of indigenous religions that
largely repeats Eco's own essay. Ventriloquated through Casaubon (p. interestingly, she does not speak entirely in her own voice), Amparo's critique condemns the rites of carnival and soccer rituals in which "the disinherited expended their combative energy and sense of revolt . . . completely
unaware of the Establishment, which wanted to keep them in a state of
ecstatic enthusiasm" (p. 163). Eco similarly remarks on the way that carnival, soccer, and indigenous religious rites further the containment of the
disinherited masses," yet he valorizes the rites themselves for being "wiser .
. . truer, bound more to elementary pulsations, to the mysteries of the
body and of nature."[19]

In *Foucault* Amparo herself stands in for this valorization, yet she also
carries the semiotic load of negative personal and political consequences
which come with such "elementary pulsations." In the "mysteries" of a
naturalized, primitive female flesh, Amparo's politics and feminism collapse. Though her possession in Brazil introduces a nostalgia for meaningful political discourse that Casaubon details in the Italy to which he returns, Amparo's own departure is sparely noted, much less mourned.

LIA

If Amparo rejects "natural" bodily meanings she can neither escape nor
control, Lia, in comparison, appears to embrace, even to relish, the corporeal significance that Casaubon's narrative assigns to her. Lia is represented
principally *as* a body. It is her corporeal presence that Casaubon continually records: how she sits (inelegantly, in a "housewifely pose" "with her
spread legs drawing her skirt tight" [p. 361]), how she touches herself, pat-
ting her belly, the "swelling taut vessel" in which Casaubon's "good primal
matter" is transmuted (p. 437). Hers is, moreover, no ordinary belly;
rather, it is an archetypal, a paradigmatic belly, instructing Casaubon that
the "secretum secretorum no longer needed to be sought" because it is there
"in the bellies of all the Lias of the world" (p. 438). "Wet nurse" and "matri-
archal authority"–Casaubon even responds to her with "Yes, Mama" (p.
362)–Lia speaks "with the wisdom of life and birth" (p. 365).

Among the various hermetic myths and systems in which the three
Garamond editors dabble, Casaubon chooses the highly gendered discourse
of alchemy to figure the story of his personal life.[20] His inscription of the
procreative process as an alchemical transmutation makes Lia's body the
vessel in which his grail, his philosopher's stone is produced. Casaubon's
mythologizing of Lia in these terms is thoroughly consistent with the symbols and metaphors of alchemical mysteries, which established analogies

between the forces of life and creation in human beings and in the cosmos and encoded these analogies in a valorized sexual symbolism.

Casaubon's construction of Lia as the alchemical vessel and of the procreation of his child as the perfecting of the philosopher's stone inevitably invokes the entire gendered structure of alchemical discourse. The basic alchemical plot tells of the efforts of the alchemist to gain control over a female nature, a process in which the material feminine is identified as a source of creative power. Yet alchemy also portrays a dark side of feminine nature, its multiplicity and its otherness.[21] Despite the "egalitarian conjunction of opposites upon which the process of alchemical transmutation is theoretically founded," alchemical discourse distinguishes a fundamental hierarchy of masculine and feminine symbols and substances, which provides the basic structure of the human psyche and the cosmos.[22] A modern-day alchemical enthusiast describes it this way:

> As all active knowledge belongs to the masculine side of the soul, and all passive being to its feminine side, thought-dominated . . . consciousness can in a certain sense be ascribed to the masculine pole, while all involuntary powers and capacities connected with life as such, appear as an expression of the feminine pole. . . . The fundamental masculine and feminine powers are anchored in the unconscious and instinctive nature of man. The two powers experience their full development on the plane of the soul, but realize their fulfilment only in the spirit, for only here does feminine receptivity attain its broadest breadth and its purest purity, and is wholly united to the victorious masculine Act.[23]

At moments Casaubon's commentary on the alchemical gestation of his son sounds like the triumphant assertion of the "victorious masculine Act." It makes him superior to the taxidermist Salon, who only stuffs dead animals, while he creates "living animals" (p. 445). As he becomes increasingly caught up in his own enabling creativity ("My Stone that was slowly coming out of exile, from the sweet oblivious hypnotic exile of Lia's vessel; my Stone, beautiful and white" [pp. 444-45]), Lia delivers the child, alone, and undercuts the pretensions of his mythic reveries. Her response to his praise of her sets the record straight on their alchemical collaboration: "'The credit is yours, darling; it all depends on the vessel,'" he tells her. "'Of course the credit is mine, you shit,'" she replies (p. 447).[24]

In this instance Lia reappropriates her body from the inscriptions of diabolical discourse, asserting a measure of verbal agency that Gnostic oppositions and spiritual possession deny to Lorenza and Amparo. This is one of several gestures that mark her as a wisdom figure in the novel, a sort of funky Lady Philosophy, who is introduced (p. 226) with an epigraph from Purgatorio 27, in which Virgil lures Dante into and through the purgative fire that prepares him for his entry into Eden and his encounter with Beatrice.[25]

As a wisdom figure, Lia offers in the novel the only countervailing voice to diabolical language and interpretation and to the Plan. When, as the oracle of corporeality, she explains to Casaubon that "archetypes don't exist; the body exists" (p. 362), she effectively dismisses any grand metaphysical origin for the Templar plot and the syncretic features of all the world's philosophy and religion; she posits instead the common origin of distinctive mythic systems in the human body (pp. 362-65). The hermeneutic priorities Lia shows in her own version of "writing from the body" also prevail in her reading of the Plan. She deconstructs it by decoding the "secret" message on which it depends: it isn't a blueprint for the Templars' control of the world; it's a laundry list. Manipulating the multi-layered codes of the Templar message, Lia also manages to find communicated there a sentiment that not only undercuts the authority of the document but also expresses what the reader of *Foucault* must feel by this point in the novel: "Merde j'en ai marré de cette steganographie"–"Shit, I'm sick of this hermetic writing" (p. 540).

If it appears that Lia's voice is privileged in the novel, that may be because her critique of the Diabolicals' approach to the coded Templar message borrows substantively from Eco's own analysis of what he calls "Hermetic drift."[26] Eco himself has said that Lia represents an order of "common sense," "a logic of the body, a logic of nature," which both counters and limits the interpretive excess of the Diabolicals.[27] But Lia's critique of the metaphysical pretensions of the symbolic systems and hierarchical binaries of hermeticism nevertheless preserves the gender coding of the very hierarchical oppositions she seeks to undo, as does her ambiguous fate in the novel. Casaubon leaves her and Giulio to pursue events set in motion by the Plan, yet he is haunted by her words and her memory until his own words cease. But even her privileged voice disappears into some unidentified space.

The semiotics of female bodies in *Foucault's Pendulum* contributes to that work's larger interest in the material body itself. At his most transcendent moment Belbo dies from his own mortal weight; Diotallevi experiences in his wayward cancerous cells the consequences of his hermeneutic transgressions because, as he points out, the body is a book.[28] The corporeal preoccupations of *Foucault's Pendulum* replay, with a difference, an aspect of *The Name of the Rose*: Adso's meditations on linguistic meaning regularly turn to a focus on the human body. Thus he comes to reflect on the impassioned flesh of sexuality, the tortured and broken bodies of poverty and heresy, and the life-giving and death-ridden materiality of human existence itself. "It is cold in the scriptorium, my thumb aches," he says in his final retreat from language.

The corporeal turn in both of Eco's novels is linked to ways of knowing. In *The Name of the Rose* Adso grounds textuality in bodily experience, while *Foucault's Pendulum* warns that people seeking transcendence outside the material realm can die. Yet if the body is a ground of experience, a generator and end point of meanings, it is upon female bodies that this experience of signification is most fully played out. The pattern of those signs is unmistakable: even with an excess of interpretation, when we read gender, a dualistic model prevails: men seek transcendence through mind; women are bodily immanence and nature. Lorenza, Amparo, and Lia are contained by several naturalizing discourses: Lorenza's sexual body is that of the virgin and temptress; Amparo's racial body is that of a woman possessed; Lia's procreative body is that of the earth mother. In terms of these naturalizations, making the body the ground of experience and interpretation proves troublesome, for it precisely the category "nature" that has reified women's bodies for so long.

In their defining corporeal otherness, the women of *Foucault's Pendulum* ultimately incarnate silence. Their bodies and their voices succumb to death, flight, and absence. As is the case in *The Name of the Rose*, in *Foucault* men write, women are written. The object of desire is still a male-authored text, albeit a contorted, transhistorical version of Western intellectual tradition. Women occupy multiple discursive spaces but they have no agency. The price of subjectivity is silence. Garamond's Gudrun is exemplary once more: at the end of the novel she is "the only one left who tells the truth." But, as Casaubon observes, she "was never part of our story" (p. 617).

The novel's reinscription of the dominant gender binaries of western thought–the idea of women, "for better or worse," as agents of disorder–is particularly vexing in light of the unremitting reflexivity of all of Eco's textual productions, including and perhaps most especially, his novels. For if, as Hutcheon suggests, the ironic vision of *Foucault's Pendulum* in the end keeps it from being simply an exemplar of the very hermetic semiosis it aims to critique, the novel's representations of women can be only uneasily and incompletely explained by that vision.[29]

The collapsing of the individual's significance, the absorption of the feminine into nature and myth that *Foucault* enacts, is oddly at variance with the larger impulse of the novel to expose the ahistorical hermeneutic retreat into similarity for the semiotic and the human risks it incurs.

Theresa Coletti

Irony-clad Foucault

In certain critical circles, from the moment the title of Umberto Eco's second novel was announced, the speculation began. *The Name of the Rose* had been chock full of more semiotic theories than most competent readers could ever hope to discern. Did this mean that the more helpfully named *Foucault's Pendulum* would come complete with long discourses on sexuality, knowledge, and power? It was true that Eco had not often mentioned Michel Foucault by name in his theoretical work before this, but the title was certainly directive, was it not? Then we began to read the novel. And-- only then–did many of us begin to recall (with the novel's assistance) other Foucaults, especially Jean Bernard Léon Foucault, the nineteenth-century physicist whose famous pendulum hangs even today in the Conservatoire des Arts et Métiers in Paris. Foregoing our initial knee-jerk association with Michel and perhaps feeling not a little ahistorical and even foolish at being tricked, we concentrated on Jean Bernard Léon's pendulum which, after all, does have an important role in the plot. Nevertheless, Michel Foucault–especially his early work–continued to haunt this complex and learned novel for me, albeit in a very ironic fashion.

Learned novels are Eco's specialty, for like few others in our contemporary world, he can bring together his two worlds as creative writer and critical theorist, media darling and dissertation fodder. But Eco has also made it difficult for reviewers and critics to engage with those novels, despite the tantalizing lures (such as that title), because he self-reflexively ironizes the position not only of author but also of reader, thus reminding critical commentators of their secondary, even parasitic role. Given that, what do we do with a novel like *Foucault's Pendulum* that ironizes all attempts at either deconstruction or construction of meaning? What happens when pages of contradictions get welded into a totalized vision of order, when life imitates art, when the narrative structure–while seemingly loose and baggy–is in fact obsessively ordered around the form of the occult Tree of the Sefirot? And what has any of this to do with the Foucault named Michel?

Foucault's Pendulum, despite its press, is not really an adventure story, a thriller, or a detective story, like *The Name of the Rose*: it ends, rather than begins, with the requisite deaths; there is a plot–or rather, there is a plethora of plots, all brought together into something called the "Plan". Michael Holquist has argued (p. 135) that the detective story is to postmodernism what myth and depth psychology were to modernism. In Eco's perverse version of the postmodern, however, the detective as the metaphor of order and logic is ironized–by the decisive presence of chance or accident (in *The Name of the Rose*) or by hyperbolic expansion and inversion (in *Foucault's Pendulum*). In this latter novel, the "belief that the mind, given enough time, can understand everything" (Holquist 1971:141) is taken to an overstated, and I would argue, ironic extreme: in a way, it is the portrait of the totalizing mind imploding. Eco's ultra-plotted plot about plots operates much like Pynchon's paranoia in *Gravity's Rainbow*. But it is not the "scientifically charted and organized familiarity of the totalized world" (Spanos 1972:155) that gets ironically subverted here: it is rather the flip side of positivism–hermetic thought. Its self-confirming, circular mode of including mutually contradictory elements is at one and the same time put in motion and called into question. For the mystic adept, every word becomes a sign of something else, the truth of what is not said. Therefore one must learn to read with suspicion, lest something be missed. Irony, of course, is also a sign of something else, the not said, and to be sensitive to irony is to read with suspicion. *Foucault's Pendulum* shows what happens to hermetic thought when it confronts the irony that is structurally its double.

Among Eco's scholarly interests has been the idea of hermetic semiosis, and in 1986 he gave a course on this topic at the University of Bologna's Istituto di Discipline della Comunicazione, in which he studied the interpretive practice of seeing both the world and texts in terms of relations of sympathy and resemblance. His time frame ranged from prehistoric times to the present. Now, perhaps, we can begin to see what all this has to do with Michel Foucault–or at least with his early work. In *The Order of Things* (*Les Mots et les choses*), Foucault had argued that this kind of thought was historically limited: a Renaissance paradigm which gave way over time to a modern, scientific one. The epistemological space up to the end of the sixteenth century was one Foucault saw as governed by a rich "semantic web of resemblance" (p. 17). In his course, Eco clearly wanted to challenge this temporal periodization, to argue that this kind of thought never really disappeared, that there was no final epistemic break. In his view, the hermetic semiosis discernible in documents from the early centuries of the Christian era (e.g. *Corpus Hermeticum*) developed clandestinely in the medieval period, triumphed in the humanistic rediscovery of hermetic writings in the Renaissance and Baroque periods, but continues to exist in parallel to the quantitative science that then developed–often crossing it, more often opposing it (Eco, "Introduzione" 1989:9-10). Newton, for example, is known to have combined modern science and cabalistic speculation. More recently, he points out that Gilbert Durand, in his *Science de l'homme et la tradition*, has linked contemporary structuralist and post-structuralist thought with the same logic that accepts the plurivocal nature of both interpretation and texts. We might recall, in this vein, Derrida's notion that "[b]etween rationalism and mysticism there is. . .a certain complicity" (p. 80). In other words, the pendulum has continued to swing between the extremes of some form of reason and some form of mysticism–and this is one of the many meanings of the titular pendulum. But there are many others, and for these other contexts are helpful.

The story of *Foucault's Pendulum* is narrated by a young Italian scholar named, simply, Casaubon, in the hours following the climax of the Plan's plotting, as he awaits what he imagines to be his death. It is in this light–knowing the end of the story, so to speak–that he fills in the background. He recounts how, while writing a dissertation on the medieval Knights Templar, he had become an unofficial consultant to Jacopo Belbo and his colleague, Diotallevi, editors for a small, serious press, when a certain right-wing Colonel Ardenti had approached the press about publishing a problematic book. According to its author, this book would act as a call to pool knowledge and solve the mystery of the Templar plan to conquer the world, a plan that involved a secret about some immense power source. Such a publication would enable contact with others "in the know" that might lead to picking up the thread of the plot that had been lost because of a missed meeting and thus a missing piece of the puzzle. When Ardenti disappears under mysterious circumstances, possibly murdered, the book remains unpublished–but its contents lie dormant in the minds of the editors and their consultant, Casaubon.

The young scholar completes his dissertation on the Templars, goes to Brazil, falls in love with the beautiful Amparo, attends some Afro-Brazilian religious rites, and meets a singular Signor Agliè who seems to be the Comte de Saint-Germain *redivivus*. It is in Brazil that Casaubon begins to be lulled, as he puts it, by the notion of resemblance, by the feeling that everything might be related to everything else. When he returns to Italy, we are told, he converts this "metaphysics" into "mechanics"–with the help of Belbo and Diotallevi, who employ him to do research for their publishing house's vanity press division. From his initial task–finding illustrations for a science book on the history of metals–Casaubon finds that magic and science go hand in hand; soon he feels he has one foot in the cabala and the other in the laboratory. Eco's pendulum has begun to swing. The two presses decide to publish a new series of hermetic texts, and Signor Agliè is brought in as a consultant to help them deal with the vast number of manuscripts written by their "Diabolicals," as they suggestively name them.

A chance encounter with the police inspector in charge of the earlier Ardenti case reminds Casaubon of the theory of the Templar plot to rule the world, and this leads to the three editors' conceiving of what they call "the Plan" out of their formalist (even modernist?) "desire to give shape to shapelessness, to transform into fantasized reality that fantasy that others wanted to be real" (p. 337). Out of data and desire, with the aid of a computer program to randomize information, they set out deliberately and ironically to deploy–rather than decode–the hermetic semiosis. Feeding hermetic data into the computer, along with connectives and neutral data, they randomize the order and then create connections: "Any fact becomes important when it's connected to another. The connection changes the perspective; it leads you to think that every detail of the world, every voice, every word written or spoken has more than its literal meaning, that it tells us of a Secret. The Rule is simple: Suspect, only suspect" (p. 378). The ironic play in English on E.M. Forster's "Connect, only connect" marks its exaggeration, not its negation. Starting with Ardenti's notion of the Templar plot, they "narrativize" isolated data, making connections–causal, temporal, spatial. They start with verifiable facts; the fictionalizing is in the Foucaultian "order of things", so to speak. Soon, everything from the cabala to Bacon to Shakespeare to the Templars to the Rosicrucians to the Masons to the Jesuits to Hitler are linked in a plot whose climax should–by the Plan's reasoning–take place in Paris at the Conservatoire des Arts et Métiers where hangs Foucault's pendulum–the laboratory proof of the earth's diurnal rotation. Nothing they discuss or consider remains innocent; all is interconnected, once this hermetic thinking is set in motion. In tandem with this male creation of artifice, Casaubon's child is gestating in the womb of Lia, his partner, who is endowed with the "wisdom of life and birth" [365]. The pendulum swings.

Parallel to this narrative is the revelation of the contents of Belbo's computer files which Casaubon has recently read. Having decided he was one of life's spectators, not actors, and thus having chosen to be an editor not a writer, Belbo nevertheless uses his new computer to record stories of his childhood in the war-time Italian countryside, to work out his feelings for the beautiful Lorenza, and to write, to create. But what he creates is a parody of Eco's own radical intertextual play in the novel itself, as we shall see shortly. The three Planners have to keep reminding themselves that the idea is to *create* not discover the Templars' secret, that their Plan is a fake (pp. 387; 391): "We consoled ourselves with the realization–unspoken, now, respecting the etiquette of irony–that we were parodying the logic of our Diabolicals" (p. 467). But the problem is that their "brains grew accustomed to connecting, connecting, connecting everything with everything else, until [they] did it automatically, out of habit" (p. 467). Gradually they lose the ability to tell the similar from the identical, the metaphoric from the real (p. 468). They come to decide that their "story was plausible, rational, because it was backed by facts, it was true" (p. 493). Unfortunately, others also decide likewise: Agliè believes them and, when they will not reveal the Secret they claim to know about, he vanishes.

Things then begin to go badly for the Planners. As Belbo works Hitler into the Plan, Diotallevi (who wants to be Jewish) takes sick. Convinced that he has developed cancer because they have "sinned against the Word" (p. 564) by mocking knowledge, Diotallevi sees his cancer cells as inventing a Plan of their own in a diabolical allegory of their hermetic Plan (p. 566). As Diotallevi lies dying, Belbo falls into the trap of belief. Desperate to be an actor instead of a spectator, an author instead of an editor, he thinks himself a god-like creator: "Inventing, he had created the principle of reality" (p. 531). Given the importance the Plan had granted to the Conservatoire and the pendulum in Paris, Belbo leaves to fulfill his destiny on the day of the summer solstice. An interrupted call from Belbo to Casaubon sends the latter to Belbo's apartment to read his computer files and, from there, to follow him to Paris, where he hides in a periscope in the Conservatoire and waits for the stroke of midnight on this, the solstice.

The Templi Resurgentes Equites Synarchici (the TRES)–an invention of the Planners, or so they thought–appear on time and almost the entire cast of characters of the novel is to be found among these reborn Templars. As Casaubon says: "if you invent a plan and others carry it out, it's as if the Plan exists. At that point it does exist" (p. 619). Belbo and the pendulum are the centre of the bizarre ceremony that Casaubon witnesses, as they try to wrest from him the Secret. Since there is no Secret, of course, Belbo dies— refusing "to bow to unmeaning" (p. 623). Early in the novel, we had read one of Belbo's computer files in which a slip of the finger is said to have the power to erase memory: "I have no Message to reveal. But later on–who knows?–I might" (p. 27). But if he does, he does not reveal it, even later on: he dies, hanging by and from the pendulum. Casaubon flees back to Italy, to Belbo's country house, and waits. He finds the "Key Text" there–the story of the most glorious moment of Belbo's life–but one way of interpreting what he learns from this key is that there is nothing to learn: he understands that there is nothing to understand. He waits in peace, offering a self-reflexive warning to the reader (earlier referred to, in a parody of Baudelaire via Eliot, as "apocryphe lecteur, mon semblable, mon frère" [p. 200]): "I would like to write down everything I thought today. But if They were to read it, They would only derive another dark theory and spend another eternity trying to decipher the secret message hidden behind my words. It's impossible, They would say; he can't only have been making fun of us. No" (p. 641). Then he adds: "It makes no difference whether I write or not. They will look for other meanings, even in my silence". And so They will.

So do we all: it is the job of critics–and readers–to "derive another dark theory" and "decipher the secret message hidden behind" the words of texts. This is what I meant by the notion that Eco makes his works hard to write about. But I would still want to argue that, although this is a novel about connections and resemblances that is structured, obsessively so, on connections and resemblances, it is irony–the canker (or cancer?) beneath overt resemblance–that makes Eco's plot different from Casaubon's Plan. Without irony, Eco's novel would be an exemplar of hermetic semiosis; with irony, it becomes simultaneously a critique as well as an exemplar.

This is "both/and" thinking of the first order and, as the temporal pendulum swings, medieval hermeticism and contemporary postmodernism share the ability to juggle "complexity and contradiction" in what postmodern architect Robert Venturi calls "the difficult unity of inclusion" (p. 16). *Foucault's Pendulum*–structured as tightly, indeed rigidly, as any modernist novel–carries structure to such an extreme that it implodes; it ironically turns in on itself and metamorphoses into an "open" work, by Eco's own definition. It both continues and contravenes the modernist project. The pendulum swings. And it is irony that provides the magnetic field to make it swing. In calling *The Name of the Rose* postmodern, Eco himself once foregrounded this double-talking trope: "Irony, metalinguistic play, enunciation squared. Thus, with the modern, anyone who does not understand the game can only reject it, but with the postmodern, it is possible not to understand the game and yet to take it seriously. Which is, after all, the quality (the risk) of irony" (*Postscript* 68). In *Foucault's Pendulum*, it is the ironizing of the twin modernist elements of reflexivity and intertextuality that activates the particular game of connections and resemblances.

The operation of textual reflexivity can be seen on so many levels of this novel and in such an obvious way that a few examples will give a flavor of the whole. Each of the 120 sections of the work begins with a citation–presumably one of the 120 that Casaubon found in Belbo's computer files and in the light of which he interprets "the whole story" (p. 43). The 120 sections are divided into 10 chapters of uneven length, each labeled according to one of the parts of the mystic Tree of the Sefirot and each explained within the text itself. The first (Keter), for instance, is called "the Crown, the beginning, the primal void" (p. 18); the second (Hokhmah) is strangely described as the sign of wisdom in a box–strangely, that is, until we realize that this is the section in which Casaubon finds out how to enter Belbo's computer system and achieve, if not wisdom, at least information. It is also the source of much of the story line to follow, just as Hokhmah is said to hold "the essence of all that will emanate from it" (p. 41). This patterning continues throughout the rest of the novel.

Eco actually printed a visual representation of the Tree of the Sefirot as the frontispiece to the novel–not merely to help us follow the order, for that is not particularly difficult. I think it is there, rather, to help us visualize the swing, the rhythm–for the movement of the order of the named chapters is, not surprisingly, that of the horizontal swing from side to side on the diagram. It also forms an overall elliptical shape, if viewed vertically, rather than horizontally.

The famous pendulum of Foucault, of course, does exactly the same thing. In naming his novel as he did, then, Eco was pointing us to multiple, complex levels of reflexivity. The actual pendulum, hung from "the only Fixed Point in the universe, eternally unmoving" (p. 5), but representing, indeed demonstrating, the working of time (Vita-Finzi 1989:225; Berardinelli 1988:5), is itself as inherently paradoxical a symbol as the place in which it hangs still today. The Conservatoire des Arts et Métiers in Paris is a post-revolutionary museum, deliberately set up in a church (St-Martin-des-Champs); it is a run-down museum of industry and technology housed in part in a gothic priory, here used as the setting for a climactic occult ritual. Of course, it is an apt place for Eco's climax for other reasons than these ironic paradoxes: it is situated in front of former Templar towers and it is historically connected to a figure important to the Plan–Bacon–and his House of Solomon in the *New Atlantis*, where all the inventions of human-kind are found collected together.

The pendulum itself is presented from the first pages of the novel in language both mystic and scientific, both overblown and precise, signaling in language the swing between magic and reason. What we might call pendular thinking, oscillating between opposites, has always characterized Eco's work–both creative and theoretical. We need only remember the importance of non-order to order, instability to stability, in his semiotic theorizing, or the undercutting of reason by chance in *The Name of the Rose*. That pendular binaries also end up moving more or less in circles, like Foucault's pendulum, is not unrelated to Eco's theory of the self-reflexive circularity of semiotic systems in his *Theory of Semiotics*. The titular pendu-lum, in other words, becomes a plurivalent sign whose allegorical meanings proliferate in the text to form a complex set of reflexive mises-en-abyme. At the climax of the novel, as Belbo hangs from the pendulum, however, something seems to change. While the pendulum is described in binary terms both as Belbo's Sinai and as his Calvary (p. 600), the ironic paradoxes that have constituted its identity seem to resolve, as it is identified with Belbo's moment of understanding. It is described as "no symbol, no sign, symptom, allusion, metaphor, or enigma: it was what it was. It did not stand for anything else" (p. 633). Yet, it is hard not to notice that this reso-lution into non-paradox, non-irony comes (ironically) at the moment in which a literalization of the so-called postmodern death of the subject re-sults in the affirmation of subjectivity, when the so-called postmodern cri-sis in representation is resolved–doubly resolved, in both literary and scien-tific terms: the very next section opens with a letter from a scientist explaining precisely how a pendulum would swing if a man were hanging from it–a literal re-presentation of the scene we have just read. And yet, and yet, what one critic calls the charm of a pendular mind (Berardinelli 1988:4) still seems to endure, no matter what the thematic and structural resolution that might seem to stop the pendulum's swing temporarily. These ideological ironies, these undercuttings of contemporary theoretical truisms, constitute yet another layer of reflexive and deconstructing mirrorings.

Still others abound, of course. The naming of characters, as well as of the novel itself, functions ironically. As I mentioned at the start, for me, at least, the Foucault of the title is both that French physicist, Jean Bernard Léon Foucault (1819-1868), and Michel Foucault (1926-1984), the French theorist of the "order of things". Similarly, Casaubon, as the text itself tells us, is the name of both a character in George Eliot's novel, *Middlemarch*, and a Renaissance philologist. Eliot's "learned provincial clergyman" bears little physical resemblance to Eco's narrator, who is no "dried bookworm towards fifty", but on another level, he may not be unrelated to the man whose aim is to find the "Key to all Mythologies". Eliot's own ironies at her character's expense, of course, are also a warning to the reader of Eco's text about trusting anything, even the final discovery of what is ominously referred to as the "Key" text. By explicitly sending his readers to a text that ironizes totalizing thinking, underlining its "constructedness", Eco points not only to the Plan's obvious fabrication, but to the equally suspiciously constructed nature of all totalizing systems of thought–including, of course, his own.

The other series of cultural intertexts behind the name of Casaubon are likewise ironized. That Renaissance philologist, Isaac Casaubon (1559-1614), was known for his apposite but profuse illustrative commentaries on texts. Here I'd like to think that it is Eco himself as much as his character who is being ironized. But the historical Casaubon also wrote a book which challenged the authenticity of certain hermetic texts which were crucial to Renaissance occultism and also forced a change in the idea of when hermetic thought originated. With the proliferation of apt intertextual echoes like these, Eco enacts both what he has called "hermetic drift" and Peirce's "unlimited semiosis". In fact, he uses each to ironize the other. Here is his definition of the similarity and difference between the two terms: "There is a fundamental principle in Peirce's semiotics: 'A sign is something by knowing which we know something more' (8.332). On the contrary, the norm of Hermetic semiosis seems to be: 'A sign is something by knowing which we know something else'" (*Limits* 28). The ironic literalization and the exaggeration (that is, the not only unlimited but rampant semiosis) of the Plan provide the "something else" which becomes the "something more"–much to the Planner's shock.

Peirce's theories are as important intertexts to *Foucault's Pendulum* as they were to *The Name of the Rose*, though often the ironies are more pronounced. For example, the immediate contact of signs and their referents that is not part of Peirce's semiotic theory is what the climax of the novel is all about: the autonomy of the semiotic system (the Plan) is jeopardized by the occult believers' need to link signs and world. The system becomes a "true philosophy" according to Eco's description in Semiotics and the Philosophy of Language: "A philosophy is true insofar as it satisfies a need to provide a coherent form to the world so as to allow its followers to deal coherently with it" (p. 11). Here, however, there are fatal consequences of that urge toward coherent form. The flip side of this is that the Plan itself becomes the ironic literalization of the structuralist theory that sign systems exist independently of reality and are thus autonomous of any referent. The opening parodic words of the prologue of *The Name of the Rose* become ironic in this context: "In the beginning was the Word. . ." (p. 11).

As in his first novel, there are so many other reflexive recalls of Eco's own theorizing, as well as that of others, in *Foucault's Pendulum* that it is hard to know where to start. For example, the Planners' (and Eco's) holistic thinking is relatable to Eco's notion of the encyclopedia and of how we make meaning by tracing units of signification through wonderfully varied and tangled possible avenues of connections. It also suggests his description of the Deleuzian rhizome: "every path can be connected to every other one. It has no center, no periphery, no exit, because it is potentially infinite", for it is "the space of conjecture" (*Postscript* 57). Is it not also possible to read *Foucault's Pendulum* as an example of abduction run amok, with the Planners making too much meaning by connections and relations between signs? It is certainly an example of what Eco has wittily called "cogito interruptus", a mode of thought common "both to the insane and to the authors of a reasoned 'illogic'" (*Travels* 222) that sees the world as inhabited by symbols or symptoms.

In "Dreaming the Middle Ages", an earlier essay, Eco provided a succinct description of a particular literary use of that period that he links to "so-called Tradition" or occult philosophy. This description functions as perhaps the best possible summary of his own later novel. He writes of

an eternal and rather eclectic ramshackle structure, swarming with Knights Templars, Rosicrucians, alchemists, Masonic initiates, neo-Kabbalists. . .mixing up René Guénon and Conan the Barbarian. . ... Antiscientific by definition, these Middle Ages keep going under the banner of the mystical weddings of the micro- with the macrocosm, and as a result they convince their adepts that everything is the same as anything else and that the whole world is born to convey, in any of its aspects and events, the same Message. Fortunately the message got lost. . .. [*Travels* 71]

Here Eco provides an example of this kind of ironically reversed thinking ("propter hoc ergo ante hoc"). In *Foucault's Pendulum*, this kind of thinking by the adepts of the occult, as ironized and literalized by the Planners, turns on resemblances and connections. As Casaubon the narrator claims (in a Foucaultian insight into power relations): "No piece of information is superior to any other. Power lies in having them all on file and then finding the connections. There are always connections; you only have to want to find them" (p. 225)–or they will find you, as he learns. Indeed, Casaubon's description of the plan as "a great feast of analogies, a Coney Island, a Moscow May Day, a Jubilee Year of analogies" (p. 361) is an apt way to describe Eco's entire novel.

This proliferation of relations is not, I think, simply for the sake of play, despite Casaubon's hypothesis about the New Testament: "Matthew, Mark, Luke, and John are a bunch of practical jokers who meet somewhere and decide to have a contest. They invent a character, agree on a few basic facts, and then each one's free to take it and run with it" (p. 200). In casting doubt on the "naturalness" of the narrative of one of the most sacred of texts, the Bible, as well as of the infamous Plan, Eco's irony points to the un-natural, constructed nature of all narrative, including his own. The Plan is an ordered, narrativized, connected account of historical data; the fiction-alizing is in the construction, in the connections–and these are ironically man-made (not, significantly, woman-made). As in many postmodern "historiographic metafictions" (Hutcheon), history and fiction are both re-vealed as constructions, as fictionalizations. In both showing and ironizing the process of construction within the novel itself, Eco has produced an aesthetically self-reflexive mise-en-abyme of his own novelistic act and, at the same time, an ideologically de-naturalizing allegory of the structuralist insight that language constructs reality, rather than reflecting it.

Eco here does not only to allude to, but also makes ironic–again through the device of literalizing–Michel Foucault's exact description of sixteenth-century thought: "The heritage of Antiquity, like nature herself, is a vast space requiring interpretation; in both cases there are signs to be discovered and then, little by little, made to speak" (pp. 33-4) by using either divinatio (magic, maybe fiction) or eruditio (learning, history). Both are part of the same hermeneutic, however. According to Foucault, the esoterism of the sixteenth century is a phenomenon of the written word. The spoken is seen as the "female part of language" (p. 39), the sign of the passive intellect. In Eco's version, the pregnant Lia's common-sensical talk to Casaubon about the "mysteries" of the human body provides the antidote to the male-gener-ated Plan. Yet, the irony is that it is Lia who is literally creative and (re)productive, and not the males, even if the "male principle" of language--that is, writing–is said to harbour "the truth" (Foucault 1970:139). But Eco provides yet another ironic twist here. Because of what Foucault calls "a non-distinction between what is seen and what is read" (p. 39), the Planners make this writing into their own "truth"–but so too do their occult enemies.

Parodies continue to proliferate. The very linear form of writing is itself parodied in the novel as the Planners construct their plot from data drawn from the computer, which they have named Abulafia. So the plotting literally moves from a (Abulafia) to b (Belbo, the computer operator) to c (Casaubon, the narrator) to d (Diotallevi, the man whose cancerous body enacts its own diabolical plan). But Abulafia, the computer itself, takes on allegorical–and ironic–functions. In fact, it comes to stand for the sign of the true Secret of world power: therefore, not telluric currents, as the planners speculate, but information is the real source of power today. Information is what "nourishes, heals, wounds, blinds, strikes down. . ." (p. 141). If this is a Grail, it is an ironized Grail.

The ironic play on this theme does not stop there: the computer's binary thinking is both emblematic of the pendular thought of the novel and tied in with the occult numerology of the Plan. And Abulafia has a role in the ironizing of the Foucault as well as the pendulum of the title. In *The Order of Things*, Foucault wrote: "man is only a recent invention, a figure not yet two centuries old, a new wrinkle in our knowledge, and. . .he will disappear again as soon as that knowledge has discovered a new form" (p. xxiii). In the age of information technology, many have wanted to see the computer as that "new form" of knowledge. But, as it is presented in the novel, the computer can never replace "man", for it cannot create knowledge, only combine and randomize knowledge that is given to it–and even that is done more effectively by a human, the press's assistant, Gudrun (p. 373). It isn't even used to make cross-referenced connections: Casaubon uses index cards to help him do that (p. 225). Belbo, the main user of the computer in the story, says he will employ it to order, to edit the work of others, not to create or write about himself. He names it Abulafia after the man who dedicated his life to the science of the combination of the letters of God's name, and one of his first exercises on the computer is to work out all those 720 combinations–duly printed in the text we read. Despite his stated intentions, Belbo does use it to write about his own life and even to fictionalize, beginning with: "O what a beautiful morning at the end of November, in the beginning was the word, sing to me, goddess, the son of Peleus, Achilles now is the winter of our discontent" (p. 24). Obviously the opening parodies, with a kind of Joycean euphoria, the multiple texts of many others, including Eco himself.

The greatest and the most Foucaultian irony in the novel's presentation of the computer, however, is that its limitations–its ability to randomize, to use only what is fed to it–turn out to be the limits that Foucault ascribes to the mechanisms of resemblance in pre-seventeenth-century hermetic thought, when he writes of "the plethoric yet absolutely poverty-stricken character of this knowledge" (p. 30), always working with the same things: "Hence those immense columns of compilation, hence their monotony". (Some reviewers have said similar things about *Foucault's Pendulum*, of course.) Though Eco, as I mentioned earlier, has not often referred openly to Michel Foucault's work, the ironic intertextual allusions to that work in the novel abound: "Knowledge. . .consisted in relating one form of language to another form of language. . ..Language contains its own inner principle of proliferation" in the Renaissance (Foucault 1970:40), leading to commentaries, interpretations of interpretations. Eco's novel literalizes and ironizes at the same time many such statements about occult thought based on a theory of resemblance: the Plan is its literal enactment and the irony comes from both its overtness of construction and its temporal dislocation. If Foucault were right, this mode of thought should have died out by the end of the Renaissance. But has it? Herein lies Eco's challenge to Foucault's early periodizing.

This kind of parody, or ironized intertextuality, is clearly one of the major modes of reflexivity in *Foucault's Pendulum*, making it a kind of "intertextual collage"–Eco's term to describe the film Casablanca. Likewise his novel could share that film's label as "a palimpsest for future students of twentieth-century religiosity, a paramount laboratory for semiotic research into textual strategies" (*Travels* 197). It is hard to read any of Eco's essays of the last decade or so without seeing intertextual allusions or reflexive mises-en-abyme of the novel he was then writing. Certain passages have been fictionalized and dropped, almost verbatim, into the novel. And other intertexts, besides the author's own works, have been picked up by reviewers who made connections to Calvino and Del Giudice (Berardinelli 1988:4), as well as to the films featuring both Sam Spade and Indiana Jones. That these latter are overt in the novel itself makes this task somewhat straightforward: again, Eco makes his critics feel secondary! Other films mentioned by name and usually cited ironically are *Star Wars*, *A Man Called Horse*, *Gone with the Wind*, *Hellzapoppin*, *Rosemary's Baby*, and the Pink Panther films–not all film classics, to be sure, but all equally fodder for Eco's broad echoic cultural play. Popular culture and high art meet in all of Eco's work, theoretical and novelistic, and in all cases the allusions are not usually hidden. The intertextual scenarios are repeated, discussed, recalled, even if inverted. As Casaubon–and Eco–know (p. 588), any story about a pendulum inevitably suggests Poe's "The Pit and the Pendulum," and indeed Eco tries to one-up Poe in the macabre and the terrifyingly fatal. Similarly any tale about the occult, with references to the Tetragrammaton, the names of Yahweh (p. 31), and the aleph (p. 41) recalls such stories by Jorge Luis Borges as "Death and the Compass" and "The Aleph."

The character Belbo, even more than the narrator Casaubon, is the one who is the past master, so to speak, of intertextual ironies. His computer files, obsessively examining childhood memories, are appropriately full of references to Proust's fiction. So too are they replete with allusions to T.S. Eliot and Conrad, not to mention Joyce. While each intertextual echo functions in a different way, what these cumulative references add up to is a chain of allusions to the specifically *modernist* masters. And one way

(Hugh Kenner's [1962]) of looking at the modernist aesthetic and linguistic paradigm is to see it as a combinatory process within a closed field, where what is important is the relations of elements with each other. From this perspective, modernism too reveals itself to be modeled on hermetic semiosis. If Belbo is the modernist, does that make his collaborative reader, Casaubon, the postmodernist? Certainly he sounds like it, at times. He alludes to Derridean themes in associating Hermes, the god of trickery, with "writing, which is the art of evasion and dissimulation, a navigation that carries us to the end of all boundaries" (p. 185). At the climax of the novel, Casaubon ironically recalls what Roland Barthes had proclaimed in his famous essay announcing "The Death of the Author": "the author has to die in order for the reader to become aware of his truth" (p. 633). In the end, then, Belbo becomes an author, a dead one.

The reason it's so hard to decide precisely what kind of allegorical fun Eco is having with the tenets of either modernism or postmodernism is the persistent, almost scatter-gun effect of his irony. While irony is clearly a frequent trope of the postmodern today, it also characterizes much modernist writing. I have been arguing that *Foucault's Pendulum* is an obsessively formalist novel that is about the implosion of formalism in upon itself. But it is also a novel that foregrounds its own ironies–be they about Foucault or about hermetic thought. The rug is constantly pulled out from under the figurative feet of the reader. In a novel full of images of inversion, of upside-down worlds, of mirrored reversals, it may not be surprising to find allegories of the hermeneutics of irony. I mentioned at the start that irony demands an attitude of suspicion as much as does hermetic thought. Casaubon describes two Rosicrucian manifestoes in terms that also function to allegorize the need for markers that tell us to interpret, not literally, but ironically: "Taken literally these two texts were a pile of absurdities, riddles, contradictions. Therefore they could not be saying what they seemed to be saying. . ... They were a coded message. . ... I had to read with mistrust" (p. 394). If *The Name of the Rose* is, by Eco's own admission, "ironclad" in its obvious scaffolding (in Rosso 1983:7), then *Foucault's Pendulum* must be "irony-clad." Hence my title.

This pervasive irony means that ambiguity reigns, even unto the end. How are we to read Belbo's death? Is it murder or suicide? Is it accidental or planned? Even the language of his Conservatoire death scene, as narrated by Casaubon, is an ambivalent one of science overlaid with magic, as mentioned earlier. Its choice of words plays off (and with) the names of the inventions of that other Foucault (after whom were named, not only a pendulum, but magnetic currents, mirroring prisms, a polarizer, and a "knife-edge" test–all of which figure in the language of the scene). But Michel Foucault isn't far away either. In fact, this scene and the remainder of the novel that follows it can be read, once again, as ironic literalizations of the latter Foucault's description of the Renaissance semiosis of resemblance, specifically as described in the chapter on "The Prose of the World" in *The Order of Things*.

In this section Foucault analyses the four principal figures that determine the knowledge of resemblance. The first, spatial adjacency or resemblance by contact, is called "convenientia" and is represented by the image of an "immense, taut, and vibrating chain" (p. 19). In Eco's novel, this is literalized in the pendulum's very physical form. The second figure of hermetic knowledge is "aemulatio", or mirroring across distances, polarized into imbalanced weak and strong forces: "Similitude then becomes the combat of one form against another–or rather of one and the same form separated from itself by the weight of matter or distance in space" (p. 20). The importance of the "one and the same form" for the novel is clearer in conjunction with Foucault's third epistemological figure, analogy. Here the principles of resemblance include reversibility and polyvalency in a universal field of application which is drawn together through a "privileged point" saturated with analogies: man's body, "the fulcrum upon which all these relations turn" (p. 22). Belbo dies by being hanged from the pendulum by the neck. The effect this has on the movement of the pendulum is that it starts to move from Belbo's body downward. His body becomes the point of suspension, "the Fixed Pin, the Place from which the vault of the world is hung" (p. 597). As the scientific epigraph of the next chapter explains, a body hanging from a pendulum becomes the fulcrum, thus literalizing in a horrific image Foucault's "privileged point". But Belbo's body, at first jerked about by the pendulum's movement (that is, before it becomes its fulcrum), is said to describe a shape in the air–the shape of the Tree of the Sefirot, the shape that is visible on the novel's frontispiece and that structures the entire novel, in fact.

In *The Order of Things*, the fourth and final figure of resemblance is called "sympathies", the powerful play of the "Same" in a free state throughout the universe: "It is a principle of mobility: it attracts what is heavy to the heaviness of the earth. . ." (p. 23)–not unlike the other Foucault's eternally moving pendulum. But this is a dangerous figure: it has the power to assimilate, to make all things the same, destroying individuality–unless counterbalanced by "antipathy" (p. 23). The pendular thought of the entire novel offers countless examples of this binary figure at work, just as the plot structure opposes the Planners' totalizing assimilation of everything into their Plan against the factionalism and divisiveness of the various credulous occult groups. There is more than one Foucault's pendulum, in other words, just as there is more than one Foucault.

Irony is a trope to which Michel Foucault himself turns when discussing the need for visible marker or "signatures" of these various kinds of often secret resemblances operating in hermetic thinking–not accidently, a need shared by irony itself: "Now there is a possibility that we might make our way through all this marvelous teeming abundance of resemblances without even suspecting that it has long been prepared by the order of the world, for our greater benefit" (p. 26). In Eco's ironic literalizing (of Foucault's irony), the Plan is not "prepared by the order of the world" but is prepared very much by the order of man. And resemblance, as Foucault describes it, becomes the inversion of the trope of irony: both "require signatures" to be interpreted, so that "the space inhabited" by both "becomes like a vast open book; it bristles with written signs;. . .. All that remains is to decipher them" (p. 27). This image of the "signature" is also that which Eco has chosen to describe the interpretive habit of hermeticism in a recent essay–but with no direct reference to Foucault: "It is through similitudes that the otherwise occult parenthood between things is manifested and every sublunar body bears the traces of that parenthood impressed on it as a *signature*" (*Limits* 24).

In Eco's hands, irony becomes a kind of inverted extension or perverse variant of hermetic similitude, exploiting the inevitable if "slight degree of non-coincidence between the resemblances" of which Foucault speaks (p. 30). This slight degree of non-coincidence provides the space for and of irony. What Foucault writes about the process of deciphering similitude also defines the intent of ironic reading: "to find a way from the visible mark to that which is being said by it and which, without that mark, would lie like unspoken speech, dormant" (p. 32). Eco has with good reason been called "an author who has irony in his soul" (Vita-Finzi 1989:618).

Michel Foucault was describing his own affiliation when he talked about the "great warm and tender Freemasonry of useless erudition" (1980:79), but Eco seems to be part of that same cabal, and the coincidence of hermetic images is irresistible. The pendulum has come full swing again, but with another of those "slight degrees of non-coincidence" that turns resemblance into irony, hermetic semiosis into postmodern semiosis. Foucault characterized sixteenth-century language as that which "simultaneously promises and postpones" (1970:41), as what offers all signs as "written matter for further discourse" (p. 41). But for Eco, what he calls the "perennial shift and deferral of any possible meaning" (*Limits* 27), the unstoppable slippage of meaning (Eco, "Introduzione" 1989:14) that constituted hermetic thought, has been transformed into the postmodern deferral of meaning, the intertextually ironic, deferring deference to other texts, other commentaries, other discourses. In Foucault's words–which describe so well Eco's novel–it is "the traversal of this futile yet fundamental space that the text of literature traces from day to day" (p. 44).

However, perhaps this space is not really futile at all. Just as, in Eco's own words, "[i]f Lacan is interesting it's because he resumes Parmenides" (*Travels* 127), so I would argue that Eco is interesting–and particularly provocative today–in part because he resumes Foucault–as well as many others. Though he has rarely discussed Foucault's work in detail, Eco did once tellingly define the postmodern as "the orientation of anyone who has learned the lesson of Foucault, i.e., that power is not something unitary that exists outside us" (in Rosso 1983:4). With this hint and with the example of *Foucault's Pendulum*, much more will undoubtedly be written in the future–indeed, in this very volume–about the impact on Eco of Foucault's theorizing of the relationship between power and knowledge. In a postmodern world that is paradoxically witnessing the consequences of the revival of "master narratives" of nation, ethnicity, race, and religion (not to mention the continuing ones, including that of capitalism), Foucault's theories of the mobile, unstable, even contradictory nature of power relations–both within and outside us–cannot help but provoke fruitful debate. Thanks to Eco and his critical ironies, that debate may not only take place in the academy. Herein lies the social role of the cultural critic and theorist writing as *novelist*, for it is perhaps on the best sellers' lists that broader impact can be registered.

Linda Hutcheon

The Swing of the 'Pendulum': Eco's Novels*

Umberto Eco is a phenomenon. The range of his erudition, the centrality of his influence in a number of academic disciplines and discourses, the originality, insight, diversity and sheer volume of his writings defy comparison among his contemporaries. So does the size of his audience. *The Name of the Rose*, written in the popular narrative mode of the analytical detective story, made Umberto Eco a household word in the U.S., Europe, and Latin America. The novel seemed effortlessly to breach the usually impenetrable line between elite and mass culture in this country - a feat achieved by only a few writers in recent years, most notably by Latin American novelists (Gabriel García Márquez, Isabel Allende) and the occasional English academic–Iris Murdoch, professor of philosophy at Oxford, and J. R. R. Tolkien, late professor of medieval literature at the same university. *The Name of the Rose* was an academic crossover dream come true: here was a serious novel by a professor of semiotics, filled with dense historical and theological material, being sold in airports, malls, drugstores (Rollin 1988). *Foucault's Pendulum* also luxuriated for months on the 1990 best-seller charts, but I venture to guess that it will be enjoyed by far fewer of its purchasers than was *The Name of the Rose*. The temptation to compare Eco's novels is inevitable, so I yield here at the outset.

Like its predecessor, *Foucault's Pendulum* is a novel in which both content and form address the problem of interpretation, decipherment, and detection. Its main characters, like those in *The Name of the Rose*, are *de facto* detectives, semioticians whether they know it or not. They are confronted with conjectural structures that ramify into further conjectures that are ultimately linked to the structure of conjecture as such. Hermeneutical delirium is the subject of these novels, and the principle condition of their narrative structures. The desperate difficulties of disclosure. the awareness of obstacles to interpretive effort, are the notes upon which the novels conclude. In this regard, Eco's novels are of a piece.

There are, though, essential differences as well. Unlike *The Name of the Rose*, the sleuths in *Foucault's Pendulum* do not enlist the reader as their ally in their quest for understanding. They do not because they cannot: they are not realized novelistic characters. Nothing is more basic to the novel as a genre than the reader's cherished illusion that characters' lives and experiences exist in some meaningful relation to our own. However obviously fictional characters are made of print and paper, of strings of letters and empty spaces, they must eventually defy their silent two-dimensional space to emerge (a most magical mental operation) into the noisy four-dimensional world of the reader. Even 'self-conscious' novels whose characters call attention to their status as (mere) language recognize and engage (as they undermine) the reader's natural impulse to 'identify' with fictional characters. Here I think of Nabokov's brilliant narrative tricks, or Calvino's, which insist upon their characters as verbal constructs at the same time that they encourage the reader to endow those constructs with flesh and blood, with a local habitation and a name. In *Foucault's Pendulum*, these two contradictory messages are not coordinated; the author's plotted erudition and his characters' 'lived experience' are not integrated. We are asked to follow their moves, but not to feel them. Their search does not transcend the mere execution of its own processes, the playing out of the patterns of the textual game. In *Foucault's Pendulum*, we watch Belbo, Diotallevi, and Casaubon move through labyrinths like stick figures, operating/operated by remote control.

What I am saying may, perhaps, be simply summarized: *The Name of the Rose* is Eco's modernist novel, *Foucault's Pendulum* his postmodernist novel. The former, with its use of the symbols and narrative strategies of Biblical apocalypse, does suggest the possibility of some occulted system beyond the welter of phenomena encountered by the characters. In *The Name of the Rose*, Eco maintains till the end the possibility of a viable master code such as those typical of the great modernists works (James Joyce's *Ulysses*, William Faulkner's *Absalom, Absalom!*, Thomas Mann's *The Magic Mountain*). The seven trumpet woes of Revelation that seem to William of Baskerville to explain the murders, and Adso's narrative positioning as an apocalyptist who retrospectively surveys the cataclysmic history of an entire world, suggest the pursuit of truths beyond the murder mystery as such (Zamora 1988). Adso believes that signs may still be read, and therefore that meaning may still exist—no matter how elusive, tragic, terminal. The narrative structure of *The Name of the Rose*, with its causal, progressive, and explanatory relations, reiterates the youthful Adso's Neoplatonic faith in a level of meaning beyond the objects and events he perceives. The older narrator Adso expresses nominalist doubts about this: he has, it seems, during the half century between the events he narrates and his narration, come to question the existence of any level of transcendental signification, to wonder whether there is any meaning beyond the name of things. But the novel's conclusion clearly embodies the younger Adso's Neoplatonic position. Its apocalyptic ending judges, hence assigns significance, to all that has happened before.

In *Foucault's Pendulum*, there is no mythic master code, no potential or occulted truth validated by the narrative, no conclusion that contains or reflects upon the meaning of the whole. There is only information. Eco's narrative structure in this second novel also embodies a hermeneutic theory but it differs radically from *The Name of the Rose* and corresponds to a basic postmodernist literary notion: texts circulate, all is already said, ironic quotation is our only resort. From the outset, the narrator of *Foucault's Pendulum*, Casaubon, occupies the nominalist position of the disillusioned older Adso, though he (and Eco) still flirt with the possibility of some vestigial system of meaning in the world. A mythic master code–the Kabbalah–is presented in the novel, but its truth claims are discredited or, more accurately, never really engaged in the first place. Eco's description of postmodern culture in *Travels in Hyperreality* describes the world of *Foucault's Pendulum*: "a centerless universe where all is margin and there is no longer any 'heart' of anything" (*Travels* 255).

Eco's novelistic project in *Foucault's Pendulum* again recalls James Joyce - not the modernist Joyce of *Ulysses*, but the postmodernist Joyce of *Finnegins Wake*. The shifts in form and spirit are both profound and palpable. Eco published a study of Joyce, *Le Poetiche di Joyce* (1966), early in his career. The study was, in fact, originally a part of *Opera aperta* (1962), and it was translated into English as *The Aesthetics of Chaosmos: The Middle Ages of James Joyce* (1982). Eco's comments on Joyce's 'chaosmos' in *Finnegans Wake* may be seen (with the hindsight that literary critics count on) as prefiguring Eco's own 'chaosmos' in *Foucault's Pendulum*. I cite Eco's observations at some length, so as to suggest the parallels:

> . . . *Finnegans Wake* is the book of an epoch of transition, a time in which science and the evolution of social relations propose a vision of the world that no longer obeys the schemas of other, more secure epochs yet lacks any formula for clarifying its own situation. *The Wake* attempts paradoxically to define the new world by assembling a chaotic and dizzy encyclopedia from the old one and filling it with explanations that once seemed mutually exclusive. Through this clash and the 'Big Bang' of these oppositions, something new is born.
> *Finnegans Wake* rebels against the narrow-mindedness of modern methodologies which permit us to define only partial aspects of reality, thus eliminating the possibility of an ultimate and total definition. *The Wake* attempts to compensate for this with an assemblage of partial and provisional definitions that syncretically collide and combine in an enormous 'world theater', a clavis universalis in which these ideas are so arranged that the structure of the work results in a 'mirror' of the cosmos. . . .*Finnegans Wake* makes the proud claim to bend language to express 'everything'. To this aim, language selects terms

from the most disparate cultural heritages and makes possible their coexistence through the connective tissue of a language capable of grafting one thing to another and of tying together, by etymological violence, the most disparate references.

. . . Joyce accumulated materials whose form captivates him but whose substance does not elicit his belief. It is as if Joyce offers us the entire wisdom of mankind, without determining whether or not it reflects a unique Eternal truth. He is concerned only with the cultural repertoire assembled by the whole of History . . ..

. . . Joyce engages a reality composed of all that has been said of it and organizes this world according to rules which are derived, not from the things themselves but from words that express things. He proposes a form of the world in language, a hypothesis offered from within the linguistic format. The world as such is not Joyce's concern. (*Chaosmos* 83-84; italics added)

I have emphasized passages where Eco points to the encyclopedic, totalizing impulse of *Finnegans Wake*, to its vision of the world as a vast theater of ideas, as a non-hierarchical aggregation of texts. Throughout, the highlights Joyce's debate between Neoplatonist and nominalist Hermeneutics. Eco cannot disguise a wistful longing (which he projects, correctly, I think, onto Joyce) for some central and centering system of meaning - some *clavis universalis*, as he puts it in the text cited above. So, Eco argues, Joyce's literary 'chaosmos' is a rebellion against its own 'chaosmic' structuring principles, a totalizing linguistic structure constructed to defend again proliferating linguistic structures, to counteract the 'narrowmindedness of modern methodologies which permit us to define only partial aspects of reality. 'Eco places himself and us (along with Joyce) in a postmodern 'neo-medieval' world where all is margin, where power, along with meaning, has become unlocatably diffused. In the spirit of *Finnegan's Wake* (if not in its richly inventive language), *Foucault's Pendulum* is Eco's 'chaosmos'–a cosmos based on, and constructed from, chaos. Its characters and plot are compelled by the contradiction between order and disorder inherent in this neologism. Eco and his characters long for *logos*, and in so doing, both celebrate and bury it.

The novel's central image, the pendulum designed by Jean Bernard Léon Foucault (1819-1868) to demonstrate the rotation of the earth, is the slippery sign of a centering logos. Or so the narrator Casaubon tells himself in the first scene of the novel. As he hides in the Conservatoire des Arts et Métiers located in the church of Saint-Martin-des-Champs in Paris, he contemplates the Pendulum (always capitalized),

whose own plane never changed direction, because up there, along the infinite extrapolation of its wire beyond the choir ceiling, up toward the most distant galaxies, lay the Only Fixed Point in the universe, eternally unmoving. So it

was not so much the earth to which I addressed my gaze but the heavens, where
the mystery of absolute immobility was celebrated. *The Pendulum* told me
that, as everything moved - earth, solar system, nebulae and black holes, all the
children of the great cosmic expansion - one single point stood still: a pivot,
bolt or hook around which the universe could move. And I was now taking
part in the supreme experience. I, too, moved with the all, but I could see the
One, the Rock, the Guarantee. . . (p. 5)

Eco's *Pendulum* points unabashedly to some transcendental signified--
the unmasking and discrediting of which will provide the energy that drives
the plot forward. I will not be giving away too much in saying that the
Pendulum is ultimately reduced to a mere physical pendulum - to an object
signifying only itself - in its final grisly use at the end of the novel.

Eco's potential *Pendulum*, the mystical Metapendulum that his character initially projects, derives from Kabbalistic sources. If *The Name of the
Rose* depends upon a mythic structure that addresses the nature of historical
interpretation (apocalypse), so *Foucault's Pendulum* is auspiciously based
upon the Kabbalah, a medieval mystical hermeneutic system devised to interpret sacred Jewish texts. The Kabbalah claims great antiquity (the word
means 'tradition'), but is basically the product of the Middle Ages, arising
in the seventh century and lasting into the eighteenth in response to the
need to spiritualize Judaism, which had become formal, legalistic. Kabbalistic interpretations, which influenced Christian as well as Jewish mysticism,
are based upon the belief that the Scriptures contain deeply hidden divine
mysteries, and that every word, letter, number, and even accent of the sacred writing has occult meaning. The Kabbalists conceived of God as the
source from which emanates His entire creation, and God in turn as an
emanation of holy writ.

Eco's characters sometimes derive their names, and his novel its narrative structure, from the Kabbalah, particularly the *Sefer Yesirah (Book of
Creation)*. Each of the novel's ten sections is titled by one of the ten Sefirot
described in the *Sefer Yesirah* as eternal emanations of the godhead, each of
which corresponds to a region of heaven, a name of God, a commandment
of the decalogue, a part of the human body, and a class of angels. A diagram
of the sacred tree of the Sefirot (unlabeled) serves as the frontispiece of
Foucault's Pendulum, and the epigraph of the first chapter–in Hebrew, and
again, unlabeled–is in fact a citation from the sixteenth-century Kabbalist
Isaac Luria (Muniz-Huberman 1990:38). The withheld translation of the
Hebrew epigraph is: 'And here as the infinite light continues in a straight
line across the vacuum mentioned above, it does not immediately go downward but continues little by little. That is, at first it begins to emit a line of
light and immediately the line expands until it changes into something like
a spherical wheel'. The first line of Casaubon's narration (and the novel)
follows hard upon this epigraph. Casaubon begins: 'That was when I saw

the Pendulum' (p. 3). The Kabbalistic description of the penetration of the light of the divine emanations corresponds to the spatial movement of the Pendulum as Casaubon construes it. Eco's *Pendulum* begins as no ordinary pendulum, then, not even as an ordinary Foucauldian pendulum. By association with the untranslated Hebrew epigraph from the Kabbalah, it stands for divine wisdom.

In the opening scene of the novel, which I have just described, Casaubon gazes ceilingward, then pulls himself up short: visions of cosmic unity, he realizes, cannot be maintained for long in a computer age. As if to address the illusion inherent in his earlier lyricism, he tells himself: 'You cannot escape one infinite . . . by fleeing to another; you cannot escape the revelation of the identical by taking refuge in the illusion of the multiple' (pp. 6-7). But multiplicity turns out to be no illusion. So Eco's *Pendulum* swings between Casaubon's desire for unitary truth and his knowledge that there is none. His namesake is not only George Eliot's arid intellectual in *Middlemarch*, but also the Kabbalist Isaac Casaubon, who in 1614 proved that hermetic texts had been falsely attributed to Hermes Trismegisto (Yates 1964:398). Casaubon's discoveries deconstruct authority and dismiss the Author.

Another principal character, Jacopo Belbo, also seems to be a displaced modernist in a postmodernist world. He is, among other things, a hacker, and has named his computer Abulafia, after the thirteenth-century Kabbalist from Aragón, Abraham Abulafia. When Belbo disappears, kidnapped by members of a conspiracy (the contemporary incarnation of the Knights Templar) that aims to rule the world, Casaubon manages to find the password into Belbo's computer. As he sits in front of Abulafia's screen, he thinks, 'now, having breached the secret of Abulafia and, with it, Belbo's soul, I see that what I thought was disenchantment and a philosophy of life was a form of melancholy. His intellectual disrespect concealed a desperate thirst for the Absolute' (p. 56). He concludes about the reclusive Belbo: 'As long as you remain in your private vacuum, you can pretend you are in harmony with the One' (p. 57). This character too appears to be impelled by the energy of Neoplatonic idealism, and appalled by his growing recognition that there are no Forms behind the signs. His fate at the end of the novel confirms that recognition - too late for him, but not for the reader.

In fact, Belbo chooses the name for his computer because he sees it, with its combinatory powers, as the postmodern analogue of the medieval Kabbalist. Diotallevi, the third of the novel's trio of sleuths, warns Belbo:

> Abraham Abulafia's *Hokhmath ha-Zeruf* was at once the science of the combination of letters and the science of the purification of the heart. Mystic logic, letters whirling in infinite change, is the world of bliss, it is the music of thought, but see that you proceed slowly, and with caution, because your machine may bring you delirium instead of ecstasy. (p. 34).

Belbo's disastrous end suggests the wisdom of the warning. Again Eco's Pendulum swings between poles, even as his characters search for a cosmic plan that will embrace all opposites.

Foucault's Pendulum, like *The Name of the Rose*, is animated by its author's passion for history. The medieval hermeneutic systems with which he structures his novels have their medieval political and cultural contexts, of course, and Eco makes good novelistic use of them in both novels: the popular apocalyptic movements in *The Name of the Rose*, the political history of the Knights Templar in *Foucault's Pendulum*. In *The Name of the Rose*, Eco allows his reader to enter the world of the fourteenth century and stay there. He does not superimpose contemporary reality upon the past, though he has commented on his sense of the parallels between the fourteenth century depicted in his novel and our own times.[1] Those parallels emerge with stunning clarity. In *Foucault's Pendulum*, on the other hand, he constantly moves between the postmodern present and the remembered (or reconstructed) medieval past.

In *Foucault's Pendulum*, Eco places his historical material within a contemporary narrative framework in order to address postmodern conditions and assumptions. But do we, in the last analysis, feel that the novel manages to do so? Eco's peripatetic temporality seems designed to rupture the reader's sense of a coherent fictional world (in accordance, I suppose, with our experience of rupture in a postmodern world): here, indeed, we travel in hyperreality. But there are costs associated with the trip. In *Foucault's Pendulum*, Eco sacrifices what he achieved so well in *The Name of the Rose* and what is indispensable to good fiction: a concrete sense of time(s) and place(s), and the plotting of attendant cultural categories. Eco's first novel is proof positive that the novelist can reflect upon modern questions without explicitly describing the modern world. In his second novel, he does not invest his historical materials with their own imaginative energy, or allow the reader to remain in the historical past long enough for the parallels to postmodernism to emerge. The continual temporal juxtapositions and anachronisms detract from the novel's cultural content, and from the impact of the plot's unfolding. Too much is told, too little dramatized Eco's characters are garrulous on the subject of their historical displacement, and on the impossibility of penetrating their postmodern textual labyrinth–so much so that the problems (and pleasures) that might proceed from their interpretive engagement with their world are vitiated. Along the way, Eco's readers are also deprived of our function as interpreters, and hence of the sheer fun that armchair detection might provide.

In the study of Joyce from which I have quoted above, Eco writes of the process whereby the author withdraws 'from the world of things into a universe of words in order to reconstruct the form of the world' (*Chaosmos* 77). Eco argues that in *Finnegans Wake*, Joyce "establishes the possibility of defining our universe in the 'transcendental' form of language. He provides a laboratory in which to formulate a model of reality and, in so doing, withdraws from *things* to *language*' (*Chaosmos* 84-85). In his anti-realist work, Joyce invents an oneiric language to project the nonverbal, symbolic landscape of dreams. Eco recognizes Joyce's affinity to two central Kabbalistic ideas: the symbolic textuality of creation and, conversely, the world-generating capacity of language. But unlike God, novelists must connect their 'universe of words' to the realities of lived experience (whether in a postmodern Paris or a dreamed Dublin). And unlike the Kabbalists, whose interpretive satisfactions rest on faith, contemporary readers have a right to expect the connections to be credible. Whether Joyce succeeds is beside the point here, but Eco's success is not. In *Foucault's Pendulum*, communication becomes an end in itself, its narrative structure a kind of floating brain filled with data but without central content. The world as such is not Eco's concern.

In *Foucault's Pendulum*, Eco strains to create an 'open work', which he describes as a work where "an ordered world based on universally acknowledged laws is being replaced by a world based on ambiguity, both in the negative sense that directional centers are missing and in a positive sense because values and dogma are constantly being placed in question" (*Role* 54). *Foucault's Pendulum* clearly conforms to the first part of this definition: it lacks 'directional centers' (The novel's title and principal - image - Foucault's pendulum, with the symbolic symmetry of its spatial inscription - is deeply ironic). And the second part of the definition: does it place 'values and dogma' in question? Eco's characters are perpetually posing questions, all right, but their questions are less about values and dogma than about texts *per se*. Some of their texts have ethical and social implications, of course, but others (the pages of reproduced computer variables, for example) have only spatial extension. In either case, it is textual *form* rather than textual *content* that interests them. Nor are we readers encouraged to interrogate the ontological and existential situation of the fictional world, or our own. We, too, follow the patterns of the text to discover in the end that those patterns are the novel's primary referent. Eco tells us that 'suggestiveness' is central to the open work, that 'a halo of indefiniteness' surrounds it and prevents definitive readings. Although the novel ends inconclusively, with Casaubon on the run to nowhere, it does not end 'openly', as Eco intends that term.

I have mentioned the eponymous (albeit absent) character of *Foucault's Pendulum* - Jean Bernard Léon Foucault. There is another absent Foucault in this novel. If Jean, nineteenth-century scientist, provides the image Eco uses ironically to mirror the lost 'directional center' in/of his novel, Michel Foucault, twentieth-century post-structuralist theorist, elaborates a theory of that loss. Eco's description of the postmodern world that I have already cited– 'a centerless universe where all is margin and there is no longer any "heart" of anything'–concludes Eco's essay, 'Language, power, force', on Michel Foucault's theory of the diffusion of power in postmodern culture. It is this second Foucault who jostles against (and ultimately unhinges) the symbolic center of Eco's novel, the pendulum of the earlier Foucault.

In his essay, Eco chooses to cite passages from Michel Foucault's writings that employ images from physics and that resonate ironically with the physics of Jean Bernard Léon Foucault. Power does not emanate from a single center, Foucault writes in *The History of Sexuality*, but in

> moving substrate of force relations which, by virtue of their inequality, constantly engender states of power, but the latter are always local and unstable. . . . There is no binary and all-encompassing opposition between rulers and ruled. . . .'The points knots, or focuses of resistance are spread over time and space at varying densities at times mobilizing groups or individuals in a definitive way, inflaming certain points of the body, certain moments in life, certain types of behavior. . . . But more often one is dealing with mobile and transitory points of resistance, producing cleavages in society that shift about, fracturing unities and effecting regroupings furrowing across individuals themselves, cutting them up and remolding them. . . . (Foucault 1978:94-96; cited in *Travels* 243, 251-52)

Moving substrate, points, knots, cleavages, fractures, furrows–everything but the swing of a pendulum measured by the former Foucault, that emblem of the 'binary and all-encompassing oppositions' discredited by the latter Foucault.

Eco asserts that his own theory of language is 'homologous' to Foucault's theory of power–an assertion that does not surprise the readers of *Foucault's Pendulum*, or the readers of Eco's semiotic theory. For that matter, indeed, Foucault's description of postmodern power relations ('points, knots, or focuses of resistance . . . spread over time and space at varying densities') aptly describes Eco's novelistic structure.

There is one more absent protagonist of postmodernism to be mentioned here. Jorge Luis Borges is embodied as a character in *The Name of the Rose*, Eco's modernist means of acknowledging influence and admiration. In *Foucault's Pendulum*, Eco postmodernizes Borges. The Argentine writer becomes in this second novel a Foucauldian power point, everywhere present, nowhere visible. In *The Name of the Rose*, Jorge of Burgos dies by eating a book. In *Foucault's Pendulum*, he has been fully digested.

It is, in particular, Burgos's detective story, 'Death and the compass', that informs *Foucault's Pendulum*. This story, written in 1942 to acknowledge the centenary of Edgar Allan Poe's 'The purloined letter', is itself a postmodernizing of the detective genre (Irwin 1990). You'll remember that Erik Lönrot, Burgos's sleuth, is out-sleuthed by the arch-criminal, Red

Scharloch. Lönrot brilliantly follows clues that are even more brilliantly planted by Scharloch. Scharloch's false clues are based on supposed readings of Kabbalistic texts (a series of murders appears to correspond to the murderer's search for the Tetragrammaton - the divine Name) and on cartographic directions. Lönrot uses his Kabbalistic research and a pair of dividers and a compass to detect the time and place of the final murder. What he fails to understand is that it will be his own.

Like the Foucauldian pendulum upon which Eco's character Belbo hangs, Lönrot's compass no longer serves to measure the postmodern world. In Burgos's story, as in Eco's novel, 'directional centers' are literally undone. Pursuer and pursued are reversed, the processes of detection are ironized, and the human hope for a 'solution' is presented as tragicomedy. So, I conclude:

J. B. L.; Foucault's pendulum + M. Foucault's points and knots + J. L. Borge's compass = Eco's Pendulum.

As a formula for postmodern culture, it works well. Whether or not it can be made to work as the 'moving substrate' of a novel needs to be further investigated. Mr. Eco's fans hope that he will continue to write novels that do so.

And he does.

What is the "moving substratet" of Eco's third novel, *The Island of the Day Before*? What are its spatial and cultural coordinates? How does it relate to the metaphoric structures of meaning of the earlier novels? The publication of *Reading Eco* gives me the unexpected (and welcome) opportunity to add to my 1992 review, which you have just read. With the passage of these four years and the publication of *The Island of the Day Before*, I can pursue further Eco's novelistic investigation of postmodernism. Once again, the author has created a detailed historical context for his characters, the better that he (and we) may consider postmodernity in terms of its premodern sources. So we are asked to see, as does his protagonist in this latest novel, "the past as a figure of the present" (p. 45).

But what past? What figure? The novel is set in the seventeenth century–1614 to 1643, to be exact; and the controlling figure of the novel is longitude. *The Island* traces the 17th century's "great anguish over longitude" (p. 508), an anguish fueled by Europe's frustrated passion to chart "the very New World": the Fijis, the Moluccas, the Austral Terra Incognita, the fabled Islands of Solomon. Longitude is to this novel as Jean Bernard Léon Foucault's pendulum and Michel Foucault's points and knots are to *Foucault's Pendulum*: a spatial metaphor with proliferating cultural and narrative implications. The myriad angles and intersecting lines of longitude and latitude–the invisible grid that wraps round the globe––

provide the subject matter and the primary metaphoric figure of *The Island of the Day Before*.

But the plot thickens: in 1642 and 1643, the final years of Eco's narrative, this grid did not yet exist with any degree of certainty. Longitude had been theorized, but the scientific means to calculate it accurately were still unknown. Longitude measures distances east or west around the variable circumference of a planet turning on its axis. What fixed point or system of spatial reference could be used to determine a ship's longitudinal position relative to its place of departure or destination? No one knew. In contrast, the determination of latitude was easy: navigators had long been able to calculate latitude at sea by using a quadrant to measure the angle of the sun or a polar star (usually Polaris) in relation to the horizon, and thus determine their position with respect to the equator.[2]

It would be more than one hundred years after the historical period dramatized by Eco in *The Island of the Day Before* before the Englishman John Harrison would invent a mechanism that could measure longitude.[3] Harrison worked during the first fifty years of the 18th century to perfect his "chronometer," a clock that could keep virtually perfect time on the high seas (as no marine timekeeper of that period could.) In 1759, Harrison gave to navigators and map makers the definitive marker with which to complete their gridded globes. Although it took another decade and more to receive official recognition of the conclusive nature of his contribution, Harrison had solved, once and for all, the problem of longitude. He had done so by using the fourth dimension–time–to link points in three-dimensional space.

For longitude is, of course, a measure of time as well as space. The earth turns on its axis every 24 hours; divide the 360 degrees of the earth's circumference by 24: one hour equals 15 degrees of distance. If you know what time it is at an agreed-upon place–a prime meridian–and you know what time it is aboard ship, you can calculate the time difference between the prime meridian and your own location, and so calculate your degrees longitude. (As the English established themselves as the master clock-makers of Europe during the 18th century, the prime meridian was increasingly calculated from the Royal Observatory at Greenwich; before the 18th century, and since the time of Ptolemy, the designated prime meridian had run through the Isla de Hierro, the Island of Iron, eighteen degrees west of Greenwich.) Ships could, then, determine high noon at sea by measuring the sun at its zenith, ten calculate their degrees longitude by the time difference from Greenwich–a difference they could know with certainty *only* if they carried Harrison's chronometer on board. By the 1780s, ships had begun routinely to carry chronometers; in 1791, the East India Company issued logbooks with columns to enter "longitude by Chronometer"; by 1815, approximately five thousand chronometers were in use worldwide and the revolution in navigation wrought by Harrison was accomplished. (Sober, 1995: 162-163)

But in the first half of the 17th century–Eco's fictional time frame in *The Island*–longitude was still a geometry of desire. Its phantom lines were debated by astronomers and mechanics (makers of clocks and all manner of other measuring devices), as well as by theologians, visionaries, and sundry quacks. The grid that now girdles our globe, and which we take for granted, represents the hermeneutic ingenuity of centuries of thinkers of every stripe. Because Umberto Eco is fascinated by just such hermeneutic ingenuity and variety, he chooses to set *The Island* at a historical moment *before* the advent of scientific certainty, *before* Harrison's chronometer, the multitude of theories surrounding the problem of longitude were reduced and contained in one working mechanism. Eco integrates into *The Island* a number of pre-Harrisonian theories about longitude: the so-called "powder of sympathy"; the ephemerides and the moons of Jupiter–astronomical observations of the relative positions of heavenly bodies at particular hours; the magnetic needle of the compass; "dead reckoning"; and most importantly, biblical passages describing geographical and natural phenomena.[4]

This welter of explanatory structures and systems is exemplified by Ecots character Father Caspar Wanderdrossel, who straddles the medieval and modern ages in 1643. This priest sets sail for the South Seas on the *Daphne*, a vessel fitted for scientific research, order to further his monumental work on the Great Flood. The narrator describes Father Caspar:

> A true man of the Church, he intended to prove that the Bible had not lied; but, also a man of science, he wanted to make the Sacred Text agree with the results of the research of his own time. And to this end he had collected fossils, explored the lands of the Orient to discover something on the peak of Mount Ararat, and made very careful calculations of the putative dimensions of the Ark, such as to allow it to contain so many animals (and, mind you, seven pairs of the clean ones), and at the same time to have the correct proportion between the exposed part and the submerged part so the ship would not sink under all that weight or be swamped by waves, which during the Flood cannot have been negligible ripples (p. 261).

The passage continues at length to demonstrate Father Caspar's ingenious synthesis of biblical texts and scientific wisdom (especially in his discussion of the source of so much water, which, he argues, could not have been rain but rather the "fountains of the deep t' mentioned in Genesis.) The narrator introduces this passage with his own discourse on the widespread conflation of science and Sacred Astronomy at that time.

Eco's chosen year, 1643, approaches the apogee of the European baroque, the period of creative chaos spanning the 17th century and marking the shifting balance from Father Caspar's medieval forms of wonder to modern forms of reason. Eco's understanding of the Middle Ages (as explained in *Art and Beauty in the Middle Ages* and dramatized in *The Name of the Rose*) attests to his admiration for the medieval conflation of wonder *and* empirical science. Eco celebrates the Christian thinkers of the medieval period who "were looking for a positive justification of earthly things, at the very least as an instrument of salvation" (*Art* 54). As an example, he gives Roger Bacon, the thirteenth-century scientist and Franciscan who "pronounced that goat's blood was not essential for fracturing diamonds. The proof: 'I saw it with my own eyes' " (p. 64).

But there are further historical distinctions to be made. Whereas the allegorical sensibility of the early Middle Ages projected symbolic significance onto observed physical phenomenon, the later Middle Age focused on the concrete forms of things themselves. Eco locates the change as occurring from the twelfth to the thirteenth centuries, with Aquinas' integration of Aristotelian categories into Christian theology. Eco writes of this paradigm shift:

> The cosmos of the early Middle Ages gave way to a universe which we could call scientific. Earlier, things had possessed a value not because of what they were but because of what they meant; but at a certain point it was realised that God's creative activity was not an organising of signs by a reifying of forms. . .
> ..All that survived of the universal allegory were the dizzying mathematics that give such power to the *homo auadratus*. So in the fifteenth century we find Alan de la Roch multiplying the ten commandments by the fifteen virtues, in order to obtain one hundred and fifty moral habits" (*Art* 64).

But in the 17th-century world of *The Island of the Day Before*, this shift is still in progress. The hegemony of European scientific materialism was far from fully established in the mid-17th century; indeed, it was still on the horizon in ways that recall the medieval period of transition just described by Eco. 1642 is the year of the death of Galileo, the great observer of physical phenomena (and inventor of the pendulum as a form of keeping time); Newton is born in that same year. And Descartes, father of analytical geometry, who intended to extend mathematical method to all forms of human knowledge, was engaged in writing his most influential speculations on scientific certainty. The pendulum was about to swing, but hadn't yet: the possibility of a transcendental signified could still be reconciled with scientific data. We have already observed this swing of Eco's pendulum between his first and second novels, between the young Adso's Neo-platonic faith in a system of meaning beyond the welter of physical phenomena in *The Name of the Rose* on the one hand, and the modern narrator's nominalist world view in *Foucault's Pendulum* on the other. In *The Island*, these world views are held in balance: Eco's pendulum is in the middle of its arc between these poles. Let us leave it there for the moment.

Here, my point is that the historical setting of this novel allows the author to exploit the intersecting hermeneutic imperatives that drive both human beings and plotted narratives. Detection is the stated business of both the protagonist and the narrator of , as it is in *The Name of the Rose*, and the result is the rich multiplicity of explanatory structures-theological and empirical and narrative–upon which I have barely touched. And like *Foucault's Pendulum*, the narrative constantly shifts between past and present, but in a different way: the events of *The Island* are set entirely in the past, but the narrator of those events is our contemporary. This dual temporal structure is not distracting, as it is in *Foucault's Pendulum*, because there is no description of the narrator's contemporary setting. Indeed, I had to wait until the final pages of the novel to be sure of the historical positioning of the narrator. There is a stilted style to the narrative that at first annoyed me, and made me think that the narrator was surely located in the 18th century. But not so. The narrator's concluding references to Hollywood, the Anxiety of Influence, and his summary of how the mystery of longitude was solved by Harrison make clear that he is our contemporary.

The story is this: Roberto della Griva is born in the duchy of Milan in 1614. We first meet him as he is caught up in the battle of Casale in Italy in 1630 (in what the narrator, not the combatants, know as the Thirty Years war). He finds his way to the French court in Paris, where he encounters his fair beloved, Lilia. By 1642, through the agency of an alter ego (who pops up throughout the novel as a kind of psychological cipher-- unsuccessfully so, in my view), Roberto meets the dying Richelieu. Richelieu has his ministers Mazarin and Colbert brief Roberto on the longitude question, and then send him off as a spy on a Dutch ship, the *Amaryllis*, to learn what he can about the scientific investigations taking place on board. The *Amaryllis* sets sail from Amsterdam, carrying a scientist (an Englishman, one Dr. Byrd) looking for the *Punto fijo*, the fixed point by which longitude may be calculated, and experimenting with other methods of longitudinal measurement as well. By this device, Roberto learns a great deal (as does the reader) about mid-17th century wisdom and error on this question.

The *Amaryllis* is shipwrecked, but Roberto saves himself by climbing aboard another ship, an almost deserted one called the *Daphne*, anchored off the island that gives the novel its title. This island is in sight of the *Daphne*, but separated, Roberto figures, by what we now call the international date line: the 180th meridian, which separates yesterday from today. Across that line, in sight but distant, the island offers Roberto his only hope of escape. Ironically, this island that holds his future exists in his past–it is "the island of the day before" that gives the novel its title. So it seems to mocks Roberto's efforts of survival, of historical continuance.

But this (recognizably postmodernist) historical disjunction is counter-balanced by what Roberto finds on board the *Daphne*. He quickly learns that the crew of the *Daphne*, like that of the *Amaryllis*, was also exploring this "very New World." From the evidence remaining on board, the scientific expedition included naturalists collecting all manner of botanical and zoological novelties, which they surely intended to sell upon their return. But their mercantile motives were nonetheless fueled by a sense of wonder. Their collecting implied connecting, a point upon which Eco is explicit. For on board the *Daphne*, there is a *Wunderkammer*, a cabinet of wonders–a room that literally contains the 17th-century Neoplatonic view of the universe as a great chain of being is which all things are linked in a complex hierarchy of correspondences. Lawrence Weschler writes that the *Wunder-kammer* as inspired by "an innate (and distinctly new–or, anyway, re-newed) belief in the fundamental perfectibility of man, his ability to tran-scend Adam's fallen destiny on his own (without necessarily having to rely on Christ's intervention). . ." (Weschler 1995: 130). The impulse during this period to collect and catalogue reflects this Neoplatonic world view: every-thing is a symbol or a reflection of something else, possibly even of other worlds as yet unknown in this one.

The cabinet of wonders was, then, a common 17th-century phenom-enon, containing all manner of oddities collected by travelers and obeying the Baroque impulse to include everything.[5] Recall Eco's celebration of the mobile, decentered, inclusive forms of the "open work": it is, Eco argues, 17th-century Baroque forms that first provide these open forms of expres-sion.[6] In the cabinet of wonders, Eco's appreciation of Baroque multiplicity and medieval empiricism meet.

Eco's narrator describes Roberto's discovery of the cabinet of wonders on board the *Daphne*:

> He discovered two other storage spaces beyond the hawser locker toward the prow, one was empty, the other completely full, its walls covered with shelves that had raised edges to prevent objects falling when the sea turned rough. He saw lizard skins dried in the sun, pits of fruit of forgotten identity, stones of various colors, pebbles polished by the sea, fragments of coral, insects pierced with a pin on a board, a fly and a spider in a piece of amber, a dried chameleon, jars filled with liquid in which young snakes or little eels floated, enormous bones (a whalets, he thought), the sword that must have adorned the snout of a fish, and a long horn which Roberto took for a unicorn's, though I believe it was a narwhal 's. In short, a room revealing a taste for erudite collection, such as could be found in those days on the vessels of explorers and naturalists (pp. 228-29).

This scene ends when a kangaroo, described in the most fantastic terms, terrorizes Roberto, until he realizes that the animal is stuffed. Of course, Roberto would never have seen such a beast before: thus, terror of the unknown cedes to wonder at the newly discovered, then to empirical observation and categorization, and eventually to colonization and exploitation.

But the politics of this process interest Eco less than its physics and metaphysics. Later, in a chapter entitled "Monologue on the Plurality of Worlds," Roberto repairs to the *Wunderkammer* on board the *Daphne* to contemplate the world in precisely the terms of Neoplatonism and nominalism that define the swing of Eco's pendulum:

> To see if and how many worlds there were in a dead thing, Roberto went into the little museum on the *Daphne*, and he lined up on the bridge, as if he had before him so many astragals, all the dead objects he found there: fossils, pebbles, fish bones; he shifted his eyes from one to the other, continuing to reflect on Chance and chances. (p. 428, my emphasis).

The oscillation between transcendental connectedness and nominalist fragmentation–between 'Chance and chances'–pervades Roberto's speculations about meaning.

Roberto survives on the *Daphne* long enough to write a long series of florid letters to his beloved Lilia in Paris, in which he reflects back over his past and speculates about his future (limited as it almost surely is.) Inevitably, he wonders whether these letters will ever reach her, for he is hardly in a position to carry them back to her, much less to mail them. What he cannot know is that they will somehow reach our narrator in the late twentieth century, who will make sense of them and recast them as a novel. Indeed, the narrator, in a concluding "Colophon," imagines the agent of the letters' discovery (presumably on board the *Daphne*, since the novel ends as Roberto sets out to attempt to swim to the island of the day before.) Perhaps, the narrator speculates, it was the Dutchman Abel Tasman, as he charted what was to become Tasmania and headed for the Tongas in 1643, who boarded the *Daphne* and came upon Roberto's papers. Perhaps Tasman (even with his poor Italian) would have seen that the papers treated the problem of longitude and would, therefore, have delivered them to the Dutch East Tndia Company, where they would have been filed away in a secret archive. And then, the narrator adds,

> a century after our story, Harrison's invention of the marine chronometer puts an end to the frantic search for the Punto Fijo. The problem of longitude is no longer a problem, and some archivist of the Company, eager to clear his cupboards, discards, gives away, sells–who knows?–Roberto's papers, now a mere curiosity for some maniacal collector of manuscripts (p. 507).

Or perhaps it was Captain Bligh who rescued Roberto's letters from oblivion, for hadn't the mutineers of the *Bounty* put him out to sea in that region in a sloop with eighteen loyal men in May of 1789? The mystery continues, and so do the narrator's hermeneutic speculations.

For if Roberto and just about everyone else in this novel is engaged in detecting longitude, the narrator is engaged in detecting Roberto. Here, the narrator's investigation is complicated by historical distance, by the need to determine the present significance and function of the received structures of the past-namely, Roberto's letters. The narrator constantly speculates about what Roberto might have been doing or thinking at a particular moment, and also about his own role in making sense of this historical moment. Casting his dilemma in terms appropriate to the story he tells, the narrator writes of Roberto: "The truth is that with the data Roberto gives us, it is not possible to determine where the *Daphne* fetched up. . ..But still I wanted to make a try. One day I would like to retrace Roberto's voyage, searching for signs of him. But my geography is one thing, and his history is another" (p. 260).

In this structure of double detection, Eco can investigate the post-modernist problem of cultural inheritance-what to do with the culturally given. In this narrative structure, the ahistorical tendency of much post-modernist theory must be balanced against the undeniable presence of the recorded past-Roberto's past. Eco refers to this kind of historicizing project as "semantic fission," which he defines as follows: "the abstraction of the sign from its original context and a reinsertion of it in a new context, which charges it with different meanings" (Eco, in Broadbent 1980: 31). Early in *The Island*, the narrator describes his project in just these terms: "the chronicler of [Roberto's] turbulent annals must read between the lines of the story. To judge by his quirks, he is the sort of author who, to postpone the unmasking of the murderer, gives the reader only the scantiest of clues. And so I must wrest hints from him, as if from a delator." (p. 20) we perceive Eco's wink at *The Name of the Rose*-and there are others along the way-but in this novel there is no murder, no murderer. There are only "wrested hints": the narrator frequently refers to the impossibility of his task of imposing order, connection, design, meaning.

Impossible, but worth the try: the novel ends on this point. The narrator asks:

> If the Creator consented to change His mind, did an order that He had imposed on the Universe still exist? Perhaps He had imposed many, from the beginning; perhaps He was prepared to change them day by day; perhaps a secret order existed, presiding over the constant change of orders and perspectives, but *we* were destined never to discover it, to follow instead the shifting play of those appearances of order that were reordered at every new experience (p. 512, my emphasis).

The narrator follows Roberto–indeed, in some ways *becomes* Roberto in his inadvertent use of "we" in this concluding meditation. Like Roberto, he asks us to entertain the paired possibilities of "Chance and chances," the Neoplatonic and nominalist poles linked, as I have argued, by the swing of Eco's pendulum. And he asks us to do so in terms of his own narrativizing activity:

> Finally, if from this story I wanted to produce a novel, I would demonstrate once again that it is impossible to write except by making a palimpsest of the rediscovered manuscript–without ever succeeding in eluding the Anxiety of Influence (p. 512).

If Harold Bloom defines the "Anxiety of Influence" in terms of the Romantic compulsion to reject the cultural past in the name of originality, this postmodernist narrator historicizes that anxiety by embracing his precursor in the name of cultural origins.

Eco's narrator is, then, well aware of the process of "semantic fission'" in which he is engaged, and he knows that he may drain Roberto's letters of their historical significance, and/or enrich them with his own historical and narrative design. He is, in short, acutely aware of the exigencies of form. As he recounts the process of transforming Roberto's 17th-century epistolary Romance into a late twentieth-century Novel (the capital letters are the narrator's), he frequently digresses to consider the meaning of these literary forms, and the meaning of form itself. It is this postmodern narrator's sensitivity to literary form that impels his use of a highly metaphoric style reminiscent of the 18th-century epistolary novel. What seemed to me at first to be no more than a highly figurative style is, I would argue, an homage to the explanatory power of metaphor.

This point is made explicit in the chapter entitled "The Aristotelian Telescope," when Eco has a character discuss the relation of science and poetry. The character is Padre Emanuele, a learned man whose wise words, the narrator tells us, Roberto emphasizes by recording them with capital letters. Padre Emanuele refers to the theories of Descartes and Galileo, then asserts that there is another way of knowing the world, "another Telescope, the same that Aristotle formerly used, and which is neither a tube nor a lens, but a Weft of Words, Perspicacious Idea, because it is only the gift of Artful Eloquence that allows us to understand this Universe" (p. 88). He asks Roberto to consider metaphor as a means of understanding the physical world:

> [Consider] the case of the savage fisherman terrified by those nocturnal Images of Fire sometimes visible in the Sky & frightening to behold; but as soon as the Meteorists, who are also Poets, dare call them Crined Comets, Bearded & Tailed, Goats, Beams, Shields, Torches & Thunderbolts, these figures of speech

clarify for you the clever Symbols through which Nature means to speak, and she uses the Images as Hieroglyphics. . .. (p. 89)

In Baroque fashion, Padre Emanuelets list continues for a page, reaching its final crescendo at "the supreme Figure of all":

Metaphor. If Genius, & therefore Learning, consists in connecting remote Notions & finding Similitude in things dissimilar, then Metaphor, the most acute and farfetched among Tropes, is the only one capable of producing Wonder, which gives way to Pleasure, as do changes of scene in the theater (p. 90).

Once again, we move from the terror of the unknown ("the case of the savage fisherman") to the Wonder of creating connections (metaphors), and ultimately to the Pleasure produced by this process.

Padre Emanuele has invented what he calls an Aristotelian Machine, described as the "strangest imaginable piece of furniture," consisting of drawers and cylinders organized according to the ten Aristotelian categories and all possible instances of those categories, and designed to combine phenomena in ways that generate metaphors. Padre Emanuele is described as he "turned his cylinders and searched through his drawers, fast as a conjurer, so the metaphors seemed to arise for him as if by enchantment, without anyone's noticing the mechanical gasping that produced them" (p. 95). In this combination of imagination and mechanics, Eco dramatizes once more the coexistence of wonder and science. Roberto concludes that "Padre Emanuele's machine seems to me an image of Genius, which does not aim at striking or seducing but at discovering and revealing connections between things, and therefore becoming a new instrument of truth" (p. 113).

We are back, it would seem, to the allegorical sensibility that aims to connect everything to everything, a sensibility that Eco has attributed to the early Middle Ages. But he also dramatizes that sensibility here, in the mid-17th century. And again in the late 20th. For we have see that the narrator–our contemporary-recognizes the need to fashion his own "Weft of Words," which will refer in palimpsest fashion to the histories and meanings that precede him and are in some sense accumulated in him. He, like Padre Emanuele, is engaged in "connecting remote Notions & finding Similitude in things dissimilar." By means of this narrator, Eco insists upon the historical nature of postmodern poetics and poets, and on their responsibility to historical meaning. What seems at first to be an anachronistic style is, in fact, a vehicle for making this point. As the novel concludes, the narrator looks more and more like Mr. Eco himself.

How, then, to formulate the swing of Eco's pendulum in this novel? Perhaps in the "tick sock" of Harrison's chronometer, an instrument that, as I have said, is mentioned only in passing and that post-dates the action of the novel by more than 100 years. Part of Harrison's genius was, after all, to *eliminate* the need for a pendulum, to create an internal timekeeping mechanism that would not be swayed by the ocean's movement. And in the "gasping" of Padre Emanuele's Aristotelian metaphor machine. And in the "metallic" notes of the pipe organ on board the *Daphne*, built there so that its crew of naturalists could investigate the sound of the Universal Harmony.

So I arrive at an interpretive formula for *The Island of the Day Before* whose elements are sounds rather than symbolic geometries. Eco composes a postmodernist ode to historical connection, based on the proposition that science and wonder may still operate in concert. This Baroque inquiry into modern reason and its technologies is Eco's most ambitious mapping yet of the moving substrate of our postmodern times.

Lois Parkinson Zamora

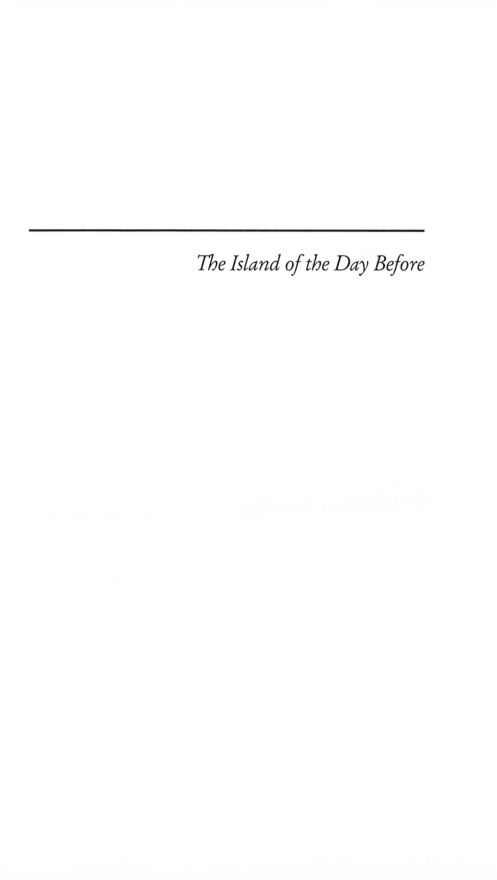

The Island of the Day Before

"Whose 'Excess of Wonder' Is It Anyway?: Reading Umberto Eco's Tangle of Hermetic and Pragmatic Semiosis in *The Island of the Day Before*"

To the reader unacquainted with Eco's work,[1] *The Island of the Day Before* is likely to be read as an historical-cum romance novel relating the adventures of a seventeenth-century man–Roberto de La Griva–reconstructed by an anonymous narrator from his letters and unfinished novel. Following an arrest in Paris, Roberto is offered a chance for freedom by the Cardinal Mazarin if he agrees to go on a mission to uncover the British attempt to find the *"punto fijo;"* the fixed point to measure the longitudes which was sought by European navigators till Harrison's invention of the maritime chronometer. Roberto accepts Mazarin's deal and embarks on the *Amaryllis* to spy on the English doctor Byrd. As Roberto discovers, the latter is taking measurements from the premise of universal attraction of like atoms and by the empirical application of the "Weapon Salve," or *"unguentum armarium,"* to a sample of blood from a dog whose wound is kept open. However, Roberto, already familiar with the use of salves from the teachings of a Carmelitan monk and the English naturalist d'Igby, cannot disclose his detection to Mazarin nor barter it with freedom since between July and August 1643 the *Amaryllis* shipwrecks in front of a small island in the South Pacific. The waves push Roberto and his float towards a second boat, the *Daphne*, apparently empty of human life but rich in secret compartments where exotic plants, animals unknown to Europeans and exotic collections of objects abound. The description of the boat's secret treasures interweave with Roberto's analeptic narration of his childhood and youth, extending from fantasies of a secret, evil brother–Ferrante–to the Casale siege during the Thirty Years War (1618-1648), and finally to an exciting Parisian tableau. This tableau is complete with the political intrigues of Richelieu, Colbert, and Mazarin. It is in one of these salons that Roberto recalls meeting Lilia, the French "précieuse" to whom he addresses his letters. After a few days aboard the *Daphne*, Roberto discovers a second passenger, the German Jesuit Caspar Wanderdrossel, who relates to him the mission of the *Daphne*'s crew and the crew's sad ending at the hands of the natives. Caspar explains to Roberto that his mission was also to find thecenter of time and he believes that it has been found; it lies between the island and the *Daphne*, dividing yesterday from today, the past from the present. Roberto's initial circumspection is quickly won by Caspar's convincing words and by his seductive descriptions of the flora and fauna of the island, including a beautiful orange dove. Yet, Roberto is not to enjoy Caspar's company for very long: in an effort to reach land inside a primitive submarine of his own making, the Jesuit drowns. Roberto, victim of solitude and confusion starts to write a novel to give order to the chaos of his life. This aesthetic reconstruction of reality proves to be fatal since Roberto crosses ontological lines and, in an attempt to save Lilia from a fictional death of his own making, enters the water to swim along the time meridian and disappears into the ocean. The novel closes with the anonymous narrator's metafictional commentary on the pedagogical worth of the tale and on the condition of writing as necessarily palimpsestic.

To readers familiar with Eco's work, *The Island of the Day Before* reads as a novel saturated by Eco's formal work on semiotics; the latest illustration of how his theoretical interests on the mechanisms and dynamics of sign production, continue to inform and shape his fictional imagination, despite a recent attempt to argue the contrary.[2] Yet, this is also a contradictory, ambivalent text; a novel which voices Eco's latest theoretical stance against aberrant, Hermetic models of semiotic creativity, while coming perhaps dangerously close to reproducing precisely a definitional expenditure, that "excess of wonder" that it had set out to critique.

As David Robey[3] has observed, Eco's specific contribution to the field of semiotics, at least up to the mid-eighties, can be summarized as a conflation of structuralist thought and Marxist historicism. This has resulted in a theory which, from *La struttura assente* (1968) to the monumental *A Theory of Semiotics* (1976) and *Semiotics and the Philosophy of Language* (1984), is descriptive of the continuous reorganization of codes under the pressures of historical and social evolution. While together these works are of course invaluable documents for any in-depth study of Eco's formal inquiry, in the context of this discussion of *The Island*, some of its fundamental concepts are perhaps more economically exemplified in a shorter and less known piece; "On the Possibility of Generating Aesthetic Messages in an Edenic Language"(*Role* 90-104).

Originally written as a journal article in 1971, and now reprinted in *The Role of the Reader*, the essay is, to tell it with Teresa de Lauretis, a parodic rewriting of the story of the Garden of Eden *"sub specie semiotica. . . a practical demonstration of the work of semiosis. . . and especially of invention as a mode of sign production"* (de Lauretis 1987:53). It playfully describes how, before God's prohibition, Adam and Eve are living in a universe organized according to a rigid taxonomy of edibility, beauty, the color red, and their binary opposites of inedibility, ugliness, and the color blue. In this harmonious world, where "Words equal things. . . and things equal words" (p. 94), their semiotic inventiveness is kept to a minimum and consists mainly of tautologically reproducing the structuralist Ur-code of the Garden. One day, however, God introduces the apple as a prohibited fruit. Being red, the apple naturally belongs to the positive side of the bar but, as an inedible food, it also includes the negative qualification of the color blue. Because no names exist to define it, Adam relies on the metaphorizing of "unlimited semiosis"–C.S. Peirce's concept for the movement of regress whereby a sign becomes the meaning of another sign, or its "interpretant"–and devises a rather simple syntagmatic compound: He calls the apple "the thing which is named red-blue" (p. 96). As Eco repeatedly emphasizes, and the story illustrates, it is the introduction of some measure of ambiguity in the closed, binary universe of the Garden that awakens Adam's semiotic faculty, forcing it to formulate other orders, and therefore produce newer structures of communications. "From that moment onwards," comments Eco, "(not from the time when Adam really ate the apple), world history commenced" (p. 103). It is also at a similar dehiscence of structures, or at least at the point of their historical weakening, that all of Eco's novels appear to begin, and his latest is certainly no exception.

As readers will recall, Eco's first fiction, *The Name of the Rose*, is set at the end of the High Middles Ages, a period when traditional orders were being overthrown, and begins when a murder has shaken the order of the abbey. Analogously, Eco's second novel, *Foucault's Pendulum*, takes place in the plural world following the 1968 cultural revolution. Not surprisingly, the background of Eco's latest is the seventeenth century. This is an epoch which, in the path of inquiry traced by Walter Benjamin (1977) and threaded, among many others, by Michel Foucault in *The Order of Things*,[4] represents one of Western history most dramatic moments of religious, social, and philosophical decenterment. In Foucault's words, "It is here that a culture, imperceptibly deviating from the empirical orders prescribed for it by its primary codes. . . discover(s) that these orders are perhaps not the only possible ones or the best ones. . ." (XX).

To put it in the anonymous narrator's words, the figure of the cosmos in which the fabula of The Island originates, is no longer the circle, "stable and round" (p. 510), but the spiral, "a snail shell, a vortex" (p. 511). Many events are contributing to this helical configuration and mention is made to the Reformation, the Nantes Edict, and the discovery of the New World as a possible cause for the crumbling of inherited models of theological representation. The Copernican revolution and the experiments of Galileo Galilei are also probing the adequacy of previous scientific models, while philosophical systems of pre-Socratic and Lucretian derivation are rising and clashing with Aristotelian substantiality and Scholastic metaphysics. Political and social decenterment is just as strong. With the Thirty Years War begins a period of alternating hegemonies of French, British, and Spanish powers, while the feudal order of society is being eroded by a flourishing mercantile mode of economic production.

Against this larger context, the story of Roberto emerges as an expanded version of Eco's parodic rewriting of Genesis, a metonymy of "On the Possibility of Generating Aesthetic Messages." To tell it with Foucault again, Roberto's story is Adam's apprenticeship novel into the breakdown of familiar models of classification; an itinerary retracing how the "tabula," or the taxomical grids enabling "thought to operate upon the entities of our world" (XVII), is becoming increasingly inadequate before the "heterotopia" of reality. Significantly, one of Roberto's first memories is a contradictory utterance voiced by his father. Almost God-like, the older Pozzo calls Roberto "my firstborn!" (p. 22), when in fact he is Pozzo's only child. This sentence, which opens a breach into Roberto's genealogical structure, is by no means an isolated case, but inaugurates a long chain of severed connections between the order of words and world, or "Les Mots et les Choses," to use Foucault's best known title. During the Thirty Years War, for example, Roberto, by now adolescent, learns how the binary, rigid division between good and bad armies, villains and heroes is not absolute. French and Spanish armies not only come to occupy both positions as the fortunes of war change but, during the Casale's siege, the besieging soldiers feed the besieged. Here again, the role of father Pozzo is instrumental, since the older man does not hesitate to kill a Spanish soldier of whom he had just spoken very approvingly. Next to the crumbling of a genealogical and ethical order, Roberto also experiences the eclipse of his theological and social representations by way of a materialist philosopher, Saint-Savin, and Señor Gaspar de Salazar. So, in the midst of crumbling structures, Roberto painfully learns that the order of the Garden of Eden, "that earthly paradise he had known at la Griva" (p. 52), is over. It has been replaced by a fluid, ambiguous space where different knowledges exist in a process of mutual relativization, or in the narrator's quasi Borgesian voice of Ficciones (1945), "a territory made up of forked paths" (p. 52). Not surprisingly, therefore, the narrative repeatedly emphasizes Roberto's problem of vision, which, more than the effect of a wound received on the Casale battlefield and the aftermath of the plague, acquires the significance of a world loosing the clarity of ordered classifications and crisply defined contours. Yet, Roberto's Bildung is to know further developments. Like Adam in a new land after his shipwreck in the New World–"An embarrassed Adam" (p. 41) as the chapter "The Seraglio of Wonders" (pp. 936-44) often emphasizes –he discovers additional, and perhaps even more troubling examples of Derridean "différance" inhabiting his semantic universe. Aboard the Daphne, he learns that the signs that his language-system has provided him with, are not only inadequate to describe an evolving European culture, but appear to be so even in relation to the physical world. In what might perhaps be an allusion to John Poinsot's Tractatus de signis (1632)–the early Iberian semiotician who broadened semiotics to include the "ens reale"–Roberto's storehouse of definitions fail before the fauna and flora of the New World: "He could not give names to these creatures, except the names of birds of his own hemisphere: That one is a heron, he said to himself, that a crane, a quail. . . But it was like calling a goose a swan" (p. 41). While in Europe plants are equated with frailty, animals with strength, and bright colors with edibility, in the New World just the opposite holds true. Frailty becomes an attribute of animals, strength of plants, and absence of color of edibility (p. 101 ff). As Roberto comments, "To live in the Antipodes, then, means. . . to learn how unstable the world is, which in one half follows certain laws, and in the other half the opposite of those laws" (p. 102). Nonetheless, it is precisely when interpretative grids fail before a culture become labyrinth–"The Labyrinth of the World" and the title of the novel's fifth chapter–that the semiotic imagination awakens, that new messages are produced by connecting signs with other signs in a process of semiosis. With the latter, however, also originate aberrant practices of interpretation. To go back to Eco's rewriting of Genesis' story, we read that Adam was not content with the trope "the thing which is named red and blue," and so began to experiment with the creative possibilities of language contained in the encyclopedia; the paradigmatic storehouse of his semantic competence. Taking pleasure in textuality, he began all sort of linkages no longer directed towards the reformulation of content, but based instead on the poetic value of words:

> At first he looses control of his own exuberance. He continually takes to pieces and puts together again this crazy gadget that he has found in his control; he composes totally implausible gibberish and then hums it admiringly for hours on end (p. 102).

Eve, Eco comments, admired Adam's virtuosity in connecting signs according to rhythm and rhymes and, had she had the appropriate critical vocabulary, would very likely have commented on the "baroque" (p. 98) flavor of her companion's messages. "Eventually, we read, "Adam calm(ed) down" (p. 102), but the potential of uncontrolled connotation remained as a legacy for future generations to actualize and study, as Eco has been doing from the late eighties onwards.

In 1986 Eco taught a course on the history of aberrant interpretative practices, or Hermetic semiosis, which he then re-echoed in the introduction to L'idea deforme (1989), and in his The Limits of Interpretation (1990) and Interpretation and Overinterpretation (1992). Together, these three works argue that as a legacy of Greek irrationalism, Hermetic semiosis is informed by a deep disregard for rules of rational logic–non-contradiction, excluded middle, and causality–and produces signifying chains propelled by flexible, illusory connectionism.[5] Its first documented emergence is traceable to the first centuries of the Christian era, with the *Corpus Hermeticum*. From then on, it has continued throughout the Renaissance and the Baroque. In the contemporary period it returns in radical reader-response and deconstructive theory of the sign, albeit with some difference: Whereas historical models of drift are tied to Gnostic beliefs in absolute, transcendental truths ultimately revealed in the course of semiosis, contemporary versions deny the existence of any teleological horizon whatsoever and therefore open the deferral of signs to the infinity of connections allowed by the paradigmatic storehouse of the encyclopedia. Since, for Eco, "these two options are both instances of epistemological fanaticism"(*Limits* 24), interpretations whose "excess of wonder leads to overestimating the importance of coincidences,"(*IO* 50) under the umbrella concept of a Pragmatic semiosis he has attempted to put limits to connotative drift. Still holding firmly to the notion that meaning is produced in and by a process of regress–"the 'nomadism' of semiosis" voiced earlier in *Semiotics and the Philosophy of Language* (p. 1), Eco has called for some measure of plausibility and contextual strictures in sign production. He has done so by proposing to combine the humanist–and for some reactionary[6]–notion of rational "modus" with Pierce's concepts of "Final Interpretant" and "Habit"(see Io 26 ff; *Limits* 39) These are provisional closures which freeze regress by narcotizing the potentially infinite connections allowed by the encyclopedia while actualizing dictionary-type definitions according to the consensus of the intersubjective community.

As Eco's early semiotic inquiry on the generation of new models of communication unfolds on this novel, so do the latest development of his theory, since *The Island* is also a novel about Hermetic-Gnostic processes of interpretation. Before the breakdown of former structures, Eco's seventeenth-century dwellers engage in a frantic process of sign production. In ways akin to Eco's description of historical practitioners of Hermetic semiosis, they are convinced of the possibility of absolute knowledge, and try to acquire it by links based on flexible system of similitudes, analogies, and resemblances. Padre Emanuele, for example, a character modeled on Emanuele Tesauro, the author of the 1655 *Cannocchiale Aristotelico*, and about whom Eco has written in a chapter of his *Semiotics and the Philosophy of Language* (p. 105 ff), attempts to understand an ever-expanding and ambiguous universe by way of an unrestrained process of metaphorizing. As a supplement to his human ability to generate tropes, he has also invented the "Aristotelian Telescope" (p. 86 ff); a prototype of the computer Abulafia from *Foucault's Pendulum*, and a tool capable of producing endless tropic equivalences both by chance and by mechanics. Similar to a slot-machine, it connects by the roll of a drum any one of the substances listed

by the inventor to each of the ten Aristotelian categories. Another character, Father Caspar Wanderdrossel, wants to contain and order the contradictions of increased information — particularly those foregrounded by
natural science in relation to the Biblical story of the Deluge (p. 261 ff)–by
engaging in interpretative processes "based on a vicious circle" (p. 289); that
is to say disregardful of rules of rational logic, and particularly causal linearity (pp. 288-89). Mirroring the metaphysical desires of Padre Emanuele,
Caspar has also put much faith in a machine, the "Specula Melitensis" (p.
306 ff), and he is convinced that, when implemented from drawings ordered by Lascaris, the Master of the Knights of Malta, it will provide its
user with total knowledge. In what might be an allusion to Eco's latest
nonfiction book, *The Search for the Perfect European Language*[7] animating
the Western mind, Caspar believes that the "Specula" will also disclose the
alphabets of the languages of the New and Antique world, including the
Edenic one whose absolute propriety and literalness he believes to be preserved in the onomatopoeias of the German tongue.

Caspar and Emanuele are not the only characters to engage in such desperate searches. Others, such as Colbert, Mazarin, and the crew of the
Amaryllis are attempting to discover the *"punto fijo"* by way of practical
applications of salves. Since such experiments derive from the theoretical
premise of universal sympathy and analogy, they are but the "empirical"
side of Hermetic semiosis. Against this ground of frantic interpreters, the
story of Roberto develops into a quixotic tale of connectionism run amuck.
To draw on Foucault's work again, *The Island* repeats the adventures of
Cervantes' *Don Quixote*; the story of the man who set out to reconnect
world and words but became *"alienated in analogy. . . the disordered player
of the Same and the Other"* (p. 49).

As Adam's descendant, as well as Padre Emanuele's pupil, Roberto seeks
meaning in metaphors, when he shipwrecks in the New World. Thus, an
unknown reptile, which is identified by the anonymous narrator as a tur-
tle, is described by Roberto as the artwork of a silversmith imprisoning in a
shield a footed serpent (p. 106). A kangaroo is a grotesque, two-headed rat
(p. 229), while palms are trees whose trunk is a star (p. 275). Yet, if the
scrambling of the Edenic Garden propels the creation of new, even poetic
forms of communication, it also causes the doom of Adam and Eve as the
story of Roberto evolves into an aberrant sign production culminating
quite likely in death. As time goes by, Roberto, who has absorbed the facile
interpretative transitivity of Padre Emanuele, Father Caspar Wanderdrossel, as well as the lesson of the *"pointe"* (p. 122) of Saint-Savin–the "act.
. . that expresses the inconceivable correspondence between two objects. . .
so that. . . any concern for substance is happily lost" (p. 122)–begins to
engage in analogical processes which reproduce some of the aberrant rela-

tions criticized by Eco in *The Limits of Interpretation*. One day, for example, Roberto associates the boat on which he is living with Lilia by way of an unrestrained journey across the encyclopedic paradigm. Since the boat is made of wood and its name is *Daphne*, by what *The Limits* call "similarity of substance" (p. 26), it can be connected with the laurel. Of course, via the "mythological contiguity" (p. 25) provided by Ovid's *Metamorphosis*, the latter stands for the nymph Daphne. Since Daphne was also a female, through "similarity of morphological traits" (p. 25) she can be equated to Lilia. This alchemical transmutation remains by no means an isolated illustration of Hermeticism, since other analogous examples of "Device. . . the expression of a correspondence" (p. 346) multiply, as when Roberto links the beautiful orange dove described by Caspar to the island, Lilia, and the lost past (p. 345). Such daily experiences of epistemic instability or, as the narrator calls it, "the magma" of "I magma, shlup, shlup shlup, I flow, fluid, plop plop slupp, I bubble bub bub" (p. 479), foment Roberto's desire for metaphysical presence and truths. An emerging *"homo rhetoricus"*–we know his story from "the papers" (p. 505) on which he has written his letters, love poems, and an unfinished novel–in an almost Proustian fashion, Roberto naturally turns to written language as a provider of order and starts a narrative. Allowing the metamorphism of Gnostic-Hermetic semiosis to fuel his writing as well, he begins a redemptive connectionism, a Gnostic interpretation to solve all contradictions of his past and present life. A childhood fantasy of an evil brother, Ferrante, which had originated at La Griva in order to explain Pozzo's comment, resurges and is now promoted to the position of a Transcendental Signifier. Therefore, it is made to explain the death of Pozzo himself, Roberto's arrest in Paris, and also Lilia's indifference. However, as Jacques Derrida has taught us, the economy of writing is "the *pharmakon*, the drug: the medicine and/or poison"(Derrida 1981:70) or, as the narrator comments in a clear allusion to this essay, "medicine teaches also about poisons" (p. 369). While the text progresses, Roberto, by now as adept as Hermes the alchemist at fortuitous connections, begins to identify fiction with reality, and crosses ontological lines: "But Roberto. . . had finally come to make the two universes flow effortlessly one into the other, and he had mingled their laws" (p. 497). Despite an epiphanic moment in which he might realize the futility of his attempt (pp. 480-81), "the conflation of universes" (p. 500) has been sanctioned by now, and so he continues in his drift. Imagining that Lilia has been abandoned by Ferrante on a float, and has now shipwrecked on one side of the island, Roberto decides to prevent her death by stopping his own time's flow as the narrator of her story. In a last analogical flight, Roberto begins swimming towards the open ocean, while thinking that his body will dissolve into atoms of air, and that these will eventually conjoin with Lilia in an eternal embrace, precisely according to the theory of sympathy voiced by the Carmelitan monk of his youth, and the natural scientists d'Igby and Byrd.

If *The Island* illustrates the dynamics and pitfalls of Hermetic models of sign production by way of the narrative demise of Roberto–a strategy not unlike that of *Foucault's Pendulum*–more forcefully even, it also voices their critique through the diegesis of the anonymous narrator. Separated from the characters not only by chronotopic barriers but, more significantly, by interpretative patterns, this is a twentieth-century narrator[8] who obtrusively comments on the various practitioners of semiosic drifts, while appearing to engage in something of a Pragmatic model of interpretation. In what certainly brings to mind Foucault's observations concerning the "Cartesian critique of resemblance" (p. 52) voiced by the analytical, rational episteme of the Classical age against the metamorphism of the Baroque mind, the narrator describes Roberto's symbolizations as metaphoric processes of "unabashed conceits" (p. 1), while the Hermetic transmutation of the *Daphne* into Lilia is the product of a "chain of thought. . . entirely inconsequent" (p. 342). Before Padre Emanuele's "Aristotelian Telescope," the narrator again reflects on the futility of unrestrained tropes by commenting how the noun "dwarf," whose definition is being sought, recedes "suffocating" (p. 97) in the labyrinth of multiplied taxonomies: "embryo, fragment of homunculus. . . the carnal appendage that begins where it ends, the line that clots in a point, the tip of a needle. . . a mustard spark. . ." (p. 97). Ultimately, the "Telescope" is said to be a phantasmagoria; a machine apt only at "revers(ing) the visible through the lens" (p. 129). It is, however, in the course of the twenty-sixth chapter titled "Delights for the Ingenious: A Collection of Emblems," that the pitfalls of actualizing the potentially infinite network of definitions is most forcefully illustrated. This section offers a practical demonstration of how, by opening the sign "dove" to the global semantic competence, one does not obtain meaning but, rather, "too many meanings (p. 352), the implosion by over-determination, as "dove" is interpreted as purity by the Egyptians, erotic sensuality by the Greeks, conjugal chastity by the Latin poets, mystic symbol by Biblical hermeneutics, and so on. In addition to foregrounding the need to segment the continuum of expressions in some sort of definition capable of putting strictures to the adventure of the sign, the narrative voice also illustrates an alternative production of meaning. Without ever claiming an infallible, absolute knowledge–we are never told precisely how the manuscripts of Roberto where transmitted nor where the events in question occur (pp. 505-09)–the narrator engages nonetheless in plausible and contextual semiosic processes. Since the story of Roberto is dispersed in several manuscripts, and is often incoherent and full of gaps, the narrator is well aware that "all must be based on conjecture" (p. 505), on regressive types of inferences, yet this is done pragmatically. For example, since Roberto's letters do not mention the time he spent floating in the ocean before being pushed against the *Daphne*, in the opening pages of the novel the narrator infers that, because of the sun and the condition of Roberto's health, it could not have been more than two days. Moreover, since Roberto was not aware of having been pushed against another vessel, it was likely nighttime. Throughout the rest of the section, additional conjectures establish with some measure of plausibility when Roberto began exploring the boat (p. 7) and following which order of actions (p. 10). Other chapters analogously engage in interpretative chains intended to settle in some definition or, to use a dictum that Eco borrows from Peirce and quotes often in *The Limits*, the narrator's signifying chains seems to be propelled by the idea that "A sign is something by knowing which we know something more" (p. 28).

Together, then, the fabula and the diegesis of this novel appear to fulfill the performative intent of a cautionary tale, the "moral lesson" (pp. 509-10) of "Colophon," marshalling Eco's Pragmatic semiosis as opposed to an Hermetic one, and illustrating the importance of "reasonable" semiotic practices; interpretative adventures which, as one section of *Semiotics and the Philosophy of Language* puts it, are provisional, yet settle in "'local'. . . systems of knowledge" (p. 84). And, yet, despite all this, the net mimetic effect of *The Island* also appears to undermine such effort and might per-haps explain the verbal gesture of the narrator, who, just before the con-cluding chapter hopes that Roberto, "before destiny, and the waters, decide for him" might have looked at the island and seen "rising in flight–like an arrow eager to strike the sun–the Orange Dove" (p. 503). More so than any of Eco's previous fictions, this novel betrays what Jonathan Culler has called Eco's "hermetical soul"[9] which draws him in to practice something very close to what he had set out to critique. The textuality of *The Island* certainly confirms Culler's intuitions, growing, as it does, by associations often motivated less towards the (re)formulation of content and more by the pleasure of the signifier. To begin with, Roberto's writing style is a pastiche of the salon poetry of "préciosité," being overloaded with hyper-bolic exaggerations and conceits. At every turn of sentence, oxymora and paradoxical antithesis multiply, and often extend well behind the legitimate illustration of a baroque *"vis rhetorica"* to point instead to the presence of a Barthesian "jouissance" escaping the author's control. More macroscopi-cally, the text itself is a fabric woven by linking as many intertextual threads as possible. It playfully trafficks with the texts common to the ba-roque culture, and abounds in quotations from the treatises of scientists, astronomers, and philosophers of the seventeenth century, as well as from the more mundane works of lyric poetry in the tradition of European Petrarchism such as Gongora, Gracian, and Marino. It also networks with the chivalric romances, Cervantes' *Don Quixote* (1605-1615), the baroque novels of M.lle de Scudéry, and the Renaissance's treatises. For example, Salazar's speeches against the ascending class of picaroes (p. 109 ff) are often double-voiced words. The reader hears not just Salazar's voice but also Ariosto's polemic in *Orlando Furioso* (1521) against the war machines which are replacing human valor and courage. Salazar's descriptions of the means of success in a world of social mobility (pp. 110-13) and the narrator's representation of "The Soul of Ferrante" in the twenty-ninth chapter (pp. 370-85), are citations from comments on fortune, simulation, prudence, and discretion by Castiglione's *Cortigiano* (1518), Machiavelli's *Principe* (1513), and Guicciardini's *Ricordi* (1530).

Cervantes' *Don Quixote* also looms large in Eco's novel. Much like the famous *hidalgo*, *Roberto* is an avid reader of chivalric romances (p. 21) and blurs boundaries of fiction and reality. For example, Roberto joins the war of Casale thinking he is a knight's errant from the times of the "fair Melisende" and the "Leper King" (p. 56); "a paladin" (p. 53) fighting for his king and his lady. In the chapter "The Passion of the Soul" (p. 114 ff), he idealizes a peasant woman, Anna Maria Novarese (pp. 114-25), into a beautiful and cultivated damsel, much like the *hidalgo*'s transformation of Aldonza Lorenzo in Dulcinea. He confuses a geographical map with a female body, as the episode of "The Map of Tenderness" (pp. 126-30) illustrates. This episode in itself is, of course, one more literary allusion; in that it refers to the famous "Carte du Tendre" from M.lle de Scudéry's baroque novel *Clélie* (1654).

Besides the references to the texts that were common knowledge to the baroque culture–which can be considered as circumstancially legitimate given the time-frame of this fiction–*The Island* also barters with works from different periods, and therefore without much respect for contextual plausibility and linearity. Besides the Proustian flavor of Roberto's enterprise in a world become a Borgesian labyrinth, *The Island* is also a texture of allusions to eighteenth and nineteenth-century narratives. As Remo Ceserani has suggested,[10] the novel engages in intertextual folds with Defoe's *Robison Crusoe* (1719), beginning with Roberto's name which, for Ceserani, is an alchemical combination of the first syllable of Defoe's title and Umberto's last. *The Island* also participates in the genre of the historical-cum-romance novel inaugurated in the Italian literary tradition by Alessandro Manzoni with *I promessi sposi* (1827).[11] Eco follows Manzoni in setting, characters, and point of view. The reader familiar with the novel will quickly recognize how *The Island*'s second, third, and fifth chapters are allusions to Manzoni's pages on the siege of Casale, completed with mention of the plague and the "Lanzi" soldiers. The romantic side of *I promessi sposi*–the tale of the obstructed love of Renzo and Lucia–bears analogies to Roberto's romance, while the name of Ferrante immediately brings to mind Manzoni's Don Ferrante (pp. 401-16) whose library represents a confusion of knowledge, being an heterogeneous collection of Aristotle's works and treatises on magic. The anonymous narrator of Eco's novel poses, just as Manzoni's, as the obtrusive and ironic editor of a found seventeenth-century manuscript, commenting on the style of the ancient text, its chaotic period, and its unenlightened author. Other texts of the period are also actualized, and include, for example, Balzac's Restoration novel *Père Goriot* (1835), whose closure–"A nous deux maintenant"[12] –is cited almost verbatim by Ferrante on his way to Paris as "Paris, à nous deux maintenant!" (p. 376). Elements drawn from the intertext of popular culture are here as well, and range from references to Captain Bligh from the *Bounty*'s mutiny to the larger pattern of detection which animates most of the novel, from the numerous quests for the *"punto fijo"* to the narrator's own signifying practices.

When faced with such rhizomatic, Joycean "riverrunning," we, like the Eve from Eco's "On the Possibility of Generating Aesthetic Messages in an Edenic Language," cannot but admire the virtuosity of the paradigmatic declinations of the archive achieved by this 1995 Adam. Moreover, since we now have a "critical metalanguage at (our) disposal" (p. 98), we can say "How very baroque" (p. 98), while remaining unable to decide whose "excess of wonder" does Eco's latest ultimately represent?

Norma Bouchard

'Dove' is the Dove?

The animals "(i) frenzied, (j) innumerable, (k) drawn with a very fine camel hair brush"–where would they ever meet, except in the immaterial sound of the voice pronouncing their enumeration, or on the page transcribing it? Where else could they be juxtaposed except in the non-place of language? (M. Foucault *The Order of Things*)

1. IS THE "NON-PLACE OF LANGUAGE" THE "PRISON-HOUSE" OF THE BIRD?

The title of this paper is not a reference to Stein's "a rose is a rose is a rose" as Stein was playing with the multiple connotations of the word "rose" in the "encyclopedia." My title plays with homophony because "dove"–which in English means "where"–in Italian stands for "colomba," and in Umberto Eco's *The Island of the Day Before*, the "dove" stands for different significations, such as an oracular bird of unusual color, a symbol of "the day before," a 17th-century emblem, an enigma to be solved, and, possibly, the key to this *roman à clef*. *The Island of the Day Before* is at the same time many novels: a seafaring novel which uses topoi from a narrative tradition spanning from the 1600's to the 1900's, a *Bildungsroman*, a text that examines scientific and epistemological arguments in the last four centuries, and a metanarrative discourse, just to mention a few. Throughout this paper my focus will be on the relationship between "semiotics" and "writing" inscribed within the text.

Roberto de La Griva, the main character of *The Island*, finds himself trapped in a completely new narrative situation: he is shipwrecked on a deserted ship, the *Daphne*. Photophobic, full of provisions, stuck on a ship that is anchored in front of an island, unable to swim, and without any books to read, his only solution is a semiotic one. Roberto's only companions are his memories of his Parisian and Monferrato past, of his dead friend Saint-Savin, of his long-lost love Lilia, and of the shipwrecked boat, the *Amaryllis*. Surrounded by absence, everything becomes a sign of the past:

and the "*Daphne*" was transformed into a Theater of Memory [. . .] as long as he remained there, every corner of that seagoing house would remind him, moment by moment, of everything he wanted to forget [. . .] And as a lover, revisiting a place, recognizes the beloved in every flower, in every rustling of leaves, every path, here, now, he could die of love, caressing the mouth of a cannon. . .. (p. 106).

On the *Daphne*, every object becomes a sign of his beloved Lilia; and so a map becomes an "analog" of his beloved's body, and the volcanoes drawn on the map will lead his own passions to erupt; even Roberto's passions are released in a semiotic way.[1] It is not just the geographical representations which ignite his amorous passion, but also his recollections[2] which are prompted by his friend Saint-Savin's warnings: "Control yourself. Do not confuse love with art" (p. 121). His relationship with the present, as well with the past, is of a semiotic nature, always mediated by an interpretative distance; and the method of mediating this distance is abduction.

As the story unfolds Roberto discovers an intruder on the *Daphne*, a German Jesuit named Caspar; he is the one who tells Roberto about the dove, explaining its presence with arguments of a textual nature:

"On the Island was the Flame Dove."
"Flame Dove? What is that?" Roberto asked, and the eagerness in his question seems to us excessive. As if the Island for some time had promised him an obscure emblem, which only now had become radiant.
Father Caspar explained how hard it was to describe the beauty of this bird: you had to see it before you could talk about it. The very day of his arrival, he had glimpsed it through his spyglass. From a distance it was like seeing a fiery sphere of gold, or of gilded fire, which from the top of the tallest tree shot up towards the sky [. . .]
That orange-colored bird, Father Caspar said, could live only on the Island of Solomon, because it was in the Song of that great king that a dove was spoken of, rising like the dawn, bright as the sun, terribilis ut castrorum acies ordinata. It had, as another psalm says, wings covered with silver and feathers with glints of gold (pp. 277-279).

From the moment Roberto sees the dove he cannot think of anything else and begins "to consider his landing on the Island as the event that would give meaning, forever, to his life" (p. 309). The readers will also not be able to think of anything else because the dove, as the narrator suggests, is the key to reading the text, the password without which the universe of the text, even though it is right before our eyes, remains incomprehensible. The dove, an orange colored tropical bird, lives on the island in front of the boat. The *Daphne* is anchored on the 180th meridian, so the island, one of the Salmon Islands, is on the other side of the time line. Both the island and the dove are, by convention, in a time zone different from Roberto's, making the dove a symbol of the day before and of Roberto's now unreachable past. In order to reach the island, he tries to learn how to swim with some help from Caspar, but not without incurring some dangers:

> What he thought of as he challenged the waves was the hope of reaching an Island that had been yesterday, and of which the symbol seemed to him the Orange Dove, beyond any capture, as if it had fled into the past (p. 310).

The orange dove, described enigmatically by the narrator in the shape of an "emblem, for Roberto [and] become[s] the symbol for going back into time and for the reader it" signifies instead the password for gaining entry into the meaning of the text, and therefore becomes the cipher of the text. Roberto and the reader would like nothing better than to reach this evasive and semiotic animal.

A "dove is a dove is a dove," and the dove, even though appears as a prisoner in the sky of language, is at the same time a guardian and a picklock of the text whose key the reader must find.

> [On the Fall River Boat] Mr. Bangs, "What makes you think he has stolen your watch?"
> "Why," said I, "I have no reason whatever for thinking so; but I am entirely confident that it is so." (C. S. Peirce "Guessing")[3]

2. The Abduction Ship

As stated, Roberto's relationship with the outside world (mediated by distance and diversity) can only be of a semiotic nature. And the outside world is anything but "natural," its winds become "capricious winds" and its sea is a rhetorical "Sea of the Contrary," where "only the rules of art count, not those of nature" (p. 101). In this strange textual universe, Roberto tries to decipher everything that appears around him, without the certainty of possessing the necessary codes. From the very beginning, strange things happen on the Daphne and Roberto must try to interpret them, mainly by using logic. Everything becomes a trace or a clue of something else: a barrel which has been moved becomes an indication of an intruder, a Latin expression–peste bubonicus–in the middle of an incomprehensible passage may be a clue to why the ship is deserted, and so on. Confined to the deserted ship, and surrounded by aqua vitae and memories, Roberto abandons himself to a world crowded with signs.

The abductive relationship that Roberto establishes with the world around him will become an example for the reader who also begins to interact abductively with the universe of the text. There are many clues–explicit and implicit–given to the Model Reader which should help him in discovering the dove's meaning, especially if he adopts an abductive investigative approach (cfr. Miranda 1996). The Model Reader, who ought to "gather with the closest approximation possible the code of the sender" (*Role* 63),[4] must be able in this case to reason abductively in order to disentangle the enigmas that the narrator has woven within the text.

On the second last page, the narrator rhetorically asks the question whether the text has a "secret order" (or a "secret code"), and whether there are many codes constantly changing?:

> If the Creator consented to change His mind, did an order that He had imposed on the Universe still exist? Perhaps He had imposed many, from the beginning; perhaps He was prepared to change them day by day; perhaps a secret order existed, presiding over the constant change of orders and perspectives, but we were destined never to discover it, to follow instead the shifting play of those appearances of order that were reordered at every new experience. Then the story of Roberto de La Griva would be merely the tale of an unhappy lover, condemned to live beneath an exaggerated sky, a man unable to reconcile himself to the idea that the earth wandered along an ellipse of which the sun was only one of the fires.
>
> Which, as many will agree, is too little to make a story with a proper beginning and a proper end (p. 512).

I agree with the narrator: if this novel is only Roberto's story, perhaps it is not enough for a story with "a proper beginning and a proper end." In fact, in this novel what is most interesting is not the story but the plot.[5] This, however, is not the only differentiation with which the narrator is playing. He is also aware of the double (narrative) Gestalt that a roman à clef implies, where the possession of the key opens the door to a parallel world that lies in the text, unperceived by a first reading. During another reading of the text, a completely different form appears, in which the same instances are reformulated by a different point of view. And so a different text–parallel to the first–appears. But, if the novel has a secret order that the reader must discover, which is veiled by the narrator through the dove-emblem, does it mean that the Model Author and the Model Reader belong to the Rortyian category of the "half hearted pragmatists"?[6] And, does it mean that both will precipitate into the purgatory of critics?[7] Now I will attempt to answer this question and to describe the theoretical difficulties and dangers every reader (even the most innocent one) of *The Island of the Day Before* must face.

> When I've said that religion and metaphysics were both branches of fantastic literature, I did not say that with hostile intentions, on the contrary. I think that Saint Thomas would like to be the greatest poet in the world. (J. L. Borges Talks with Osvaldo Ferrari)

3. Textualism or How to Do Texts with Words and Other Texts.

The orange dove, animal "beyond any capture," is not at all an innocent bird. The dove is part of a textual strategy and of a specific theoretical choice. Here I shall trace, briefly, its theoretical genealogy.

Derrida's programmatic statement "il n'y a pas de hors-texte"–the text is all we have, and all we can speak of–eliminates the possibility of any kind of relationship with the world of objective referents. It is a strong stand with regard to the connection, or, as in this case, the lack of, between the texts and its historical context. This connection is at the foundation of Eco's semiotics and his concept of "encyclopedia."

The deconstructionist practice denies the existence of a direct relationship between rationality and the world of objective referents and asserts the impossibility of interaction between literary and scientific culture (Culler 1982; Rorty 1982). These assumptions create a new way of producing (or at least of writing) philosophy–that is, "philosophy as a genre." Rorty considers this a consequence of the pragmatic dissolution of the concept of truth. Another consequence is what he calls "textualism"–grouping Derrida, Foucault and the so-called "Yale School" of deconstruction critics. They are, for Rorty, the "spiritual descendants" of idealism because they insist that it is not possible to compare thought or language with naked reality. According to Rorty: "in the last century there were philosophers who argued that nothing exists except ideas. In our century there are people who write as if there were nothing but texts" (1982:139). While the idealists took their cue from Berkeley's notion that one idea cannot be compared to another, the textualists "start off from the claim that all problems, topics and distinctions are language-relative" (Rorty 1982:140).

Rorty distinguishes between two philosophical traditions in their relationship to the concept of truth: Kantian and Hegelian; the idealists, structuralists and pragmatists belong to the second group. According to Rorty, the Kantian line of thought "thinks of truth as a vertical relationship between representations and what is represented" (1982:92), whereas the Hegelians see truth as being in direct relation to interpretative mediation, and conceived it as a reinterpretation of previous reinterpretations in an "ad infinitum" vortex. Rorty's classification designs a topology where Peirce and Eco have to share the same theoretical Hegelian space with Derrida and the American Deconstructionists. Given this territorial conflict, it is understandable that Eco's polemic against deconstruction is sparked by a different concept of what this interpretative mediation should be.

> Birds and mammals not only have territories which they occupy and defend
> against their own kind but they have a series of uniform distances which they

maintain from each other [. . .] Man, too, has a uniform way of handling distance from his fellows. (E.T. Hall The Hidden Dimension)

4. THEORY AND TERRITORY, RECEPTION AND REPARATION

This uncomfortable cohabitation within Rorty's classification is not the sole reason for Eco's mobilization. Among the reasons which motivated him to establish a limit to the openness of a work we must not overlook what I call "a sense of theoretical guilt."[8] In 1962 The Open Work opened the door to a new paradigm for the reading of texts, and in the last 30 years many undesired guests have aggregated themselves to that paradigm. We must consider that "openness" in the early 60's had a very different meaning than the one it can possibly have today, after Derrida. In this case we clearly find ourselves facing the problem of the reception of the text due to the change in the context of criticism. The concept of openness put forth by Eco in The Open Work, read out of a cultural and temporal context, risks being misunderstood and even misinterpreted (cfr. Miranda 1992).

In the "Introduction" to Lector in Fabula, Eco admits that after The Open Work, a good part of his work tended to elaborate the concepts therein contained: "all the studies I carried out between 1963 and 1975 aimed [. . .] at finding the semiotic foundation of that experience of "opening" that I had spoke of but whose rules I did not state in The Open Work." However, it was not until the end of the eighties (the height of American Deconstruction, and after Rorty's definition of deconstruction as "true pragmatism") that Eco concerned himself with clearly delineating his own theoretical space. In order to do so he had to distinguish his concept of openness from that advocated by American Deconstruction and Peirce's pragmatism–and therefore his own pragmatism from the one that Rorty spoke of. I distinguish three different levels (or moves) in the strategy used by Eco: the genealogical, the theoretical, and the narrative one.

4.1. AN EXTRAPARADIGMATIC PARADIGM

The genealogical move is the first necessary step in the Eco's strategy to clearly delineate his own theoretical space; this move consists in the construction of a new "theoretical paradigm," what he calls "hermetic semiosis." In the best tradition of the history of ideas, and from an outlook similar to that of Lovejoy (1936), Eco produces an analogy between hermeticism, which begins with the appearance of the Corpus Hermeticum in the Second century and runs through western culture, and critical thought starting with Derrida and, in particular, with American deconstructionists. The latter is based, as is Peircean semiotics, on the fundamental role of the interpretant of a sign, but does not specify any rules for the interpretative activity, leaving open the possibility for unlimited interpretations. This uncontrollability is compared by Eco to the degenerative process of cancer cells–a "theoretic metaphor" of the "cancerization of semiosis" that he developed in a theoretical context, as well as in a narrative one.

Through the creation of the "hermetic semiosis paradigm" Eco includes in the same theoretic genealogy the "hermetic" tradition and the deconstruction theories of Derrida and American deconstructionists.[9] Eco's strategy bifurcates into the theoretical and the fictional field, in *Foucault's Pendulum* (1988) and *The Limits of Interpretation* (1990). In both works Eco underlines, according to well defined and different rhetorical styles (Miranda 1992), his differentiation from those belonging to the "hermetic semiosis" paradigm. I would like to point out that normally, in the history of the sciences, the creation of a critical paradigm is carried out by the members of that paradigm (cfr. Kuhn 1962). In this case the new paradigm is proposed from the outside with the proposer's intention of differentiating himself from those belonging to that paradigm.

4.2. Consequences of Pragmaticism

In an imaginary theoretical chess game (that can be called a Peircean-chess-game), whose rules state that each move must be triadic, Eco would be an expert player. The three-oretical move is one of three in the triple strategy developed by Eco in order to differentiate his theory from other open oriented text theories. Its three steps are: (1) debating Rorty's definition of pragmatism, (2) discussing Derrida's reading of Peirce, and (3) trying to find within the texts a self-regulating mechanism that can keep in check the number of "uncontrolled" interpretations. Eco points out the differences between Rorty's pragmatism and Peirce's (1990), to which he adheres, thereby distancing himself from the Rorty pragmatists. Eco does not find any theoretical difficulty in differentiating Rortyian pragmatism from that of Peirce,[10] pointing out Peirce's pragmatism includes the realistic nuances of his idealism and the inextricable idea of a "purpose" (both of which are unacceptable for a "pragmatist," in Rorty's sense).[11] Rorty includes Peirce in the very periphery of his pragmatism. The conflict arises because Derrida, an example of "true Rortyan pragmatist," claims to have based himself on Peirce while constructing his theory of interpretation. This explains why Eco's polemics will center above all on Derrida's reading of Peirce.

The word "precursor" is indispensable in the vocabulary of criticism. [. . .] The fact is that each writer "creates" his precursors. His work modifies our conception of the past, as it will modify the future. (J. L. Borges "Kafka and His Precursors").

4.2.1. The struggle for the precursor: a discussion about "infinite semiosis."

In *De la grammatologie* Derrida transforms Peirce into his precursor, because he "goes very far in the direction that I have called the de-construction of the transcendental signified, which, at one time or another, would place a reassuring end to the reference from sign to sign (p. 49). The notion of the interpretative infinity present in Peircean semiotics is foreshadowed by Derrida, who states:

> The so-called "thing itself" is always already a representamen shielded from the simplicity of intuitive evidence. The representamen functions only by giving rise to an interpretant that itself becomes a sign and so on to infinity. The self-identity of the signified conceals itself unceasingly and is always on the move. The property of the representamen is to be itself and another, to be produced as a structure of reference, to be separated from itself. The property of the representamen is not to be proper [propre], that is to say absolutely proximate to itself (prope, proprius). The represented is always already a representamen [. . .] From the moment that there is a meaning there are nothing but signs. We think only in signs (p. 50).

On the basis of this semiotic idea, Derrida arrives at the principle "il n'y a pas de hors-texte." The Peircean concept of infinite interpretability of the sign evokes two very different interpretations in Eco and Derrida. For Derrida, a descendant of structuralism, locked-up inside the F. Jameson "prison-house of language," where the only space available is textual, this image of Peirce sets the stage for the concept of infinite interpretability of a text (that eliminates every reality from the interpretation itself). For Eco, texts are open to the context, so the Peircean concept of infinite interpretation of the sign leads him to the concept of the encyclopedia: "in light of this theory, the contents of a single word becomes very similar to an encyclopedia" (*Lector* 33). Against Derrida's use of the unlimited potential of semiosis, Eco responds with a principle of contextuality which works by reducing the infinite possibilities and limiting them to the confines of a specific universe of discourse which only works with a specific culture, time and structure of the cognitive universe:

> But if the chain of interpretation can be infinite, as Peirce maintained, the universe of discourse intervenes to limit the encyclopedia. And a text is only a

strategy that constitutes the universe of its interpretation–if not legitimate, able to be legitimate. Any other decision to use a text freely corresponds to a decision of expanding the universe of discourse. The dynamics of unlimited semiosis do not prohibit it, instead, they encourage it. One must decide whether to continue the exercise of semiosis or to interpret a text (my trans.; *Lector* 59-60)

In other words, the *encyclopedic* reading of a text, potentially unlimited, must not be confused with the *subjective* infiniteness of interpretations. The decisive factors are, in this case, the historical and social sanctions. Eco's theoretic strategy is to advance a reading of Peirce's semiotics that emphasizes the "*hors-texte*" in the interpretative process. Regardless of the obvious differences between Eco and Derrida's reading of Peirce, their co-existence was tranquil until the mid-eighties. Eco engaged in a direct attack only after Rorty's distinction between weak and strong textualists. Eco's opposition to Derrida's interpretation of Peirce was articulated in different papers and takes its definitive form in *The Limits of Interpretation*.

The first step in Eco's polemic is the creation of the sintagm "unlimited semiosis" and its application to Peirce's concept of infinite interpretability of the sign. Where Peirce discusses "infinite regression" (CP 1.339), Eco prefers to use the term "unlimited" because "infinite" is a difficult word to combat on a linguistic level. Once the concept of "unlimited semiosis" is established as a pivotal point, Eco's theoretical work moves toward demonstrating the desirability of some interpretative limits. The third step is the recovery of the "final interpretant" so as to halt the potential for infinite interpretations. Eco's fundamental objection to Derrida's reading of Peirce is that "the formation of a habit, as a disposition to act, stops (at least temporarily) the unending process of interpretation" (*Limits* 335). In fact, Peirce's theory foresees a stop device within the semiotic process: the "habit" or "final interpretant," that imposes an end to unlimited intepretants:

> The Habit is a disposition to act upon the world, and this possibility to act, as well as the recognition of this possibility as a Law, requires something which is very close to a transcendental instance: a community as an intersubjective guarantee of a nonintuitive, nonnaively realistic, but rather conjectural notion of truth (*Limits* 39).

Eco underlines that this "final interpretant" is not provided for in a deconstructionist framework, thereby making Derrida's appropriation of Peirce unfounded.

> If the doctrine of the three categories was Peirce's gift to the world, the most precious part of that gift was the insight that, because thirdness is essentially law like, it is also essentially thought-like. (Guy Debrock *Living Doubt*[12]).

4.2.2. Three Types of "lectors"

The third step of the "theoretical move" is trying to find within the texts themselves the mechanisms for self-regulation which, while allowing a co-operation between the reader and the text, would at the same time avoid interpretive "excesses" by the reader–that is, interpretations not authorized by the text. In order to do this Eco produces a triad of oppositions, the last of which is a triad itself: the first, chronologically speaking, is the opposition between "use" and "interpretation" of the text, the second is the dichotomy between "semiosic reader" and "semiotic reader," and the third is the distinction between *intentio auctoris*, *intentio operis* and *intentio lectoris*. Let's go back and look at this from a chronological perspective.

The first step was the distinction between "interpretive cooperation" and "critical interpretation" (*OW*), where the latter is produced by the critic, a type of a cooperative reader who "after having analyzed the text, recounts his cooperative steps and clarifies how the author, using his own textual strategy, led him to cooperate in that way" (*Lector* 183). The difference between these two types of readers is solely a question of degrees, due not only to the level of "clarity and lucidity" of the critical reader's interpretation, but also to his ability to explain his own reading of the text. The semiotic criteria necessary to evaluate this critical stance were not expounded then, and Eco himself admitted that "the line between these two activities is very thin" (*Lector*: 183)and that the most interesting difference was not between "critical interpretation" and "interpretative cooperation," but rather between "the modalities of textual cooperation" and criticism that uses the text to fulfill other objectives. *Lector in Fabula* was an attempt to clarify the steps involved in textual cooperation, and the theoretical categories of Model Reader and Model Author were at the time his proposal for finding a way to keep in check farfetched "uses" of the text which the text did not authorize (see also *The Role of the Reader*).[13]

Each of these differentiations are re-proposed, *mutatis mutandis* in *The Limits of Interpretation*, where "interpretation" and "use" of texts are again discussed.[14] These opposed categories are linked to two possible approaches to the reading of a text: a "semiotic or critical interpretation" or a "semiosic or semantic interpretation":

> Semantic interpretation is the result of the process by which an addressee, facing a Linear Text manifestation, fills it up with a given meaning. Every response-oriented approach deals first of all with this type of interpretation, which is a natural semiosic phenomenon. Critical interpretation is, on the contrary, a metalinguistic activity–a semiotic approach–which aims at describing and explaining for which formal reasons a given text produces a given response (and in this sense it can also assume the form of an aesthetic analysis) (*Limits* 54).

This distinction is a re-elaboration of the previous distinction made between "interpretative co-operation" and "critical interpretation." What I would like to point out is that the difference between critical "naiveté" and critical "awareness," the watershed which divides a semiosic interpretation from a semiotic one, is not pertinent in distinguishing a Model Reader from one who is not, because there can be two types of Model Readers foreseen by the text: a *Model Semantic Reader* and a *Model Semiosic Reader*. The differentiation between these two types of readers is an innovation that Eco has recently examined in his critical theory:

> I am in fact implying that many texts aim at producing two Model Readers, a first level, or a naive one, supposed to understand semantically what the text says, and a second level, or critical one, supposed to appreciate the way in which the text says so (*Limits* 55).

Eco suggests that texts whose function is aesthetic usually provide for both types of interpretation, and in so doing these texts can play with the relationship established between the two. As an example he uses Agatha Christie's *The Murder of Roger Ackroyd* which "invites the critical reader to admire the ability with which the text leads the naive reader to error" (*Limits* 29). If both a semiotic and a semiosic interpretation are foreseen by the text, then the distinction is not sufficient to differentiate between "use" and "interpretation" of a text. In fact, semiotic and semiosic interpretations belong to the field of "text interpretation." At this point the triad *intentio auctoris*, *intentio lectoris* and *intentio operis* appears to untie the critical knot. Eco examines these three positions in the history of interpretation and states that *intentio auctoris* assumes that interpreting a text means bringing to life the meaning the author had intended, and it assumes the objective nature of the text, independent of our own interpretations; whereas *intentio lectoris* assumes that there is an infinite number of interpretations of the text. The first option is exemplified by the different types of critical fundamentalism[15] and the second by the paradigm of "hermetic semiosis." Both are considered by Eco as cases of "epistemological fanaticism." Eco's own proposal would be a dialectic between *intentio operis* and *intentio lectoris*:

> The semiotic theories of interpretative cooperation, such as my theory of the Model Reader (Eco 1979), look at the textual strategy as a system of instructions aiming at producing a possible reader whose profile is designed by and within the text, can be extrapolated from it and described independently of and even before any empirical reading (*Limits* 52).

The genealogical and theoretical now meet. The interpretative area of "hermetic semiosis," and of deconstruction, is the area set out by intentio lectoris and remains quite distinct from his own interpretative proposal. Let us now look at how narrating for Eco becomes an instrument in the process of theoretical clarification.

Di ciò di cui non si può teorizzare, si deve narrare [What cannot be theorized, must be narrated]. U. Eco

4.3. WRITING AS A KIND OF PHILOSOPHY

Eco's "narrative move" consists in a subversion of the textualist logic with regard to writing. The textualist common sense tends to assimilate each type of text to literature, which becomes the point of comparison for all other disciplines. This explains why, in the topology of textualist criticism, literature tends to cover the entire semiosphere, leaving no room for the autonomy of philosophy or theory. If for Derrida all texts, even philosophy, or rather philosophy above all, become *écriture*, for Eco all texts, even novels, become theory.

In 1979, at the University of Bologna, Eco organized a seminar on Peirce and the detective story. In 1983 an anthology edited by Eco and T. Sebeok entitled *The Sign of the Three* (Holmes, Dupin, Peirce) appeared. Since the title is an intertextual allusion to Conan Doyle's *The Sign of Four*, the question that comes to mind is: who is the missing fourth? What quickly comes to mind is the perfect example of Peircean inferential semiotics, as well as of Holmes and Dupin's abductive methods: William of Baskerville, the protagonist of *The Name of the Rose* (1980).

Seven years later, we notice something similar in Eco's activities. During the 1986/87 academic year, Eco held a monographic course on hermetical semiosis at the University of Bologna. *Foucault's Pendulum*, a compendium of hermetic theory, which addresses the topic of excessive attempts at interpretation, was published in 1988. *The Limits of Interpretation*, a collection of essays written over various years, was published in 1990. The conditions of utterance, together with the theoretical context, confirm that the same semiotic lesson which is hidden in the narrative fabric of *Foucault's Pendulum* is expounded later in *The Limits of Interpretation*. The area of fiction functions in this case as a ritual area of purification, useful in exorcising theoretical phantoms and transcending contradictions implicit in theory (Miranda 1992).

Six years later, we have once again the sequence: a university seminar, a theoretical text, a novel. Now the backdrop for the seminar changes, it is no longer Bologna but Harvard, where Eco holds the Norton Lectures during the 1992/93 academic year. *Six Walks in the Fictional Woods* (1994) is the rewriting of the "Norton Lectures" and appears only few months before

The Island of the Day Before. Each of the six walks that Eco has undertaken in the woods of the novels of others authors can be used by the readers as a compass to navigate (as if it were a hyper-text) the narrative ship that is *The Island.* This novel is not only a successful subversion of the Derridian, deconstructionist and textualist topos of "philosophy as a kind of writing" (Rorty 1982), but also a clear, distinct and definitive differentiation from the textualist (and pragmatist) paradigm as defined by Rorty–an escape from other's textualism performed in the textual place *par excellence*: a novel. *The Island* is an example of "scientific writing" that takes the form of a novel, written in such a away as to reveal narrative solutions to venerable theoretical problems.

The rest of my paper will attempt to demonstrate that the dove in *The Island of the Day Before* is not only the password which opens up the novel, but also the completion to all theoretical strategies described above. How can this orange bird resolve, with the touch of a feather, years of theory?

A logical theory may be tested by its capacity for dealing with puzzles, and it is a wholesome plan, in thinking about logic, to stock the mind with as many puzzles as possible, since these serve much the same purpose as is served by experiments in physical science.(Bertrand Russell "On Denoting").

5. "Dove" Is The Meaning of The Dove?

In order to answer the question "Why is the theory of meaning so *hard*?," Putnam (1970) analyses the class of general names associated with *natural kinds*. In order to understand why is the meaning of the orange dove so hard, I will follow Putnam's path. He points out that the fact that "a natural kind may have abnormal members" is a semantic problem with which *traditional* theories of meaning are not able to deal. If we describe the meaning only by specifying a conjunction of *properties*, we cannot explain why a green lemon is still a lemon, why a three legged tiger is still a tiger and, I add, why an orange dove is still a dove. In Putnam's view of meaning, the same word can have certain series of properties for different speakers, depending on which part of the *encyclopedia* they activate in each case (1970 and 1975). For example, when I use lemon in my tea, I am not activating all the semantic properties that a lemon has for a botantist.

The narrator's choice of an orange dove (an abnormal member of a natural kind), as the emblem of the novel becomes an interesting clue. In fact, Putnam's conception of the meaning is at the basis of a semantic encyclopedia, as proposed by Eco (*SPL* Ch. 2) and in the game that the narrator of the *Island* proposes to his readers.

Halfway through *The Island,* the narrator emphasizes that the dove carries with it an enigma. Although chapter 22 is entitled "The Orange Dove," it is in chapter 26 "Delights for the Ingenious: A Collection of Emblems," where more attempts at explaining the meaning of this enigmatic animal are to be found. The narrator carries out an "Explication of the Dove" that presents the history of the multiple literary and biblical meanings of the dove: from Talmud to the Old Testament, from Egyptian writing to Virgil, from the Bestiaries of the Middle Ages to the Fathers of the Church, etc. Paradoxically, this excess of information does not aid the reader in understanding the meaning of the dove. Rather, the dove, flying over this sea of multiple meanings, remains an unknown. At the conclusion of this encyclopedic display the narrator states, "it seems so clear to me (luce lucidior) that I have decided to proceed no further with my Explication of the Dove" (p. 356). The narrator's statement can be seen as either ironic or paradoxical, it is playing both with the concept of information as well as with the concept of the s-code.

To state it in terms of *A Theory of Semiotics* (1975), according to a theory of information in which a value increases with the number of possible choices (Shannon e Weaver 1949, Eco 1975), what can be said is that the reader has received many "bits" of information about the dove. Yet, side by side with this concept of information, seen as directly proportional to the "entropy" of the system, there is another concept that sees information as something that: "means a precise amount of selected information which *has actually been transmitted and received* " (cfr. Eco TS §1.4.).

The *Model Semiotic Reader* of this novel ought to fill in the space that exists between these two concepts of information, because until the reader finds the s-code that reduces the equi-probability of the source, we cannot state that the information has been "in fact transmitted and received." The novel's Model Author demonstrates his full awareness of this differentiation when he states: "but today we are still here, asking ourselves what the Golden Bough meant. A sign that doves carry messages, but the messages are in cipher" (p. 353). If the meaning of the dove is encoded, deciphering it will be the task of the reader. Many of the citations and the references in the "Explication of the Dove" belong to the semantic area of the sacred, and the narrator himself reminds us: "No dove, no revelation." This assertion, along with many others in the novel, works on two levels; on a "narrative" level, that makes reference to the Egyptian and Greek oracles, and on a "meta-narrative" level, where the Model Author addresses his Model Reader. On this level, the assertion becomes auto-referential: no dove's cipher, no text's revelation.

My hypothesis is that the meaning of the dove fulfills the same function within Eco's theory that puzzles, according to Russell, fulfill in theories of logic and experiments in physical science. The Model Author of *The Island* shall therefore present the dove-puzzle that a theory of interpretation should be able to solve, and the *Semiotic Model Reader* then sets out to show

how Eco's theory can solve it. As we shall see, this "narrative experiment" is performed by the narrator with the cooperation of his readers.

6. The Name of the Dove

Through Eco's intertext we know that "we have only names" to decipher the meaning of the dove.[16] The dove does not have a name, but the ships and the characters do. The names of the three ships are *Daphne*, *Tweede Daphne*, and *Amaryllis*, and at a first glance we cannot tell what they have in common. Each one of these ships has a character that is linked to them: Dr. Byrd is the captain of the *Amaryllis*, Father Caspar is living on the *Daphne* when Roberto arrives, and the *Tweede Daphne* is an invention of Roberto. These three characters have something in common: a bird name. If it is generic in Dr. Byrd's case, it is instead specific for "Roberto de La Griva" ("grive" means "thrush" in French) and Father Wanderdrossel ("drossel" means "thrush" in German, and "Wanderdrossel" is a migratory thrush).[17] But, what do these polyglot textual birds have in common? In nature birds share a musical language. Now we see the connection between the names of the characters and the name of the ship, they all belong to a "musical thematic isotopy." The "*Daphne*" is also a melody, played by the only cylinder of the water organ in the cabin, as well as by the ship itself:

> That one song, whose words he did not know, if it ever had any, was being transformed into the prayer that he intended to make the machine murmur every day: "*Daphne*" played by the water and wind in the recesses of the Daphne, in memory of the ancient metamorphosis of a divine Daphne. Every evening, looking at the sky, he hummed that melody softly, like a litany (p. 342).

At this point it becomes relevant that the *Daphne* is "a Dutch fluyt, or flute, or flûte, or fluste, or flyboat, or fliebote." The "Elsevier's Nautical Dictionary" (Vandenberghe 1994) confirms that this ship, number 5308 in their code, is called that way, adding the Spanish "flauta." The Italian "flauto," the French "flute" and the Dutch "fluyt" are also the names of a musical instrument: the flute. In chapter 26 the narrator states that: "we fall in love with them [the doves] because they have this other, most tender characteristic: they weep or moan instead of singing (p. 349).[18] There is an obvious similarity between the *gemitus* of the dove and the murmur of the *Daphne* as they are described in the novel. Both are musical, repetitive and enticing (at least for the narrator), so the "*gemitus*" of the dove becomes an animal analogy of the "litany" produced by the *Daphne*.[19]

By now there is very little doubt about the relationship that exists between the ship, the musical instrument (the flute) and the dove. The Model

Semiotic Reader willing to resolve the cipher of the dove will go looking
through the 17th-century compositions for flute, once the isotopic relationship of these elements has been discovered, knowing that it is necessary
to refer to the "encyclopedia"–in this case the baroque musical encyclopedia. After some research he will find that the "Daphne," the "Tweede
Daphne" and the "Amarilli mia Bella" are all compositions for the flute
written by the Dutch composer, Jonkheer Jakob Van Eyck.

"Doen Daphne d'over schoone Maeght," the piece the bellmaster plays
for Roberto in chapter 20, is also written by Van Eyck, who was the
bellmaster at the Utrecht Cathedral from 1624 to 1648; he was also blind, as
is the bellmaster that Roberto meets in late December 1642, in a cathedral
in Amsterdam. Around the end of the third volume of his complete works
(Eyck 1984) the composition "Orainge" ("orange colored") appears. It is a
short piece in which the dominant key is the "sol maggiore." The words
used by the narrator to describe the dove "a fiery sphere of gold, or of
gilded fire" (p. 278) now acquire a new meaning, because in Italian the word
"Sol" indicates both the musical key as well as "the sun," the "fiery sphere
of gold."

What is the value if the reader discovers–that the orange colored dove is
the cipher to a seventeenth century composition for flute? Can the reader
now state that because of this, s/he understands the meaning of the text,
without transforming the reading of the novel in a mere enigmatic game?
The obvious danger lies in following the path of deviant interpreters of
Dante, those that Eco calls the "Followers of the Veil" (the *adepti del
Velame*; cfr. Pozzato 1988 and IO), who reduce the meaning of the Divine
Comedy to a Ghibelline secret game, a Masonic jargon, a Rosicrucian crossword, or a mere declaration of esoteric faith. Then, to avoid falling into
"suspicious interpretation," another check, with both the text and the
theory, becomes necessary.

7. THE SIGN OF THE DOVE

Among the quotations given by the narrator in his "Explication of the
Dove" there is a paraphrased reference to the Eraclitean notion of the sign,
which Eco uses in *Semiotics and the Philosophy of Language* to explain the
ancient difference between "words" and "signs":

> The dove is there to signify that the world speaks in hieroglyphics, and there is
> a hieroglyph that itself signifies hieroglyphics. And a hieroglyph does not say
> and does not conceal; it simply shows (p. 354).

> The names are not signs, and signs are something else. Also Eraclite says: "The
> lord, which oracle is in Delfos, not say () and does not conceal; it simply shows
> () (p. 23)

How should we interpret this clue given to us by the narrator? Is he telling us to look at the dove not as a word, but as a sign? If we overlap the two quotations the following text appears: **The dove is here to signify that the world speaks in signs and not in words.** What does this mean? For our *semiotic common sense* the words are signs. To understand this difference between signs and words suggested by the narrator, the Model Semiotic Reader (a reader of Eco's theory) should remember:

> that Greek semiotics, from the *Corpus Hippochraticum* up to the Stoics, made a clear-cut distinction between a theory of verbal language (names, *onomata*) and a theory of signs (*semeia*). Signs are natural events that acts as symptoms or indexes, and they entertain with that which they designate a relation based on the mechanism of inference (if such a symptom, then such a sickness; if smoke, then fire). Words stand in a different relation with the thing they designate [. . .] and this relation is based on mere equivalence and biconditionality (*Limits* 112-113).

The inference is the watershed for this venerable differentiation, which in Eco's interpretation outlines the distinction between biconditionality and the triadicity. It is not difficult to associate the difference between onomata and semeia to the two most noted modern definitions of the sign: that of Saussure and Peirce. In fact, in *Semiotics and the Philosophy of Language* Eco states that in order to understand the Peircean concept of the sign "we need to reconsider the initial phase of its historical development. Such a reconsideration requires the elimination of an embarrassing notion, that of linguistic sign. Since this notion is after all a late cultural product" (*SPL* 26).

Through this reference to Eco's theoretical intertext, the narrator suggests to the *Model Semiotic Reader* that the dove is not an *onoma*, but a *semeion*, and so it can be deciphered following the triadic and abductive logic of Peircean semiotics. The dove is therefore, "something which stands to somebody or something in some respects or capacity" (Peirce, CP 2.228), and the Model Reader ought to discover "that somebody or something" which is not in the text. The reader must not only find the missing element in the text but he must also be able to make "semiosis" work. For Peirce "semiosis" is "an action, an influence, which is, or involves, a cooperation of *three* subjects, such as a sign, its object and its interpretant; this tri-relative influence not being in anyway resolvable into actions between pairs (5.484 in *TS* 15). Semiosis is a device where every interpretant that follows in the process of semiosis is related to the Object by the preceding interpretant, which has become a sign. Within a triadic concept of the sign, discovering that the interpretant of the sign dove is a musical score is not enough to give us the definitive meaning of the text, because the relationship between aliquo and aliquid is never biconditional. So in this way, the interpretant of the sign "dove," as the musical score "Orainge," become in turn the sign for another interpretant, which then become a sign for another interpretant, and so forth. As seen in 4.2.2., without the final interpretant or "Habit," the process would be infinite. This is the process that Eco was thinking about, when he coined the concept of the openness of art works. We do not find elements of the triangle (sign-object-interpretant) which remain unchanged and after a while nothing remains of the first phase of the process (cfr. Proni 1990:2.3). Until the reader is able to put this process in motion, the universe of the text will seem an accumulation of information and quotations, or as an erudite postmodern writing, as seen by many critics. [20]

In *The Island of the Day Before* the *Semiotic Model Reader* must solve the mystery of the relationship between the interpretant (or interpretants) and the possible interpretation of the text–the same theoretical problem that Eco has been discussing over the last twenty years. And the reader of *The Island* must follow Eco's own reading of Peirce, as opposed to Derrida's, in order to solve the enigma. As seen in section 4.2.2., Eco opposed a principle of contextuality against the uncontrollable drifting of reading. On a theoretical level, Eco's reading of Peirce makes hors texte decisive in the interpretative process, and on a narrative level, for the Semiotic Model Reader, going back to hors texte is the only way to gain access to the meaning of the dove, and therefore, of the text. Without a recourse to the context, in this case given by Eco's intertext and by the 17th-century encyclopedia, the Model Reader will find himself immersed in a textual world so crowded with senses that risks becoming senseless.

The protagonist of *The Name of the Rose*, William of Baskerville, was a medieval Sherlock Holmes who reasoned with the tools of semiotic theory to discover that the murder was the reader (of the manuscript).[21] In *The Island of the Day Before* the role of the reader is overturned. Now it is the reader, who in order to solve the mystery of the text, must reason like Sherlock Holmes, expert, not of ashes or poison, this time, but of semiotic theories. [22] I shall end this argument "in the words of a forgotten poet": *stat columba pristina signum, signa nuda tenemus.*

8. INTERPRETING EMBLEMATIC ANIMALS

On a literal level the word "emblem" acquires its modern definition as "a picture with a motto or set of verses intended as a moral lesson or a subject of meditation that was common in the 17th-century" (Webster 1986)[23] from the work *Emblematum liber* (1531) by Andrea Alciato. This was the

meaning of the word in the 17th-century and "device" was one of its synonyms.[24] This symbolic figure can also act as either "a badge or insignia" and
it is in this sense that the term would later be used by scholars such as De
Sanctis and Croce; [25] in a figurative way an emblem is "mere appearance,
lacking in real power."

As the narrator says "the wonderful thing about the Dove, at least (I
believe) for Roberto, was that it was not only a message, like every Device
or Emblem, but a message whose message was the indecipherability of
clever messages" (pp. 352-353). In the novel, while the emblem meaning
remains hidden, all the previous meanings of "emblem" are active. The
dove is the "badge or insignia" of the novel itself; as a sign, it is also "mere
appearance," because it indicates something that (by definition) is absent in
the text, and its interpretant (a musical score) can be easily described as a
"group of symbolic figures usually accompanied by a statement in verse or
prose." In this light the explanation given by the narrator in chapter 26
acquires a new meaning:

> In short, a Device was a mysterious notion, the expression of a correspondence:
> a poetry that did not sing but was made up of a silent figure and a motto that
> spoke for it to the eyes (p. 346).

This complex assertion can be read on three different levels. The first is
a literal level, the narrator describes what a Device is, using a poetic language. The second level is self-referential, where the author gives the Model
Reader instructions on how to decipher the Device of the dove. The third
level is the description of the cipher, a musical score, "made up of silent
figures and mottoes that spoke for it to the eyes," which the reader is able
to understand only after having deciphered the meaning of the Device.

The first level is for all pragmatic readers of the text. The second and
third levels are only for the Model Reader of the text, who understand that
within this definition there is a hidden enigma which they must discover.
In the third level the narrator invites the *Model Semiotic Reader* to admire
the skillfulness with which the text lead the naive reader to err. The narrator of *The Island* behaves like A. Allais in the novel analyzed in *Lector in
Fabula*, and Agatha Christie in *The Murder of Roger Ackroyd* (*Limits* Ch. 3).
This type of discoursive strategy is proposed by the narrator many times.
Here is another example:

> We must remember that his [Roberto] was a time when people invented or
> reinvented images of every sort to discover in them recondite and revelatory
> meanings. It sufficed to see, I will not say a beautiful flower or a crocodile, but
> merely a basket, a ladder, a sieve, or a column, and one would try to build
> around it a network of things that at first glance nobody had seen there (pp.
> 345-346).

What "at first glance nobody had seen there," but what the *Model Semiotic Reader* is able to see, is that a "basket," a "ladder," a "a sieve, a column" and a "net" are the components of a pentagram; where the web of the "basket" suggests the lines of a pentagram and "ladder" stands for "musical scale." The Italian word *scala* that appears in the original allows the semantic ambiguity between "ladder" and "musical scale," which in the English translation is lost. "Column," in addition to the obvious meaning of "architectural element," in Italian *colonna* has another meaning, a "series of elements vertically disposed, specially in an orderly way, one under the other" (*serie di elementi disposti verticalmente, spec. ordinatamente l'uno sotto l'altro*) (Zingarelli 1983). The image represented by the lines of the pentagram crossed by the musical notes is expressed by *setaccio*, and in this case the English "sieve" is equally useful. The *Gestalt* game that this enumeration produces is due to the semantic ambiguity of the terms used by the narrator. In one *Gestalt* configuration the reader sees a group of heterotopic objects; it is only by over imposing the musical context over these objects that another *Gestalt*–a pentagram–appears. If we over impose another context, Eco's intertext, yet another *Gestalt* appears, because the "net" (here developed in "network") and the "ladder" were already used in *The Name of the Rose* to re-write Wittgenstein. [26] This intertextual reference emphasizes the meaning of "Orainge" as a mere clue (to be thrown away after it serves its purpose) which shows the structural musical context of the novel. Nothing better that the famous Wittgensteinian ladder to describe the rule of the *Interpretant* within the process of Peircean semiosis. Metaphor, theory and intertext are interwoven in order to construct this meaningful gestaltic game. In Eco's theoretical intertext an "emblem" is a "drawing which reproduces something, but in a stylized form, so that recognizing the object represented is less important than recognizing a content 'other' for which the represented object stands" (*SPL* 17). Emblems are iconic and arbitrary signs. Eco uses the examples of the Cross, the Crescent and the Hammer and the sickle, which stand for Christianity, Islam and Communism, respectively. He specifies that with the common use of the word they are considered as "symbols":

> They [emblems] are commonly called symbols, but in a sense opposite to that adopted for formulas and diagrams. Whereas the latter are quite empty, open to any meaning, [but according to definite rules][27] the former are quite full, filled with multiple but definite meanings (*SPL* 17)

In *The Island of the Day Before*, the emblem (the dove) is "quite full, filled with multiple but definite meanings," as we saw in section 5. Its interpretant is a musical score, a diagram (a pentagram) with formulas (musical), "open to any meaning" but "according to precise rules." In the theoretic opposition between emblems and formulas or diagrams, the problem between openness and closure of meanings is focused. In its narrative application (dove-score) the problem of openness and closure of the texts is resolved.

> During the Middle Ages, the word fuga (flight) was in musical terminology used to designate what he would call a canon. (H. T. David *Bach's Musical Offering*).

9. The Flight of Semiosis: the Fugue (fuga) of Interpretants.

The dove, even though lives inside a textual universe, is not an *onoma*, so is not at all a prisoner in the Jamesonian "prison-house" of the language, but flies freely over the sky of signs, which in Eco's semiotics is the open and boundless space of the "encyclopedia." Yet, its freedom to fly, that is the fugue of the interpretants in Peirce's unlimited semiotics, adheres to certain rules, the context is one; and in this case it is a musical, baroque and semiotic (Peircean) one.

The interpretant of the sign-dove–a musical score for the flute entitled "Orainge"–indicates to the reader a musical possible world as the context of the novel. Rethinking and re-reading the novel in a musical key throws new light on the different temporal parallels: the past and the present of the narration which coexist side by side within the structure of the novel, and the parallel times of the ship and of "the island of the day before," which are different notwithstanding their close proximity. Many things now appear through a new perspective; as it is the case for the image of the compass (also a musical term) in the poem, in chapter 16, and Roberto's vain battle to escape from his own time and to reach the day before on the island. Moreover, the specular structure of musical canon explains the many repetitions and reflected images that appear in the novel: Roberto and Ferrante, the *Daphne* and the *Tweede Daphne*, the novel within a novel, etc.

"The Poetics of the Open Work," the first chapter of *The Open Work* (1962), begins with the description of some musical compositions proposed by Eco as examples of messages neither concluded nor definite, but rather as having "a possibility of various organizations entrusted to the interpreter's initiative"; Eco proposes then an analogy between "interpretation" and "performance." In the "Introduction" to the *Tascabili Bompiani* edition of *Lector in Fabula* (1985), Eco tells us how the ideas regarding the openness of contemporary art works originated through his contact with contemporary music (Maderna, Boulez, Pousseur, Stockhausen):

> Between 1958 and 1959 I was working at Rai [a television network] in Milan. Two floors above my office there was the musical phonology laboratory, then

run by Luciano Berio [. . .] That is where a musical experiment originally titled "Omaggio a Joyce" was born; it was a sort of 40 minute radio transmission which begins reading chapter 11 of Ulysses (the one with the mermaids, an orgy of onomatopoeia and alliterations), in three languages, English, French and Italian; but then, since Joyce himself had said that the structure of this chapter was a "fuga per canonem," Berio began to overlap the texts in a fugue manner, first English over English, than English over French and so on, a kind of polylingual and Rabelaisian Fra Martino Campanaro, with big orchestral effects (p. v).

In 1994 the experiment is transposed into a textual environment, but maintaining certain basic characteristics: the musical structure, the sea isotopy, the polylingual play (the novel adds a fourth language: German), the overlapping strategy. The structure of The Island now appears as a narrative transposition of the musical laboratory experiments, of the "Rai" studio, that took place at the end of the fifties. The narrator did the same thing with the ships, the characters and the narrative levels, that Berio did with the works of Joyce–that is, to superimpose them as if they were a fugue. The result is a sort of textual analog of a vast musical composition made up of multiple texts, which the reader can also read and interpret by overlapping them differently each time.

In this case the s-code of the text (the musical code), rather than limiting the meaning to a fixed and established one, opens the door to innumerable senses. The Rortyan distinction between "weak" and "strong" textualists–– between those who think "that there really is a secret code and that once it's discovered we shall have gotten the text right" and those who do not " care about the distinction between discovery and creation, finding and making" (1982:152) is not able to classify the reader of this novel: a fantastic animal with body of "weak" textualist and head of "strong" textualist (and wings of dove). And the dove of The Island flies high over the Rortyan distinction, which is unable to explain its flight. It is an abnormal member not only of zoological classification, but theoretical as well.

The movement of the dove becomes the movement of the reader; the "flight" of the dove is a "fugue," and the reading of the text also takes a "fugue of interpretants"– a "flight" which, as we have seen, adheres to certain rules. Through its musical flight, the dove "fugues" from a closed universe of words and texts towards the boundless universe of signs; it frees itself from the "prison-house of language" to connect with the open universe of the encyclopedia. Through the creation of this "theoretic metaphor." Eco has also "fugued"; he has freed himself from any connection with post-structuralism and textualism, and has escaped from an uncomfortable classification.

"This sentence is false." Here we seem to have the irreducible essence of
antinomy: a sentence that is true if and only if it is false. (W.V. Quine *The ways
of paradox*).

10. All Writers Lie: A Fake Textual Paradox between Theory and Writing

As we have seen so far, discovering the cipher opens the text to a multiplicity of readings. *The Island* is not a *roman à clef* in the traditional sense–that
is, the reader has a definitive meaning of the text, once it has been deciphered. Instead, this is a *"roman à clef* in progress." *The Island of the Day
Before* is a paradoxical text; while it has each of the characteristics with
which an open work was defined in 1962 (generic indetermination, variety,
indefinite), it remains closed and enigmatic until the meaning of the dove is
understood. The emblem of the dove is a strategy of control of the
interpretation–it is a guardian of the text that closes the door to whomever
does not play by its rules, but once they are accepted, the text opens to the
infinite cooperation of the Model Reader.

The dove is an animal of two worlds that flies through parallel times. On
a narrative level, it is like Escher's paradoxical objects and becomes the
perfect metaphor for Eco's interpretative theory–in itself, a theoretical object that comes out from the openness and arrives at the limitation is nevertheless a single object, although difficult to perceive on a first reading. This
is the logic of the design in the figure 1, proposed by Eco (*Limits* and *Walks*)
as "a good visual metaphor of a self-voiding fiction":

> The celebrated optical illusion [. . .] which on a first "reading" gives both the
> impression of a coherent world and a feeling of some inexplicable impossibil-
> ity. On the second reading (to read it properly, one should try to design it), one
> realizes how it is bidimensionally possible but tridimensionally absurd (*Limits*
> 82).

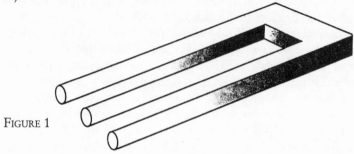

Figure 1

Many things in the novel follow the logic of figure 1: the temporal structure (suspended between the past and the present of the narration), the

space (between the time of the ship and the preceding time of the island), the logic of its reading (difficult balance between opening and closing), and even the topological description of the *Daphne*. That is why the narrator states that to understand the *Daphne* one must try to draw it.

The dialectical movement between two polarities is a characteristic of Eco's narrative theory and his general semiotic theory is an attempt to trace a semiotic "middle way." In the "Introduction" to *Semiotics and the Philosophy of Language* Eco points out that "contemporary semiotics is perturbed in front of an alternative: its own basic concept is sign or semiosis?" In this disjunction "sign" stands for the tradition of Genevan structuralism, "semiosis" the posterior interest for the interpretation of texts and for the "pleasure of semiosis" that leads to deconstruction. Eco's theoretic intention is to "go beyond the alternative" and propose a middle ground. On the one hand, trying to overcome the concept of sign as a biplanary entity, on the assumption of the concept of the triad "where the third term, interpretant, automatically generates a new interpretation, and so on, until infinity," while on the other, attempting to establish the theoretical limits of this possible infinite semiosis, keeping in check the "excesses" of interpretation.

Through the emblem of the dove, Eco solves, on a narrative level, some old theoretical problems: the dove's *difficilis* flight fixes the difficult balance between aperture and closure of the text; it exemplifies the necessary dialectic between sign and semiosis; it shows the importance of the context in the process of interpreting texts, and it demonstrates that the Peircean unlimited semiosis is limited by the *final interpretant*. Similarly, the author inhabits the theoretical space of a difficult equilibrium, suspended between historic oppositions. His creation, the dove, belongs to a narrative world of temporal intersections, suspended between the present and the past. On a representational level, this double *Gestalt* is present also in the Godelian Moebius' fence, in Escher's lithographs (cfr. Miranda 1996), and, not to leave the quotation incomplete, in Bach's fugue.

Achilles: Could we also play the Endlessly Rising canon? It's my favorite canon.
Tortoise: Reentering Introduction Creates Endlessly Rising Canon, After RICERCAR. (D. R. Hofstadter *Godel, Escher, Bach*)

11. BACK TO THE BEGINNING OR "RICERCAR"

It has already been stated that, if the story of Roberto de La Griva "would be merely the tale of an unhappy lover," it would be really "too little to make a story with a proper beginning and a proper end"(p. 512). But it is all dependent upon the type of reader we are, or chose to become. In a novel such as this, constructed with juxtapositions of other texts, the Semiosic Model Reader can choose to read the topoi tied to the tradition of the adventure stories, of seafaring novels, of *Bildungsroman*, and even of unhappy love-stories. The Semiotic Model Reader, a sort of metanarrative Sherlock Holmes, will choose to read the self-referentiality written in the text. And what both types of readers have in common is their search, potentially infinite, for meaning(s).

If the musical movement of the dove is a "fuga," the reader's is instead a movement of *ricercare*.[28] In Italian the verb *ricercare* means "to search with attention and determination" (*cercare con cura e impegno*), or "to search again" (*tornare a cercare*) (Zingarelli 1983). In this way, the image of the Model Reading of the novel is related to the origin itself of the musical fugue form originated in the "ricercar" or "ricercare."[29] As Hofstadter (1979) suggests, the musical movement of the "ricercar" is related to the movement of going back to the beginning. Nothing more relevant then for a novel whose author goes back in his own story to the late fifties, to the period of the musical laboratory in Milan, and to the beginning of his theoretical writings. And therefore, it is quite logical for the Model Reader's activity to be that of going back to the beginning and to re-read the novel, potentially *in aeternum*; but, "Would he stop one day?" (p. 501).

Claudia Miranda

Intertextuality, Metaphors, and Metafiction as Cognitive Strategies in *The Island of the Day Before*[*]

"You could be learned in a playful fashion."
(U. Eco)

The Island of the Day Before (1995) is Umberto Eco's third encyclopedic postmodern collage and essay-novel which focuses, among many other things, on the practice of semiosis, on palimpsests, on meta-narrativity, and on the connection between "knowledge and power."[1] Capitalizing on three most significant heterogeneous historical eras, the XIVth and XVIIth Centuries (two extraordinary periods of history marked by revolutionary transformations in all sectors of society),[2] and the XXth Century (an era exemplified by frequent changes and by so called postmodern pastiches and recyclings of every cultural phenomenon from the past) Eco's trilogy[3] illustrates how man's eternal quest for knowledge and power has not changed since the days of Ulysses' "folle volo."[4] In fact, his novels confirm that the epistemological and heuristic values of encyclopedic *hypertexts* continue to attract readers from the days of Dante to those of Joyce, Borges, Pynchon, and Eco.

With each of his publications, Umberto Eco seems to constantly re-elaborate his works on semiotics, mass culture, textual strategies, and interpretation. Not surprisingly, his intertextual and meta-historical "possible worlds" share several characteristics while they all underline some of the author's most familiar notions on the philosophy of language which we have seen discussed in his collection of essays and theoretical works. His narratives clearly show how authors often rewrite the same text–whether one of their own, or of others–intentionally or unintentionally, over and over again.[5] L. Dolezel summarizes it very well as he maintains (cf. *The Themata of Eco's Semiotics of Literature* in Part II of this anthology) that Eco is an author who keeps on writing on the "infinite variations" of his favorite themes.

1. FROM SIGNS AND METAPHORS TO METAFICTIONS

For nearly thirty years Eco has focused on signs, irony and metaphors as instruments for "lying"[6] –that is, for saying something and meaning something else–in both his scientific work and in his eclectic collections of essays beginning with *Opera aperta* (1962) and *Diario minimo* (1963). Since the eighties, he has chosen possible worlds which combine historical and detective fictions for discussing the same linguistic, philosophical and epistemological concerns that he had treated in his theoretical works. In short, writing novels for Eco has become an entertaining way for bringing together theories and practice. For example, in *The Island* Eco's familiar definition of texts as "machines for generating interpretations"[7] is brilliantly demonstrated through fascinating stories and engrossing dialogues.

As many critics usually do, I also resort to the term "postmodern" in describing Eco's encyclopedic fiction. I use it mainly for convenience, and probably for lack of another term.[8] Nonetheless, I should clarify that "postmodernism"–which has become a catch-all term with which many critics apply their own notion of *tout se tient*–for Eco has definite heuristic, metaphoric and performative[9] connotations that we find illustrated throughout his novels. Beginning with Postscript to 'The Name of the Rose', whenever the author has discussed postmodernism we can see that for him the interdisciplinary and encyclopedic features associated with postmodernism are appreciated not just as forms of parody, kitsch or pastiche, but also as instruments that he parallels with semiotic practices and epistemological textual metaphors. In essence, metaphor, parody, binomial structures,10 unlimited semiosis, intertextuality, citationism, or rhizoma, for Eco are all interactive cognitive vehicles for bridging (for bringing closer) different terms, images, ideas, and aspects of culture(s). By the same token his fiction is a confirmation of Peircean pragmatics of semiosis by which "interpretation of ideas by ideas, signs by signs, is the way meaning grows and evolves" (Kevelson, forthcoming). I would add that his intricate rhizomatic novels are all careful (con)textualizations of intellectual and aesthetic issues illustrated through semiotic readings of culture (Lotman 1990).

As Eco exploits parody, intertextuality, kitsch, pastiches, rhizomatic structures, palimpsests, and citationism, he shows that knowledge is dynamic, cumulative, associative, and, most of all, interactive. From *The Rose* to *The Island* he resorts very cleverly to absorbing stories, familiar frames, or prefabricated images that can best depict his basic theories on cultural trends, interpretation, pragmatics of language, philosophy, and aesthetics. Furthermore, the rhizomatic or labyrinthine intertextuality[11] at the foundation of his palimpsests–explained repeatedly by William to Adso in *The Rose*–is an excellent vehicle for demonstrating how something new can be derived by juxtaposing and embedding the old and the new, past and present.

In this article, I shall focus mainly on Eco's familiar exploitations of palimpsests and intertextuality and on his overall notion that our language and "conceptual systems" are metaphoric (Lakoff and Johnson 1980). And, just as metaphors function as vehicles for bridging concepts, images, and texts in our archeology of knowledge and culture (Foucault 1972) so does Eco's intertextual postmodernism. In fact, very much in line with Lakoff's notion of metaphor, his fiction demonstrates how we understand ideas, concepts, and realities in terms of other ideas, concepts and realities, and how we certainly understand books in term of other books, authors with other authors, and so on.

In *The Island* we find several of Eco's familiar discussions on metaphor, especially from Semiotics and Philosophy of Language (see Ch. 3 on metaphor, semiosis and the importance of Emanuele Tesauro in the study of the philosophy of language). References to Tesauro, and to other writers like Marino and Donne, underline throughout the novel of how experience, images, ars combinatoria, intelligence, and imagination combine in creating (poetic) metaphors which serve as powerful cognitive tools. At the same time, many of these considerations on metaphors (dealing with icons, ingenuity, analogies, transference of meaning, frames, intertextual scenes, etc.) make us realize that they are also applicable to (Eco's) "possible worlds" which indeed function as bridges–as they establish similarities, correlations, and analogies between texts and authors, past and present, fiction and reality. Furthermore, *The Island* suggests many interesting analogies between (neo)-baroque and postmodernism, as they both rely on various forms of metaphors as instruments of cognition, ordering, structuring, and conceptualizing, as well as elements for evoking "wonder".

Readers accustomed to the author's talent for speaking both synchronically and diachronically about specific topics will notice that while he narrates about father Emanuele's machine for creating metaphors, he is also echoing a number of theories on the "interaction view"[12] of metaphor, from Aristotle to Vico, and from Peirce to the most recent works of Lakoff or Ricoeur.[13] It may be interesting to recall that in *Semiotics and the Philosophy of Language* Eco begins his chapter on metaphor quoting G.B.Vico. My contention is that Vico's notion of metaphors as "little fables" fits quite well within Eco's application of metaphors as micro-narratives. Both seem to follow the Aristotelian notion of metaphors used to reveal meaning and to delight while learning.

Eco's "possible worlds" show how writing entails quoting, embedding and rewriting other texts. Hardly by chance all three of his novels are allegedly generated from found manuscripts. And, as he experiments with his own strategies of (re)working "palimpsests" he brings to our attention a process that in the last four decades has received plenty of attention, in a variety of forms, from writers like Borges,[14] Calvino and Pynchon; from critics such as Genette,[15] Barth[16] and Bloom;[17] and from movie directors like

Woody Allen and Spielberg. The whole ironic concept of not being able to kill our (textual) forefathers is reiterated in the conclusion of *The Island*:

> . . . if from this story I wanted to produce a novel, I would demonstrate once again that it is impossible to write except by making a palimpsest of a rediscovered manuscript–without ever succeeding in eluding the Anxiety of Influence (p. 512).

However, it should be clear that as Eco recalls Bloom, he is in fact speaking about that general "Anxiety of Influence" that accompanies the writing of most texts–especially those that flaunt the idea that all texts are by nature palimpsests and intertexts. Naturally, everybody has a precursor (a father). Among the innumerable literary analogies present in *The Island* we can take the following example: Petrarch (for his style, conceits, emblems, symbols, metaphors, etc.) is a forerunner of Marino, Donne and other 17th century poets (for their use of ingenuity, device, hyperboles, or witty puns), who in turn are some of the forerunners of postmodern writers (like Eco). This type of logic on the "anxiety of influence" is implicit for many other obvious, or not so evident, intertextual allusions to writers, thinkers and artists that we encounter throughout *The Island*.

Eco's novels are in fact an ingenious and entertaining confirmation of the principle that elements of continuity, repetition and difference, can be found in every period of history. However, in his work one must be careful not to confuse "unlimited intertextuality" and "anxiety of influence" with "hermetic drift". The author has argued against this confusion in several of his essays (see in particular *L'idea deforme* and *The Limits of Interpretation*) and especially in his second novel, *Foucault's Pendulum*.

On the surface, *The Island* is another Ecoesque international postmodern pastiche. Here we find erudite 17th century texts fused with 19th-century popular novels, such as *Robinson Crusoe*, *Treasure Island*, *The Mysterious Island*, *The Three Musketeers*, *The Man in the Iron Mask*, and *Gulliver's Travels*. And, for this neo-baroque picaresque romance that at one point in the story is accurately, and self-ironically, referred to by its narrator as "A highly acute chiasmus" (p. 500) the author goes back to the development of the genre of the novel in early XVIIth century, when Italian authors such as G.B. Manzini defined the novel precisely as a "stupendous and glorious machine."[18]

In this third entertaining, and equally challenging, possible world Eco returns to themes and topics present in *The Name of the Rose* and in *Foucault's Pendulum*, as he resumes several discussions on epistemological, philosophical, rhetorical and general semiotic questions which send us, once again, as far back into history as to Aristotle and to the *Bible*. And once again he treats linguistic and intellectual issues which continue to be debated repeatedly since the Middle Ages. Consequently, Roberto de La

Griva, like his predecessors Gugliemo, Adso and Casaubon, is deeply concerned with the practices of interpreting signs, symbols and metaphors, as
well as with issues about language, knowledge and culture. These and many
other debates in Eco's fiction are also meant to demonstrate how many of
the allegedly new postmodern practices existed long before contemporary
critics began to argue against the flattening and leveling off effects of
postmodernism. And thus, with each novel Eco portrays the unending
process of "repetition and difference" (Foucault; Deleuze; Derrida) which
best describes the ongoing practices of manifesting knowledge and artistic
creation through the ages.

The Island is overwhelmingly (but pleasantly) saturated with intertextual
echoes that readers, depending on their cultural competence, can recall
from a variety of interdisciplinary sources ranging from semiotics, philosophy and reader reception theories, to a gamut of postmodern narrative
theories–especially those expounded by John Barth in "The Literature of
Exhaustion" and "The Literature of Replenishment." Barth, Thomas
Pynchon[19] and Donald Barthelme are three key American postmodern authors who have influenced Eco during his writing of his own best-sellers.
Italo Calvino and Jorge Luis Borges remain, nonetheless, his main mentors
for a type of postmodernism that is at the same time minimalist and encyclopedic. Furthermore, Eco's polyphonic (inter)texts point to a type of
intertextuality that recall not only writers like Julia Kristeva, Roland
Barthes and Jacques Derrida (three illustrious members of the French connection to the work of Michail Bakhtin), but also American authors and
critics such as Leslie Fiedler, John Barth and Harold Bloom.

2. SAILING ON THE SEA OF INTERTEXTUALITY

Eco's witty and parodic international postmodernism sails freely around
The Island, and we can feel the presence of the model (and empirical) author
winking at us from behind every allusion to characters like Don Quixote,
Cyrano De Bergerac, the Three Musketeers, Rastignac, Captain Nemo,
Captain Bligh, Robinson Crusoe, Esmeralda, Manzoni's Brother
Cristoforo, and Indiana Jones, to mention just a few.

In the opening chapters we learn that Roberto might have an imaginary
evil twin brother named Ferrante.[20] We also notice that Roberto has a
knack for attracting many mentors from whom he learns different life skills
and ideas. Among his several teachers we must recall at least Saint-Savin (for
his lessons on love and war, and on the art of the novel) and Father
Emanuele (for his lectures on the art of inventing and using metaphors).
And we should also mention Roberto's second Signora (named Lilia, because of her lily white complexion) who teaches him that a *"préciuese* is
won only with words" (p. 161). Later in the novel Roberto learns about

swimming, theology, science, philosophy, and the creation of the universe, from his last teacher, the Jesuit Father Caspar.[21]

The Island is a ludic neo-baroque[22] "narrative machine" that opens with "unabashed conceits" (p. 1) from a narrator who is just as interested in dialoguing with his readers as he is in narrating his adventurous story. Moreover, in his demonstrations of how writing fiction is in essence an attempt to give order to a chaotic reality the author sends us frequently back and forth between "real," "possible" and "infinite worlds" in a gamut of mirror-images, echoes, doubles, micro-narratives, and *mise en abymes* reinforce. However, even with its many flashbacks, authorial parenthetical statements,[23] digressions,[24] metafictional games, clever juxtapositions of first and third person narration, and blatant illustrations of narrativity, the plot of *The Island* is for the most part remarkably captivating.

Amidst all sorts of intellectual debates, intertextual allusions, and demonstrations of textual strategies, develops a wonderful and intriguing neo-baroque *Bildungsroman*[25] of Roberto de La Griva Pozzo di San Patrizio[26] (from the age of sixteen to about thirty). His life story begins in Piedmont during the Thirty Years War–in 1630, to be exact–as Roberto accompanies his father to the battle of Casale which was to decide whether the French or the Spaniards would control that region. The pages dedicated to the battle in which Roberto's father dies as a hero are filled with humorous Quixotic echoes, swashbuckling scenes (reminiscent of a number of entertaining parodies of the astounding actions of novels like *The Three Musketeers*), and parodic heroic adventures of super-spectacular Hollywood movies.

The plot unfolds as Roberto, while in Paris (where he is getting a more complete educational, sentimental and cultural), is wrongly accused of treason, thanks to the doings of his envious and mischievous twin brother Ferrante. In order to clear his name, Roberto is forced (by Mazarin and Richelieu) to spy for France. His mission is to sail on an English ship, the *Amaryllis*, and to spy on Dr. Byrd, who is on his way to the Pacific Islands searching for the secret of the longitudes, to be found, supposedly, near the newly discovered Salomon Islands.

During his odyssey at sea Roberto is shipwrecked not on an island, like Robinson Crusoe, but, ironically, on an abandoned Dutch ship, the *Daphne*, off the cost of an unchartered island (today part of the Fijis, where the 180th meridian passes). Roberto learns this secret and other valuable information mainly from Father Caspar, an old Jesuit priest who is the only survivor aboard the *Daphne*. It is both amusing and ironic to see how whereas a scientist like Dr. Byrd uses the magical "Powder of Sympathy" for his experiments in trying to solve the mystery of the longitude, a Jesuit, Father Caspar, relies on clocks and other scientific mechanical devices, like the amazing "specula melitense," to achieve the same end.

Roberto can never reach the symbolic island because he cannot swim. This proves to be convenient for the plot as Roberto must watch and imagine life on the island from a distance. From the deck of the *Daphne* he can only try to scrutinize, through a telescope,[27] the colorful and fantastic coastline as he attempts to spot a mysterious and mystical dove–the emblematic "Orange Colored Dove" hiding in the exotic vegetation (see above all Ch. 26 "Delights for the Ingenious: A Collection of Emblems"). This chapter is loaded with numerous allusions to the semiosic process of reading signs and interpreting symbols. The references to the different possible meanings of the "Dove" will easily recall similar passages in *The Rose* (e.g. on the different meanings of the lion) and several pages from *A Theory of Semiotics* and *Semiotics and the Philosophy of Language*, where the author discusses signs, symbols, emblems, and metaphors. From this point on Tesauro's and Galileo's "telescopes" become both ingenious vehicles and metaphors for bringing together (bridging) different (distant) images and realities. And, as we would expect, the author has plenty of fun with the many playful connections and associations made possible by these "telescopes" which are frequently underlined for his readers. See for example how Roberto, as he looks through the telescope, attempts to possess at the same time the Island and Lilia (see pp. 67, 197, 363).

3. Possible Order Through Possible Worlds

In his solitude, Roberto has plenty of time for reconstructing various events in his life and for recollecting his lost love, his "Lady" Lilia (with many echoes of the Petrarca, Marino and Donne lyrical tradition). Roberto also contemplates a myriad of intellectual and existential issues that reveal his doubts about life and his concern with death (see Ch. 37). But, what proves to be most fascinating in these pages of Roberto's memoirs is the way the metafictional elements that the author had treated sporadically in the story, are brought to the foreground by a narrator who wishes to see himself as both narrator and protagonist of his own story. Now the playful interaction of authorities, intentions, point of view, omniscience, and authorial intrusions become even more blatant (and more amusing), as we notice how an ironic intrusive author (Eco) handles an intrusive narrator (Roberto) who must control an intrusive character (Ferrante). And of course, they are all being watched by some intrusive readers.

The reader is mentioned (or addressed to) at least thirteen times in the novel. In fact, Eco–the advocator of "inferential walks"–expects his readers to jump (intrude) into the story, any time they wish to. By the same token, readers are also constantly reminded that in the "Land of Romance" one "must suspend disbelief" (p. 260) [and here we see how a common sense statement about "possible worlds" is at the same time an echo of Coleridge's notion of "suspension of disbelief" that Eco has recently commented in *Six Walks in the Fictional Woods* (p. 77)]. Here is an example of how the reader is treated (and manipulated?) by the narrator:

> ... (unless the reader chooses to insinuate that because from now on I need him on deck full-time, and finding no contradiction among his papers, I am freeing him from all illness, with authorial arrogance) (p. 280).

In the first part of the novel Roberto learns a lot from Saint Savin, including some concepts about novels. In the second part some of these notions of narrativity are put into practice as Roberto transforms his initial "Theater of Memory"(p. 106), and using his thoughts, letters and diary he begins to write a story within a story. Roberto relies on his clever metafiction to spy on Ferrante; first, in Paris (where he continues to impersonate Roberto in front of Mazarin), and then, on the stolen ship, the *Daphne* II–the "*Tweede Daphne*" (yes! another case of twins)–which is on its way to find the *Amaryllis*. The pages dedicated to Ferrante's incredible escape from jail, his adventurous search for Roberto, the mutiny on the *Tweede Daphne*, and his final moments on the island, are all filled with some of the most fascinating cinematographic action-packed images in the novel. These scenes, as well as those in which Roberto's "Lady" comes to Ferrante's rescue with an army of human derelicts, clearly demonstrate Eco's talent in incorporating into his writing baroque paintings, several treatises, scenes from popular novels (especially Dumas' *The Man in the Iron Mask*), and a pastiche of movies which includes, naturally, *Mutiny on the Bounty*.

In the novel within the novel the narrator Roberto is at times a clear echo–a double–of the empirical and model author (Umberto). They employ similar storytelling techniques and seem to have the same encyclopedic competence in the area of narrativity and textual strategies:

> Perhaps conceiving Romances means living through our own characters, making them live in our world, and delivering ourselves and our creatures to the minds of those to come, even when we will no longer be able to say I . . .
> But if this is so, it is up to me alone to banish Ferrante from my own world, forever, to have his banishment governed by divine justice, and to create the conditions whereby I can be united with Lilia.
> Filled with renewed enthusiasm, Roberto decided to conceive the last chapter of his story.
> He did not know that, especially when their authors are now determined to die, stories often write themselves, and go where they want to go (p. 482).

Throughout the second part of the novel Roberto enjoys living vicari-
ously all of his brother's desires, doings, and adventures. But at the end,
once he determines that he cannot allow Ferrante, even as a character, to
replace him entirely, he decides it is time to kill his evil double and fic-
tional-self. Consequently, Ferrante ends his final hours, on the island, in a
terrifying "hellish" scenario (The same type of hell that Roberto experienced in his nightmare after he had been bitten by a poisonous stone-fish in
the corals). Unfortunately, this also implies killing part of (if not all of)
himself as a character and as a narrator. And thus, as we see in the conclusion, Roberto has very little to live for after Ferrante and his "Lady" are
gone.

4. NEO-BAROQUE AND POSTMODERNISM

The plot, the use of language(s), the style, and the structure of The Island all
confirm that Eco continues to have fun with his possible worlds.[28] For this
third narration he revisits the history and culture of the 17th century with
the same curiosity and passion that accompanied his research for the writing of The Name of the Rose and Foucault's Pendulum.[29]
    The XVIIth Century is a time when scientific discoveries contribute to
the loss of a "center" in the universe. It is also a period characterized by
political struggles for power and control of the "new world" among European nations, by conflicts between Church and states, and by Baroque aesthetics. The label Baroque is generally associated with the clever usages of
language (especially the ingenious applications of metaphors and "mots
precieux") and with different games of visual effects involving light, shadows, reflections, and perception. Moreover, baroque art and literature
thrive on images of sensuality and hedonism, on psychological games, on
masks, doubles, intrigues, deus-ex-machina, simulation, performance, hyperboles, and, in short, on everything theatrical.[30] The Island certainly capi-
talizes on all of these baroque elements (as well as on the clichés connected
with them). This may also explain why all the characters talk and act as if
they were on a stage, and why Roberto transforms his floating island into a
theater:

> . . .and the Daphne was transformed into a Theater of Memory, as such theaters
> were conceived in his day, where every feature recalled to him an episode,
> remote or recent, in his story. . .(p. 106).

From beginning to end The Island confirms that Eco has carefully studied the XVIIth Century paying close attention to its overall culture and

especially to epistemological and ontological issues that continue to assail man today. Of course Eco exploits Baroque elements just as he does any other intertextual echo that can help him present his views on semiotic practices, and on writing, reading and interpreting texts. We recall that in *The Name of the Rose* Eco makes references to Aristotle, Saint Augustine, Roger Bacon and William of Occam as he alludes repeatedly to the development of the science of signs. In *The Island* the author discusses signs, symbols and metaphors, and gets much closer to Peirce's semiotics as he makes references to the works of authors like Tesauro, Galileo, Locke, and Vico, who were also concerned with language, semantics, knowledge, and the overall interpretation of signs. In *The Search for the Perfect Language* Eco had pointed out how in the XVIIth century we find some major milestones in the development of the science of signs. In *The Island* he reiterates this notion with allusions to T. Hobbes, Sir Francis Bacon, and above all to J. Locke's *Essay Concerning Human Understanding*[31]

In addition to scientific discoveries, baroque aesthetics, and overall concerns with the nature of language, the 17th century also witnesses the development of the novel. In fact, baroque and picaresque "romances" have a lot in common with Eco's art of mixing genres, topics, plots, languages, and styles. Naturally Eco is fully aware that except for a relatively small group of XVIIth Century specialists, to the general public, narratives such as Manzini's *Cretideo* (1637) are neither as popular nor as well known as XIXth and XXth century novels. Nonetheless, at a time when the expression "postmodern" has become so general (especially in reference to contemporary narratives), the author feels that it is time to show how literary and artistic pastiches were conceived and practiced in the past.

My contention is that with *The Island* Eco feels that it is timely to narrate some of the same elements that critics like Omar Calabrese have examined in making several analogies between baroque aesthetics and postmodernism (Calabrese 1992). As it is also timely to narrate elements of other brilliant critical studies on Baroque, such as those of Mario Praz on seventeenth century imagery and on the relationships between literature and the visual arts.[32] These are some of the studies that may have also expanded Eco's own encyclopedic competence on English metaphysical poets like Donne and Crashaw. Studies that readers may want to consult for a better appreciation of a century that the author, in the closing lines of the novel, capitalizing on a cliché about the "mannered exercises" of baroquism, ironically, comments: "You know how they wrote in that century. . . . People with no soul" (p. 513).

The baroque novel provides Eco with some of the best models of thematic and stylistic compositions through which one can teach, entertain, and make readers "marvel" in front of a work of art. Marvelous constructions which at the same time draw attention to the competence and erudition of the author.

In his own demonstration of the art of making readers "wonder"[33] and marvel, Eco resorts to a variety of appropriations from the works of the great masters of baroque art. Among the numerous Italian protagonists of the era we distinguish two well known writers, G. Marino and E. Tesauro, and a scientist, Galileo–all three known for their fascination with metaphors and other rhetorical devices. Baroque scholars will immediately recognize the allusions to the poet of the "marvelous"[34] from the innumerable references to ingenuity, wit, conceit, and wonder (See above all Ch. 20, "Wit and the Art of Ingenuity"), even though the titles of Marino's works are not mentioned. Of course when John Donne's poem "A Valediction: Forbidding Mourning" (lines 21-32) is so shrewdly quoted by D'Igby (p. 163)[35] the British poet is also not named. The same case could be made for Gassendi and for many other writers and scientists alluded to in *The Island*. And one could argue that the appropriations of well known authors and artists are so obvious that they do not need to be named. Nonetheless, it is different with Emanuele Tesauro. Eco spends many pages on *The Aristotelian Telescope*, 1654 (see especially Ch. 9, "The Aristotelian Telescope") making sure that his protagonist, Father Emanuele, comes through as a clear *dramatis persona* of the XVIIth century writer under examination.

The central importance of Marino and Tesauro is easily understood after a few pages. The art of inventing metaphors, the practice of *ars combinatoria* and the overall process of creating images (especially by evoking synesthesia) are unquestionably some of the key motifs of this novel. Innumerable examples appear in chapters 9 through 11. Moreover, in the conclusion of Ch. 11, "The Art of Prudence," readers will find the whole discussion on "simulating" and "dissimulating" both amusing and enlightening, as I am sure that while Eco is talking about the power of metaphors he is also making allusions to the art (his own?) of fiction:

> Padre Emanuele's machine seems to me an image of Genius, which does not aim at striking or seducing but at discovering and revealing connections between things, and therefore becoming a new instrument of truth(p. 113).

In the discussions on Tesauro's "Aristotelic telescope" and in chapters 9 to 11, we get a definite impression that Eco is making a series of analogies between metaphors and meta-fictions, metaphors and *ars combinatoria*, metaphors and encyclopedic competence, and metaphor and postmodernism. In fact, as we understand the dynamics and the art of generating metaphors we also appreciate how Eco creates his intertexts as instruments or vehicles for knowing something more, and something else, about the subject(s) under examination. And thus, it is not surprising that in *The Is-land* metaphors are celebrated continuously:

> . . . the supreme Figure of all: Metaphor. If Genius, & therefore Learning, consists in connecting remote Notions & finding Similitude in things dissimi-lar, then Metaphor, the most acute and farfetched among Tropes, is the only one capable of producing Wonder, which gives birth to Pleasure, as do changes of scene in the theater. And if the Pleasure produced by Figures derive from learning new things without effort & many things in small volume, then Meta-phor, setting our mind to flying betwixt one Genus and another, allows us to discern in a single Word more than one Object (p. 90).
> There were gusts of wind, and for the first time he realized that he was in a floating house, which rocked like a cradle, as a slamming of doors enlivened the considerable bulk of that wooden womb.
> He savored this metaphor and wondered how Padre Emanuele would have read the ship as a source of enigmatic Devices. Then he thought of the Island and defined it as unattainable proximity. This fine conceit showed him, for the second time that day, the dissimilar similitude between the Island and the Lady, and he stayed awake into the night to pen the pages I have drawn on for this chapter (p. 100)

The study of the metaphor, as we can see in *Semiotics and the Philosophy of Language*, has always been at the center of Eco's linguistic and semiotics essays, and from the seventies on has become one of his main topic for discussing epistemological issues. As illustrated by Emanuele, but also by Roberto, metaphors are not just rhetorical devices; they are wonderful mechanisms which help us delve into the archeology of knowledge and aid us in understanding the very nature of language. Throughout the novel Eco makes sure that the function of metaphors is seen as applied to art, litera-ture and science–the way painters, poets, writers and scientists made exten-sive use of metaphors in the XVIIth Century. Consequently Aristotle, Cer-vantes, Marino, Donne, Tesauro, Galileo, as well as Góngora and *les précieux*, are all echoed in *The Island*. The various linguistic issues examined throughout the novel would in fact require a full length study dedicated exclusively to Eco's treatment of rhetorical figures such as syllogism, iso-morphism, chiasmus, and, above all, metaphors. And experts in music, such as Luciano Berio,[36] could show that throughout the novel Eco has integrated into his text many of the musical elements which exemplify the XVIIth Century.

The spirit of intertextuality and encyclopedia that gives life to the novel can be spotted even in the titles of each chapter. Each title is either a direct quote or a paraphrase of titles of texts from the Baroque era, such as *Wit and the Art of Ingenuity* (1639) of Matteo Pellegrini (Ch. 29), or *Dialogues of the Maximum Systems* (1632) of Galileo (Ch. 27). And in chapter 30,

"Anatomy of Erotic Melancholy" we notice how Eco combines very cleverly both R. Burton's and J. Ferrand's treatises on love.

In the same fashion that *The Name of the Rose* posits a clever juxtaposition of elements from the Middle Ages with those from our own postmodern era, in *The Island of the Day Before* there are implicit analogies between baroque and contemporary techniques of pastiche, intertextuality and kitsch that show how the past continues to be related (and to be pertinent) to our present culture. As we recall, in the *Postscript to The Name of the Rose* Eco presented some of his own notions of postmodernism:

> [. . .] We could say that every period has its own postmodernism. . . The past conditions us, harries us, blackmails us.
> [. . .] The postmodern reply to the modern consists of recognizing that the past, since it cannot really be destroyed, because its destruction leads to silence, must be revisited: but with irony, not innocence.[37]

Once again, this explains why authors like Cervantes, Galileo, Marino, Tesauro, Locke, or Donne, artists like Velasquez, Caravaggio or Arcimboldo, and thinkers such as Gassendi, Descartes, or Pascal, are all present in *The Island*. Many of the works associated with these illustrious names are in fact at the foundation of contemporary authors (like Saussure, Peirce, Bakhtin, Wittgenstein. Foucault, Barthes, Derrida, or Eco) concerned with signs, communication, interpretation and the overall process of semiosis,

As clearly suggested in the conclusion of *The Island*, today there is practically nothing new, not only in the world of fiction but also in our culture in general. And just as postmodernism plays with the whole idea that everything is *déjà vu, déjà lu, or déjà* heard, the author openly admits that in his novel(s), for the most part, he is repeating, recalling, quoting, or reconstructing issues, texts and events from our world encyclopedia. Of course we are also aware that Eco knows that in a parody, or in a pastiche, texts, names or works which are placed in a new context, automatically, through interaction, set in motion a chain of new meanings and interpretations. Naturally, it is up to the reader/interpreter to extract out of a text what he perceives to be new among so much imitation and repetition; just as it is up to the reader to use the text as a dynamic intertext–or, if we wish, as a metaphoric bridge–between the past and the present, the old and the new.

In *The Island* the search for a "punto fijo"[38] is not much different than the search for a metaphoric fixed point, or center, or "cosmic plan" that we had seen in Eco's previous narratives. Granted, here the need of a fixed point, or the allegorical search for God, are not as cerebral and esoteric as in *Foucault's Pendulum*. However, the quest for scientific and magical secrets is very much in line with the idea of gaining power by protecting secret texts, or by claiming to have a secret plan. As he exploits the universal appeal for the eternal quest for a metaphoric Grail, Eco resorts once again to familiar elements of detective novels, adventure stories, and challenging mind-games between detectives and spies, narrators and readers.

The debates with the Jesuit Father Caspar on God and his infinite powers go on for several pages, at times giving the sensation that they are perhaps a little too excessive. The same could be said for numerous passages where the narrator ponders on death, nothingness, infinity, and atomism. But because we are dealing with Eco we must ask if such blatant "excesses" of style and content are not deliberate. And in fact, they are essential elements of the author's art in portraying, faithfully, the aesthetic of hyperboles and exaggerations commonly associated with baroque imagination and baroquism in general. This is all part of recreating a particular *Zeitgeist* through careful representations of characters, language and key cultural issues of the times.

The Island, as it focuses on nature and science, does not appear to deal explicitly with libraries and labyrinths. However, this third novel is just as intertextual as Eco's other two encyclopedic narratives where we also find an ingenious parodic pastiche of erudite and popular culture. Moreover, it too is a palimpsest–a narrative to the "second degree" (to recall Genette) in which a narrator must combine the material of a found manuscript with his own inferences as he recounts the events of the novel. Therefore, once again we are confronted with an essay-novel in which the author has orchestrated a ludic (con)fusion and interaction of history, fiction, science, philosophy, theology, narrativity, semiotics, and cinema, for various levels of readers with different degrees of competence(s). Hollywood, which is alluded to on a number of occasions, is actually mentioned in the closing pages of the story (p. 509). This is a reminder that just as in the industry of fiction, in our contemporary postmodern film and TV industry parody, pastiches and recyclings have become a common practice. As we know, Eco has discussed the process of intertextuality in films on a number of occasions and in particular in his well known articles on *Casablanca*.[39]

5. POSTMODERNISM AND MODEL READERS

In *The Role of the Reader* Eco has discussed extensively how authors have their readers in mind as they write their texts and construct their "possible worlds." In writing *The Island* he must have had in mind, again, international model readers with an encyclopedic culture. For example, Eco took into consideration that English speaking readers would recognize intertextual echoes of XIXth century English and American novelists such as Defoe, Sterne, Stevenson, and Poe. At the same time, readers with a background in comparative and interdisciplinary studies would recall European writers like Cervantes, Donne, Marino, Tesauro, Ferrand, Scudery, Góngora, D'Urfé, Dumas, Verne, or Manzoni, as well as the works of scientists and philosophers such as Keppler, Galileo, Gassendi, Descartes, Pascal, and Spinoza. Moreover, some readers may see in the story of Roberto and Ferrante a variant on the theme of *The Strange Case of Dr. Jekyll and Mr. Hyde*, or perhaps will think of analogies with a Shakespearean play (such as *Much Ado About Nothing*) dealing with rivaling brothers. On the other hand, Italian readers may think of the tradition of baroque plays exemplified by Della Porta's *I due fratelli rivali* ("The Two Rival Brothers"), or of narratives by authors like G. Manzini.[40] And I would think that Eco has also calculated that to some, the split between Roberto and Ferrante, will bring to mind Calvino's fantastic *roman philosophique* of a divided-self in *The Cloven Viscount*.

In short, in *The Island* Eco is once again exemplifying through the use of implicit and explicit quotations the general principle of "unlimited intertextuality and semiosis"[41] at the foundation of writing and reading texts. Furthermore, all uses and abuses of quotations and of appropriations that might be constructed as a practice that verges on plagiarism are also part of a controlled ludic technique used to captivate the readers' attention. Eco has been discussing strategies of palimpsests, intertextuality and appropriation for a number of years. We need only to recall how in *The Limits of Interpretation* he speaks about the postmodern practice of exploiting, parodying, quoting, or merely alluding to previous texts and authors:

> There are imperceptible quotations, of which not even that author is aware, that are the normal effect of the game of artistic influence. There are also quotations of which the author is aware but which should remain ungraspable by the consumer. In these cases we are usually in the presence of a banal case of plagiarism.
> What is more interesting is when the quotation is explicit and recognizable, as happens in postmodern literature and art, which blatantly and ironically play on the intertextuality. . . .. There is a procedure typical of the postmodern narrative that has been much used recently in the field of mass communication: it concerns the ironic quotation of the commonplace (topos) (*Limits* 88).

As William of Baskerville argued so well in *The Name of the Rose*, texts do not stand alone and often they speak about other texts and among each other. Our own readings and interpretations of a text (as we mentally rewrite it) are conditioned by our previous readings and by our overall cultural encyclopedic competence which includes TV, cinema, advertising, comic books, and fairytales. But, I would add, we are also conditioned by our over all knowledge of the author of the text that we are reading.

6. A CONCLUSION

Umberto Eco continues to discuss interdisciplinary cultural issues that are relevant to academics and to the general public. At the same time he is not afraid to display his amazing encyclopedic competence as he presents his well documented research along with his personal views. In his usual witty and intelligent manner, Eco continues to apply his fundamental belief of "docere et delectare"–"to teach and to entertain at the same time." This is precisely what Roberto learns: "You could be learned and playful at the same time" (p. 431). And it is the same lesson that Umberto Eco repeats to his readers and critics, first in *The Name of the Rose* and then in the *Postscript*, where he speaks about breaking down the barrier between "art and enjoyability." This suggestion may echo American postmodernists such as L. Fiedler, T. Pynchon and J. Barth, [42] but it is mainly meant to recall a number of topics linked to the works of authors such as Galileo, C.P. Snow, W. Benjamin, or L. Fiedler, on the concept of bridging the "two cultures"[43] of science and the humanities.

The Island succeeds very well as an intertext in our cultural encyclopedia. To use again the metaphor of a bridge, Eco's novel is an effective ludic device which helps to close the gap between science, philosophy, linguistics, art, literature, and popular culture. In addition to being a most entertaining fiction, it is also a playful device that entices readers to brush up on Baroque aesthetics, and on XVIIth Century history in general. At the same time, in a typically Ecoesque fashion, *The Island* reminds us through a variety of amusing tricks of intertextuality of the many novels/texts that we have read, should have read, may have heard about, or may have seen adopted for TV or movies.

Umberto Eco's novels are ludic postmodern *hypertexts*. They are insightful examples of how culture is structured like an intricate web, like a rhizomatic encyclopedia of signs, images and texts. For readers who are willing, and capable, of playing Eco's games of intertextuality the fun continues as we close the cover of his texts and begin our quest for other texts in our own library. Whether or not we are able to move on from the obvious allusions to nineteenth century popular novels and to writers like Cervantes, Donne, Tesauro, or Ferrand, is entirely up to us. Eco has planted plenty of traces which lead us to these and many other authors who can teach us a great deal about Baroque aesthetics and postmodern techniques. However, in this type of quest the satisfaction should not come merely from our validation of a number of Eco's wealth of sources. Each "epiphany" (in discovering the relevance of a text, author, or event) should lead to the intellectual pleasure of acquiring new or additional knowledge from these sources.

Eco's heuristic fictions are ingenious metaphoric machines–epistemological bridges–that can link us to the universal encyclopedia of culture. In his novels we are constantly reminded of at least two of Peirce's well known definitions of a sign: "something which stands to somebody for something in some respect or capacity" (CP 2.228); and, "something [in Eco's case we can easily substitute text/novel for sign) by knowing which we know something more" (CP 8.332). If Eco's texts can be used as a (pre)text–as a vehicle for knowing something more (and something else) in the encyclopedia of knowledge–it is because the author conceives his works as intertexts.

Reading Eco is first and foremost a pleasurable cognitive experience (of *docere et delectare*) that reveals a great deal of knowledge about the rhizomatic structures of our culture. Umberto Eco chooses to examine signs/texts which are clearly embedded within a cultural context. Culture, for our author, is always interactive at play and in an endless continuum.

Rocco Capozzi

Part IV

References

Notes

1.2

* From *Daedalis* 114 (Fall 1985), pp. 161-184.

1. On the opposition between innovation and repetition, see my works *Opera aperta* (Milan: Bompiani 1962) and *Apocalittici e Integrati* (Milan: Bompiani, 1964). Partial English translations appear in *The Role of the Reader* (Bloomington, Indiana: Indiana University Press, 1979).
2. I repeat here some of my old remarks in "The Myth of Superman" (1962), now in *The Role of the Reader*, op. cit.
3. Cf., for the idea of "the model reader," my *The Role of the Reader*, op. cit.
4. "Dal leggibile all'illegibile," in Luigi Russo, ed., *Letteratura tra consumo e ricerca* (Bologna: Mulino, 1984).
5. The "manifesto" of this new aesthetics of seriality is the special issue of the journal *Cinema & Cinema* 35-36, 1983, pp. 20-24.
6. "I replicanti," *Cinema & Cinema*, op. cit., pp. 25-39,
7. "JR: vi presento il racconto," *Cinema & Cinema*, op. cit., pp. 46-51.

1.3

* From *Poetics Today,* Vol. 2:1a (1980), pp. 145-161.

1. Cf. Greimas (1966:52-53). Cf. also van Dijk "Aspects d'une théorie générative du texte poétique" in Greimas ed., *Essais de semiotique poétique*, Paris: Larousse, 1972, pp. 180-206, "It can be said that the central isotopy of a text is made up of the lowest seme or classeme dominating the greatest number of lexemes of the text."
2. The distinction between isotopies with paradigmatic disjunction and those with syntagmatic disjunction corresponds to the one between vertical and horizontal isotopies proposed by Rastier and discussed in Kerbrat-Orecchioni, 1976:24-25.
3. The text was proposed by Alain Cohen in the course of a colloquium on modalities held at Urbino at the International Semiotics Center in July 1978. Cohen's analysis, however, aimed at different goals from ours, and concerned only the discourse on Power referred to below.
4. Cf. e.g. our studies on James Bond, Les mystères de Paris, Superman, etc. in Eco, 1965a, 1965b, 1968, 1976.

1.4

* Yuri M. Lotman. 1990. Universe of the Mind. A Semiotic Theory of Culture. Trans. by Ann Shukman. London-New York: I.B. Tauris & Co. Ltd.

1. Victor Elrich. 1954. Russian Formalism. New Haven: Yale University Press.
2. Théorie de la littérature - Textes des formalistes russes. Paris: Seuil. 1965.
3. 'La structure et la forme. Reflexions sur un ouvrage de Vladimir Propp". Cahiers de l'Institut de Science Economique et Appliquée 99, 1960.
4. 'O semioticestom mechanizme kul'tury', Trudy 5(1971): 144-76.
5. 'K probleme tipologii kul'tury', Trudy 3(1967):30-8.
6. 'Oh oppociii 'cest'-'slava' v svetskich tekstach kievskogo perioda', Trudy 3(1967):100-12.

1.5

1. "Umberto Eco. Imja Roso" in Sovriemiennaja hodoziestviennaja litieratura za rubiezom 5 (1982):101 ffg.
2. "La camicia del nesso," Quaderni medievali 27 (1989).

2.1

1. Henry James, Views and Reviews, p. 18.
2. Umberto Eco, *The Open Work* (London: Hutchinson Radius, 1989), p. 4. All subsequent page references to *The Open Work* incorporated in the text
3. Roland Barthes, "From Work to Text," in *Textual Strategies. Perspectives in Post-Structuralist Criticism*, p. 80.
4. *Reflections on The Name of the Rose*, 1985, p. 8.
5. Raymond Federman, "Surfiction-Four Propositions in Form of an Introduction, in his *Surfiction. Fiction Now . . . And Tomorrow*, p. 11.
6. See, e.g., Jerzy Kutnik, *The Novel as Performance: The Fiction of Ronald Sukenick and Raymond Federman*.
7. Rudolph Arnheim, *Entropy and Art. An Essay on Disorder and Order* (1974), pp. 11-12. "Entropy" is collected in Pynchon's *Slow Learner* (1985). I have discussed the different meanings to the term in Order in Thomas Pynchon's "Entropy", in Harold Bloom, ed., *Thomas Pynchon: Modern Critical Views* (1986), pp. 157-174.
8. "Narrative Structures in Fleming" is collected as chapter 6 of *The Role of the Reader* (London: Hutchinson, 1987), pp. 144-172.
9. "*Casablanca*, or the Clichés Are Having a Ball," in *On Signs*, ed. by Marshall Blonsky Oxford: 1985, p. 38. A slightly different form of this essay has been published under the title "*Casablanca*: Cult Movies and Intertextual Collage" in Eco's *Faith in Fakes* (1986), pp. 197-212.
10. *Reflections*, pp. 54, 57.
11. Cf. e.g.: "It is not a free appropriation and assimilation of the word itself that authoritative discourse seeks to elicit from us; rather, it demands our uncondi-tional allegiance" (M.M. Bakhtin, *The Dialogic Imagination*, 1981), p. 343. Like Eco Bakhtin associates plurality and openness of discourse with freedom and choice; and monoglossia with authoritarian prescription.
12. Eco, *The Middle Ages of James Joyce: The Aesthetics of Chaosmos* (London: Hutchinson Radius, 1989), p. 2.
13. *The Middle Ages*, p. 26.
14. *The Middle Ages*, p. 45.
15. Eco, *The Aesthetics of Thomas Aquinas* (London: Hutchinson Radius, 1988), p. ix.
16. Edward Mendelson, "Encyclopedic Narrative: From Dante to Pynchon," *MLN* 91.

17. Joseph Frank, "Spatial From in Modern Literature" (1945), now in *The Widening Gyre*, 1963.
18. *The Middle Ages*, p. 73.

2.2

1. See Eco's comments in his "Prefazione" to the original volume (1975:6).
2. David Robey introduces English readers to *The Open Work* (1989) by assuring them glibly that "the terms 'semiotics' and 'semiology' can be used interchangeably".
3. Thus Michael Dirda, reviewing Eco's latest novel for the *Washington Post Book World* for October 22, 1995, ignorantly defines semiotics as "the study of cultural 'signs'"—a definition strictly applicable only to semiology as subalternate to, as a part only of, the much vaster study of sign action in the universe at large properly called semiotics.
4. Sebeok 1971: 56. The author had preceded this remark by noting, in the same paragraph, that "While every contributor to *Semiotica*"—he names the journal of the International Association for Semiotic Studies, but the latinate formation will serve just as well to name "whatever matters semiotical", or "semiotic affairs"—may indulge his personal taste [the text is pre-gender-neutral] when attaching a label to the theory of signs, his terminology within the same piece of discourse will not oscillate *ad libitum*, for his initial selection will have signaled to his sophisticated readership whether he has chosen to align himself with the Locke-Peirce-Morris tradition, the Mead variation, or the Saussurean pattern of thought and action."
5. In this curious feature, as we shall have further occasion to note if but in passing, Eco achieves an authorial status parallel to that of Kant, who also could not realize the idealist status of his theory. See Kant 1787: "Preface to the Second Edition", esp. note *a*, pp. 34-35; discussion in Deely 1992a.
6. Eco's wonderful term from *Limits*: 32.
7. For the historical details in particular, see Deely 1994a.
8. I do not mean the clarity of easy reading. In this respect, my original characterization of the book as a "readable account" was quite misleading. The book is anything but that, as generations of students have learned. I mean the clarity of a theoretical conception rigorously formulated and adhered to in its logical consequences throughout. In my original review, I described Eco's book as a "more readable account of semiotics in the current market". More readable than what? At its time the work was *sui generis*, and "readable" means "able to be read easily" (*Merriam Webster's Collegiate Dictionary*), which cannot be truthfully said of this book. I have always wanted to correct this false characterization, and I am grateful to Professor Capozzi for affording me the public opportunity to do so.
9. In the inadequacy of their nomenclature, the Latins had blurred the profound difference between the idea as sign and the dinosaur bone as sign, for example. In speaking of the *signum naturale* as both *formale* and *instrumentale*, and, as *instrumentale*, *ex consuetudine* as well, they had covered over (cf. Deely 1978a)— or glossed over—the profound need for what Eco calls a theory of sign-production, even though without losing a profound sense of the permeability of nature to culture and vice-versa (cf. esp. Poinsot 1632: Book II, Questions 5 and 6; and see note 36 below). And, connected with this last point, they had not developed

at all their rudimentary understanding of the third term of the sign relation, what we now call the *interpretant*, even though their semiotic treatises had explicitly reached the point of demonstrating that the sign consists not only in a relationship as such, but in a relationship irreducibly triadic—the point where Peirce picked up the Ariadne's thread of late Latin-early modern discussion to give us what we call "semiotics" today (see Beuchot and Deely 1995).

10. E.g., see Diagram 10, "Semiotic condensation of the natural philosophy tradition", and Diagram 26 on "The place of structuralism in the study of signs", in *Introducing Semiotic* (Deely 1982: 41 and 197, respectively).

11. Deely 1982 and 1990: 108–114; Eco, Lambertini, Marmo, and Tabarroni 1986; and Manetti 1993.

12. See "Locke's Proposal for Semiotic: What Was New and What Was Not", in Deely 1994a: 109ff.; see also the discussion of "a distinction which unites" in Deely 1982: 62–64.

13. See the fold-out Synoptic Table in Deely 1985: 371-375.

14. Mauricio Beuchot and I are able at this time to name ten Latin authors of neglected semiotic treatises; when I arrived in México in September of 1994 we knew only of four.

15. The earliest mapping of the terms at play was provided by Sebeok 1971, an essay we have already had occasion to quote. The clearest marking of the decisive paradigm-shift as such within contemporary sign studies was made in the anthology, *Frontiers in Semiotics* (Deely, Williams, and Kruse 1986). See in particular the Editors' Preface, "Pars Pro Toto", pp. xviii–xxii. Also Deely 1990: 1–8.

16. See Sebeok 1971; Beuchot and Deely 1995: 539–545; Deely 1995. A more thorough investigation of the details of the terms and issues I hope to bring to publication soon under the title *Why Semiotics?*

17. Cf. Deely 1973: 33n53, 49, and passim.

18. See Sebeok 1976; Deely 1982a and 1986.

19. See Deely 1990: xi–xii, and 1992; Campos Figueiredo 1995: XIX note.

20. Compare Eco's remark, dated July of 1974, in the "Prefazione" to the original edition of his *Trattato de semiotica generale*, p. 6: "Se qualcuno non avesse già avuto un'idea analoga, mi sarebbe piaciuto intitolarlo *Critica della semiotica pura e della semiotica practica*: tale titolo avrebbe reso abbastanza bene le mie intenzione, ma sfortunatamente timore reverenziale, senso dell misura e senso dell'umorismo si sono congiurati per sconsigliarmi tanta impudenza." The reverence for Kant is touching, but perhaps reveals more than was realized. Recall too Kant's own protestations that his work had escaped idealism (Deely 1992a).

21. Cf. the discussion of the point in Maritain 1921.

22. It was for naming the foundational area so conceived that the -ic form (semiotic), in English at least, makes perhaps the most appropriate usage. See Deely 1976; 1982.

23. Again speaking in the strictly English language context, for this—the study of how signs are produced and function in diverse contexts and areas—the -ics form (semiotics) makes a more appropriate designation. But as this way of putting the matter is not available within the semantic fields of many other contemporary languages, I no longer think much should be made of what amounts to an English provincialism.

24. For it is not only a question of the action of signs within and across anthroposemiotic structures, but of the action of signs in other species, both

animal and plant, and even in nature as an evolutionary whole. See Sebeok 1963, 1972, 1975, 1977, 1978, 1986; Sebeok and Rosenthal 1981; Krampen 1981; Deely 1990: 94–103; 1994a: 183–200.

25. But if the author means the *actual* social existence of the universe of signification, we must demur from his formula; the formula holds only if what is meant is the *in principle* social existence of the universe of signification—i.e., the public-in-principle character of objects signified, whether in part physical also or objective only.

26. But, in the second place, it is also difficult to know on what grounds even a supposedly "ordinary" or "naive" notion of sign could be non-relational—unless it were very naive indeed—since such a notion would be self-contradictory, the semiotician's version of a square circle. Such a muddled notion, more than naive, would be pseudo. This predicament is not impossible in the play of common speech, but it should be *shown* rather than merely *asserted* to exist; and, even then, it would remain beside the point both for the history and the theory of semiotics.

27. "... recentiores ... quotidianis disputationibus agitare solent", Poinsot observed (1632: 194/38–40). And see the recent anthology on this point by Beuchot Ed. 1996.

28. Poinsot 1632: 117/13–14: "quia nihil seipsum significat, licet se repraesentare possit". See 116/14–117/11 and 121/19–123/32, for fuller discussion of the point. Also Deely 1980.

29. Deely 1994: ¶32: "The first and most radical misconception to be addressed is the notion that there are other things besides signs, as if signs were an item within our experience which has its place among other things besides. For, when we speak from the strict standpoint of experience (which of course we must in all contexts where we hope to avoid delusion), the sign is not by any means one thing among many others: the sign is not any thing at all, nor is it even first of all a distinct class of objects. As a type of object or objective structure contrasting with other objective structures, the sign is singularly unstable and derivative, precisely because signs are not objects first of all. Signs are presupposed to there so much as being whatever objects there are in the content of experience in general and at any given time."

30. Even as a political matter, this particular boundary of semiotics has not survived in all respects over time, as the introduction of the notion of physiosemiosis may serve to illustrate. See Sebeok 1968, 1974a; Deely 1990: 83–95.

31. Notice the parallel in Eco's theory, excepting only the expansion of "arbitrary link" to "cultural link", to Saussure's "remark in passing" (i.1906–11: 68): "when semiology becomes organized as a science, the question will arise whether or not it properly includes modes of expression based on completely natural signs, such as pantomime. Supposing that the new science welcomes them, its main concern will still be the whole group of systems grounded on the arbitrariness of the sign. In fact, every means of expression used in society is based, in principle, on collective behavior or—what amounts to the same thing—on convention. Polite formulas, for instance, though often imbued with a certain natural expressiveness (as in the case of a Chinese who greets his emperor by bowing down to the ground nine times), are nonetheless fixed by rule; it is this rule and not the intrinsic value of the gestures that obliges one to use them. Signs that are wholly arbitrary realize better than the others the ideal of the semiological process." The

parallel runs all the way to the consideration of natural signs primarily patterned on indexicality to the point of omission of indexicality as a distinctive base of connection. See further Eco 1972 and 1977 (with the comments in Deely 1994a: ¶168).

32. That the sign relation, the relation constituting a sign as such, is always different from physical relations of cause and effect, even in the case of signs called "natural", has long been a matter of explicit recognition. The late Latin sense on this question was expressly summarized by Poinsot in Book I, Question 2 of his *Tractatus de Signis*. See esp. 137/7, note 4. What no Latin author known to me went on to explain, however, was the exact manner in which the relation of effect to cause or cause to effect that arises as a result of the habilitation—the *motivation*, in recent terms—of sign-vehicle to object signified in the case of natural signs (e.g., smoke to fire or clouds to rain), and which relation is in itself a dyadic relation at the level of brute secondness, becomes incorporated into the triadic relation of renvoi in which alone any sign as such, whether natural or conventional, actually consists. For an explanation of this incorporation the topic of "the modes of sign production" is one of the essential topics to be thematized for the advance of semiotic consciousness. See the remarks in note 9 above.

33. A remark Peirce made (c.1906: 5.555) apropos of the relativizing the true to the human by pragmatism (as opposed to pragmaticism, it should go without saying) would apply equally, *mutatis mutandis*, to the theory Eco would have us adopt: "there are certain mummified pedants who have never waked to the truth that the act of knowing a real object alters it. They are curious specimens of humanity, and as I am one of them, it may be amusing to see how I think. It seems that our oblivion to this truth is due to our not having made the acquaintance of a new analysis that the True is simply that in cognition which is Satisfactory [or, now, which conforms to our conventions]. As to this doctrine, if it is meant that True and Satisfactory [or true and conventionalized] are synonyms, it strikes me that it is not so much a doctrine of philosophy as it is a new contribution to English lexicography."

34. "In cognitione simplici sine hoc, quod transeat ad discursum vel collationem, potest attingi non solum obiectum, quod immediate proponitur seu apponitur sensui, sed quod in eo continetur; sicut videt visus externus Herculem in statua et species repraesentans coloratum etiam repraesentat figuram et motum aliaque sensibilia communia ibi contenta et adiuncta, nec tamen ob hoc desinit esse simplex cognitio, licet cognitum non sit simplex, sed plura, alioquin non possemus simplici visione plura obiecta videre. Quodsi possumus, cur non etiam ordinata et unum per aliud, et consequenter signatum per signum et ut contentum in signo?" (Poinsot 1632: 212/41-7; see also 208/34-47, 207/18-39, and Book I, Question 6 generally). See further Deely 1996.

35. See Deely, 1975b: esp. 96-99.

36. See note 32 above.

37. Nor, twenty years later, are the days of this gross misunderstanding yet past. Lecturing abroad in the winter of 1995, I introduced my audience to the notion of interpretant with the remark that this was a term invented by Peirce which had no previous counterpart in the modern languages. At this point my translator interrupted my remarks to inform me that I was mistaken, since the word

already existed, if not in English, at least in Spanish. Pray tell, I asked, what is this Spanish term which corresponds to Peirce's notion of interpretant. He replied without a moment's blush, "Intérprete" ("interpreter"!), well illustrating the persistence of the semiotically naïve mindset with which the *Trattato di semiotica generale* had to contend already in the 1970s.

38. Deely 1994, 1994a, 1996.

39. "Aliae differentiae rerum ut res, aliae ut obiecti et in esse obiecti", *Tractatus de Signis*, 270/39–41; see also 149/44–46, 187/32–35, and throughout.

40. But any comparison of this case where thing and object intertwine with the phoneme analysis of Jakobson-Halle 1956, such as Eco goes on to make (p. 114), is limited by the truth that phonemes as such are *primarily* within, whereas whales as such are only *secondarily* within, the universe of discourse as such (or, more generally, the human Lebenswelt in its contrast as objective with the physical environment as such). This point can well be generalized, and it is one that philosophical attempts at understanding language (such as that of Haas 1968) can ill afford systematically to avoid (we are back to the problem of the semiosis of sensation and the assimilation to perception of the physical relations involved as such in *signa naturalia*).

41. See also Hjelmslev 1961: 22–23—with whom, however, Eco is well familiar; and Deely 1996a.

42. For relevant considerations on the notions of "fact" presupposed here, see the indexical entry in Deely and Nogar 1973.

2.4

1. The evolution of Eco's themata is a logical, rather than a chronological progression. The chronology of his writings is something of a mess. Since Eco became a hot commodity for American university presses, his book collections mix older and newer papers, some in several versions, some translated from Italian, others written originally in English. It will require special textological studies to sort it out.

2. It is instructive to note that Eco emphasizes most strongly the text's authority when analyzing a most open text, James Joyce's *Finnegan's Wake* (1990, ch.9).

3. Eco has been trying to enlist a helper in this task, a helper called the Model Reader. The concept recurs again and again in Eco's writings, but it remains indefinite. It fluctuates between being the author's construct, the text's device, a set of felicity conditions and the personified "competent" judge of interpretations. I suspect that the Model Reader is Eco's contribution to the thriving market of readers offered by the various reader-reception theories. But Eco cannot quite decide what to do with this superfluous entity, and so his Model Reader remains suspended midway between the eaminence grise of the Konstanz school and the actual reader whose reading practices are amenable to empirical study. In the end, Eco, now a Model Author, treats the Model Reader with some irony, having discovered that he/she/it will not read and interpret as expected (IO 76, 83, 84).

4. Eco's concept stimulated my proposal to make encyclopedic knowledge relative to worlds. The actual-world encyclopedia is just one among numerous encyclopedias of possible worlds which text producers and receivers can acquire. Fictional encyclopedia is the knowledge about a possible world constructed by a

fictional text. Simultaneously with the construction of a fictional world, every fictional text compiles a corresponding fictional encyclopedia (Dolezel 1985:206-08).

5. Chisholm considers the term 'actual' ambiguous and proposes instead 'the world that obtains' or 'the prevailing world' (1981:129); this might be a useful terminological suggestion, but it only confirms the need for assigning to one possible world an exclusive ontological status.

2.5

1. We are also living in a time of what must be called anti-archic, if not anarchic, permissiveness in the academic practice of literary interpretation.

2. Cf. my *Semiotics From Peirce to Barthes* (1988), *A Semeiotics of Literature For the Good Reader* (in press), and *Plato's Dialogues One by One* (1984).

3. C.Morris *Foundations of the Theory of Signs* (1938) (FTS). See also his *Signification and Significance* (1964) for his psychologistic and narrow redefinition of Peirce's "interpretant of a sign" as "a disposition, caused by the sign, to respond in a certain kind of way" (p.49).

4. "Pragmatics" in Morris's sense is also a term or notion *not* to be found in Peirce. Eco, as we shall see, nonetheless uses the notion repeatedly.

5. My "Has Eco Understood Peirce," *The American Journal of Semiotics* (1989), 251-264, also addresses this problem in Eco's semeiotics.

6. The application of these principles is, by coincidence, illustrated in a recent essay completed by this reviewer before he had read Eco's book: "On the Form and Authenticity of the 'Lysis'," in *Ancient Philosophy* X.2 (1990). The translators, for instance, have never succeeded in registering these attributes in their versions of the dialogues. What's more, the tradition of transmission has habitually seen the dialogues as having the properties of works purporting to advance a system of doctrine. This causes readers to apply the *non-literary* test of the consistency of doctrines present in the pseudo- epigraph Oj with those *supposedly* being advanced in Oa2, Oa3 or Oa4.

7. J.Buchler *Metaphysics of Natural Complexes* (1966) (MNC). *Toward a General Theory of Human Judgment* (1951); *Nature and Judgment* (1955); *The Main of Light* (1974).

8. The reader should note that, in Buchler's systematic view, there are no simples except by stipulation, so that unities, as integrities, are rightly seen to be complex or plural. Things or processes that are unities are not unities as such, but unities in some respect.

9. Not that Eco leaves this out of account: Chapter 6 on "Interpreting Drama" is rich in formulations that address the phenomenon of multivoicedness in the literary arts.

10. "The metalanguage of interpretation is not different from its object language" (*Limits*: 60).

11. In Chapter 13, on "Semantics, Pragmatics, and Text Semiotics." W.V.Quine "Two Dogmas of Empiricism," *From a Logical Point of View* (1953).

12. "Networking" because in Eco's theory "the content of a single term becomes something similar to an encyclopedia" (*Role* 185). This is because the sign, or the term, contains all the texts in which it can be inserted. This follows, for Eco, from the understanding that the meaning of a sign is the sum of its interpretants. But doesn't this inflate the notion of meaning into an absurdity? Namely, a sign

has different integrities in different orders or contexts, and the continuity among these integrities is its contour or "gross integrity." But (i) grasping the meaning of a term does not, in practice, require a mapping of all its uses, and (ii) an *occurrence* of a term is not its definition: its identity is the continuous relation that obtains between its contour and any of its integrites. So if the definition of a term is its identity, it is distinct from its integrities or occurrences in various orders or contexts. And (iii) "if the content of a single term becomes something like an encyclopedia" (*Role* 185), then won't what we require be *both* an encyclopedia with entries equal to the number of words in the language *and* an enyclopedic volume for each word? Eco, obviously, is talking about the Saussurean construct "language" and not about speech or language in use.

13. For a clarification of what Eco means by a rhizomatic structure, see my *Semiotics From Peirce to Barthes*; p.122f.

14. For Van Gogh see P.Heelan *Space-Perception and the Philosophy of Science* (1983); for the early Presocratics, see my *Modes of Greek Thought* (1971), and *Three Poetic Thinkers* (in press).

15. In both Anglo-analytic philosophizing and Continental phenomenology. Though this assumption and other neopositivist or essentialist dogmas are what generate the language which Eco too often borrows from rationalist empiricism, his novels show that he is easily capable of full detachment from them. Readers of Eco's theoretical works who omit reading his novels are liable to take the skewed terminology and the distinctions that block fruitful inquiry more categorically than they deserve.

16. See the most helpful presentation in Theresa Coletti's *Naming the Rose* (1988). The case is much like that of G.B.Shaw in which it is hard to decide which are more truly his views–as between what he says about millionaires in the Prefaces to *Major Barbara* and *The Millionairess* in the assertive mode, and what emerges about them from the exhibitive judgments effectuated by the plays. As wholes, *The Name of the Rose* and *Foucault's Pendulum* are *exhibitive judgments* of the assertions made by the characters within them; so, if the parts of a work are subordinate to the whole, then the work-of-art gets the last word.

17. "Niweing": an O.E. neologism borrowed from G.M. Hopkins; niwe = new, newly; the verb niwan = renew, recur, repeat; the adverb niwan = lately, recently.

18. Cf. my *Semiotics from Peirce to Barthes*, 132f.

19. The principle of contradiction does not apply because, as we've already noted, metaphor is not an assertive syntagm, but an exhibitive judgment.

2.6

* This is a new and expanded version of my article "Does Semiotics Lead to Deconstruction?" published in *Semiosis*, 17-1-4 (1992).

1. C.S.Peirce: *Manuscripts*. MS 292

2. Umberto Eco: *A Theory of Semiotics*, op.cit. Vide the title of the part I of the book.

3. C.S.Peirce: *Semiotics and Significs*. 1977:31-32.

4. C.S.Peirce: *Manuscripts*. MS 290.

5. VIDE: Max Bense: *Semiotics Process undo System* (1975) and *Vermittlung der Realitaeten*rlag (1976).

2.8

1. This seems true of all definitions of intertextuality despite important differences between them (Ruprecht 1983, Bruce 1983, Morgan 1984, and worton and Still 1990:1-44, less ideologically committed than H. F. Plett 1990). To invoke intertextuality would be pointless, however, if it were just meant as a fancier term for the traditional study of influence and sources (on this all-important distinction: Riffaterre 1978, 1980a, 1980b,1983a, and 1984).

2. On this definition, *Role* 180-191. Peirce re-defined his concept many times; see esp. his letters to Lady Welby (Hardwick 1977).

3. For its applicability to Biblical criticism, see Boyarin 1990 and Philipps 1991 (the latter unfortunately seems to confuse interpretant and interpreter).

4. On meaning defined as a habit or law, Savan 1976:30, 35; *Role* 192.

5. Since the representation of things in literature refers to imaginary ones, the sign determines the object rather than the reverse procedure that characterizes signs referring to a reality.

6. Alice herself emphasizes the "innocence" of her bottle by musing aloud on the fact thatthe label does *not* say "Poison."

7. On *ground* as related to meaning, Savan 1976:11; *Role* 182-183.

8. Cf. Peirce CP 2.303. This reversal, or backtracking, has for its consequence that the interpretant recorded by feedback from the mental interpretant mediates between theoriginal sign (now functioning as an interpretant) and its unchanged intertext-object, while in the case of the mental interpretant, the sign is what mediates between object and interpretant.

9. Peirce CP 1.339, 2.92, 2.303 (a sign) is "anything which determines something else (its interpretant) to refer to an object to which itself refers (its object) in the same way, the interpretant becoming in turn a sign, and so in *ad infinitum*;" TS 121-122; *Role* 89, etc.

2.9

1. Italo Calvino, "Comment j'ai écrit un de mes livres."

2. Cf. Greimas and Courtés (1982), p. 369.

3. "Two other better-known manuals appeared prior to Mazarin's: *The Manual Oracle or Art of Prudence* (1647) by Baltasar Gracian, and *On Honest Dissimulation* (1641) by Torquato Accetto." (p. 4)

4. As Sender, the American people at the same time delegates a power and sanctions. It also interdicts any illegal act by the President. As the Receiver it is governed (acted upon) by the President and receives his speech.

5. It should be noted that Eco's analysis is so convincing that Marshall Blonsky, the editor of this volume, in a note feels obliged to comment and moralize the President's (Villain) actions one year later, in dysphoric terms: "In the light of Nixon's successful attempt to stage a *surreptitious* come-back, it is illuminating to recall the *method of madness* and *media downfall*." (Italics ours)

6. "And every muscle of Nixon's face betrayed embarrassment, fear, tension. . .Nixon's speech was the visual representation of insecurity, acted out by the 'guarantor of security'"(p. 11).

7. In the first footnote M. Blonsky writes: "This article was written in 1973, while Eco was a visiting professor at the Graduate Center of the City University of New York", whereas the second series of photos of Nixon deal specifically with his August 1974 speech.

2.11
* Review article of *L'idea deforme. Interpretazioni esoteriche di Dante*, ed. by Maria Pia Pozzato. With an introduction by Umberto Eco (1989).
1. All the quotations, including this one, are translated by the reviewer.
2. Eco himself shows the distance that divides Peirce from Derrida in the last chapter of *I limiti dell'interpretazione*.
3. Critics have to further consider this problem: the coexistence of different interpretations of the same text that different readers, in different ages or cultural contexts, propose, as Segre underlines in his recent *Notizie dalla crisi* (Segre 1993:292).

2.12
* This is a revision of two lectures which had appeared, completely unedited, in *Signifying Behavior* 1 (1994), pp.176-200.
1. Faced with an "unprecedented case" of a writer whose first novel became an instant international bestseller, many critics in Italy spoke of Eco's success story as the "caso Eco." The so-called "caso" becomes even more intriguing with the publication of Eco's second novel. Two Italian studies which trace Eco's success story are: Francesca Pansa e Anna Vinci's *Effetto Eco* and Margherita Ganeri's *Il caso Eco*. For a documentation of how *Foucault's Pendulum* was initially accepted in Italy, by writers and critics (from the day that the novel was first announced to the appearance of its first reviews) see my "Troppi movimenti intorno al Pendolo di Eco," in *Quaderni d'italianistica*.
2. *Interpretation and Overinterpretation* is the publication of "The 1990 Cambridge Tanner Lectures" which took place just before Eco published *The Limits of Interpretation*. The Italian version, *I limiti dell'interpretazione*, does not contain the same essays as *The Limits of Interpretation*. For our discussion it is worth mentioning that in *The Limits of Interpretation* we find at least two essays which had appeared before *Foucault's Pendulum*. "Abduction in Uqbar" had appeared in German and in Italian, in 1983 and 1985 respectively; "Joyce, Semiosis, and Semiotics" was written for a James Joyce Symposium (Venice, 1988). Both essays deal specifically with topics that we see illustrated in Eco's novels: Borges, encyclopedia, labyrinth, abduction, detective novels, unlimited semiosis, and hermetic drift.

   Throughout this paper, unless otherwise specified, my comments on *Interpretation and Overinterpretation* are also applicable to *The Limits of Interpretation*.
3. See *The Role of the Reader;* also see "Two Problems in Textual Interpretation," in particular p. 146.
4. Originally published in 1968. In 1983 this important collection of essays on aesthetics, cinema, literature, art, experimentalism, "neoavanguardia," and interdisciplinary criticism, was reprinted with a revised introduction (Milano: Garzanti, 1983), and then (Milano: Mursia, 1990).
5. The title "Apocalyptic and Integrated" refers to critics who either accept or reject *a priori* the neoavanguardia and postmodernism. In this work we can appreciate Eco's first treatment of postmodern theories (presented long before most Italian critics discover "postmodernism"). Today we can read Eco's observations on popular culture and postmodernism in an essay first published in *Sugli specchi e altri saggi* and later translated for *The Limits of Interpretation*, see chap. 5 "Interpreting serials," pp. 83-100. A selection of translated essays now appear in *Apoca-*

lypse Postponed (1994).

6. In his introduction to *Lector in fabula* Eco reconstructs the days of *Opera aperta* insisting that "Quando nel 1962 pubblicavo *Opera aperta* mi ponevo il problema di come un'opera d'arte da un lato postulasse un libero intervento interpretativo da parte dei propri destinatari, e dall'altro esibisse caratteristiche strutturali che insieme stimolavano e regolavano l'ordine delle sue interpretazioni. Come ho appreso più tardi, facevo allora senza saperlo della pragmatica del testo. . . .affrontavo un aspetto, l'attività cooperativa che porta il destinatario a trarre dal testo quel che il testo non dice (ma presuppone, promette, implica ed esplicita), a riempire spazi vuoti, a connettere quello che vi è in quel testo con il tessuto dell'intertestualità da cui quel testo si origina e in cui andrà a confluire. . . mi preoccupavo. . . di stabilire cosa, nel testo, stimolasse e regolasse a un tempo la libertà interpretativa" (*Lector* 5). These are exactly the key issues which return in *The Limits of Interpretation*. In the opening statement of the first Tanner Lecture, "Interpretation and History," Eco summarizes the above statement for his English-speaking readers, first reminding them that what he is about to discuss goes back to *Opera aperta*, and then stating: "I was studying the dialectics between the rights of texts and the rights of their interpreters. I have the impression that, in the course of the last decades, the rights of the interpreters have been overstressed" (*Limits* 23).
    Here I would also remind that *Opera aperta* appear six years before Roland Barthes' "The death of the author" (1968).

7. In the preface, Hartman claims that the essays in *Deconstruction and criticism* do not wish to constitute neither a "polemical book nor a manifesto in the ordinary sense" (p. vii). However, from its first appearance, this text represented for many readers the beginning of American deconstructionism. For some of the objections which can be directed against deconstructionism (I am speaking of those objections that Eco also voices) see the recent study of John M. Ellis, *Against Deconstruction*.

8. Robert Scholes does not deal with *Interpretation and Overinterpretation*, but his review of *The Limits of Interpretation* contains excellent suggestions on why Eco's main target should have been S. Fish and R. Rorty, rather than J. Derrida. See "Eco's Limits," *Semiotica* (1992).

9. See Luigi Pareyson's *Verità e interpretazione* (1971); for our discussion, see especially, *Estetica. Teoria della formatività* (1974). Estetica was first published in 1954 and later reprinted in 1960 (Bologna: Zanichelli).

10. "Two Problems in Textual Interpretation," p. 154. See entire article in Part I of this anthology.

11. One of the best examples remains *Postscript to The Name of the Rose*, where Eco discusses the genesis of *The Rose* and in so doing deprives many of his critics the pleasure of claiming to have discovered by themselves some of the themes, topics and intertextual echoes planted in the novel.

12. This question of an author who foresees his own readers is amply discussed in *The Role of the Reader*. From the days of *La definizione dell'arte* to those of *The Limits of Interpretation* Eco appears to reformulate Pareyson's definition of the author's "formazione" ["giving form"] and the reader's "esecuzione" ["executing"]: "L'esecuzione del lettore è talmente essenziale all'opera d'arte, che l'artista, nell'atto in cui esegue la sua opera. . . in quell'atto stesso se ne

preoccupa, e cerca di regolarla con i mezzi che ha a sua disposizione, diversi a seconda delle arti" (*Estetica* 224). "Esecuzione" is then linked to "interpretation" and to the notion that a work of art –or a text– regulates its own *esecuzione*: ". . . sarà necessario ricorrere al concetto d'interpretazione, che spiega non solo come l'esecuzione possa essere molteplice e infinita, e anche questa sua infinità non metta in pericolo l'identità dell'opera, ma piuttosto la garantisca" (*Estetica* 225).

13. Recently Eco has reminded his readers that he owes a lot to Pareyson. In *The Open Work* our author includes an essay in which he "revisits" Pareyson's theories of interpretation. In *The Limits of Interpretation* (see note 3, p. 63) Eco makes it a point to underline this essay and it seems that he wants to remind his readers that although in the past he may have not been very generous towards his teacher, now it's time to pay his debt to a great theorist of aesthetics, not very well known outside of Italy, who deserves much more attention than he has received up to now both in Italy and abroad.

14. Not surprisingly, in the introduction to *Semiotics and the Philosophy of Language* Eco does not mention Derrida's notion that there is nothing "outside the text"[the "*hors d'oeuvre* discussed in *Dissémination*] and quotes instead Valéry: "the principle of interpretation (in its Peircean sense) has not to be identified with farfetched assumptions that, as Valéry said, *il n'y a pas de vrai sens d'un texte*" (SPL 3).

15. *The Limits of Interpretation*, p. 33. The art of using endless chains of signifiers, popularized by Roland Barthes' *Le plaisir du texte*, becomes quite fashionable in the Sixties and Seventies. In Italy narrators and poets had fun illustrating these theories. With the decreasing popularity of the "Neoavanguardia" many readers and critics became tired of a literature that focused almost exclusively on the notion of texts as ways of playing games with words, or with texts presented as "meccano sets" with which ("do it yourself") readers could write/create/generate their own texts.

16. "Eco has arrived at that favorite picture for the 1980s, a signifier (or "representamen" or "interpretant") that leads to another signifier that leads to another signifier and so on and on, never coming to rest in any signified or meaning. It is very like Derrida's endless play of language. . . As always in these maneuvers, the psychology of the intender or the interpreter has been replaced by what the philosopher, critic, or semioticist is good at and feels more comfortable with "texts." *The Critical I* , p. 182.

17. Nor does Eco disagree with many of Paul de Man's remarks on the text's ambiguity, ambivalence and self-referentiality (in *Blindness and Insight)*. The question is whether Eco and de Man would accept these elements, which are inscribed in the text, by the author, as evidence of the author's presence–of his intentional self-reflexiveness?

18. See for example *The Limits of Interpretation*, pp. 32-34. It must added that Eco does not refute all of Derrida's work, in fact, in these pages we see Eco actually defending Derrida against some of Searle's remarks (*Limits* 36).

19. *Interpretation and Overinterpretation*, p. 48. See also the sections "Unlimited semiosis and deconstruction" and "Derrida on Peirce" in *The Limits of Interpretation*, pp. 33-37. In *Interpretation and Overinterpretation* see the entire lecture two, "Overinterpreting texts."

20. "To identify these frames the reader had to 'walk', so to speak, outside the text,

in order to gather intertextual support (a quest for analogous 'topoi', themes, or motives). I call these interpretative moves inferential walks." *(Role* 32)

21. In order to send his readers to the encyclopedia of culture, whereas in his essays and theoretical writings Eco uses quotations, footnotes and bibliographies, in his novels he uses intertextual echoes, as well as parodic or ironic quotations. Nontheless, in both forms of writing he illustrates his ideas with examples (often humorous) extracted from popular and erudite literature, from mass media, from scientific knowledge, and, in short, from different sources which make up a "global encyclopedia of knowledge."

22. See also *Postscript to The Name of the Rose,* p. 28. The first Italian translation of *Ficciones* appears in Italy in 1955 (translated by Lucentini and with a preface of M. Blanchot). In Italy, as it had happened in France, Borges soon became one of the most imitated narrators. Calvino had read Borges as early as the Fifties (we can see the influence of the Argentinean narrator from *Cosmicomics* on). Eco became an avid reader of Borges when the reprint of *Finzioni* was already drawing a lot of attention from writers and critics around the world.

23. Speaking of Borges, it is interesting to see how Calvino opens *If On a Winter Night a Traveler* (see p.5) with an allusion to "The Library of Babylon" where all the books are contained, including those which are yet to be written.

24. Two of my earlier articles on *The Rose* were revised in "Palimpsests and Laughter: The Dialogical Pleasure of Unlimited Intertextuality in *The Name of the Rose*," now in *Italica* (1989).

25. In an interview which appeared shortly after his death, in the daily, *La Nazione* (12 august 1986), Calvino affirms that "divertire è una cosa seria" ("to entertain is a serious business"). The whole issue of Aristotle's second book of poetics, on humor and laughter, at the center of *The Name of the Rose,* gives us an excellent indication of how Eco has always felt about humor in general.

26. A notion parodied very well in the conclusion of *The Island of the Day Before.*

27. Of Moishe Idel see especially: *Kabbalah* and *Language, Torah, and Hermeneutics in Abraham Abulafia.* For Harold Bloom, see *A Map of Misreading,* and *Kabbalah and Criticism.*

28. *The Search for the Perfect Language* is the result of a series of lectures and seminars in which Eco analyzed with his students historical, sociological, legendary, apocryphal works on the origin of a primordial and perfect language. In the opening chapters we see that Eco is discussing some of the central issues at the center of *Foucault's Pendulum.*

29. Norman N. Holland, even if one disagrees with his psychological perspective, offers some interesting alternatives which include a consideration of the author's intentions and of the referentiality of signs. In addition to *The Critical I*, see also *The Dynamics of Literary Response* and *Five readers reading.*

30. In "An Author and his Interpreters" Eco defends his intention of using his character Casaubon against the (mis) interpretation of readers who assumed that he was using George Eliot's Mr. Casaubon, from *Middlemarch.* As we know Eco had in mind Isaac Casaubon who in *De rebus sacris et ecclesiasticis* (1614) challenges the original attribution of the *Corpus Hermeticum.* For an historical analysis of the *Corpus Hermeticum* originally attributed to Hermes Trismalgistes see *Hermetica. The Greek Corpus Hermeticum* (Cambridge, New York: Cambridge UP, 1992). This recent new translation has excellent bibliographical references.

3.1

* Reprinted from *Technologies of Gender. Essays on Theory, Film, and Fiction* (Bloomington: IUP, 1987), pp. 51-69. Written in various versions, English and Italian, between 1983 and 1985. A first English version with a different title, was presented at the symposium: "The Question of the Postmodern: Literature/Criticism/Culture" organized by M. Hays at Cornell University in April 1977. First published in the present expanded version as a contribution to the special issue of *SubStance* 47 (1985), on Eco's *The Name of the Rose*.

1. In Umberto Eco, *Le forme del contenuto* (1971). The English version of this essay, 'On the Possibility of Generating Aesthetic Messages in an Edenic Language," is in Umberto Eco, *The Role of the Reader: Explorations in the Semiotics of Texts* (1979), pp. 90-104.

2. Umberto Eco, *Il diario minimo* (1976 [1963]), p. 96; translation mine.

3. Elsa Morante, *La storia* (Torino: Einaudi, 1974); *History, A Novel*, trans. William Weaver (New York: Knopf, 1977).

4. See "Pierre Menard, Author of the Quixote," in Jorge Luís Borges, *Labyrinths*, ed. Donald A. Yates and James E. Irby (New York: New Directions, 1964).

5. Sir Arthur Conan Doyle, *The Hound of the Baskervilles* (Garden City, NY: Doubleday, 1974), p. 47.

6. Umberto Eco, "Ore 9: Amleto all'assedio di Casablanca," *L'Espresso* (17 agosto 1975); translation mine. See also his contribution to this issue, "*Casablanca*: Cult Movies and Intertextual Collage."

7. Maria Corti, "È un'opera chiusa," *L'Espresso* (19 ottobre 1980); translation mine.

8. See Louis Althusser, *Lenin and Philosophy*, trans. Ben Brewster (New York and London: Monthly Review Press, 1971), p. 176. I have suggested elsewhere that the circularity of the argumentation and the reappearance of critical imagery and concerning recurrent in structuralist writers like Lévi-Strauss and Greimas point to a kind of retrenchment, on Eco's part, to the positions which he himself wag among the first to criticize in *La struttura assente* and which his *Theory of Semiotics* subsequently argued to be untenable. I have offered a reading of the possible reasons for such unhappy return in chapter 6 of my *Alice Doesn't: Feminism, Semiotics, Cinema* (1984).

9. For Derrida's critique of Lévi-Strauss, see *Of Grammatology*, trans. Gayatri Chakravorty Spivak (1976), Pt. II, chap. I.

10. Umberto Eco, "Postille a Il nome della rosa," *Alfabeta*, 49 (giugno 1983), pp. 19-22; translation mine. This work has been recently published in English by Harcourt Brace Jovanovich.

11. Jacques Derrida, *Eperons. Les styles de Nietzsche*, English trans. Barbara Harlow (Venezia: Corbo e Fiore, 1976), p. 69.

12. Gayatri Chakravorty Spivak, "Displacement and the Discourse of Woman," in *Displacement: Derrida and After*, ed. Mark Krupnick (Bloomington: Indiana University Press, 1983), p. 177.

13. The significance of the latter can be inferred from the apparent effort made to maintain gender neutrality in a language, Italian, that is strictly two-gendered. In Weaver's excellent translation, the three references to that person are rendered as: "a dear friend," "my beloved," and "the person with whom I was traveling" (*Rose* 1-2). The Italian text is even more controlled in the second reference: "una persona cara," "la persona attesa," and "la persona con cui viaggiavo" (*Rosa* 11)

14. Cited by Craig Owens, "The Discourse of Others: Feminism and Postmodernism," in *The Anti-Aesthetic: Essays on Postmodern Culture*, ed. Hal Foster (1983), p. 77.

15. Owens, "The Discourse of Others," p. 67.

16. Jean François Lyotard, *La Condition postmoderne* (1979). An unusual essay by Lyotard, "One of the Things at Stake in the Women's Struggle," *SubStance* 20 (1978), pp. 9-17, may be usefully considered in this regard. An intervention in the feminist debate, or so it purports, the essay appears to speak for women ("It is a philosopher who is speaking here about relations between men and women. He is trying to escape what is masculine in the very posing of such a question; . . . [he] is tempted to give his pen over to the antonym of the inquisitive adult male, to the little girl"). But the argument is in fact a peroration *pro domo sua*, an effort to build the notion of a generalized libidinal economy on the model of what the philosopher understands as female sexuality: "a puzzle of erotic potentialities (fertility, passivity, sensitivity, jealousy)." The conception of such a different sexual space would put an end to "the signifier's *imparium* over the masculine body," would free "the master-warrior-speaker . . . from his armor of words and death." In short, the women's struggle is reclaimed as a tool for the philosopher's discourse, a stake to be driven into the heart of metalanguage and metaphysics.

17. Umberto Eco, *La struttura assente: Introduzione alla ricerca semiologica* (1968), pp. 357-358; translation mine.

18. *The Boston Globe*, 5 April 1984, p. 2.

19. Dorothy L. Sayers, *Gaudy Night* (New York: Avon Books, 1968 [first published in 1936]).

3.2

* A different version of this essay was published in *Studies in 20th Century Literature*, Vol. 10, No. 2, (Spring, 1986).

1. See Rocco Capozzi, "Palimpsests and Laughter: The Dialogical Pleasure of Unlimited Intertexuality in *The Name of the Rose*." *Italica* 66:4 (1989): 413. After Eco's own works, Borges is probably the most commonly cited intertext in *The Name of the Rose*, but English-speaking critics had a surprising tendency to cite Dickens; see for example Robert Caserio, "The Name of the Horse: Hard Times, Semiotics and the Supernatural" in *Novel* 20:1 (1986) 5-23 and Gerhard Joseph, "The Labyrinth and the Library en abyme: Eco, Borges, Dickens," in Mary Ann Caws, ed., *City Images* (New York: Gordon and Breach, 1991), 42-59.

2. Umberto Eco, "Reflections on *The Name of the Rose*," *Encounter* 64: 4 (April 1985), p. 7. Same article as *Postscript to the 'Name of the Rose'* (1984).

3. Alain is given the Latin form of his name, Alanus ad Insulis, in *Rose* 23.

4. The "William" doubtless honors William of Ockham [1285?-1349?], the Franciscan philosopher whose rejection of essentialism and devotion to clarity and simplicity of causal explanation William of Baskerville shares.

5. We are given selections from Holmes's essay, "The Book of Life," which Watson reads skeptically, unaware of its authorship, in *A Study in Scarlet*, chapter 2. Sir Arthur Conan Doyle. *A Study in Scarlet* and *The Sign of Four* (New York: Berkley Books, 1975).

6. Peirce may be regarded as one of the founders of semiotics–which may account for the interest taken in him by semioticians like Thomas Sebeok and Eco him-

self. In his private life Peirce (like Doyle himself) was an accomplished amateur
detective. See Thomas A. Sebeok and Jean Umiker-Sebeok. " 'You Know My
Method': A Juxtaposition of Charles S. Peirce and Sherlock Holmes," in U. Eco
and T.A. Sebeok. eds.. *The Sign of Three: Dupin, Holmes, Peirce.* (1984), pp. 11-54.
7. A minor emendation to the translation is placed in brackets.
8. François Arouet de Voltaire, *Zadig, or Fate,* trans. Tobias Smollett in *Candide
and other Tales* (London: Dent. 1937). p. 11.
9. One of the readers of this essay adds that Wittgenstein's "ladder image comes
from a philosopher of language, Fritz Mauthner, who is famous for his 'gottlose
Mystik'–the mystery of what sustains the world of speaking and of how words
'fit' their referents. This reference-within-reference is, of course, one of Eco's
techniques elsewhere."
10. Barbara Tuchman, *A Distant Mirror* (New York: Knopf, 1978) p. xviii.
11. To say that the political theme detracts *formally* from *The Name of the Rose* is not
to say that I would wish it away. Quite the contrary: as a textural element it is
very largely responsible for the novel's success–especially on a second reading
when mysteries so often fail to hold the reader's attention. I mean only that the
theme functions neither to advance nor retard the conclusion–it neither makes
the solution of the mystery clearer nor distracts us with red herrings–and is
therefore structurally independent of the central mystery around which the
novel is composed.
12. See *The Pursuit of Crime* (New Haven: Yale University Press. 1981), p. 37.
13. Msgr. Ronald Knox published a "Detective Story Decalogue" and S. S. Van Dine
a set of "Twenty Rules" for writing whodunits, both in 1928. They are reprinted
in Howard Haycraft, ed., *The Art of the Mystery Story* (New York: Carroll and
Graf, 1983), pp. 189-96.
14. "The Detective Novel as Game," from *Le Roman Policier* (Buenos Aires: Sur,
1941), reprinted in Glenn W. Most and William W. Stowe, eds., *The Poetics of
Murder* (New York: Harcourt Brace-Jovanovich, 1983), pp. 1-12.
15. Eco has included a rich pattern of allusions to Borges within *The Name of the
Rose,* most obviously in the name of the antagonist, Jorge of Burgos, his sightless
condition, and the nearly infinite, labyrinthine library (like that in Borges's
"The Library of Babylon") in which so much of the memorable action in the
novel takes place.

3.3
*This is the English version, with English references, of an article, with appropriate
Japanese references, written for a book in Japanese, dedicated to Umberto Eco,
titled in English *Ayukawa and the 13 Mysteries of 1900,* published by Tokyo
Shogen sha (Tokyo, 1990). A previous version appeared in *The American Journal
of Semiotics,* 4 (1991), pp. 41-52.

3.4
*A version of this essay will appear in my *Umberto Eco: Signs for These Times* (Cambridge: Cambridge University Press, 1996).
1. "La semiosi ermetica e il 'paradigma del velame'". Introduction to Pozzato 1992.
2. English translation by various hands, Bloomington: Indiana University Press,
1989.

3. Umberto Eco, *Interpretation and Overinterpretation with Richard Rorty, Jonathan Culler and Christine Brooke-Rose*, ed. Stefan Collini; Italian translation *Interpretazione e sovrainterpretazione: Un dibattito con Richard Rorty, Jonathan Culler e Christine Brooke-Rose*, ed. Stefan Collini (Milan: Bompiani, 1995). The Italian edition contains a "Postfazione" by Sandra Cavicchioli (pp. 183-208) that analyzes the Cambridge debate following Eco's Tanner lectures.

4. For examples of these highly amusing views of Dante, see the various essays in Pozzato 1992, or the far more schematic discussion in IO 53-60.

5. Similar arguments may also be found in both *L'idea deforme* and *The Limits of Interpretation*.

6. Eco cites the original Latin (IO 26). I cite from Horace, *The Complete Works of Horace*, trans. and ed. By Casper J. Kraemer (New York: Random House, 1936), p. 6.

7. The strongest argument for a connection between Michel Foucault and Eco's title is made by Thomas Stauder in "*Il pendolo di Foucault*: l'autobiografia segreta di Umberto Eco," *Il lettore di provincia*, 23 (1991), pp. 3-22. Stauder (p. 5) argues that Foucault died in Paris on the 25th of June 1984; Belbo, one of Eco's protagonists, dies between 23 and 24 June of the same year, while Casaubon passes his final night in the novel between 26 and 27 June of 1984. Stauder refuses to believe that these dates are accidentally related and also points to the fact that Michel Foucault's *Les mots et les choses* (first published in 1966; translated into English as *The Order of Things*) was required reading for the seminar Eco offered in Bologna.

8. *L'idea deforme*, p. 37 (author's translation).

9. Roberto Controneo's brief essay, *La diffidenza come sistema: Saggio sulla narrativa di Umberto Eco* (Milan: Anabasi, 1995), plus earlier essays upon which this brief but enlightening book was based, provide the most important discussion of Eco's use of autobiographical data in his second novel, a problem that will be discussed further along in this chapter.

10. For Oulipo, see Warren F. Motte Jr.'s previously cited anthology, *Oulipo: A Primer of Potential Literature* (Lincoln: University of Nebraska Press, 1985). Queneau's book was published by Gallimard in Paris; the English translation by Barbara Wright was published in New York by New Directions in 1958. Eco's own translation of Queneau is *Esercizi di stile* (Turin: Einaudi, 1983) and remains in print in Italy.

11. McHale's book devotes an entire chapter to *Foucault's Pendulum* and is highly recommended reading. For other important interpretations of this novel, see Rocco Capozzi, "*Il pendolo di Foucault*: Kitsch o neo/post-moderno?," *Quaderni d'Italianistica* 11 (1990), 225-37; JoAnn Cannon, "The Imaginary Universe of Umberto Eco: A Reading of *Foucault's Pendulum*," *Modern Fiction Studies* 4 (1992), 895-909; and Giosuè Musca, " La camicia nel nesso: ovverro *Il pendolo di Foucault* di Umberto Eco," *Quaderni medievali* 27 (1989), 104-49; plus the articles by Cristina Degli-Esposti and Norma Bouchard noted below.

12. Talamo 1989:81-99 provides an indispensable outline of the structure of the novel, including the breakdown of the narrative blocks from Belbo's computer files. Equally useful is another similar reference book by Luigi Bauco and Francesco Millocca, *Dizionario del pendolo di Foucault*, ed. Luciano Turrini (Ferrara: Gabriele Corbo, 1989).

13. For example, Bloom declares that " a reading, to be strong, must be a misreading for no strong reading can fail to insist upon itself" (Bloom 1975a:125); or again when Bloom lists four illusions about poetry–that poetry possesses or creates 1) a real presence; 2) a kind of unity; 3) a definite form; and 4) meaning (Bloom 1975a:122). In *Kabbalah and Criticism*, many of Bloom's ideas about textual interpretation, taken to their logical conclusions, would result in the kind of Deconstructionist destruction of meaning that Eco attacks in the followers of Derrida. One of the earliest manifestos of Deconstruction in the United States was a collection of essays containing works by Harold Bloom, Paul De Man, Jacques Derrida, Geoffrey H. Hartman, and J. Hillis Miller: *Deconstruction and Criticism* (New York: Continuum, 1979). Bloom made an important contribution to this collection, an essay entitled "The Breaking of Form" (pp. 1-38), even though in the introduction to the collection, Geoffrey H. Hartman describes Derrida, Miller, and De Man as true deconstructionists, while he claims that Bloom and he are "barely deconstructionists" and "may even write against it on occasion" (p. ix).

14. For example, Bauco and Millocca's *Dizionario del pendolo di Foucault* (pp. 12-13) argues that the plot structure "non è casuale: l'ordine corrisponde a quello previsto dell'Alberto delle sifiroth (e dall'Adam Qadmon) ed esprime un graduale passaggio, una discesa nei vari gradi del divino, dall'Eterno verso il Mondo (Malkut)." In the Kabbalistic theories of Isaac Luria (1534-72), the ten parts of the Sefirot form, in the particular order followed by Eco, the divine figure of Adam Qadmon or the Celestial Adam: the first three sefirot comprise the head, the fourth and the fifth the body; the sixth the trunk; the seventh and the eighth the legs, the ninth the sexual organs; and the tenth the totality of the image (p. 19). That Eco knew of this doctrine and followed its order in his novel there is no doubt. That it means anything other than a general invitation to delve deeply into Kabbalistic readings of the work, thereby producing in the Model Reader the same kinds of paranoid readings experienced by Eco's characters, would be difficult to prove.

15. For a very different interpretation of these Sefirot which are accepted as a true narrative pattern, see Cristina Degli-Esposti, "The Poetics of Hermeticism in Umberto Eco's *Il pendolo di Foucault*," *Forum Italicum* 25:2 (1991), 190.

16. I have supplied English translations for the story about Murat, which is in French even in the English version of the novel.

17. "If anyone should want to know my name,
    I am called Leah. And I spend all my time
    weaving garlands of flowers with my fair hands,
    to please me when I stand before my mirror;
    my sister Rachel sits all the day long
    before her own and never moves away.
    She loves to contemplate her lovely eyes;
    I love to use my hands to adorn myself:
    her joy is in reflection, mine in act."
    Cited from Dante, *The Divine Comedy*- Vol. II: Purgatory. Trans. M. Musa (New York: Penguin, 1985), p.293.

18. Were I a Diabolical critic, I would interpret the reference to Lia/Rachel in *Foucault*'s pendulum as a clear reference to Michel Foucault's postmodern clas-

sic, *The Order of Things: An Archaeology of the Human Sciences*, which begins
with a very famous discussion of Velàzquez's *Las Meninas*, a painting containing
an image reflected in a mirror that Foucault selects as the archetypal example of
the effacement of the subject and representational mimesis.

19. See *The Aesthetics of Chaosmos: The Middle Ages of James Joyce*, pp. 23-32, for Eco's
discussion of epiphany. Eco sees Joyce's concept of epiphany as being derived
not only from the aesthetics of Walter Pater but also from Gabriele d'Annunzio,
whose work Joyce knew well and whose novel *Il fuoco* contains a chapter entitled "Epifania del fuoco."

3.5

1. Jacques Le Goff, "Forcement médiévale et terriblement moderne," *Magazine
Litteraire*, 262 (1989):30-33. This issue was devoted to Umberto Eco. On the role
of the Middle Ages in Eco's first novel, see my *Naming the Rose: Eco, Medieval
Signs, and Modern Theory* (1988).

2. "Le Moyen Age a été une epoque d'hommes, Georges Duby le rappelait
recemment–les romans d'Umberto Eco sont des romans d'hommes. C'est
évident dans *Le nom de la rose*. C'est aussi, me semble-t-il, le cas dans *Le pendule de
Foucault*, malgré la présence de plusieurs personnages féminins dotes de
vigoureuses personnalités et qui représentent souvent la force de la raison face a
la faiblesse des personnages masculins. Pourtant, ce sont eux les heros, bien qu'en
général emportés par le flux de l'histoire. Les femmes n'en sont pas pour autant
ni de simples repoussoirs, ni de purs ressorts romanesques. Elles sont, comme au
Moyen Age, ce qui apporte, pour le meilleur et pour le pire, le trouble dans ce
monde masculin"; Le Goff, "Forcément médiévale," p. 32.

3. See, for example, the works cited in Joseph Consoli, "Navigating the Labyrinth:
A Bibliographic Essay of Selected Criticism of Works of Umberto Eco," *Style*, 27
(1993):478-514.

4. An earlier version of this essay was published under the title "Pinball, Voodoo,
and 'Good Primal Matter': Incarnations of Silence in *Foucault's Pendulum*," in
MLN, 107 (1992):877-91. Since the time of its writing late in 1990, a large body of
theoretical work in feminist and gender studies has critiqued constructions of
gender as both products and processes of the representational, discursive, and
material practices of culture. This work has established that relationships between gender, sexuality, and subjectivity are fluid and complex. In revising the
MLN article for inclusion in the present volume, I think it important to point out
that this essay understands the category of women as referring to subjectivities
constituted by and in systems of culture and representation. My aim here is to
suggest that the dominant western version of that category is reproduced and, I
believe, naturalized by the cultural discourses of gender employed in *Foucault's
Pendulum*.

5. For a discussion of the role of the peasant girl in the several narratives of the
novel, see my *Naming the Rose: Eco, Medieval Signs, and Modern Theory* (1988).
See also Teresa de Lauretis's discussion of the girl in "Gaudy Rose: Eco and Narcissism," *SubStance*, 14.2 (1985):23. This essay also appears in her *Technologies of
Gender: Essays on Theory, Film, and Fiction*.

6. de Lauretis, "Gaudy Rose," pp. 23-24. Although I do not agree with de Lauretis's
observation that in *The Name of the Rose* Eco poses the "question of meaning

production" within a "purely discursive dimension" outside "the field of social practices in their materiality and historicity" (pp. 25-26), I am persuaded by her analysis of gender in the novel, a subject that was largely occluded from my own earlier study of the *Rose*.

7. The quotation in this sentence is from de Lauretis, "Gaudy Rose," pp. 26-27. In his formal response to my comments on Lauretis's position on this matter, Eco says that the "erasure of gender was an evident feature" of his effort to "represent the point of view of medieval monastic society"; "Reading My Readers," *MLN*, 107 (1992):820.

8. Le Goff, "Forcément médiéval," p. 32.

9. On the instability of medieval and modern as categories of difference see *Postscript to "The Name of the Rose*," trans. William Weaver (1984), pp. 13-18, 65-72.

10. My critique of the problem of gender in *Foucault's Pendulum* seeks to go beyond assessments like that of Victoria Nelson, who asserts "that the women characters in this novel are truly awful, if only because Eco tries so earnestly to make them the intellectual equals of their men while still bestowing on them their ancient role as embodiments of the life principle"; "The Hermeticon of Umbertus E." *Raritan*, 13 (1993):98.

11. When this essay was first written, concepts of essentialism had recently become the site of important debate in feminist and gender theory. See, for example, Diana Fuss, *Essentially Speaking: Feminism, Nature, and Difference* (New York: Routledge, 1989); Teresa de Lauretis, "Upping the Anti (sic) in Feminist Theory," *Conflicts in Feminism*, ed. Marianne Hirsch and Evelyn Fox Keller (New York: Routledge, 1990), pp. 255-270; Jane Gallop, Marianne Hirsch, and Nancy K. Miller, "Criticizing Feminist Criticism," in *Conflicts in Feminism*, pp. 349-369; Elizabeth V. Spelman, *Inessential Woman: Problems of Exclusion in Feminist Thought* (Boston: Beacon Press, 1988).

12. I am following the options suggested by Eco in his "*Intentio Lectoris*: The State of the Art," *The Limits of Interpretation* (1990), pp. 44-63. For some excellent discussions of the intersections of Eco's theories and *Foucault's Pendulum* see JoAnn Cannon (1992), 895-909; Rocco Capozzi (1990), 225-37; Linda Hutcheon (1992), 2-16.

13. I borrow this reading of pinball from Robert Artigiani (1992):855-76.

14. Eco has elsewhere explained the incident on which his story of Amparo's possession is based; see Thomas Stauder, (1989), 6. The example of the German psychologist also appears in Eco's account of a visit to Brazil, which bears many other similarities to this episode in the novel; see "Whose Side are the Orixa On?" in *Travels in Hyperreality*, 103-112.

15. It is difficult to distinguish Casaubon's eroticized politics from a politicized eroticism. In one instance as Aglie and Amparo debate the effects of European tradition on the Brazilian slave population, Casaubon interjects this observation into his account of Amparo's remarks about a slave revolt: "Smiling like an angel, she drew her beautiful hand straight across her throat. For me, even Amparo's teeth aroused desire" (186).

16. Hutcheon notes that it is in Brazil that Causabon first succumbs to the "notion of resemblance, . . . the feeling that everything might be related to everything else"; "Eco's Echoes," p. 4.

17. Stauder, 1989, "Un colloquio. . .," pp. 6-7. Since I arrived at these conclusions

before reading the Stauder interview, I was happy to discover that Eco agreed with me!

18. "Whose Side are the Orixa On?" cited in note 12 above.

19. "Whose Side are the Orixa On?" p. 112. This statement bears comparison to a remark Aglie makes when discussing the fate of Brazilian slaves with Amparo: "These children of slaves pay a price in returning a sense of expectation to a West paralyzed by well-being; perhaps they even suffer, but still they know the language of the spirits of nature, of the air, the waters, and the winds. . ." (186).

20. On the gendered discourse of alchemy, see Titus Burckhardt, *Alchemy* (Shaftsbury, Dorset: Element Books, 1986), especially pp. 69, 79, 116-122; C. A. Burland, *The Arts of the Alchemists* (New York: Macmillan, 1988); F. Sherwood Taylor, *The Alchemists: Founders of Modern Chemistry* (London: William Heinemann Ltd., 1951). As I discovered in my effort to learn something about alchemy, much material on the subject is written from the Diabolicals' perspective.

21. Sally G. Allen and Joanna Hubbs, "Outrunning Atalanta: Feminine Destiny in Alchemical Transmutation," *Signs*, 6.2 (1980): 212-213; Burckhardt, *Alchemy*, p. 116.

22. Allen and Hubbs, "Outrunning Atalanta," p. 219.

23. Burckhardt, *Alchemy*, pp. 151, 154.

24. As Allen and Hubbs have shown, one of the alchemical works twice cited in the novel, Michael Maier's *Atalanta Fugiens* (28, 195), suggests that the alchemical collaboration between man and nature "is achieved by denying the independent status of the feminine and by containing and arrogating her creative powers"; "Outrunning Atalanta," p. 215.

25. The advent and triumph of Beatrice occurs in *Purgatorio* 29-31; Dante Alighieri, *The Divine Comedy: Purgatorio*, trans. and commentary by Charles S. Singleton (Princeton: Princeton University Press, 1973).

26. See Eco's several discussions of Hermetic Platonism in *The Limits of Interpretation*, pp. 10, 18-20, 24-32. On the relationship between unlimited semiosis and hermetic drift, see also Cannon, "Imaginary Universe." For an illuminating discussion, from a different perspective, of the ways in which alchemical discourse raises the "problem of the verbal representation of truth," see Lee Patterson, "Perpetual Motion: Alchemy and the Technology of the Self," *Studies in the Age of Chaucer*, 15 (1993):25-57, especially pp. 39 and 44-48.

27. Stauder, "Un Colloquio con Umberto Eco," p. 5. Eco has elsewhere intimated that the stance Lia takes in the novel comes close to his own position on this issue; see his "Reading my Readers," p. 825. Linda Hutcheon suggests that the novel's depiction of the pregnant Lia's commonsense antidote to male diabolicism ironizes Foucault's characterization of sixteenth-century thought, which makes esotericism "a phenomenon of the [male] written word" and sees the spoken female word as a "sign of the passive intellect"; "Eco's Echoes," p. 10.

28. Eco makes a similar point in his response to the larger critique advanced by this essay; "Reading My Readers," pp. 824-25.

29. Hutcheon, "Eco's Echoes," p. 5.

3.7

* Part of this article appeared as "Eco's Pendulum," in *Semiotica* 91:1/2 (1992), 149-159, review-article of *Foucault's Pendulum*.

1. With respect to the parallels between the fourteenth and twentieth centuries, Eco commented in an interview in *Die Zeit*: "What joins the two epochs is exactly this: the feeling of living in a dangerous time of transition" (cited in *Time Magazine*, 23 December 1985:32). In his essay in *Beatus of Liébana*, which accompanies the reproductions of the tenth-century illuminated manuscript of the Beatus commentary on Revelation, Eco reiterates his sense of the apocalyptic character of the two centuries.

2. See also Eco's essays, "Living in the new Middle Ages" and "Dreaming of the Middle Ages," in *Travels in Hyperreality*, in which the author proposes convincing similarities between postmodern and medieval cultural landscapes.

3. *The Island* contains a scene at Richelieu's court in which Colbert explains latitude to Roberto in precise and accurate terms: " 'With instruments that made the ancient astronomers illustrious, the altitude of a star above the horizon is established, its distance from the zenith is deduced; and knowing its declination, and since zenith distance plus or minus declination determines latitude, you know immediately on which parallel you are, that is, how much you are north or south of a known point. That is clear I think.' 'A child could understand it, ' Mazarin said" (p.189).

4. It is an exceedingly happy coincidence that as I was reading *The Island*, I came across Dava Sobel's recent nonfiction account of Harrison's conquest of longitude. Sobel's book, entitled *Longitude*, is a brilliant discussion of what its subtitle describes as "the true story of a lone genius who solved the greatest scientific problem of his time." Although her focus is Harrison, she also discusses the myriad ways of (inaccurately) determining longitude that are dramatized in Eco's novel.

5. Eco gives this list to his fictional Colbert, and has him foresee the need for Harrison's chronometer: "'There is of course one sure method: keep on board a clock that always tells the time of the Paris meridian, then determine the local time at sea, and from the difference in times deduce the difference of longitude. This is the globe on which we live, and you can see how the wisdom of the ancients divided it into three hundred and sixty degrees of longitude, usually starting from the meridian that crosses the Isla de Hierro in the Canaries. In its celestial course, the sun. . .covers fifteen degrees of longitude in one hour, so when in Paris it is midnight, as it is at this moment, then at one hundred eighty degrees of meridian from Paris it is noon. So if you know for sure that in Paris the clocks say, for example, noon, and you can determine that in the place where you are now it is six in the morning, you calculate the difference in time, translate every hour into fifteen degrees, and you will learn that you are ninety degrees from Paris. . . .*But while it is not hard to determine the time in the place where you are making your calculation, it is quite difficult to keep a clock that will continue to tell the correct time after months of navigation on board a ship tossed by the winds, such movement causing error even in the most ingenious of modern instruments, not to mention hourglasses and water clock, which to function properly must rest on an immobile plane* (pp. 191-92, my italics).

6. Another happy conjunction of historical thematics with Eco's novel is Lawrence Weschler's *Mr. Wilson's Cabinet of Wonder: Pronged Ants. Horned Humans, Mice on Toast and Other Marvels of Jurassic Technology*. As Weschler's title suggests, this book discusses the 17th-century *Wunderkammer* and the Baroque naturalism that inspired it.

7. I have already cited Eco's essay "The Poetics of the Open Work" which appears in *The Role of the Reader*. In this essay, he contrasts classical and Renaissance forms, with their frontal perspective, central axis, symmetrical lines and closed angles, to the mobility, dynamism and multiplicity of Baroque forms. Whereas Renaissance perspective "cajoles the eye toward the center in such a way as to suggest an idea of 'essential' eternity rather than movement, [Baroque perspective] tends to an indeterminacy of effect in its play of solid and void, light and darkness, with its curvature, its broken surfaces, its widely diversified angles of inclination. . ..The Baroque work of art never allows a privileged, definitive, frontal view. . ." (*Role* 52).

3.8

1. This is a substantially revised version of my earlier "Umberto Eco's *L'isola del giorno prima*: Postmodern Theory and Fictional Praxis," *Italica* 72 (1995):193-207.
2. Roberto Cotroneo, in *La diffidenza come sistema* (Milano: Anabasi, 1995) proposes reading *The Island* without establishing metonymic relations between Eco's narratives and theoretical inquiries.
3. David Robey, "Introduction" to Umberto Eco, *The Open Work* XX ff. See also Teresa de Lauretis' discussion of Eco's semiotic theory in *Umberto Eco* (Firenze: La Nuova Italia, 1981).
4. In Italy, the debate has been particularly lively in the last decade. See, for example, Luciano Anceschi's *L'Idea del barocco*. Studi su un problema estetico (Bologna: Nuova Alfa, 1984); Guido Guglielmi's "Barocchi e moderni," *Il Verri* 1-2 (1987):97-110; Ezio Raimondi's *Barocco moderno: Carlo Emilio Gadda e Roberto Longhi* (Bologna: CUSL, 1990).
5. For a more detailed explication of analogical flexibility, see *The Limits of Interpretation* 24 ff, where Eco, drawing upon Giulio Camillo Delminio's *Idea del Theatro* (1567) and Cosma Rosselli's *Thesaurus Artificiosae Memoriae* (1579), classifies various forms of similarity.
6. From the theoretical vantage point of Cultural Studies, and drawing upon Teresa de Lauretis' *The Technologies of Gender*, Mieke Bal, in "The Predicaments of Semiotics," *Poetics Today* 13 (1992):543-52, has argued that Eco's appeal to a notion of ground shared by the social group is based on an "unproblematically unified social community," (p. 547) or one which has not been traversed by issues of "gender, class, ethnicity, and age. . ." (p. 548).
7. The author discusses the utopias, informing much European thought from the Middle Ages onwards, of recovering the symbolic propriety and literality of the Adamic language.
8. I am inferring this point from some of the narrator's quotation, and notably the reference to the *Bounty*'s mutiny (p. 507) and to the Bloomian "Anxiety of influence" (p. 512).
9. Jonathan Culler, "In Defence of Overinterpretation," in Eco's *Interpretation and Overinterpretation* 110. Two other critics, Linda Hutcheon and Claudia Miranda, have made analogous arguments in reference to *Foucault's Pendulum*. For additional discussion, see Linda Hutcheon, "Eco's Echoes: Ironizing the (Post)Modern," *Diacritics* 22 (1992):2-6; Claudia Miranda, "Oscillazione fra teoria semiotica e scrittura nel 'Pendolo di Foucault'," *Semiotica: Storia Teoria*

Interpretazione, a cura di Patrizia Magli, Giovanni Manetti, Patrizia Violi (Milano: Bompiani, 1992) pp. 283-303.

10. Remo Ceserani, "Nuotare in un mare pescoso," *L'Indice* (December 1994):6.

11. Alessandro Manzoni, *I promessi sposi* (Milano: Mursia, 1989).

12. Honoré de Balzac, *Le Père Goriot* (Paris: Garnier-Flammarion, 1966) p. 254.

3.9

1. "The Passions of the Soul" and "The Map of Tenderness," chapters 12 and 13, belong to the pastiche, and to the "satire." The implicit text is the "Carte de Tendre" included in the novel *Clelie: histoire romaine* (1654) by M.lle Madeleine de Scudery, which is a paradigmatic example of a *roman à clef*, a product of the Parisian Salon culture during the time of the *précieuses*, and M.lle de Scudery is one of the most famous of the time. In the studies of the literary culture of the seventeenth century the novel appears as an example of the *roman à clef*, whereas recently it has become a topic of study of the semiotic of passions, born within the field of the French semiotic school (Greimas-Fontanille 1991), an example of "figurativization of passions" in Greimasian terms (cfr. Pezzini 1990). To readers aware of these theoretical developments, the satirical intention with regard to the "*sémiotique des passions*" is inescapable, when the narrator rewrites his own personal *Carte de tendre* of Monferrato.

2. The novel has continuous temporal shifts between Roberto's past (his recollections) and his present on the *Daphne*.

3. Quoted in Thomas A. Sebeok and Jean Umiker-Sebeok "You know my method," in *The Sign of Three*, p. 12.

4. There are major differences between Eco's original texts and the English versions, mostly of them change structurally by adding or suppressing paragraphs and even chapters. For that reason, sometimes the quotation appears only in the original text, others in the English version.

5. I use "fabula" in the sense of the traditional opposition between "fabula" and "plot" formulated by the Russian formalists (cfr. Victor Erlich. *Russian Formalism*. The Hague: Mouton, 1954). Eco's formulation of these concepts is that the fabula or story "is the fundamental scheme of the narration, the logic of the actions and the syntax of the characters, the course of events in chronological order" while the plot "is the way in which the story is told, its structure, and its temporal dislocations, flashbacks, flashforwards (or rather foreshadows and flash-backs), descriptions, digressions, parenthetical reflections. In a narrative text the plot is identified with the discursive structures" (*Lector* 102).

6. The half-hearted pragmatist, for Rorty, is a "kind of textualist who claims to have gotten the secret of the text" who thinks that there really is a secret code and that once it's discovered we shall have gotten the text right. He believes that criticism is discovery rather than creation (1982:152).

7. It is possible to make an analogy of the topology of writing outlined by Rorty's classification and Dante's three worlds. In this *Critical Comedy* the "true pragmatists" would be in the Paradise of Writers, the "half-hearted pragmatists" would be floundering in the Purgatory of Critics, and the "realists of common sense" and the "Kantians" would be in Hell. If in the first case we spoke of "writers," in the second, of "critics" and in the third, of "philosophers," it is because, according to Rorty, for the true pragmatist, there is no difference between read-

ing and writing, theory and writing, literature and philosophy, nor in any of the categories in any combination. They live in the undifferentiated universe of "writing." The inhabitants of Purgatory, on the other hand, still differentiate between writing and criticism, discovery and creation, but this notwithstanding, they are on the path that can lead them to higher places. The inhabitants of Hell however, they are the damned who believe that human thought culminates in the application of the "scientific method."

8. I am not referring to a mere psychological level, but to an imaginary "Theoretical Metapsychology" that would analyze the pathemic structures that lies beneath each theoretical construction.

9. I would like to point out that, within the deconstructionist framework, Eco makes a clear distinction between Derrida and American deconstruction. He points out "pretextual reading" is something Derrida does "not in order to interpret the text but to show how much language can produce unlimited semiosis," and this type of interpretation has a philosophical function. Eco's fundamental theoretical objection is against the transposition of this method of reading texts to the field of literary criticism

10. As Eco points out "the pragmatism of which Rorty speaks is not the pragmaticism of Peirce. Rorty knows that Peirce only invented the word pragmatism but remained the most Kantian of thinkers" (*Limits* 161)

11. For Eco "The idea of a *purpose*, pretty natural for a pragmaticist, is pretty embarrassing for a 'pragmatist' (in Rorty's sense). A purpose is, without any shade of doubt, and at least in the Peircean framework, connected with something which lies outside language. Maybe it has nothing to do with a transcendental subject, but it has to do with referents, with the external world, and links the idea of interpretation to the idea of interpreting according to a given meaning. When Peirce provides his famous definitium of "lithium" as a packet of instructions aimed at permitting not only the identification but also the production of a specimen of lithium, he remarks: 'The peculiarity of this definition it that it tells you what the word "lithium" denotes by prescribing what you are to do in order to gain a perceptive acquaintance with the object of the word' 2.330)." (*Limits* 38).

12. The interesting reflections of Debrock about Peirce's thinking can be seen in the "Introduction" to Debrock & Hulswit 1994.

13. Eco discusses about the abstract categories of Model Author and Model reader as examples of textual strategies troughout the opening chapters of *Role*.

14. Though Eco admits the difficulty in distinguishing between "use" and "interpretation," in *The Limits of Interpretation* he presents a strong case of "interpretation" of texts in opposition to the "use" of texts that deconstructionists seem to favor.

15. In *The Limits of Interpretation* (Ch. 2) Eco identifies a type of interpretation that runs through the centuries and that assumes that to interpret a text means to find out the meaning intended by its original author, or–in any case–its objective nature or essence, an essence which, as such, is independent of our interpretation [. . .] [this type of interpretation] is instantiated by various kinds of fundamentalism and of various forms of metaphysical realism (let us say, the one advocated by Aquinas or by Lenin in *Materialism and Empiriocriticism*). Knowledge is *adaequatio rei et intellectus*. The most outrageous example of the alternative option is certainly [. . .] the paradigm of the *Hermetic semiosis* (*Limits* 24).

16. As we recall, *The Name of the Rose* ends with a verse from Bernardo Morliacense's *De contemptu mundi*: stat rosa pristine nome, nomina nuda tenemus (the primogenial rose exists as a name, we have only names).

17. The Italian verb for the German "wandern" is "passeggiare" and "Sei passeggiate nei boschi narrativi" is the Italian title for *Six walks in the fictional woods*, transcription of the "Norton Lectures" Eco held at Harvard University during the academic year 1992-1993, the same period of time he was writing the novel. I think that "Wanderdrossel" is a very good name for Father Caspar, because this character is a *rara avis* found by Eco during one of his "wandern" (walks) in the fictional woods of the *Bildungsroman*. In the figure of Father Caspar, one of Roberto's three teachers on the novel, there are echoes of characteristics of the Jesuit Lowe Naphta, one of Hans Castorp's teachers in Thomas Mann's *Magic Mountain*. Playing Escherian Metamorphosis, Eco has transformed the Mannian lion (Löwe) into a bird (Drossel).

18. One could state that il *gemitus significativus* of the dove in *The Island of the Day Before* is only a late and collateral effect of a bad translation of Aristotle. In *De Interpretatione* he spoke of the noises (agrammatoi psophoi) of animals, distinguishing clearly between noises and sounds. That nuance gets lost in the Boethius's translation of Aristotle. As Eco states: "unfortunately, from Boethius onward, the medieval commentators translated the Aristotelian *phone'* (sound) with *vox*, and *psòphos* (noise) with *sonus*. Thus from the medieval commentators animals without lungs emit sounds, but animals with lungs emit voices, and *voces* can be *significativae*" (*Limits* 114). The road is open for a significant *gemitus* of the dove.

19. Hidden behind this analogy there is a long semiotic history. The *gemitus infirmorum* has been the object of multiple classifications from Boethius to Bacon, the history of this has recently been traced by Eco in "Interpreting Animals" (*Limits* Ch. 7).

20. Coe (1995) and Lumley (1995) are good examples of this type of reading, unable to identify any meaning in the text. Capozzi (1996) mentions other examples of this type of reading among the Italian critics.

21. In *Postscript to the Name of the Rose,* trying to explain the possible origin of the novel's idea, Eco says "It seems that the Parisian Oulipo group has recently constructed a matrix of all possible murder-story situations and has found that there is still to be written a book in which the murderer is the reader" (*Postscript* 78).

22. The relationship between abduction and interpretation and between detective work and interpretation of a text is outlined in greater depth in Eco's semiotic theory. A noted example is the anthology of the texts *The Sign of the Three*.

23. The Italian dictionary's definition is "symbolic figure usually accompanied by a motto, a statement, or an explanation in verse or in prose" (Zingarelli 1983).

24. I want to underline that the same word that in a theoretical field Eco uses to refers to "semiosis": "device," is the synonym of "emblem," used by the (translator of the) narrator of the novel to refers to the dove's enigma. I ask myself if it is only an innocent "effect of translation," or another clue given to us by a Model Author, who is able to play his puzzle-game foreseeing the translation of his own text.

25. In the fifth volume of the *Grande Dizionario della lingua italiana* (Battaglia 1968), under the entry "emblem" there are the following examples: *De Sanctis*, II-15-67: Those Calabrians that then yelled "death" to the liberals, raised to 48 the

first cry of freedom in Europe; and the Calabrian hats, then insignia for Holy
Faith, made the rounds of Europe, emblem of liberty for the people who were
rising up. *B. Croce*, I-1-249: Sharply he [Vico] returning to . . . figurative language,
not only the hieroglyphics, but emblems, chivalric deeds, arms and coats of
arms, which said the "Medieval hieroglyphics."

26. During the night of the seventh day, while the library is burning, Guglielmo says
Adso: "The order that our mind imagines is like a net, or like a ladder, built to
attain something. But afterward you must throw the ladder away, because you
discover that, even if it was useful, it was meaningless. Er muoz gelîchesame die
leiter abewerfen, soêr an ir ufgestigen. . .Is that how you say it?
That is how it is said in my language. Who told you that?'
A mystic from your land . He wrote it somewhere, I forget where.'" (*Rose* 492).
Guglielmo doesn't remember that this is one of the last statements in
Wittgenstein's *Tractatus Logicus Philosophicus*, in order not to commit an anach-
ronism.

27. "But according to definite rules" is our translation for the clause "ma secondo
regole precise" that appears on page 8 of original text , yet was not carried over in
the English translation (SPL 17).

28. According to David, the *ricercar* was in Bach's mind, a kind of fugue (David
1945).

29. This musical form was developed in the 17th-century by Flamish masters who
worked in Italy, among them Adrian Willaert and Jacques Buus. Later was developed by Venetians Claudio Merulo and Andrea Gabrielli, and obtained its definitive form in the Frescobaldi's *ricercari*, admired by Bach (David 1945:28-30).

3.10
* The first draft of this article appeared in *Rivista di studi italiani* 1(1996):158-189.
1. I am using the Foucault binomial "knowledge and power" because Michel
Foucault's writings are often present in Eco's work. On Foucault's "archeology
of knowledge" see in particular, *The Order of Things*, trans. by Alan Sheridan-
Smith (1970) and, *Power/Knowledge: Selected Interviews and Other Writings*
(1980), ed. by Colin Gordon. Also, see *Irony-clad Foucault*, Hutcheon's contribution to this anthology.
2. The many analogies between The Middle Ages and the Seventeenth Century's
aesthetics, philosophy and overall artistic manifestations, have been amply studied by critics such as Mario Praz. See above all *Studies in Seventeenth Century
Imagery* (1939). Eco's encyclopedic competence/presentation of the Middle
Ages in *The Name of the Rose* can be compared to his equally enlightening illustration of the Seventeenth Century world in *The Island*.
3. In my review of *L'isola del giorno prima*, in *Rivista di Studi Italiani* (June 1995),
pp. 216-222, I have mentioned an analogy between Italo Calvino's trilogy *I nostri
antenati* (1960, "Our Ancestors") and Eco's novels (trilogy?)–in the way they
both use historical metafictions to show the similarities that exist between the
old and the new, ancients and moderns. Moreover since my first article on Eco's
Rose I have maintained that Calvino may also be partly responsible for Eco's
deep appreciation of Borges. For some of my views on Eco's fiction see *"Il*

pendolo di Foucault: Kitsch o neo-/post-moderno" (Capozzi 1990), and "Palimpsests and Laughter: The Dialogical Pleasure of Unlimited Intertextuality in *The Name of the Rose*" (Capozzi 1989).

4. Dante dedicates Canto XXVI of the *Inferno* to Ulysses' allegoric mad or foolish flight (the "folle volo") and to his symbolic thirst for knowledge. Eco continues to demonstrate how, throughout the centuries, from the days of the Templars to the present, knowledge and secrets are also equated with power and control.

5. For Eco's theories on language, semiotics and metaphor, see *Semiotics and the Philosophy of Language* and *The Search for the Perfect Language*. For his notions on narratology and on reader's reception theories see *The Role of the Reader* and *The Limits of Interpretation*. These are four basic texts that could be considered as Eco's key intra/intertextual palimpsests from/on which he traces his novels.

6. It is worth recalling that in the opening pages of *A Theory of Semiotics* we find Eco stating: "Thus semiotics is in principle the discipline studying everything which can be used in order to lie"(p. 7). In *Semiotics and the Philosophy of Language,* speaking about the creation of metaphors, Eco affirms: "It is obvious that when someone creates metaphors, he is, literally speaking, lying–as everybody knows"(p. 89).

   Moreover, in one of Eco's most important eclectic collections of essays, *Dalla periferia dell'impero* (1977) we find essays on lying, such as "Morfologia della bugia" ("The morphology of lying"), pp. 167-172, and "Mentire con la foto" ("Lying with photos"), pp. 289-293; two topics that we see discussed in Eco's semiotic essays. I must thank Paul Perron for bringing to my attention that in M. Blonsky's *On Signs* (1985:3-11) appears Eco's article "Strategies of Lying"–a slightly revised and translated version of the 1976 articles which are most pertinent to our discussion on *The Island*. The discussions on Mazarin, lying, spying, and on the art of dissimulation [see Perron and Debbèche in this anthology] are, in fact, all present, in narrative form, in *The Island*.

7. This key notion already present in *The Open Work* (1989; the Italian original, *Opera aperta*, was published in 1962) is further developed and emphasized in *The Role of the Reader* and *Six Walks in the Fictional Woods*.

8. Elsewhere I have discussed how Eco's "postmodernism" must be qualified in terms of its content, methodology and intentionality. Eco's fiction has very little in common with most of the so-called Italian postmodern narratives of the eighties. Eco's postmodernism is much more in line with postmodern American theories and practices promoted by writers such as Fiedler and Barth, and with the encyclopedic postmodernism of narrators such as Borges, Calvino and Pynchon (see Capozzi 1993).

9. In my work in progress on Eco's narrative strategies I investigate how in Eco's postmodernism we see a clever interaction of theoretical writings of Peirce, Lotman, Austin, Foucault, and Baudrillard. In this interaction the element of "performance" stands out as a key vehicle for manifesting aspects of knowledge and modern culture.

10. There is a whole field of research on metaphor as cognitive structures that Eco is well aware of and that he certainly alludes to in *The Island* and naturally in his essays. See especially G. Lakoff and M. Johnson *Metaphors we live by* (1980).

11. For a global presentation of various aspects of intertextualities see Heinrich F. Plett's article "Intertextualities," in his outstanding collection of essays, *Intertextuality* (1991:3-29).

12. Black's definition of "interaction-metaphors" seems quite *á propos* to Eco's application of interactive metaphors, intertextuality and postmodern pastiches:

    Too speak of the "interaction" of two thoughts "active together"(or, again, of their "interillumination" or "co-operation") is to use a metaphor emphasizing the dynamic aspects of a good reader's response to a nontrivial metaphor (1962:9).

    Their mode of operation requires the reader to use a system of implications (a system of "commonplaces"–or a special system established for the purpose in hand) as a means for selecting, emphasizing, and organizing relations in a different field. This use of a "subsidiary subject" to foster insight into a "principal subject" is a distinctive intellectual operation (through one familiar enough through our experiences of learning anything whatever), demanding simultaneous awareness of both subjects but not reducible to any comparison between the two (p. 46).

13. For an overall view of the interactive role of metaphor see Richards 1936; Black 1962, 1990; Conte 1972; and Cabot Haley 1988.

14. Borges' short story "Pierre Menard Author of Don Quixote," from *Fictions*, has received a great deal of attention from critics who examine the parodic act of rewriting palimpsests. Eco is no exception as he continues to pay his debts to Borges in *The Island*. For example, when we see Ch. 5 "The Labyrinth of the World" and on its first page we read "peregrination in a territory made up of forked paths" (p.49), an "inferential walk" in Borges' fiction is quite normal, and perhaps even expected.

15. See *Palimpsestes: La littérature au second degré* (1982), and *Seuil* (1987).

16. Barth's articles were first published in *The Atlantic*, August 1967 and January 1980, respectively. Now they appear with many other interesting essays on literature in *The Friday Book. Essays and Other Nonfiction*. For more recent views on postmodernism see also his *Further Fridays. Essays, Lectures and Other Nonfiction 1984-94*.

17. Here Eco speaks specifically of *The Anxiety of Influence* (1973), but in *The Name of the Rose* and, even more so, in *Foucault's Pendulum* the author had made numerous allusions also to *A Map of Misreading* (1975), *Poetry and Repression* (1976), and *Kabbalah and Criticism* (1975).

18. "Questo genere di componimento che romanzo è chiamato dai moderni, scriveva Giovanni Battista Manzini nella prefazione al suo *Cretideo* nel 1637, è la più stupenda e gloriosa macchina che fabbrichi l'ingegno. È più nobile dell'Istoria. . . contiene poi di vantaggio tutti i meriti della Poetica. . . egli supera la stessa epopea" [This type of composition that moderns call romance, wrote G.B. Manzini, in the preface to his *Cretideo* in 1637, is the most stupendous and glorious machine that ingenuity can create. It is more noble than History.. It has the advantage of all the merits of Poetics. . . it surpasses even the epic"–my trans.] As quoted in *La più stupenda e gloriosa macchina. Il romanzo italiano del sec. XVII.* Ed. by Marco Santoro (1981).

19. The analogies between Eco's fiction and Pynchon's encyclopedic novels like *V* and *Gravity's Rainbow* are far too many to be discussed here. In both authors

readers find a plethora of references to movies, TV and other pop culture and mass media sources of entertainment and information.

20. Just as with Roberto's name, Eco has a field day with possible allusions related to the name Ferrante, among which we must include the XVIIth century author Ferrante Pallavicino. However the most witty allusion emerges when the narrator asks jokingly if the name was Ferrante or Ferrand, and thus openly playing with the intertextual echo of Jacques Ferrand, author of *A Treatise on Love Sickness*. For Ferrand's treatise (clearly appropriated by Eco for his discussion on Roberto's love melancholy) see the translation edited by Donald A. Beecher and Massimo Ciavolella (1990). It is important to note that J. Ferrand's treatise appears also in *The Name of the Rose* in conjunction with Adso's love sickness.

21. Father Caspar is a "persona." Eco is inspired by Father Caspar Schott, a student of Athanasius Kircher.

22. I am using the term "neo-baroque" not only because of the historical and literary frame within which Eco's story takes place, but also in reference to Omar Calabrese's definition of postmodernism, argued so convincingly in *Neo-Baroque. A Sign of the Times* (1992)–with a preface by Eco. For the baroque notion of instilling "wonder" in a work of art, as well as for some excellent views on metaphor, on Marino, on Tesauro, and on the XVIIth century "wonderful narrative machines," I have found the studies of Ezio Raimondi of immense help. See above all *Il mondo della metafora. Il seicento letterario italiano* (1987); also: *Letteratura barocca* (1982) and *Trattatisti e narratori del seicento* (1961). I would also suggest the works of Mario Praz for an insightful presentation of the general imagery of mannerism and baroque, as well as for a study of metaphysical poets like John Donne and their relations to Italian baroque writers.

Again I would like to bring to our attention the article by Perron and Debbèche in which we see Eco's expression "a piece of High Baroque theatre" (Blonsky p. 5) and numerous other terms discussed by the authors (i.e., on power, deceit, dissimulation, Dumas, and so on) applied to "Strategies of Lying" which are all *à propos* for *The Island*. Also, the two XVIIth Century authors mentioned by Perron and Debbèche in their endnote 3, Gracián and Accetto, in Eco's novel play an important role for the topics of "Prudence" and "Dissimulation".

23. At least 200 of them are enclosed within actual parentheses and there are many more authorial interventions which can be recognized in ironic statements and other means of indirect addressing to readers.

24. The model for the art of narrative digressions remains Laurence Sterne's *Tristram Shandy*. In *The Island* the debt to Sterne becomes even more interesting if we think of how Sterne quotes in his own novel Robert Burton on medicine and love sickness (from *The anatomy of melancholy*, 1622). The relation between Burton and Ferrand is also one of intertextuality and appropriation if we consider that Burton allegedly plagiarized some pages from Ferrand. For this discussion see Beecher's and Ciavolella's introduction in J. Ferrand *Treatise on Love Sickness, op. cit.*

25. In Roberto's learning/formative experiences we can find plenty of resemblances with Adso's cultural, semiotic and romantic education in *The Name of the Rose.*

26. Roberto's name is a brilliant and witty baroque construction. The name, in addition to recalling an Italian saying: "it is like the Pozzo of San Patrizio" (meaning it is endless), becomes much more symbolic if we think specifically of the famous

well in Orvieto. The historical "Pozzo di San Patrizio" (commissioned by Pope Clement VII) is an architectural wonder. The well is known for its incredible depth, its numerous internal windows, its unusual light source, and above all for its complementary symmetrical spiral staircases.

27. Given the historical moment it is easy to understand how Eco dwells at great length on the benefits derived from the discovery of the telescope. *The Island* exploits a number of scientific discoveries that at the same time echo Jules Verne's fiction. In *The Name of the Rose* we had seen Eco do the same thing with scientific inventions like William's eye glasses.

28. From Eco's interviews we learn that he had fun doing the scientific research, on location, in the Fiji Islands. We also learn why he had shaved his famous beard for a few months. See Eco's comments in: Antonella Rampini's "L'Eco del futuro," *Capital* (Nov. 1994), pp. 17-24; Silvia Sereni's "C'è un segreto in fondo al mio nuovo libro," *Epoca* (9 ottobre 1994), pp. 57-59; Roberto Barbolini's "La carica del Seicento," *Panorama* (7 ottobre 1994), pp. 79-84.

29. Speaking of Eco as an incredible voracious reader with an encyclopedic mind, I would recall that whereas he was already well educated in the history and literature of the Middle Ages, for the writing of *Foucault's Pendulum* and of *The Island of the Day Before* the author must have consulted hundreds of sources that "competent readers" will recognize and have fun with while reading the novel. For *The Island* we should take into consideration Eco's central role in the development of the "Encyclomedia CD *Il Seicento*-a remarkable multimedia encyclopedia of the Italian XVIIth Century.

30. Readers will certainly notice the frequent appearances of words like spectacle, spectator, theater, and theatrical from the beginning to the end of the story.

31. See Eco's discussion on the importance of Leibniz, Locke and John Wilkins in *The Search for the Perfect Language* and in *The Limits of Interpretation*. Some excellent pages on John Locke's role in the development of semiotics are found in John Deely's *New Beginning. Early Modern Philosophy and Postmodern Thought* (1994:109-144).

32. Of Mario Praz see above all: *Studies in Seventeenth-century imagery* (1939); *Mnemosyne: The Parallel between literature and the visual arts* (1939); *Il giardino dei sensi: studi sul manierismo e sul barocco* (1975), and *La poesia metafisica del seicento. John Donne* (1945).

33. As Eco has pointed out in *Semiotics and the Philosophy of Language*, for Aristotle "wonder induces persons to philosophize" (p. 19). Two things that Adso in *The Rose* and Roberto in *The Island* do very well.

34. For an informative study of Marino and his work (with several references to Tesauro) see James V. Mirollo, *The Poet of the Marvelous. G. Marino* (1963).

35. In a novel about loss of a "center" and about separated "souls" (brothers and lovers), Donne's lyrics, in which he uses the image of the "compass," could not have been more appropriate as a fitting metaphor of Roberto's condition–I am referring to both, his love for Lilia and his love-hate relationship with Ferrante.

36. In one of the first reviews of *L'isola del giorno prima*, Luciano Berio claims that Eco's third novel is one of the most musical narratives he has ever read. See: "Leggetelo, anzi ascoltatelo: è musica," in *L'Espresso* (7 Oct. 1994), 28. Eco certainly had fun with musical intertextuality. For example the boats in *The Island* are shaped like "fluyte"–flutes. And, hardly by coincidence, the boats' names are

"*Daphne*," "*Tweene Daphne*" and "*Amaryllis*," which are seventeenth century flute compositions by Jackob van Eyck (I thank Eco for confirming this witty piece of trivia).

An excellent encyclopedic account of music and the XVIIth Century (with specific references to Marino) is given by Lorenzo Bianconi in *Il Seicento* (1982).

37. This is all part of Eco's view on postmodernism, defined and explained in "Postmodernism, Irony, The Enjoyable." See *Postscript to The Name of the Rose* (1984), pp. 65-72.

38. In addition to the obvious allusion to "a" (and not necessarily "the") fixed point from which one can make specific references, Eco may also be alluding more specifically to the "punto fijo" that Cervantes mentions in his " El Coloquio de los perros" (I thank Eco for confirming this bit of information). In this witty picaresque story Cervantes not only speaks of a metaphoric "punto fijo" that can be found anywhere, but, more pertinent to *The Island*, he makes use of intertextual literary echoes and exploits a pun on the "quest for the Holy Grail" in quoting "la Historia de la demanda del Santo Brial"; see M. De Cervantes, *El Coloquio de los perros* (Madrid: Zaragoza, 1938), p.119.

The importance of this passage on the "punto fijo" can be seen also in relation to *The Rose* and *Foucault's Pendulum* where the main protagonist searched in vain for a center, a fixed point, or a secret plan:

I've been looking, for the fixed point for twenty-two years, and within an ace of finding it; and when I think I've found it and that it can't escape me come what may, all of a sudden I find I'm so far away from it that I'm absolutely amazed. The same thing happens to me over squaring the circle: I've got so near finding the final answer, that I don't know and can't think how I haven't already got it in my pocket, and so I suffer the tortures of Tantalus, who was within reach of fruit and yet dying of hunger, and right beside water and yet perishing of thirst (Cervantes *Exemplary Stories*, p. 249).

39. "Casablanca. A Cult Movie," in *SubStance*, 47 (1985). Also, "Casablanca: Cult Movies and Intertextual Collage," in *Travels* 197-212.

40. For some interesting observations on the development of the novel in Italy, in the 17th century, see *La più stupenda e gloriosa macchina. Il romanzo italiano del sec. XVII*, op. cit.; M. Capucci, *Romanzieri del seicento* (1974); and, Albert Mancini, *Romanzi e romanzieri del seicento* (1981).

41. In "Palimpsests and Laughter: The Dialogical Pleasure of Unlimited Intertextuality," *op. cit.*, I have discussed how in *The Name of the Rose* Eco demonstrates some analogies between the Peircean concept of unlimited semiosis and the practice of unlimited intertextuality which also send us to Bakhtinian and Derridean notions of intertextuality. Among the many excellent texts which have appeared on the postmodern applications of intertextuality in the last twenty years I would again point out the collection of essays edited by Heinrich F. Plett: *Intertextuality* , op. cit..

42. See "Postmodernism, Irony, The Enjoyable," *op. cit.*. Also see Leslie Fiedler's famous article "Cross the Border–Close the Gap," now in *The Collected Essays of Leslie Fiedler* (1971).

43. Snow, *The Two Cultures and The Scientific Revolution* (1959). Walter Benjamin, "The Work of Art in the Age of Mechanical Reproduction," now in *Illuminations*, ed. by Hanna Arendt (1968), pp. 217-251.

Integrated Bibliography

Adams, Robert M. 1974. Theories of Actuality. *Noûs* 8:211-31.

Agosti, Stefano. 1989. *Enunciazione e racconto.* Bologna: Il Mulino.

Alazraki Jaime. 1988. *Borges and the Kabbalah.* Cambridge: Cambridge University Press.

Allèn, Sture, ed. 1989. *Possible Worlds in Humanities, Arts and Sciences.* Berlin and New York: Walter de Gruyter.

Almansi, Guido, and Guido Fink. 1976. *Quasi come.* Milan: Bompiani.

Anceschi, Luciano. 1984. *L'idea del barocco.* Bologna: Nuova Alfa.

Apel, Karl-Otto. 1970. *Der Denkweg von Charles S. Peirce.* Frankfurt am Main: Suhrkamp, Verlag.

Apel, Karl. 1964. Peirce's theory of perception. In: *Studies in the Philosophy of Charles Sanders Peirce,* ed. Edward C. Moore and Richard Robin, pp. 165-189. Amherst: University of Massachusetts Press.

Appleyard, Bryan. 1995. U. Eco is a rare thing: a high priest of semiotics who sells novels by the million. (Review of *The Island of the Day Before*). *Independent* (Oct. 6):10-11.

Ardener, Edwin. 1971a. The new anthropology and its critics. *Man* n.s. 6:449-67.

Ardener, Edwin. 1971b. Social anthropology and language. In: *Social Anthropology and Language.* A.S.A. Monographs 10, ed. Edwin Ardener, pp. ix-cii. London: Tavistock Press.

Arnheim, Rudolph. 1971. *Entropy and Art. An Essay on Disorder and Order.* Berkley: University of California Press.

Aristotle. 1909. *Poetics,* trans. I Bywather. Oxford: Oxford University Press.

Artigiani, Robert. 1992. Image-Music-Pinball. *Modern Language Notes.* 107 (5):855-76.

Asad, Talal. 1979. Anthropology and the analysis of ideology. *Man* n.s. 14:607-27.

Atlan, H. 1987. Uncommon Finalities. In: *Gaia,* ed. W. I. Thompson. Great Barington, Mass.: Lindisfarne.

Austin, J. L. 1962. How To Do Things With Words. London: Oxford University Press.

Baer, Eugen. 1992. Via Semiotica. *Semiotica* 92:351-57.

Black, Max. 1962. Models and Metaphors: Studies in Language and Philosophy. Ithaca: Cornell University Press.

Bailey, R. W., L. Matejka and P. Steiner, eds. 1978. The Sign Around the World. Ann Arbor, Michigan: Michigan Slavic Publications.

Bakhtin, M. M. 1963. Problems of Dostoevsky's Poetics, trans. R. W. Rotsel. Ann Arbor: Ardis.

Bakhtin, M. M. 1968. Rabelais and His World, trans. Helene Iswolsky. Cambridge, Mass.: The MIT Press.

Bakhtin, M. M. 1979. Estetika slovesnogo tvorcestva. Moscow: Isskustvo. The principal essay of this work, 'Author and hero in aesthetic activity', is scheduled to appear in English translation under the University of Texas imprint.

Bakhtin, M. M. 1981. The Dialogic Imagination: Four Essays by M. M. Bakhtin, trans. Caryl Emason and Michael Holquist; ed. Michael Holquist. Austin: University of Texas Press, Slavic Series 1.

Bakhtin, M. M. 1984. Problems of Dostoevsky's Poetics, trans. Caryl Emerson (ed.) Minneapolis: University of Minnesota Press, Theory and History of Literature Series 8.

Bakhtin, M. M. 1986. Speech Genres and Other Late Essays, trans. Vern W. McGee; ed. Caryl Emerson and Michael Holquist. Austin: University of Texas Press, Slavic Series 8.

Bakhtin, Mikhail and Vološinov, Valentin N. 1927. Frejdizm: Kriticeskij ocerk. Moscow-Leningrad: Gosizdat. [1987. Freudianism: A Critical Sketch, trans. I. R. Titunik, ed. I. R. Titunik and N. H. Bruss. Bloomington and Indianapolis: Indiana University Press.]

Bakhtin, Mikhail and Vološinov, Valentin N. 1930 [1929]. Marksizm i filosofija: Osnovnye problemy sociologiceskogo metoda v naüke o jazyke. Leningrad. [1973. Marxism and the Philosophy of Language, trans. L. Matejka and I. R. Titunik. New York and London: Seminar Press.]

Bal, Mieke. 1992. The Predicaments of Semiotics. Poetics Today 13:543-52.

Balzac, Honoré de. 1966. Le Père Goriot. Paris: Garnier-Flammarion.

Bang, Preben, and Preben Dahlstrom. 1972. Collins Guide to Animal Tracks and Signs: A Guide to the Tracking of All British and European Mammals and Birds. London: Collins.

Barsky, Robert F. and Holquist, Michael, eds. 1990. Bakhtin and Otherness. Discours social/Social Discourse 3 (1/2). Special issue.

Barthes, Roland. 1957. Mythologies. Paris: Éditions du Seuil.

Barthes, Roland. 1964. Eléments de sémiologie. Communications 4.

Barthes, Roland. 1964. Eléments de sémiologie. Paris: Éditions du Seuil. [1967. Elements of Semiology, trans. Annette Lavers and Colin Smith. New York: Hill and Wang.]

Barthes, Roland. 1966. L'analyse structurale du récit. Communications 8. Paris: Seuil.

Barthes, Roland. 1967. Système de la mode. Paris: Éditions du Seuil.

Barthes, Roland. 1970a. New preface to Mythologies, pp. 7-8. Paris: Éditions du Seuil.

Barthes, Roland. 1970b. S/Z. Paris: Éditions du Seuil. [1974. S/Z, trans. Richard Miller. New York: Hill and Wang.]

Barthes, Roland. 1974. L'aventure sémiologique. Le Monde, June 7.

Barthes, Roland. 1975. Roland Barthes par Roland Barthes. Paris: Éditions du Seuil. [1977. Roland Barthes by Roland Barthes, trans. Richard Howard. New York: Hill and Wang.]

Barthes, Roland. 1977. Image-Music-Text. New York: Hill and Wang.

Barthes, Roland. 1980. From Work to Text. In: *Textual Strategies. Perspective in Post-Structuralist Criticism*, ed. By J. V. Harari. London: Methuen.

Barthes, Roland. 1981. *Le grain de la voix, Entretiens 1962-1980*. Paris: Éditions du Seuil.

Barthes, Roland. 1982. *L'Obvie et l'obtus. Essais critiques III*. Paris: Éditions du Seuil.

Barthes, Roland. 1986. *The Rustle of Language*, trans. Richard Howard. Oxford: Basil Blackwell.

Bauco, Luigi, and Millocca, Francesco. 1989. *Dizionario del pendolo di Foucault*. Ferrara: Gabriele Corbo.

Bean, Susan S. 1981. Toward a semiotics of 'purity' and 'pollution' in India. *American Ethnologist* 8:575-95.

Beebee, Thomas O. 1992. The Legal Theaters of Bertold Brecht. In: *Law and Aesthetics*, ed. R. Kevelson, pp. 37-68. New York: Peter Lang Publishing.

Belleau, Andre. 1970-71. Bakhtine et le multiple. *Etudes françaises*, 4-V1:481-86.

Ben-Porat, Ziva. 1976. The Poetics of Literary Allusion. *PTL* 1:105-28.

Bennett, T. 1979. *Formalism and Marxism*. Methuen and Co. Ltd.

Benjamin, Walter. 1977. *The Origin of the German Tragic Drama*. London: Lowe & Brydone Printers.

Bense, Max. 1975. *SemiotischeProzesse und Systeme*. Baden-Baden: Agis Verlag.

Bense, Max. 1976. Vermittlung der Realitaeten. Baden-Bade: Agis Verlag.

Benveniste, Emile. 1966. De la subjectivité dans le langage. In: *Problémes de linguistiques générale*, pp. 258-66. Paris: Gallimard.

Berardinelli, Alfonso. 1988. Eco, o il pensiero pendolare. *Linea d'ombra*, 31 Oct., pp. 3-6.

Bernstein, Basil. 1972. Social class, language and socialization. In: *Language and Social Context*, ed. Pier Paolo Giglioli, pp. 157-78. Harmondsworth: Penguin Books.

Bernstein, Basil, ed. 1973. *Class Codes and Control*, Vol. 2. *Applied Studies toward a Sociology of Language* (Primary socialization: language and education). London: Routledge and Kegan Paul.

Bernstein, Richard J. 1964. Peirce's theory of perception. In: *Studies in the Philosophy of Charles Sanders Peirce*, ed. Edward C. Moore and Richard Robin, pp. 165-89. Amherst: University of Massachusetts Press.

Betti, Emilio. 1955. *Teoria generale della interpretazione*, voll. 1-2. Milano: Dott. A. Giuffrè.

Bauchot, Mauricio and J. Deely. 1995. Common Sources for the Semiotic of C. Peirce and J. Poinsot. *Review of Metaphysics* XLVIII-3:539-66.

Bauchot, Mauricio and J. Deely, ed. 1996. *Algunas Teorías del Signo en la Escolastica Iberica Post-Medieval*. Maracaibo y Caracas: University Del Zulia y University Católica Andres.

Bickerton, D. 1990. *Language and Species*. Chicago: University of Chicago Press.

Bird, Otto A. 1987. John of St. Thomas redivivus ut John Poinsot. *The New Scholasticism* LXI-1:103-07.

Black, Max. 1962. *Models and Metaphors: studies in language and philosophy*. Ithaca: Cornell University Press.

Black, Max. 1990. *Perplexities*. Ithaca: Cornell University Press.

Blanchot, Maurice. 1955. *L'espace littéraire*. Paris: Gallimard.

Blanchot, Maurice. 1969. *L'entretien infini*. Paris: Gallimard.

Bleicher, Josef. 1980. *Contemporary Hermeneutics*. London: Routledge and Kegan Paul.

Bloch, Ernst. 1988 [1974]. *The Utopian Functions of Art and Literature*, trans. J. Zifes and F. Meecklenburg. Cambridge: The MIT Press.

Blonsky, Marshall, ed. 1985. *On Signs*. Baltimore: The Johns Hopkins Press.

Bloom, Harold. 1973. *The Anxiety of Influence: A Theory of Poetry*. New York: Oxford University Press.

Bloom, Harold. 1975a. *A Map of Misreading*. New York: Oxford University Press.

Bloom, Harold. 1975b. *Kabbalah and Criticism*. New York: The Seabury Press.

Bloom, Harold et al. 1979. *Deconstruction & Criticism*. New York: The Seabury Press.

Blumenberg, Hans. 1986. *Die Lesharkeit der Welt*. Frankfurt am Main Sullrkamp.

Bochenski, J. M. 1965. *The Methods of Contemporary Thought*. Dordrecht: Reidel.

Bochenski, J. M. 1970. *A History of Formal Logic*. New York: Chelsea Pub. Co.

Bohr, N. 1961. *Atomic Theory and the Description of Nature*. Cambridge: Cambridge University.

Boler, John F. 1964. Habits of thought. In: *Studies in the Philosphy of Charles Sanders Peirce*, ed. Edward C. Moore and Richard Robin, pp. 382-400. Amherst: University of Massachusetts Press. Brown, W. M.

Boler, John F. 1983. The economy of Peirce's abduction. *Transactions of the Charles Peirce Society* 19:397-411.

Bonfantini, Massimo A. 1981. Le tre tendenze semiotiche del Novecento. *Versus*, 30:2

Bonfantini, Massimo A. 1984. *Semiotica ai media*. Bari: Adriatica.

Bonfantini, Massimo A. 1987. *La semiosi e l'abduzione*. Milan: Bompiani.

Bonfantini, Massimo A., G. Mininni and A. Ponzio. 1985. *Per parlare dei segni/ Talking About Signs*, trans. S. Petrillli. Bari: Adriatica.

Bonfantini, Massimo A. and Ponzio, Augusto. 1986. *Dialogo sui dialoghi*. Ravenna: Longo.

Bonfantini, Massimo A. and Arturo Martone, eds. 1993. *Peirce in Italia*. Naples: Liguori.

Booth, Wayne. 1961. *A Rhetoric of Fiction*. Chicago: Chicago University Press.

Borges Jorge Luis. 1964. Death and the compass. In: *Labyrinths*, trans. Donald A. Yates and James E. Irby, pp. 76-87. New York: New Directions.

Borges Jorge Luis. 1962 [1956]. *Ficciones*. New York: Grove Press. Buenos Aires: Emecé Editores.

Born, M. 1968. *My Life and My Views*. New York: Scribners.

Bouchard, Norma. 1995. Umberto Eco's *L'isola del giorno prima*: PostmodernTheory and Fictional Praxis. *Italica* 72-2:193-208.

Bouchard, Norma. 1995. Critifictional Epistemes in Contemporary Literature: The Case of *Foucault's Pendulum*. *Comparative Literature Studies*. Forthcoming.

Bouissac, Paul. 1983. Figurative versus objective semiotics: An epistemological crossroads. In: *Semiotics 1981*, ed. John N. Deely and Margot D. Lenhart, pp. 3-12. New York: Plenum Press.

Bourdieu, Pierre. 1977. *Outline of a Theory of Practice*, trans. Richard Nice. Cambridge: Cambridge University Press.

Boyarin, Daniel. 1990. *Intertextuality and the Reading of Midrash*. Bloomington: Indiana University Press.

Bridgeman, Roger. 1969. Horses and Hounds. *The Sherlock Holmes Journal* 9-2:59-61.

Broadbent, G., R. Bunt and C. Jenks, eds. 1995. *Signs, Symbols and Architecture.* New York: John Wiley and Sons.

Brower, Reuben A. 1959. *Alexander Pope: The Poetry of Allusion.* Oxford: Clarendon Press.

Brown, W. M. 1983. The economy of Peirce's abduction. *Transactions of the Charles Peirce Society* 19: 397-411.

Bruce, Don. 1983. Bibliographie annotée: écrits sur l'intertextualité. *Texte: Revue de critique et de théorie littéraire* 2:217-58.

Buber, Martin. 1954. *Die Schriften über das dialogische Prinzip.* Heidelberg: Verlag Lambert Schneider.

Buchler, J. 1939a. *Charles Peirce's Empiricism.* New York: Harcourt.

Buchler, J. 1939b. *Selected Writings of C. S. Peirce. Logic as Semiotic: The Theory of Signs.* New York: Dover Rpt.

Buchler, J. 1974. *The Main of Light.* Oxford: Oxford University Press.

Buchler, J. 1979 [1951]. *Toward a General Theory of Human Judgment.* New York: Dover Rpt.

Buchler, J. 1985 [1955]. *Nature and Judgment.* Lanham: University Press of America.

Buchler, J. 1990 [1966]. *Metaphysics of Natural Complexes.* Albany: SUNY Press.

Buczynska-Garewicz, Hanna. 1978. Sign and continuity. *Ars Semeiotica* 2: 3-15

Buczynska-Garewicz, Hanna. 1979. The degenerate sign. *Semiosis* 13: 5-17.

Buczynska-Garewicz, Hanna. 1981. The Interpretant and a System of Signs. *Ars Semiotioca* 4:187-200.

Buczynska-Garewicz, Hanna. 1992. Does Semiotics Lead to Deconstruction? *Semiotics,* pp. 65-68.

Calabrese, Omar. 1987. *L'età neo-barocca.* Rome, Bari: Laterza. (1992. *Neo-Baroque. A sign of the Times,* trans. Charles Lambert. Princeton: Princeton University Press.)

Calabrese, Omar. 1981. La sintassi della vertigine: Sguardi, specchi e ritratti. *VS* 29.

Calvino, Italo. 1984 [1965]. *Cosmicomiche vecchie e nuove.* Turin: Einaudi. (1968. *Cosmicomics,* trans. William Weaver. New York: Harcourt Brace Jovanovich.)

Calvino, Italo. 1967. *T con zero.* Turin: Einaudi. (1969. *T-Zero,* trans. William Weaver. New York: Harcourt Brace Jovanovich.)

Calvino, Italo. 1972. *Città invisibili.* Turin: Einaudi. (1972. *Invisible Cities,* trans. William Weaver. New York: Harcourt Brace Jovanovich.)

Calvino, Italo. 1979. *Se una notte d'inverno un viaggiatore.* Turin: Einaudi. (1981. *If on a Winter Night, a Traveller,* trans. William Weaver. New York: Harcourt Brace Jovanovich.)

Calvino, Italo. 1984. Comment j'ai écrit un de mes livres. Actes sémiotique-documentes VI, 54. Documents de recherche, Centre national de la recherche scientifique.

Cannon, JoAnn. 1992. The Imaginary Universe of U. Eco: A Reading of *Foucault's Pendulum. Modern Fiction Studies* 4:895-909.

Capozzi, Rocco. 1983. Intertextuality and Semiosis: Eco's éducation sémiotique. *Recherches sémiotiques/Semiotic inquiry* 3:284-96.

Capozzi, Rocco. 1988. Troppi movimenti intorno al *Pendolo* di Eco. *Quaderni d'italianistica.* 2:301-13.

Capozzi, Rocco. 1989. Palimpsests and Laughter: The Dialogical Pleasure of Unlimited Intertextuality in *The Name of the Rose*. *Italica* 4:412-28.

Capozzi, Rocco. 1990. *Il pendolo di Foucault*: Kitsch o neo/postmoderno. *Quaderni d'italianistica*. 2:225-37.

Capozzi, Rocco. 1993. Apocalittici e integrati nell'industrtia culturale postmoderna. *Scrittori, tendenze letterarie e conflitto delle poetiche in Italia* (1960-1990). Ravenna: Longo.

Capozzi, Rocco. 1994. Eco's Theories and Practices of Interpretation. The Rights of the Text and the (implied) Presence of the Author. *Signifying Behavior*, 1:176-200.

Capozzi, Rocco. 1996. Metaphors and Intertextuality in Eco's Neo-Baroque Narrative Machine: *The Island of the Day Before. Rivista di Studi Italiani.* 1(1996):158-89.

Carlyle, Thomas. 1987 [1833]. *Sartor Resartus*. Oxford: Oxford University Press.

Carnap, Rudolf. 1937a. Testability and Meaning. *Philosophy of Science 4*.

Carnap, Rudolf. 1937b. *The Logical Syntax of Language*, trans. Amethe Smeaton. London: Routledge & Kegan Paul.

Carnap, Rudolf. 1967c. *The Logical Structure of the World and Pseudoproblems in Philosophy*, trans. Rolf A. George. Berkeley and Los Angeles: University of California Press.

Carreri, Giorgio. 1984. *Order and Disorder in Matter*. Menlo Park: Benjamin/Cummings.

Cartwright, N. 1983. *How the Laws of Physics Lie*. Oxford: Clarendon.

Cervantes, M. 1984. The Dogs' Colloquy. In: *Exemplary Stories*, trans. C. A. Jones. Harmonsworth Middlesex: Penguin Books.

Ceserani, Remo. 1994. Nuotare in un mare pescoso. (Review of *L'isola del giorno prima*). *L'Indice* (December):11.

Chatman, Seymour. 1978. *Story and Discourse. Narrative Structure in fiction and film*. Ithaca: Cornell University Press.

Chatman, Seymour. 1990. *Coming to Terms. The Rhetoric of Narrative in fiction and film*. Ithaca: Cornell University Press.

Cherry, Colin. 1957. *On Human Communication*. Cambridge, Mass.: The MIT Press.

Chisolm, Rderick M. 1981. *The First Person: An Essay on Reference and Intentionality*. Brighton: Harvester Press.

Chomsky, Noam. 1966. *Cartesian Linguistics*. New York: Harper and Row.

Chomsky, Noam. 1972. *Language and Mind*. New York: Harcourt Brace Jovanovich.

Cixous, Helene. 1976. The laugh of the Medusa, trans. Keith Cohen and Paula Cohen. *Signs: Journal of Women in Culture and Society* 1-4:875-93.

Clark, Herbert H. and Eve V. Clark. 1977. *Psychology and Language. An Introduction to Psychlinguistics*. New York: Harcourt, Brace, Jovanovich.

Clark, Katerina and Michael Holquist. 1984. *Mikhail Bakhtin*. Cambridge: Harvard University Press.

Clark, M. 1978. The word of God and the language of man: Puritan semiotics and the theology and scientific 'plain styles' of the seventeenth century. *Semiotic Scene: Bulletin of the Semiotic Society of America* 2, No. 2.

Clifford, James. 1983. On ethnographic authority. *Representations* 2:118-46.

Clutton-Brock, Juliet. 1981. *Domesticated Animals from Early Times*. London British Museum [Natural History].

Cohen, Michael. 1988. The Hounding of Baskerville: Allusion and Apocalypse in Eco's *The Name of the Rose*. In: *Naming the Rose: Essays on Eco's The Name of the Rose*, ed. M. Thomas Inge, pp. 65-76. Jackson: University Press of Mississippi.

Coe, Jonathan. 1995. Disorientation. (Review of *The Island of the Day Before*). *London Review of Books* (Oct. 3):8.

Coletti, Theresa. 1988. *Naming the Rose: Eco, Medieval Signs and Modern Theory*. Ithaca: Cornell University Press.

Coletti, Theresa. 1992. Pinball, Voodoo and 'Good Primal Matter': Incarnations of Silence in *Foucault's Pendulum*. *Modern Language Notes* 107-5 (December):877-91.

Colombo, Furio. 1994. L'isola di Eco. (Review of *L'isola del giorno prima*). *La rivista dei libri* (Oct.):4-7.

Colson, F. H. 1919. The Analogist and the Anomalist Controvery. *The Classical Quarterly* XIII:24-36.

Consoli, Joseph. 1993. Navigating the Labyrinth: A Bibliographical Essay of Selected Criticism of Works of Umberto Eco. *Style* 27:478-514.

Conte, Giuseppe. 1972. *La metafora barocca*. Milan: Mursia.

Corry, Leo. Jorge Borges, Author of *The Name of the Rose*. *Poetics Today* 13-3:425-45.

Corti, Maria. 1980. È un'opera chiusa. *L'Espresso* 19 October.

Corti, Maria. 1989. Le metafore della navigazione, del volo e della lingua di fuoco all'episodio di Ulisse (Inferno, XXVI). In: *Miscellanea di studi in onore di Aurelio Roncaglia*. Modena: Mucchi Editore. (1990. On Metaphors of Sailing, Flight, and Tongues of Fire in the episode of Ulysses (*Inferno XXVI*). *Stanford Italian Review* IX:33-47.)

Corvino, Francesco et al. 1983. *Linguistica medievale*. Bari: Adriatica.

Cotroneo, Roberto. 1995. *La diffidenza come sistema. Saggio sulla narrativa di Umberto Eco*. Milan: Anabasi.

Creasy, John. 1959. *Death of a Racehorse*. New York: Scribner's.

Crutchfield, J. P., J. D. Farmer, N. H. Packard, and R. S. Shaw. 1986. Chaos. *Scientific American* 255:38-49.

Culler, Jonathan. 1975. *Structuralist Poetics: Structuralism Linguistics and the Study of Literature*. Ithaca: Cornell University Press.

Culler, Jonathan. 1981. *The Pursuit of Signs. Semiotics, Literature, Deconstruction*. Ithaca: Cornell University Press.

d'Amico, Masolino. 1983. Medieval Mirth. *Times Educational Supplement* (Nov. 18):22.

Daddesio, Thomas D. 1990. William of Baskerville Or The Myth of the Master of Signs. In: *Semiotics 1989*, ed. John Deely, Karen Haworth and Terry Prewitt, pp. 45-50. Lanham: University Press of America.

Dallenbach, Lucien. 1976. Intertexte et autotexte. *Poétique* 27:282-96.

Danow, David. 1988. Word, utterance, text. *Semiotica* 72:179-86.

Darnton, Robert. 1971a. Reading, writing, and publishing in eighteenth-century France: A case study in the sociology of literature. *Daedelus*, pp. 214-56.

Darnton, Robert. 1971b. In search of enlightenment: Recent attempts to create a social history of ideas. *Journal of Modern History* 43:113-32.

Darnton, Robert. 1971c. The high enlightenment and the low-life of literature in pre-revolutionary France. *Past and Present* 51:81-115.

Darnton, Robert. 1979. *The Business of Enlightenment. A Publishing History of the* Encyclopédie *1775-1800.* Cambridge: Harvard University Press.

Darnton, Robert. 1982. *The Literary Underground of the Old Regime.* Cambridge: Harvard University Press.

Darnton, Robert. 1984. *The Great Cat Massacre and Other Episodes in French Cultural History.* New York: Basic Books.

Darnton, Robert. 1986. The symbolic element in history. *Journal of Modern History* 58-1:218-34.

Davidson, Donald. 1986. *Truth and Interpretation.* Oxford: Clarendon Press.

de Beaugrande, R. 1978. Information, expectation and processing: on classifying poetic texts. *Poetics* 7-1:3-44

de Couto, H. H. 1973. *Speech and Phenomena and other Essays on Husserl's Theory of Signs.* Evanstown: Northwestern University Press.

de Laurentis, Theresa. 1981. *Umberto Eco.* Firenze: La Nuova Italia.

de Laurentis, Theresa. 1982. *Alice Doesn't. Feminism, Semiotics, Cinema.* Bloomington: Indiana University Press.

de Laurentis, Theresa. 1985. Gaudy Rose: Eco and Narcissism. *SubStance.* 47:13-29.

de Laurentis, Theresa. 1987. *Technologies of Gender.* Bloomington: Indiana University Press.

de Man, Paul. 1971. *Blindness and Insight.* New York: Oxford University Press.

Deely, John N. 1965-6. Evolution: Concept and Content. Part I, *Listening* (Autumn) 1965:27-50. Part II, *Listening* (Winter) 1966:35-66.

Deely, John N. 1973. The Impact of Evolution on Scientific Methods. In: *The Problem of Evolution,* ed. John N. Deely and R. J. Nogar, pp. 3-82. New York: Appleton-Century-Crofts.

Deely, John N. 1975b. Modern Logic, Animal Psychology, And Human Discourse. *Revue de l'Université d'Ottawa* 45-1:80-100.

Deely, John N. 1976. The Doctrine of Signs: Taking Form at Last. *Semiotica,* 18:171-93.

Deely, John N. 1980. Antecedents to Peirce's Notion of Iconic Signs, *Semiotics* 1980:109-120.

Deely, John N. 1981. Cognition from a Semiotic Point of View. *Semiotics* 1981:21-28.

Deely, John N. 1982. *Introducing Semiotic: Its History and Doctrine.* Bloomington: Indiana University Press.

Deely, John N. 1986a. A context for Narrative Universals. *The American Journal of Semiotics* 4:53-68.

Deely, John N. 1986b. John Locke's Place in the History of Semiotic Inquiry. *Semiotics* 1986:406-18.

Deely, John N. 1988. The Semiotics of J. Poinsot: Yesterday and Tomorrow. *Semiotica* 69: 31-127.

Deely, John N. 1990. *Basics of Semiotics.* Bloomington: Indiana University Press.

Deely, John N. 1994a. *The Human Use of Signs; or Elements of Anthroposemiosis.* Lanham: Rowan & Littlefield.

Deely, John N. 1994b. *New Beginnings. Early Modern Philosophy and Postmodern Thought.* Toronto: University of Toronto Press.

Deely, John N. 1996. The Intersemiosis of Perception and Understanding. *The American Journal of Semiotics,* forthcoming.

Deely, John N. and R. J. Nogar, eds. 1973. *The Problem of Evolution*. New York: Appleton-Century-Crofts.

Deely, John N., J. N. Brooke and F. E. Kruse, eds. 1986. *Frontiers in Semiotics*. Bloomington: Indiana University Press.

Degli Espositi, Christina. 1991. The Poetics of Hermeticism in Umberto Eco's *Il Pendolo di Foucault*. *Forum Italicum* 1:185-204.

Deledalle, Gérard. 1990. *Charles S. Peirce: An Intellectual Biography*, trans. S. Petrilli. Amsterdam: John Benjamins.

Derrida, Jacques. 1967a. *De la Grammatologie*. Paris: Éditions de Minuit. (1976. *Of Grammatology*, trans. Gayatri C. Spivak. Baltimore: Johns Hopkins University Press.)

Derrida, Jacques. 1967b. Structure, signe et jeu dans les discours des sciences humaines. In: *L'Écriture et la différence*. Paris: Éditions du Seuil. (1978. *Structure, Sign, and Play*. In: *The Discourse of the Human Sciences. Writing and Difference*, trans. Alan Bass. Chicago: University of Chicago Press.)

Derrida, Jacques. 1972. *La dissémination*. Paris: Éditions du Seuil. (1981. *Dissemination*, trans. Barbara Johnson. Chicago: Chicago University Press.)

Derrida, Jacques. 1972. *Positions*. Paris: Éditions de Minuit. (1981. *Positions*, trans. Alan Bass. Chicago: University of Chicago Press.)

Derrida, Jacques. 1973. *Speech and Phenomena and other Essays on Husserl's Theory of Signs*. Evanstown: Northwestern University Press.

Derrida, Jacques. 1978. *La Vérité en peinture*. Paris: Flammarion.

Derrida, Jacques. 1979. *Survivre*. * (Living On: Borderlines. In: *Deconstuction and Criticism*, ed. Harold Bloom et al., pp. 75-176. New York: Seabury Press.)

Derrida, Jacques. 1982. *Margins of Philosophy*. Chicago University Press.

Dewey, J. 1987 [1934]. *Art as Experience*. Carbondale: Southern Illinois University Press.

Dewey, J. 1938. *Logic: The Theory of Inquiry*. New York: Holt.

Dewey, J. 1946. Peirce's Theory of Linguistic Signs, Thought and Meaning. *Journal of Philosophy* 43-4.

Dipple, Elizabeth. 1988. A novel, which is a machine for generating interpretaions: Umberto Eco and *The Name of the Rose*. In: *The Unresolveable Plot*. pp. 119-139. New York, London: Routledge.

Doležel, Lubomir. 1980. Eco and his Model Reader. *Poetics Today* 1-4:181-88.

Doležel, Lubomir. 1980. Truth and Authenticity in Narrative. *Poetics Today* 1-4:7-25.

Doležel, Lubomir. 1989. Possible Worlds and Literary Fictions. In: *Possible Worlds in Humanities, Arts and Sciences*, ed. Allèn, Sture, pp. 221-42. Berlin and New York: Walter de Gruyter.

Doležel, Lubomir. 1993. The Limits of Interpretation (Review). *Journal of Pragmatics* 19:585-601.

Doležel, Lubomir. 1995. Fictional Worlds: Density, Gaps and Inference. *Style* 29: 201-14.

Doležel, Lubomir. Forthcoming. *Fiction and Possible Worlds*.

Douglas, Mary. 1975. *Implicit Meanings: Essays in Anthropology*. London: Routledge and Kegan Paul.

Doyle, Arthur Conan. 1967. *The Annotated Sherlock Holmes*. Vols. 1-11, ed. William S. Baring-Gould. New York: Clarkson N. Potter.

Durand, Gilbert. 1979. *Science de l'homme et la tradition*. Paris: Berg.

Ebner, Ferdinand. 1921. *Das Wort und die geistigen Realitaten.* Regensburg.

Eco, Umberto. 1962. *Opera aperta.* Milan: Bompiani.

Eco, Umberto. 1962. *Diario minimo.* Milan: Mondadori.

Eco, Umberto. 1962. Del modo di formare come impegno sulla realtà. *Il Menabò* 5:198-237.

Eco, Umberto. 1964. *Apocalittici e integrati.* Milan: Bompiani.

Eco, Umberto. 1966. *Le poetiche di Joyce.* Milan: Bompiani.

Eco, Umberto. 1966. James Bond: une combinatoire narrative. In: R. Barthes. *Communications 8*, pp. 83-99. Paris: Seuil.

Eco, Umberto. 1968. *La definizione dell'arte.* Milan: Mursia.

Eco, Umberto. 1968. *La struttura assente.* Milan: Bompiani.

Eco, Umberto. 1971. *Le forme del contenuto.* Milan: Bompiani.

Eco, Umberto. 1972. Social Life as a Sign System. In: *Structuralism: An Introduction*, ed. David Robey, pp. 57-72. Oxford: Claredon Press.

Eco, Umberto. 1973. *Segno.* Milan: ISEDI.

Eco, Umberto. 1974. Is the present king of France a bachelor? *Versus* 7:1-53.

Eco, Umberto. 1975. *Trattato di semiotica generale.* Milan: Bompiani.

Eco, Umberto. 1975. Looking for a Logic of Culture. In: *The Tell-Tale Sign: A survey of semiotics*, ed. T. A. Sebeok, pp. 9-17. Lisse: Peter de Ridder.

Eco, Umberto. 1976. *A Theory of Semiotics.* Bloomington: Indiana University Press.

Eco, Umberto. 1976. *Il superuomo di massa.* Milan: Bompiani.

Eco, Umberto. 1977. *Dalla periferia all'impero.* Milan: Bompiani.

Eco, Umberto. 1977. Semiotics of Theatrical Performance. *Drama Review* 21-1:110.

Eco, Umberto. 1977. On Levels of Literary Form. *Yale Italian Studies* 1-3:269-80.

Eco, Umberto. 1977. The Code: Metaphor or Interdisciplinary Category? *Yale Italian Studies* 1-1:24-52.

Eco, Umberto. 1978. Semiotics: A Discipline or an Interdisciplinary Method? In: *Sight, Sound, and Sense*, ed. T. A. Sebeok, pp. 73-83. Bloomington: Indiana University Press.

Eco, Umberto. 1979. Concluding remarks. In: *A Semiotic Landscape: Proceedings of the First Congress of IASS.* Milan, June 1974, ed. Seymour Chatman, pp. 251-65. The Hague: Mouton.

Eco, Umberto. 1979. *Lector in fabula.* Milan: Bompiani.

Eco, Umberto. 1979. *The Role of the Reader.* Bloomington: Indiana University Press.

Eco, Umberto. 1980. *Il nome della rosa.* Milan: Bompiani. (1983. *The Name of the Rose.* trans, William Weaver. New York: Harcourt Brace Jovanovich.)

Eco, Umberto. 1980. Two Problems in Textual Interpretation. *Poetics Today* 2-1:145-61.

Eco, Umberto. 1981. Guessing: From Aristotle to Sherlock Holmes. *Versus* 30:3-20.

Eco, Umberto. 1983. *Sette anni di desiderio.* Milan: Bompiani.

Eco, Umberto. 1983. Horns, Hooves, Insteps: Some Hypotheses on Three Types of Abduction. In: *The Sign of Three: Dupin, Holmes, Peirce*, ed. U. Eco and T. A. Sebeok, pp. 198-220. Bloomington: Indiana University Press.

Eco, Umberto. 1983. Postille a Il nome della rosa. *Alfabeta* 49:19-22.

Eco, Umberto. 1984. The frames of comic 'freedom'. In: *Carnival*, ed. U. Eco, V. V. Ivanov and M. Rector, pp. 1-9. Berlin, New York: Mouton.

Eco, Umberto. 1984. *Semiotica e la filosofia del linguaggio.* Milan: Bompiani. (1984. *Semiotics and the Philosophy of Language.* London: McMillan.)

Eco, Umberto. 1984. *Postcript to* The Name of the Rose. New York: Harcourt Brace Jovanovich.

Eco, Umberto. 1985. *Sugli specchi e altri saggi.* Milan: Bompiani.

Eco, Umberto. 1985. Innovation and Repetition: Between Modern and Post-Modern Aesthetics. *Daedalus* 114:161-184.

Eco, Umberto. 1985. Strategies of Lying. In: *On* Signs, ed. M. Blonsky, pp. 4-11. Baltimore: The Johns Hopkins Press.

Eco, Umberto. 1985. *Casablanca*: Cult Movies and Intertextual Collage. *SubStance* 47:3-12.

Eco, Umberto. 1985. Casablanca, or the Clichés Are Having a Ball. In: *On Signs*, ed. M. Blonsky. Baltimore: The Johns Hopkins Press.

Eco, Umberto. 1985. *Reflections on* The Name of the Rose. London: Secker and Warburg.

Eco, Umberto. 1986. *Arte e bellezza nell'estetica medievale.* Milan: Bompiani. (*Art and Beauty in the Middle Ages.* New Haven: Yale University Press.)

Eco, Umberto. 1986. *Travels in Hyperreality.* New York: Harcourt Brace Jovanich.

Eco, Umberto. 1986. *Faith in Fakes.* London: Secker and warburg.

Eco, Umberto. 1987. Notes sur la sémiotique de la réception, Actes sémiotique-documents, IX, 81. Documents de recherche. Centre national de la recherche scientifique.

Eco, Umberto. 1988. *Il pendolo di Foucault.* Milan: Bompiani. (1989. *Foucault's Pendulum*, trans. William Weaver. New York: Harcourt Brace Jovanovich.)

Eco, Umberto. 1989. *The Open Work*, trans. Anna Cancogni. Cambridge: Harvard University Press. (Selected translation of *Opera aperta*.)

Eco, Umberto. 1989. *The Aesthetics of Chaosmos. The Middle Ages of James Joyce.* Cambridge: Harvard University Press.

Eco, Umberto. 1990. *The Limits of Interpretation.* Bloomington: Indiana University Press.

Eco, Umberto. 1990. Some paranoid readings. *Times Literary Supplement* (June 29-July 5):705-6.

Eco, Umberto. 1990. Introduction. In: J. Lotman. *Universe of the Mind. The Semiotic Theory of Culture*, trans. Ann Shukman, pp. vii-xiii. London -New York: I. B. Tauris & Co. Ltd.

Eco, Umberto. 1992. *Interpretation and Overinterpretation.* Cambridge: Cambridge University Press.

Eco, Umberto. 1992. Reading my Readers. *Modern Language Notes* 107-5:819-27.

Eco, Umberto. 1993. *Misreadings*, trans. William Weaver. London: Jonathan Cape. (Selected translation of *Diario minimo*.)

Eco, Umberto. 1993. *La ricerca della lingua perfetta.* Rome-Bari: Laterza. (1993. *The Search for the Perfect Language*, trans. James Fentress. Oxford: Blackwell.)

Eco, Umberto. 1994. *Apocalypse Postponed*, ed. Robert Lumley. Bloomington: Indiana University Press. (Selected translation of *Apocalittici e integrati*.)

Eco, Umberto. 1994. *Il secondo Diario minimo.* Milan: Bompiani. Eco, Umberto. (1994. *How to Travel with a Salmon and Other Essays*, trans. William Weaver. N. Y., San Diego: Harcourt Brace Jovanovich.)

Eco, Umberto. 1994. *Sei passeggiate nei boschi narrativi.* Milan: Bompiani. (*Six Walks in the Fictional Woods.* Cambridge: Harvard University Press.)

Eco, Umberto. 1994. *L'isola del giorno prima*. Milan: Bompiani.

Eco, Umberto. 1995. *The Island of the Day Before*, trans. William Weaver. N. Y., San Diego: Harcourt Brace Jovanovich.

Eco, Umberto. 1995. Fuction and Sign: The Semiotics of Architecture. In: *Signs, Symbols and Architecture*, ed. G. Broadbent, R. Bunt and C. Jenks, pp. 11-70. New York: John Wiley and Sons.

Eco, Umberto and Seymour Chatman, and Jean-Marie Klinkenberg, eds. 1979. *Panorama sémiotique/A Semiotic Landscape*. Proceedings of the First Congress of the International Association for Semiotics. Milan. The Hague: Mouton.

Eco, Umberto and Thomas A. Sebeok, eds. 1983. *Il segno dei tre: Holmes Dupin, Peirce* Milan: Bompiani. (*The Sign of Three: Dupin, Holmes, Peirce*. Bloomington: Indiana University Press.)

Eco, Umberto and Ivanov, V. V. and Rector, Monica. 1984. *Carnival!*, ed. T. A. Sebeok. Berlin, New York: Mouton.

Eco, Umberto and Patrizia Magli. 1985. Semantique Greimassienne et encyclopédie. In: *Exigences et perspectives de la semiotique. Recueil d'hommage pour Algirdas Julien Greimas*, ed. Herman Parret and Hans-George Ruprecht, pp. 161-78. Amsterdam: John Benjamins.

Eco, Umberto and R. Lambertini, C. Marmo and A. Tabarroni. 1986. Latratus Canins or: The Dog's Barking. In: *Frontiers in Semiotics*, ed. John N. Deely, J. N. Brooke and F. E. Kruse, pp. 63-73. Bloomington: Indiana University Press.

Eco, Umberto, Marco Santabrogio and Patrizia Violi, eds. 1988. *Meaning and Mental Representations*. Bloomington: Indiana University Press.

Eco, Umberto and Constantino Marmo, eds. 1989. *On the Medieval Theory of Signs*. Amsterdam: John Benjamins.

Eco, Umberto and Patrizia Magli. 1989. Gremaissian Semantics and the Encyclopedia. *New Literary History* 20:707-721.

Eco, Umberto and Maria Pia Pozzato. 1989. *L'idea deforme: interpretazioni esoteriche di Dante*. Milan: Bompiani.

Eliot, George. 1956. *Middlemarch*. Boston: Houghton Mifflin.

Eliot, T. S. 1920. *The Sacred Wood: Essays on Poetry and Criticism*. London: Methuen.

Ellis, John M. 1989. *Against Deconstruction*. Princeton: Princeton University Press.

Ellman, Richard. 1983. Murder in the Monastery? *New York Review of Books* (July 21):11.

Encyclopedic dictionary of semiotics. 1994 [1986]. Berlin, N. Y.: Mouton de Gruyter.

Ennion, E. A. R., and N. Tinbergen. 1967. *Tracks*. Oxford: Clarendon Press.

Evans-Pritchard, E. E. 1940. *The Nuer: A Description of the Modes of Livelihood and Political Institutions of a Nilotic People*. Oxford: Clarendon Press.

Ewing, Adelaide P. and Robert R. Patrick. 1965. A Sherlockian Zoo. In: *West By One and By One*, pp. 113-124. San Francisco: Privately printed.

Fabian, Johannes. 1983. *Time and the Other. How Anthropology Makes its Object*. New York: Columbia University Press.

Fann. K. T. 1970. *Peirce's Theory of Abduction*. The Hague: Nijhoff.

Fano, Giorgio. 1992. *Origins and Nature of Language*, trans. S. Petrilli. Bloomington: Indiana University Press.

Fawcett, R. P. 1980. *Cognitive Linguistics and Social Interaction: Towards an integrated model of a systemic functional grammar and the other components of a com-*

municating mind. Heidelberg: Julius Groos Verlag and Exeter University.

Federman, Raymon. 1986. *Surfiction. Fiction Now ... And Tomorrow.* Chicago: Swallow Press.

Feibleman, James K. and Russell, Bertrand. 1970. *An Introduction to the Philosophy of Charles S. Peirce.* Cambridge, Mass.: The MIT Press.

Feyerabend, P. 1975. *Against Method.* London: Verso.

Fiedler, Leslie A. 1968. *The Dynamics of Literary Response.* New York: Oxford University Press.

Fiedler, Leslie A. 1971. *The Collected Essays of Leslie Fiedler.* Vol. II. New York: Simon and Schuster.

Fillmore, C. 1968. The case for the case. In: *Universals in Linguistic Theory*, ed. E. Bach and R. Harms. New York: Holt.

Fillmore, C. 1971 [1968]. Verbs of judging: an exercise in semantic description. In: *Studies in Linguistic Semantics*, ed. C. J Fillmore and D. T. Langendoen. New York: Holt.

Fisch, M. 1978. Peirce's general theory of signs. In: *Sight, Sound, and Sense*, ed. T. A. Sebeok. Bloomington: Indiana University Press.

Fisch, M. 1986. *Peirce, Semiotic, and Pragmatism*, ed. K. Ketner and C Kloesel. Bloomington: Indiana University Press.

Fish, Stanley. 1980. *Is There a Text in This Class?* Cambridge: Harvard University Press.

Fleissner, Robert F. 1989. *A Rose by any other Name. A survey of flora from Shakespeare to Eco.* West Cornwall: Locust Hill Press.

Foucault, Michel. 1966. *Les Mots et les choses.* Paris: Éditions Gallimard. (1970. *The Order of Things: An Archaeology of the Human Sciences.* New York: Random House.)

Foucault, Michel. 1969. *L'Archéologie du savoir.* Paris: Éditions Gillmard. (1972. *The Archeology of Knowledge*, trans. A. M. Sheridan Smith. New York: Pantheon.)

Foucault, Michel. 1978. *The History of Sexuality, vol. 1: An Introduction*, trans. Robert Huxley. New York: Pantheon Books.

Foucault, Michel. 1980. *Power Knowledge: Selected Interviews and Other Writings, 1972-1977*, trans. Colin Graham, Leo Marshall, John Mepham, and Kate Soper; ed. Colin Gordon. New York: Pantheon Books.

Fowler, R. 1981. *Literature as Social Discourse.* Bloomington: Indiana University Press.

Fowler, R. 1982. How to see through language: perspective in fiction. *Poetics* 11-3:213.

Francis, Dick. 1990. *Longshot.* New York: G. P. Putnam.

Frank, Joseph. 1945. Spatial Form in Modern Literature. In: *The Widening Gyre.* New Brunswick: Rutgers University Press, 1963.

Frege, Gottlob. 1892. Über Sinn und Bedeutung. *Zeitschrift für Philosophie und philosophische Kritik*, p. 100.

Frye, Northrop. 1957. *Anatomy of Criticism: Four Essays.* Princeton: Princeton University Press.

Gadamer. Hans-Georg. 1975. *Truth and Method.* Bloomington: Indiana University Press.

Ganeri, Margherita. 1991. *Il caso Eco.* Palermo: Palumbo.

Garroni, Emilio. 1977. *Ricognizione della semiotica.* Rome: Officina.

Geertz, Clifford. 1988. *Works and Lives. The Anthropologist as Author*. Stanford, California: Stanford University Press.

Gellner, E. 1988. *Plough, Sword, and Book*. Chicago: University of Chicago Press.

Genette, Gérard. 1972. *Figures III*. Paris: Seuil.

Genette, Gérard. 1979. *Introduction à l'architexte*. Paris: Éditions du Seuil.

Genette, Gérard. 1982. *Palimpsestes: La Littérature au second degré*. Paris: Éditions du Seuil.

Genette, Gérard. 1987. *Seuils*. Paris: Éditions du Seuil.

Giddens, Anthony. 1984. *The Constitution of Society. Outline of The Theory of Structuration*. Cambridge: Polity Press.

Giles, Kenneth. 1967. *Death at the Furlong Post*. New York: Walker.

Giovannoli, Renato, ed. 1985. *Saggi sul Nome della rosa*. Milan: Bompiani.

Giuliani, Alessandro. 1976. Vico's rhetorical philosophy and the New Rhetoric. In: *Giambattista Vico's Science of Humanity*, ed. Giorgio Tagliacozzo and Donald Phillip Verene, pp. 31-46 Baltimore: The Johns Hopkins University Press.

Golino, Enzo. 1994. Carosello Barocco. (Review of *L'isola del giorno prima*) *La Repubblica* (Oct. 4):22.

Goodman, Nelson. 1968. *Language of Art: an approach to a theory of symbols*. Indianapolis: Bobbs Merrill.

Goody, Jack. 1977. *The Domestication of The Savage Mind*. Cambridge: Cambridge University Press.

Gregory, B. 1990. *Inventing Reality: Physics and Language*. New York: Wiley.

Greimas, A. J. 1966. *Sémantique structurale*. Paris: Larousse.

Greimas, A. J. 1966. Eléments pour une théorie de l'interprétation mythique. In: R. Barthes. *Communications 8*, pp. 34-65. Paris: Seuil.

Greimas, A. J. 1970. *Du Sens*. Paris: Éditions du Seuil.

Greimas, A. J. and I. Courtés. 1979. *Sémiotique. Dictionnaire raisonné de la rhétorie du langage*. Paris: Librairie. (1982. *Semiotics and Language: An Analytical Dictionary*, trans. by Larry Crist et al. Bloomington: Indiana University Press.)

Greimas, A. J. 1987. *On Meaning. Selected Writings in Semiotic Theory*, trans. P. Perron and F. H. Collins. Minneapolis: University of Minnesota Press.

Greimas, A. J. 1987 En guise de préface, *Actes sémiotique-documents* IX, 81:3-4. Documents de recherche. Centre national de la recherche scientifique.

Greimas, A. J. 1990. *The Social Sciences. A Semiotic view*, trans P. Perron and F. H. Collins. Minneapolis: University of Minnesota Press.

Greimas, A. J. and Jacques Fontanille. 1993. *The Semiotic of Passions*, trans P. Perron and F. H. Collins. Minneapolis: University Of Minnesota Press.

Gritti, Jules. 1991. *Umberto Eco*. Paris: Editions Universitaires.

Gruber, Frank. 1942. *The Gift Horse*. New York: Farrar and Rinehart.

Guglielmi, Guido. 1987. Barocchi e moderni. *Il Verri*, 1-2:97-110.

Gullentops, David. 1995. Pour une Sémantique de l' espace poétique. *Degrés* (Brussels) 84:1-18.

Haas, Robert. 1968. The Theory of Translation. In: *The Theory of Meaning*, ed. G. H. R. Parkinson, pp. 86-108. London: Oxford.

Hacking, I. 1983. *Representing and Intervening*. Cambridge: Cambridge University Press.

Haley, Michael Cabot. 1988. *The Semeiosis of Poetic Metaphor*. Bloomington: Indiana University Press.

Halle, M. 1978. Roman Jakobson's contribution to the modern study of speech sounds. In: *Sound, Sign and Meaning. The Quinquagenary of the Prague Linguistic Circle*, ed. L. Matejka. Ann Arbor, Michigan: Michigan Slavic Contributions 6.

Halliday, M. A. K. 1973. Linguistic function and literary style: an enquiry into the language of William Golding's *The Inheritors*. In: *Literary Style: A Symposium*, ed. S. Chatman. New York: Oxford University Press.

Halliday, M. A. K. 1975. *Learning How to Mean - Explorations in the Development of Language*. London: Arnold.

Halliday, M. A. K. 1978. *Language as Social Semiotic: the Social Interpretations of Language and Meaning*. London: Arnold.

Halliday, M. A. K. 1980. Text semantics and clause grammar: some patterns of realisation. In: *The Seventh Lacus Forum*, ed. J. E. Copeland and P. W. Davis. Columbia: Hornbeam Press.

Halliday, M. A. K. 1981. Options and functions in the English clause. In: *Readings in Systemic Linguistics*, ed. M. A. K. Halliday and J. R. Martin. Bristol: Batsford.

Halliday, M. A. K. 1982. *A Short Linguistic Introduction to Functional Grammar*, Parts I and II. Mimeo: Linguistics Dept., University of Sydney.

Halliday, M. A. K. and R. Hasan. 1976. *Cohesion in English*. London: Longman.

Hamburg, Max. 1971. *Theories of Differentiation*. New York: America Elsewhere.

Hanson. Norwood Russell. 1958. *Patterns of Discovery*. Cambridge: Cambridge University Press.

Hardwick, Charles, ed. 1977. *Semiotic and Significs. The Correspondence Between Charles S. Peirce and Victoria Lady Welby*. Bloomington: Indiana University Press.

Hasan, R. 1973. Code, register and social dialect. In: *Class, Codes and Control*, ed. B. Berstein, Vol. 2. London: Routledge and Kegan Paul.

Hasan, R. 1980. What's going on: a dynamic view of context in language. In: *Seventh Lacus Forum*, ed. J. E. Copeland and P. W. Davis. Columbia: Hornbeam Press.

Hasan, R. 1984. Coherence and cohesive harmony. In: *Understanding Reading and Comprehension: Cognition, Language and the Structure of Prose*, ed. J. Flood. Delaware: International Reading Association. -

Hawkes, Terence. 1977. *Structuralism and Semiotics*. Berkeley: University of California Press.

Hayles, N. K. 1984. *The Cosmic Web*. Ithaca: Cornell University Press.

Hayles, N. K. 1990. *Chaos Bound*. Ithaca: Cornell University Press.

Heelan, P. 1983. *Space-Perception and the Philosophy of Science*. Berkeley: University of California Press.

Heidegger, Martin. 1927. *Sein und Zeit*. 10th edition. Tubingen: Niemeyer, 1963.

Heisenberg, W. 1955. The Representation of Nature in Contemporary Physics. *Daedalus* 3:95-108.

Hendricks, William O. 1973a. Verbal art and the structuralist synthesis. *Semiotica* 8:239-62.

Hendricks, William O. 1973b. *Essays on Semiolinguistics and Verbal Art* (Approaches to Semiotics 37). The Hague: Mouton.

Hendricks, William O. 1975a. The work and play structures of narrative. *Semiotica* 13:281-328.

Hendricks, William O. 1975b. Style and the structure of literary discourse. In: *Style and Text: Studies Presented to Nils Erik Enkvist*, ed. H. Ringbom et al., pp. 63-74.

Stockholm: Skriptor.

Hendricks, William O. 1977a. 'A Rose for Emily': A syntagmatic analysis. *Poetics and Theory of Literature* 2:257-95.

Hendricks, William O. 1977b. Prolegomena to a semiolinguistic theory of character. *Poetica* 7:1-49.

Herculano de Carvalho, Jose G. 1969. Segno e Significazione in Joao de Sao Tomás. *Estudos Linguisticos* (vol 2):129-68. Coimbra: Atlantida Editora.

Herculano de Carvalho, Jose G. 1973 [1970]. *Teoria da linguagem. Natureza do fenomeno linguístico e a análise da linguas.* Coimbra: Atlantida.

Herzfeld, Michael. 1987. Semiotics of theory or theory as a semiotic of practice? In: *Developments in Linguistics and Semiotics; Language Teaching and Learning Communication Across Cultures,* ed. Simon P. X. Battestini, pp. 239-254. (GURT '86). Washington, DC: Georgetown University Press.

Hill, Archibald. 1948. The Use of Dictionaries in Language Teaching. *Language Learning* 1:9-13.

Hillis, W. D. 1988. Intelligence as an Emergent Characteristic; Or, The Songs of Eden. *Daedalus* 117:175-90.

Hintikka, Jaakko. 1990. Exploring Possible Worlds. In: *Possible Worlds in Humanities, Arts and Sciences,* ed. Allèn, Sture, pp. 52-73. Berlin and New York: Walter de Gruyter.

Hirsch, E. D., Jr. 1967. *Validity in Interpretation.* New Haven, CT: Yale University Press.

Hjelmslev, Louis. 1943. *Prolegomena to a Theory of Language,* trans. F. J. Whitfield. Madison: University of Wisconsin, 1961.

Hjelmslev, Louis. 1959. *Essais linguistiques.* Copenhagen: Nordisk Sprog-og-Kulturforlag.

Hodge, B., G. Kress and T. Trew. 1979. *Language and Control.* London: Routledge and Kegan Paul.

Holland, Norman N. 1968. *The Dynamics of Literary Response.* New York: Oxford University Press.

Holland, Norman N. 1978. A transactive account of transactive criticism. *Poetics* 7:177-89.

Holland, Norman N. 1992. *The Critical I.* New York: Columbia University Press.

Holquist, Michael. 1971. Whodunit and Other Questions: Metaphysical Detective Stories in Post-War Fiction. *New Literary History* 3:135-56.

Holquist, Michael. 1978. Bakhtin, Mikhail Mikhailovich. In: *Modern Encyclopaedia of Russian and Soviet Literature,* pp. 52-59.

Holquist, Michael. 1990. *Dialogism: Bakhtin and His World.* London and New York: Routledge.

Holstein, L. S. 1970. Holmes and Equus Caballus. *The Baker Street Journal* n.s. 20-2:112-16.

Hrushovski, B. 1979. The structure of semiotic objects: a three-dimensional model. *Poetics Today* 1:1-2.

Huellen, Werner. 1987. Semiotics narrated: Umberto Eco's *The Name of the Rose. Semiotica* 64:41-57.

Hutcheon, Linda. 1988. *A Poetics of Postmodernism: History, Theory, Fiction.* New York: Routledge.

Hutcheon, Linda. 1992. Eco's Echoes: Ironizing the (Post)Modern. *Diacritics* 22:2-

16.

Huxley, Thomas. 1881. On the Method of Zadig: Retrospective Prophecy as a Function of Science. In: *Science and Culture and Other Essays*, pp. 128-48. London: MacMillan.

Idel, Moise. 1988. *Kabbalah*. New Haven: Yale University Press.

Idel, Moise. 1989. *Language, Torah and Hermeneutics in Abraham Abulafia*. Albany: SUNY Press.

Ikegami, Yoshihiko. 1984. Review article: U. Eco's semiotics. *Kodikas/Code* 4:163-74.

Inge, Thomas M, ed. 1988. *Naming the Rose*. Jackson: University Press of Mississippi.

Irwin John T. 1990. Mysteries we reread, mysteries of rereading Poe, Borges and the analytic detective story; also Lacan, Derrida, and Johnson. In: *Do the Americas Have a Common Literature?*, ed. Gustavo Perez Firmat, pp. 198-242. Durham, NC: Duke University Press.

Ivanov, Viach. Vs. 1974. The significance of M. M. Bakhtin's ideas on sign, utterance, and dialogue for modern semiotics. In: *Semiotics and Structuralism*, ed. Henryk Baran, pp. 310-67. White Plains, NY: International Arts and Sciences Press.

Jacob, F. 1982. *The Possible and the Actual*. New York: Pantheon Books.

Jakobson, Roman. 1956. The Metaphoric and Metonymic Poles. In: R. Jakobson and M. Halle, *Fundamentals of Language*. The Hague: Mouton.

Jakobson, Roman. 1960. Closing Statement: Linguistics and Poetics. *Style in language*, ed. T. A. Sebeok, pp. 350-77. Cambridge, Mass.: The MIT Press.

Jakobson, Roman. 1968. Poetry of grammar and grammar of poetry. *Lingua* XXI: 597-609.

Jakobson, Roman. 1974. Coup d'oeil sur le devélopement de la sémiotique. In: *Panorama sémiotique/A Semiotic Landscape*. Proceedings of the First Congress of the International Association for Semiotics. Milan, ed. S. Chatman, U. Eco and J. M. Klinkenberg, pp. 3-18. The Hague: Mouton 1979.

James, Henry 1969 [1908]. *Views and reviews*, ed. Le Roy Phillips. New York: AMS Press.

Jameson, Frederick. 1987. Foreword. *On Meaning. Selected Writings in Semiotic Theory*, trans. P. Perron and F. H. Collins, pp. vi-xxii. Minneapolis: University of Minnesota Press.

Jenny, Laurent. 1976. La stratégie de la forme. *Poétique* 27:257-81.

Jewison, D. B. 1983. The Architecture of Eco's *The Name of the Rose*. *Perspectives on Contemporary Literature*. 13:2-16.

Johansen, Jorgen D. 1993. *Dialogic Semiosis. An essay on sign and meaning*. Bloomington: Indiana University Press.

Karcevskij, Sergej. 1929. Du dualisme asymétrique du signe linguistique. *Travaux du Cercle linguistique de Prague I*, pp. 88-93.

Katz, Jerrold J. and Jerry A. Fodor. 1963. The structure of a semantic theory. *Language* 39:170-210.

Kelly, Robert. 1995. Castaway. (Review of *The Island of the Day Before*). *The N.Y. Times Book Review* (Oct. 22):7-9.

Kelly, John and John Local. 1989. *Doing Phonology. Observing, Recording, Interpreting*. Manchester: Manchester University Press and New York: Pantheon.

Kenner, Hugh. 1962. Art in a Closed Field. *Virginia Quarterly Review* 38:397-413.

Ketner, K. L. 1981. Peirce's ethics of terminology. *Transactions of the Charles S. Peirce Society* 17-4:327-47.

Kevelson, Roberta. 1965. *Play: Anarchic Comedy and Counterculture*, ms., unpublished.

Kevelson, Roberta. 1975. *The Play as Interpretant*, ms, unpublished.

Kevelson, Roberta. 1987. *Charles S. Peirce's Method of Methods*. Amsterdam: J. Benjamins.

Kevelson, Roberta. 1990. *Peirce, Praxis, Pradox*. Amsterdam: Mouton de Gruyter.

Kevelson, Roberta. 1993. *Peirce's Esthetics of Freedom*. New York: Peter Lang Pub.

Kevelson, Roberta. 1995. *Peirce, Science, Signs*. New York: Peter Lang Pub.

Kevelson, Roberta. Forthcoming. *Codes, Crypt and Incarnations: Peirce's rhetorical Turn*.

Köller, Wilhelm. 1980. Der Peircesche Denkansatz als Grundlage rur die Literatursemiotik. In: *Literatursemiotik I Methoden—Analvsen—Tendenzen*, ed. Achim Eschbach and Wendeiin Rader, pp. 39-64. Tubingen: Gunter Narr Verlag.

Krampen, Martin, and Klaus Oehler, Roland Posner, Thomas A. Sebeok, Thure von Uexküll, eds. 1987. *Classics of Semiotics*. New York: Plenum.

Krausser, Peter. 1960. Die drei fundamentale Strukturkategorien bei Charles S. Peirce. *Philosophia Naturalis* 6:3-38.

Kress, G., ed. 1976. *Halliday: System and Function in Language*. Oxford University Press.

Kripke, Saul A. 1972. Naming and Necessity. In: *Semantics of Natural Language*, D. Davidson and G. Harman, pp. 253-355. Dordrecht: Reidel.

Kripke, Saul A. 1963. Semantical Considerations on Modal Logic. *Acta Philosophica Fennica* 16:83-94.

Kristeva, Julia. 1969. *Recherches pour une sémanalyse*. Paris: Éditions du Seuil.

Kristeva, Julia. 1970. Une poétique ruinée. In: M. M. Bakhtin. *La poétique de Dostoievski*, pp . 5-27. Paris: Éditions du Seuil.

Kristeva, Julia. 1975. *La Révolution du langage poétique: L'Avant-garde à la fin du XIXe Siecle: Lautréamont et Mallarmé*. Paris: Éditions du Seuil. (*Revolution in Poetic Language*. trans. Margaret Waller. New York: Columbia University Press.)

Kristeva, Julia. 1976. Signifying practice and mode of production. *Edinburgh Magazine*, pp. 64-73.

Kristeva, Julia. 1977. *Polylogue*. Paris: Éditions du Seuil.

Kristeva, Julia. 1980. *Desire in Language: A Semiotic Approach to Language and Art*, trans. Thomas Gora, Alice Jardine, and Leon S. Roudiez; ed. Leon S. Roudiez. New York: Columbia University Press.

Kristeva, Julia. 1986. About Chinese women, trans. by Sean Hand. In: *The Kristeva Reader*, ed. Toril Moi, pp. 138-59. New York: Columbia University Press.

Kuhn, Thomas S. 1962. *The Structure of Scientific Revolution*. Chicago: Chiacago University Press.

Kutnik, Jerry. 1986. *The Novel as Performance: The Fiction of R. Sukenick and R. Federman*. Carbondale: Southern Illinois University Press.

Lacan, J. 1975 [1953]. Le séminaire (1). In: *Le séminaire de J. Lacan*. Paris: Éditions du Seuil.

Lacan, J. 1966. *Écrits*. Paris: Éditions du Seuil.

LaCapra, Dominick. 1982. *Madame Bovary on Trial*. Ithaca: Cornell University Press.

LaCapra, Dominick. 1983. *Rethinking Intellectual History: Texts, Contexts, Language*. Ithaca: Cornell University Press.

LaCapra, Dominick. 1985. *History and Criticism*. Ithaca: Cornell University Press.

LaCapra, Dominick. 1987. *History, Politics and the Novel*. Ithaca: Cornell University Press.

LaCapra, Dominick. 1988. Chartier, Darnton and the great symbol massacre. *Journal of Modern History* 6-1:95-112.

Lakoff, George. 1987. *Women, Fire, and Dangerous Things: What Categories Reveal about the Mind*. Chicago: University of Chicago Press.

Lakoff, George and Mark Johnson. 1980. *Metaphors we live by*. Chicago: University of Chicago Press.

Langacker, Ronald. 1987. *Foundations of Cognitive Grammar I: Theoretical Perspectives*. Stanford: Stanford University Press.

Laszlo, E. 1987. *Evolution*. Boston: New Science Library.

Lauritzen, Henry. 1959. *Holmes og Heste*. Aalborg: Silkeborg Bogtrykker.

Lawrence, Elizabeth Atwood. 1985. *Hoofbeats and Society: Studies of Human-Horse Interactions*. Bloomington: Indiana University Press.

Leach, Edmund R. 1969a. Vico and Lévi-Strauss on the origins of humanity. In: *Giambattista Vico. An Inernational Symposium*, ed. Giorgio Tagliacozzo and Hayden V. White, pp. 309-18. Baltimore: Johns Hopkins University Press.

Leach, Edmund R. 1969b. *Genesis as Myth and Other Essays*. London: Johnathan Cape.

Leach, Edmund R. 1976. Vico and the future of anthropology. *Social Research* 43:807-17.

Leach, Edmund R. 1984. Glimpses of the unmentionable in the history of British social anthropology. *Annual Reviews of Anthropology* 13:1-23.

Leibniz, G. W. F. 1704. *Nouveaux Essais sur l'entendement humain*. Amsterdam 1765. (1981. *New Essays on Human Understanding*, trans and ed. P. Remnant and J. Bennett. Cambridge University Press.)

Lepschy, Giulio. 1977. Review of a *Theory of Semiotics*. *Language* 53:711-14.

Levinas, Emmanuel. 1993 [1987]. *Outside the Subject*, trans. M. B. Smith. London: Athlone Press.

Lévi-Strauss, Claude. 1955. *Trites tropiques*. Paris: Librairie Plon. (1978. *Tristes tropiques*, trans. John and Doreen Weightman. New York: Atheneum.)

Lévi-Strauss, Claude. 1955. The structural study of myth. *Journal of American Folklore* 68:428-44.

Lévi-Strauss, Claude. 1958. The Structural Study of Myth. In: *Myth: A Symposium*, ed. T. A. Sebeok, pp. 81-106. Bloomington: Indiana University Press.

Lévi-Strauss, Claude. 1962. *La Pensée sauvage*. Paris: Librairie Plon. (1966. *The Savage Mind*. Chicago: University of Chicago Press.)

Lévi-Strauss, Claude. 1964. *Le Cru et le cuit*. Paris: Librairie Plon. (1970. *The Raw and the Cooked: Introduction to a Science of Mythology*, trans. John and Doreen Weightman. New York: Harper and Row.)

Levin, S. R. 1973. *Linguistic Structures in Poetry*. The Hague: Mouton.

Lévinas, Emmanuel. 1961. *Totalité et infini*. La Haye: Nijhoff.

Lewis, David. 1983. *Philosophical Papers* Vol. 1. New York Oxford University Press.

Lewis, David. 1986. *On the Plurality of Worlds.* London: Blackwell.

Locke, J. 1959. *An Essay Concerning Human Understanding.* vol. 2. New York: Dover Publications.

Lodge, D. 1984. *Small World.* New York: Penguin.

Longoni, Anna. 1993. Hermetic Criticism and the Legitmacy of Interpretation. *Semiotica* 95:93-199.

Lorenz, Konrad. 1973. Introduction. In: *The Sexual Code: Social Behavior of Animals and Men.* Wolfgang Wickler, pp. xi-xix. Garden City: Anchor Books.

Lotman, Juri. 1976. *Analysis of the Poetic Text,* trans. D. Barton Johnson. Ann Arbor: Ardis.

Lotman, Juri. 1977. *The Structure of the Artistic Text,* trans. Gail Lenhoff and Ronald Vroon. Ann Arbor: University of Michigan Press.

Lotman, Juri. 1990. *Universe of the Mind. A Semiotic Theory of Culture,* trans. Ann Shukman. London -New York: I.B. Tauris & Co. Ltd.

Lumley, Robert. 1995. The sea and the mirror. (Review of *The Island of the Day Before*). *New Statesman* (Oct. 6):39-40.

Lyotard, François Jean. 1979. *La Condition postmoderne.* Paris: Minuit.

MacCabe, Colin. 1978. *James Joyce and the Revolution of the World.* London: MacMillian.

MacCannell, Dean and Juliet Flower. 1982. *The Time of the Sign: A Semiotic Interpretation of Modern Culture.* Bloomington: Indiana University Press.

MacCannell, Dean and Juliet Flower. 1986. Letter to Mihai Nadin, April 18.1.

Macksey, Richard A., ed. 1976. The C. S. Peirce Symposium on Semiotics and the Arts. *Modern Language Notes* 91:1424-539.

Magazine Littéraire. 1989. February issue, n. 262, dedicated to Eco.

Magli, Patrizia, Giovanni Manetti and Patrizia Violi, ed. 1992. *Semiotica: Storia, teoria, interpretazione.* Milan: Bompiani.

Manetti, Giovanni. 1987. Le teorie del segno nell'antichità classica. Milan: Bompiani. (1993. *Theories of the Sign in Classical Antiquity,* trans. Christine Richardson. Bloomington: Indiana University Press.)

Maritain, Jacques. 1921. *Theonas, ou les entretiens d'un sage et deux philosophes sur diverses materes ingegalment actuelles.* Paris: NLN.

Maritain, Jacques. 1957. Language and the Theory of Sign, in *Language: An Enquiry into Its Meaning and Function,* ed. R. Nanda Anshen, pp. 86-101. N.Y.: Harper And Bros.

Marrone, Gianfranco, ed. 1986. *Dove va la semiotica?. Quaderni del circolo semiologico siciliano* 24.

Martin, J. R. 1984. Politicalising ecology: the politics of baby seals and kangaroos. In: *Semiotics: Language and Ideology,* ed. E. Gross, M. A. K. Halliday, G. Kress and T. Threadgold. Sydney (1985).

Martin, L. D. 1979. Changing the past: theories of influence and orignality 1680-1830. *Dispositio* 4/11-12:189-212.

Matejka, L. and K. Pomorska, eds. 1978. *Readings in Russian Poetics: Formalist and Dtructuralist Views.* Ann Arbor: Michigan Slavic Publications.

McCarthy, Jeremiah E. 1984. Semiotic idealism. *Transactions of The Charles Peirce Society* 20:385-433.

McHale, Brian. 1992. *Constructing Postmodernism*. London: Routledge.

Medvedev, I. N. (M. Bakhtin). 1928. *Formal'nyi metod v literaturovedenii*. Leningrad: Priboi.

Mendelson, Edward. 1976. Encyclopedic Narrative: From Dante to Pynchon, *MLN* 91:1267-75.

Merrell, Floyd. 1984. Deconstruction Meets a Mathematician: Meta-semiotic Inquiry. *American Journal of Semiotics* 2:125-52.

Merton, Robert K. 1993. *On the Shoulders of Giants: A Shandean Postscript. The Post-Italianate Edition*. Chicago: University of Chicago Press.

Messick, Brinkley. 1987. Subordinate discourse: Women, weaving, and gender relations in North Africa. *American Ethnologist* 14:210-25.

Mincu, Marin, ed. 1982. *La semiotica letteraria italiana*. Milan: Feltrinelli.

Miranda, Claudia. 1992. Oscillazione fra teoria semiotica e scrittura nel *Pendolo di Foucault*. In: *Semiotica: Storia, teoria, interpretazione*, ed. P. Magli, G. Manetti and P. Violi. Milan: Bompiani.

Miranda, Claudia. 1996 Das Schiff der Theorie im Meer der Schrift. In: *Staunen uber das Sein: Internationale beitrage zu Umberto Ecos Insel des Vorigen Tages*, ed. T. Stauder. Darmstadt: WissenschaftlicheBuchGesellschaft.

MLN. Modern Language Notes. 1992. 107:5 Comparative Literature Issue dedicated to *Foucault's Pendulum*.

Morgan, Thaïs E. 1985. Is there an intertext in this text? Literary and interdisciplinary approaches to intertextuality. *American Journal of Semiotics* 3-4:1-40.

Morris, C. 1927. Unpublished letter to E. A. Burtt. Morris archives at the Peirce Edition Project. Indiana University-Purdue University at Indianapolis.

Morris, C. 1938a. Scientific empiricism. In *Encyclopedia and Unified Science*. Chicago: University of Chicago Press.

Morris, C. 1938b. *Foundations of the Theory of Signs*. Chicago: University of Chicago Press.

Morris, C. 1964. *Signification and Significance*. Cambridge, Mass.: The MIT Press.

Motte, Warren F. Jr. 1985. *Oulipo: A Primer of Potential Litterature*. Lincoln Nebraska: University of Nebraska Press.

Muñiz-Huberman, Angelina. 1990. Las trampas de Umberto Eco. *La cultura en México* (February 28):38.

Musca, Giosué. 1989. La camicia nel nesso: ovvero *Il pendolo di Foucault* di U. Eco. *Quaderni medievali* 27:104-49.

Nicolis, G. and I. Prigogine 1989. *Exploring Complexity*. San Francisco: Freeman.

Nicolis, J. 1986. *Dynamics of Hierarchical Systems*. New York: Springer.

Noakes, Susan. 1982. An English translation of Emilio Betti's *Teoria generale della interpretazione*. *Modern Language Studies* 12:35-43.

Noakes, Susan. 1984. An Introduction to Emilio Betti's hermeneutics. *Hermeneutics: Questions and Prospects*, ed. Gary Shapiro and Alan Sica. Amherst: University of Massachusetts Press.

Noakes, Susan. 1982. Hermeneutics and Semiotics: Betti's Debt to Peirce. *Semiotics* 1982. New York: Plenum.

Noakes, Susan. 1985. Literary Semiotics and Hermeneutics: Towards a Taxonomy of the Interpretant. *American Journal of Semiotics* 3-3:109-19.

O'Toole, L. M. 1975. Analytic and Synthetic Approaches to Narrative Structure: Sherlock Holmes and 'The Sussex Vampire'. In: *Style and Structure in Literature*, ed. R. Fowler, pp. 143-76. Oxford: Blackwell.

Ogden, C. K. and I. A. Richards. 1923. *The Meaning of Meaning. A Study of the Influence of Language upon Thought.* New York: Harcourt Brace.

Oliver, Andrew, ed. 1983. *L'intertextualité: Intertexte, Autotexte, Intratexte.* Special issue, *Texte* 2.

Olshewsky, Thomas M. 1983. Peirce's pragmatic maxim. *Transactions of the Charles Peirce Society* 19:200-10.

O'Neill, Patrick. 1990. *The Comedy of Entropy. Humour, Narrative, Reading.* Toronto: University of Toronto Press.

Ousby, Ian, ed. 1988. *The Cambridge Guide to Literature in English.* Cambridge: Cambridge University Press.

Owens, Craig. 1983. The Discourse of Others: Feminism and Postmodenism. In: *The Anti-Aesthetic: Essays on Postmodern Culture,* ed. Hal Foster. Port Townsend, Was.: Bay Press.

Painter, C. A. 1982. The development of language in the first two years: a case study. Unpub. M.A thesis. Dept. of Linguistics, University of Sydney.

Palmer, Richard. 1969. *Hermeneutics.* Evanston: Northwestern University Press.

Palmer, Stuart. 1937. *The Puzzle of the Red Stallion.* Garden City.

Palmer, Stuart. 1941. *The Puzzle of Happy Hooligan.* New York: Doubleday.

Parmentier, Richard. 1994. *Signs in Society. Studies in Semiotic Anthropology.* Bloomington: Indiana University Press.

Pansa, F. and Vinci, A. 1992. *Effetto Eco.* Roma: Nuova Edizioni del Gallo.

Pareto, V. 1896-97. *Cours d'économie politique.* Lausanne: Rouge.

Pareyson, Luigi. 1954. *Estetica. Teoria della formatività.* Bologna: Zanichelli. Also, 1974. Milan: Sansoni.

Pareyson, Luigi. 1971. *Verità e interpretazione.* Milan: Mursia.

Peirce, Charles Sanders. 1866. The Logic of Science, or, Induction and Hypothesis, presented in the Lowell Lectures of 1866, and which appears in the *Collected Papers of Charles Sanders Peirce.* Cambridge, MA: Harvard University Press, 1974, 7.591-7.595.

Peirce, Charles Sanders. 1868. Some Consequences of Four Incapacities. *Journal of Speculative Philosophy* 2:140-57. Reprinted in the *Collected Papers* 5.264-5.137.

Peirce, Charles Sanders. 1898. Philosophy and the Conduct of Life , unpublished manuscript.

Peirce, Charles Sanders. 1899c. FRL , MS 285, published in entirety in *Collected Papers* 1.135-1.140.

Peirce, Charles Sanders. 1905. The Basis of Pragmaticism, MS 283.

Peirce, Charles Sanders. 1906b. Pragmatism, MS 318, published in the *Collected Papers* 5.11-13, 5.464-496.

Peirce, Charles Sanders. 1906c. Reflexions upon Pluralistic Pragmatism and upon Cenopythagorean Pragmaticism, CP 5.555-564.

Peirce, Charles Sanders. 1982-90. *Writings of Charles Sanders Peirce: A Chronological Edition.* Vols. 1-6 eds. M Fish et al. Bloomington: Indiana University Press.

Peirce, Charles Sanders. 1931-1958. *Collected Papers of Charles Sanders Peirce.* Vols. 1-8, ed. C. Hartshorne, P. Weiss, and A. W. Burks. Cambridge: Harvard University Press.

Peirce, Charles Sanders. 1931. *Collected Papers.* Vols I-VI, ed. Charles Hartshorne and Paul Weiss. Cambridge: Harvard University Press.

Peirce, Charles Sanders. 1958. *Collected Papers.* Vols. VII-VIII, ed. Arthur W. Burks. Cambridge: Harvard University Press.

Peirce, Charles Sanders. 1966. *Selected Writings,* ed. Philip P. Wiener. New York: Dover Publications.

Peirce, Charles Sanders. 1977. *Semiotics and Significs.* Bloomington, London: Indiana University Press.

Peirce, Charles Sanders. 1980. *Semiotica,* ed M. A. Bonfantini, L. Grassi, G. Proni. Turin: Einaudi.

Peirce, Charles Sanders. 1984. *Le leggi dell'ipotesi,* ed. M. A. Bonfantini, R. Grazia, G. Proni. Milan: Bompiani.

Perri, Carmela. 1978. On Alluding. *Poetics* 713:289-307.

Perrone-Moisés, Leyla. 1976. L'intertextualité critique. *Poétique* 27:372-84.

Peter of Spain. 1985. *Tractatus. Summule logicales,* trans. A. Ponzio. Bari: Adriatica.

Petersen, A. 1963. The Philosophy of Neils Bohr. *Bulletin of the Atomic Scientists,* XIX-7:8-14.

Petrilli, Susan, ed. 1984. *Dialogue, Iconicity, and Meaning. Readings.* Bari: Adriatica.

Petrilli, Susan. 1988. *Significs semiotica significazione.* Bari: Adriatica.

Petrilli, Susan. 1990a. Introduction. In: A. Ponzio. *Man as a Sign: Essays on the Philosophy of Language,* trans. and ed. S. Petrilli. pp. 1-13. Berlin and New York: Mouton De Gruyter.

Petrilli, Susan. 1990b. The problem of signifying in Welby, Peirce, Vailati, Bakhtin. In: A. Ponzio. *Man as a Sign: Essays on the Philosophy of Language,* trans. and ed. S. Petrilli. pp. 313-63. Berlin and New York: Mouton De Gruyter.

Petrilli, Susan. 1990c. On the materiality of signs. In: A. Ponzio. *Man as a Sign: Essays on the Philosophy of Language,* trans. and ed. S. Petrilli. pp. 365-401. Berlin and New York: Mouton De Gruyter.

Petrilli, Susan. 1990d. Dialogue and chronotopic otherness: Bakhtin and Welby. *Discours social/Social Discourse* 3-1/2:339-50.

Petrilli, Susan. 1990e. On the semiotics of interpretation: Introduction. In: Deledalle. *Charles S. Peirce: An Intellectual Biography,* trans. S. Petrilli, pp. xi-xxvii. Amsterdam: John Benjamins.

Petrilli, Susan , ed. 1992a. Social Practice, Semiotics and the Sciences of Man: The Correspondence Between Charles Morris and Ferruccio Rossi-Landi. *Semiotica* 88-1/2, Special issue.

Petrilli, Susan. 1992b. Iconicity at the origin of language: C. S. Peirce and G. Fano. Introduction. In: Fano. *Origins and Nature of Language,* trans. S. Petrilli, pp. xvii-xxvii. Bloomington: Indiana University Press.

Petrilli, Susan. 1992c. The unconscious, signs and ideology. *Semiotica* 90:379-87.

Petrilli, Susan. 1992d. Linguistic production, ideology and otherness: Contributions by Augusto Ponzio to the philosophy of language. *Scripta semiotica* 1:89-117.

Petrilli, Susan. 1993. Dialogism and Interpretation in the Study of Signs. *Semiotica* 97:103-18.

Petrilli, Susan. 1995a. *Materia segnica e interpretazione.* Lecce: Milella.

Petrilli, Susan. 1995b. *Che cosa significa significare?.* Bari: Edizioni dal Sud.

Pezzini, Isabella. 1990. *La carte de tendre*: un modello figurativo della passione. In: *Espaces du Texte,* ed. P. Frohlicher, G. Guntert, F. Thurlemann. Neuchatel: A la Baconnière.

Phillips, Gary A. 1991. Sign/Text/Différance. In: *Intertextuality,* ed. H. F. Plett. pp.

78-97. Berlin: W. De Gruyter.

Philips, Judson Pentecost [Hugh Pentecost]. 1961. *Murder Clear, Track Fast*. New York: Dodd, Mead.

Piaget, Jean. 1970. *Structuralism*, trans. and ed. Chaninah Maschler. New York: Harper Torchbooks.

Piaget, Jean. 1973. *Main Trends in Inter-Disciplinary Research*. New York: Harper Torchbooks.

Plantiga, Alvin. 1974. *The Nature of Necessity*. Oxford: Claredon.

Plato. 1973. *The Collected Dialogues*. Princeton: Princeton University Press. (*Sophist*, trans. F. M. Cornford; *Philebus*, trans. R. Hackforth)

Platt, Kin. 1973. *The Princess Stakes Murder*. New York: Random House.

Plett, Heinrich F, ed. 1991. *Intertextuality*. Berlin: W. De Gruyter.

Plottel, Jeanine P. and Hanna Charney, eds. 1978. *Intertextuality: New Perspectives in Criticism*. New York: New York Literary Forum.

Poinsot, John. 1632. Tractatus de Signis, disengaged from the Artis Logicae Secunda Pars (Alcalá, Spain) and published in the bilingual edition, *The Semiotic of John Poinsot*, arranged by J. Deely. Berkley: University Of California Press, 1985.

Ponzio, Augusto. 1970. *Linguaggio e relazioni sociali*. Bari: Adriatica.

Ponzio, Augusto. 1973. *Produzione linguistica e ideologia sociale*. Bari: De Donato.

Ponzio, Augusto. 1974. *Filosofia del linguaggio e prassi sociale*. Lecce: Milella.

Ponzio, Augusto. 1976. *La semiotica in Italia. Fondamenti teorici*. Bari: Dedonato.

Ponzio, Augusto. 1977. Ed. By. *Bachtin. Semiotica, teoria della letteratura e marxismo*. Bari: Dedalo.

Ponzio, Augusto. 1978. *Marxismo, scienza e problema dell'uomo*. Verona: Bertani.

Ponzio, Augusto. 1980. *Michail Bachtin*. Bari: Dedalo.

Ponzio, Augusto. 1981. *Segni e contraddizioni. Fra Marx e Bachtin*. Verona: Bertani.

Ponzio, Augusto. 1983. *Tra linguaggio e letteratura*. Bari: Adriati.

Ponzio, Augusto. 1984. Semiotics between Peirce and Bakhtin. *Recherches Sémiotique/Semiotic Inquiry* 4-3/4:273-91.

Ponzio, Augusto. 1985a. *Filosofia del linguaggio*. Bari: Adriatica.

Ponzio, Augusto. 1985b. Signs to talk about signs. In: *Per parlare dei segni/Talking About Signs*, trans. S. Petrilli; ed. M. A. Bonfantini, G. Mininni, and A. Ponzio, pp. 77-145. Bari: Adriatica.

Ponzio, Augusto. 1986a. *Interpretazione e scrittura*. Verona: Bertani.

Ponzio, Augusto. 1988. *Rossi-Landi e la filosofia del linguaggio*. Bari: Adriatica.

Ponzio, Augusto. 1989. *Soggetto e alterità. Da Lévinas a Lévinas*. Bari: Adriatica.

Ponzio, Augusto. 1990. *Man as a Sign: Essays on the Philosophy of Language*, trans. and ed. S. Petrilli. Berlin and New York: Mouton De Gruyter.

Ponzio, Augusto. 1991. *Filosofia del linguaggio 2: Segni, valori e ideologie*. Bari: Adriatica.

Ponzio, Augusto. 1992. *Fra semiotica e letteratura. Introduzione a Michail Bachtin*. Milan: Bompiani.

Ponzio, Augusto. 1993a. *Signs, Dialogue, and Ideology*, trans. and ed. S. Petrilli. Amsterdam: John Benjamins.

Ponzio, Augusto and M. A. Bonfantini. 1986. *Dialogo sui dialoghi*. Ravenna: Longo.

Ponzio, Augusto, S. Petrilli and O. Calbrese. 1993. *La ricerca semiotica*. Bologna: Esculapio.

Ponzio, Augusto, S. Petrilli and P. Calefato. 1994. *Fondamenti di filosofia del linguaggio.* Bari: Laterza.

Popper, K. R. 1982. *Quantum Theory and the Schism in Physics.* Totowa, N.J.: Rowman and Littlefield.

Pozzato, Maria Pia, ed. 1992. *L'idea deforme.* Milan: Bompiani.

Praz, Mario. 1925. *Secentismo e marinismo in Inghilterra. J. Donne e R. Crashaw.* Firenze: La Voce.

Praz, Mario. 1939. *Studies in Seventeenth-Century Imagery.* London:Warburg Institute.

Praz, Mario. 1958. *The Flaming Heart.* New York: Doubleday & Co.

Prieto, Luis J. 1966. *Messages et signeaux.* Paris: Presses Universitaires.

Prigogine, I. 1980. *From Being to Becoming.* San Francisco: Freeman.

Prigogine, I. 1989. Presidential Address, ISSS Conference, Edinburgh.

Prigogine, I. and I. Stengers. 1984. *Order Out of Chaos.* New York: Bantam.

Prodi, Giorgio. 1977. *Le basi materiali della significazione.* Milan: Bompiani.

Proni, Giampaolo. 1990. *Introduzione a Peirce.* Milan: Bompiani.

Proni, Giampaolo. 1993. Umberto Eco: An Intellectual Biography. *The Semiotic Web* 3-22.

Propp, Vladmir. 1969. *Morphology of the Folktale.* Austin: University of Texas Press.

Pynchon, Thomas. 1984. *Slow Learner: Early Stories.* Boston: Little Brown.

Putnam, Hilary. 1970. Is Semantics Possible? In: *Language, Belief and Metaphisics,* ed. H. E. Kiefer and M. K. Munitz. New York: New York University Press.

Putnam, Hilary. 1975. *Mind Language and Reality.* Vol. 2. London: Cambridge University Press.

Quillian, M. Ross. 1971. Un modello di memoria semantica. *Versus* 1:61-104

Quine, W. V. 1953. *From a Logical Point of View.* Cambridge: Harvard University Press.

Radcliffe-Brown, A. R. 1952. *Structure and Function in Primitive Society.* London: Cohen and West.

Raimondi, Ezio. 1961. *Trattatisti e narratori del seicento.* Milano: Ricciardi.

Raimondi, Ezio. 1982. *Letteratura barocca.* Firenze: Olschki.

Raimondi, Ezio. 1987. *Il mondo della metafora. Il seicento letterario italiano.* Bologna: CUSL.

Raimondi, Ezio. 1990. *Barocco moderno: C.E. Gadda e R. Longhi.* Bologna: CUSL.

Rand, Benjamin, ed. 1927. *The Correspondence of John Locke and Edward Clarcke.* London: Oxford University Press.

Ransdell, J. 1977. Some leading ideas of Peirce's semiotic. *Semiotica* 19:3-4.

Ransdell, J. 1983. Semiotic and linguistics. In: *The Signifying Animal: the Grammar of Languae and Experience,* ed. I. Rauch and G. Cann. Bloomington: Indiana University Press.

Rauch, Irmengard. 1984. 'Symbols Grow': Creation, Compulsion, Change. *American Journal of Semiotics* 3:1-23.

Rauch, Irmengard. 1991. Semiotics: (No)canon (no)theses. *Semiotica* 86:85-92.

Rauch, Irmengard. 1992. Deconstruction, Prototype Theory and Semiotics. *American Journal of Semiotics* 9:131-40.

Rauch, Irmengard, et al. 1995. BAG IV: Phonological Interference. In: *Berkeley/ Michigan Germanic Linguistics Roundtable.*

Rescher, Nicholas. 1975. *A Theory of Possibility.* Oxford: Blackwell.

Rescher, Nicholas. 1976. Peirce and the economy of research. *Philosophy of Science*

43:71-96.

Revzin, I. I. 1978. Notes on the Semiotic Analysis of Detective Novels: With Examples from the Novels of Agatha Christie. *New Literary History* 9:385-88.

Rey-Debove, J. 1973. Introduction. In: *Recherches sur les Systèmes Signifiants*, ed. Rey-Debove, pp. 5-8. The Hague: Mouton.

Richards, I. A. 1936. *The Philosophy of Rhetoric*. London: Oxford University Press.

Richter, David H. 1985. Eco's Echoes: Semiotic Theory and Detective Practice in *The Name of the Rose*. *Studies in 20th Century Literature* 10-2:213-36.

Ricoeur, Paul. 1969. *Le Conflit des Interpretations*. Published as *The Conflict of Interpretations*, trans. Kathleen McLoughlin. Evanston: Northwestern University Press.

Ricoeur, Paul. 1978. *The Rule of Metaphor: Multi-Disciplinary Studies of the Creation of Meaning in Language*. Trans. R. Czerny, K. McLaughlin, and J. Costello. Toronto: University of Toronto Press.

Ricoeur, Paul. 1986 [1984]. *Time and Narrative I, II, III*. Chicago: University of Chicago Press.

Ridgeway, William. 1964 [1915]. *The Dramas and Dramatic Dances of the Non-European Races*. New York: B. Blom.

Riffaterre, Michael. 1966. Describing poetic structures: Two approaches to Baudelaire's *Les Chats*. *Yale French Studies* 36-37:200-42.

Riffaterre, Michael. 1973. The Self-sufficient Text. *Diacritics* (Fall):39-45.

Riffaterre, Michael. 1978. *Semiotics of Poetry*. Bloomington: Indiana University Press.

Riffaterre, Michael. 1979. Sémiotique intertextuelle: l'interprétant. *Revue d'esthétique* pp. 128-50.

Riffaterre, Michael. 1979. *La Production du texte*. Paris: Éditions du Seuil. (1983. *The Production of the Text*, trans. Térese Lyons. New York: Columbia University Press.)

Riffaterre, Michael. 1979. *Sémiotique intertextuelle: L'interprétant. Rhétoriques sémiotiques*. Paris: Union Générale d'Éditions.

Riffaterre, Michael. 1979. La Syllepse intertextuelle. *Poétique* 40:496-501.

Riffaterre, Michael. 1980. Syllepsis. *Critical Inquiry* 6-4:625-38.

Riffaterre, Michael. 1980. La Trace de l'intertexte. *La Pensée: Revue du rationalisme moderne* 215:4-18.

Riffaterre, Michael. 1981. Interpretation and Undecidability. *New Literary History* 1212:227-42.

Riffaterre, Michael. 1983. *Text Production*. New York: Columbia University Press.

Riffaterre, Michael. 1983. Hermeneutic Models. *Poetics Today* 4:7-16.

Riffaterre, Michael. 1984. Intertextual Representation: On Mimesis as Interpretive Discourse. *Critical Inquiry*, 11:141-62.

Riffaterre, Michael. 1985. The Interpretant in Literary Semiotics. *American Journal of Semiotics*, 3-4:41-55.

Riffaterre, Michael. 1991. The Reconstruction of Intertextuality. In: *Intertextuality*, ed. H. F. Plett, pp. 60-77. Berlin: W. De Gruyter.

Robey, David. 1984. Umberto Eco. In: *Writers and Society in Contemporary Italy*, ed. M. Caesar and P. Hainsworth, pp. 63-88. Warwickshire: Berg Publishers.

Robey, David. 1989. Introduction. In: *The Open Work*.

Rochberg-Halton, and Kevin McMurtrey. The foundations of Modern Semiotic:

Charles Peirce and Charles Morris. *American Journal of Semiotics* 2:129-56.

Rollin, Roger. 1988. Postscript: *The Name of the Rose* as popular culture. In: *Naming the Rose. Essays on Eco's* The Name of the Rose, ed. M. Thomas Inge, pp. 157-72. Jackson and London: University Press of Mississippi.

Romeo, Luigi. 1977. The Derivation of Semiotics through the History of the Discipline. *Semiosis* 6-2:37-49.

Rorty, Richard. 1982. *Consequences of Pragmatism*. Minneapolis: University of Minnesota Press.

Rorty, Richard. 1989. *Contingency, Irony, and Solidarity*. Cambridge: Cambridge University.

Rorty, Richard. 1991a. *Objectivity, Relativism, and Truth*. Cambridge: Cambridge University Press.

Rorty, Richard. 1991b. *Essays on Heidegger and Others*. Cambridge: Cambridge University Press.

Rosch, Eleanor and Carolyn Mervis. 1975. Family Resemblances. *Cognitive Psychology* 7:573-605.

Rossi-Landi, Ferruccio. 1953. *Charles Morris e la semiotica novecentesca*. Milan: Feltrinelli; 2nd. Edition, 1975.

Rossi-Landi, Ferruccio. 1961. *Significato, comunicazione e parlare comune*. Padova: Marsilio 1980.

Rossi-Landi, Ferruccio. 1968. *Il linguaggio come lavoro e come mercato*. Milano: Bompiani. (1983. *Language as Work and Trade*. South Hadley: Bergin or Garvey.)

Rossi-Landi, Ferruccio. 1972. *Semiotica e ideologia*. Milano: Bompiani.

Rossi-Landi, Ferruccio. 1975. *Linguistics and Economics*. The Hague: Mouton.

Rossi-Landi, Ferruccio. 1976. On Some Post Morrisian Problems. *Ars semiotica* 3:3-32.

Rossi-Landi, Ferruccio. 1978. *Ideologia*. Milan: Mondadori. Eng. trans. as *Marxism and Ideology*. by R. Griffin. Oxford: Clarendon Press, 1990.

Rossi-Landi, Ferruccio. 1979. Ideas for A Manifesto of Materialistic Semiotics. *Kodikas/Code*, 2:1211

Rossi-Landi, Ferruccio. 1983. A Correspondence with U. Eco, trans. C. Springer. *Boundary 2* 12-1:1-13.

Rossi-Landi, Ferruccio. 1985. *Metodica filosofica e scienza dei segni*. Milan: Bompiani.

Rossi-Landi, Ferruccio. 1988. A fragment in the history of Italian semiotics *Semiotic Theory and Practice: Proceedings of the Third International Congress of the IASS*, pp. 243-261. The Hague: Mouton de Gruyter.

Rossi-Landi, Ferruccio. 1992. *Between Signs and Non-signs*, ed. S. Petrilli. Amsterdam: John Benjamins.

Rubino, C. A. 1985. The Invisible Worm, *SubStance* 14:54-63.

Ruprecht, Hans-George 1983 Intertextualité. *Texte: Revue de critique et de théorie littéraire* 2:13-22.

Salthe, S. 1985. *Involving Hierarchical Systems*. New York: Columbia University.

Salthe, S. 1990. Sketch of a Logical Demonstration. *Journal of Ideas* 1:54-59.

Sangster, R. B. 1982. *Roman Jakobson and Beyond: Language as a System of Signs*. Janua Linguarum, Series Maior 109. The Hague: Mouton.

Santaella-Braga, Lucia. 1991. John Poinsot's Doctrine of Signs: The Recovery of a Missing Link. *The Journal od Speculative Philosophy* 5-2:151-59.

Santaella-Braga, Lucia. 1994. The Way to Postmodernity. In: Deely 1994b. *New Beginnings. Early Modern Philosophy and Postmodern Thought, pp.* xv-xvi. Toronto: University of Toronto Press.

Saunders, George R. 1984. Contemporary Italian cultural anthropology. *Annual Review of Anthropology* 13:447-66.

Saussure, Ferdinand de. 1915. *Cours de linguistique générale,* ed. Charles Bally, Albert Sechehaye, et al. Geneva. (1966. *Course in General Linguistics,* trans. Wade Baskin. New York: McGraw Hill.)

Savan, David. 1976. *An Introduction to C. S. Peirce's Semiotics.* Toronto: Victoria University.

Shannon, C. E. & Weaver, W. 1949. *The Mathematical Theory of Communication.* Urbana: Illinois University Press.

Scheglov, Yu. K. and A. K. Zholkovsky. 1975. Towards a 'The me-(Expression Devices)-Text': Model of Literary Structure. *Russian Poetics in Translation* 1:1-77.

Schillemans, Sandra. 1992. Umberto Eco and William of Baskerville: Partners in abduction. *Semiotica* 92:259-85.

Scholem, Gershom G. 1954. *Major Trends in Jewish Mysticism,* trans. by Ralph Manheim. New York: Schocken Books.

Scholem, Gershom G. 1960. *The Kabbalah and Its Symbolism,* trans. by Ralph Manheim. New York: Schocken Books.

Scholes, Robert. 1989. *Protocols of Reading.* New Haven Yale University Press.

Scholes, Robert. 1989. 1992. Eco's Limits. *Semiotica* 89:83-88.

Schrodinger, E. 1954. *Nature and the Greeks.* Cambridge: Cambridge University.

Searle, John R. 1969. *Speech Acts.* London: Cambridge University Press.

Sebeok, Thomas A. 1971. Semiotic and Its Congeners. In: *Linguistic and Literary Studies in Honor of A. Hill,* ed. M. A. Jazayery, E. C. Polomé and W. Wintr, pp. 283-95. Lisse: Peter de ridder Press.

Sebeok, Thomas A. 1972a. *Perspectives in Zoosemiotics.* The Hague: Mouton.

Sebeok, Thomas A. 1972b. Problems in Classification of Signs,in Sebeok 1985:95-110.

Sebeok, Thomas A. 1974a. *Structure and Texture.* The Hague: Mouton.

Sebeok, Thomas A. 1974b. Semiotics: A Survey of the State of the Art. In: *Current Trends in Linguistics* Vol. 12, ed. T. A. Sebeok. The Hague: Mouton.

Sebeok, Thomas A. 1975a. Zoosemiotics: At the Intersection of Nature and Culture. In: *Tell-Tale Sign,* ed. T. A. Sebeok, pp. 85-95. Lisse: Peter de Ridder.

Sebeok, Thomas A. 1975b. The Semiotic Web: A Chronicle of Prejudices. *Bulletin of Literary Semiotics,* 2:1-65.

Sebeok, Thomas A. 1976a. Final Report to the National Endowment for the Humanities on the Pilot Program in Semiotics in the Humanities at Indiana University, Bloomington, August 1, 1975-July 31, 1976. June 1, 1976. Research Center for Language and Semiotic Studies, Indiana University, Bloomington, Indiana.

Sebeok, Thomas A. 1976b. *Contributions to The Doctrine of Signs.* Bloomington: Indiana University Press.

Sebeok, Thomas A. 1979. *The Sign and Its Masters.* Austin and London: University of Texas Press.

Sebeok, Thomas A. 1981. *The Play of Musement.* Bloomington: Indiana University Press.

Sebeok, Thomas A. 1985. *Contributions to the Doctrine of Signs.* Lanham: University

Press of America.

Sebeok, Thomas A. 1986. *I Think I Am a Verb.* New York and London: Plenum Press.

Sebeok, Thomas A. 1986a. A Signifying Man. Feature Review of *Tractatus de Signis. The New York Times Review,* 30 March 1986, pp. 14-15.

Sebeok, Thomas A. 1990a. *A Sign Is Just A Sign.* Advances in Semiotics Series, ed. T. A. Sebeok. Bloomington: Indiana University Press.

Sebeok, Thomas A. 1990b. *American Signatures.* Norman: University of Oklahoma Press.

Sebeok, Thomas A. 1990c. *Essays in Zoosemiotics.* Toronto Semiotic Circle, Monograph Series #5.

Sebeok, Thomas A. 1991a. *Semiotics in the United States. The View from the Center.* Bloomington: Indiana University Press.

Sebeok, Thomas A. 1991b. Give Me Another Horse. *American Journal of Semiotics* 4:41-52.

Sebeok, Thomas A. 1991c. Indexicality. *American Journal of Semiotics* 7:7-28.

Sebeok, Thomas A. 1992. Sguardo sulla semiotica americana. *Il campo semiotico,* ed. U. Eco. Milan: Bompiani.

Sebeok, Thomas A, ed. 1960. *Style in Language.* New York: John Wiley and Sons.

Sebeok, Thomas A, ed. 1968. *Animal Communication: Techniques of Study and Results of Research.* Bloomington: Indiana University Press.

Sebeok, Thomas A, ed. 1977. *A Perfusion of Signs.* Advances in Semiotics Series. Bloomington: Indiana University Press.

Sebeok, Thomas A, ed. 1978. *Sight, Sound, and Sense.* Bloomington: Indiana University Press.

Sebeok, Thomas A, ed. 1981. *The Clever Hans Phenomenon: Communication with Horses, Whales, Apes and People.* New York: The N.Y. Academy of Sciences.

Sebeok, Thomas A., et al. 1986b. *Encyclopedic Dictionary of Semiotics.* Berlin: Mouton de Gruyter.

Sebeok, Thomas A. and Jean Umiker-Sebeok. 1974. 'You Know My Method': A Juxtaposition of Charles S. Peirce and Sherlock Holmes. *Semiotica* 26:203-50.

Sebeok, Thomas A. and Jean Umiker-Sebeok. 1980. *You Know My Method. A Juxtaposition of Charles S. Peirce and Sherlock Holmes.* Bloomington: Gaslight Publications.

Sebeok, Thomas A. and Umiker-Sebeok, Jean. 1982. *Du kennst meine Methode. Charles S. Peirce und Sherlock Holmes.* Frankfurt am Main: Suhrkamp.

Sebeok, Thomas A. 1975. Six species of signs: Some propositions and strictures. *Semiotica* 13:233-60.

Seed, David. 1986. Order in T. Pynchon's 'Entropy'. In: Thomas Pynchon. *Modern Critical Views,* ed. Harold Bloom. New York: Chelsea House.

Seed, David. 1991. The Poetics of the Open Work. *Essays in Criticism,* 41:87-96.

Segre, Cesare. 1973. *Semiotics and Literary Criticism.* The Hague: Mouton.

Segre, Cesare. 1979. *Structures and Time.* Chicago: University of Chicago Press.

Segre, Cesare. 1993. *Notizie dalla crisi.* Torino: Einaudi.

Sercarz, Eli, et al., eds. 1988. *The Semiotics of Cellular Communication in the Immune System.* Berlin: Springer.

Shaeffer, John D. 1992. Eco and Vico. *New Vico Studies* 10:73-77.

Shannon, C. E. and Weaver, Warren. 1949. *The Mathematical Theory of Communica-*

tion. Urbana: University of Illinois Press.

Shapiro, Michael. 1983. *The Sense of Grammar.* Bloomington: Indiana University Press.

Shklovsky, V. 1925. Novella tain. In: *O teorii prozy.* Moscow: Federacija.

Silverman, Kaja. 1983. *The Subject of Semiotics.* New York: Oxford University Press.

Simon, Yves. 1970. *The Great Dialogue of Nature and Space.* New York: Magi.

Sinclair, J. McH., S. Jones and R. Daley. 1970. *English lexical studies.* OSTI Report on Project C/LP/08. Dept. of English, University of Birmingham, #15.

Singer, Milton. 1984. *Man's Glassy Essence.* Bloomington: Indiana University Press.

Sobel, Dava. 1995. Longitude: *The True Story of a Lone Genius Who Solved the Greatest Scientific Problem of his Time.* New York: Walker Company.

Sontag, Susan. 1970. The anthropologist as hero. In: *Claude Lévi-Strauss: The Anthropologist as Hero,* ed. E. Nelson Hayes and Tanya Hayes, pp. 184-196. Cambridge, Mass.: The MIT Press.

Spanos, William V. 1972. The Detective and the Boundary: Some Notes on the Postmodern Literary Imagination. *Boundary* 2 1.1:147-68.

Stalnaker, Robert. 1984. *Inquiry.* Cambridge, Mass.: Bradford Books.

Stauder, Thomas. 1989. Un colloquio con U. Eco su *Il pendolo di Foucault, Il lettore di provincia* 75:3-11.

Stauder, Thomas. 1991. *Il pendolo di Foucault*: L'autobiografia segreta di Eco. *Il lettore di provincia* 23:3-22.

Steiner, George. 1975. *After Babel Aspects of language in translation.* London: Oxford.

Steiner, Wendy. 1976. Point of view from the Russian point of view. *Dispositio* 1, 3:315-326.

Steiner, Wendy. 1978. Language as Process: Sergej Karcevskij's Semiotics of Language. In: *Sound, Sign and Meaning. Quinquagenary of the Prague Linguistic Circle,* ed. L. Matejka, pp. 291-300. Ann Arbor: Michigan Slavic Publications.

Stephens, Walter, E. 1983. Ec(h)o in fabula. *Diacritics,* pp. 51-64.

SubStance. 1985. Vol. 47. Issue dedicated to U. Eco's *The Name of the Rose.*

Suino, M. E. 1976. Communication and culture. *Dispositio* 1-3:349.

Szondi, Peter. 1970. L'herméneutique de Schleiermacher. *Poétique* 1-2:141-55.

Tagliacozzo, Giorgio, ed. 1983. *Vico and Marx. Affinities and Contrasts.* Atlantic Highlands, NJ: Humanities Press; London: Macmillan.

Talamo, Mario. 1989. *I segreti del pendolo: percorsi e giochi intorno a 'Il pendolo di Foucault'.* Naples: Simone.

Tani, Stefano. 1984. *The Doomed Detective: The Contribution of the Detective Novel to Postmodern American and Italian Fiction.* Carbondale: Southern Illinois University Press.

Tarnas, Richard. 1990. The Western Mind at the Threshold. Paper presented to the Center for Psychological Studies in the Nuclear Age. Cambridge, MA: Affiliate of Harvard Medical School at The Cambridge Hospital.

Taylor, John R. 1989. *Linguistic Categorization: Prototypes in Linguistic Theory.* Oxford: Oxford University Press.

Tejera, Vittorino. 1965. *Art and Human Intelligence.* New York: Appleton-Century.

Tejera, Vittorino. 1971. *Modes of Greek Thought.* New York: Appleton-Century.

Tejera, Vittorino. 1984. *Plato's Dialogues One by One.* New York: Irvington.

Tejera, Vittorino. 1986. Community, Comunication, and Meaning: the Theories of Buchler and Habermas. *Symbolic Interaction* 9/1.

Tejera, Vittorino. 1988. *Semiotics from Peirce to Barthes.* Leiden: Brill.

Tejera, Vittorino. 1989. Has Eco Understood Peirce? *The American Journal of Semiotics*, 6:251-64.

Tejera, Vittorino. 1990. On the Form and Authenticity of the 'Lysis'. *Ancient Philosophy* IX. 2.

Tejera, Vittorino. 1991. Eco, Peirce and Interpretationism. Semiotics, Literary Theory and the Limits of Interpretation. *American Journal of Semiotics* 8:149-68.

Thibault, Paul J. 1991. *Social Semiotics as Praxis.* Minneapolis: University of Minnesota Press.

Thomas, Bill. 1985. *Talking with the Animals: How to Communicate with Wildlife.* New York: William Morrow.

Thomson, Clive. 1983. The Semiotics of M. M. Bakhtin. *The University of Ottawa Quarterly* 5:11-22.

Threadgold, Terry. 1986. The Semiotics of Vološinov, Halliday and Eco. *American Journal of Semiotics* 4:107-42.

Titunik, I. R. 1986. The Bakhtin problem: Concerning Katerina Clark and Michael Holquist's Mikhail Bakhtin. *Slavic and East European Journal* 30-1:91-95.

Todorov, Tzvetan. 1981. *Mikhail Bakhtine: le principe dialogique suivi de Écrits du Cercle de Bakhtine.* Paris: Éditions du Seuil.

Todorov, Tzvetan. 1982. *Theories of the Symbol.* Trans. C. Porter. Oxford: Basil Blackwell.

Todorov, Tzvetan. 1984. *Mikhail Bakhtin: The Dialogical Principle*, trans. Wlad Godzich. Theory and History of Literature Series 13, Minneapolis: University of Minnesota Press.

Toscani, Claudio. 1988. Review of *Il pendolo di Foucault. Critica letteraria* 16:617-20.

Troubetzky, N. S. 1939. Gedanken über das Indogermanenproblem. *Acta Linguista* 1:81-89.

Turner, G. J. 1973. Social class and children's language of control at blend five and age seven. In:. *Class Codes and Control,* Vol. 2. *Applied Studies toward a Sociology of Language* (Primary socialization: language and education), ed. B. Bernstein. London: Routledge and Kegan Paul.

Umiker-Sebeok, Jean and Thomas A. Sebeok 1981. Clever Hans and smart imians: The self-fulfilling prophecy and kindred methodological pitfalls. *Anthropos* 76:89-165.

Uspensky, B. 1973. *A Poetics of Composition: the structure of the artistic text and typology of a compositional form*, trans. V. Zavarin and S. Wittig. Berkeley: University of California Press.

Uspensky, B., V. V. Ivanov, V. N. Toporov and A. M. Pjatigorsky. 1975. *Theses on the Semiotic Study of Culture.* Netherlands: Peter de Ridder.

Vandenberghe, J. P. and M. Johnen. 1994. *Elsevier's Nautical Dictionary.* Amsterdam: Elsevier Science.

Van Dijk, T. 1977. *Text and Context. Explorations in the Semantics and Pragmatics of Discourse.* London and New York: Longman.

Van Dine, S. S. [Willard Huntington Wright]. 1935. *The Garden Murder Case.* New York: Scribner.

Van Zoest, Aart. 1978. *Semiotiek. Over tekens hoe ze werken en wat we ermee doen.* Baarn: Ambo.

Vattimo, G. 1988. *The End of Modernity.* Baltimore: Johns Hopkins.

Veatch, Henry. 1952. Intentional Logic. New Haven: Yale University Press.

Veatch, Henry. 1969. *Two Logics.* Evanston, Ill.: Northwestern University Press.

Venturi, Robert. 1977. *Complexity and Contradiction in Architecture.* New York: Museum of Modern Art.

Veltrusky, J. 1964. Man and Object in the theater. In: *A Prague School Reader on Aesthetics, Literary Structure and Style,* ed. P. Garvin, pp. 83-91.

Versus. Quaderni di studi semiotici. 1988. Signs of Antiquity/Antiquity of Signs. 50/51, trans S. Petrilli; ed. G. Manetti.

Vico, Giambattista. 1975/1990. *A Study of the New Science,* ed. Leon Pompa. Cambridge: Cambridge University Press.

Violi, Patrizia. 1982. Du coté du lecteur. *Versus* 31/32:3-34.

Vita-Finzi, Claudio. 1989. Omnivorous fantasy. (Review of *ll pendolo di Foucault*). *Times Literary Supplement* (3 March):225.

Vološinov, V. N., and M. Bakhtin. 1929. *Marksizm i filosofija jazyka.* Leningrad: Priboi, 1929. (1973. *Marxism and the Philosophy of Language,* trans. L. Matejka and I. R. Titunik. New York, London: Seminar Press.)

Vološinov, V. N., and M. Bakhtin. 1976. Discourse in life and discourse in art concerning sociological poetics. In: *Freudianism: A Marxist Critique,* trans. I. R. Titunik; I. R. ed. Titunik and Neal H. Bruss, pp. 93-116. New York: Academic Press.

Voltaire. 1926. *Zadig and Other Romances,* trans. H. I. Woolf and W. S. Jackson. New York: Dodd, Mead.

Von Uexküll, Jakob. 1940. *Bedeutungslehre.* BIOS IO.

Vygotsky L. S. 1962 [1934]. *Thought and Language,* trans. E. Haufmann; ed. G. Vakar. Michigan: The MIT Press.

Vygotsky L. S. and A. Luria. 1930. The function and fate of egocentric speech. *Proceedings of the Ninth International Congress of Psychologists: New Haven, 1929.* Princeton: Psych. Rev. Company.

Wagner, Roy. 1975. *The Invention of Culture.* Englewood Cliffs, NJ: Prentice-Hall.

Waite, A. E. 1929. *The Holy Kabbalah.* Secaucus, NJ: University Books.

Wallace, Edgar. 1922. *The Flying Fifty-Five.* London: Hutchinson.

Wallace, Edgar. 1930. *The Green Ribbon.* New York: Doubleday.

Walras, L. 1874-77. *Eléments d'économie politique pure.* Lausanne: Guillaumin.

Weber, Samuel. 1982. *The Legend of Freud.* Minneapolis: University of Minnesota Press.

Weizsacker, E. and C. F. von Weizsacker. 1987. How to Live with Errors. *World Futures* 23:225-35.

Wertsch, J. V. 1984. The role of semiosis in L. S. Vygotsky's theory of human cognition. In: *Sociogenesis of Language and Human Conduct,* ed. B. Bain. Calgary: The University of Alberta.

Weschler, Lawrence. 1995. *Mr. Wilson's Cabinet of Wonder.* New York:Pantheon.

Williams, Brooke. 1985. Challenging Signs at the Crossroads. In: T. A. Sebeok. *Contibutions to the Doctrine of Signs,* pp. xv-xlii. Lanham: University Press of America.

Wittgenstein, Ludwig. 1958. *Philosophical Investigatios,* 3rd ed. G. E. M. Anscombe.

New York: Macmillan.

Wittgenstein, Ludwig. 1971. *Tractatus Logico-Philosophicus*, trans. D. F. Pears and B. F. McGuinness. London: Routledge & Kegan Paul.

Wohlnuth. P. 1988. Nested Realities, *World Futures* 25:199-236.

Worton, Michael and Still, Judith. 1990. *Intertextuality. Theories and practices*. Manchester University Press.

Yates, F. E. 1986. Semiotics as Bridge Between Information (Biology) and Dynamics (Physics). *Recherches Sémiotiques/Semiotic Inquiry* 5:347-60.

Yates, Frances A. 1964. *Giordano Bruno and the Hermetic Tradition*. Chicago: University of Chicago Press.

Zamora, Lois Parkinson. 1988. Apocalyptic visions and visionaries in *The Name of the Rose*. In: *Naming the* Rose, ed. T. Inge, pp. 31-47. Jackson: University Press of Mississippi.

Zamora, Lois Parkinson. 1992. Eco's Pendulum. *Semiotica* 91:149-59.

Zholkovsky, Alexander. 1984. *Themes and Texts: Toward a Poetics of Expressiveness*. Ithaca: Cornell University Press.

Zingarelli, Nicola. 1983. *Dizionario enciclopedico della lingua italiana*. Bologna: Zanichelli.

Contributors

PETER BONDANELLA is Distinguished Professor of Comparative Literature, Film Studies and West European Studies at Indiana University. His publications include *Italian Cinema: From Neorealism to the Present* (Continuum, 1990), *The Cinema of Federico Fellini* (Princeton University Press, 1992), *The Film of Roberto Rossellini* (Cambridge University Press, 1993), *Umberto Eco: Signs for These Times* (Cambridge University Press, 1996). He is the editor of *Dictionary of Italian Literature* (Greenwood Press, 1996).

HANNA BUCZYNSKA-GAREWICZ is Professor of Philosophy at College of the Holy Cross in Worcester, Massachusetts's (formerly a Professor at Warsaw University and Polish Academy of Science). She is the author of ten books on contemporary philosophical problems, a recent volume on C.S. Peirce's semiotics and of numerous articles on Peirce and semiotics in several international semiotic journals.

ROCCO CAPOZZI is Professor of Italian Literature at the University of Toronto. Author of *Bernari. Tra realtà e fantasia* (SEN, 1984) and *Scrittori, critici e industria culturale* (Manni, 1991). Some of his other publications include the editing of: *A Homage to Moravia* (Stony Brook, 1992) and *Scrittori e Le poetiche letterarie in Italia* (Longo, 1993). He has published in major journals on Bernari, Calvino, Moravia, Morante, Volponi, and Eco.

THERESA COLETTI is Professor and Chairperson of the English Department at the University of Maryland College Park. She is the author of *Naming the Rose: Eco, Medieval Signs and Modern Theory* (Cornell: University Press.1988), and essays on medieval English Literature that have appeared in journals such as *Studies in Philology*, *Medievalia et Umanistica*, and *Chaucer review*. She is currently working on the book-length studies on the Middle English Innocents plays and the figure of Mary Magdalene in the late medieval England.

PATRICK DEBBÈCHE is a graduate student in the department of French at the University of Toronto and completing a thesis on the semiotics of Beaumarchais' Comic Theater.

JOHN DEELY is Professor in the Dept. of Philosophy at Loras College, Dubuque, Iowa. He is the author of several texts which include: *Introducing Semiotic, Its History and Doctrine* (Indiana University Press, 1982); *Basics of semiotics* (Indiana University Press, 1982); *New Beginnings. Early Modern Philosophy and Postmodern Thought* (University of Toronto Press, 1994). *The Human Use of Signs; or Elements of Anthroposemiosis* (Lanham: Rowan & Littlefield, 1994).

TERESA DE LAURETIS is Professor of the History of Consciousness at the University of California, Santa Cruz. She is the author of several books including *Umberto Eco* (1980), *Alice Doesn't: Feminism, Semiotics, Cinema* (1984), *Technologies of Gender* (1987), *The Practice of Love* (1994), and *Sui generis. Scritti di teoria femminista* (Milan: Feltrinelli, 1996).

LUBOMIR DOLEŽEL, F.R.S.C., is Professor Emeritus of Slavic and Comparative Literature at the University of Toronto. He was educated at Charles University and received his Ph.D. from the Czechoslovask Academy of Sciences in Prague. His interdisciplinary interests comprise stylistics, poetics, semiotics, narratology and fiction theory. His book publications include *Narrative Models in Czech Literature* (University of Toronto Press, 1973), *Occidental Poetics: Tradition and Progress* (University of Nebraska Press, 1990), and *Fiction and Possible Worlds* (forthcoming).

UMBERTO ECO is ECO!

LINDA HUTCHEON is Professor of English and Comparative Literature at the University of Toronto. Author of 8 books on contemporary literature and critical theory, including *Narcissistic Narrative* (1980), *A Theory of Parody* (1985), *Poetics of Postmodernism: History, Theory, Fiction* (Routledge, 1988), and the latest, *Irony's Edge: The Theory and Politics of Irony* (London: Routledge, 1995).

ROBERTA KEVELSON is Distinguished Professor of Philosophy at Penn State University. Her publications include *Charles S. Peirce's Method of Methods* (J. Benjamins, 1987); *Peirce, Praxis, Paradox* (Mouton de Gruyter, 1990); *Peirce's Esthetics of Freedom* (Peter Lang Pub., 1993); *Peirce, Science, Signs* (Peter Lang Pub., 1995).

ANNA LONGONI has studied and is working with Maria Corti at the University of Pavia. She is has done extensive work on Dante's *Convivium* and its philosophic sources. She is presently working on the Arabic sources in Dante's *Divine Comedy*. Her scholarship in contemporary Italian Literature can be appreciated in her study of the *opera omnia* of Ennio Flaiano. With Diana Rüesch has co-edited, *Soltanto le parole. Lettere di E. Flaiano* (Milan: Bompiani, 1996).

CLAUDIA MIRANDA is a research assistant at the University of Bologna. Her previous contributions to the field of Umberto Eco's narrative include an article on *Foucault's Pendulum* in *Semiotica: Storia, teoria, interpretazione* (Milano, 1992). An article on *The Island of the Day Before* appears in Thomas Studer, ed. *Stunen uber das Sein: Inteernationale beitrage zu Umberto Ecos Insel des Vorigen Tages* (Darmstadt, 1996).

PAUL PERRON is Professor of French at the University of Toronto. Co-author of Balzac. *Sémiotique du personnage romanesque* (1980) and A.J. *Greimas and Narrative Cognition* (1993). He has co-edited a number of books on semiotics including: *Le dialogue* (1985); *The Biological Foundation of Gesture: Motor and Semiotic Aspects* (1986); *Le conte* (1987); *Paris School Semiotics. I: Theory & II: Practice* (1989); *A.J. Greimas: On Meaning* (1987); *A.J. Greimas: The Social Sciences. A Semiotic View* (1990).

SUSAN PETRILLI is Associate Professor of Philosophy of Language at the University of Bari. Has published *Significs, semiotica e significazione* (Adriatica, 1988), *Il significato del significare. Itinerari nello studio dei segni* (1966). With Prof. A. Ponzio is the co-author of *Man as a Sign* (Mouton de Gruyter, 1990) and *Signs, Dialogue and Ideology* (John Benjamins, 1993). Has edited Ferruccio Rossi-Landi's *Between Signs and Non Signs* (John Benjamins, 1992). For the Journal *Semiotica* has edited *The Correspondence between Morris and Rossi-Landi* (1992) and *Semiotcs in the U.S. and Beyond: Problems, People and Perspective* (1993).

IRMENGARD RAUCH is Professor of Germanic Linguistics at the University of California at Berkely. Author of *The Old High German Diphthongization: A Description of a Phonemic Change*; of *The Old Saxon Language: Grammar, Epic Narrative, Linguistic Interference*, and of numerous articles and chapters on linguistics and semiotics. She is founder of the Interdisciplinary *Journal for Germanic Linguistics and Semiotic Analysis* and co-editor of the Proceedings of the Fifth Congress of the International Association for Semiotic Studies.

Michael Riffaterre is University Professor at Columbia University. He served three terms as Director of the School of Criticism and Theory at Dartmouth. A second edition of his most recent book *Fictional Truth* has just been published and the French translation of it will appear in 1996. He conducted the Christian Gauss Seminars at Princeton in 1992, the text of which will be published as a book on the *Discourse of Criticism*.

David Seed is a Reader in the English Department at Liverpool University. His publications include *The Fictional Labyrinths of Thomas Pynchon* (1988), *The Fiction of Joseph Heller: Against the Grain* (1989), *Rudolph Wurlitzer, American Novelist and Screenwriter* (1992) and *James Joyce's A Portrait of the Artist as a Young Man* (1992). Forthcoming a book on "Cold War and Science Fiction." He is the Editor of the Liverpool University Press: Science Fiction Texts and Studies Series.

Victorino Tejera is Professor of Humanities Emeritus at SUNY at Stony Brook. His publications include *Art and Human Intelligence* (N.Y.: Appleton-Century, 1965); *Modes of Greek Thought* (Appleton-Century, 1971); *Plato's Dialogues: A Dialogical Interpretation* (N.Y.: Irvington, 1984); *Nietzche and Greek Thought*, 1987; *History as a Human Science*, 1984; *Semiotics from Peirce to Barthes* (Leiden: Brill, 1988); *Literature, Criticism and the Theory of Signs*, (Amsterdam: J. Benjamins, 1995); *Aristotle's Organon in Epitome: The Poetics, The Rhetoric, the Analytics* (Mellen, 1995).

Lois Parkinson Zamora is Professor of Comparative Literature at the University of Houston. Her books include *Writing the Apocalypse: historical Visions in Contemporary U.S. and Latin American Fiction* (Cambridge University Press, 1989) and *Image and Memory: Latin American Photography, 1880-1892* (Rice University Press, 1996). She is co-editor of *Magical Realism: Theory, History, Community* (Duke University Press, 1995).